BANNING BRANCHES

Revised Edition

Leroy F. Banning

HERITAGE BOOKS
2007

HERITAGE BOOKS

AN IMPRINT OF HERITAGE BOOKS, INC.

Books, CDs, and more—Worldwide

For our listing of thousands of titles see our website
at
www.HeritageBooks.com

Published 2007 by
HERITAGE BOOKS, INC.
Publishing Division
65 East Main Street
Westminster, Maryland 21157-5026

Other books by the author:

Banning Branches
Regimental History of the 35th Alabama Infantry, 1862-1865

International Standard Book Number: 978-0-7884-0726-0

INDEX TO THE BRANCHES

A SHORT HISTORY OF THE BANNINGS

The name of Banning is one of great antiquity and is of Danish origin. It applied to a class of people called "hero worshippers", and signified a home or dwelling. The name is found in Scottish songs. One of the earliest ballads or epic poems on record is "Widsith" and contains the line "Over the Bannings Becca ruled". Becca was a prince of an independent tribe and had many warriors. He was a hero or ruler of the Banning clan of Vikings. The manuscript was found in an Irish monastery and is thought to date back to 600-700 A.D. Banning, or Baningum in Old English, means "son of the slayers", if pronounced with a long "A". With a short "A" the meaning is "the righteous, hospitable". The Bannings are not identified with any other known tribe. In any event, our name is one of the first 1200 words written in the English language.

The Anglo-Saxon termination "ing", has always marked the name and has suffered little change throughout many hundred years of existence as well as movement into many countries. Whatever changes have occurred are due to misspelling or to the natural accommodation of a new language. In Holland the name is spelled Banninsh, Banningk or Bannick. Earlier in Holland it was also Benningh, Bennigk and Bennick.

In Denmark you will find many Bannings living today. England has many Bayninge, Banninge and Baninge. In Germany the name is spelled Bonning, Banninger, Baninger, Behning, Benning. In France it is De Branning, which is becoming Branning. Ireland gives us Bannon, Bannin, Branigan and others.

In the 4th or 5th century, some Bannings migrated from what is now Denmark to Holland. They lived there for 1000 years before coming into prominence. There is no trace of the name in history until 1386 when "Gerrit Banningh", a cloth merchant of Wienwendyk, who came from a hamlet called Banningh by the Stadt of De Venter, moved to Amsterdam. He is mentioned as the progenitor of the Banningh families in Holland, who helped govern that country to a greater or lesser extent for 300 years.

Rembrandt's "Night Watch", painted in 1642 has as its central figure, Captain Franz Banning-Coq, who although dying, made his power and influence felt. Franz Banning's mother was a Banning of noble birth and married an apothecary named Coq from Bremen, against the wishes of her parents. Their son, Franz, on his own, prefixed his mother's name, Banning, giving him a hyphenated name. Franz left Holland, studied law, returned to Amsterdam, became Alderman, then Magistrate and then Burgomaster. The King of Frankreich reigned him to the nobility. He built the city hall or Governor's Headquarters, which later became the King's Palace. He died young and childless in the midst of a promising career.

Jacob Banning, the standard bearer, is the central figure in the painting by Van Der Helst "Celebrating the peace of Munster" or "Conclusion of the 30 year war", painted in 1648.

The Banning family in Holland was of great prominence from 1386 to 1655 when their influence began to decline. From time to time efforts were made to regain former power, but with no lasting success. Influence was finally lost when some Bannings considered the government to be to harsh on Catholics and made an effort to interfere on their behalf. This caused various Banning families to fight among themselves, and resulted in many of them migrating around 1600. Some settled near Techlenberg in what is now the province of Westphalia, Germany. Other branches of the family went to England, Ireland, Scotland, America and elsewhere.

Sometime around 1500-1600 Bannings settled an area in England now known as

Banningham in Norfolk. No trace of them can now be found in that area, but they are traceable to Midland and London, from which the different branches there seem to have come.

The Bannings in England became prominent in military and social life in the l6th century. They were active in the Crusades to the Holy Land, for which a coat of arms was granted in 1588. Two peerages were created, both of which became extinct in the l7th century. The first peerage was granted to Sir Paul Bayning, Lord Mayor of London, who in his patent of nobility, reverted to the original spelling, and became Viscount Banning.

The Bannings came to America in the 17th century. From just where is uncertain, but the early names are Edward, James, John and Samuel, so they probably came from England. Sometime prior to 1678, Edward Banning settled in Talbot County, Maryland, shortly after Lord Baltimore was granted a charter for colonization by the King of England.

James Banning of Talbot County, Maryland is like a great number of people who came to the USA in the early days, in that the location from which he came is unknown, but tradition states that James came from England. This is not unlikely, but it is also possible that he was the son of Edward Banning, the first Banning in America. Edward was in Talbot County prior to 1678 and James is known to have been in Talbot County around 1700.

Edward Banning was in this country several years prior to 1678, because his name is mentioned in the archives of Maryland, Vol. 7, covering 1678 to 1683, under the heading, "An act for the payment and accessing the publick charges of the province", in which the assembly, in November 1678, paid him 300 pounds of tobacco to reimburse him for "charges to the province." It is not unlikely that he was the father of James Banning and possibly the father of John and Samuel Banning, who settled in Lyme, Connecticut about 1700. Tradition states that James, Samuel and John were brothers and probably sons of Edward.

Forty years later Benoni Banning came from Dublin, Ireland and settled in Talbot County, Maryland, so it is said.

The Bannings in Delaware, it is thought, came from those in Maryland, but may have migrated from Holland. Most descendants of the first James Banning of Maryland live in Ohio, Indiana, Delaware and Maryland, but some live elsewhere. Descendants from the two Connecticut branches have scattered to all parts of the U.S., many becoming early settlers of new states and territories.

One branch started in New York state and tradition indicates they came from Northern Ireland. They then went to Canada and from there they migrated to the central and western United States. Today there are towns named Banning in Pennsylvania, Georgia and California.

This, the 2nd edition of "Banning Branches", is largely due to the many excellent contributors and researchers that were kind enough correspond and give me the benefit of their knowledge and finding. As a result errors have been corrected, descendants added and additional information added to most of the lines. The source list has grown from 61 to 99. Every letter received has contained much valued information and many folks have been especially helpful. Among the latter are Virgil Fast of Orange, CA, Lois Herth of Tacoma, WA, Carolyn Malmberg of Dover, DE, Flora Baxter of Rochester, NY John Banning of San Antonio, TX, and Laurel Harris of Malaga, Western Australia, to name a few.

This edition reflects a change and realignment of the early members of the "E" and "F" lines, thanks to a great deal of outstanding research by Mary Friedlander of Milwaukee, WI. She proved her point with wills, deeds, etc. Thank you very much Mary. Thanks is also due to P.W. Banning, who's "First Banning Genealogy", issued in 1908, was my starting point.

 As a general rule I have given full information on the children of Banning daughters, but only name, date and place of birth for their grandchildren. The source of the information on each person has been indicated. Much effort has gone into trying to make this work as accurate as possible, however at times a choice had to be made concerning conflicting information. Any errors are therefore mine. Should any reader come across an error or omission, kindly bring it to my attention for correction in any future edition.

Leroy F. Banning (E19052)
11807 Broadwood
San Antonio, Texas 78249

April 1997

EDWARD BANNING OF MARYLAND

A1 STEPHEN BANNING alive in 1714. (See K71) Source: 1,24,28,29

        A2 John Banning
        A3 Edward Banning
        A4 Not used

A2 JOHN BANNING married 1694 (See K126) Source: 1,27,24

        K231 Elizabeth Banning (See K231)
        K232 Mary Frances Banning (See K232)
        K234 John Banning   (See K234)
        K235 Martha Banning   (See K235)
        K236 Susan Banning   (See K236)

A3 EDWARD BANNING (See K127) He is said to have moved to Talbot Co. Md. from England about 1650. He is supposed to have been a cousin to John Banning who settled in Lyme, Conn. Edward was said to be a sea captain. He purchased 50 acres of land known as "Goose Neck" on the N, side of the Choptank River on Jan. 13, 1690. He married 1st, ???? and 2nd, Susannah ???, about 1698. Susannah was the widow of ??? Nutwell by whom she had a son , John. Edward's will was signed in 1704, submitted for probate Aug. 7, 1710 and proved 1712 in Talbot Co. Md. Source: 1,12,24,45,47,49

        A5 William Banning (See B1)
        A5a John Banning   (See B2)
        A5b Edward Banning
        A5c Andrew Banning
        A5d Thomas Banning
        A5e Elizabeth Banning
        A5f Charles Banning
        A5g Susannah Banning

A5 WILLIAM BANNING (BANDY) (Also see B1) He was of age by 1704 and married Jane Spencer about 1722. This may have been his 2nd or 3rd marriage. She was born about 1696 in Maryland. William's name recorded as "BANDY" from time to time. He sold 50 acres of land called "Goose Neck" April 30, 1745 and leased it back for the live of William and Jane, his wife on May 8, 1745. The rent was one ear of corn per year. He died 1745-46. The record states, "Nicholas Goldsbrough, son of Robert and Elizabeth Goldsbrough and twin brother of Robert, married on April 7, 1746, Jane Banning, widow of William (or James in some incorrect books) Banning and died November 14, 1756" of Small Pox. Nicholas was born Feb. 17, 1704. Having no children, he adopted those of his wife and in his will, dated October 20, 1756 left them his property. He was a man of wealth for his time. Source: 1,12,21,22,24,28,29,40,43,44,49

Jane Spencer was married to William not James. The error can be traced to a book "Old Kent, The Eastern Shore of Maryland" published in 1876. The error was due to an incorrect reading of the Administrative letters of the estate of James Banning, who was her SON not husband. That Jane was married to William is established by church records and deeds. She was buried at the home of her son Jeremiah (A10).

Source: 12,24,28,47,49

> A8 James Banning (See B4)
> A9 Andrew Banning
> A10 Jeremiah Banning
> A11 Henry Banning
> A12 Anthony Banning

A5a JOHN BANNING (See B2) He was of age by 1704, married the daughter of
   Richard Parnell, who gave then 1/2 of "Golden Lyon" in Q.A. County in 1715. He
   was dead by 1718. His will is on file in Queen Ann Co., Md. His children A6, A6a &
   A7 were orphans, given 1st to Thomas Banning then their uncle, Andrew. Source:
   12,13,24, 28,47

> A6 William Banning (A6)
> A6a John Banning (See B3)
> A7 Richard Banning (See C3)

A5b EDWARD BANNING, JR. he was of age by 1704 and lived on 3rd Haven Creek.
   Source: 12,13,24,27,28,47

> A12e Charles Banning (same as A5f ?)
> A12f Susanna Banning (same as A5g?)
> A12g Edward Banning III

A5c ANDREW BANNING (BANDE) he was of age by 1704, and died 1767. He
   married Deborah Willson Dudley April 25, 1720. She was probably his 2nd wife.
   Deborah was the daughter of John Willson and the widow of Richard Dudley, whom
   she married in 1718.   Richard Banning (C3) was living with Andrew in 1733.
   Andrew had became the guardian of Richard, John & William Banning in 1724.
   They were the heirs of John Banning, his brother. Andrew did the inventory of the
   estate of William Banning in 1763. Andrew paid tax on "Kingston" from 1738 to
   1770. His grandson was the administrator of Andrew's estate. Source: 12,22,
   24,28,47,49

> Al2j Phillip Banning

A5d THOMAS BANNING born 1684-1704. Married Hannah Jones. She was the
   daughter of William Jones, who gave the couple land known as "Lane's Forrest" in
   1721. Thomas was in charge of his brothers estate and children for a time. His will
   is dated 1726 in Queen Ann Co., Md. She married 2nd James Bell. Source:
   12,24,28,47

A5e ELIZABETH BANNING born 1688-1704. She married Joshua Clark on July 27,
   1730 in St. Peters Parish, Talbot Co., Md. Source: 12,24, 28,47

A5f CHARLES BANNING (Nutwell says born about 1700)(if son of A3 why not in will)
   Source: 47

A5g SUSANNAH BANNING born after 1704 (Nutwell says born about 1702) and
   married ??? Gordin. This information as per gift from Susannah Bannin of Talbot
   Co. dated Dec. 12, 1727. (If born 1702 and daughter of A3, why not in will?)
   Source: 12,47

A12k John Gordin

A6 WILLIAM BANNING born pre 1714. Source: 47

A6a JOHN BANNING born pre 1718 and married Mary ??? (See B3) Source: 24

        B5 John Banning (See B5)
        B6 Asa Banning (See B6)

A12a Thomas Banning (Best guess as to where they go)

        A12b James Banning (Best guess as to where they go)

A7 RICHARD BANNING born 1715-16 (See C3) Source: 24

        C4 Richard Banning Jr. (See C4)
        C5 John Banning (See C5)
        C6 Phineas Banning (See C6)

A8 JAMES BANNING (See B4) born about 1724 in Maryland and married Angelica
Frazier. She was the daughter of Benoni and Cecilia Frazier, born about 1726.
They lived in Dorchester Co., Md. He died by July 27, 1767. Source: 3,12,18,
21,22,24,27,28,29,35,44,47,49

        B7 Benoni Banning (See B7)
        B8 James Banning (See B8)
        A13 Angelica Banning
        A14 Jeremiah Banning
        A15 Alexander Banning
        A16 Sarah Banning
        A16a Sarah Banning
        A16b Sarah Banning

A9 ANDREW BANNING born about 1726 and married Deborah Perry. He was a
school teacher in 1754 in that part of Dorchester Co. that became part of Caroline
Co. Records again indicate he was teaching at the "Oaks School" in 1793. He was
dead by 1797. Source: 12,21,22,28, 29,47

        A17 Anthony Banning
        A18 Henry Banning
        A19 James Banning
        A20 Andrew Banning
        A21 Deborah Banning
        A21a Jane Banning

A10 JEREMIAH BANNING born March 25, 1733 in Talbot County, Maryland. He
married Mary Gossage. Died 1798. His home was called "The Isthmus. The early
days of his life were spent at sea, carrying cargo to and from Europe and elsewhere
in connection with mercantile interests he had ashore and under contract to
merchants in London. He also traded in slaves, but at his death, his will made
provision that each of his slaves then living should be set free and educated at the
expense of the estate. He was a man of daring and greatly enjoyed adventure,
which he often found upon the sea. He became wealthy and settled at "The
Isthmus", his home, where he entertained many early historical people.

An old book states, "The home of Jeremiah Banning, "The Isthmus", was the scene of great hospitality during the early period preceding the revolution. Here Washington, Lafayette, William Morris, the financier and others of fame during that period, held nightly gatherings. The rooms of the noble old mansion could tell many tales of stately society. The owner was a man of daring mind and adventurous tendencies, which later got him into trouble over smuggling into this country Zachary Hood (*) and other piratical people. The Isthmus was one of the finest homes of that early period and the youth and beauty of Maryland gathered there during the early days of this country." * Zachary Hood was a Marylander sent from England to collect the "Stamp Tax" on Tea.

The archives of Maryland, Vol. 14, page 419- 1761 to 1771 records that Governor Sharp on September 3, 1767, stated that Captain Banning, who was to have sailed from London in Mid June, was bringing something to him.

He was captured by a French Privateer in 1761, imprisoned at St. Pierre and was only one of 2 men out of more than 300 to survive. He escaped after several months.

Jeremiah Banning was commissioned a Lieutenant Colonel of the 38th Battalion of Talbot Co. Militia in the revolution on April 9, 1778, the same day, his brother Henry was appointed Captain. He represented Talbot County at the General Assembly in Annapolis, to ratify and confirm the Federal Government of the United States. He was a Magistrate until 1778 and was commissioned by George Washington to be the collector of the port of Oxford on Aug. 3, 1789. He was also on the Board of Supervisors that had to attend and witness the printing of paper money. He became a Major in the army in 1775-76, and was 6' 5" tall. The 1776 Census indicates he owned 10 slaves. He died in 1798.

It is said that A22 through A24 were his wife's children by another marriage, and that he adopted them. For more information on Jeremiah see Jeremiah Banning, Mariner and Patriot, Jane F. Tucker, Economy Printing Co., Easton, Md. 1977, and The Log and Will of Jeremiah Banning published by W.F. Austin of N.Y. in 1932. Source: 1,3,12, 21,22, 24,28,29,35,40,45,47,49

> A22 Robert (Gossage) Banning
> A23 Freeborn (Gossage) Banning
> A24 Clementina T. (Gossage) Banning

A11 HENRY BANNING born 1736 in Talbot Co., Md. and married Araminta ----? She was born in July 1751. He lived on his plantation known as "Royal Oak", which was near Hopkin's Neck, Talbot County, Maryland. He had four children. He became judge of Talbot County by 1774 and held many other important offices. April 9, 1778, he was appointed Captain in the army. The 1790 census shows his name on page 111. The names also appears on page 113, but it is another person, probably belonging to the Benoni Banning branch. She Died Sept 18, 1807 and is buried in the Banning Graveyard in Hopkin's Neck, Talbot Co. He died at "Royal Oak" Aug. 20, 1818. He may have had 8 children, see the 1776 census. Source: 1,3,4,12, 21,22,28,29, 30,35,40,45,47,49

> A25 Anthony Banning
> A26 Thomas Banning
> A27 (John) Wesley Banning
> A28 Jane Banning
> A28a Ann Banning

A12 ANTHONY BANNING born in 1740 in Talbot Co., Maryland. Married Anna Calder, the daughter of James and Anna Katherine (Murray) Calder and was born about 1748 in Talbot Co., Md. They had three children. They lived on his plantation near Chestertown, Kent County, Maryland. He was associated in business with his brother Jeremiah. Anthony died Feb. 27, 1787 in Chestertown. His wife died Dec. 1, 1773 in Kent Co., Md. He served in the Maryland Militia during the Revolution and was a large slave owner. He also made several voyages with his brother. NOTE: Some sources, including his will indicate his only legitimate child is A30. Source: 1,3,12,21,22, 28,29,35,40,45,47,49

> A29 James Mansfield Anthony Banning
> A30 Katherine Banning
> A31 Annie Banning

A12a THOMAS BANNING born Aug. 26, 1724 in St. Peters Parish, Talbot Co., Md. (I am not sure I have the right parents, this is my best guess at this point.) Source: 12,13,27

> A32 for children

A12b JAMES BANNING no information. (I am not sure I have the right parents, this is my best guess at this point.)

> A33 for children

A12e CHARLES BANNING, (Nuttall says he is the son of A3, if so why not in will?) Born Aug. 1, 1700 and christen May 11, 1701 in Talbot Co., Md. He married 1st, Sarah Jane Marshall on Feb. 5, 1721 in Talbot Co. She was the daughter of William Marshall. John Beesley, who was living with Charles in 1733 had married Jane's sister. He married 2nd, Rachel Humphreys on Jan. 9, 1739 in St. Peters Parish, Talbot Co. His will was dated Aug. 16, 1742 in Talbot Co. Sources: 12,13,14,24, 27,47

> A34 Rachel Banning
> A34a John Banning
> A34b Thomas Banning
> A34c Charles Banning
> A34d Elizabeth Banning
> A34e Jane Banning
> A34f Sarah Banning

A12f SUSANNAH BANNING born Feb. 1702 and christen May 20, 1703 in Talbot Co., Md. Source: 12,13,49

> A35 for children

A12g EDWARD BANNING III served in Thomas Porter's co. of the Talbot County Militia in 1748. Source: 47

A12j PHILLIP BANNING (BANNEN) He was of age by 1718 and married Mary (???). He owned several plantations, including "New Designe" "Falkner's Square" and Banin"s Hazard. He died 1735-38. Source: 12,24,47,49

A36 Philman Banning
A36a Mary Banning
A36b William Banning
A36c Quilton Banning
A36d Henry Banning

A12k JOHN GORDIN he paid tax in 1733 and was in the Queen Ann Militia in 1748.

A13 ANGELICA BANNING born Dec. 17, 1749 Source: 12,18,27,28,29,35

A37 for children

A14 JEREMIAH BANNING born March 5, 1756. Source: 12,18,27,28,29,35

A38 for children

A15 ALEXANDER BANNING born Sept. 16, 1759. Source: 12,18,27,28, 29,35

A39 for children

A16 SARAH BANNING born May 2, 1743. She died by 1748. Source: 12,18

A16a SARAH BANNING born Oct. 10, 1748. She died by 1752. Source: 18

A16b SARAH BANNING born May 25, 1752. Source: 12,18,27,28,29,35

A39f for children

A17 ANTHONY BANNING married Nancy Augdon Aug. 9, 1796 in Talbot Co. Md.
Source: 12,13,47

A40 for children

A18 HENRY BANNING no information Source:47

A40f for children

A19 JAMES BANNING married Sarah Coleman Oct. 24, 1791 in Caroline Co. Md.
Source: 12,13,47

A40j for children

A20 ANDREW BANNING married Sally Bowdle Sept. 26, 1806 in Caroline Co. Md.
They lived in Dorchester Co. He died Dec. 18, 1825 and she died Feb. 20, 1826.
Source: 13,30,47

A40p William Banning Jr.

A21 DEBORAH BANNING no information Source: 47

A21a JANE BANNING Married a Mr. Sterat. Source: 47

A22 ROBERT (GOSSAGE) BANNING born 1776 in Maryland. Married twice: lst. to
Miss. Susan Thomas on April 27, 1799. She descended from the Oldham family.

Married 2nd, Mary Macky, and had two children. He was a man of prominence, being the Collector of the Port of Oxford, a member of the House of Delegates and became a Captain in the Militia in 1812, as well as standing high in the business community. He died Sept. 17, 1845 in Miles river Neck, Talbot Co. Md. Source: 1,21,29,40

> A41 Robert Banning
> A42 Alexander Banning
> A43 Maria Banning
> A44 Katherine F. Banning
> A45 Susan Banning
> A46 Matilda Banning (with wife 2)
> A47 Mary Elizabeth Banning (with wife 2)
> A48 Jeremiah Banning

A23 FREEBORN (GOSSAGE) BANNING Born March or May 24, 1777 in Talbot Co., Maryland. Married two times, lst to Harriett Thomas on Jan. 22, 1803 in Talbot Co. She was descended from the Oldham family. After the death of his wife, he married Sarah Geddes Nov. 14, 1814. She was born about 1778 and was the daughter of Captain Henry Geddes and Margaret (Latimer) Geddes. Her father was an officer in the British Navy commanding several vessels, on one of which Freeborn Banning served. April 30, 1798 Freeborn entered the U.S. Navy as a midshipman and on June 1, 1799 he was made a Lieutenant. He resigned his commission on Feb. 9, 1802. He died in 1826. She was living in Wilmington, Del in 1840 and with her son Henry in 1850. She died May 19, 1855, in Talbot Co. Source: 1,21,40,49

> A49 Emily Banning
> A50 Samuel Banning
> A51 Henry Geddes Banning

A24 CLEMANTINA TURNER (GOSSAGE) BANNING Born in Maryland and married Jeremiah Hopkins on Sept. 26, 1795 in Talbot Co. Source: 1,13, 21,49

> A52 through A54 unknown children

A25 ANTHONY BANNING Born April 2, 1768 at "Woodley" Royal Oak, Maryland. He married three times: lst to ? Spencer of Kent, Maryland. They had one daughter. 2nd, Mrs. Sophia Charlotte Edmundson on May 15, 1810. Sophia was born in 1775 and died in 1821. They had no children together. 3rd, Maria Nicholson who was born about 1782. They lived in Royal Oak, Maryland. He was in the war of 1812 and died on May 3, 1843. Maria died July 8, 1850 and is buried in the Banning Graveyard in Hopkin's Neck, Talbot Co. Source: 1,2,11,28,35,40,47,49

> A55 Emma Banning
> A56 Annie M. Banning
> A57 Caroline H. Banning
> A58 James C. Banning

A26 THOMAS BANNING born in Maryland about 1770. He married and had 2 boys and 1 girl by 1790. He died in 1840. Source: 1,21,28,35, 40,47,49

> A59 through A61 unknown children

A27 (JOHN) WESLEY BANNING He died Dec. 18, 1823. No additional information.

Source: 1,21,28,35,40,47,49

A62 through A65 unknown children

A28 JANE BANNING born in Maryland and married 1st Richard Parrott Jr. He died in 1823 in Washington, D.C. She married 2nd Stephen Bloomer Balch in 1830. He died in 1833. She married 3rd William Rassell (Razell) of Mt. Holly, N.J. on May 5, 1826 in Auburn, N.J. She was dead by 1847. Source: 1,21,28, 35,47,49

    A66 Eliza Parrott
    A66a William Henry Parrott

A28a ANN BANNING married 1st Hugh Watts and 2nd, James Earle Denny. She died in 1805. Source: 47

    A66b Martha Banning Watts
    A66c Mary Denny
    A66d Catherine Denny

A29 (JAMES MANSFIELD ?) ANTHONY BANNING born May 13, 1768 in Talbot County, Maryland. Moved to Fayette Co., Pa. in 1785/86. Married Sarah Murphy (Pierce) on June 30, 1791 at Connellsville, Pennsylvania. She was the daughter of Jacob and Elizabeth (Mason) Murphy, born Dec. 7, 1766 and was a "native of the Eastern Shore of Maryland". At the time of their marriage, she was the widow of George Pierce. Her marriage to Pierce was the result of a duel fought between a Col. Paul and Pierce, while standing on barrels in the river at Connellsville. Col. Paul had his thumb shot off, and therefor Miss. Murphy became the bride of Pierce.

One source states: "Sarah Murphy came from Ellicot's Mill, Baltimore Co. Md. and was the daughter of William & Anne Murphy."

One source states: "At an early age Anthony was left an orphan and went to live with his grandparents, who apprenticed him to a tailor. At the age of 10 he joined the Methodist Episcopal Church, for which he was disowned." A History of Fayette Co. Pa. states: "He ran away from home at the age of 16 (1784) after having experienced religion at a Methodist campmeeting ---." He became a minister in 1789, and upon his marriage, settled in Connellsville Pa. He became a business man, leader in public affairs and was appointed Judge in 1827. With his son, Jacob, he owned mills, tan yards, Indian trading post and cattle. Moved to Knox Co. Ohio about 1812 and was one of the founders of Mount Vernon, Ohio. He drowned Feb. 5, 1844, while crossing the ice on the Vernon River at Mt. Vernon. His estate papers were filed in Knox Co., Oh. She died June 4, 1844, at Mount Vernon, Ohio. Both are buried in Mound View Cemetery in Mt. Vernon. There is much more on him in the microfilm. NOTE: Some sources seem to indicate he is the illegitimate son of A12 and Sarah Mansfield. There was anger in the family at the time of his death. His will was burned by a family member and was reconstructed by the Ohio Supreme Court. Source: 1,2, 3,4,12,15,21,28,29, 30,35,40,49

    A67 Sarah B. Banning
    A68 Jacob Murphy Banning
    A69 Rachel Banning
    A70 James Smith Banning
    A71 Elizabeth (Betsy) Banning
    A72 Mary B. Banning

A73 Priscilla Banning
A74 Anthony Banning Jr.

A30 KATHERINE BANNING born July 6, 1770 in Chestertown, Maryland. Married
Benjamin Chew Jr., the son of Chief Justice Benjamin Chew and his 2nd wife
Elizabeth Oswald of Germantown, Pa. on Dec. 11, 1788, at "The Isthmus". They
lived at Germantown where she died in March 1855. He was born Sept. 30, 1758
became a lawyer and died April 30, 1844. Source: 1,21,22,28,35,49

A75 Samuel Chew
A76 Eliza Chew
A77 Benjamin Chew
A78 Samuel Chew
A79 John Chew
A80 Eliza Margaret Chew
A81 Henry Banning Chew
A82 William White Chew
A83 Anna Sophia Chew
A84 Joseph Turner Chew
A85 Anthony Banning Chew
A86 Catherine Maria Chew
A87 Oswald Chew

A31 ANNIE BANNING born in Chestertown, Md. Died as an infant in 1774. Source:
1,21,28,35,49

A32 and A33 unknown children of A13 and A14

A88 through A93 unknown children

A34 RACHELL BANNING born Oct. 2, 1723 in St. Peters Parish, Talbot Co., Md. She
married 1st Isaac Edwards on Oct. 9, 1740 and 2nd, William Moor(e) on Dec. 4,
1744, both in St. Peters Parish. Source: 12,13,14,24,49

A94 for children

A34a JOHN BANNING no information. Source: 12,24

A95 for children

A34b THOMAS BANNING born March 2, 1728 in St. Peters Parish, Talbot Co., Md.
Source: 12,24

A96 for children

A34c CHARLES BANNING born April 4, 1730 in St. Peters Parish, Talbot Co., Md.
He married the daughter of Charles Gannon. He served in Thomas Porter's co. of
Talbot Co. Militia in 1748. Source: 12, 24,47

A97 for children

A34d ELIZABETH BANNING born March 21, 1731 in St. Peters Parish, Talbot Co.,
Md. Source: 12,13,27

A98 for children

A34e JANE BANNING born May 2, 1734 in St. Peters Parish, Talbot Co., Md. Source: 12,13,24,27

A99 for children

A34f SARAH BANNING born Sept. 2, 1736 in St. Peters Parish, Talbot Co., Md. Source: 12,13,24,27

A100 for children

A35 children of 12f

A101 for children

A36 PHILMAN (PHILIPMON, PHILEMON) BANNING born about 1720. He was not of age by 1735. Source: 12,24,47

A102 for children

A36a MARY BANNING born about 1720. She was not of age by 1735. She married Littleton Ward. He died by 1748 Source: 12,24

> A102j Phillip Ward
> A102K James Ward
> A102L Rachel Ward

A36b WILLIAM BANNING born about 1720 and was not of age by 1735. He married Ann Walker, the daughter of James Walker. They lived in Queen Ann Co. Md. He developed and sold new plantations on vacant land and was the administrator of his grandfathers estate. William died 1780 in Caroline Co. Md. Source: 14,24,47,49

> A103 William Banning
> A103a John Banning
> A103b Elianor Bell Banning
> A103c Thomas Banning
> A103d Nancy Banning

A36c QUILTON BANNING born 1715-35 Source: 12,24,47

A104 for children

A36d HENRY BANNING born after 1715 and was not of age by 1735. He was apprenticed to his brother-in-law, Littleton Ward Source: 12, 24,47

A37 through A40 children of A13 through A21

A105 through A116 unknown children

A40p WILLIAM BANNING Jr. born 1808 and died Feb. 20, 1826. Source: 13,30,47

A41 ROBERT BANNING born 1806 in Md. and married his 2nd cousin, Emma Banning, (A55, daughter of Anthony Banning), on Oct. 30, 1828 in Talbot Co., Md.

He was a farmer and died in 1865.   Source: 1,5, 12,13,27

> A117 Henry Banning
> A118 Susan Antonia Banning

A42 ALEXANDER BANNING he was born 1812 in Md. and married Maria S. Birkhead on Nov. 10, 1842 in St. Michael's Parish, Talbot Co., Md. She was born about 1821. He was a farmer. Source: 1,5,12,13,27,40

> AI19 William Birkhead Banning
> A120 Robert Freeborn Banning
> A121 through A123 unknown children

A43 MARIA BANNING no information   Source: 1

> A124 through A128 unknown children.

A44 KATHERINE BANNING died unmarried. Source: 1

A45 SUSAN BANNING no information. Source: 1

> A129 through A134 unknown children.

A46 MATILDA BANNING   died young. Source: 1

A47 MARY ELIZABETH BANNING born in 1820 at Miles River Neck, Md. and lived in Winchester, Va. where she died, unmarried, Feb. 28, 1803. Source: 1

A48 JEREMIAH BANNING born in 1800 in Maryland. Entered the Navy and was killed by chain-shot in 1820. He never married. Source: 1,40

A49 EMILY BANNING born Sept. 1804 in Talbot Co., Md. She died Oct. 2, 1806 and is buried in he Banning Graveyard in Hopkin's Neck. Source: 1

A50 SAMUEL S. BANNING married Susan Sherwood on Sept. 30, 1834 in St. Michael's Parish, Talbot Co., Md.   Source: 1,12,13,27,40

> A135 through A143 for unknown children

A51 HENRY GEDDES BANNING born March 8, 1816 in Talbot Co. Md. Married Emily Eschenburg on April 7 or 17, 1847. She was born April 8, 1825 in Buenos Aires. He was President of the National Bank of Delaware in Wilmington for 33 years. He was a member of the Del. House of Representatives and held other important positions. He died March 12, 1906 in Wilmington. She died Sept. 3, 1897. Source: 1, 5,40

> A144 James Latimer Banning
> A145 John Henry Banning

A52 through A54 unknown children of A24

A55 EMMA BANNING born 1807 in Md. She married the grandson of Jeremiah Banning, Robert Banning (A41). She died in 1878. Source: 1,5,21

A56 ANNIE M. BANNING born 1827 in Maryland and married Gustavus Skinner on Nov. 16, 1847 in St. Michael's Parish, Talbot Co., Md. He was a Lawyer. They lived at the old homestead "Woodley" at Royal Oak, Md. She died March 9, 1908. Source: 1,13,21

> A146 Lawrence Albert Skinner

A57 CAROLINE H. BANNING married Dr. Christopher C. Harper on Feb. 13, 1849 in Talbot Co., Md., and lived at Centerville, Md. She died in 1844. Source: 1,21

> A147 Susan Antonia Harper

A58 JAMES C. BANNING he lived on a farm near Easton, Md. Source: 1, 21,40

> A148 through A156 unknown children

A59 through A65 unknown children of A26 and A27

> A157 through A219 unknown children

A66 ELIZA PARROTT she married a Mr. williams. Source: 1,21

A66a WILLIAM HENRY PARROTT born 1801 in Washington D.C. He went to La. some time after 1823. Source: 47

A66b MARTHA BANNING WATTS married John Lodman Elbert. She died in 1815. He married 2nd Harriett Troth. Source: 47

A66c MARY DENNY married Samuel (?) Horsley on Aug. 3, 1818. Source: 47

A66d CATHERINE B. DENNY married 1st Thomas Sherwood and 2nd Hilary Baker. Source: 47

A67 SARAH B. BANNING born June 13, 1792 in Connellsville, Pa. She married Daniel Sheldon Norton of Uniontown, Pa. on Aug. 11, 1816 at Mount Vernon, Ohio. She was his 2nd wife. He was the son of Philo Norton (born 1762) and Ann Baldwin (born 1760), born April 10, 1788 in Newton Ct. They lived in Mount Vernon. She died March 12, 1874 and he died on Oct. 25, 1859 in Mount Vernon. Source: 1,2, 21,49

> A220 Mary Banning Norton
> A221 Abram Baldwin Norton
> A222 Anthony Banning Norton
> A223 Maria Banning Norton
> A224 George Kenyon Norton
> A225 Daniel Sheldon Norton
> A226 Sarah Banning Norton

A68 JACOB MURPHY BANNING born June 22, 1794 in Connellsville, Pa. He married Sophia Eva Zimmerman on May 10, 1818 in Mount Vernon, Ohio. She was born July 12, 1798 in Hagerstown, Md. and was the daughter of Gottlieb (1762-1843) and Eva (Hahn) Zimmerman of Frederickstown, Md. They lived in Kenton, Ohio. He was a Doctor and was in business with his father, including Indian trading post in

Sandusky and Tymochtee, and was Pres. of the Owl Creek Bank. He died Feb. 20, 1836 while driving cattle across the Ohio River. Jacob plunged into the river and finally got them across, but the icy water was to much and lead to his death. She died Jan. 22, 1883 (or 1879). They are buried in the Mound View Cemetery. His estate papers are on file in Knox Co. Oh.   Source: 1,4,5,12,15,21,29,30,40,49

> A227 Louise Ann Banning
> A228 Nancy Moore Banning
> A229 Anthony Banning
> A230 Rachel Banning
> A231 Maria Coloric Banning
> A232 Raymond Banning
> A233 George Banning
> A234 Ben Franklin Banning
> A235 Norton Sheldon Banning
> A236 Blucher Banning
> A237 Sophia Eva Banning
> A238 Jacob Murphy Banning Jr.

A69 RACHEL BANNING born Nov. 12, 1796 in Connellsville, Pa. She married Rev. Elnathan Raymond of Norwalk, Conn. on May 18, 1819 at Mount Vernon, Ohio. He was a Methodist Minister. They lived in Brooklyn and in 1834 they moved to Mount Vernon, Oh., 213 W. High St., where she died July 17 (or 23), 1880. Source: 1, 21,30,49

> A239 Sarah Banning Raymond
> A240 Mary Banning Raymond
> A241 Anthony Banning Raymond
> A242 Elizabeth Raymond
> A243 Delia Maria Raymond
> A244 George Elnathan Raymond

A70 JAMES SMITH BANNING born Jan. or June 11, 1800 in Connellsville, Pa. He married Eliza A. Blackstone on March 12, 1822. She was the daughter of James Blackstone of Connellsville, born 1805 in Pa. and a descendent of Sir William Blackstone. She was a gifted woman. In 1812 he moved to Mount Vernon, Oh. where he engaged in farming, milling and other Mercantile business. The 1850 census has them in Knox Co. and indicates he was a miller and farmer with real estate valued at $25,000. He died May 22, 1867 in Mount Vernon. She died Sept. 29,1878. Source: 1,4,5,21,40,49

> A245 Anna Banning
> A246 Sarah Davidson Banning
> A247 James Blackstone Banning
> A248 Anthony Rogers Banning
> A249 Priscilla Banning
> A250 William Davidson Banning
> A251 Henry Blackstone Banning
> A252 Elizabeth Blackstone Banning
> A253 Thomas Davidson Banning
> A254 Mary Blackstone Banning

A71 ELIZABETH (BETSY) BANNING born May 13, 1803 in Connellsville, Pa. She married Charles Cotesworth Pinkney Bronson on March 4, 1828 at Mount Vernon,

Ohio. He was born May 23, 1800 in Litchfield, Conn. and died June 12, 1866 in New York City. They lived in Mount Vernon where she died July 12, 1866. Source: 1,15,21,49

> A255 Mary Elizabeth Bronson
> A256 Alice Bronson
> A257 Charles Anthony Bronson

A72 MARY B. BANNING born Feb. 14, 1805 in Connellsville, Pa. She married Henry Caswell of Sandusky City, Ohio on June 5, 1828 in Mount Vernon, Ohio. He was the uncle of Jay Cook. They had one child and lived in Mount Vernon where she died May 9, 1878. She is buried in Mound View Cemetery. Source: 1,15,21,49

> A258 --------? Caswell

A73 PRISCILLA BANNING born May 8, 1807 in Connellsville, Pa. She married Sewell Gray of Maine on Nov. 2, 1845 in Mount Vernon, Ohio. He was born April 9, 1806. They had no children and lived in Mount Vernon where she died Sept. 14, 1893. He died May 2, i862. They are buried in Mound View Cemetery. Source: 1,15,21,49

A74 ANTHONY BANNING JR. born Oct. 10, 1809 in Connellsville, Pa. He married Jane Dadley on Nov. 27, 1843 at Mount Vernon, Ohio. She was born in 1816 in London, England and died Nov. 16, 1881 in Mount Vernon. They lived at 200 W. High St. The 1850 census places them in Knox Co. with real estate valued at $5,000. He died Sept. 28, 1879 in Mount Vernon. Both are buried in Mound View Cemetery. Source: 1,5,21,40,49

> A259 William Dadley Banning
> A260 Sarah Banning
> A261 Henry Banning
> A262 George Banning
> A263 Frank Banning

A75 SAMUEL CHEW born Dec. 8, 1789 and died March 21, 1795. Source: 1,49

A76 ELIZA CHEW born May 4, 1791 and died March 31, 1795. Source: 1,49

A77 BENJAMIN CHEW born Dec. 5, 1793 and married Elizabeth M. Tilghmam, the daughter of Chief Justice William Tilghmam of Pa. in July 1816. Benjamin was a lawyer and served in the Army in the War of 1812. They had one son who died at age 3. Source: 1,49

A78 SAMUEL CHEW born June 19, 1795. He was a Lawyer and died unmarried on Aug. 21, 1841. Source: 1,49

A79 JOHN CHEW born Jan. 23, 1797. Was a Midshipman in the U.S. Navy and was lost at sea in 1815. Source: 1,49

A80 ELIZA MARGARET CHEW born Nov. 18, 1798 and married James M. Mason. He became a U.S. Senator. She died Feb. 11, 1874. Source: 1,49

A81 HENRY BANNING CHEW born Dec. 1, 1800 and married lst Harriet Ridgely. She was the daughter of Charles Ridgely, Governor of Maryland. They had 3 children, Charles, Benjamin and Samuel. He married 2nd, Elizabeth Ralston. Henry was a merchant in Philadelphia and died Dec. 12, 1866. Source: 1,49

A82 WILLIAM WHITE CHEW born April 12, 1803. He was Secretary of the American Legation to Russia 1837-1840. He died unmarried Nov. 13, 1851. Source: 1,49

A83 ANNA SOPHIA PENN CHEW she lived unmarried at "Cliveden" in Germantown. Source: 1,49

A84 JOSEPH TURNER CHEW born Dec. 12, 1806 and died in 1835 in Butler Co., Pa. Source: 1,49

A85 ANTHONY BANNING CHEW born Jan. 24, 1809 and died unmarried Feb. 1854. Source: 1,49

A86 CATHERINE MARIA CHEW born May 12, 1811 and died Oct. 27, 1811. Source: 1,49

A87 OSWALD CHEW born May 23, 1813 and died June 1824. Source: 1,49

A88 through A102 unknown children of A32 through A36

          A264 through A278   for children

A102j PHILLIP WARD No information. Source: 12,47

A102k JAMES WARD no information. Source: 12,47

A102l RACHEL WARD no information. Source: 47

A103 WILLIAM BANNING born March 17, 1750 in Queen Ann Co., Md. and married Rebecca Cheezum on June 21, 1774 in Caroline Co., Md. He died in 1796 with his estate going to his brother & sister. Source: 12,14,24,47

          A279 for children

A103a JOHN BANNING born Sept. 5, 1755 and died Oct. 8, 1756 in Queen Ann Co., Md. Source: 14,24,47

A103b ELIANOR BELL BANNING born Feb. 2, 1756. Source: 14,24,47

          A280 for children

A103c THOMAS BANNING date of birth unknown, died July 14, 1756. Source: 12, 14,24,47

A103d NANCY BANNING born Oct. 20, 1754. Source: 47

          A281 for children

A104 & A116 unknown children of A36d through 40

          A282 through A284 children

A117 HENRY BANNING christen Sept. 25, 1831 in St. Michael's Parish, Talbot Co.,

Md. He married Maria Louisa Waters on March 26, 1857 in St. Michael's Parish. They lived in Baltimore. Source: 1,5,13

> A285 Thomas Banning
> A286 Wesley Banning
> A287 Jane Banning
> A288 Robert Henry Banning
> A289 Richard Anthony Banning
> A290 through A292 for children

All8 SUSAN ANTONIA BANNING christen Sept. 16, 1846 in St. Michael's Parish Talbot Co., Md. and married Charles Martin. Source: 1,5,13

> A293 through A300 for children

A119 WILLIAM BIRKHEAD BANNING christen June 15, 1845 in St. Michael's Parish, Talbot Co. Md. Source: 1,5,13

> A301 through A307 for children

A120 ROBERT FREEBORN BANNING christen June 6, 1847 in St. Michael's Parish, Talbot Co., Md. Source: 5,13

> A308 through A315 for children

A121 through A123 for children of A42

> A316 through A371 for unknown children

A124 through A134 unknown children of A43 & A45

A135 through A143 for children of A50

> A372 through A412 for children

A144 JAMES LATIMER BANNING born April 8, 1848 in Wilmington, Del. He married Emma Harris, the daughter of Alexander and Maria Spencer Harris, on June 3, 1879. They lived in Wilmington where he became prominent in local affairs. He died April 8, 1914 in Wilmington. Source: 1,5

> A413 Henry Geddes Banning
> A414 James Latimer Banning

A145 JOHN HENRY BANNING born Oct. 31, 1863. He lived in Wilmington, Del., where he was connected with the National Bank of Delaware. Source: 1

> A415 through A423 for children

A146 LAWRENCE ALBERT SKINNER lived at the old homestead, "Woodley". Had 6 children. Source: 1

A147 SUSAN ANTONIA HARPER married a Mr. Martin. She died leaving 3 sons & 1 daughter. Source: 1

A148 through A219 unknown children of A58 through A65

A424 through A624 for children

A220 MARY BANNING NORTON born 1817 and married Judge Rollin Hurd of Mount Vernon, Ohio. They had 7 children. She died in 1894. Source: 1,49

A221 ABRAM BALDWIN NORTON born 1819 in Connellsville, Pa. where he married Sarah Davidson. They had one son. He was a Major in an Ohio Regiment during the Civil War. He died in 1868. Source: 1,49

A222 ANTHONY BANNING NORTON born May 6, 1821. He was married 3 times, one time to Ellen Burr. He wrote 8 books including several histories on Ohio and it's matters. Anthony ran a newspaper in Mansfield, Oh and was "ridden out of town on a rail because of his pro-slavery position." He moved to Dallas, Texas and started the first newspaper in that city. He is said to have had the longest beard ever recorded. He died Jan. 2, 1894 in Dallas. They had 2 sons. Source: 1,2,49

A223 MARIA BANNING NORTON born 182? and died as an infant. Source: 1,49

A224 GEORGE KENYON NORTON born 1827 and married Mrs. Elizabeth Raymond Merrick (see A242) in 1861. They had one daughter. He died in 1877. She died April 30, 1910 in Cleveland, Oh. at age 83. Source: 1,30,49

A225 DANIEL SHELDON NORTON born 1829 and married Elizabeth Sherman in Mount Vernon, Ohio. He died in 1868 while a member of the U.S. Senate. Source: 1,2,49

A226 SARAH BANNING NORTON born 1831 and died unmarried in 1850. Source: 1,49

A227 LOUISE ANN BANNING born in 1817 at Mount Vernon, Ohio. She married Col. John Stevens of New York in 1834 in Mount Vernon. They lived in Kenton, Ohio where she died in 1845. Source: 1, 21,49

        A625 Anthony Banning Stevens
        A626 Almary Stevens

A228 NANCY MOORE BANNING born May 27, 1819 in Mount Vernon, Ohio. She married Rev. Silas Dunning Seymour on Oct. 17, 1844 in Kenton, Oh. He was born in Johnstown, N.Y. and died 1896. She died April 16, 1856 in Fairfield, Ohio. Source: 1,21,49

        A627 Louise Ann Seymour
        A628 Rhoda Sophia Seymour
        A629 Rachel Maria Seymour
        A630 Nancy Banning Seymour

A229 ANTHONY BANNING born Nov. 17, 1820 in Mount Vernon, Ohio. He married Louise Cessna on Dec. 6, 1844 in Kenton, Ohio. She was the daughter of William T. Cessna, born 1823. The 1850 census places them in Hardin Co., Oh. where he was a farmer. They lived in Kenton where he died Oct. 6, 1889. Source: 1,5, 21,40,49

```
                    A631   Jonathan  Cessna Banning
                    A632   Nancy  Seymour Banning
                    A633   Catherine  Banning
                    A634   Sophia  Eva Banning
                    A635   Caroline  Banning
                    A636   Amos  Jacob Banning
                    A637   Helen  Banning
```

A230 RACHEL BANNING born March 27, 1822 in Mount Vernon, Knox Co., Ohio. She
married Edwin Fisher Oct. 27, 1841 in Mount Vernon. He was the son of Asa and
Rebecca (Waite) Fisher born about 1814 in Mass. or N.Y. They lived in Kenton,
Ohio, where he was an attorney. She died shortly after Sept. 7, 1859 at LaRue,
Ohio. He died May 15, 1874. Source: 1,21,29,49

```
                    A638 Edwin Banning Fisher
                    A639 Ray Fisher
                    A640 Anthony Banning Fisher
                    A641 Sallie Fisher
                    A642 Clara Fisher
                    A643 Alfred Fisher
                    A644 Blucher Fisher
                    A645 George Fisher
```

A231 MARIA COLORIC BANNING born Jan. 27, 1824 in Mount Vernon, Ohio. Moved
to Hardin Co. Oh. in 1827. She married Lieut. Amos Wheeler Nov. 27, 1847. He
was born Dec. 1819 in Ohio. They lived in Dudley, Oh. She died in 1905 at Pfeiffer
Station, Oh. from a ruptured artery. He was in the 65th Div. Source: 1,21,30,49

```
                    A646 Sophia E. Wheeler
                    A647 Portius Wheeler
                    A648 Frank Wheeler
                    A649 Alice Maria Wheeler
                    A650 Eva Wheeler
                    A651 Amy Wheeler
                    A652 Maud Wheeler
```

A232 RAYMOND BANNING born Aug. 20, 1825 in Mount Vernon, Ohio. He married
Jane Edgar in 1854 at Painter's Creek, Ohio. They Lived in Dudlay township, Hardin
Co., Ohio, where he was a farmer and died in 1877. Source: 1,5,21 40,49

```
                    A653 Jacob Murphy Banning
                    A654 Louise Ann Banning
                    A655 Mary Banning
                    A656 Maria Inez Banning
                    A657 Edgar Banning
                    A658 Clum Banning
                    A659 Sophia Banning
                    A660 Minda Banning
                    A661 Jane Banning
                    A662 Infant Banning
```

A233 GEORGE BANNING born April 25, 1827 in Mount Vernon, Ohio. He married
Nancy Smith in 1865 at Kenton, Ohio. She was born about 1845. They lived in
Pfeiffer's Station, Ohio where he died in 1889. Source: 1,5,21,40,49

A663 Jacob Nelson Banning
A664 Norton Nathan Banning
A665 Mary Maria Banning
A666 George Banning
A667 Howard Smith Banning
A668 William McLain Banning
A669 Frank Banning
A670 Avis Banning
A671 Inez Banning
A672 John Banning

A234 BEN FRANKLIN BANNING born Feb. 8, 1829 in Mount Vernon, Ohio. He
married Minerva Melvin in 1863 at LaRur, Oh. They lived in Dudley, Oh. where he
died in 1873. Another source states that he was unmarried, was kicked by a horse
while returning from Pikes Peak, Col. and died in Hardin Co., Oh. in 1859. See
A236. Source: 1,5, 21,40,49

A673 Blucher Banning
A674 Frank Banning

A235 NORTON SHELDON BANNING born Sept. 20, 1830 in Mount Vernon, Ohio. He
married Irminda Jane Frederick in 1864 at LaRue, Oh. She was born June 1, 1846
in Knox Co., Oh. They lived at LaRue, where he died in 1873. She moved to Del. in
1882 and in Oct. 1904 and married John A. Bennett of Shelbyville, Mo. She died in
Dec. 1906. Source: 1,5,13,21,30,40,49

A675 Blanch Banfield Banning
A676 Emmet Vore Banning
A677 Avis G. Banning

A236 BLUCHER BANNING born July 9, 1832 in Mount Vernon, Ohio. He died
unmarried in 1859 as the result being kicked by a horse on his return from Pikes
Peak, Col. See A234. Source: 1,5,21,40,49

A237 SOPHIA EVA BANNING born July 31, 1834 in Mount Vernon, Ohio. She married
William Columbus De Long Dec. 17, 1857 in Marion Co. , Oh. They lived in Marion,
Ind. He died in 1879 and she moved to Santa Anna, Calif. In 1808 she was living in
Tustin, Calif. Source: 1, 5,13,21,30,49

A678 Norton Sheldon De Long
A679 Blucher De Long
A680 Birdie Maria De Long
A681 Frank Banning De Long
A682 William Columbus De Long

A238 JACOB MURPHY BANNING born June 9, 1835 in Mount Vernon, Ohio. He
married Mary Arnett in 1870 in Bellefountain, Oh. They lived in Marrion, Ind. He
died 188? in Missouri. He was a Major in the l2lst Ohio Vol. Infty. They had one
child. Source: 1,5,21,30, 40,49

A683 -------? Banning

A239 SARAH BANNING RAYMOND born 1820. She married Gen. Goshen A. Jones of Mount Vernon, Ohio. They lived at 219 W. High St. in Mt. Vernon, had 5 children, four of which were Gertrude, Mary, Addie and Fred. She died in 1885. Source: 1, 21,49

A240 MARY BANNING RAYMOND born 182l in Brooklyn, L.I. She died unmarried in 1898 in Los Angles, Calif. Source: 1,21,49

A241 ANTHONY BANNING RAYMOND born 1823 in Brooklyn, L.I. He died unmarried in 1871 in Mount Vernon, Ohio. He served in the Mexican and Civil Wars. Source: 1,21,49

A242 ELIZABETH RAYMOND born 1828 in Brooklyn, L.I. She married lst, William H. Merrick and 2nd, George Norton, the historian of Ohio (see A224). They had two children and lived in Canton, Ohio. She aided in gathering information for the First Banning Genealogy and died April 30, 1910. Source: 1,30

A243 DELIA MARIA RAYMOND born 1832 in Brooklyn, L.I. and married James Blanchard of Mount Vernon, Ohio. They had two children. She died in 1896 in Los Angles, Calif. Source: 1,21,49

A244 GEORGE ELNATHAN RAYMOND born 1834 in Brooklyn, L.I. He married lst, a Ms. Craft and 2nd, Miss Russell. They had two children. He died in 1906. Source: 1,49

A245 ANNA BANNING born in 1824 in Mount Vernon, Ohio and died as an infant. Source: 49

A246 SARAH DAVIDSON BANNING born 1826 in Mount Vernon, Ohio. She lived unmarried and was known for her literary ability and artistic taste. She died in 1881 at "Buttonwood" in Mount Vernon. Source: 5,49

A247 JAMES BLACKSTONE BANNING born April 5, 1825 (or 1827) in Mount Vernon, Ohio. He married Mrs. Mary Williams (Curtis). They lived in Mount Vernon where he died Aug, 28, 1897. He was in the Civil War. They had no children. Source: 5,40,49

A248 ANTHONY ROGERS BANNING born Aug. 1831 (or 1828) in Mount Vernon, Ohio. He married Mrs. Catherine Torrence of Connellsville, Pa. They had no children and lived in Connellsville, where he owned much coal land and on one of his farms he started the town of Banning, Pa. For many years, he was on the board of directors of the B & O Railroad. He died in Banning Sept. 10, 1905. Source: 1,5,40,49

A249 PRISCILLA BANNING born Jan. 5, 1829 (or 1831) in Mount Vernon, Ohio. She married John D. Thompson of Dublin, Ireland Feb. 18, 1854 in Mount Vernon, Knox Co., Oh. They had no children and lived in Mount Vernon where she died in 1895. Source: 1,5,13,49

A250 WILLIAM DAVIDSON BANNING born July 29, 1830 (or 1831) in Mount Vernon, Ohio. He married Mary Lake of Wooster, Oh. on March 4, 1863 in Wayne Co. Oh. He joined the Knox Co. Militia in May 1867. They lived in Mount Vernon where he died Sept. 9, 1908. Source: 1,5,13,40,49

A684 Eliza Banning

A685 Priscilla Banning
A686 Mary Lake Banning
A687 Anna Lake Banning
A688 Lake Banning
A689 William Davidson Banning

A251 HENRY BLACKSTONE BANNING born Nov. 10, 1836 (or 1834) in Mount
Vernon, Ohio. He married Julia Kerby, the daughter of Timothy Kirby of Cincinnati
on Sept. 9, 1868 in Cincinnati. He was a lawyer and a man of prominence in
Cincinnati, where they lived. He died there Dec. 10, 1881. For a time he practiced
law in Mount Vernon with the firm of Dunbar & Kirby. He was Capt. of Co. B of the
4th Ohio Vol. Infty. and was then promoted to Major in the 52nd O.V.I., but before he
could join the 52nd, he was placed in command of the 87th. After 3 months, he was
promoted to Lieut. Col. of the 125th O.V.I. and served as such until 1863 when he
was transferred to the l2lst. He was promoted to the rank of Brev. Brig. General
during the Atlanta Campaign. In the spring of 1865 he was placed in charge of the
Port of Alexandria, Va., where he remained until Dec. 2, 1865, when he was
mustered out. While in the service, he was elected to the Ohio Legislature from
Knox county. In 1872 he defeated ex-president Hayes for Congress. He was
re-elected several times. Source: 1,5,40,49

A690 Kirby Banning
A691 Harry Bryon Banning
A692 Ella Kirby Banning
A693 Clinton Kirby Banning

A252 ELIZABETH BLACKSTONE BANNING born Aug. 21, 1837 in Mount Vernon,
Ohio. She married William Burr Brown of Mount Vernon, Oct. 14, 1862 in Mount
Vernon, where they lived. Source: 1,5,49

A694 Bessie Brown
A695 James Brown
A696 William Brown
A697 Eliza Brown

A253 THOMAS DAVIDSON BANNING born 1840 (or 1842) in Mount Vernon, Ohio.
He joined the Knox Co. Militia in May 1867 and lived unmarried in Mount Vernon
where he died Nov. 21, 1913. Source: 1,5,40,49

A254 MARY BLACKSTONE BANNING born July l1, 1843 (or 1844) in Mount Vernon,
Ohio. She married Frank William Watkins of Steubenville on Dec. 12, 1875 at
Mount Vernon. They lived in Springfield, Mass. Where she died July 27, 1911. He
died Oct. 29, 1914 in Los Angeles, Calif. Source: 1,5,49

A698 Lila Banning Watkins

A255 MARY ELIZABETH BRONSON born Aug. 4, 1829 in Mount Vernon, Ohio. She
married James LeDuc of Hastings, Minn. They had 4 children and she died in 1904.
Source: 49

A256 ALICE BRONSON died as an infant. Source: 49

A257 CHARLES ANTHONY BRONSON born March 7, 1839 in Mount Vernon, Ohio.
He died unmarried June 12, 1866 in Hastings, Minn. He was in the Civil War.

Source: 49

A258 ————? CASWELL died as an infant.

A259 WILLIAM DADLEY BANNING born Sept. 14, 1844 in Mount Vernon, Ohio. He married Ida Augusta McCreary May 10, 1885 at Mount Vernon. She was the daughter of Dr. Jacob and Mary Matilda (Skeen) McCreary, born in Mount Vernon on Feb. 18, 1855. She died May 23, 1907 and he died Dec. 29, 1912. Both are buried in the Mound View Cemetery. Source: 5,21,49

> A699 William McCreary Banning
> A700 Harold Banning

A260 SARAH BANNING born Nov. 20, 1846 in Mount Vernon, Ohio. She married Isaac Errett in Mount Vernon, Where they lived. She died there in Nov. 1919. Source: 5,49

> A7O1 Jane Errett
> A702 Ike Errett
> A703 Banning Errett
> A704 Charles Errett
> A705 Harry Errett

A261 HENRY BANNING born Nov. 3, 1849 in Mount Vernon, Ohio, where he died in a fireworks accident in July 1855. Source: 1,5,49

A262 GEORGE BANNING born in 1843 (or 1848) in Mount Vernon, Ohio where he lived unmarried and died May 2, 1896. Source: 1,49

A263 FRANK BANNING born March 9, 1861 in Mount Vernon, Ohio. He married Fanny Raymond in Mount Vernon in May 1885. She was born in 1861. He died March 14, 1931. Source: 1,49

> A706 Hazel Banning
> A706a Carolton Banning
> A707 Darrell (Paul Darrell ?) Banning
> A708 Francis R. Banning

A264 through A284 for unknown children of A88 through A116

> A709 through A759 for children

A285 THOMAS BANNING born in Baltimore, Maryland. Source: 1

> A760 through A765 for children

A286 WESLEY BANNING born in Baltimore, Md. Source: 1

> A766 through A770 for children

A287 JANE BANNING born in Baltimore, Md. Source: 1

> A771 through A776 for children

A288 ROBERT HENRY BANNING born in 1858 in Baltimore, Md. He lived in New York City where he was a partner in the firm of Tucker & Banning, Leather Goods. Source: 1

A777 through A782 for children

A289 RICHARD ANTHONY BANNING born in 1859 in Baltimore, Md. where he lived and engaged in the Manufacture of carriages. Source: 1

A783 through A788 for children

A290 through A292 unknown children of A117

A789 through A799 for children

A293 through A300 for children of A118

A301 through A371 unknown children of A119 through A123

A800 through A939 for children

A372 through A412 unknown children of A135 through A143

A940 through A1039 for children

A413 HENRY GEDDES BANNING born June 28, 1880 in Easton, Maryland. He died unmarried Jan. 15, 1914 in Wilmington, Del. Source: 1

A414 JAMES LATIMER BANNING born Jan. 13, 1882 at Easton, Maryland. He lived unmarried in Wilmington, Del. Source: 1

A415 through A423 children of A145

A1040 through A1060 for children

A424 through A624 unknown children of A148 through A219

A1061 through A1561 for children

A625 ANTHONY BANNING STEVENS born in 1836 and died unmarried in 1903 in Calif. Source: 21

A626 ALMARY STEVENS born 1838. Married Edwin Potts in 1855. They had 3 children. Source: 21

A627 LOUISE ANN SEYMOUR born Feb. 14, 1846 in Fortoria, Seneca Co., Iowa. She lived in Santa Paula, Calif. unmarried and died 19??. Source: 21

A628 RHODA SOPHIA SEYMOUR born Feb. 24, 1849 in Licking Co., Iowa. She married George Washington Faulkner in 1875. Their children's names are Alpha Lulu, Stella Martin, George Seymour and Rhoda Evangeline. Source: 21

A629 RACHEL MARIA SEYMOUR born Nov. 3, 1850 in East Union, Ohio. She married Charles Milton Drake in 1887. They lived in Berkley, Calif. and had no children. Source: 21

A630 NANCY BANNING SEYMOUR born March 22, 1854 and died Dec. 26, 1854. Source: 21

A631 JONATHAN CESSNA BANNING born in 1845 in Dudley T/S, Hardin Co. , Ohio. He married Sadie Parker at Round Head, Ohio. They lived in Bell Center, Ohio where he practiced medicine. He was a great hunter and had a fine collection of Indian battle axes. Source: 5,21

> A1562 Louise Banning

A632 NANCY SEYMOUR BANNING born 1848 in Ohio. She married Hiram Sowers of Battle Creek, Ohio in Kenton, Ohio in 1874. They had no children and lived in Battle Creek. Source: 5,21

A633 CATHERINE BANNING born in 1851 in Dudley T/S, Hardin Co., Ohio. She married Wesley Strong of Tiffin, Ohio in 1872 in Kenton, Ohio. They lived in Orange, Calif. He died in 1905 in Kenton, Oh. due to an accident. He was in the Civil War. Source: 21

> A1563 Paul Strong
> A1564 Roger Wesley Strong
> A1565 Nellie Strong
> A1566 Gertrude Strong

A634 SOPHIA EVA BANNING born 1855 in Hardin Co., Ohio. She married Conn Harris in 1878 in Kenton, OH., where they lived. Source: 21

> A1567 Eugene Harris

A635 CAROLINE BANNING born in 1856 in Hardin Co., Ohio. She married Edward Boulton in 1879 in Kenton, Oh., where they lived. She died in 1949. Source: 21,49

> A1568 Kittie Boulton
> A1569 Allen Boulton
> A1570 Louisa Boulton

A636 AMOS JACOB BANNING born in 1859 in Kenton, Ohio and married Clara Ansleman. They lived in Ottawa, Ohio. Source: 21

> A1571 Helen Banning

A637 HELEN BANNING died 1889 in Kenton, Ohio. Source: 21

> A1572 through A1576 for unknown children

A638 EDWIN BANNING FISHER born 1842/44 in Hardin Co, Oh. and was killed in the battle of Lost Mountain in Georgia, near Atlanta, on June 14, 1864. He was unmarried. Source: 21

A639 RAY FISHER born July 31, 1845 in Ohio and died in 1865 from exposure in the Civil War. He was unmarried. Source: 21

A640 ANTHONY BANNING FISHER born 1848 in Ohio and died in 1864. He was unmarried. Source: 21

A641 SALLIE FISHER born in 1850/51 in Ohio and married Arthur Melvin in 1878. She died in 1883. They had one child, Madge. Source: 21

A642 CLARA FISHER born 1852/56 in Ohio and married Albert Lingo in 1879. She died in 1882/85. They had 2 children, Edna & James. Source: 21

A643 ALFRED FISHER born Sept. 6, 1853 in Hardin Co., Oh. and married Mary Rose Haley Jan. 27, 1881 in Hardin Co. She was the daughter of John and Sarah Lurinda (Barrett) Haley. She died April 14, 1898 in Kenton. They had 6 children, Almary, John, Blucher, Raymond, Alfred & Althea. He died Feb. 15, 1890 in Ohio. Source: 21

A644 BLUCHER FISHER born Sept. 7, 1859 in Hardin Co., Oh. and married Idella "Del', Robbins. She was born Nov. 24, 1864 and died Feb. 7, 1913. They had one child. He died June 22, 1930 in Orange Co., Calif. Both are buried in Fairhaven Cemetery. in Orange Co. Source: 21

A645 GEORGE FISHER he was the twin of Blucher. He never married. Source: 21

A646 SOPHIA E. WHEELER born in 1846 and died in 1848. Source: 21,30

A647 PORTIUS WHEELER born 1849 and married Emma McCreary in 1873. They had 4 children, Vernon, Blanch, Rolla & Frank. He was alive in 1905. Source: 21,30

A648 FRANK WHEELER born 1853 and lived in Hepburn, Ohio. He was alive in 1905. Source: 21,30

A649 ALICE MARIA WHEELER born 1851 and lived in Anaheim, Calif. She was alive in 1905. Source: 21,30

A650 EVA WHEELER died as an infant. Source: 21

A651 AMY WHEELER born 1862 and alive in 1905. Source: 21

A652 MAUD WHEELER born 1864 and died 1889. Source: 21

A653 JACOB MURPHY BANNING born 1855 in Hardin Co., Ohio. He lived on the old Banning farm in Hardin Co. He died unmarried in i9??. Source: 21

A654 LOUISE ANN BANNING born 1856 in Hardin Co., Ohio. She died unmarried in 1890. Source: 21

A655 MARY BANNING born 1858 in Hardin Co., Ohio. She married and lived in W. Va. where they had 5 children. Source: 21

A1577 through A1581 for children.

A656 MARIA INEZ BANNING born 1860 in Hardin Co., Ohio. She married Mr. Auselman in 1888 in Kenton, Ohio. They lived in Logan Co. Ohio. Source: 21

A1582 Ernest Auselman

A657 EDGAR BANNING born 1859 and died unmarried in 1875. Source: 21

A658 CLUM BANNING born 1862 in Ohio and died 1875. Source: 21

A659 SOPHIA BANNING born 1864 in Hardin Co., Ohio. She was a nurse and lived in
Marion, Ind. She died in 19??. Source: 21

A1583 through A1588 for children.

A660 MINDA BANNING born 1866 and lived unmarried in Kenton, Ohio. Source: 21

A661 JANE BANNING born 1868 and died as an infant. Source: 21

A662 INFANT BANNING unnamed child died as an infant. Source: 21

A663 JACOB NELSON BANNING born 1866 at Pfeiffer's Station, Ohio. He married
Emma Shaffner. Source: 1,21

A1589 Amy Banning
A1590 Ruth Banning
A1591 Mary Banning
A1592 Jacob Banning

A664 NORTON NATHAN BANNING born 1868 at Pfeiffer's Station, Ohio. He lived
unmarried in Hepburn, Ohio. Source: 1,21

A665 MARY MARIA BANNING born in 1871 at Pfeiffer's Station, Ohio. She married
Milton Everheart in 1890. They lived in Mount Victory, Oh. Source: 1,21,30

A1593 Mildred Everheart

A666 GEORGE BANNING born 1870 in Pfeiffer's Station, Ohio, and married Eva
Pfeiffer. They lived in Hepburn, Oh. Source: 1,
21,30

A1594 Son---? Banning
A1595 Merle Banning
A1596 Son---? Banning

A667 HOWARD SMITH BANNING born 1875. He married Anna ------? in 1905 in
Indiana. Source: 1,21

A1597 through A1602 for children

A668 WILLIAM McLAIN BANNING born 1876 in Pfeiffer's Station, Ohio. He lived
unmarried in Hepburn, OH. Source: 1,21

A669 FRANK BANNING born 1878 in Pfeiffer's Station, Ohio. He lived in Buena Park,
Calif. Source: 1,21

A1603 through A1608 for children.

A670 AVIS BANNING born 1880 in Pfeiffer's Station, Ohio. She married Edgar Dixon in 1904 in Hepburn, Oh. Source: 1

A1609 through A1614 for children.

A671 INEZ BANNING she was the twin to Avis. Source: 1,21

A1614 through A1619 for children

A672 JOHN BANNING born 1886 in Pfeiffer's station, Ohio. Source: 1,21

A1620 through A1625 for children

A673 BLUCHER BANNING born 1868 in Hardin Co. Ohio. He married Gertrude Ellison in Kenton, Ohio. They had 2 children and lived in Hepburn, Oh. Source: 1

A1626 Son---? Banning
A1627 Son---? Banning

A674 FRANK BANNING born 1873 in Hardin Co., Ohio. He married Nettie Handlin. They lived in Hepburn, Oh. and by 1908, they had 2 children. Source: 1

A1628 through A1631 for children

A675 BLANCH BANFIELD BANNING born in 1865 in LaRue, Oh. She married William Pratt in 1884 in Chicago. They had 5 children and lived in Chicago. Source: 1,30

A1632 Blanch Pratt
A1633 Howard Pratt
A1634 unknown child.

A676 EMMETT VORE BANNING born in 1868 in LaRur, Oh. He married Maria ----? in 1895 in Chicago. They lived in Cleveland, Ohio. Source: 1,30

A1635 Blanch Banning
A1636 Hope Banning
A1637 Minda Banning
A1638 Emmett Banning

A677 AVIS G. BANNING born June 8, 1870 in Marion Co., Oh. and died as an infant. Source: 1,13

A678 NORTON SHELDON DeLONG born 1857 and died 1876. Source: 1

A679 BLUCHER DeLONG born 1858 and died 1860. Source: 1

A680 BIRDIE MARIA LeLONG born 1860 and lived in Tustin, Calif. Source: 1

A681 FRANK BANNING DeLONG born 1865, lived in Tustin, Calif. He married, had one child and died in 1908. Source: 1

A682 WILLIAM COLUMBUS DeLONG born 1874 in Marion, Ind. and lived in Tustin, Calif. Source: 1

A683 ------? BANNING died as an infant Source: 1 Source: 21 states this person was a Major in the 121st. OVL and lived in Marion, Ind.

A684 ELIZA BANNING born Jan. 23, 1871 and died April 5, 1872. Source: 1,49

A685 PRISCILLA BANNING born Jan. 6, 1873 in Mount Vernon, Ohio. She married Harry Sanderson of Mount Vernon on Sept. 12, 1900 in Mount Vernon, where they lived. Source: 1,49

> A1639 Anna Minerva Sanderson
> A1640 Howard Sanderson
> A1641 and A1642 for children

A686 MARY LAKE BANNING born Aug. 1, 1875 in Mount Vernon, Oh. where she died April 5, 1886. Source: 1,49

A687 ANNA LAKE BANNING born Aug 1, 1875 in Mount Vernon, Oh. where she married Philo Hankey of Bowling Green, Oh. on June 25, 1902. She died Feb. 13, 1903 in Mount Vernon. No children. Source: 1,49

A688 LAKE BANNING born June 8, 1882 in Mount Vernon, Oh. where he married Elizabeth W. Harper of that city on Dec. 19, 1905. They lived in Mount Vernon. Source: 1,49

> A1643 Mary Margaret Banning
> A1644 Charles Banning
> A1645 through A1647 for children

A689 WILLIAM DAVIDSON BANNING born June 8, 1882 in Mount Vernon, Oh. He died Dec. 25, 1884. Source: 1

A690 KIRBY BANNING born Aug. 29, 1869 in Cincinnati, Oh. where he lived unmarried. He was an Attorney and died in Cincinnati on May 17, 1894. Source: 1

A691 HARRY BRYON BANNING born Nov. 2, 1870 in Cincinnati, Oh. where he lived unmarried as of 1908. Source: 1

A692 ELLA KIRBY BANNING born i87? in Cincinnati, Oh. where she lived unmarried as of 1908. Source: 1

A693 CLINTON KIRBY BANNING born May 17, 1880 in Cincinnati, Oh. where he lived. Source: 1

> A1648 through A1652 for children

A694 BESSIE BROWN born 1864 in Mount Vernon, OH. She married Dr. J.W. Taylor of Chicago and had one daughter, Clara. She died in Chicago. Source: 1,49

A695 JAMES BROWN born 1868 in Mount Vernon, Oh. He died unmarried in Dallas, Texas. Source: 1,49

A696 WILLIAM BROWN born 1868 in Mount Vernon, Oh. where he married Ethel Campbell in 1911. Their children are William (1913 - 1928) and Barbara (1917).

Source: 1,49

A697 ELIZA BROWN died as an infant. Source: 1,49

A698 LILA BANNING WATKINS born Feb. 25, 1878 in Mount Vernon. She married
Pierson Worrall Banning (from the "B" line, and the author of this book in 1908) on
May 16, 1913 in Los Angeles, Calif. She was a talented pianist. See B598 for
children. Source: 1,30,40

A699 WILLIAM McCREARY BANNING born June 29, 1886 in Mount Vernon, Oh. He
married Lula Edna Vaughn on Sept. 26, 1905. She was born Feb. 16, 1887 in
Garrett, Ind. He died March 8, 1931 and she passed away July 22, 1967. Both are
buried in Mound View Cemetery. Source: 21,49

> A1653 William Vaughn Banning
> A1654 Augusta Banning
> A1655 Flora Corinne Banning
> A1656 & A1657 for children

A700 HAROLD DADLEY BANNING born Sept. 5 or 7, 1889 in Mount Vernon, Oh. He
died in 1966. Source: 1,49

> A1658 through A1660 for children

A701 JANE ERRETT born 1885 and married Edwin Lee. Source: 1,49

A702 ISAAC ERRETT born 1876 and died 1912. Source: 1,49

A703 BANNING ERRETT married Minnie Breutlinger. They had one son, Banning Jr.
Source: 1,49

A704 CHARLES ERRETT born 1868, married Blanch Robinson and had one child,
Virginia born 1902. He died 1952. Source: 1,49

A705 HARRY ERRETT born 1866, married Elizabeth Tudor and had one child,
Geoffrey. He died in 1918. Source: 1,49

A706 HAZEL BANNING born Aug. 5, 1889 in Mount Vernon, Oh. and married 1st.
Oliver L. Conklin in 1924 in Mount Vernon. They lived in Fla. Source: 1,49

> A1661 through A1665 for children.

A706a CAROLTON BANNING died as an infant. Source: 49

A707 PAUL DARRELL BANNING born Aug. 17, 1892 in Mount Vernon, Oh. and
married Elizabeth Bessie Bartlett in 1913 in Mount Vernon where they lived. He was
a lawyer and worked for the government in Washington, D.C. They were living in
Lakeworth, Fla. in 1979. Source: 1,30,49

> A1666 Elizabeth Banning
> A1667 through A1670 for unknown children

A708 FRANCIS R. BANNING born July 9, 1895 in Mount Vernon, Oh. and married Iva
Perrin on Nov. 21, 1917 in Mount Vernon. She was born 1899 in Mount Vernon and

he was a Machinist. He died in 1979 and is buried in Mound View Cemetery. Source: 1,30,49

A1671 Rodney Banning
A1672 Robert Banning

A709 through A770 unknown children of A264 through A286

A1673 through A1826 for children

A771 through A776 unknown children of A287

A777 through A788 unknown children of A288 & A289

A1827 through A1857 for children

A789 through A1039 unknown children of A290 through A412

A1858 through A2460 for children.

A1040 through A1561 unknown children of A415 through A624

A2461 through A3461 for children

A1562 LOUISE BANNING born 18?? and married Mr. Ramsey in Bell Center, Oh., where they lived. Source: 1

A3462 William Banning Ramsey
A3463 through A3465 for children

A1563 PAUL STRONG born 1874 and lived in Kenton, Oh., where he was the County Surveyor. Source: 1

A1564 ROGER WESLEY STRONG born 1875 and lived in Orange, Calif. Source: 1

A1565 NELLIE STRONG born 1878 and married Elon Smith in 1900. They lived in Kenton, Oh. Source: 1

A1566 GERTRUDE STRONG born in 1880 and lived in Kenton, Oh., where she was a teacher. Source: 1

A1567 EUGENE HARRIS born 1880. He married in 1906 and was a Dr. in Seattle, Wash. Source: 1

A1568 KATHERINE (KITTIE) BOULTON born in 1880 and married a Mr. Scott. Source: 49

A1569 ALLEN BOULTON born in 1888. Source: 49

A1570 LOUISA BOULTON born in 1892. Source: 49

A1571 HELEN BANNING lived in Kenton, Oh. and had 6 children. Source: 1

A3466 through A3471 for children.

A1572 through A1581 unknown children of A637 & A655

A1582 ERNEST AUSELMAN no information

A1583 through A1588 unknown children of A659

A1589 AMY BANNING no information

    A3472 through A3477 for children

A1590 RUTH BANNING no information

    A3478 through A3483 for children

A1591 MARY BANNING no information

    A3484 through A3489 for children

A1592 JACOB BANNING no information

    A3490 through A3495 for Children

A1593 MILDRED EVERHEART born in 1904

A1594 SON ----? BANNING no information

    A3496 through A3500 for children

A1595 MERLE BANNING born i902 and died 1904

A1596 SON----? BANNING no information

    A3501 through A3505 for children

A1597 through A1608 unknown children of A667 & A669

    A3506 through A3536 for children

A1609 through A1619 unknown children of A670 & A671

A1620 through A1631 unknown children of A672 through A674

    A3537 through A3567 for children

A1632 BLANCH PRATT no information

A1633 HOWARD PRATT no information

A1634 for unknown Pratt child

A1635 BLANCH BANNING no information

    A3568 through A3573 for children

A1636 HOPE BANNING no information

A3574 through A3579 for children

A1637 MINDA BANNING no information

A3580 through A3585 for children

A1638 EMMETT BANNING born 1904

A3586 through A3590 for children

A1639 ANNA MINERVA SANDERSON born Sept 4, 1904 in Mount Vernon, Oh. and
married Charles Salisbury April 1929. He was born in 1902. Source: 49

A1640 HOWARD SANDERSON born 1908. Source: 49

A1641 and A1642 unknown Sanderson children

A1643 MARY MARGARET BANNING born Nov. 24, 1906 in Mount Vernon, Oh. and
married Olin Pritchard June 8, 1929. Source: 49

A3591 Eugene Pritchard
A3592 Janith Pritchard

A1644 CHARLES BANNING born 1915 and married Louise ??? Source: 49

A3593 Charles Banning
A3594 Elizabeth Banning
A3595 Albert Banning

A1645 through A1652 unknown children of A688 and A693

A3596 through A3656 for children

A1653 WILLIAM VAUGHN BANNING born July 13, 1906 in Mount Vernon, Oh. He
was a Capt. in the U.S. Army Medical Corps, 1942-46 and married Edna Roth of
Shreve, Oh in 1946. She was born Jan. 27, 1909 and was the daughter of Joseph
P. Roth. They moved to Newark, Oh. in 1956 where he died Dec. 6, 1972. He is
buried in Mound View Cemetery in Mount Vernon. Source: 30,49

A3657 Jon Wilroth Banning

A1654 AUGUSTA BANNING born March 1, 1908 in Mount Vernon, Ohio and married
Edwin Sheppard Miller Aug. 5, 1930. He was born Sept. 23, 1904. They moved to
Columbia, Mo. in 1934 and lived at various times in Japan, Italy and the Netherlands.
She died May 26, 1980 in Columbia. Source: 30,49

A3658 Diana Miller

A1655 FLORA CORINNE BANNING born April 18, 1917 in Mount Vernon, Oh. and
married Robert Clarkson Baxter July 20, 1941. He was born March 22, 1916. They
live in Rochester, N.Y. She is the source of much information on this line. Source:

A3659 Robert Banning Baxter
A3660 Lawrence Joel Baxter

A1656 through A1660 for unknown Banning children.

A1666 ELIZABETH BANNING born 1927 in Mount Vernon, Oh. Source: 49

A1671 RODNEY BANNING born 1919 and lived in Cleveland, Oh. He was alive in 1989. Source: 30,49

A1672 ROBERT BANNING born Nov. 21, 1921 in Mount Vernon, Ohio and married Rosemary Kempton June 16, 1945 in Mount Vernon where they lived. She was born 1923 in Starta, Oh. Source: 1,30,49

A3700 Rosanne Banning
A3701 Michael Banning
A3702 Mary Banning
A3703 Rebecca Banning
A3704 Jane Banning

A3591 EUGENE PRITCHARD born 1931 and married in 1951. He had 2 children. Source: 49

A3592 JANITH PRITCHARD born 1938. Source: 49

A3593 CHARLES BANNING no information Source: 49

A3594 ELIZABETH BANNING no information Source: 49

A3595 ALBERT BANNING no information Source: 49

A3657 JON WILROTH BANNING born Oct. 17, 1947 in Shreve, Wayne Co., Oh. and married Karla Courtwright. They lived in Johnson City, Tenn. Source: 49

A9951 Aminda Banning
A9952 Kami Jon Banning

A3658 DIANA MILLER born June 3, 1935 (in Japan ?) and married George Broughton Delano June 12, 1956. He was born Jan 19, 1931. Their children are Sylvia Rose (1960), and Elizabeth Christina (1966). They live in Virginia Beach, Va. Source: 30,49

A3659 ROBERT BANNING BAXTER born Aug. 26, 1946 and married Sandra Weber in 1973. Their children are Matthew (1977), Darcy (1981) and Jeffrey (1986). Source: 49

A3660 LAWRENCE JOEL BAXTER born July 31, 1949 and married Sandra Rapkin on Dec. 23, 1979. Their children are Victoria (1981) and William Vaughn (1987). Source: 49

A3700 ROSANNA BANNING no information Source: 49

A3701 MICHAEL BANNING no information Source: 49

A3702 MARY BANNING no information Source: 49

A3703 REBECCA BANNING no information Source: 49

A3704 JANE BANNING died at age 3 months. Source: 49

A9951 AMINDA BANNING born 1976. Source: 49

A9952 KAMI JON BANNING born 1978. Source: 49

BENONI BANNING of MARYLAND

A3 EDWARD BANNING (See A3 & K127) He is said to have moved to Talbot Co. Md. from England about 1650. He is supposed to have been a cousin to John Banning who settled in Lyme, Conn. Edward was said to be a sea captain. He purchased 50 acres of land known as "Goose Neck" on the N, side of the Choptank River on Jan. 13, 1690. He married 1st, ???? and 2nd, Susannah ???, about 1698. Susannah was the widow of ??? Nutwell by whom she had a son , John. Edward's will was signed in 1704, submitted for probate Aug. 7, 1710 and proved 1712 in Talbot Co. Md. Source: 1,12,24,45,47,49

> A5 William Banning (See B1)
> A5a John Banning (See B2)
> A5b Edward Banning (See A5b)
> A5c Andrew Banning (See A5c)
> A5d Thomas Banning (See A5d)
> A5e Elizabeth Banning (See A5e)
> A5f Charles Banning (See A5f)
> A5g Susannah Banning (See A5g)

B1 WILLIAM BANNING (BANDY) (Also see A5) He was of age by 1704 and married Jane Spencer about 1722. This may have been his 2nd or 3rd marriage. She was born about 1696 in Maryland. William's name recorded as "BANDY" from time to time. He sold 50 acres of land called "Goose Neck" April 30, 1745 and leased it back for the live of William and Jane, his wife on May 8, 1745. The rent was one ear of corn per year. He died 1745-46. The record states, "Nicholas Goldsbrough, son of Robert and Elizabeth Goldsbrough and twin brother of Robert, married on April 7, 1746, Jane Banning, widow of William (or James in some incorrect books) Banning and died November 14, 1756" of Small Pox. Nicholas was born Feb. 17, 1704. Having no children, he adopted those of his wife and in his will, dated October 20, 1756 left them his property. He was a man of wealth for his time. Source: 1,12,21, 22,24,28,29,40,43,44,49

Jane Spencer was married to William not James. The error can be traced to a book "Old Kent, The Eastern Shore of Maryland" published in 1876. The error was due to an incorrect reading of the Administrative letters of the estate of James Banning, who was her SON not husband. That Jane was married to William is established by church records and deeds. She was buried at the home of her son Jeremiah (A10). Source: 12,24,28,47,49

> B4 James Banning (Same as A8)
> A9 Andrew Banning (See A9)
> A10 Jeremiah Banning (See A10)
> A11 Henry Banning (See A11)
> A12 Anthony Banning (See A12)

B2 JOHN BANNING he was of age by 1704, married the daughter of Richard Parnell, who gave then 1/2 of "Golden Lyon" in Q.A. County in 1715. He was dead by 1718. His will is on file in Queen Ann Co., Md. His children A6, B3 & C3 were orphans, given 1st to Thomas Banning (A5d) then their uncle, Andrew (A5c). Source: 12,13, 24,28,47

> A6 William Banning (See A6)
> B3 John Banning (Same as A6a)

C3 Richard Banning (Same as A7, see C3)

B3 JOHN BANNING (Same as A6a) Born pre 1718 and married Mary ???. Source: 24

> B5 John Banning
> B6 Asa Banning
> A12a Thomas Banning (See A12a)
> A12b James Banning (See A12b)

B4 JAMES BANNING (same as A8) born about 1724 in Maryland and married Angelica
Frazier. She was the daughter of Benoni and Cecilia Frazier, born about 1726.
They lived in Dorchester Co., Md. He died by July 27, 1767. Source: 3,12,18,21
,22,24,27,28,29,35,44,47,49

> B7 Benoni Banning
> B8 James Banning
> A13 Angelica Banning (See A13)
> A14 Jeremiah Banning (See A14)
> A15 Alexander Banning (See A15)
> A16 Sarah Banning   (See A16)
> A16a Sarah Banning   (See A16a)
> A16b Sarah Banning   (See A16b)

B5 JOHN BANNING (See C5) He was a Capt. in the Virginia Militia from 1779 to 1781.
There is a slight chance he could be the same person a E8 or E18.

B6 ASA BANNING said to have been born about 1742 and died in 1818. Asa was an
Ensign in the 28th Battalion of Militia of Caroline Co. Md. He was born in Talbot Co.,
Md. and died in 1818 in Rockbridge Co. Va., where he had purchased 136 acres of
land on March 16, 1805. He married 1st Sabina Smith in 1762. She was the
daughter of William and Abigail Smith Sr. of Dorchester Co., Md., born in 1742 and
died Jan. 5, 1791. Her father gave her some slaves in 1787. Asa married 2nd,
Ester Acton, the widow of John Acton, on Sept. 19, 1796 in Rockbridge. He owned
land in Caroline Co. Md. in 1778. Source: 3,24,28,32,40,47,63

> B9   John Banning
> B10 Hannah Banning
> B11 Abigale Banning
> B12 Thomas Banning

B7 BENONI BANNING born June 26, 1744. He married Ann Clark on Jan. 3, 1769 in
Dorchester Co., Maryland. She was the daughter of Abraham and Elizabeth
(Williams) Clark, born Dec. 3, 1749 in Dorchester Co. They moved to Washington
Co., Va. where he was in Capt. Campbell's Va. Militia. He was a soldier in the
American Rev. War and was stabbed 3 times by British bayonets on Oct. 7, 1780 at
the Battle of King's Mountain, and only survived due to the efforts of William
Fulwood (B14). They sold 78 Acres of land in Washington Co., Va. in 1799 and
moved to Burke Co., N.C. Tax records indicate he owned 275 acres in Burke Co.
They were living in Burke Co. in 1820. She died March 3, 1824 in McDowell (Burke
?) Co., N.C. He died Feb. 25, 1827 in Old Fort, N.C. and is buried in Ebeneazer
Cemetery in McDowell Co., N.C. Source: 1,2,4,12,18,24,27,28,29,32,40,43,44,
45,46,47

> B13 Clark Banning

B14 Elizabeth Banning
B15 Angelica banning
B16 Sarah Banning
B17 Frazier Banning
B18 James Banning
B19 Alexander Banning
B20 Jeremiah Banning
B21 Henry Banning
B22 Philadelphia Banning

B8 JAMES BANNING born Nov. 30, 1746 in Md. Married Mercy Coffin of Edgartown, Mass. on July 21, 1774 in Edgartown. She was born April 5, 1753 and was the daughter of Enoch & Jane (Jean ?) Coffin. They lived in Edgartown where he was a "sea-faring man". She died on Nov. 6, 1833. He died Nov. 9, 1826 from "universal decay", both in Edgartown. Source:1,2,12,18,24,27,28,29,39,40,45

B23 James Banning
B23a Infant Banning
B24 Henry Banning
B25 William Banning
B26 Frazier Banning
B27 Mercy Banning
B28 Jeremiah Banning

B9 JOHN BANNING born March 23, 1764 in Talbot Co., Md. Married Elizabeth Black, the daughter of Henry & Martha Black, on Oct. 24, 1797, in Rockbridge Co., Va. He died March 5, 1833 or 1839 in Rockbridge Co., Va. She died in McDonough Co., Ill. in 1843-44. Source: 1,2,4,24,32,63

B29 William Banning
B30 Henry Banning
B31 Salina Banning
B32 John Banning
B33 Martha Banning
B34 Asa Banning
B35 Ephraim Banning
B36 Mary Banning

B10 HANNAH BANNING married William Acton on Aug. 6, 1800 in Rockbridge Co. Va.

B37 through B39 for children

B11 ABIGALE BANNING born prior to 1776. She married Henry Rippy on June 22, 1797 in Rockbridge Co. Va. Source: 32

B40 through B42 for children

B12 THOMAS BANNING born about 1775 and married Keziah Gillfer Nov. 3, 1801 in Rockbridge Co. Va. She was the daughter of Thomas Gillfer. Source: 19,32,63

B43 Stephen Banning
B44 through B46 for children

B13 CLARK BANNING born Sept. 25, 1769 in Talbot Co., Md. Married Ann Wiley about 1790. She was born 1765-75. They lived in Md. and W. Va., then moved to Cumberland Co. Ky in 1806 where he is listed as a farmer in 1810 and 1820. He was a Methodist Minister and died in Ill. probably Greene Co. Source: 1,2,3,4,18, 27,28,29,40,44,45,46,49,59,67

B47 James Banning
B48 Thomas Wiley Banning
B49 Ann Banning
B50 John K. Banning
B51 Benoni Banning
B52 Alexander Banning
B53 Clark Banning
B54 Frazier Banning
B55 Mary Banning
B56 Jeremiah Banning
B57 Williamson Banning
B58 Elizabeth Banning
B59 Nancy Banning
B60 Henry Banning

B14 ELIZABETH BANNING born March 18, 1772 in Talbot County, Md. Married William Fullwood on April 6, 1797 in Washington Co. Va. or Maryland. He was a Methodist minister born Nov. 10, 1763 in S.C. They lived in Burke County, N. Carolina. She died Oct. 27, 1851. He applied for a pension in 1844 at the age of 80. He died Oct. 27, 1851. They are both buried in Obeth Cemetery. Source: 1,2, 12,13,18,27,28,29,32,44,45,46,63

B61 John Mason Fullwood
B61a William Fullwood
B61b Samuel Marion Fullwood
B61c Elizabeth Fullwood
B61d Sarah Fullwood
B61e Ann Fullwood
B61f Martha Fullwood

B15 ANGELICA BANNING born April 26, 1775 (76?) in Talbot Co. Md. and married Jonathan Bird Jan. 9, 1798 in Washington Co., Va. He was the son of Benjamin and Elizabeth Bird, born Jan. 22, 1764 in Wilkes N.C. He became a minister and died July 12, 1848 in McDowell Co., N.C. She died Oct. 5, 1863 in McDowell Co., N.C. They are buried in Ebinezer Cemetery. Source: 2,12,18,27, 28,29,32,44,46

B62 Lemuel Bird
B62a Clark Bird
B62b Green Bird
B63 Mirnda Bird
B63a Thomas Bird
B63b Williamson "Wilson" Bird
B63c Harbert "Harbord" Bird
B64 Elizabeth Bird
B64a Benjamin Bird
B64b Sarah Ann Bird
B64c Asbury Bird

B16 SARAH BANNING born May 2, 1778 in Talbot Co., Md. She married John (or Abram) Hill Nov. 25, 1815 in Burke Co., N.C. He was the son of Swinfield Hill and was born about 1801. She died between 1840 and 1843 in Carter Co., Tn. He married 2nd, Elizabeth Hains and had two additional children. He died about March 1877 in McMinn Co., Tn. Source: 4,12,13,18,27,28,29,44,46,54

> B65 R. B. Hill
> B65a Charles Hill
> B66 Stephen Hill
> B66a Elizabeth Hill
> B67 Absolem Hill
> B67a Nancy A. Hill

B17 FRAZIER BANNING born Jan. 1, 1781 in Washington Co. Va. He married Elizabeth Allison about 1804. She was the sister of Jemima (B18) and the daughter of Thomas and Cassandra (Bird) Allison, born about 1784 in N.C. He owned 50 acres of land in Burke Co. N.C. in 1805. They moved to Shelby Co., Ill. in 1828 with his brothers Alexander and Jeremiah. In addition to farming, Frazier, Alexander and Jeremiah made hand looms, wool and flax spinning wheels, chairs and wagons for their own use and for others. The brothers also help to build the first church in Dry Point Township. Elizabeth died May 9, 1863 in Shelby Co., Ill. and is buried in the Neal Cemetery. He died Aug. 6, 1844 in Shelby Co. Ill. She was living with her son (B72) in 1850 & 1860. Source: 2,4,5,6,18,27,28,29,30,44,46,75,79,91,92

> B68 Lorenzo Banning
> B69 Thomas Banning
> B70 Clark Banning
> B71 Benjamin A. Banning
> B72 Adolphus A. Banning
> B73 Barbara Banning
> B74 Sassy Kelly Banning
> B75 Daughter
> B76 Daughter

B18 JAMES BANNING born March 31, 1783 in Washington Co. Va. He married Jemima Allison about 1808. She was born about 1791, and was the sister to Elizabeth, (B17). They were living in Burke Co., N.C. in 1810. He was a carpenter. He died 1860-70 in N.C. and she died 1870-80 in Henderson Co., N.C. Source: 4,18,27,28,29,30,44,46,92

> B77 Thomas Banning
> B77a Mahalia Banning
> B78 Cassandra Banning
> B79 Rufus Banning
> B80 James Banning
> B81 Benjamin Banning

B19 ALEXANDER BANNING, born Oct. 20 or 25, 1785 in Washington Co., Va. He married Lucinda (???). They were living in Burke Co., N.C. in 1820-30. They moved to Shelby Co. Ill. about 1828 with his brothers Frazier and Jeremiah. In addition to farming, Frazier, Alexander and Jeremiah made hand looms, wool and flax spinning wheels, chairs and wagons for their own use and for others. The brothers also help to build the first church in Dry Point Township. Lucinda died in 1842 and is buried in Neil Cemetery about 1/2 mile North of Cowden, Ill. He married 2nd, Nancy C. Petty on Sept. 9, 1846 in Fayette Co. Ill. She was born about 1802 in Tenn. He died in 1848 in Shelby Co., Ill. and is buried in Neil Cemetery. She married 2nd, Hudson Cothron on June 9, 1853 in Shelby Co. Source: 2,4,12,18,27

,28,29,30,43,44,46,92

> B82 Ann Banning
> B83 Elizabeth Banning
> B84 Machac (Mashack) Banning
> B85 Benoni Banning
> B86 William Banning
> B87 James Banning
> B88 Alexander Banning
> B88A Banning son
> B88b Banning daughter

B20 JEREMIAH BANNING born Aug. 26, 1788 or 89 in Washington Co., Va. He married 1st, Elizabeth Ann Brooks in 1811 in Buncombe Co., N.C. She was the daughter of William Brooks, born 1785-94 in Ky. They had 6 children. In addition to farming, Frazier, Alexander and Jeremiah made hand looms, wool and flax spinning wheels, chairs and wagons for their own use and for others. The brothers also help to build the first church in Dry Point Township. Jeremiah was elected Justice of the Peace in 1838. He died May 1861 in Shelby Co. Ill. They were living in Cumberland Co. Ky. in 1820, moved to Jackson Co. Ala and then to Dry Point Township, Shelby Co., Ill. in 1828 with his brothers Frazier and Alexander. By 1850 he was in Wakefield, Shelby Co., Ill. where he had land valued at $650. He married 2nd, Ann Redmon on Sept. 4, 1849 and 3rd, Sarah Simmerman (or Ammerman) on Jan. 26, 1858 in Shelby Co.   Source: 2,4,5,6,12,13,18,27,28,29,30,32,43,44,46,92

> B89 Jonathan Bird Banning
> B89a Clark Banning
> B90 Mary E. (Margaret) Banning
> B90a William Banning
> B91 Rhoda (Rhody) Banning
> B91a daughter
> B91b son
> B91c Ann E. Banning

B21 HENRY BANNING born March 19, 1790 or 91 in Washington Co. Va. He married Nancy Glass. She was born about 1798. They were living in Burke Co., N.C. in 1820 & 30. He died in 1869. Source: 4,18,27,28,29,44,46

> B92 Philadelphia Banning
> B93 Joseph Banning
> B94 Elijah Banning

B22 PHILADELPHIA BANNING born Feb. 4, 1794 in Washington Co. Va. She married John Kelly on Sept. 12, 1850 in McDowell Co., N.C. and died 1874. Source: 13,18,27,28,29,44,46

> B95 through B97 for children

B23 JAMES BANNING born Jan. 2, 1776 or 78 in Edgartown, Mass. Died at sea in Aug. 1794 of "Georgia Fever". Source: 1,39,45

B23a Infant Banning died 8 hours and 17 minutes after birth on June 10, 1775. Source: 1

B24 HENRY BANNING born May 28, 1782 in Edgartown, Mass. Source: 1,45

B98 through B100 for children.

B25 WILLIAM BANNING born May 2, 1784 in Edgartown, Mass. Source: 1,45

B101 through B103 for children.

B26 FRAZIER BANNING born May 25, 1786 in Edgartown, Mass. He died at sea during passage from England in March 1805. Source: 1,39,45

B27 MERCY BANNING born July 11, 1790 in Edgartown, Mass. She married Henry Pease Worth Oct. 21, 1813. He was born Aug. 24, 1790 and was the son of Jethro & Velina (Pease) Worth. She died in Fishbury, Dukes County, Mass. Source: 1, 39,45

B104 for children.

B28 JEREMIAH BANNING born Oct. 31, 1792 in Edgartown, Mass. Married on Dec. 16, 1821, Abigail Merchant of Edgartown, where they lived until 1835 when they moved to Goshen, Ind. She was born July 31, 1804 and was the daughter of George & Abigail (Butler) Merchant. In 1839 they moved to South Bend, and by 1850 he was postmaster in St. Joseph Co. He died in Goshen, Ind. on Oct. 2, 1872. Source: 1,4,5,39,45

B105 James Henry Banning
B106 Charles L. Banning
B107 Alexander Frazier Banning
B108 Elizabeth Griffith Banning
B109 James Henry Banning

B29 WILLIAM BANNING born May 8, 1799 in Rockbridge Co., Va. Source: 1,2,40

B110 through B111 for children

B30 HENRY BANNING born March 24, 1801 in Rockbridge Co., Va. and died June 24, 1834. Source: 1,2,40

B112 for children

B31 SALINA BANNING born March 22, 1803 in Rockbridge Co., Va. and died June 28, 1836. Source: 1,2

B1l3 for children

B32 JOHN BANNING born Nov. 13, 1804 in Rockbridge co. Va. He married Eliza Ann Anderson April 10, 1834 in Wheeling, Ohio Co., Va. and moved to Henry Co. , Iowa about 1838, settling on the Skunk River 15 miles from Mount Pleasant. She was born in Oct. 1815 in (West) Virginia and died in Henry Co., Iowa Feb. 7, 1855. He married 2nd, a widow, Mary ??? by 1860. She was born 1818 in Ohio. The 1860 Census indicates that Mary brought several children to this marriage. They had one child together. He was a farmer and died Sept 7, 1864 in Iowa. Source: 1,2,4, 5,6,13,32,40,63

B1l4 Horatio Banning
B1l5 John Anderson Banning

B116 William Henry Banning
B117 James Edgar Banning
B118 Abraham Sampson Banning
B118a Susan Jami Banning
BI19 Mary E. Banning
B12O Jane Banning
B121 Emma Banning
B121a Harriet Banning
B122 Morgan Banning

B33 MARTHA BANNING born July 30, 1806 in Rockbridge Co., Va. Source: 1,2

B123 thur B128 for children

B34 ASA BANNING born March 16, 1808 in Rockbridge Co., Va. He married
Margaret Clark on Feb. 23, 1829 in Ohio Co., Va. and moved to Graves Creek near
Wheeling. Later he moved to Marshall Co., Va., where he became a man of
prominence. Source: 1,2,13,40,49

B129 John Banning
B130 Elizabeth Banning
B131 Ephraim Banning
B132 Charlotte Banning

B35 EPHRAIM BANNING born April 17, 1811 in Rockbridge Co., Va. He received the
name Ephraim in honor of Ephraim Doty who had saved his father from drowning
just before Ephraim's birth. In 1824 he went to Wheeling where he remained for 10
years. He then moved to McDonough Co., Ill. near the town of Bushnell. He
married Mary Potter (or Porter) on Jan. 26, 1836 in Wheeling, returned to Ill. and for
the next 22 years he lived in Walnut Grove, about 8 miles S.E. of Macomb. They
had 3 children. She died Oct. 10, 1840 and he married Louisa Caroline Walker on
May 12, 1842 in McDounough Co. She was the daughter of Joseph Gilmer Walker
and Martha Scott (born 1795 in Ky.) and was born near Columbia, Adair Co., Ky on
Jan. 15, 1817. They moved to Douglas Co. Kansas in 1855. Ephraim was active in
the movement to admit Kansas to the Union as a free state. Their home was the
meeting place for the "Free Soilers" during the border warfare. They moved again in
1860, to Brookfield, Missouri, where he died Nov. 8, 1878. She died Aug. 10, 1887.
He was a leader in civic matters, helped bring State hood to Kansas and held
several public offices. The 1860 census has him in Pettis Co. Mo. as a farmer.
Source: 1,2,6,13,24,40,63,75

B133 William Frederick Banning
B134 John Banning
B135 James Henry Banning
B136 Joseph Gilmer Banning
B137 Pinkney Asa Banning
B138 Elizabeth Mary Banning
B139 Ephraim Banning
B140 Thomas Allen Banning
B141 Cyrus Walker Banning
B142 Hubert Ashley Banning
B143 Cynthia Ellen Banning
B144 Martha Bell Banning

B36 MARY BANNING born April 17, 1813 in Rockbridge Co. Va. She married Morgan

Keys circa 1835-37 and moved to the Willamette Valley, Ore. where she died, in Linn Co. in 1883. They had no children. Source: 1,2

B37 through B42 children of B11 & B12

B43 STEPHEN BANNING born May 15, 1815 in Ohio. Moved to Ill in 1837 and settled near Chambersburg, Ill. on Dec. 10, 1839. He married Elizabeth D. Riggs on Dec. 19, 1838 in Pike Co. Ill. She was born about 1819. He was a school director and also owned 160 Acres of Land in Sect. 26. They had 8 children, but only 3 girls lived to marry. Source: 5,13,19

> B331 Martha A. Banning
> B332 Nancy J. Banning
> B333 Rhoda Banning
> B334 Sarah E. Banning
> B335 through B336 for children

B44 through B46 for children of B12

> B145 and 146 for children

B47 JAMES BANNING born Dec. 6, 1792 in West Va. He died Oct. 13, 1817. Source: 1,27,40

> B147thur B149 for children

B48 THOMAS WILEY BANNING born March 19, 1794 in West Va. He married Rebecca Griffin Sept. 22, 1814 in Cumberland Co., Ky., where his family had moved in 1806. She was born 1795 in S.C. They moved to Macon Co., Missouri about 1821 where he died April 30, 1873. He was a farmer in Cumberland Co. Ky. in 1820. Source: 1,4,5,13,27, 40,44

> B150 Sally Banning
> B151 James Banning
> B152 Nancy Banning
> B153 Catherine Banning
> B154 Betsy Jane Banning
> B155 Matilda Banning
> B156 Thomas Franklin Banning

B49 ANN BANNING born Oct. 23, 1795 in West Va. She married a Mr. Scrogins. Source: 1,27,44

> B157 thur B162 for children

B50 JOHN K. BANNING born Aug. 26, 1797 in West Va. He died Nov.6, 1798. Source: 1,27,40,44

B51 BENONI BANNING born Jan. 11, 1794 or 1799 in West Va. He married Mary ???. She was born 1801 in Va. They were married by 1820 and living in Cumberland Co., Ky. The 1850 census places them in Macoupin Co. Ill. as a farmer. Source: 1,4,5,27,40,44

> B163 Nancy Banning
> B164 Catherine Banning

47

B165 through B168 for children

B52 ALEXANDER BANNING born May 20, 1800 in West Va. He married Elizabeth Smith in 1822 in Ruth Co., Tenn. and moved to Missouri, near the town of Keytsville in Chariton Co., Mo. She was born in 1802 in Tenn. or N.C. They were living in Chariton Co. in 1840 and had 4 boys and 3 girls at that time. Source: 1,4,13,27, 40,44,87

> B169 William Banning
> B170 Jane Banning
> B171 Alexander Banning
> B172 Louis P. Banning
> B173 LaSatt Banning
> B174 for children

B53 CLARK BANNING born Feb. 12, 1802 in West Va. He married Jane Beaty March 7, 1822. She was born Sept. 7, 1800 in Tenn. and died Dec. 15, 1871. They lived in Lynn Co., Mo. where he died Feb. 23, 1882. They were living in Chariton Co. Mo. in 1840. The 1860 census has them in Lynn Co. Mo. as a farmer with $3,000. land value. Clark is buried in the "Banning Cemetery" in Brookfield township, Linn County, Mo. located in the NE1/4 of Sect. 31, T58, R19. Source: 1,4,5,6,15, 27,40,44,87

> B175 Pleasant Wilson Banning
> B176 Annie Banning
> B177 Williamson Banning
> B178 Andrew Banning
> B179 James Henry Banning
> B180 Catherine Banning
> B180a Pleasant Snow Banning

B54 FRAZIER BANNING born Aug. 14, 1804 in Cumberland Co. Ky. He married Rebecca Watson in Chariton Co., Mo. on July 11, 1827. She was born 1811 in Va. or Ky. The 1860 census show's him as a farmer in Macon Co. Mo. with land valued at $2,500. The 1850 and 1860 census indicates he was born in Va. He died Feb. 22, 1874 in Chariton Co. Mo. Source: 1,4,5,6,27,40,44

> BI81 Missouri Banning
> B182 James Franklin Banning
> B183 Thomas Jasper Banning
> B184 Melissa Viola Banning
> B185 John Banning
> B186 Martha C. "Mattie" Banning

B55 MARY BANNING born April 4, 1806 in Ky. and married a Mr. Johnson. Source: 1,27,44

> B187 through B192 for children

B56 JEREMIAH BANNING born Dec. 31, 1807 in Cumberland Co. Ky. He married Isabel Matilda Campbell Dec. 24, 1829 in Chariton Co. Mo. She was born about 1814 in Va. In 1840 they were in Daviess Co., Mo. By 1860 they were living in Gainsville, Cooke Co., Texas where he died June 19, 1883.. Source: 1,4,6,7,8,12, 27,40,44,67

B193 Vianah R. Banning
B194 Catherine Ellen Banning
B195 Samuel C. Banning
B196 William W. Banning
B197 Jancy V. Banning
B198 Jeremiah Dallas Banning

B57 WILLIAMSON BANNING born Sept. 23, 1809 in Ky. He married Nancy Johnson. She was born about 1813 in Ill. He was a farmer in Greene Co., Ill. in 1850. Source: 1,4,5,27,40,44,59

B199 Elizabeth Banning
B200 Julia Banning
B201 John Banning
B202 Clark Banning
B203 James Banning
B204 Andrew Banning
B205 Joel Banning
B206 Mary Ann Banning

B58 ELIZABETH BANNING born May l5, 1811. She married William Johnson. Source: 1,27,44

B207 Julia Edna Johnson
B208 & B209 for children

B59 NANCY BANNING born March 10, 1813. Source: 1,44

B210 through B212 for children

B60 HENRY BANNING born April 16, 1814 in Ky. He married Mary ??? who was born about 1822 in Tenn. He was a farmer living in Green Co. Ill. in 1850. They moved to Huntsville, Mo. where he died in 1892. They had 2 children who were living in Ill. when he died. Source: 1,4,5,27,40,44

B213 Elizabeth Ann Banning
B214 Francis M. Banning

B61 JOHN MASON FULLWOOD married Elizabeth Howard on Sept. 10, 1818 and had a son, Robert. John died in 1843. Source: 1,44,46

B61a WILLIAM FULLWOOD He had no children. Source: 1,44,46

B61b SAMUEL MARION FULLWOOD Born about 1811 and married Ann Bell Howard in 1831. She was the daughter of William and Rebecca Blythe Howard. Ann was born in 1812 and died in 1884. He died in 1896. Their known children are John, William, Samuel, Robert and Sarah Elizabeth. Source: 1,32,44,46,63

B61c ELIZABETH FULLWOOD Source: 1,44,46

B61d SARAH FULLWOOD married William T. Austin and had a son, William Thomas. Source: 1,44,46

B61e ANN FULLWOOD married John Estes. They had at least one child, Sarah. Source: 1,44,46

B61f MARTHA FULLWOOD married William M.D. Howard. He was the son of William and Rebecca Blythe Howard. Their known children are Cecillia, Robert, William, Margaret, Edward and Mortimer. Source: 1,44,46

B62 LEMUEL BIRD born Jan. 22, 1799 in Washington, Va. and married Lavisa (???). She was born 1802. He died about 1865. Their children are Jonathan (1826), William (1828) and Rolie (1838). Source; 44,46

B62a CLARK BIRD born Dec. 18, 1800 in Burke Co., N.C. and married Mary Pauline "Polly" Curtis on Dec. 7, 1820. She was born March 26, 1804. He died July 18, 1885 in Macon, N.C. Their children are James Harvey (1821), Asbury (1823), John Williamson (1824), Mary Ann (1825), Joshua Curtis (1828), Elizabeth "Betty" Jane (1829), Louisa Delilah (1831), Ceila Brittain (1832), Rebecca "Becky" Melinda (1835), Jonathan Lafayette (1837), Eleanor "Ellen" Merinda (1838), Jessie Richardson (1840), Martha "Matt" Ovian (1842), Carmine "Carr" Sevier (1844), Benjamin Andrew (1846) and Bird. Source: 16, 44,46

B62b GREEN BIRD born Feb. 2, 1802 in Burke Co., N.C. and died May 8, 1802. Source: 44,46

B63 MIRNDA BIRD born Feb. 22, 1803 in Burke Co. N.C. and died June 5, 1803. Source: 44,46

B63a THOMAS BIRD born March 19, 1804 in Burke Co., N.C. and died April 26, 1804. Source: 44,46

B63b WILLIAMSON "WILSON" BIRD born April 15, 1806 in Burke Co., N.C. and married Rebecca (???). He died July 11, 1828 in Burke Co. Source: 44,46

B63c HARBERT "HARBORD" BIRD born Feb. 5, 1809 in Burke Co., N.C. and married Delilah "Liley" (???) about 1835. She was born in 1817. He died about 1880. Their children are Mary R. (1836), John W. (1839), Benton (1840), Elizabeth "Cindy" (1844), Catherine (1850), Joseph (1852), George W. (1858) and Sarah M. (1861). Source: 44,46

B64 ELIZABETH BIRD born July 8, 1811 in Burke Co., N.C. and married Josiah Askew Curtis Jan. 2, 1832 in Burke Co. He was born 1810. They moved to Macon Co., N.C. When gold was discovered in Calif., he left his family to be a "49er" and never returned. He died in Calif. in Sept. 1866. She died June 4, 1909 in Macon, N.C. and is buried in Asbury Cemetery in Otto, N.C. Their children are Angelica (1832), Emily (1834), John Spencer (1836), George Washington (1838), Washington Lafayette (1841), Mary A. (1843), Jonathan Bird (1845), Elizabeth (1848) and Moses Hightower (1852). Source: 19,44,46

B64a BENJAMIN BIRD born Feb. 2, 1814 in Burke Co., N.C. and married Clairssia Minerva Conley on Aug. 16, 1843 in Macon, N.C. She was born 1823 and died in 1903. He died May 5, 1892 in McDowell Co., N.C. Their children are Harriet V. (1844), Margaret A. (1846), Augusta F. (1849), Joseph Lenox Clingman (1854), Hood A. (1856), Charles A. (1859) and Mary Conley (1866). Source: 32,44,46,63

B64b SARAH ANN BIRD born June 2, 1816 in Burke Co., N.C. and died July 19, 1816. Source: 44,46

B64c ASBURY BIRD born June 15, 1817 in Burke Co., N.C. and died Sept. 11, 1817.

Source: 44,46

B65 R. B. HILL No information. Source: 12,54

B65a CHARLES HILL Married Elizabeth Stephens on May 23, 1846 in Carter Co., Tn.
Source: 12,54

B66 STEPHEN HILL born about 1821 and married Mary Stewart on Feb. 21, 1849 in
McMinn Co., Tn. Source: 5,12,54

B66a ELIZABETH HILL born about 1829 in Burke Co., N.C. and married James
Harvey VanZant on Feb. 21, 1846 in McMinn Co., Tn. She died prior to Jan. 1894 in
Webster Co., Mo. They had at least one child, Sarah. Source: 5,12,54

B67 ABSOLEM HILL born about 1833. Source: 5,12,54

B67a NANCY A. HILL born about 1836 and married John VanZant on Oct. 10, 1853 in
McMinn Co., Tn. She died prior to Oct. 22, 1879. Source: 12,54

B68 LORENZO BANNING born Sept. 27, 1805 in N.C. and married 1st, Susanna
(???)(Bryson?) who was born May 3, 1804 in N.C. He married 2nd, Mary E. Baker
on April 23, 1857 in Shelby Co. Ill. She was born about 1811 in Ohio. He was a
farmer in Shelby Co. in 1850 & 60. Source: 5,6,12,27,43,44,75,79,91

> B215 John C. Banning
> B216 Elizabeth Ann Banning
> B217 Frazier Azbury Banning
> B217a William W. Banning
> B218 James D. Banning
> B219 Margaret J. Banning
> B220 Martha Louisa Banning
> B221 Thomas M. Banning
> B222 Benjamin B. Banning

B69 THOMAS BANNING born about 1808 in N.C. He married 1st, Jane A. Samson
(or Liverson) on July 23, 1832 in Shelby Co., Ill. She was born April 1, 1807 and
died March 5, 1847. She is buried in Elebert Cemetery in Shelby Co. He married
2nd, Elizabeth Martin on July 23, 1854 in Shelby Co. Elizabeth was born about
1823 in N.C. He was farming in Shelby Co. in 1850 & 1860 where he died July 22,
1864. Source: 4,5,6,12,27,43,44,79,91

> B223 William Bird Banning
> B224 Elizabeth Ann Banning
> B225 Joseph T. Banning
> B226 Dolphus Banning
> B227 Clark Banning
> B227a Jane Banning
> B228 David Banning
> B229 Barbara Banning

B70 CLARK BANNING born Nov. 28, 1821 in Bumcombe Co. (?) N.C. He married
Mary Daniel Feb. 15, 1852 in Shelbyville, Shelby Co. Ill. She was the daughter of
Robert Daniel, born about 1834 in Ill. He died Nov. 21, 1865 in Shelby Co. and is
buried in Neal Cemetery in Cowden, Ill. Mary married 2nd Samuel J. Severe on Oct.
11, 1866 and 3rd Gilman Severe (born 1816, see B231) (source 27 states no 3rd

marriage). She died in Shelby Co.   Source: 4,6,12,13,27,43,44,79,91

> B230 Robert Banning
> B231 Martha Jane Banning
> B232 Thomas Banning
> B233 James R. Banning

B71 BENJAMIN ANDREW BANNING born 1815-20 in N.C. and married Caroline Matilda Cordin on Jan. 13, 1837 in Shelby Co., Ill. She was born about 1821 in Tenn. He married 2nd, Sarah C. Bevins on June 17, 1845 in Shelby Co., Ill. She was born about 1820 in Tn. They moved to Polk Co., Mo. in 1857-60. They were were living in Benton Township in 1860, where he is listed as a wagonmaker. (The name is spelled "Barnny".) There are still in Benton Township in 1870 and 1880, where he is listed as a farmer. Both were alive in 1881 when they sold 40 acres of land in Polk Co., Mo. Source: 5,6,7,8,12,27,43,44,75,79

> B233a Lorenzo B.A. Banning
> B234   Dolphus Banning
> B235   Solomon Banning (Rimes)
> B235a Frazier Banning (?)
> B236   Jacob Banning
> B237   Franklin Banning
> B237a Willis Banning
> B237b Malenda Banning
> B237c Elizabeth Banning
> B237d John Banning

B72 ADOLPHUS A. (DOSS) BANNING born Nov. 15, 1824 in Buncombe Co., N.C. He moved to Shelby Co., Ill with his parents in 1828-32, and married Malinda C. Sullivan on Jan. 24, 1849 in Shelby Co. She was born June 14, 1827 in Tenn. to William B. and Jane S. Sullivan. He is listed as a farmer in Shelby Co. in 1850 & 60. He served in the Mexican war. Doss died Jan. 15, 1901 and she died June 8, 1909, both in Shelby Co. where they are buried in Neal Cemetery. Source: 5,6, 12,27,30,43,44,92

> B238 Clark Banning
> B239 Martha Banning
> B240 Annie Banning
> B241 William F. Banning
> B242 Catherine (Kate) Banning
> B243 John Franklin Banning

B73 BARBARA BANNING born 1828 in N.C. She died July 21, 1849 in Shelby Co., Ill. and is buried in Neal Cemetery. Source: 27

> B244 through B248 for children

B74 SASSY KELLY BANNING born 1820-25. Source: 27,44

> B249 through B253 for children

B75 Daughter born 1810-15. Source: 27

B76 Daughter born 1815-20. Source: 27

B254 through B257 for children

B77 THOMAS BANNING born July 1818 to 1825 and married Sarah Allison Allen. She was born 1830 and died Sept. 19, 1914. He died about 1900. Source: 27,44,46

> B258 William Hicks Banning
> B259 Mary D. Banning
> B260 James Marcus Banning
> B261 Martha J. Banning
> B262 Mahalia Banning
> B263 David Jasper Banning

B77a MAHALIA BANNING born 1814 and married William Allison. He was born July 10, 1811. They liven near Old Fort, MacDowell Co., N.C. She died in 1869 of Typhoid Fever and he died about 1874. Source: 44,46

> B264 Alexander Turner Allison
> B265 Ellen Allison
> B266 James Allison
> B267 Thomas Allison
> B268 Jemima Allison
> B269 Richard Isaac Allison
> B270 Benjamin Allison

B78 CASSANDRA BANNING born about 1826 and died after 1850. Source: 27,44,46

> B271 for children

B79 RUFUS P. BANNING born about 1836, and married Sarah A. Rickman on Jan. 10, 1866. They had two children. Rufus married 2nd, N.C. Scruggs on Oct. 19, 1872. Source: 27,44,46,97

> B272 Alice Banning
> B272A Unknown son
> B273 Julia Banning
> B274 Nancy Banning

B80 JAMES BANNING born Oct. 1, 1820 and married Rebecca Swayingame. She was born April 30, 1816. Source: 27,44,46

> B275 Elvira Banning
> B276 Joseph R. Banning
> B277 Sophia Emma Banning
> B278 John Sullins Banning
> B279 James Banning
> B280 Sarah Rebecca Banning

B81 BENJAMIN BANNING born 1810 or 1813 and married Dice Ann (???). She was born about 1818. Source: 27,44,46

> B281 Richard Banning
> B282 Victoria Banning
> B283 Malinda Banning

B82 ANN BANNING born 1804-10 and married Rutherford Tennison in Shelby Co., Ill.
Source: 12,27,43

B284 through B287 for children

B83 ELIZABETH BANNING born 1815-16 {married Clark (M.?) Banning (B89a ?) on
Feb.26, 1832 in Shelby Co., Ill. She died before 1850. (this info is suspect)}
Source: 12,27,43

B84 MACHAC (MASHACK ?) BANNING born about 1809 in N.C. (S.C.?) He married
Minerva Waller on July 8, 1834 in Fayette Co. Ill. She was the daughter of Joseph
Waller. He died July 8, 1851 in Fayette Co., Ill. She died prior to Aug. 1850.
Source: 5,16,27,43

> B288 Joseph Banning
> B289 Elizabeth Banning
> B290 Henry Banning
> B291 Alexander Banning
> B292 & B293 unused

B85 BENONI BANNING born 1810-15 and married Tempy Harris on March 5, 1835 in
Shelby Co. Ill. He died before a will was probated in Feb. 1842 in Shelby Co.
Source: 4,12,27,43

> B294 Elias Banning
> B295 Emeling Banning
> B296 Ann Banning

B86 WILLIAM BANNING born about 1817 in N.C. and married Eliza Jane Barr on
March 15, 1840 in Shelby Co., Ill. She was born about 1820. Source: 4,5,12,27,43

> B297 Elizabeth Banning
> B297a Delila Banning
> B298 William J. Banning
> B298a Levi W. Banning
> B299 Ann Banning
> B300 Alexander Banning

B87 JAMES BANNING born 1810-15 and married Martha Yountlae (Youthler ?) in
Shelby Co., Ill. She was born 1821. He died before a will was probated in March
1847. She married 2nd, Tillman A. Johnson on Aug. 5, 1847 in Shelby Co. Source:
12,27,43

B301 Melissa Banning

B88 ALEXANDER BANNING Jr. born Oct. 9, 1827 in N.C. He married 1st, Katherine
(???) and 2nd, Mary Jane Murray. He died on Oct. 16, 1874 in Shelby Co. and is
buried in Neil Cemetery, 1/2 mile North of Cowden, Ill. The 1860 census indicates
that his wife is Lucinda, born about 1834 in Ill. I may have a mix up between his
mother (B19) and his wife. Source: 6,27,43,79

> B302 Mary M. Banning
> B303 Melissa E. Banning
> B304 William S. Banning
> B305 Julian Banning

54

B306　Eliss Banning
B307　Sherman Banning
B308　Charles Newton Banning
B309　Sylvester Banning
B309a　Allen Banning

B88A　BANNING son born 1820-25 probably in N.C.　Source: 4,27

B88B　BANNING daughter born 1820-25 probably in N.C.　Source: 4.27

B89　JOHATHAN BIRD BANNING born July 15, 1834 in Shelby Co., Ill. He married
　　　1st Jane Davis on May 6, 1856 in Shelby Co. She was the daughter of W.H. and
　　　Mary (Johnson) Davis, born Sept. 21 (or 12), 1837 in Marion Co., Oh. Both of her
　　　parents were born in Del. Jonathan was farming in Shelby Co., in 1860. He and
　　　Jane moved to Webster Co., Mo. in 1871. They had 9 children, 4 of which were
　　　alive in 1900. She died May 17, 1919 in Marshfield, Mo. He married 2nd, Angelica
　　　(???). He was a farmer and died June 6 or 23, 1917 in Marshfield, Webster Co.,
　　　Mo. and is buried with his wife Jane. Source: 5,8,6,10,12,15,27,29,30,32,43,44,
　　　53,79,92

　　　　　　　　　B310　Maria Ella Banning
　　　　　　　　　B310a　Eva Dora Banning
　　　　　　　　　B311　Herman E. Banning
　　　　　　　　　B311a　Clara Banning
　　　　　　　　　B311b　Charley Banning

B89a　CLARK (M. ?) BANNING born about 1813 in Ky. See B83.　Source: 27

　　　　　　　　　B312　John Banning
　　　　　　　　　B312a　Mary A. Banning
　　　　　　　　　B312b　Wilson P. Banning
　　　　　　　　　B312c　Sarah J. Banning
　　　　　　　　　B312d　Harvey Banning
　　　　　　　　　B312e　Jeremiah Banning
　　　　　　　　　B312f　Nancy Banning
　　　　　　　　　B312g　Burrell Banning
　　　　　　　　　B312h　Lucy Banning

B90　MARY E. (MARGARET) BANNING born March 14, 1829 in Shelby Co., Ill. She
　　　married Harvey E. Thompson on July 29, 1849 in Shelby Co. The Shelby County
　　　Historical Soc. states that she was the 1st Banning born in the county. Source:
　　　12,27,43,44

　　　　　　　　　B313 for children

B90a　WILLIAM BANNING born about 1816 in Ky. and married Jane E. Rogers on April
　　　2, 1848 in Shelby Co. Ill. She was born about 1816 in Tn. He was farming in
　　　Shelby Co. in 1860. It is said he owned a mill on the Kaskaskia river, just east of
　　　Cowden in Shelby Co. Source: 5,6,12,27,43,79,89

　　　　　　　　　B314　Louisa Banning
　　　　　　　　　B314a　Nancy Melvira Banning
　　　　　　　　　B314b　William Jackson Banning
　　　　　　　　　B314c　James A. Banning
　　　　　　　　　B314d　Brooks Banning

B314e Dennis F. Banning
B314f Enos F. Banning
B314g Robert J. Banning

B91 RHODA (RHODY) BANNING born 1830-34 in Shelby Co., Ill. She was living with the Rogers family in Shelby Co. in 1850 and married John R. Askins on Dec. 21, 1854 in Shelby Co. Source: 5,12,27,43,44

B315 for children

B91a BANNING Daughter born 1820-25 in Ky. Probably married Mr. Atteberry. Source: 27,30,92

B91b BANNING Son born 1820-25 in Ky. Source: 27

B91c ANN E. BANNING born 1827 in Ky. and married James F. Rogers on March 16, 1848 in Shelby Co., Ill. Source: 12,27,43

B92 PHILADELPHIA BANNING born about 1833 and married James M. Bradley in McDowell Co. N.C. on Aug. 22, 1859. He was born about 1840. Source: 13,27,44

B316 Francis M. Bradley
B316a Nancy E. Bradley
B316b James H. Bradley
B317 Henry S. Bradley
B317a Prudence B. Bradley
B317b Ella M. Bradley

B93 JOSEPH BANNING born April 19, 1822 in Burke Co., N.C. He married Elizabeth Curtis on Dec. 25, 1845. She was born on Oct. 11, 1820 in Burke Co. She died on Aug. 12, 1886. He died July 14, 1888 in McDowell Co., N.C. They are buried in Bethlehem Cemetery near Old Fort, N.C. Source: 27,44

B318 Nancy Matilda Banning
B319 Thomas Clark Banning
B320 Mary Lucinda Banning
B321 James Henry Banning
B322 John C. Banning
B323 Rebecca Edolene Banning
B324 Joseph Ivy Banning

B94 ELIJAH BANNING born about 1832. Source: 27

B325 through B330 for children

B95 through B97 unknown children of B22

B98 through B103 for children of B24 and B25

B337 through B419 for children

B104 Child of B27

B105 JAMES HENRY BANNING born March 24, 1824 in Edgartown, Mass. He died May 15, 1828. Source: 1

B106 CHARLES L. BANNING born Oct. 28, 1825 in Edgartown, Mass. and died April 5, 1826. Source: 1

B107 ALEXANDER FRAZIER BANNING born Jan. 16, 1826 in Edgartown, Mass. He died unmarried March 6, 1845 in South Bend, Ind. Source: 1

B108 ELIZABETH GRIFFITH BANNING born July 22, 1830 or 1833 in Edgartown, Mass. She was living with her parents in St. Joseph Co. Ind. in 1850. She married Henry Gaylord in 1857 in Goshen, Ind. They lived in Summit Co., Ohio. She died March 26, 1907 in Stow, Ohio. They had no children. Source: 1,5

B109 JAMES HENRY BANNING born Dec. 9, 1843 in South Bend, Ind. He married Mary E. Hardman on June 6, 1872 in South Bend. They had 3 children and she died in 1878. He married 2nd, Charlotte L. Henshaw on June 23, 1880 in Summit Co., Ohio. They had no children. He was one of the founders of the South Bend Daily Tribune. They moved to Indianapolis in 1886 and in 1901 they moved to Cuyahoga Falls, Ohio. Source: 1,5,13,40

> B420 Katherine Woodward Banning
> B421 Frank Merchant Banning
> B422 Bessie Maxon Banning

B110 through B113 for unknown children of B29 through B31

> B423 through B516 for children

B114 HORATIO BANNING born about 1834 in Ohio Co., (West) Virginia. He and his parents moved to Henry Co., Iowa where he married Sarah J. ----? on Nov. 16, 1865. She was born about 1843 in Iowa. They lived in the New London Iowa area. He was a farmer. Source: 5, 6,7,8,63

> B517 Olive L. Banning
> B518 Maggie Elvira Banning
> B519 Ross E. Banning
> B520 Alice Banning
> B521 Ida Banning
> B522 Winnie Banning

B115 JOHN ANDERSON BANNING born Aug. 18, 1836 in Ohio Co. (West) Virginia. He lived in Denver, Col. Source: 1,5,6,40,63

> B523 through B529 for children

B116 WILLIAM HENRY BANNING born July 21, 1838 in Burlington, Iowa. In 1867 he moved to Union, Neb. Source: 1,5,6

> B530 through B534 for children

B117 JAMES EDGAR BANNING born Aug. 19, 1840 in Henry Co., Iowa. He married Anna Hurst June 19, 1865. She was born in June 1847 and died Nov. 20, 1874 in Otoe County, Neb. He lived in Mount Pleasant, Iowa where he went into business hauling freight to Neb. and Col. In 1870 he entered the milling business in Factor, Neb. and sold out in 1887. By 1880 he was married to Parthenia (Elkins ?), who was born 1844 in Miss. He then went into the elevator business in Nehawka, Neb.

which is where he died January 1, 1895. Source: 1,5,6,8,13,32,40,63

> B535 James Edward Banning
> B536 Emma Banning
> B537 Charles William Banning
> B538 Rhoda Banning
> B539 James Banning

B118 ABRAHAM SAMPSON BANNING born about 1848 in Iowa. Source: 1,5,6

> B540 through B544 for children

B118a SUSAN JAMI BANNING born 1846 in Iowa. She was living with her brother in Henry Co. Iowa in 1860. Source: 5,6

> B545 through B547 for children

B119 MARY E. BANNING born 1844 in Henry Co., Iowa and married a Mr. Bouler. She died shortly after her marriage at age 30. Source: 1,5,6,63

> B548 through B550 for children

B120 JANE BANNING died as an infant. Source: 1

B121 EMMA BANNING died as an infant. Source: 1

B121a HARRIETT A. BANNING born Aug. 1854 (1856?) in Henry County, Iowa. After the death of her mother, it appears moved to Colorado one of her older siblings. She married John McLennan Ross about 1876, probably in Colorado. He was born in Stanley Bridge, Prince Edward Island, Canada on June 3, 1844. "Jack" Ross went to Col. to mine for gold and silver in Russell Gulch near Central City. Harriett was about 4'11" tall and John was well over 6'. It is said that he spoke with a Scottish accent and died about 1920. "Hattie" married 2nd Lewis M. Hickox on Dec. 6, 1922 in Golden, Col. They had no children. Lewis was an excellent woodworker. He built a desk which is still in the family. Harriett died late about 1925. Source: 6,63

> B551 Ellen Gertrude Ross
> B551a Clara Bell Ross
> B552 John Banning Ross
> B552a Charles Stanley Ross
> B553 George McLennan Ross
> B553a Hattie Eliza Ross
> B553b Robert Anderson Ross

B122 MORGAN BANNING born about 1860 in Henry Co., Iowa. He was a half brother to the others. Source: 1,63

> B554 through B556 for children.

B123 through B128 unknown children of B33

B129 JOHN BANNING born 1830 in Marshall Co., W. Va. He married Eliza Bowman in 1848 and in 1849 they moved to Keokuk Co., Iowa near the town of Lancaster. They moved to Kansas in 1855 and returned to Iowa in 1860, where he died.

B557 Laura Banning

B130 ELIZABETH BANNING born 1836 (or Feb. 7, 1843) in Marshall Co., W. Va. She married Donald Franklin Aug. 23, 1860 in Marshall Co. where they lived until she died on April 24, 1899. He was born Nov. 18, 1835 and died May 23, 1908. Source: 1,49

B558 William Franklin
B559 Ira Banning Franklin
B560 Asa Franklin
B561 Margaret Franklin
B562 Emma Franklin
B563 John Franklin
B564 Clarence Franklin
B565 Edith Franklin
B566 James Franklin

B131 EPHRAIM BANNING born 1834 in Marshall Co.. W. Va. He married Ruth Reed in 1857 in Marshall Co. where they lived until 1871 when they moved to Wheeling. They had 7 children and she died in 1878 in Wheeling. In 1883 he moved to Custer Co., Neb. where he took up a homestead. He married 2nd, Mary Mack of N. Dakota in 1885. They had no children. He died April 12, 1901 in Lillian, Custer Co., Neb. He served 3 years during the Civil War with Co. H of the 11th Va. Reg. The 1890 census of veterans has him in Johnstown, Brown Co., Neb. Source: 1,9,13,40, 49,63

B567 Samantha Banning
B568 Maletha Banning
B569 Clark Banning
B570 Asa Ephraim Banning
B571 Elsie Banning
B572 Charlotte Banning
B573 Donald Banning

B132 CHARLOTTE BANNING born 1825 in Marshall Co. W. Va. She married Jasper (or Joseph) Jackson in 1848 in Marshall Co., where they lived. Source: 1,49

B574 Charlotte Jackson
B575 Theresa Jackson
B576 Ephraim Jackson
B577 Alonzo Jackson
B578 Orange Jackson
B579 Lee Jackson
B580 Oscar Jackson
B581 Samuel Jackson
B582 Vista Jackson

B133 WILLIAM FREDERICK BANNING born Jan. 6, 1837 in McDonough Co. , Ill. He never married. About 1860 he moved to the southwest, staying in Az., N.M. and southern Calif. where he had varied interest. He was listed as a farmer in Prescott, Az. in 1870. He was in the transportation business at the time of his death in 1902 in Tombstone, Az. He is buried on the San Pedro, where his brother, John, erected a monument at the grave site. Source: 1,2, 7,40

B134 JOHN BANNING born Feb. 15, 1838 (1839?) in McDonough Co., Ill. He moved to Kansas in 1855 with his parents, and married Hetty Jane Roberts of Shawnee Co., Kansas on Sept. 7, 1862. In 1869 they took up a homestead on the Sac & Fox Reservations in Osage Co. near Lyndon where they remained until his death. Source: 1,2,63

> B583 Josephine Theresa Banning
> B584 Ephraim Newton Banning
> B585 Mary Matilda Banning
> B586 Ella Bell Banning
> B587 John Wesley Banning
> B588 Hetty May Banning
> B589 William Burgess Banning
> B590 Thomas Hubert Banning

B135 JAMES HENRY BANNING born Oct. 3, 1840 in McDonough Co., Ill. where he died as an infant. Source: 1,2

B136 JOSEPH GILMER BANNING born March 8, 1843 in McDonough Co., Ill. He moved with his parents to Kansas in 1855 and on to Missouri in 1860. When Civil War broke out, he and his brother Pinkney enlisted in the "Home Guards" at Brookfield, Mo. where he was then living, and served until Sept. 19, 1864. At that point in the Civil War, he went into the l2th Mo. Vol. Cavalry and fought under Gen. Wilson. He went with the Reg. on the Indian Campaign in 1865-66. He mustered out April 9, 1866. He married Letitia Ann Miller on Nov. 3, 1870 in Linn Co., Mo. She was the daughter of Thomas and Margaret Miller and was born Oct. 21, 1850 in County Antrim, Ireland. Mr. Millar died in 1888 in Pittsburgh, Pa. Joseph was active in local matters and held offices of responsibility and influence. He died May 9, 1908 in Brookfield, Mo. Source: 1,2,6,13,63

> B591 Ephraim Pinkney Banning
> B592 Margaret Ellen Banning
> B593 Letitia Louise Banning
> B594 Thomas Gilmer Banning
> B595 Caroline Agnes Banning

B137 PINKNEY ASA BANNING born July 22, 1845 in McDonough Co, Ill. He enlisted in the "Home Guards" at Brookfield, Mo. with his brother. On Sept. 19, 1864 they joined the l2th Mo. Vol. Cavalry. Pinkney was wounded in a cavalry charge on Dec. 15, 1864 at the Battle of Nashville, Tenn. He died unmarried in the Army Hospital on Jan. 27, 1865. He is buried in the National Cemetery in Nashville. Source: 1,2,6

B138 ELIZABETH MARY BANNING born Jan. 31, 1847 in McDonough Co., Ill. and moved with her parents in 1855 to Douglas Co., Kansas and moved again in 1860 to Brookfield, Missouri. She married Charles H. Vertrees of Walnut Grove T/S, McDonough Co. on Sept. 15, 1881 in Brookfield, Mo. She died at her home in Harrisonville, Mo. on June 17, 1902. Source: 1,2,6,13,63

> B596 Edwin Alfred Vertrees
> B597 Ernest Vertrees

B139 EPHRAIM BANNING born July 21, 1849 near Bushnell, McDonough Co. , Ill. His parents moved to Douglas Co., Kansas in 1855 and then to Brookfield, Mo. in 1860. He went to Chicago in 1871 and joined the law firm of Rosenthal & Pence.

He married Lucretia Thalia Lindsley on Oct. 22, 1878 at the home of her uncle, William P. Pierson, in Onarga, Ill. She was the daughter of Myron B. Thales Lindsley (born June 14, 1818) and Caroline Lucertia Pierson and was born June 5, 1853 near LeRoy, N.Y. They had 3 children. She died in Chicago Feb. 5, 1887. He married 2nd, Emilie Bartlett Jenne of Elgin, Ill. on Sept. 5, 1889. No children were born to this marriage. She was the daughter of Otis Bartlett and Hannah Amelia (McClure) Jenne, and a descendant of John Jenney, who came to the U. S. July 1623 on the Ship "Little James" which landed at Plymouth, Mass. There was no issue from this marriage. He died in Chicago on Dec. 2, 1907, as the result of a streetcar accident. He was a prominent lawyer and well known philanthropist. About 1872 Ephraim and his brother, Thomas, formed the law firm of Banning & Banning. They specialized in patent & corporation law. Source: 1,2,6,24,63

> B598 Pierson Worrall Banning
> B599 Walker Banning
> B600 Ephraim Banning

B140 THOMAS ALLEN BANNING born Jan. 16, 1851 in McDonough Co., Ill. The family moved in 1855 to Kansas and then Missouri. He followed his brother to Chicago in 1872, and there he married Sarah Jane Hubbard on Dec. 21, 1875 in Highland, Ks. She was born in Bowling Green, Ky. on July 23, 1854. He was a partner with his brother Ephraim in the Chicago law firm of Banning & Banning until his death. They were both patent attorneys of some note. Source: 1,2,6

> B601 Samuel Walker Banning
> B602 Edith Banning
> B603 Helen Ruth Banning
> B604 Thomas Allen Banning
> B605 Sarah Louise Banning
> B606 Dorothea Esther Banning

B141 CYRUS WALKER BANNING born Jan. 4, 1853 in McDonough Co., Ill. He married Nancy Ellen Miller on April 18, 1878 in Wayne Co., Iowa. She was the daughter of Thomas J. and Almira (Patterson) Miller and was born Jan. 31, 1861, in Wayne Co., Iowa. They lived in Seymour, Iowa until 1911, when they moved to Milford, Utah. He was a Physician. Source: 1,2,6

> B607 Bertha Lucille Banning
> B608 Jennie Malvern Banning
> B609 Thomas Ephraim Banning
> B610 Alma Louise Banning
> B611 Cyrus Walker Banning
> B612 Hubert Charles Banning
> B613 Wayne Elson Banning

B142 HUBERT ASHLEY BANNING born June 7, 1855 in Douglas Co., Kansas. He is said to be the first child born in Kansas after its organization as a free territory. The family moved to Missouri in 1960. He married Viola H. Suydam on Nov. 23, 1881 in New York City. He was an attorney and died in New York Jan. 3, 1916. Source: 1,2,6,63

> B614 Hubert Temple Banning

B143 CYNTHIA ELLEN BANNING born March 6, 1858 in Douglas Co., Kansas and moved with her parents to Missouri in 1860. She married Hiram Almanson Smith of

Chicago, Ill. on Nov. 16, 1882. She died in Chicago June 24, 1902. Source: 1,2,6,63

B615 Cynthia Ellen Smith
B616 Alice Marion Smith
B617 Helen Almanson Smith

B144 MARTHA BELL BANNING born June 12, 1860 in Pettis Co., Mo., near Georgetown. Her parents moved to Brookfield, Mo. in 1862. She married George Augustus Lawton on Sept. 6, 1887 in Chicago. He was the son of George Augustus (born 1829) and Sophia Pauline (Mitchell) Lawton of Green Bay, Wisc., born Jan. 6, 1862. He died in Daphne, Alabama on Aug. 17, 1915. Source: 1,2,63

B618 Sophia Louise Lawton
B619 Helen Margaret Lawton
B620 Grace Lawton
B621 & B622 twin Boys
B623 George Augustus Lawton
B624 William Ephraim Lawton
B625 Walter Banning Lawton
B626 Ruth Lawton

B145 through B149 unknown children of B44 through B47.

B627 through B657 for children

B150 SALLY BANNING born Nov. 18, 1815 in Cumberland Co., Ky. She married Mr. Fisher Rice. Source: 1

B658 through B663 for children

B151 JAMES BANNING born May 12, 1818 in Cumberland Co., Ky. He married Margaret (Margarita) Hammett Sept. 30, 1838 in Randolph Co., Mo. They were living in Macon Co. Mo. where he is listed as a farmer in 1850. He died in 1907 in Kansas. Source: 1,4,5,12,13,40

B664 James Banning
B665 Gardiner Banning
B666 Alonzo Banning
B666a Mary C. Banning
B667 Rebecca Banning
B668 Catherine Banning
B669 Cornelia Banning

B152 NANCY BANNING born Aug. 12, 1820 in Macon Co., MO. She married William B. Powell on Dec. 31, 1843 in College Mound, Macon Co., Mo. She died Jan. 24, 1892 in Macon Co., Mo. Source: 1,13

B670 Peter Powell
B671 Thomas Powell
B672 Baswell Powell
B673 Louise Powell
B674 James Powell
B675 John Powell

B153 CATHERINE BANNING born Aug. 7, 1823 in Wayne Co., Ky. She married
   Smith Gipson on April 18, 1839 (or April 5, 1838) in Macon Co., Mo. They lived and
   she died in Macon City, Mo. on July 10, 1908. Source: 1,12

> B676 Margaret Gipson
> B677 Grace Gipson
> B678 Mary Gipson
> B679 Sarah Gipson
> B680 Melissa Gipson
> B681 Martha Gipson
> B682 Nannie Gipson
> B683 Stephen Gipson
> B684 James Gipson
> B685 Thomas Gipson
> B686 Binda Gipson
> B687 Elijah Gipson
> B688 Louisa Gipson
> B689 ? infant Gipson
> B690 D. B. Gipson
> B691 William Gipson
> B692 Susie Gipson
> B693 Grant Gipson
> B694 Smith Gipson

B154 BETSY JANE BANNING born Aug 19, 1827 in Cumberland Co., Ky. She married
   Joseph Singleton. They lived in Macon Co., Mo and had 2 children. Source: 1

> B695 & B696 for children

B155 MATILDA BANNING born Nov. 16, 1831 in Mo. She was the first white child
   born in Macon Co. She married George Green and died March 31, 1862. Source:
   1,5

> B697 Matilda Green

B156 THOMAS FRANKLIN BANNING born Sept. 15, 1834 in Macon Co., Mo. He
   married Christina Green on July 24, 1855 in Macon Co. They lived at College
   Mound, Mo. Source: 1,5,40

> B698 Mary Lowry Banning
> B699 William Tolman Banning
> B700 Susie Banning
> B701 George Banning

B157 through B162 for unknown Scrogins children (B49)

B163 NANCY BANNING born 1829 in Ill. Source: 5

> B702 through B705 for children

B164 CATHERINE BANNING born 1831 in Ill. Source: 5

> B706 through B709 for children

B165 through B168 for unknown children of B51

B710 through B729

B169 WILLIAM BANNING born about 1834. Source: 87

B730 through B735 for children

B170 JANE BANNING born about 1838. Source: 87

B736 through B740 for children

B171 ALEXANDER (ELEXANDER) BANNING born about 1841. Source: 87

B741 through B746 for children

B172 LOUIS P. BANNING born Dec. 1845 in Missouri and married Sarah Ann
Elizabeth Rogers on Feb. 25, 1872 in Chariton Co., Mo. She was the daughter of
Joshua and Lydia (Rickey) Rogers, born May 2, 1856 in Indiana. He died Nov. 15,
1903 and is buried in the Elmwood Cemetery in Marceline, Mo. She died June 17,
1946 in Excelsior Springs, Clay Co., Mo. Source: 87

> B747 Zara Jackson Banning
> B748 Dora Banning
> B749 Adelia E. Banning
> B750 John Richard Banning
> B751 Louis Edward Banning
> B752 William Chrisley Banning

B173 LaSATT BANNING born about 1849. Source: 87

B753 through B757 for children

B174 for children of B52

B758 through B762 for children

B175 PLEASENT WILSON BANNING born April 13, 1824 in Cumberland Co., Ky. He
married lst, Rebecca Terrill on Dec. 27, 1849. She was born 1830 in Ky. The 1850
census has them living in Chariton Co., Mo. where he was a farmer. She died May
8, 1859. The 1860 census has P.W. and his children living with his parents in Linn
Co. He was an Ass't Marshall and helped take the census. He married 2nd, Harriet
C. Hubbard on Nov. 27, 1862 in Linn Co., Mo. He died Sept. 18, 1870. P.W. and
Rebecca are buried in the "Banning Cemetery" in Brookfield township, Linn County,
Mo. located in the NE1/4 of Sect. 31, T58, R19. Source: 1,5,6,13,15, 40,87

> B763 Laura Amner Banning
> B764 William Alonzo Banning
> B765 Maria Luella Banning
> B766 Samuel Terrill Banning
> B767 Rebecca Jane Banning
> B767a Rhoda Banning
> B767b Moses Banning
> B768 Cora Bell Banning

B176 ANNIE BANNING born Nov. 5, 1826 in Green Co., Ill. (or Ky.) She was living with her parents in Linn Co. Mo. in 1860. She died unmarried on April 25, 1905 in Brookfield, Mo. She is buried in the "Banning Cemetery" in Brookfield township, Linn County, Mo. located in the NE1/4 of Sect. 31, T58, R19. Source: 1,5,6,15,87

B177 WILLIAMSON BANNING born May 18, 1829 in Ill. and married Agnes Terrill on Sept. 15, 1857 in Howard Co. Mo. She was born about 1834 in Ky. The 1860 census has them in Linn Co. Mo. where he was a farmer with land valued at $3240. He died in Randolph Co., Mo. on Feb, 21, 1878. Source: 1,5,6,40

        B769 Milton H. Banning
        B770 Bodie Banning
        B771 John Banning
        B772 Susan Andrew Banning
        B773 Elizabeth Banning
        B774 Annie Banning
        B775 Williamson Banning
        B776 Thomas Pleasant Banning
        B777 Charles Clark Banning
        B778 Martha Jane Banning
        B779 Susan Agnes Banning

BI78 ANDREW BANNING born June 5, 1832 in Green Co., Ill. He married his cousin, Melissa Viola Banning (B184) on March 6, 1855 in college Mound, Mo. They were living in Linn Co. Mo., next to his parents, in 1860. He was a farmer with land valued at $1200. They lived in Brookfield, Mo. where he died on July 29, 1888. Andrew is buried in the "Banning Cemetery" in Brookfield township, Linn County, Mo. located in the NE1/4 of Sect. 31, T58, R19. Source: 1,5,6,15,40,87

        B780 Eugene Banning
        B781 Clark Banning
        B782 Fay Banning

B179 JAMES HENRY BANNING born Aug. 5, 1835 in Mo. He was living with his parents in Linn Co. Mo. in 1860. He died, unmarried, on July 5, 1865, and is buried in the "Banning Cemetery" in Brookfield township, Linn County, Mo. located in the NE1/4 of Sect. 31, T58, R19. Source: 1,5,6,15,87

B180 CATHERINE BANNING born Aug. 2, 1838 in Mo. She was living with her parents in 1860 in Linn Co. Mo. She married Madison Lee Smith on April 28, 1864 in Linn Co., Mo. and died on Nov. 11, 1887 and is buried in the "Banning Cemetery" in Brookfield township, Linn County, Mo. located in the NE1/4 of Sect. 31, T58, R19. Source: 1,5,6,13,15,87

        B783 Flora June Smith
        B784 Anna Nellie Smith
        B785 Allen Lee Smith
        B786 Mary Amner Smith

B180a PLEASANT SNOW BANNING born 1840 in Mo. Source: 5,6

B181 MISSOURI A. BANNING born 1835 in Mo. (1850 census indicates she was born 1832 in Ill.) She married Joseph Wirts. They had one child and lived in Iowa. Source: 1,5

B182 JAMES FRANKLIN BANNING born 1836 in Macon Co., Mo. (1850 Census indicates he was born 1834) He married and moved to Monrovia, Calif. They had no children and he died in Jan. 1906. Source: 1,5

B183 THOMAS JASPER BANNING born 1838 in Macon Co., Mo. and married Pauline Williams. They lived in Salisbury, Mo. where he was a Physician. The 1860 census has him living with his brother (B178) in Linn Co. Mo and indicates he is a Physician. Source: 1,5,6,40

B788 Mary Banning

B184 MELISSA VIOLA BANNING born April 12, 1837 in Macon Co., Mo. She married her cousin. See B178. Source: 1,5,6

B185 JOHN BANNING born 1842 in Macon Co., Mo. and married Mary Bradley. They had no children and he died in Jan. 1907 in Carson City, Nevada. He served with the Confederates States of America in the Civil War. Source: 1,5,6

B186 MARTHA C. "MATTIE" BANNING born about 1849 in Mo. She married Joseph Combs and had 3 children. Source: 1,5,6

B789 through B791 for children

B187 through B192 for unknown children of B55

B193 VIANAH R. BANNING born Sept. 10, 1830 in Mo. and married Joseph Miller. He was born July 26, 1816 and died April 19, 1885. She died in Gainesville, Cooke Co., Tx Oct. 31, 1900. Both are buried in Gainesville Cemetery. Source: 7,8,67

> B792 Mary E. Miller
> B792A Elizabeth J. Miller
> B793 James R. Miller

B194 CATHERINE ELLEN BANNING born about 1832 in Mo. and married John C. Oxford on July 12, 1855 in Gainesville, Cooke Co. Tx. He was born in Mo. about 1833. Source: 6,7,8,10,67

> B794 Mary Will Oxford
> B794A Emily Jane Oxford
> B795 William Jerry Oxford
> B795A M.L. Oxford
> B796 Jessie C. Oxford
> B796A James Richard Oxford
> B797 John W. Oxford
> B797A Joseph Henry Oxford
> B798 Margaretta E. Oxford

B195 SAMUEL C. BANNING born about 1834 in Mo. Source: 6,67

B799 through B802 for children

B196 WILLIAM W. BANNING born about 1847. Source: 6,67

B803 through B806 for children

B197 JANCY V. BANNING born about 1852 in Mo. and married W. Ben F.
Benningfield on Jan. 28, 1868 in Gainesville, Cooke Co., Tx. He was born about
1844. After his death, some time after 1878, she married 2nd, F. W. Woody on
Aug. 11, 1883 in Gainesville. Source: 7,8,67

> B807 James C. Benningfield
> B808 Charles H. Benningfield

B198 JEREMIAH DALLAS BANNING born about 1853 in Texas and married N.A.
Nicholes on Oct. 12, 1878 in Gainesville, Cooke Co., Tx. Source: 6,7,67

> B809 through B812 for children

B199 ELIZABETH BANNING born 1835 in Ill. Source: 5,27

> B813 through B816 for children

B200 JULIA BANNING born 1836 in Ill. Source: 5,27

> B817 through B820 for children

B201 JOHN BANNING born 1838 in Ill. Source: 5,27

> B821 through B824 for children

B202 CLARK BANNING born 1840 in Ill. Source: 5,27

> B825 through B828 for children

B203 JAMES BANNING born 1842 in Ill. Source: 5,27

> B829 through B832 for children

B204 ANDREW BANNING born 1844 in Ill. Source: 5,27

> B833 through B836 for children

B205 JOEL BANNING born 1846 in Ill. Source: 5,27

> B837 through B840 for children

B206 MARY ANN BANNING born Aug. 1850 in Ill. and married Benjamin Franklin
Smith. She died May 6, 1877. Source: 5,27,59

> B841 through B844 for children

B207 JULIA EDNA JOHNSON married Henry Clinton DeShasier on Dec. 21, 1881 in
Carrolton, Greene Co. Ill. Source: 27

B208 through B212 for unknown children of B58 & B59

B213 ELIZABETH ANN BANNING born 1843 in Greene Co. Ill. Source: 5,27

B845 through B849 for children

B214 FRANCIS M. BANNING born 1845 in Green Co. Ill. Source: 5,27

B850 through B854 for children

B215 JOHN C. BANNING born July 17, 1830 in N.C. Source: 5,16,27,91

B855 through B859 for children

B216 ELIZABETH ANN BANNING born May 3, 1833 in N.C. She died Aug. 3, 1928.
Source: 5,16,27,91

B860 through B864 for children

B217 FRAZIER AZBURY BANNING born Nov. 10, 1835 in N.C. (See B235a)
Source: 5,16,27,91

B865 through B869 for children

B217a WILLIAM W. BANNING born July 8, 1836. Source: 16,91

B218 JAMES D. BANNING born 1839 in Tenn. He died prior to June 28, 1862.
Source: 5,27

B870 through B874 for children

B219 MARGARET J. BANNING born Dec. 9, 1840 in Ga. and married William J. Cook
on Feb. 24, 1861 in Shelby Co. Ill. Source: 5,13,16,27,43,91

B875 through B879 for children

B220 MARTHA LOUISA BANNING born May 2, 1843 in Ga. She married Reuben
Scoles on Oct. 12, 1871 in Shelby Co, Ill. She died May 2, 1931. Source: 5,12,
16,27,43,91

> B880 Melvin Scoles
> B881 John William Scoles
> B882 Charles Wesley Scoles
> B883 Reuben Ezra Scoles
> B884 Martha Evaline Scoles

B221 THOMAS M. BANNING born July 28, 1845 in Tenn. and married Adeline F.
(Spracklin) Banning, the widow of Clark Banning (B227). Thomas died Jan. 20,
1920. Source: 5,6,16,12,27,43,91

B885 through B889 for children

B222 BENJAMIN B. BANNING born July 7, 1850 in Ill. He died in April, 1912.
Source: 6,16,27,91

B890 through B894 for children

B223 WILLIAM BIRD BANNING born about 1834 in Shelby Co. Ill. He married 1st,

Harriet Hayward (Davis?) on Dec. 20, 1860 (?) in Shelby Co.   Source: 5,6,12,27,43

B895 through B899 for children

B224 ELIZABETH ANN BANNING born about 1837 in Ill. She married Josiah Martin on Nov. 27, 1856 in Shelby Co. Ill.   Source: 5,6,12,27,43

B900 and B901 for children

B225 JOSEPH T. BANNING born Aug. 14, 1837 in Ill. and married Mary E. Herrington on May 30, 1857 in Shelby Co. Ill. He married 2nd, Charlotte Ellen Herrington on July 18, 1867 in Shelby Co., Ill. He died Feb. 15, 1911. (He may have been counted twice in the 1860 census.)   Source: 5,6,12,27,43

B902 through B906 for children

B226 DOLPHUS BANNING born about 1839 in Ill.   Source: 5,6,27

B907 through B911 for children

B227 CLARK BANNING born about 1844 in Ill.   Source: 5,6,27

B912 through B916 for children

B227a JANE BANNING born about 1846 in Ill.   Source: 5,6,27

B917 and B918 for children

B228 DAVID BANNING born about 1856 in Ill.   Source: 6,27

B919 through B923 for children

B229 BARBARA BANNING born about 1858 in Ill.   Source: 6,27

B924 through B926 for children

B230 ROBERT BANNING born 1854 in Shelby Co. Ill.   Source: 6,27

B927 through B929 for children

B231 MARTHA JANE BANNING born Nov. 12, 1855 in Shelby Co., Ill. and married Jessie Severe Dec. 28, 1872 in Shelby Co. He was the son of Gilman and Arene (Breece) Severe, born March 11, 1854 in Shelby Co., Ill. He died March 9, 1932 in Shelby Co. She died May 24, 1940 in Shelby Co. Source: 6,12,13,27,43

B930 George Severe
B930a Charles Severe
B930b Marry A. Severe
B931 Ottie Filena Severe
B931a Cordia May Severe
B931b Cenia Josephine Severe
B932 Ollie Grace Severe
B932a Vernon Severe

B232 THOMAS BANNING born about 1858 in Shelby Co. Ill.   Source: 6,27

B933 through B935 for children

B233 JAMES R. BANNING born about 1863 in Shelby Co., Ill. Source: 27

B936 through B938 for children

B233A LORENZO B. A. BANNING born Aug. 8, 1838 in Ill. He was living with his parents in Polk Co., Mo. in 1860 (Barnny) where he was listed as a wagon maker. He married Nancy Jane Thomas on March 28, 1861 in Shelby Co., Ill. (The family bible indicates marriage on March 28, 1860.) She was born Nov 13, 1844 in Ill., and died March 5, 1908. They were living in Benton Township, Polk Co., Mo. in 1870 & 1880, where he was listed as a farmer. By 1900 they were living in Independence Co., Ark. Lorenzo died there in Nov. 1917, and is buried in Anderson, Izard Co., Ark. Source: 6,7,8,10,12,18,43,75,79

> B939 Mary Malisse Banning
> B939a James F. Banning
> B940 William R. Banning
> B940a Caroline M. Banning
> B940b Cynthia Ann Banning
> B940c Sarah Ellen Banning
> B941 John Benjamin Banning
> B941a Martha M. Banning
> B942 Andrew Lorenzo Banning
> B942a Infant Son
> B942b Nancy J. Banning
> B943 Charlie Weaver Banning
> B943a Juda Elizabeth Banning
> B943b Jemima Florence Banning

B234 DOLPHUS BANNING born about 1840 in Ill. He was living with his parents in Benton Township, Polk Co., Mo. in 1860, under the last name of Banny. Source: 6,27,79

B944 through B947 for children

B235 SOLOMON BANNING born about 1841 in Tenn. He may have been a Step-Son to his father. He was living with his parents (Barnny) in Benton Township, Polk Co., Mo. in 1860, where his last name is listed as Rimes. Source: 5,6,27,79

B948 through B951 for children

B235a FRAZIER BANNING (?) born about 1840 in Ill. He may have been a Step-Son to his father. He was living with his parents (Barnny) in Benton Township, Polk Co., Mo. in 1860. He married 1st, Mary Ann Johnson in 1858 in Ill. (I think she died in 1862.) He married 2nd, Nancy Reves on Nov. 30, 1865 in Polk Co. Mo. Source: 6, 7,12,13,43,75,79

> B952 Nancy Banning
> B953 Sarah J. Banning

B236 JACOB BANNING born about 1842 in Ill. and married Delilah F. Davison on Nov. 5, 1869 in Polk Co. Mo. Source: 5,12,13,27,75,79

B954 through B957 for children

B237 FRANKLIN BANNING born June 1850 in Ill. Source: 5,27

B958 through B961 for children

B237a WILLIS BANNING born about 1855 in Ill. He was living with his parents
(Barnny) in Benton Township, Polk Co., Mo. in 1860 and 1870. He married Tempie
J. Neel on July 16, 1891 in Izard Co. Ark, where they were living in 1900. Source:
6,7,10,75,79

B962 Minnie A. Banning
B962a Sarah N. Banning
B963 Willis F. Banning
B963a Byrd A. Banning
B963b Dola E. Banning
B964 Francis R. Banning
B964a Ida L. Banning
B964b Martha M. Banning

B237b MALENDA BANNING born about 1857 in Ill. She was living with her parents
(Barnny) in Benton Township, Polk Co., Mo. in 1860, 70 and 80. Source: 6,7,8,79

B965 for children

B237c ELIZABETH BANNING born 1860 in Mo. She was living with her parents
(Barnny) in Benton Township, Polk Co., Mo. in 1860, 70 and 80. Source: 6,7,8,79

B966 for children

B237d JOHN C. BANNING born about 1862 in Mo. He was living with his parents in
Benton Township, Polk Co., Mo. in 1870 and 1880. By 1900 he is living in Izard Co.
Ark. with his wife, Dora A. who was born about 1864. Source: 7,8,10,79

B967 Albert E. Banning
B967a Lena L. Banning

B238 CLARK BANNING born July 1850 in Shelby Co. Ill. Source: 5,6,27

B968 through B970 for children

B239 MARTHA BANNING born about 1854 in Shelby Co. Ill. and married George
Compton. Source: 6,27

B971 through B972 for children

B240 ANNIE BANNING born about 1857 in Shelby Co. Ill. Source: 6,27

B973 through B974 for children

B241 WILLIAM F. BANNING born Dec. 26, 1858 in Shelby Co. Ill. and married
Margaret E. Carr. He died Nov. 27, 1941 in Shelby Co. and is buried in Neal
Cemetery. Source: 6,27

B975 through B979 for children

B242 CATHERINE ISABELLA (Kate) BANNING born April 26, 1862 in Droppoint Twp. Shelby Co. Ill. and married Wells Tallman on Nov. 21, 1880 in Shelby Co. He was the son of Benjamin Franklin Tallman (1804-1877) and Nancy C. Tallman ((his Cousin) 1824-1877), born Feb. 22, 1858. Source: 27,33

> B980 Stella Cecil Tallman
> B981 Carl Benjamin Tallman
> B982 Edith Ora Tallman
> B983 Lora Estella Tallman
> B984 Ernest Wells Tallman

B243 JOHN FRANKLIN BANNING born Dec. 21, 1865 in Shelby Co., Ill and married Clara Mae Oller. She was born Sept. 18, 1866 and was the daughter of Henry J and Martha E. Himes Oller. She died of Pneumonia while pregnant on March 30, 1908. He died Dec. 22, 1930 in Shelby Co. Both are buried in Neal Cemetery near Cowden, Ill. Source: 16,27,92

> B985 Henry Banning
> B985a Frank "Copie" Banning
> B985b Carl Banning
> B986 William "Bill" Banning
> B986a Annie Mae Banning
> B986b Infant Son

B244 through B257 for children of B73 through B76

B258 WILLIAM HICKS BANNING born 1853. Source: 44,46

> B987 and B988 for children

B259 MARY D. BANNING born 1858 and married Thomas Clark Allison. Source: 44,46

> B989 Oliver Allison
> B290 Asher Allison
> B990a Oscar Allison

B260 JAMES MARCUS BANNING born March 2, 1861 and married Nancy Jane Simpson. He died Jan. 13, 1926. Source: 44,46

> B991 Thomas D. Banning
> B991a James Virgil Banning
> B991b Dovie A. Banning
> B992 Sophie E. Banning
> B992a Mary E. Banning
> B992b Loree J. Banning

B261 MARTHA J. BANNING born 1863 and married Matthew Townsend. Source: 44,46

> B993 Jessie H. Townsend
> B994 for children

B262 MAHILA BANNING born 1867. Source: 44,46

B995 and B996 for children

B263 DAVID JASPER BANNING born 1870 and married Lillie Cox. She was born 1882 and died in 1972. He died in 1954 and both are buried in Boylston Church Cemetery. Source: 44,46

B997 Exa Banning
B997a Edith banning
B997b Jones Banning
B997c Ralph Banning
B997d Owen Banning
B998 Mary Banning
B998a Alma Banning
B998b Ina Banning
B998c Annie Lou Banning

B264 ALEXANDER TURNER ALLISON born 1840. Source: 44,46

B265 ELLEN ALLISON born 1842. Source: 44,46

B266 JAMES ALLISON born 1845. Source: 44,46

B267 THOMAS ALLISON born 1849. Source: 44,46

B268 JEMIMA ALLISON born 1851. Source: 44,46

B269 RICHARD ISAAC ALLISON born 1856 in Old Fort, McDowell Co., N.C. and married Sarah Banning, B280. Source: 44,46

B270 BENJAMIN ALLISON born 1857. Source: 44,46

B271 For children of B78

B999 and B1000 for children

B272 ALICE BANNING born Dec. 6, 1866 and married Benjamin Logan Whitaker on Dec. 13, 1885. She died Sept. 29, 1892. Source: 44,46,97

B1001 Maude Whitaker
B101A Ethel Whitaker
B1002 Myrtle Whitaker

B272a UNKNOWN BANNING SON. Born 186? And was a deaf-mute. Source: 97

B273 JULIA BANNING born 1877. Source: 44,46,97

B1003 and B1004 for children

B274 NANCY BANNING born 1879. Source: 44,46,97

B1005 and B1006 for children

B275 ELVIRA (ALVIRA ?) BANNING born Nov. 26, 1847 and married Taylor Williams on Feb. 20, 1867. He had a tannery in Henderson Co., N.C. She died in Aug. 1889 and he married 2nd, Elizabeth M. (Johnson) Banning, B278, in June 1893. Source: 44,46

B1007 Ella Williams
B1008 James Williams
B1009 T.C. Williams

B276 JOSEPH R. BANNING born May 4, 1849. He never married and died in Aug. 1889. Source: 44,46

B277 SOPHIA EMMA BANNING born Sept. 26, 1850 and married Benjamin Swayingame on March 30, 1876. Source: 44,46

B1010 Edgebert Swayingame
B1011 Earl Swayingame

B278 JOHN SULLINS BANNING born Nov. 16, 1852 and married Elizabeth M. Johnson on Nov. 20, 1879. He died July 24, 1889 and she married 2nd, Taylor Williams, (B275). Source: 44,46

B1012 and B1013 for children

B279 JAMES BANNING born Nov. 8, 1854 and married Julia A. Gallamore. She was the daughter of John Alexander and Mary Mintz Gallamore. He died Dec, 12, 1925 and she followed July 23, 1949. Source: 44,46

B1014 Rebecca Pearl Banning
B1014a Mary Josephine Banning
B1014b Rose Edna Banning
B1015 James Alexander Banning

B280 SARAH REBECCA BANNING born March 8, 1857 and married Richard Isaac Allison (B269). They moved to Henderson Co. then on to Transylvania Co., N.C. where he died. She died Jan. 20, 1940. Source: 44,46

B1016 for children

B281 RICHARD BANNING born 1844. Source: 44,46

B1017 and B1018 for children

B282 VICTORIA BANNING born 1847. Source: 44,46

B1019 for children

B283 MALINDA BANNING born 1849. Source: 44,46

B1020 for children

B284 through B287 for children of B82

B288 JOSEPH BANNING born 1832 and died March 11, 1854 in Ill. during the probate of his father's estate. Source: 5,16,43

B1021 through B1024 for children

B289 ELIZABETH BANNING born June 26, 1834 in Shelby Co., Ill. She married
Griffin Tipsword on Nov. 23, 1853 in Shelby Co. He was the son of John Tipsword
(1805-1870) and Frances Carlyle (1805-?), born Aug 30, 1831 in Shelby Co. She
died Sept. 23, 1926 in St. Louis Mo. He was a farmer, died March 19, 1913 in
Philips Co., Mo. and is buried in Goodall Cemetery in Newburg, Mo.   Source: 12,
16, 27,43

        B1025 Sarah Anne Tipsword
        B1026 John J. Tipsword
        B1027 Mary Hester Josie Tipsword
        B1028 James Merida Tipsword
        B1029 Juresin Frances Tipsword
        B1030 Isaac VanLandingham Tipsword
        B1031 Christopher C. Tipsword
        B1032 Joseph C. Tipsword
        B1033 Minda Tipsword
        B1034 Walter Tipsword

B290 HENRY BANNING born 1835. Source: 5,16,43

        B1035 through B1039 for children

B291 ALEXANDER BANNING born 1837. Source: 5,16,43

        B1040 through B1044 for children

B292 and B293 unused

B294 ELIAS BANNING born 1835-40 Source: 27

        B1045 through B1049 for children

B295 EMELING BANNING born 1835-41 Source: 27

        B1050 through B1054 for children

B296 ANN BANNING born 1835-41 Source: 27

        B1055 through B1059 for children

B297 ELIZABETH BANNING born about 1841 in Ill. She is the twin to B297a. She
married Michael Cockenower (Cokenower ?) on Sept. 15, 1859 in Shelby Co. Ill.
Source: 5,12,27,43

        B1060 through B1062 for children

B297A DELILA BANNING born 1841 in Ill. She is the twin to B297. She married
Joseph Smith Jr. on Jan. 3, 1861 in Shelby Co. Ill. Source: 5,12,27,43

        B1063 through B1065 for children

B298 WILLIAM J. BANNING born 1843 in Ill. and married Pamela A. Spracklin on
June 20, 1866 in Shelby Co. Ill. Source: 5,12,27,43

B1066 through B1069 for children

B298a LEVI W. BANNING born 1845 in Ill.   Source: 5,27

B1070 through B1073 for children

B299 ANN BANNING born 1849 in Ill. She is the twin to B300.   Source: 5,27

B1074 through B1077 for children

B300 ALEXANDER BANNING born 1849 in Ill. He is the twin to B299.   Source: 5,27

B1078 through B1081 for children

B301 MELISSA BANNING born about 1847 in Shelby Co. Ill. Source: 27

B1082 through B1087 for children

B302 MARY M. BANNING born about 1851 in Ill. Source: 6,27

B1088 through B1093 for children

B303 MELISSA E. BANNING born 1855 in Ill. Source: 6,27

B1094 through B1099 for children

B304 WILLIAM S. BANNING born 1856 in Ill. Source: 6,27

B1100 through B1104 for children

B305 JULIAN BANNING born March 31, 1857 in Ill. and died Sept. 25, 1904. Source:
6,27

B1105 through B1109 for children

B306 ELISS BANNING born Feb. 21, 1863 and died Oct. 27, 1930. Source: 27

B1110 through B1114 for children

B307 SHERMAN BANNING born 1864 and died 1922. Source: 27

B1115 through B1119 for children

B308 CHARLES NEWTON BANNING born Dec. 24, 1869 and married Arwilda Oller.
He died in 1943. Source: 27

B1120 through B1124 for children

B309 SYLVESTER BANNING no information Source: 27

B1125 through B1129

B309a ALLEN BANNING no information Source: 27

B1130 through B1134 for children

B310 MARIA ELLA BANNING born 1858-59 in Shelby Co., Ill. and married Greenville F. Nichols on Sept. 4, 1879 in Shelby Co. He was the son of Levi D. and Lena Ann (Waggoner) Nichols, born 1854 in Shelby Co., Ill. She married 2nd, Stephen Douglas Nichols, the brother of Greenville. She died July 22, 1937 in Herrick, Ill. Source: 6,12,27,29,32,44,53

> B1135 Herman E. Nichols
> B1136 Clara B. Nichols
> B1137 Evelyn Nichols
> B1138 Lewis Ellsworth Nichols
> B1139 Robert E. Nichols

B310a EVA DORA BANNING born Aug. 18, 1857 in Shelby Co. Ill. (or Ohio) and married Andrew N. Burke Haynes (Haymes) on Dec. 28, 1876 in Mo. He was born in Marshfield, Mo. on Feb. 26, 1858 and died in Springfield, Mo., April 24, 1933. Eva died June 13, 1927 in Marshfield, Webster Co., Mo. Source: 6,10,27,29,32, 53,63

> B1140 Albert Howard Haymes
> B1141 William E. Haymes
> B1142 Ethel D. Haymes
> B1143 John Clarence Haymes

B311 HERMAN E. BANNING born May 4, 1873 in Mo. and married Cora A. Preston in 1899. She was born in Oct. 1875 and died before 1949. He died Sept. 16, 1949 in Marshfield, Webster Co., Mo. Source: 8,10,12,16,27,29,53

> B1144 Leda (Leoa?) Banning
> B1145 Merrill Banning
> B1146 Jewel Banning
> B1147 John Banning

B311a CLARA BANNING born in 1862 in Ill. Source: 8,53

B311b CHARLEY BANNING born in 1878 in Mo. Source: 8,53

B312 JOHN BANNING born about 1841 in Ill. Source: 27

B1148 through B1151 for children

B312a MARY A. BANNING born about 1846 in Ill. Source: 27

B1152 through B1155 for children

B312b WILSON P. BANNING born about 1848 in Ill. Source: 27

B1156 through B1159 for children

B312c SARAH J. BANNING born about 1850 in Ill. and married Michael Whiteside on April 8, 1875 in Shelby Co., Ill. Source: 12,27,43

B1160 through B1163 for children

B312d HARVY BANNING born about 1852 in Ill. Source: 27

B1164 through B1167 for children

B312e JEREMIAH BANNING born about 1854 in Ill. Source: 27

B1168 through B1171 for children

B312f NANCY BANNING born about 1856 in Ill. Source: 27

B1172 through B1175 for children

B312g BURRELL BANNING born about 1858 in Ill. Source: 27

B1176 through B1179 for children

B312h LUCY BANNING born about 1860 in Ill. Source: 27

B1180 through B1183 for children

B313 for children of B90

B1184 through B1187 for children

B314 LOUISA BANNING born about 1836 in Ill. and married a Mr. Thompson. They later ran the Banning mill on the Kaskaskia River. Source: 27,89

B1188 through B1191 for children

B314a NANCY MELVIRA BANNING born March 27, 1837 in Ill. She married John M. Fortner and they lived near Beecher City, Ill. She died Aug. 24, 1873, in childbirth, at the home of her parents and was buried in the Neal Cemetery. Source: 27,89

B1192 Ethel Fortner
B1192a Douglas Fortner
B1193 Josephine Fortner
B1193a William Fortner
B1194 Alfred Fortner
B1194a Lucy Fortner
B1195 Robert Fortner

B314b WILLIAM JACKSON BANNING born about 1840 in Ill. Source: 6,27

B1196 through B1199 for children

B314c JAMES A. BANNING born about 1846 in Ill. Source: 6,27

B1200 through B1203 for children

B314d BROOKS BANNING born about 1848 in Ill. Source: 27

B1204 through B1207 for children

B314e DENNIS F. BANNING born about 1851 in Ill. As an adult he lived about a mile Northwest of the Banning mill on the Kaskaskia River. Source: 27,89

B1208 through B1211 for children

B314f ENOS F. BANNING the twin of Robert, born about 1854 in Ill. Source: 6,27

B1212 through B1215 for children

B314g ROBERT J. BANNING the twin of Enos, born about 1854 in Ill. Source: 6,27

B1216 through B1219 for children

B315 for children of B91

B316 FRANCIS M. BRADLEY born 1861. Source: 44

B316a NANCY E. BRADLEY born 1862. Source: 44

B316b JAMES H. BRADLEY born 1865. Source: 44

B317 HENRY S. BRADLEY born 1867. Source: 44

B317a PRUDENCE B. BRADLEY born 1869. Source: 44

B317b ELLA M. BRADLEY born 1874. Source: 44

B318 NANCY MATILDA BANNING born June 15, 1847. Source: 27,44

B1220 through B1222 for children

B319 THOMAS CLARK BANNING born Dec. 7, 1849. He married Rebecca Liticia Burgin and died before 1900. Source: 27,44

B1223 through B1226 for children

B320 MARY LUCINDA BANNING born June 25, 1852 and died Dec. 30, 1911. Source: 27,44

B1227 through B1229 for children

B321 JAMES HENRY BANNING born Sept. 4, 1854 and died Oct. 31, 1854. Source: 27

B322 JOHN C. BANNING born April 15, 1857 and died March 10, 1865. Source: 27

B323 REBECCA EDOLENE BANNING born April 21, 1860. She married George F. Burgin on Sept. 19, 1886. Source: 27,44

B1230 through B1234 for children

B324 JOSEPH IVY BANNING born July 2, 1864. He married Rutha York and died Jan. 6, 1940. Source: 27

B1235 through B1239 for children

B325 through B330 children of B94

79

B1240 through B1287 for children

B331 MARTHA A. BANNING born 1840 in Pike Co., Ill. She married Thomas J. Tharp on Nov. 6, 1870 in Pike Co. (See B43) Source: 5

B1288 through B1290 for children

B332 NANCY J. BANNING born 1842 in Pike Co., Ill. She married Thomas B. Dunn on April 5, 1866 in Pike Co. (See B43) Source: 5

B1291 through B1293 for children

B333 RHODA BANNING born 1843 in Pike Co., Ill. (See B43) Source: 5

B1294 through B1296 for children

B334 SARAH E. BANNING born 1846 in Pike Co., Ill. She married Joshua P. Ingram on Nov. 22, 1868 in Pike Co. (See B43) Source: 5

B1297 through B1299 for children

B335 through B419 children of B43 & B98 through B104

B1300 through B1343 for children

B420 KATHERINE WOODARD BANNING born Feb. 3, 1874 in South Bend, Ind. Source: 1

B1344 through B1349 for children

B421 FRANK MERCHANT BANNING born March 24, 1876 in South Bend, Ind. He died in South Bend on Oct. 6, 1876. Source: 1

B422 BESSIE MAXON BANNING born Dec. 22, 1877 in South Bend, Ind. She married Dr. Harry R. Snyder of Barbertown, Ohio in 1907. They lived in Barbertown. Source: 1

B1350 through B1355 for children

B423 through B516 for unknown children of B110 through B113

B1356 through B1586 for children

B517 OLIVE L. BANNING born 1866-1870 in Henry Co., Iowa. Source: 7,8

B1587 through B1592 for children

B518 MAGGIE ELVIRA BANNING born May 26, 1872 in Henry Co., Iowa. She married Theodore Kissinger on Oct. 5, 1890. Source: 8,31

B1593 through B1598 for children

B519 ROSS E. BANNING born about 1874 in Henry Co., Iowa and died Jan. 2, 1898. Source: 8,31

B1599 through B1604 for children

B520 ALICE BANNING died an infant. Source: 31

B521 IDA BANNING died an infant. Source: 31

B522 WINNIE BANNING born 186? and died an infant.

B523 through B534 unknown children of B115 & B116

B1618 through B1667 for children

B535 JAMES EDWARD BANNING born 186?. No other information.

B1668 through B1673 for children

B536 EMMA BANNING born Sept. 13, 1867 in Otoe Co., Neb. and married Frank
   Pollard Sheldon on Feb. 25, 1891. He was born Oct. 11, 1866 and was the son of
   Lawson Sheldon (1827-1907) and Julia Ann Pollard (1834-1907). He died Aug. 31,
   1930. Source: 8,32,40

B1674 Isadore Sheldon
B1675 through B1679 for children

B537 CHARLES WILLIAM BANNING born Dec. 5, 1869 in Wyoming, Otoe Co. , Neb.
   He married Effie Morrow on June 22, 1898 in Plattmouth, Cass Co., Neb. Source:
   8,40

B1680 Fannie M. Banning
BI68I through B1685 for children

B538 RHODA BANNING born Jan. 17, 1873 in Otoe Co., Neb. and married Henry
   Peter Strum on Nov. 18, 1896-98. He was born April 27, 1865 in Nehawka, Neb.
   Rhoda died in Nehawka on Jan. 12, 1940. Henry died there on Sept. 30, 1950.
   Source: 8,32,63

B1686 Dorothy Evelyn Sturm
B1687 through B1690 for children

B539 JAMES BANNING born in 1880 in Neb. Source: 8

B1691 through B1695 for children

B540 through B550 unknown children of B118 through B119

B1696 through B1715 for children

B551 ELLEN GERTRUDE ROSS born June 11, 1878 in Gilpin Co., Colorado. She
   married John Abner Russell on June 15, 1904. He was a native of Fort Scott,
   Kansas born June 13, 1873 to Cyrenus and Ann Teagarden Russell. Ellen was a
   strong-willed woman. She enrolled in Colorado University against the wishes of her
   father and was one of the first female graduates. After their marriage they moved to
   Pershing Co., Nevada and later to Auburn, Calif., where John practiced medicine for
   40 years. John died June 21, 1950 in Auburn. About 1965 Ellen moved to Walnut

Creek, Calif. to live with her daughter, Marion, where she died Dec. 21, 1968. John and Ellen are entombed in the Eastlawn Mausoleum in Sacramento, Calif. There children are Eugene Seward, born Aug., 19, 1905; Florence Irene, born May 3, 1909; John Paul, born March 26, 1913 and Marion Gertrude, born Dec. 8, 1917. Source: 63

B551a CLARA BELLE ROSS born Jan. 22, 1880 in Gilpin Co., Col. She married Ebenezer Perry and they lived in Torrington, Wyoming, where they adopted a son. Source: 63

B552 JOHN BANNING ROSS born May 2, 1881 in Gilpin Co., Col. He graduated from the Colorado School of Mines and married Margaret (???). They had children. Source: 63

B552a CHARLES STANLY ROSS Born Nov. 30, 1882 in Gilpin Co., Col. and died Jan. 29, 1886. Source: 63

B553 GEORGE McLENNAN ROSS born July 16, 1885 in Gilpin Co., Col. He graduated from the Colorado School of Mines. He went to Mexico on an engineering project during the time of the revolution and died of disease. Source: 63

B553a HATTIE ELIZA ROSS born Jan. 23, 1887 in Gilpin Co., Col. and died Feb. 18, 1887. Source: 63

B553b ROBERT ANDERSON ROSS born Jan. 30, 1888 in Gilpin Co., Col. and died March 8, 1888. Source: 63

B554 through B556 unknown children B122

B1716 through B1730 for unknown children

B557 LAURA BANNING born 185? in Keokuk Co. Iowa, moved with her parents to Kansas and back to Iowa. She married Wiley Reynolds and they lived in Lancaster, Iowa. Source: 1,63

> B1731 Allen Reynolds
> B1732 Clemon Reynolds
> B1733 Minnie Reynolds
> B1734 Arthur Reynolds
> B1735 Mira Reynolds
> B1736 Floyd Reynolds
> B1737 Earl Reynolds
> B1738 Clarence Reynolds

B558 WILLIAM FRANKLIN no information Source: 1

B559 IRA FRANKLIN no information Source: 1

B560 ASA BANNING FRANKLIN born Nov. 12, 1864 in Bannon, W. Va. and married Laura Carney on July 5, 1890 in W. Va. She was born Dec. 3, 1870 in Bannon and died in Dec. 1925. He died Dec. 4, 1916. Both are buried in Mannington, W. Va. They had at least 1 son, Ward Burdette, born Dec. 30, 1890. Source: 1,49

B561 MARGARET FRANKLIN no information Source: 1

B562 EMMA FRANKLIN no information   Source: 1

B563 JOHN FRANKLIN no information   Source: 1

B564 CLARENCE FRANKLIN no information   Source: 1

B565 EDITH FRANKLIN no information   Source: 1

B566 JAMES FRANKLIN no information   Source: 1

B567 SAMANTHA BANNING born 1858 in Marshall Co. West Va. She died there in 1872.   Source: 1

B568 MALETHA BANNING born July 5, 1860 in Marshall Co. W. Va. She married James H. Phillips on Nov. 14, 1882 in Wheeling, W. Va. They lived in Akron, Ohio.
Source: 1,63

> B1739 Homer Phillips
> B1740 Elda M. Phillips
> B1741 Custer Phillips
> B1742 Bessie L. Phillips
> B1743 H. Melvin Phillips
> B1744 Pearl Phillips
> B1745 Howard Phillips
> B1746 Carl Ivan Phillips

B569 CLARK BANNING born Dec. 11, 1864 in Marshall Co. , W. Va. and moved with his parents to Custer Co., Neb. Latter he moved to Seymour, Iowa, where he married Lizzie Wilson in 1891. They lived in Seymour.   Source: 1,63

> B1747 John Banning
> B1748 Clay Ogle Banning
> B1749 William Banning

B570 ASA EPHRAIM BANNING born May 14, 1865 in Marshall Co., W.Va. and moved with his parents to Neb. and later to Iowa. He married Rhoda Boyington on Sept. 5, 1894 in Iowa Falls, Iowa. They moved from Wright Co., Iowa to Skaget Co., Washington, near Mt. Vernon in 1899.   Source: 1,63

> B1750 Hugh Banning
> B1751 Ephraim Banning
> B1752 Max Banning

B571 ELSIE BANNING born 1869 in Marshall Co. W. Va. She died in 1892 in Taney Co., Mo.   Source: 1

B572 CHARLOTTE BANNING born in 1871 in Marshall Co. W. Va. and moved with her parents to Custer Co., Neb., where she remained as an adult. She married Stephen Maple in 1888 in Custer Co., Neb. They lived in Custer Co.   Source: 1,63

> B1753 Jessie Maple
> B1754 Mary Maple
> B1755 Lulu Maple
> B1756 Claire Maple
> B1757 Howard Maple

B573 DONALD BANNING born in 1875 in Ohio Co. W. Va. He lived unmarried (as of 1908) in Custer Co. Kansas. Source: 1

B574 CHARLOTTE JACKSON no information Source: 1

B575 THERSA JACKSON no information Source: 1

B576 EPHRAIM JACKSON no information Source: 1

B577 ALONZO JACKSON no information Source: 1

B578 ORANGE JACKSON no information Source: 1

B579 LEE JACKSON no information Source: 1

B580 OSCAR JACKSON no information Source: 1

B581 SAMUEL JACKSON no information Source: 1

B582 VISTA JACKSON no information Source: 1

B583 JOSEPHINE THERESA BANNING born Aug. 23, 1863 in Big Springs, Douglas Co., Ks. She married D. B. Sherry from Indiana in June 1887 in Ks. They lived in Eaton, Ind. where she died in Oct. 1894. Source: 1

> B1758 Homer Kent Sherry
> B1759 Inez Bell Sherry
> B1760 Edith Hope Sherry
> B1761 Cameron Banning Sherry

B584 EPHRAIM NEWTON BANNING born Dec. 23, 1864 in Big Springs, Douglas Co., Ks. He lived unmarried in Lyndon, Ks. Source: 1

B585 MARY MATILDA BANNING born Sept. 10, 1866 in Big Springs, Douglas Co., Ks. She married John Sherry from Indiana in Sept. 1891 in Ks. She died Dec. 1, 1892. They had no children. Source: 1

B586 ELLA BELL BANNING born March 11, 1869 in Douglas Co., Ks. She married J.P. Bryson of Osage Co., Ks. on July 17, 1892 in Lyndon, Ks. They lived in Osage Co. Source: 1

> B1762 Raymond A. Bryson
> B1763 Earl Bryson

B587 JOHN WESLEY BANNING born Feb. 22, 1871 in Osage Co., Ks. He lived unmarried (1908) on his farm near Worden, White Co., Ark. Source: 1

B588 HETTY MAY BANNING born Aug. 15, 1873 in Osage Co. , Ks. She died unmarried Feb. 10, 1894 in Lyndon, Ks. Source: 1

B589 WILLIAM BURGESS BANNING born July 20, 1876 in Osage Co., Ks. He married Florence E. Ballou of Ottawa Co., Ks. on Sept. 5, 1906. They both were graduates of the class of 1904, Kansas College. They lived in Lyndon, Ks. Source: 1

B1764 through B1768 for children

B590 THOMAS HUBERT BANNING born Sept. 17, 1882 and died June 28, 1887.
Source: 1

B591 EPHRAIM PINKNEY BANNING born Jan. 25, 1872 in Linn Co., Mo. He lived,
unmarried (1908), in Brookfield, Mo. He enlisted in Co. A of the 6th Mo. Vol. Inft. on
July 11, 1898. In Dec. 1898 he embarked at Jacksonville, Fla. for Havana, Cuba,
under Gen. Fitz Hugh Lee. He served 5 months near Havana as lst Duty Sergeant.
He mustered out May 6, 1899 in Savannah, Ga. Source: 1,2

B592 MARGARET ELLEN BANNING born Feb. 17, 1873 in Linn Co. , Mo. She
married William E. Cloud on April 18, 1894 in Brookfield, Mo. They lived in Canton,
S. Dakota. Source: 1,2

> B1770 David Gilmer Cloud
> B1771 Francis Millar Cloud
> B1772 William Ephraim Cloud
> B1773 Margaret Irene Cloud

B593 LETITIA LOUISE BANNING born March 27, 1877 in Linn Co., Mo. She died
March 7, 1883. Source: 1,2

B594 THOMAS GILMER BANNING born March 13, 1881 in Linn Co., Mo. He married
Louise Frazier of Brookfield, Mo. on June 3, 1908 in Brookfield. He was in the
business of growing and selling produce. Source: 1,2

B1774 through B1782 for children

B595 CAROLINE AGNES BANNING born May 1, 1884 in Linn Co., MO. She married
John Ernest Burch of Brookfield, Mo. on Nov. 8, 1908 in Canton, South Dakota.
They lived in Brookfield. He died Dec. 29, 1956 and she died Sept. 2, 1963. They
are buried in the Rose Hill Cemetery in Brookfield, Mo. Source: 1,2,16

B1783 John Shirley Burch

B596 EDWIN ALFRED VERTREES born July 2, 1882 and he died in 1900. Source:
1,2

B597 ERNEST VERTREES born in 1884 and he died in 1891. Source: 1,2

B598 PIERSON WORRALL BANNING born Sept. 13, 1879 in Chicago. He was a
member of the class of 1910 at the Kent College of Law. He married Lila Banning
Watkins (A698), on May 16, 1913 in Los Angeles, Calif. Pierson is the author of the
1908 "1st Banning Genealogy". Source: 1,2,30,63

B1784 through B1788 for children

B599 WALKER BANNING born Feb. 9, 1882 in Chicago. He married Clara Louise
Wahrer on July 30, 1902 in Chicago. She was the daughter of Frank and Elizabeth
(Biersdorfer) Wahrer, of Salino, Ohio. He was an attorney, received his Law degree
form Northwestern University in 1904 and became a member of the firm of Banning
& Banning. He died Jan. 19, 1918. Source: 1,2

B1789 Clara Louise Banning
B1790 Walker Banning

B600 EPHRAIM BANNING, III born Aug. 7, 1885 in Chicago. He married Beatrice
White Smith of Oak Park, Ill. on June 22, 1909 in Chicago. She was the daughter of
William Fulton and Viola May (Loud) Smith of Weymouth, Mass. He received his
law degree from Princeton University in 1908 and became an attorney with the firm
of Banning & Banning, specializing in patents and trade-marks. Source: 1, 2,61

B1791 Emilie Jenne Banning
B1792 Ephriam Banning, IV
B1793 Thalia Banning

B601 SAMUEL WALKER BANNING born Nov. 16, 1878 in Chicago. He received his
law degree from the Kent College of Law in 1903 and joined the firm of Banning &
Banning. He married Grace Edson of Chicago on Aug. l2, 1903 in Wheaton, Ill.
Source: 1,2

B1794 Son ----? Banning

B602 EDITH BANNING born Jan. 11, 1881 in Chicago. She went to school in
Fairbaugh, Minn. Source: 1,2

B1795 through B1800 for children

B603 HELEN RUTH BANNING born Dec. 16, 1883 in Chicago. She died Oct. 15,
1899 in Brussels, where the family was staying for a time. She is buried in LaPerto,
Ind. USA. Source: 1,2

B604 THOMAS ALLEN BANNING born April 12, 1886 in Chicago. He was an
Electrical Engineer and worked for the Chicago Street Railway dept. Source: 1,2

B1801 through B1805 for children

B605 SARAH LOUISE BANNING born Jan. 25, 1888 in Chicago. Source: 1,2

B1806 through B1810 for children

B606 DOROTHEA ESTHER BANNING born Aug. 11, 1894 in Chicago. Source: 1,2

B1811 through B1815 for children

B607 BERTHA LUCILE BANNING born Jan. 3, 1880 in Cincinnati, Iowa. She was a
school teacher in Chicago. Source: 1,2,63

B1816 through B1820 for children

B608 JENNIE MALVERN BANNING born in 1882 in Genoa, Iowa and died as a child.
Source: 1,2

B609 THOMAS EPHRAIM BANNING born May 4, 1884 in St. John, Mo. and married
Sarah Eleanor Pichforth in Sept. 19??. He lived in Milford, Utah where he was the
agent for the Salt Lake Railroad. Source: 1,2,30

B1821 Daughter Banning

B1822 Thomas Ephraim Banning
B1823 through B1825 for children

B610 ALMA LOUISE BANNING born Sept. 21, 1886 in Genoa, Iowa. She married Harley Condra of Seymour, Wayne Co., Iowa on Nov. 22, 1906 in Seymour. Source: 1,2

B1826 Carolyn Condra

B611 CYRUS WALKER BANNING born Aug. 21, 1888 near Genoa, Iowa, and lived at Choney, Iowa. Source: 1,2

B1827 through B1832 for children.

B612 HUBERT CHARLES BANNING born Feb. 24, 1890 near St. John, Mo. He lived in Seymour, Iowa. Source: 1,2

B1833 through B1838 for children

B613 WAYNE ELSON BANNING born June 9, 1893 in Genoa, Iowa. He lived in Seymour, Iowa. Source: 1,2

B1839 through B1844 for children

B614 HUBERT TEMPLE BANNING born Oct. 24, 1882 in New York City. He was a member of the Columbia University class of 1904, and received his Ph. D. from the University of Berlin in 1908. He married Olga Kurzrock, daughter of Ernest August Friedreich Kurzrock and Theresa Alvina (Wolf) of Berlin, Germany, on Sept. 17, 1909 in Bavaria. He was one of the three or four greatest linguists of his time and was highly proficient in more than 20 modern and dead languages. They made their home in New York City. Source: 1,2

B1845 Hildegard Banning

B615 CYNTHIA ELLEN SMITH born Feb. 5, 1884 in Joliet, Ill. She died Feb. 8, 1884. Source: 1,2

B616 ALICE MARION SMITH born Aug. 13, 1885 in Chicago where she was living in 1908. Source: 1,2,63

B617 HELEN ALMANSON SMITH born June 12, 1893 in Chicago and died June 14, 1893. Source: 1,2

B618 SOPHIA LOUISE LAWTON born June 20, 1888 in Winnetka, Ill. She attended the University of Wisc. Source: 1,2

B619 HELEN MARGARET LAWTON born Sept 10, 1889 in Chicago and died in June 1890 in Chicago. Source: 1,2

B620 GRACE LAWTON born Sept. 19, 1890 in Chicago and lived in River Forest, Ill. Source: 1,2

B621 & B622 TWIN LAWTON BOYS born Dec. 20, 1891 in Chicago and both died Dec. 22, 1891. Source: 1,2

B623 GEORGE AUGUSTUS LAWTON born June 11, 1893 in Afton, Wisc. He lived in River Forest, Ill. Source: 1,2

B624 WILLIAM EPHRAIM LAWTON born July 27, (or Aug. 20) 1896 in Opdyke, Ill. He lived in River Forest, Ill. Source: 1,2

B625 WALTER BANNING LAWTON born June 21, 1898 or 99 in Chicago and died 1901 in Chicago. Source: 1,2

B626 RUTH LAWTON born April 5, 1903 in Chicago and died as an infant. Source: 1,2

B627 through B657 unknown children of B145 through B149.

B1846 through B1906 for children

B658 through B663 unknown children of B150.

B664 JAMES BANNING born in Mo. and lived in Cripple Creek. Source: 1

B1907 through B1911 for children

B665 GARDINER BANNING no information Source: 1

B1912 through B1916 for children

B666 ALONZO BANNING no information Source: 1

B1917 through B1921 for children

B666a MARY C. BANNING born 1840 in Mo. Source: 1,5

B1922 through B1926 for children

B667 REBECCA BANNING born 1841 in Mo. Source: 1,5

B1927 through B1930 for children

B668 CATHERINE (CASSENDARA ?) BANNING born 1844 in Mo. Source: 1,5

B1931 through B1934 for children

B669 CORNELIA BANNING born 1848 in Mo. Source: 1,5

B1935 through B1937 for children

B670 PETER POWELL born May 24, 1846. Source: 1

B671 THOMAS POWELL born March 26, 1850. Source: 1

B672 BASWELL POWELL born Oct. 4. 1853 and died Nov. 8, 1908. Source: 1

B673 LOUISE POWELL born Dec. 19, 1855. Source: 1

B674 JAMES POWELL born July 25, 1859. Source: 1

B675 JOHN POWELL born Jan. 15, 1865. Source: 1

B676 MARGARET GIPSON born Aug. 31, 1841. Source: 1

B677 GRACE GIPSON born Sept. 22, 1842. Source: 1

B678 MARY GIPSON born June 12, 1843. Source: 1

B679 SARAH GIPSON born Oct. 12, 1844. Source: 1

B680 MELISSA GIPSON born March 7, 1846. Source: 1

B681 MARTHA GIPSON born April 25, 1847. Source: 1

B682 NANNIE GIPSON born April 25, 1847. Source: 1

B683 STEPHEN GIPSON born April 25, 1849. Source: 1

B684 JAMES GIPSON born Oct. 12, 1851. Source: 1

B685 THOMAS GIPSON born March 12, 1852. Source: 1

B686 BINDA GIPSON born Dec. 18, 1854. Source: 1

B687 ELIJAH GIPSON born June 7, 1856. Source: 1

B688 LOUISA GIPSON born Sept. 18, 1857. Source: 1

B689 ? INFANT GIPSON died at birth. Source: 1

B690 D. B. GIPSON born Sept. 2, 1860. Source: 1

B691 WILLIAM GIPSON born Sept. 8, 1862. Source: 1

B692 SUSIE GIPSON born July 18, 1864. Source: 1

B693 GRANT GIPSON born May 27, 1866. Source: 1

B694 SMITH GIPSON born June 8, 1868. Source: 1

B695 & B696 for unknown children of B154

B697 MATILDA GREEN she married but had no children. Source: 1

B698 MARY LOWRY BANNING born May 26, 1856 in Mo. and died Oct.18, 1856. Source: 1

B699 WILLIAM TOLMAN BANNING born March 24, 1863 in College Mound, Mo. and died Aug. 8, 1866. Source: 1

B700 SUSIE BANNING born July 8, 1867 in College Mound, Mo. She married Charles R. Terry on Jan. 22, 1891 in College Mound. They lived in Huntsville, Mo. Source: 1

B701 GEORGE BANNING born Nov. 29, 1877 in College Mound, Mo. He Married
Adolphia Cox on Sept. 14, 1898. They had no children by 1908. Source: 1

B702 through B746 for unknown children of B163 through B171

B1939 through B2035 for children

B747 ZARA JACKSON BANNING born April 4, 1873 in Westfield, Chariton Co., Mo.
He married 1st, Anna Morris on Feb. 9, 1900 in Brookfield, Linn Co., Mo. She was
the daughter of John Henry and Sarah (McCollum) Morris, born March 1885 in Mo.
She died about 1910 in Brookfield. He married 2nd, Maude Mary Carson
Dusenberry in 1910. He died Feb. 23, 1957 in Brookfield, Mo. and is buried in Old
New Garden Cemetery. Source: 87

> B2036 John Edward Banning
> B2037 Oliver Jackson Banning
> B2038 Mable Anna Marie Banning

B748 DORA BANNING born Sept 27, 1875 and married 1st, Henry Phelps who was
born about 1870. She married 2nd John Roland. Source: 87

> B2040 Pearl Phelps
> B2041 Goldie Phelps
> B2042 Orville Phelps
> B2043 Frank Phelps
> B2039 Buddy Roland

B749 ADELIA E. BANNING born Aug. 18, 1879 and married Robert Turpin in Jan.
1900. He was born Nov. 18, 1879. She married 2nd George Morris. There were no
children from the 2nd marriage. Source: 87

> B2044 Lola Turpin
> B2045 Orlando L. Turpin
> B2046 Elsie Turpin
> B2047 Pearl Turpin

B750 JOHN RICHARD BANNING born 1881 and married Mable (???). She was born
in 1886 and died in 1963. Source: 87

> B2048 Iva Mae Banning

B751 LOUIS EDWARD BANNING born about 1883 and married Edith (???) on Dec.
24, 1910 in Brookfield, Linn Co. Mo.. Source: 87

> B2049 Jonny Bill Banning
> B2050 Ben Banning
> B2051 Helen banning
> B2052 Marguerite Banning
> B2053 Dorothy Banning
> B2054 Mary Ann Banning
> B2055 Betty Banning

B752 WILLIAM CHRISLEY BANNING born 1886 and married Ona Alice Tomlinson.

She was born Sept. 11, 1897 and died in Excelsior Springs, Clay Co. Mo. on Sept. 18, 1974. He died Oct. 31, 1957 in Excelsior Springs. Both are buried in Crown Hill Cemetery. Source: 87

> B2056 Francis Banning
> B2057 William C. Banning Jr.
> B2058 Kenneth Richard Banning

B753 through B762 for unknown children of B173 & B174

B2059 through B2089 for children

B763 LAURA AMNER BANNING born July 17, 1851 in Brookfield, Mo. She died unmarried on March 6, 1930, and is buried in the "Banning Cemetery" in Brookfield township, Linn County, Mo. located in the NE1/4 of Sect. 31, T58, R19.. Source: 1,6,15,87

B764 WILLIAM ALONZO BANNING born March 3, 1853 in Brookfield, Mo. He died Feb. 1, 1863 in Brookfield. William is buried in the "Banning Cemetery" in Brookfield township, Linn County, Mo. located in the NE1/4 of Sect. 31, T58, R19. Source: 1, 6,15,87

B765 MARIA LUELLA BANNING born July 21, 1855 in Brookfield, Mo. She died unmarried April 13, 1873 in Brookfield. Source: 1,6

B766 SAMUEL TERRILL BANNING born April 7, 1857 in Brookfield, Mo. He died Nov. 7, 1857. Source: 1,6

B767 REBECCA JANE BANNING born May 4, 1859 near Brookfield, Mo. and died March 2, 1865. She is buried in the "Banning Cemetery" in Brookfield township, Linn County, Mo. located in the NE1/4 of Sect. 31, T58, R19. Source: 1,6,15,87

B767a RHODA BANNING born in Sept. 1863 and died Sept 21, 1865. She is buried in the "Banning Cemetery" in Brookfield township, Linn County, Mo. located in the NE1/4 of Sect. 31, T58, R19. Source: 15,87

B767b MOSES C. BANNING born in April 1866 and died Sept 29, 1867. He is buried in the "Banning Cemetery" in Brookfield township, Linn County, Mo. located in the NE1/4 of Sect. 31, T58, R19. Source: 15,87

B768 CORA BELL BANNING born Nov. 26, 1868 near Keatsville, Mo. She married Thomas R. Hamilton on Nov. 24, 1894. He was cashier at the bank in Dalton, Mo. Source: 1

B2090 through B2095 for children

B769 MILTON H. BANNING born July 8, 1858 in Howard Co., Mo. He died Dec. 14, 1859. Source: 1

B770 BODIE BANNING born May 21, 1861 in Howard Co., Mo. and died Aug. 16, 1862. Source: 1

B771 JOHN BANNING born Nov. 20, 1862 in Howard Co., Mo. and died June 27, 1872. Source: 1

B772 SUSAN ANDREW BANNING born Nov. 30, 1859 in Howard Co., Mo. She married John E. Fray on July 28, 1877 in Moberly, Randolph Co., Mo. They lived in Howard Co. Source: 1,6

> B2096 Edgar Fray
> B2097 Estelle Fray

B773 ELIZABETH BANNING born May 4, 1865 in Howard Co., Mo. Source: 1

> B2098 through B2103 for children

B774 ANNIE BANNING born Sept. 29, 1866 in Howard Co., Mo. She married Ambrose Burton on Dec. 5, 1902 in Huntsville, Mo. They lived in Higbee, Mo. Source: 1

> B2104 through B2109 for children

B775 WILLIAMSON BANNING born March 2, 1868 in Howard Co., Mo. He married Bessie Robb on Dec. 27, 1888 in Howard Co. Source: 1

> B2110 Bessie Banning
> B2111 through B2114 for children

B776 THOMAS PLEASANT BANNING born Oct. 20, 1869 in Howard Co., Mo. He married Alma Smith on Oct. 1, 1902. They lived in Yates Co., Mo. Source: 1,30

> B2115 Dorothy Banning
> B2116 Lester T. Banning
> B2117 Martha Agnes Banning
> B2118 Mary Susan Banning
> B2119 Ina B. Banning
> B2120 Alpha Banning

B777 CHARLES CLARK BANNING born Jan. 12, 1872 in Howard Co., Mo. He lived in College Mound, Mo. Source: 1

> B2121 through B2125 for children

B778 MARTHA JANE BANNING born April 3, 1874 in Howard Co., Mo. She married Burch Kirby on Dec. 9, 1903. They lived in Armstrong, Mo. Source: 1

> B2126 through B2130 for children

B779 SUSAN AGNES BANNING born June 11, 1876 in Howard Co., Mo. She lived in Yates, Mo. Source: 1

> B2131 through B2135 for children

B780 EUGENE BANNING born March 8, 1863 near Brookfield, Mo. He married Abnie Pfister and they lived in Brookfield. Source: 1

> B2136 Bertha Banning
> B2137 Hazel Banning
> B2138 Johnnie Banning

B781 CLARK BANNING born Sept. 30, 1867 in Brookfield, Mo. He died Sept l1, 1870. Clark is buried in the "Banning Cemetery" in Brookfield township, Linn County, Mo. located in the NE1/4 of Sect. 31, T58, R19. Source: 1,15,87

B782 FAY BANNING born May 9, 1874 in Brookfield, Mo. and died July 1, 1889. He is buried in the "Banning Cemetery" in Brookfield township, Linn County, Mo. located in the NE1/4 of Sect. 31, T58, R19. Source: 1,15,87

B783 FLORA JUNE SMITH no information Source: 1

B784 ANNA NELLIE SMITH no information Source: 1

B785 ALLEN LEE SMITH Died Feb. 27, 18?? at age 7 years and 2 days. He is buried in the "Banning Cemetery" in Brookfield township, Linn County, Mo. located in the NE1/4 of Sect. 31, T58, R19. Source: 1,15,87

B786 MARY AMNER SMITH born Aug. 3, 1876 and died Feb. 16, 1881. She is buried in the "Banning Cemetery" in Brookfield township, Linn County, Mo. located in the NE1/4 of Sect. 31, T58, R19. Source: 1,15,87

B787 Unknown WIRTS child, no information Source: 1

B788 MARY BANNING married Louis Braun. Source: 1

                         B2139 Hazel L. Braun

B789 through B791 unknown children of Bl86

B792 MARY E. MILLER born about 1850 in Mo. Source: 6,7,67

B792A ELIZABETH J. MILLER born about 1859 and married B.E. Scarge. They had at least one child, Joseph Henry, born May 26, 1881 and died Feb. 28, 1882. Source: 7,67

B793 JAMES R. MILLER born in Texas about 1867 and married Victoria (???). Their children were Bascomb E. (born March 28, 1889 and died Aug 28, 1889); and Arra (born June 27, 1908 and died the next day). Source: 7,67

B794 MARY WILL OXFORD born Jan. 25, 1856 in Tx. and died June 3, 1938 in Oswalt, Loce Co., Okla. She married Benjamin Carlile on April 19, 1875 in Hunt, Tx. He was born Aug. 5, 1853 in Ark. and died Sept. 1926 in Oswalt, where they both are buried. Their children are: 1. Ellen, 1875-1956; 2. Edgar L., Oct. 12, 1881 - Jan. 23, 1962; 3. Laura, born 1883; 4. Scott, born March 1890; 5. Mattie, born 1893; 6. Eula M, March 17, 1895 - June 9, 1976; 7. Leonard, born Feb. 1900. Source: 6,7, 8,10,67

B794A EMILY JANE OXFORD born in Tx. March 14, 1859 and married J.W.R. Callaway on Feb. 13, 1880 in Red River, Tx. He was born in Ark. Feb. 1852. Source: 6,7,8,67

B795 WILLIAM JERRY OKFORD born in Tx. Oct. 15, 1860 and married Ida Osteen in Denton, Denton Co., Tx on Sept. 13, 1879. She was born in Ark. in Dec. 1855 and died April 14, 1929 in Collinsville, Grayson Co., Tx. where she was buried. William died about 1903 in Gainesville, Cooke Co., Tx. Their children were: 1. James G.

born March 1880; 2. Mary Elizabeth, Dec. 9, 1881 - March 29, 1969; 3. Laura G. born July 1882; 4. John Wesley, born about 1885; 5. Martha, born March 1886; 6. Robert W., born Dec. 1887; 7. Alonzo, born Feb. 1890; 8. Charles Edgar Carl, Aug. 3, 1891 - Nov. 4, 1963; 9. Elkins, born Jan. 1894; 10. Oscar Lee, Jan. 29, 1895 - Dec. 11, 1966. Source: 6,7,8,10,67

B795A M. L. OKFORD born in Tx. April 20, 1862. Source: 67

B796 JESSIE C. OXFORD born in Tx. April 12, 1865 and died in Gainesville, Cooke Co., Tx. on March 1, 1894. He married 1st, Mollie Cates on June 13, 1889 in Gainesville. He married 2nd, Sallie F. Todd on Aug. 31, 1893 also in Gainesville. Source: 7,8,67

B796A JAMES RICHARD OXFORD born in Tx. March 11, 1868 and died in Ardmore, Carter Co., Ok. Feb. 10, 1932, where he is buried. He married Mary Emma McCan on Nov. 22, 1887 in Lamar, Tx. She was born May 23, 1869 and died in Ardmore, Ok. Aug. 7, 1948, where she is buried in the Rose Hill Cemetery. Their children are; 1. John Henry, Oct. 28, 1888 - May 15, 1926; 2. James Richard, born Dec. 31, 1889; 3. A.V., born Aug. 11, 1891; 4. Lora A., Jan. 23, 1893 - June 7, 1894; 5. Jessie J., born Sept 27, 1895; 6. Joney, Aug. 14, 1898 - June 11, 1903; 7. George Tommy, born Jan. 29, 1900; 8. Amanda, born Dec. 11, 1902; 9. Emma A., born April 27, 1903; 10. Carrie, born Feb. 20, 1905; 11. Carl B., born and died Feb. 20, 1905; 12. Iley Erwin, born Aug. 23, 1907; 13. Albert Sidney; 14, Frank G., born June 8, 1916. Source: 7,8,67

B797 JOHN W. OXFORD born in Tx. on March 16, 1870. Source: 7,67

B797A JOSEPH HENRY OXFORD born in Tx. on June 18, 1871 and died in Norman, Cleveland Co., Ok. on May 31, 1946. By 1900 he was in the Indian Territory of Ok. He is buried in Oswalt, Love Co., Ok. Source: 8,10,67

B798 MARGARETTA E. OXFORD born in Tx. on Feb. 7, 1874 and married J.M. Harrison in Gainesville, Cooke Co., Tx. on Jan. 5, 1894. Source: 8,67

B799 through B806 unknown children of B195 and B196

B2140 through B2159 for children

B807 JAMES C. BENNINGFIELD born in Gainesville, Cooke Co., Tx about 1868. Source: 7,67

B808 CHARLES H. BENNINGFIELD born in Tx. about 1878. Source: 8,67

B809 through B812 unknown children of B198

B2160 through B2179 for children

B813 through B820 unknown children of B199 and B200

B821 through B840 unknown children of B201 through B205

B2180 through B2240 for children

B841 through B854 unknown children of B205 through B214

B855 through B879 for unknown children of B215 through B219

B2241 through B2300

B880 MELVIN SCOLES born June 24, 1872. Source: 16,91

B881 JOHN WILLIAM SCOLES born Feb. 23, 1874 and died Nov. 21, 1931. Source: 16,91

B882 CHARLES WESLEY SCOLES born Feb. 18, 1877 and died Sept. 16, 1901. Source: 16,91

B883 REUBEN EZRA SCOLES born June 19, 1881 and married Cora Alice Dowell on June 19, 1901. She was born in May 1883 and was the daughter of William Manfred and Millie (Askins) Dowell. They had a son, Kenneth Nelson born Sept 24, 1920. Reuben died Sept. 21, 1956. Source: 16,91

B884 MARTHA EVALINE SCOLES born June 19, 1881. Source: 16,91

B885 through B899 unknown children of B221 through B223

B2301 through B2350 for children

B900 and B901 unknown children of B224

B902 through B929 unknown children of B225 through B230

B2351 through B2475 for children

B930 GEORGE SEVERE born June 27, 1874 in Shelby Co., Ill. and married Bertha Fisher. He died Nov. 29, 1969. Source: 16,27

B930A CHARLES SEVERE born Feb. 20, 1877 in Shelby Co., Ill. and married Catherine Russell. He died in 1946. Source: 16,27

B930B MARY A. SEVERE born April 28, 1880 in Shelby Co., Ill. Source: 16,27

B931 OTTIE FILENA SEVERE born June 25, 1883 in Shelby Co., Ill. and married John Calvin Howe on Nov. 30, 1905. She died May 7, 1973 in Shelbyville, Ill. Source: 16,27

B931A CORDIA MAY SEVERE born Oct. 17, 1886 in Shelby Co., Ill. and married Alfred Washburn. She died May 5, 1977. Source: 16,27

B931B CENIA JOSEPHINE SEVERE born Feb. 22, 1891 in Shelby Co., Ill. and married Clark Smith in Nov. 1908. She died Feb. 1, 1972. Source: 16,27

B932 OLLIE GRACE SEVERE born May 31, 1895 in Shelby Co., Ill and married Harvey Smith. She died March 1, 1956. Source: 16,27

B932A VERNON SEVERE born Nov. 22, 1898 in Shelby Co., Ill. and married Helen Morton July 30, 1956. Source: 16,27

B933 through B938 unknown children of B232 and B233

B2476 through B2496 for children

B939 MARRY MALISSE BANNING born Sept.6, 1861 in Ill. Source: 7,8,18,75

B2497 for children

B939a JAMES F. BANNING born Aug. 8, 1862. Source: 18,75

B2498 & B2499 for children

B940 WILLIAM R. BANNING born Feb. 19, 1864. Source: 18,75

B2500 & B2501 for children

B940a CARLINE M. BANNING born Feb. 6, 1866 in Mo. and died March 1912.
Source: 7,8,18,75

B2502 for children

B940b SINDA ANN BANNING   born Jan. 13, 1868 in Mo. and was the twin of
Sarah Ellen. She married C. W. Lewis of Barren Fork on Dec. 12, 1900. He was
born July 30, 1859 and died Dec. 12, 1952. She died April 18, 1953. Both are
buried in the Barren Fork Cemetery, now known as the Mt. Pleasant Cemetery.
Source: 7,8,18,75

B2503 Homer Osmer Lewis
B2503a Monnie S. Lewis
B2503b Minnie Ola Lewis
B2503c Lillian Omegia Lewis

B940c SARAH ELLEN BANNING born Jan. 13, 1868 in Mo. and was the twin of Sinda
Ann. She married Jesse Waldew of DeWitte Co, Ill. on Nov. 25, 1888 in Halfway,
Polk Co. Mo. Sarah died April 28, 1908. Source: 7,8,12,18,75,79

B2504 for children

B941 JOHN BENJAMIN BANNING born Dec. 18, 1870 in Mo. He married 1st, Nancy
E. Rose on Oct. 2, 1895 in Izard Co., Ark. She was born in Jan. 1875 in Ark. He
married 2nd, Rosa (Pareba ?) McVey on June 13, 1909. He died Nov. 10, 1939.
Source: 8,10,12,18,75,78

B2505 Mamie Banning
B2505a Sherman Banning
B2505b Murril Banning
B2505c Carl L. Banning
B2506 Joseph Banning
B2506a Charity Banning
B2506b John R. Banning

B941a MARTHA M. BANNING born Nov. 21, 1873 in Mo. Source: 8,18,75

B2507 for children

B942 ANDREW (ANDY) LORENZO BANNING born March 14, 1877 in Mo. He
married Sarah (???) who was born Nov. 1874 in Ark. By 1900 he was in

Independence Co., Ark. Source: 8,10,18,75

> B2508 Edna Banning
> B2508a Hettie Banning
> B2509 for children

B942a INFANT SON born Oct. 13, 1875. Source: 18,75

B942b NANCY J. BANNING born Nov. 15, 1878 in Mo. Source: 8,18,75

> B2510 for children

B943 CHARLIE WEAVER BANNING born Aug. 5, 1880 and died Oct. 1949. Source: 18,75

> B2511 & B2512 for children

B943a JUDA ELIZZIEBETH "JULIA ELIZABETH" BANNING "Lizzie" was born Dec. 14, 1883 in Halfway, Mo. She married George Washington Cooper on Nov. 25, 1900 in Mt. Pleasant, Ark. He was born Dec. 31, 1877 in Cushman, Ark and died March 13, 1962 in Black Oak, Ark. She died in Waldenburg, Ark. on May 12, 1968. Source: 18,75,79

> B2513 James Edwin Cooper
> B2513a Emily Imogene Cooper
> B2513b Mary Ola Cooper
> B2513c Nola Jane Cooper
> B2513d Fred D. Cooper
> B2513e Burl Lonzo Cooper
> B2513f Minnie Ester Cooper
> B2513g Ruth Cooper
> B2513h William Jennings Cooper

B943b JEMIMA FLORENCE BANNING born Jan. 16, 1887 in Halfway, Benton Township, Polk Co., Mo. She married a Mr. Wilkinson and died March 29, 1958. Source: 12,18,75

> B2514 for children

B944 through B951 unknown children of B234 and B235

> B2515 through B2519 for children

B952 NANCY BANNING She married Michael Bishop on Feb. 28, 1882 in Polk Co. Mo. Source: 12,75

> B2520 for children

B953 SARAH J. BANNING born about 1867 in Mo. She was living with her parents in Polk Co., Mo. in 1870. Source: 7

> B2521 for children

B954 THRU B961 unknown children of B236 & B237

B2522 through B2527 for children

B962 MINNIE A. BANNING born about 1884 and was living with her parents in Izard Co., Ark. in 1900. She married John W. Vest in Izard Co. on July 11, 1901. Source: 10,12,75

B2528 for children

B962a SARAH N. BANNING born about 1886 and was living with her parents in Izard Co., Ark. in 1900. Source: 10,75

B2529 & B2530 for children

B963 WILLIS F. BANNING born about 1888 and was living with his parents in Izard Co., Ark. in 1900. Source: 10,75

B2531 through B2533 for children

B963A BYRD A. BANNING born about 1890 and was living with his parents in Izard Co., Ark. in 1900. Source: 10,75

B2534 through B2537 for children

B963b DOLA (Nona?) E. BANNING born about 1892 and was living with his/her parents in Izard Co., Ark. in 1900. Nona Banning married William B. Vest on Aug. 2, 1906 in Izard Co. Source: 10,12,75

B2538 & B2539 for children

B964 FRANCIS R. BANNING born about 1894 and was living with her parents in Izard Co., Ark. in 1900. Source: 10,75

B2540 & B2541 for children

B964a IDA L. BANNING born 1897 and was living with her parents in Izard Co., Ark. in 1900. Source: 10,75

B2542 & B2543 for children

B964b MARTHA M. BANNING born about 1899 and was living with her parents in Izard Co., Ark. in 1900. Source: 10,75

B2544 & B2545 for children

B965 and B966 unknown children of B237b and B237c

B967 ALBERT E. BANNING born about 1893 and was living with his parents in Izard Co., Ark. in 1900. Source: 10,75

B2546 through B2549 for children

B967a LENA L. BANNING born about 1895 and was living with her parents in Izard Co., Ark. in 1900. Source: 10,75

B2550 for children

B968 through B970 unknown children of B238

B2551 through B2557 for children

B965 through B974 unknown children of B239 and B240

B975 through B979 unknown children of B241

B2558 through B2566 for children

B980 STELLA CECIL TALLMAN born June 15, 1882 in Shelby Co. Ill. and died May 12, 1900. Source: 33

B981 CARL BENJAMIN TALLMAN born March 21, 1884 in Shelby Co., Ill. Source: 33

B982 EDITH ORA TALLMAN born May 17, 1886 in Shelby Co., Ill. Source: 33

B983 LORA ESTELLA TALLMAN born March 10, 1890 in Shelby Co., Ill. Source: 33

B984 ERNEST WELLS TALLMAN born Nov. 18, 1893 in Beecher City, Ill. Source: 33

B985 HENRY BANNING born July 28, 1895 near Cowden, Ill., and married Nelly Barton. He was a Sgt. in the U.S. Marine Corp during WW I. He died July 6, 1963. Source: 16,92

B2567 & B2568 for children

B985a FRANK (COPIE) BANNING born April 28, 1897 near Cowden, Ill. and married Eido F. (Doty) Aoss. He died June 9, 1975. Source: 16,92

B2569 & B2570 for children

B985b CARL BANNING born March 26, 1899 near Cowden, Ill. and married Ethel Chism on June 29, 1924. Source: 16,92

B2571 & B2572 for children

B986 WILLIAM (BILL) BANNING born May 27, 1901 near Cowden, Ill. He was married twice. His first wife was Ella (???). Bill died Nov. 15, 1968. Source: 16,92

B2573 & B2574 for children

B986a ANNIE MAE BANNING born Jan. 9, 1904 near Cowden, Ill. and married Glen Dewey Holley on July 6, 1924 in Cowden, Shelby Co., Ill. He was born July 25, 1898 to Henry and Addie Mae Fortner Holley. Glen died Dec. 13, 1952 of a hart attack and is buried in the Mound Cemetery at Cowden, Ill. Annie died July 25, 1992 of hart failure in the Shelbyville Hospital and is buried in the Mound Cemetery. Source: 16,92

B2575 Gerald Dean Holley
B2575a Clara Mae Holley
B2576 Ronald Eugene Holley

B2576a Charles Franklin Holley
B2576b Shirley Jean Holley
B2576c Patsy Lou Holley
B2577 Larry Phil Holley
B2577a Steven Joe Holley

B986b INFANT SON BANNING born & died April 4, 1894 and is buried in Neal Cemetery near Cowden, Ill. Source: 16,92

B987 and B988 unknown children of B258

B2578 through B2600 for children

B989 OLIVER ALLISON buried in Ky. Source: 46

B990 ASHER ALLISON buried in Ky. Source: 46

B990a OSCAR ALLISON buried in Boylston Church Cemetery in N.C. Source: 46

B991 THOMAS D. BANNING born May 1885 in N.C. Source: 46

B2601 through B2605 for children

B991a JAMES VIRGIL BANNING born Oct. 1886 in N.C. Source: 46

B2606 through B2610 for children

B991b DOVIE A. BANNING born Oct 1889 in N.C. and married Mr. T. Bishop. Source: 46

B2611 through B2615 for children

B992 SOPHIA E. BANNING born May 1891 in N.C. Source: 46

B2616 through B2620 for children

B992a MARY E. BANNING born Feb. 1894 in N.C. and married Walter Cairnes. Source: 46

B2621 through B2625 for children

B992b LOREE J. BANNING born July 1896 in N.C. and married Walter Reese. Source: 46

B2626 through B2628 for children

B993 JESSE H. TOWNSEND born 1900 in N.C. Source: 46

B994 through B996 for children of B261 and B262

B997 EXA BANNING born 1904 in N.C. and married Walter Perkins. She died 1974. Source: 46

B2629 through B2631 for children

B997a EDITH BANNING born 1906 and married David Holiday at Brevard. Source: 46

B2632 through B2634 for children

B997b JONES BANNING born 1909 in N.C. and married May Belle Orr. Source: 46

B2635 through B2639 for children

B997c RALPH BANNING born 1911 in N.C. and married Estelle Moffitt. He was a Baptist Minister. Source: 46

B2640 through B2644 for children

B997d OWEN BANNING born 1914 in N.C. and married Dorothy Dalton. Source: 46

B2645 through B2649 for children

B998 NARY BANNING born 1916 in N.C. and married Foy Holden. Source: 46

B2650 through B2652 for children

B998a ALMA BANNING born 1919 in N.C. and married Fisco Sentelle. Source: 46

B2653 through B2655 for children

B998b INA BANNING born 1922 in N.C. and married Donald Jackson. Source: 46

B2656 through B2658 for children

B998c ANNIE LOU BANNING born 1924 in N.C. and married Howard Pace. Source: 46

B2659 through B2661 for children

B999 and B1000 for children of B271

B1001 MAUDE WHITAKER. No information. Source: 97

B1001A ETHEL WHITAKER. No information. Source: 97

B1002 MYRTLE WHITAKER. No information. Source: 97

B1004 through B1006 children of B273 and B274

B1007 ELLA WILLIAMS born 1868 in N.C. Source: 46

B1008 JAMES WILLIAMS born 1871 in N.C. Source: 46

B1009 T.C. WILLIAMS born 1873 in N.C. Source: 46

B1010 EDGEBERT SWAYINGAME born 1877 in N.C. Source: 46

B1011 EARL SWAYINGAME born 1879 in N.C. Source: 46

B1012 & B1013 children of B278

B2662 through B2671 for children

B1014 REBECCA PEARL BANNING born Oct.29, 1889 in N.C. and married H.G. Johnson. Source: 46

B2672 through B2674 for children

B1014a MARY JOSEPHINE BANNING born May 8, 1892 in N.C. and married John Collins. Source: 46

B2675 through B2677 for children

B1014b ROSE EDNA BANNING born Nov. 7, 1895 in N.C. and married Brownlow Morris Pack. Source: 46

B2678 through B2680 for children

B1015 JAMES ALEXANDER BANNING born Nov. 10, 1907 in N.C. and married Winifred Willing. Source: 46

B2681 through B2684 for children

B1016 through B1024 unknown children of B280 through B288

B2685 through B2700 for children

B1025 SARAH ANNE TIPSWORD born Dec. 24, 1863 in Effingham Co., Ill. and married Isaiah Jones Doty on Dec. 9, 1890 in Effingham Co. It was his 2nd marriage. He was the son of Moses Doty (1816-1892) and Mary Jane Cavanee (1819-1898), born Feb. 2, 1857 in Effingham Co. Isaiah died Sept. 14, 1912 in Effingham Co. and is buried in the Tipsword Cemetery. Sarah Ann died Jan. 1, 1949 in Effingham Co. and is buried in the Tipsword Cemetery. Source: 16,43

    B2701 Owen Leslie Doty
    B2702 Laura Mabelle Doty
    B2703 Jennings Bryan Doty
    B2704 Cecil Griffin Doty
    B2705 Isaiah Donald Doty
    B2706 Victoria Regina Maris Doty
    B2707 Lucille Doty

B1026 JOHN J. (JOHNNIE) TIPSWORD born 1854 in Ill. and married 1st, Marion McNeeley in 1876 and 2nd, Mary P. Parkinson. He died in Mo. Source: 16,43

B1027 MARY HESTER JOSIE TIPSWORD born 1857 and married Will Chambers. Source: 16,43

B1028 JAMES MERIDA TIPSWORD born Feb. 18, 1859 and married 1st Catherine Younger on April 7, 1887 and 2nd, Louise Morse. Source: 16,43

B1029 JURESIN FRANCES TIPSWORD born 1862. She married Sept 12, 1890 and died Nov. 1891. She is buried in the Tipsword Cemetery in Effingham, Ill. Source: 16,43

B1030 ISAAC VANLANDINGHAM TIPSWORD born 1867 and married Anna Ellie Kinsey on Aug. 9, 1888 in Mo. Source: 16,43

B1031 CHRISTOPHER C. TIPSWORD born May 1869 in Ill. Source: 16,43

B1032 JOSEPH C. TIPSWORD born Feb. 1872 in Ill. Source: 16,43

B1033 MINDA TIPSWORD born 1874 and married James Eldridge. Source: 16,43

B1034 WALTER TIPSWORD born May 1878. Source: 16,43

B1035 through B1049 for children of B290 through B294

B1050 through B1059 unknown children of B295 and B296

B1060 through B1094 unknown children of B297 through B304

B???? for children

B1095 through B1104 unknown children of B305 and B305a

B1105 through B1134 unknown children of B306 through B309a

B???? for children

B1135 HERMAN ERVIN NICHOLS born Jan. 6, 1882 in Herrick, Ill. and married Elma Helen Parmeter on Dec. 15, 1910 in Springfield, Mo. She was born Sept. 8, 1891 in Big Rapids, Mich. They had 2 son's, Paul Lewis, born Nov, 26, 1911 in Ozark, Mo. and Norman Eugene, born June 24, 1916 in Chadwick, Mo. Herman died Aug. 30, 1969 in Reno Nv. Elma died Sept. 6, 1981 in Elko, Nv. Source: 29

B1136 CLARA B. NICHOLS married a Mr. Donohue. Source: 29

B1137 EVELYN NICHOLS born Nov. 1900 and married 3 times. She married 1st, Mr. Myers and had two sons, Joseph and Steven. both children live in Ill. She married 2nd Mr. Iwanski Source: 29

B1138 LEWIS ELLSWORTH NICHOLS born May 30, 1890 and married Esther ???. He served in the U.S. Navy in WWI and died March 17, 1944. Source: 29

B1139 ROBERT E. NICHOLS he was single and died prior to 1978. Source: 29

B1140 ALBERT HOWARD HAYMES born Feb. 26, (or 22) 1883 in Marshfield, Webster Co., Mo. and married Nelle Irene Smith Oct. 24, 1915 in Jonesboro, Tex. She was the daughter of George W. and Lulu (Tichenor) Smith, born July 26, 1893 in Bloomfield, Stoddard Co., Mo. She died April 8, 1963 in Houston, Texas and is buried at Haymes Chapel in Webster Co., Mo. He was an Attorney and a 1st Lt. in the Army in W.W.I. They moved to Houston in 1927, where he died Dec. 12, 1956. He was buried at Haymes Chapel, Mo. Source: 16,32,53,63

B3000 Albert Burke Haymes
B3001 Paul Warren Haymes

B1141 WILLIAM E. HAYMES born April 3, 1881 and married Sarah Viola Waugh on

Jan. 12, 1905. She was born Dec. 15, 1884 and died Sept. 30, 1930 in Webster Co., Mo. He died Jan. 20, 1962 and is buried at Haymes Chapel in Webster Co. Mo. Their children are Charles K., born 1903; Stella Marjorie, born 1919 and Dwight William born 1922. Source: 16,53

B1142 ETHEL D. HAYMES born March 12, 1890 and married Jasper E. Bales. They were living in Newburg, Yamhill Co., Ore. in 1965. Their children are Dora Elizabeth, born March 25, 1915 and George M., born Nov. 5, 1920. Source: 16,53

B1143 JOHN CLARENCE HAYMES born Jan. 25, 1896 and married Esther Redmond. She was born Oct. 14, 1896 in Niangua, Mo. She died March 19, 1980 in Springfield, Mo. where she was buried in the Maple Park Cemetery. They had a daughter, Nancy Jane, born July 12, 1927. Source: 16,53

B1144 LEDA (Leoa?) E. BANNING born 1901 in Webster Co., Mo. and married a Mr. Chenoweth and was living in Rochester, Minn. in 1949. Source: 12,16,29,53

B1145 MERRILL BANNING living in St. Paul, Minn. in 1949. Source: 12,29,53

B1146 JEWEL BANNING married a Mr. Alrich and was living in Topeka, Ks. in 1949. Source: 12,29,53

B1147 JOHN BANNING living in St. Paul, Minn. in 1949. Source: 12, 29,53

B1148 through B1191 unknown children of B312 through B314

B1192 ETHEL FORTNER married a Mr. Taylor. They Homesteaded in Okla, near Blackwell. They had several children. Source: 89

104B1192a DOUGLES FORTNER he was crippled as a child and never married. He lived with his brother, Robert, and lived to be an old man. Source: 89

B1193 JOSEPHINE (JOSE) FORTNER married Oliver Sproat. They lived in Fayette Co., about 4 miles South of Shelby Co. Ill. They had no children. Source: 89

B1193a WILLIAM FORTNER He married 1st, Mary Eceles and had two children, Steve and Lola. He married 2nd, Minnie Devore. They children are Edith, Fred, Raleigh and a daughter. Source: 89

B1194 ALFRED FORTNER He married 1st Estella Koster. They had a son that died at age 16. He married 2nd, Carrie Burris. They had no children. Source: 89

B1194a LUCY FORTNER She married Nathaniel Clark. They had one daughter, Iona. Late in life she married 2nd, Clemit Vallandingham Tipsword. Source: 89

B1195 ROBERT FORTNER He married Eliza Jane Wood. Their children are Eva Elnora (9-12-99 to 1991), Jossie Banning (8-9-01 to 1-12-1993), Raymond (about 1904 to 1908), Edna Estella (7-6-11 to 12-25-1961). Jossie B. Fortner married Leo C. Tipsword and their son, Roland Fortner Tipsword is source 89. Source: 89

B1196 through B1219 unknown children of B314b through B314g

B1220 through B1279 unknown children of B318 through B330

B1280 through B1299 unknown children of B331 through B334

B1300 through B1343 unknown children of B335 through B419

B1344 through B1355 unknown children of B420 and B422

B1356 through B1586 for unknown children of B423 through B516

B1587 through B1598 unknown children of B517 & B518

B1599 through BI604 unknown children of B519

B1605 through B1617 unused numbers

B1618 through B1667 unknown children of B524 through B534

B1668 through B1673 unknown children of B535

B1674 ISADORE SHELDON born in Nehaka, Cass Co., Neb. and married Norris
Tucker. Source: 32

B1680 FANNIE M. BANNING born Aug. 28, 1900 in Nehawka, Cass Co., Neb.

B1681 through B1685 children of B537

B1686 DOROTHY EVELYN STURM born Nov. 14, 1910 in Nehawka, Neb. She
married Chester Bruce Stone on March 5, 1930. He was born Oct. 4, 1901 in
Nehawka. They had at least 1 child, Dorothy Jean, born Aug. 5, 1933 in Nebraska
City, Neb. Source: 32,63

B1687 through B1730 for unknown children of B538 through B546

B1731 ALLEN REYNOLDS no information   Source: 1

B1732 CLEMON REYNOLDS no information   Source: 1

B1733 MINNIE REYNOLDS no information   Source: 1

B1734 ARTHUR REYNOLDS no information   Source: 1

B1735 MIRA REYNOLDS no information   Source: 1

B1736 FLOYD REYNOLDS no information   Source: 1

B1737 EARL REYNOLDS no information   Source: 1

B1738 CLARENCE REYNOLDS no information   Source: 1

B1739 HOMER PHILLIPS no information   Source: 1

B1740 ELDA M. PHILLIPS no information   Source: 1

B1741 CUSTER PHILLIPS no information   Source: 1

B1742 BESSIE L. PHILLIPS no information   Source: 1

B1743 H. MELVIN PHILLIPS no information Source: 1

B1744 PEARL PHILLIPS no information Source: 1

B1745 HOWARD PHILLIPS no information Source: 1

B1746 CARL IVAN PHILLIPS no information Source: 1

B1747 JOHN BANNING born Dec. 29, 1893 in Seymour, Iowa. Source: 1

B1748 CLAY OGLE BANNING born April 19, 1895 in Seymour, Iowa. Source: 1

B1749 WILLIAM BANNING born Jan. 11, 1897 in Seymour, Iowa. Source: 1

B1750 HUGH BANNING born March 25, 1896 in Wright Co., Iowa. He died Aug. 14, 1896. Source: 1

B1751 EPHRAIM BANNING born Nov. 12, 1898 in Wright Co., Iowa. Source: 1

B1752 MAX BANNING born April 30, 1906 near Seattle, Wash. Source: 1

B1753 JESSIE MAPLE no information Source: 1

B1754 MARY MAPLE married a Mr. Dreessen and had at least one son, Richard. Source: 1

B1755 LULU MAPLE no information Source: 1

B1756 CLAIR MAPLE no information Source: 1

B1757 HOWARD MAPLE no information Source: 1

B1758 HOMER KENT SHERRY born Oct. 30, 1888 in Brownsburg, Ind. Source: 1

B1759 INEZ BELL SHERRY born Feb. 11, 1890 in Brownsburg, Ind. Source: 1

B1760 EDITH HOPE SHERRY born June 27, 1891 in Ness Co. , Ks. Source: 1

B1761 CAMERON BANNING SHERRY born Dec. 14, 1892 in Ness Co., Ks. Source: 1

B1762 RAYMOND A. BRYSON born Aug. 5, 1893 in Osage Co., Ks. Source: 1

B1763 EARL BRYSON born Aug. 15, 1898 in Osage Co., Ks. Source: 1

B1764 through B1769 for unknown children of B589

B1770 DAVID GILMER CLOUD no information Source: 1

B1771 FRANCIS MILLAR CLOUD no information Source: 1

B1772 WILLIAM EPHRAIM CLOUD no information Source: 1

B1773 MARGARET IRENE CLOUD no information Source: 1

B1774 through B1782 for unknown children of B594

B1783 JOHN SHIRLEY BURCH born April 18, 1920 and married Martha Victoria Berquist on Sept. 7, 1945 in Loomis, Neb. They were living in Dickinson, Tx in 1993. Their children are John Robert, born Oct. 20, 1947 in Texas City, Tx; Pamela Jean, born April 4, 1949 in Texas City; Linda Kathleen born July 13, 1951 in Texas City; and Karen Elizabeth, born Sept. 29, 1952 in Texas City. Source: 16

B1784 through B1788 for unknown children of B598

B1789 CLARA LOUISE BANNING born April 13, 1903 in Chicago. Source: 1

B1790 WALKER BANNING born Oct. 23, 1904 in Chicago. Source: 1

B1791 EMILIE JENNE BANNING born June 21, 1910 in Oak Park, Ill. Source: 1

B1792 EPHRIAM BANNING, VI born Dec. 21, 1913 in Chicago. He married Estell York. She was the daughter of John Willard and Gertrude (Phipps) York, born Sept. 13, 1935. They had no children. Source: 1,61

B1793 THALIA BANNING born Nov. 24, 1916 in Chicago. Source: 1

B1794 Son ----? BANNING died at birth. Source: 1

B1795 through B1800 for unknown children of B602

B1801 through B1805 for unknown children of B604

B1806 through B1820 for unknown children of B605 through B607

B1821 Daughter BANNING born June 8, 1910 in Milford, Utah. Source: 1

B1822 THOMAS EPHRAIM BANNING born June 25, 1918 in Farmington, Davis Co., Utah. Source: 1

B1823 through B1825 for unknown children of B609

B1826 CAROLYN CONDRA born June 10, 1908 in Seymour, Iowa. Source: 1

B1827 through B1844 for unknown children B611 through B613

B1845 HILDEGARD BANNING born Nov. 19, 1913 in Ayas Pasha, Constantinople, Turkey.

B1846 through B1906 for unknown children of B627 through B657

B1907 through B1922 for unknown children of B664 through B666

B1923 through B1937 for unknown children of B667 through B669

B1938 HERSCHELL BANNING TERRY born Dec. 5, 1891 in Mo. Source: 1

B1939 through B2035 for unknown children of B702 through B746

B2036 JOHN EDWARD BANNING born Aug. 25, 1902 in Lingo, Linn Co., Mo. and married Zoe Lee Terrell on Oct. 1, 1925 in Brookfield, Linn Co., Mo. She was the daughter of James Tuttle and Josie May (Tomlinson) Terrell, born Dec. 8, 1906 in Mo. They lived in Prathersville, Mo. John was 5' 10" tall and worked as a coal miner and roofer. He died of a heart attack in Excelsior Springs, Clay Co., Mo. on Jan. 22, 1968 and was buried in Crown Hill Cemetery. Zoe Lee died Feb. 12, 1976 in Excelsior Springs. Source: 87

      B9600 John Richard Banning
      B9601 Anna Mae Banning
      B9602 Aletha Allene Banning
      B9603 Peggy Lee Banning
      B9604 Barbara Sue Banning
      B9605 James Edward Banning

B2037 OLIVER JACKSON BANNING born Aug. 4, 1904 and married Mary Green in 1922. He married 2nd, Mildred Nester on July 10, 1943. He died Aug. 1, 1961 in Brookfield, Linn Co., Mo. and was buried in Rose Hill Cemetery. Source: 87

      B9606 Noah Oliver Banning
      B9607 Clyde Eugene Banning

B2038 MABLE ANNA MARIE BANNING born Dec. 22, 1906 and married William (Bill) Hiland in 1924. They were divorced and she married 2nd, Bud Williams on Oct. 24, 1936. Source: 87

      B9608 William Eugene Hiland
      B9609 Earl Jackson Hiland
      B9610 James Edward Hiland
      B9611 Billie Lee Williams
      B9612 Edgar Eloise Williams
      B9613 Carolyn Sue Williams
      B9614 Dapheny Ann Williams
      B9615 Jerry Dean Williams

B2039 BUDDY ROLAND no other information. Source: 87

B2040 PEARL PHELPS no other information. Source: 87

B2041 GOLDIE PHELPS no other information. Source: 87

B2042 ORVILLE PHELPS no other information. Source: 87

B2043 FRANK PHELPS no other information. Source: 87

B2044 LOLA TURPIN born Sept. 27, 1901 in Marceline, Linn Co. Mo. and married Harry M. Young about 1921. Source: 87

B2045 ORLANDO L. TURPIN born 1905 and married Mollie Ann (???). Source: 87

B2046 ELSIE TURPIN born 1909 and married Jacob Louis Seweitzer. Source: 87

B2047 PEARL TURPIN born about 1911 and married Frank Jaboe. Source: 87

B2048 IVA MAE BANNING married Alva Elgon "Punch" Brittain. She died Feb. 5,

1991. Source: 87

B9616 through B9618 for children

B2049 JONNY BILL BANNING No information. Source: 87

B9619 through B9621 for children

B2050 BEN BANNING married Irene (???) and died Nov. 5, 1978 in Henderson Nevada. Source: 87

B9622 Louis Wayne Banning

B2051 HELEN BANNING No information. Source: 87

B9623 through B9625 for children

B2052 MARGUERITE BANNING married Roy Ogle. Source: 87

B9626 through B9628 for children

B2053 DOROTHY BANNING married Bud Stapleton. Source: 87

B9629 through B9631 for children

B2054 MARY ANN BANNING no information. Source: 87

B9632 through B9634 for children

B2055 BETTY BANNING married Harvey Carrouthers. Source: 87

B9635 through B9637 for children

B2056 FRANCIS BANNING married Gale Pulham. Source: 87

B9638 through B9640 for children

B2057 WILLIAM C. BANNING JR. died about 1921. Source: 87

B2058 KENNETH RICHARD BANNING married Viva Marriott. Source: 87

B9641 Leann Banning
B9642 Melissa Banning
B9643 Richard Banning
B9644 William Banning

B2059 through B2089 for unknown children of B753 through B762

B2090 through B2095 for unknown children of B768

B2096 EDGAR FRAY born 1880. Source: 1

B2097 ESTELL FRAY born 1890. Source: 1

B2098 through B2109 for unknown children of B773 & B774

B2110 BESSIE BANNING born Jan. 23, 1893. Source: 1

B2111 through B2114 for unknown children of B775

B2115 DOROTHY BANNING married a Mr. Stewart and lived in Charleston, Mo. Source: 30

B2116 LESTER T. BANNING born Dec. 21, 1908 and married Pauline Wood in 1937. He served in WWII. Source: 30

> B9700 Beverly B. Banning
> B9701 Betty Banning
> B9702 William Banning

B2117 MARTHA AGNES BANNING born July 29, 1903 and died prior to 1979. Source: 1,30

B2118 MARY SUSAN BANNING born May 18, 1905, married Mr. Robertson and live in St. Louis, Mo.. Source: 1,30

B2119 INA B. BANNING born March 21, 1907, married Mr. Fidler and live in Troy, Idaho. Source: 1,30

B2120 ALPHA BANNING married a Mr. Manson and lived in Martinsville, Va. Source: 30

B2121 through B2125 for unknown children of B777

B2126 through B2135 for unknown children of B778 & B779

B2136 BERTHA BANNING born April 10, 1892 in Brookfield, Mo.

B2137 HAZEL BANNING born July 26, 1895 in Brookfield, Mo.

B2138 JOHNNIE BANNING born July 19, 1897 in Brookfield, MO.

B2139 HAZEL L. BRAUN born 1887.

B2503 HOMER OSMER LEWIS born Oct. 21, 1893. Source: 18,75

B2503a MONNIE E. LEWIS born March 30, 1900 and died March 12, 1911. Source: 18,75

B2503b MINNIE OLA LEWIS born Dec. 19, 1901 and married J.D. Chandless on Feb. 9, 1927. Their children were Jetta Ann, born Nov. 30, 1927 and Jadine (Bobbie), born May 27, 1931. Minnie died Sept. 4, 1934. Source: 18,75

B2503c LILLIAN OMEGIA LEWIS born Feb. 23, 1904 and died March 12, 1905. Source: 18,75

B2505 MAMIE BANNING born April 1892 in Ark. Source: 10,75

B2505a SHERMAN BANNING born July 1896 in Ark. Source: 10,75

B2505b MURRIL BANNING born 1899 in Ark. Source: 75,78

B2505c CARL L. BANNING born 1906 in Ark. Source: 75,78

B2506 JOSEPH BANNING born 1911 in Ark. Source: 75,78

B2506a CHARITY BANNING born 1913 in Ark. She married Earl Chadwick on Oct. 4, 1933 in Izard Co. Ark. Source: 12,75,78

B2506b JOHN R. BANNING born 1916 in Ark and married Velda Carter on Dec. 5, 1946 in Izard Co. Ark. Source: 12,75,78

B2508 EDNA BANNING born Dec. 1898 in Ark. Source: 10,75

B2508a HETTIE BANNING born May 1900 in Ark. Source: 10,75

B2513 JAMES EDWIN COOPER born Oct. 20, 1901 in Cushman, Ark and married Alta Frances Pierce on April 24, 1920 in Randolph Co. Ark. She was born Aug. 8, 1903 in Evening Shade, Ark. and died on March 5, 1960 in Los Angles, Ca. Their children were; Irene, born 1921, died 1923; Nola Bernice, born 1924, died 1987; Myrtle Eunice, born 1929; James Edwin Jr, born 1930, died 1940; Edwina Frances, born 1934 and Wanda Lorena born 1938. James married 2nd, Golda Marie Page on May 17, 1940 in Batesville, Ark. She was born on May 30, 1918 in Cushman, Ark. Their children were Oveta Marie, born 1943 and James Morris, born 1948. Source: 79

B2513a EMILY IMOGENE COOPER born Oct. 9, 1904 in Anderson, Ark. and married Richard Simpson on June 14, 1925 at Long Creek School near Grubbs, Ark. He was born Jan. 7, 1897 in Ill. He died in Black Oak, Ark and she died Jan. 24, 1994 in Caraway, Ark. Their children were Ola Wandalea, born 1931 and Emily, born and died March 1, 1941. Source: 79

B2513b MARY OLA "TOM" COOPER born April 7, 1907 in Mt. Pleasant, Ark. and died Dec. 27, 1971 in Newport, Ark. At an early age, she suffered a crippling disease and did not walk until she was 4 years old. She spent her life helping the sick or new born babies. She was the "second Mama" to many nieces and nephews. Source: 79

B2513c NOLA JANE "BILL" COOPER born April 7, 1907 in Mt. Pleasant, Ark and married Robert Qualls on Nov. 2, 1924. They had one child, Kenneth Edwin, born Aug. 20, 1927 in Tuckerman, Ark. They were divorced in 1927. Nola married 2nd, Charles Hubert Stoner on Sept. 30, 1930 in Tuckerman, Ark. He was born on March 23, 1910 and died Jan. 5, 1989. Nola died Feb. 26, 1961 in Waldenburg, Ark. Source: 79

B2513d FRED D. COOPER born Sept. 5, 1909 in Anderson, Ark. and married Retha Edith Dowell on Dec. 20, 1928 in Tuckerman, Ark. She was born March 24, 1913 in Tuckerman and died Nov. 6, 1993 in Manila, Ark. Their Children were Ora Lee, born 1932 and Gwen Dee, born 1933. Fred died Sept. 28, 1961 in Memphis, Tn. Source: 79

B2513e BURL LONZO COOPER born Dec. 20, 1911 in Anderson, Ark. and married Florence May Perry on Oct. 25, 1930 near Tuckerman, Ark. She was born on July

11, 1915 in Swifton, Ark. and died Nov. 29, 1994 in Spokane, Wa. Their children are William Lavern, born Aug. 20, 1931 and Burl Lavon, born Aug. 28, 1935. Burl died Oct. 27, 1994 in Spokane, Wa. Source: 79

B2513f MINNIE ESTER COOPER born Sept. 3, 1914 in Anderson, Ark. and married Oliver Millard Greeno on Oct. 21, 1934 in Harrisburg, Ark. He was born Oct. 17, 1913 in Weatley, Ark. Their children are, Malcolm Lynn, born 1935; Rowena Jean, born 1939; George Edward, born 1943 and only lived a few days; Camelia Gayle, born 1945; Roger Dale, born 1949 and Wynella Karen, born 1953. Oliver died Dec. 29, 1960 at Blytheville, Ark. and Minnie died Nov. 17, 1993 at Kimberling City, Mo. Source: 79

B2513g RUTH COOPER born Feb. 4, 1918 in Anderson, Ark and married Edgar Wayne Greeno on Jan. 1, 1936 in Weiner, Ark. He was born Jan. 17, 1909 in Poinsett Co. Ark. Their children are Edgar Wayne, Jr., born 1937; Eddie Ruth, born 1938; Peggy Angelina, born 1939; Elizabeth Waynette, born 1944; Edgar Bruce, born 1947 and Judy Carol, born 1951. Edgar died Sept 27, 1954 in Waldenburg, Ark. Ruth married 2nd Harmon Dunlap in Sept. 1958 in Lake City, Ark. and died March 19, 1982 in Ellington, Mo. Source: 79

B2513h WILLIAM JENNINGS COOPER born May 25, 1920 in Sidney, Ark. and married Della Blaine Jackson on Feb. 17, 1946 in Stuttgart, Ark. Blain was born Aug. 21, 1925 in Stuttgart. Their children are William David, born July 20, 1950 in Lawrenceburg, Tn. and James Dudley, born Oct. 14, 1952 in Corinth, Ms. They were living in Crestview Fla. in 1996. Blaine is source 79. Source: 79

B2575 GERALD DEAN HOLLEY born April 26, 1925 and married Wanda Jane Williams. Source: 16,92

B2575a CLARA MAE HOLLEY born Oct. 1, 1927 and married Charles Raymond Miller. She died of natural causes on May 5, 1993. Source: 16,92

B2576 RONALD EUGENE HOLLEY born Nov. 6, 1929 in Findley, Ill. and married Darlene Faye Phillips on Nov. 3, 1957 in Beecher City, Ill. She was the daughter of Joseph Kenneth and Cleo Frances Phillips, born Sept. 24, 1932 in Beecher City. Source: 16,92

        B14000 Sherri Frances Holley
        B14001 Bradley Gene Holley
        B14002 Julie Ann Holley

B2576a CHARLES FRANKLIN HOLLEY born Oct. 19, 1933 and married Caroline Pearce. Source: 16,92

B2576b SHIRLEY JEAN HOLLEY born March, 17 1937 and married Larry Dean Wade. She died Nov. 21, 1995. Source: 16,92

B2576c PATSY LOU HOLLEY born April 18, 1939 and married William Joe Thompson. Source: 16,92

B2577 LARRY PHIL HOLLEY born July 28, 1941 and married Joan Smith. They were divorced. Source: 16,92

B2577a STEVEN JOE HOLLEY born May 12, 1947 and married Cheryl (Sherry) Jones. Source: 16,92

B2701 OWEN LESLIE DOTY born June 28, 1892 in Effingham Co. Ill. and married
1st. Elizabeth Patterson and 2nd Donna Stonecipher. He die about 1950 in
Indianapolis, Ind. and is buried in the VA Cemetery. Source: 16,43

B2702 LAURA MABELLE DOTY born Feb. 12, 1894 in Effingham Co., Ill. and married
Franklin Willey Tipsword on Nov. 11, 1913 in Louisville, Clay Co. Ill. He was the son
of Isaac Benton and Lillian (Randolph) Tipsword, born Nov. 30, 1891 in Effingham
Co. He was a teacher, mail carrier, sales man and deputy sheriff. She was a sales
clerk and died Dec. 24, 1953 in Effingham. He died March 5, 1975 in Effingham.
Both are buried in Moccasin, Effingham Co., Ill. Their children are, Keith Warren,
born 1914; Deane Wiley, born 1915; Gail Lillian, born 1917 and source of much
information; Hugh Dwight, born 1919; Frances Jeanne, born 1924; Elizabeth Fae,
born 1933 and Vera Dalyne, born 1936. Source: 16,43

B2703 JENNINGS BRYAN DOTY born May 18, 1896 and married 1st Ada (???) and
2nd, Katie (???). Source: 16,43

B2704 CECIL GRIFFIN DOTY born Aug. 1898 and died about 1901. Source: 16,43

B2705 ISAIAH DONALD DOTY born Dec. 11, 1900 in Effingham Co., Ill. and married
Gladys (???). He died in 1988 in Greenup, Cumberland Co., Ill. in is buried in the
Tipsword Cemetery in Effingham, Ill. Source: 16,43

B2706 VICTORIA REGINA MARIS DOTY born Jan. 24, 1904 in Effingham Co., Ill.
and married Clarence Guthrie. Source: 16,43

B2707 LUCILLE DOTY born Jan. 9, 1907 in Effingham Co., Ill. and married 1st
Thomas Phillips and 2nd, Jeff. Lilley. Source: 16,43

B3000 ALBERT BURKE HAYMES born July 18, 1916 in Rector, Clay Co., Ark. and
married Sylvia Corrine (Corinn?) Popp on Nov. 15, 1941 in New Braunfels, Comal
Co., Tx. She is the daughter of Bruno Walter and Olga L. (Habermann) Popp, born
May 16, 1916 in New Braunfels, Tx. Albert served in the Army Air Corps Prior to
World War II. He is a member of the Sons of the American Revolution, # 126723.
They live in Houston, Tx. where he is a CPA. Source: 16,32,53,63

B19000 Kathryn Nelle Haymes
B19001 Pamela Jeanne Haymes

B3001 PAUL WARREN HAYMES born May 15, 1926 in Sikeston Mo. and married
Norma Juanice Simons on July 20, 1950 in Houston, Harris Co., Tx. She is the
daughter of George W. and Bertha A. (Blevins) Simons, born Jan. 10, 1925 in
Waco, Tx. He works for the FBI. They were divorced May 5, 1977. Their children
are, Paul Howard, born Oct. 15, 1954 in Montebello, Ca.: Mark Burke, born Oct. 21,
1960 in Montebello and they adopted Cynthia Ann, born Aug. 30, 1945. Source:
16,53

B9600 JOHN RICHARD BANNING born Sept. 7, 1926 in Marceline, Linn Co., M. He
married Hazel Lorraine Clinton on April 7, 1947 in San Antonio, Bexar Co., Tx. She
is the daughter of Edward McGary and Elsie Helen (Herring) Clinton, born Feb. 24,
1927 in San Antonio, Tx. He is 5' 10" tall and was an accountant for City Public
Service for 33 years. Source: 16,87

B26000 Richard Allen Banning

B26001 Kenneth Ray Banning

B9601 ANNA MAE BANNING born Nov. 19, 1928 in Marceline, Linn Co., Mo. She married Lee Tillman Swope on July 24, 1952 in Excelsior Springs, Clay Co., Mo. He was born April 22, 1932. She was 5' 2" tall, a nurse and died of a stroke in Jan. 1969. in Excelsior Springs and was buried in Crownhill Cemetery. Source: 16,87

> B26002 Beverly Banning Ward
> B26003 Jessie Lee Swope
> B26004 Sherry Ann Swope
> B26005 Catherine Renee Swope

B9602 ALETHA ALLENE BANNING born July 19, 1933 in Excelsior Springs, Clay Co., Mo. She married Don Dwyer Crowley on Oct 21, 1950 in Eureka Springs, Carroll Co., Ark. He was the son of Millard Earl and Obie Jane (Rice) Crowley, born June 21, 1930 in Rayville, Ray Co., Mo. He is a Minister, barber and Ray County Assessor. She was a postmaster, 5' 5" tall and lives in Rayville, Mo. Source: 16,87

> B26006 David Allen Crowley

B9603 PEGGY LEE BANNING born Sept. 12, 1937 in Marceline, Linn Co., Mo. She married Charley Farrell Swope on Aug. 26, 1953 in Liberty, Clay Co., Mo. He is the son of Charles William and Bitha Pearl (Clevenger) Swope, born Dec. 8, 1934 in Caldwell Co., Mo. She was 5' 2" tall and lives in Prathersville, Mo. He worked for TWA for 34 years. Source: 16,87

> B26007 Ronnie Eugene Swope
> B26008 Michael Lee Swope
> B26009 Theresa Lynn Swope

B9604 BARBARA SUE BANNING born Feb. 21, 1941 in Excelsior Springs, Clay Co., Mo. She married Michael Bryan on Aug. 18, 1969 in Miami, Miami Co., Okla. He was born Nov. 30, 1946 and worked for Hallmark Cards. They lived in Prathersville, Mo. She died from a stroke on Nov. 12, 1990 in Excelsior Springs, Clay Co., Mo. and is buried in Crownhill Cemetery. He died May 5, 1993 of cancer in Excelsior Springs. Source: 16,87

> B26010 Clarence Edward Bryan
> B26011 Charles Andrew Bryan

B9605 JAMES EDWARD BANNING born Aug. 3, 1945 and died Nov.17, 1950, both in Excelsior Springs, Clay Co. Mo. He accidentally hung himself while playing cowboys. He is buried in Crownhill Cemetery. Source: 16.87

B9606 NOAH OLIVER BANNING born July 1, 1923 and married Ruby Kathryn (???) on Dec. 20, 1940. He married 2nd, Bea (???). He died April 7, 1982 in Excelsior Springs, Clay Co., Mo. and is buried at the Pisgah Baptist Church. Source: 16,87

> B26012 Kay Banning
> B26013 Terry Banning
> B26014 Dale Banning

B9607 CLYDE EUGENE BANNING born Sept. 22, 1924 in Brookfield, Mo. and married Doreen (???). They were later divorced. He died March 31, 1996 in Brookfield. Source: 16,87

B26015 Raymond Banning
B26016 Kathryn Banning

B9608 WILLIAM EUGENE HILAND born Dec. 15, 1926 and married Rose Mary Lewis on March 29, 1945. Their children are Linda sue, born 1948 and Peggy Lee, born 1951. Source: 16,87

B9609 EARL JACKSON HILAND born May 15, 1928. Source: 16,87

B9610 JAMES EDWARD HILAND born Oct. 2, 1929. Source: 16,87

B9611 BILLIE LEE WILLIAMS She was born Aug. 15, 1934. Source: 16,87

B9612 EDGAR ELOISE WILLIAMS He was born Oct. 13, 1938. Source: 16,87

B9613 CAROLYN SUE WILLIAMS born Nov. 21, 1942. Source: 16,87

B9614 DAPHENY ANN WILLIAMS born April 10, 1945. Source: 16,87

B9615 JERRY DEAN WILLIAMS born Aug. 14, 1946. Source: 16.87

B9616 through B9621 for children of B2049 and B2049

B26017 through B26026 for children

B9622 LEWIS WAYNE BANNING no information. Source: 87

B26027 through B26030 for children

B9623 through B9637 for children of B2052 through B2055

B9638 through B9640 for children of B2056

B26031 through B26035 for children

B9641 LEANN BANNING born Aug. 31, 1944 and married Dean Eldon Stoll on June 3, 1962 in Excelsior Springs, Clay Co. Mo. Dean was born April 12, 1941 in Wichita, Ks. They are living in Owassio, Okla. Source: 16,87

B26036 Wendy Lynn Stoll
B26037 Mitchell Kent Stoll
B26038 Jennifer Leigh Stoll

B9642 MELISSA BANNING married Orville Clevenger. Source: 16,87

B9643 RICHARD BANNING no information. Source: 16,87

B9644 WILLIAM BANNING no information. Source: 16,87

B9700 BEVERLY B. BANNING living in Radford, Va. in 1979. Source: 30

B9701 BETTY BANNING married Mr. Batschelett and were living in Clinton, Mo. in 1979. Source: 30

B9702 WILLIAM BANNING living in Columbia, Mo. in 1979. Source: 30

B14000 SHERRI FRANCES HOLLEY born April 17, 1959 in Effingham, Ill. and married Scott Jerome Hilmes on June 6, 1981. He was born Feb. 8, 1959 in East St. Louis, Ill. They were living at Robins A.F.B. Ga. in 1996. Their children are Ryan Scott, born Aug. 19, 1982 in Belleville, Ill. and Taryn Holley, born April 29, 1985 at Whiteman A.F.B. in Mo. Sherri is source 92. Source: 16,92

B14001 BRADLEY GENE HOLLEY born July 4, 1960 in Vandalia, Ill and married Gerilyn Meier on Feb. 3, 1986. Source: 16,92

B14002 JULIE ANN HOLLEY born June 28, 1961 in Vandalia, Ill. Source: 16,92

B19000 KATHRYN NELLE HAYMES born April 15, 1945 in Nashville, Shelby Co., Tn. and married Jeffrey Alan Dinkin on March 25, 1979 in Oakland, Alameda Co., Ca. They have a daughter, Sophie Allison, born March 17, 1987 in Berkley, Ca. Source: 16,53

B19001 PAMELA JEANNE HAYMES born Oct. 14, 1948 in Houston, Harris Co., Tx. and married Michael Paul Graham on Feb. 21, 1976 in Houston. He is the son of Kenneth L. and Norma Doris (Whiteside) Graham, born May 15, 1948 in Leavenworth, Ks. He is an attorney and they live in Houston. Their children are Sarah Kathryn, born Nov. 13, 1980 in Houston and Patrick Edward, born March 11, 1983 in Houston. Source: 16,53

B26000 RICHARD ALLEN BANNING born Feb. 16, 1948 in San Antonio, Bexar Co., Tx. and married Laurel Jean Barrett on June 17, 1971 in San Antonio. She is the daughter of David M. and Jean D. (Bull) Barrett, born about 1947 in Los Angeles, Calif. He married 2nd Patty Louise Reisz on Oct. 2, 1976 in San Antonio. They are divorced. He served in the U.S. Army and is now a printer. Richard had no children. Source: 16,87

B26001 KENNETH RAY BANNING born April 28, 1950 in San Antonio, Bexar Co., Tx. He lives in Austin, Tx. and is an Advisory Scientist for IBM. Source: 16,87

B26002 BEVERLY BANNING WARD born March 29, 1951 in Kansas City, Jackson Co., Mo. She married Jim Durham in 1972. Their children are Mollie, born about 1973 and Jimmy born about 1975. Source: 16,87

B26003 JESSIE LEE SWOPE born Feb. 15, 1961. Source: 16,87

B26004 SHERRY ANN SWOPE born March 21, 1962 and married Frank Boatright on June 28, 1980. He was born April 28, 1947. Her children are Lois Swope, born Aug. 23, 1976, Frank, Jr. born June 14, 1981 and Angela, born June 23, 1984. Source: 16,87

B26005 CATHERINE RENEE SWOPE born May 14, 1963 and married Jewell Cates on Feb. 28, 1981. He was born April 13, 1961. Their children are James Luther, born Aug. 24, 1981; Tawyna, born Feb. 1984 and Eddie, born May 27, 1986. Source: 16,87

B26006 DAVID ALLEN CROWLEY born Nov. 11, 1952 in Excelsior Springs, Clay Co., Mo. He married Becki Mae Rogers on Aug. 5, 1972 in Rayville, Ray Co., Mo. She was born Nov. 2, 1951 in Excelsior Springs. He works for UPS and they live in Excelsior Springs. Their children are, Matthew David, born Dec. 17, 1973; Drew

Alan, born Sept. 3, 1976; Jacob Edward, born Dec. 8, 1978 and Elizabeth Jolynn, born April 3, 1981. Source: 16,87

B26007 RONNIE EUGENE SWOPE born Jan. 15, 1955 in Prathersville, Clay Co., Mo. He married Deborah L. Owens on June 28, 1974 in Prathersville. She was the daughter of Buddy Richard and Mary Elizabeth (Brand) Oens, born Jan. 19, 1958 in Excelsior Springs, Clay Co., Mo. Ronnie is a construction worker, 5' 11" tall. Their children are Christopher Eugene, born Oct. 19, 1978 and Mindy Rachelle, born Aug. 20, 1981. Source: 16,87

B26008 MICHAEL LEE SWOPE born Jan. 11, 1956 in Excelsior Springs, Clay Co., Mo. He married Cheryl Denise Summers on Mar. 28, 1981 in Excelsior Springs. She is the daughter of Raymond Joseph and Viola Maxine (Collins) Summers, born April 24, 1956 in Excelsior Springs. He is a boilermaker, 5' 6" tall. They have a son, Nathan Michael, born March 4, 1983. Source: 16,87

B26009 THERESA LYNN SWOPE born April 25, 1957 in Excelsior Springs, Clay Co., Mo. and married Randy K. Morris on March 22, 1976. They are divorced. They had two children, Melissa Dawn, born June 15, 1977 and Rachel Ann, born Aug. 2, 1978. Source: 16,87

B26010 CLARENCE EDWARD BRYAN born March 21, 1970 in Kansas City, Jackson Co., Mo. Source: 16,87

B26011 CHARLES ANDREW BRYAN born April 27, 1973 in Excelsior Springs, Clay Co., Mo. He married Shelley Renee Bishop on June 26, 1993 in Rayville, Ray Co., Mo. He is a construction worker. They have a son, William Michael Bryan, born in 1994. Source: 16,87

B26012 KAY BANNING no information. Source: 87

B26013 TERRY BANNING no information. Source: 87

B26014 DALE BANNING no information. Source: 87

B26015 RAYMOND BANNING no information. Source: 87

B26016 KATHRYN BANNING no information. Source: 87

B26017 through B26035 for children of B9616 through B9640

B26036 WENDY LYNN STOLL born Jan. 12, 1963 and married John Thomas Cline on Sept. 26, 1981 in Owasso, Tulsa Co. Okla. He was born Aug. 24, 1962 in Bartlesville, Okla. They had one child, Rachel Lynn, born June 12, 1983. They were divorced May 24, 1984 in Tulsa. She married 2nd, John Gillispie Foerster, Jr. on July 29, 1988 in Miami, Ottawa Co. Okla. He was born Feb. 24, 1959 in Athens, Henderson Co. Tex. They had two children, John G. born March 23, 1989 and Chase Banning, born July 23, 1990. Source: 87

B26037 MITCHELL KENT STOLL born Aug. 29, 1964 in Wichita, Sedgewick Co. Ks. He married Marion Audrey Powell on Aug. 16, 1986 in Jacksonville, Duvall Co. Fla. She was born Aug. 16, 1968 in Tampa, Fla. They have two children, Joshua Daniel born Nov. 20, 1987 and Nicholas Dean born Dec. 21, 1992. Source: 87

B26038 JENNIFER LEIGH STOLL born Dec. 27, 1995 in Tulsa, Okla. She married

Chad Ray Barnard on July 1, 1995 in Owasso, Tulsa Co. Okla. He was born Jan. 6, 1974 in Norman, Okla. Source: 87

RICHARD BANNING of DELAWARE

B2 JOHN BANNING (Same as A5a) He was of age by 1704, married the daughter of Richard Parnell, who gave then 1/2 of "Golden Lyon" in Q.A. County in 1715. He was dead by 1718. His will is on file in Queen Ann Co., Md. His children A6, A6a & A7 were orphans, given 1st to Thomas Banning then their uncle, Andrew. Source: 12,13,24,28,47

> A6 William Banning   (See A6)
> B3 John Banning   (Same as A6a, see B3)
> C3 Richard Banning

C3 RICHARD BANNING (Sr.) born 1715/16. He had two brothers, William & John and his grandfather was Stephen. He married Ester Wilson, the daughter of John and Mary Wilson from Tuckahoe, Queen Ann Co., Md. on Nov. 30, 1737 in St. Peters Parish, Talbot Co., Md. and then moved to Del. He was living with Andrew Banning A50) in 1733. After His death, before May 28, 1742, she married Matthew Jarratt (Jarrad or Jarrall). Source: 2,12,13,21,22,24,27,28,29,35,45,47,58

> C4 Richard Banning Jr.
> C5 John Banning
> C6 Phineas Banning

C4 RICHARD BANNING Jr. born prior to 1755 173?) and died between March 6 and Oct. 3, 1811, when he signed his will and it was approved by the court. His wife, Mary Russell was deceased by 1779. She was the daughter of William (dead by 1779) and Elizabeth Russell, born between 1755 and 1765 (?). He was a juror in a murder trial in Kent Co. Del. on May 5, 1783. His will indicates he had no surviving children by 1811. Source: 2,3,12 22,24,47

> C7 Charles Banning
> C8 James Banning
> C9 Ester Banning
> C10 White Banning
> C11 Sanford Banning

C5 JOHN BANNING born 1738/39 in Dover, Del. He married Mrs. Elizabeth (Alford) Casson between 1781 and 1785. She was the widow of John Casson and the daughter of Philip and Charity Allston Alford (1731-1783) of Philadelphia. He joined the Kent Co. Militia on April 2, 1776, a member of the Council of Safety and was on the "Committee of Correspondence" in Aug. 1775 and was one of the founders of the state of Delaware. He was a wealthy man, owned a saddle shop and other business. A House he built in 1766 still stands at 529 S. State St. in Dover. He was a member of the 1st Electoral College that made George Washington President and a member of the Del. Assembly from 1777 till his death on Feb. 15, 1791 in Dover. He is buried there in Christ Churchyard. She then married Dr. William McKee, died Jan 5-17, 1812 and is buried next to John. Source: 2,12,15,22,24,27,32,34,45,47,57,58

> C12 John Alford Banning
> C13 Sarah Banning

C6 PHINEAS BANNING born 1740 and lived in Kent Co., Del. He married 1st, Priscilla Cardeen. She was the daughter of William (died Jan. 1778) and Rachel Cardeen. He married 2nd, Phebe -----? He was a member of the Council of Safety in the Revolution. His last name is sometime indicated as "Bandy". He died before March 29, 1791 in Del. Phebe then married Joseph Baker. Source: 1,2, 12,21,22,24,47

        C14 Elizabeth Banning
        C15 Ester Banning
        C16 Nathaniel Banning (wife 2 ?)
        C17 Priscilla Banning (wife 2 ?)
        C18 Gartery Gertrude Banning

C7 CHARLES BANNING He was a private in Capt. Joseph Vaughn's Co. of Col. John Haslet's Del. Regiment of Continental Troops. He joined Jan. 22, 1776 and was "in barracks" at Dover on April 12, 1776. He again joined Capt. Vaughan's Co. at Amboy, Nov. 22, 1776. Source: 2

        C30 through C34 for children

C8 JAMES BANNING no information Source: 2

        C35 through C39 for children

C9 ESTER BANNING born between 1784 and 1794. Source: 2

        C40 through C44 for children

C10 WHITE BANNING no information Source: 2

        C45 through C49 for children

C11 SANFORD BANNING no information Source: 2

        C50 through C54 for children

C12 JOHN ALFORD BANNING born in 1790 at Dover, Kent Co., Del. He married on March 2, 1813, Elizabeth Lowber the daughter of William Lowber and Alice Ponder (Pender, Pindar), born 1794 in Del. They were descendants of Peter Lowber of Amsterdam, Holland. John Alford was engaged in shipbuilding and farming and lived on Oak Hill Farm about 3 miles from Wilmington. They were Episcopalians. He graduated from Princeton University (then the College of New Jersey) as a Bachelor of Arts in 1810. He was living in Christian Hundred, New Castle Co., in Sept 1850. He died April 13, 1854 in New Castle Co., Del. She died Nov. 1861. Source: 1,2,4,5,12,22,24,27,32,47,57,58

        C19 John Alford Banning
        C20 William Lowber Banning
        C21 Elizabeth Alice Banning
        C22 Sallie Banning
        C23 Mary Lowber Banning
        C24 Henry Banning
        C25 Richard Banning
        C26 Alice P. Banning

C27 Phineas Banning
C28 Francinia Alice Banning
C29 Cole Lowbar Banning

C13 SARAH BANNING born Feb. 18, 1787 and lived in Dover, Del. She married Henry Moore Ridgely of Dover on Nov. 21, 1803. He was born Aug. 6, 1779 and was the son of Charles Greenbury Ridgely and his wife, Ann Moore. He died Aug. 6, 1847. He was a descendant of Robert Bruce, King of Scotland. Sarah died Jan. 14, 1837.   Source: 2,12,22,24,27,32,34,47,58

C55 Charles George Ridgely
C56 Nicholas Ridgely
C57 John Banning Ridgely
C58 Williamina Ridgely
C60 Elizabeth Ridgely
C61 Anna Ridgely
C62 Henry Ridgely
C63 Juliet Ridgely
C64 Nicholas Ridgely (2nd)
C65 Eugene Ridgely
C66 Mary Ridgely
C66a Infant Ridgely
C67 Williamina Ridgely (2nd)
C68 Edward Ridgely

C14 ELIZABETH BANNING married Daniel Lowber and was alive in 1791   Source: 2,12,22,24,47

C69 through C71 for children

C15 ESTER BANNING married Thomas Baker, and moved to Ky. She was alive in 1811.   Source: 2,12,22,24,47

C72 through C74 for children

C16 NATHNIEL BANNING born 1788 in Kent Co., Del and married Nancy A. Hall on Jan. 5, 1815 in Muskingum Co., Ohio. She was the daughter of David Hall and Rachel Veach born March 1796 in Del. They lived in Decorah, Iowa. They were living in Knox Co., Ohio in 1820, 1840 & 1850 where he was a farmer. He died Sept. 11, 1862 and she died May 11, 1891, both in Winnishiek Co., Iowa and are buried in Centennial Cemetery.   Source: 2,4,5,12,13,22,24,47

C75 Phineas Banning
C76 John Banning
C77 Rachel Banning
C78 Priscilla Banning
C79 William A. Banning
C80 Nathaniel Banning
C80A Polly J. Banning
C80B Michael Banning
C80c Nancy Banning
C80d Ellen Banning

C17 PRISCILLA BANNING born May 20, 1786/90 in Del. and married Isaac Turner

Feb. 4, 1805 in Kent Co., Del. He was the son of William Turner, born about 1780 in Del. They moved to Ohio about 1815. He died May 3, 1843 in Muskingum Co., Ohio. She died April 27, 1872 in Hardin Co., Ohio and is buried in Chandler Cemetery, 4 miles N.W. of Ada, Oh. Source: 2,21,22,24,47

> C81 Sally (Sarah) Turner
> C82 Elizabeth Turner
> C83 Samuel Turner
> C84 Isaac Banning Turner
> C85 Matilda Turner
> C86 Ann Turner
> C86A Nancy Turner
> C86B John Turner
> C87 Phineas Turner

C18 GARTERY (GERTRUDE) BANNING she died unmarried before May 7, 1801. Source: 2,12,22,24,47

C19 JOHN ALFORD BANNING born about 1820 in Wilmington, Del. He lived in Wilmington and Philadelphia, Pa. where he was a lawyer. I think he married Sarah A. _____?, who was born about 1830. She may have been his 2nd wife. They were living in Christian Hundred in New Castle Co., Del. in Sept. 1850. Source: 1,2,4,5,40,58

> C94 Alice Banning
> C95 Ellen Banning
> C96 William S. Banning
> C96A Mary Banning

C20 WILLIAM LOWBER BANNING born 1814 in Wilmington, Del. By 1844 he was a lawyer in Philadelphia, where he married Mary Alice Sweeney on Jan. 20, 1850. She was born Dec. 2, 1830 in Penn. and was a direct descendant of Donal of Arnagh, the 173rd monarch of Ireland, who died A.D. 978. Donal was the son of Murkertagh and the grandson of Neall Glundubh, the 170th monarch of Ireland, who was killed in battle with the Danes A.D. 919. William fought in the civil war. He built and became president of the Lake Superior & Mississippi River Railroad. They lived in St. Paul, Minn. where he died Nov. 26, 1893. She died Feb. 4, 1910 in Los Angeles, Calif. They were living in Philadelphia in 1850. Source: 1,2,5,27, 30,32,34,40,57,58

> C97 Ellen Barrows Banning
> C98 Evans Banning
> C99 William Lowber Banning
> C100 Mary Alice Banning
> C101 Frederick Dunlevy Banning
> C102 William Lowber Banning
> C103 Katherine Stewart Banning

C21 ELIZABETH ALICE BANNING born Wilmington, Del. She married Isaac Elliott. They had 4 children. Source: 1,2,58

> C104 through C107 for children

C22 SALLIE BANNING born 1822 in New Castle Co., Del. She married Isaac L. Elliott in New Castle Co. where they lived. She died Dec. 1891. Source: 1,2,58

C108 Eliza Elliott
C109 Fanny Banning Elliott
C110 Isaac C. Elliott

C23 MARY LOWBER BANNING born Feb. 12, 1820 in New Castle Co., Del. She
married William Armstrong on March 28, 1854. They lived in New Castle Co. and
she died there Dec. 1, 1877. Source: 1,2,58

C111 Richard Banning Armstrong
C112 Annie B. Armstrong
C113 William John Banning

C24 HENRY BANNING he was born in Wilmington, Del. and lived in Minn. He was
farming in Platte Co., Mo in 1850. He died unmarried in 1860. Source: 1,2,5,58

C25 RICHARD BANNING born Nov. 22, 1822 in New Castle Co., Del. He married
Emily P. Nash May 20, 1865 in Transitville, Ind. She was born Nov. 30, 1847 in Ft.
Wayne, Ind. He was farming in Platte Co., Mo in 1850. Source: 1,5,40,58

C114 Arthur Calvin Banning
C115 Effie Viola Banning
C116 Walter F. Banning

C26 ALICE P. BANNING born about 1836 in Del. Source: 1,2,5,58

C117 through C122 for children

C27 PHINEAS BANNING born on Aug. 19, 1830 on Oakhill Farm in Wilmington, Del.)
He married Rebecca Sanford on Nov. 16, 1854 at Rancho San Jose de Buenos
Aires, just west of Los Angeles, Calif. She was born 1834/35 in Randolph Co., Mo.
They had 8 children and lived in Wilmington, Calif. She died Jan. 7, 1868 in
Wilmington. He then married Mary Hollister on Feb. 14, 1870 in Santa Barbara,
Calif. She was born 1846 and died in 1919, They had 3 children. He left home at
the age of 13 to work in the law office of his brother William in Philadelphia. By age
16 Phineas was learning the freight business as a shipping clerk on the Philadelphia
wharves. He sailed to Calif. in 1851 via Panama and landed at San Pedro Bay, near
Los Angeles. By 1853 he was a Jr. partner in a firm hauling freight between San
Pedro and Los Angeles. As the business grew, he bought out his partner and
expanded. He ran stagecoaches from Banning, Calif., which he founded, to the
State capitol. Soon his freight and stage lines extended in northern Calif., Arizona
and Utah. He built the telegraph line between Los Angeles and Yuma, Az. as well as
the first railroad in Southern California linking what was to become Los Angeles
Harbor with the downtown of that city. 1864 was the year that saw the building of
the home that became Banning Park and Museum in 1927. He had many steam
ships working up and down the Pacific coast, one of which, the "Ada Hancock" blew
up killing his brother-in-law, several Banning children and injuring Phineas, his wife
and her mother. He was elected Ca. State Senator in 1865, where he signed
California's ratification of the 13th amendment to the U.S. Constitution abolishing
slavery. Phineas was very prominent in the state and held the rank of Brigadier
General of the 1st Brigade of the Calif. State Militia. He worked for many years to
develop his harbor into what would become Los Angeles Harbor. In 1990 this port
surpassed New York as the busiest port in the nation. Phineas was well liked, had a
booming voice and was a large and powerful man standing over 6' tall. He also loved

children. Phineas raised horses, cattle & sheep, owned much real estate including several saw mills, warehouses, a shipyard, contracting firm, soap factory, lumber yards and founded the Pioneer Oil Co., in addition to his shipping, wharves and transportation interest. He died March 8th or 10th, 1885 from the aftereffects of a street car accident in San Francisco a year earlier. He was buried in Wilmington beside his 1st wife and six children. Mary, his 2nd wife, had the body moved several years later to Rosedale Cemetery in Los Angeles. After his death, his wife lived at her North Broadway home on top of Fort Moore Hill in downtown Los Angeles. Source: 1,2,13,27,30,40,51,57,58

> C123 William Banning
> C124 Joseph Brent Banning
> C125 Hancock Banning
> C126 Fanny A. Banning
> C127 Vincent Edgar Griffith Banning
> C128 John Griffin Banning
> C129 Bessie Banning
> C130 _____? Banning
> C131 Mary Holister Banning
> C132 Ellen Merrman Banning
> C133 Lucy Tichenor Banning

C28 FRANCINIA ALICE BANNING born 1833 in Wilmington, Del. and married John Horn on Sept. 1, 1859 in St. Paul, Minn., where they lived. She died April 25, 1904. He was an Attorney. Source: 1,2,58

> C134 John H. Horn
> C135 Mary B. Horn
> C136 William Banning Horn
> C137 Henry John Horn
> C138 Alexander E. Horn
> C139 Priscilla F. Horn
> C140 Laura B. Horn
> C141 Mable B. Horn

C29 COLE LOWBER BANNING born March 6, 1834 in New Castle Co., Del. He married Mrs. Hulda Ann Foulk Steward on Aug. 16, 1855. She died Sept. 15, 1874. He married Helen Oliver on April 18, 1886. They lived in Kansas City, Mo. He was alive in 1908. She died May 15, 1893. Source: 1,2,30,58

> C142 Henry Banning
> C143 Nicholas Lowber Banning
> C144 Alice Banning
> C145 Mammie Banning
> C146 Jessie Fremont Banning
> C147 Henry (Harry ?) Banning
> C148 Katherine Wallace Banning

C30 through C39 unknown children of C7 & C8

> C149 through C188 for children

C40 through C44 unknown children of C9

C45 through C54 unknown children of C10 & C11

C189 through C225 for children

C55 CHARLES GEORGE RIDGELY born Aug 12, 1804. He married Elizabeth Biddle Brincklee, who was a widow. Source: 17,47

C56 NICHOLAS RIDGELY born Jan. 27, 1806 and died about April 1806. Source: 17,47

C57 JOHN BANNING RIDGELY born Jan. 22, 1807 and died March 20, 1808. Source: 17,47

C58 WILLIAMINA RIDGELY born Jan. 5, 1809 and died Sept 3, 1810. Source: 17,47

C59 ABRAHAM RIDGELY born Feb. 10, 1811 and died Sept. 22, 1812. Source: 17, 47

C60 ELIZABETH RIDGELY born Feb. 27, 1813 and died Feb. 12, 1833. Source: 17,47

C61 ANNA RIDGELY born Feb. 21, 1815 and married Charles Irene DuPont of Wilmington, Del. on May 11, 1841. They lived in New Castle Co. She died Oct. 20, 1898. They had a daughter, Amy E. DuPont. Source: 17,27,32,34,47,58

C62 HENRY RIDGELY he was born April 15, 1817, became a Dr. and married Virginia Jenkins (or Emerson ?) in 1843. They lived in Dover, Del. and had a daughter, Ruth Anna Ridgely, born in Dover. Henry died Sept. 17, 1904. Source: 17,32,47

C63 JULIET RIDGELY born Jan. 20, 1819 and died Nov. 8, 1820. Source: 17, 47

C64 NICHOLAS RIDGELY born Dec. 18, 1820 and married Mary H. Tilden in 1845. They lived in Wilmington, Del. They had a daughter, Mary Tilden Ridgely, born in Wilmington, Del. He died Dec. 1, 1849. Source: 17,32,47

C65 EUGENE RIDGELY born May 4, 1822 and married Marry Mifflin on Dec. 20, 1853. He died Jan. 11, 1894. Source: 17,47

C66 MARY RIDGELY born Sept. 17, 1824 and died June 10, 1825. Source: 17,47

C66A INFANT RIDGELY died at birth in Jan. 1826. Source: 17,47

C67 WILLIAMINA RIDGELY born May 29, 1827 and married Alexander Johnson on June 10, 1847. She died June 25, 1859. Source: 17, 47

C68 EDWARD RIDGELY born Jan. 30, 1831 and married Elizabeth Comegys on June 22, 1859. He died Oct. 17, 1900. Source: 17,47

C70 through C74 unknown children of C14 & C15

C75 PHINEAS BANNING born Oct. 17, 1815 in Muskingum Co., Ohio. He married Mahala Frances Blue on Dec. 10, 1840. She was the daughter of Abraham Blue and Susannah Shinsberry, born Jan. 17, 1821 in Wayne Co., Oh. He died April 10, 1863 and she died Oct. 30, 1892 in Winneshiek Co., Iowa. Both are buried in Centennial Cemetery. Source: 13,24

C226 Elizanne Banning
C227 John William Banning
C228 Abraham Banning
C229 Nathaniel Banning
C230 Elizabeth Jane Banning
C231 David Banning
C232 Peter S. Banning
C233 Susanna Banning
C234 Richard Banning
C235 Nancy Asbury Banning
C236 Mary Frances Banning
C237 Phineas Michael Banning

C76 JOHN BANNING born Jan. 1825 in Ohio. He lived in Chickasaw Co., Iowa.
Source: 24

C238 through C243 for children

C77 RACHAEL BANNING born Jan. 1830 in Ohio and married Alexander Hall.
Source: 24

C244 through C249 for children

C78 PRICILLA BANNING born in 1832 in Ohio and married Mr. Rice. Source: 5,24

C250 through C255 for children

C79 WILLIAM A. BANNING born Aug. 28, 1817 in Ohio and married Mary Ann Lasch
(Losh?) Oct. 16, 1840 in Bladenburg, Knox Co., Oh. She was the daughter of
Stephen Losch, born July 10, 1826 in Ohio. 1860 they were living in Marshall Co.,
Ks. where he was a farmer. He died Nov. 28, 1889 and she died March 22, 1909,
both in Baxter Springs, Cherokee Co., Ks. Source: 6,24

C256 Lydia Ann Banning
C257 Elizabeth Banning
C258 Rebecca Banning
C259 Jonathan Banning
C260 Phineas Banning
C261 Sophia Missouri Banning
C262 Nancy Helen Banning
C263 Mary Ellen Banning
C264 Sarah Jane Banning
C265 Ruth Loretta Banning

C80 NATHANIEL BANNING born Jan. 24, 1837 in Ohio and married Mary P. Wood in
July 1866. He died Feb. 16, 1910. Source: 5,24

C266 through C269 for children

C80A POLLY J. BANNING married Stephen R. Dennis. Source: 24

C270 through C272 for children

C80b MICHAEL BANNING born 1842 in Ohio. Source: 5

> C273 through C275 for children

C80c NANCY BANNING born 1843 in Ohio. Source: 5

> C276 through C277 for children

C80d ELLEN BANNING born 1849 in Ohio. Source: 5

> C278 through C279 for children

C81 SALLY (SARAH) TURNER born June 17, 1806 in Del. and died Jan. 1, 1883, probably in Hardin Co., Ohio. Source: 24

C82 ELIZABETH TURNER born Sept. 20, 1811 and married John Spriggs. Source: 24

C83 SAMUEL TURNER born Jan. 23, 1812/15 and married Elizabeth Hostler. He died in 1898. Source: 24

C84 ISAAC BANNING TURNER born June 17, 1817 and married Elizabeth Wood on Dec. 1, 1845. He died in 1902. Source: 24

C85 MATILDA TURNER born July 23, 1820 and married Joseph Evans. They had no children. She died Feb. 12, 1842. Source: 24

C86 ANN TURNER died as an infant. Source: 24

C86A NANCY TURNER died as an infant. Source: 24

C86B JOHN TURNER died as an infant. Source: 24

C87 PHINEAS TURNER born March 26, 1827 in Zanesville, Ohio. He married Mariah Ann Fleming on Nov. 7, 1850 in Muskingum Co., Oh. She was the daughter of Abner and Mary Ann (Spriggs) Fleming, born Sept. 11, 1831 in Muskingum Co. She died Aug. 8, 1905 in Murray, Clark Co., Iowa. He died Sept. 21, 1913 in Guide Rock, Neb. and is buried in Murray, Iowa. Their children were Mary Josephine, Minna Alice, Ovid Homer, Annie Maria and Otis Howard. Source: 21,24

C88 through C93 unused numbers

C94 ALICE BANNING no information. Source: 1

> C280 through C281 for children

C95 ELLEN BANNING no information. Source: 1

> C282 through C284 for children

C96 WILLIAM A. BANNING born about 1841 in Del. Source: 1,5,40

> C285 through C289 for children

C96A MARY BANNING born about 1843 in Del. Source: 5

C97 ELLEN BURROWS BANNING born May 14, 1853 in Philadelphia, Pa. She
married Frederick Ayer Jr. of Lowell, Mass. on July 15, 1884 in St. Paul, Minn. He
was born Dec. 8, 1822 in Ledyard, Conn. She was his 2nd wife. They lived in
Boston, Mass. He died March 14, 1918 and she passed away April 3, 1918, both in
Thomas Co., Ga. Source: 1,27,30,32,34,57,58

> C290 Beatrice Banning Ayer
> C291 Frederick Banning Ayer

C98 EVANS BANNING died at age 2. Source: 1,27,34,40,58

C99 WILLIAM LOWBER BANNING he drowned in the Mississippi River at age 11 in
the early 1860's. Source: 1,27,34,57,58

C100 MARY ALICE BANNING she lived in St. Paul, Minn. and La Crescenta, Calif.
She died unmarried. Source: 1,27,34,57,58

C101 FREDERICK DUNLEVY BANNING born 1865 in St. Paul, Minn. and married
Lucy Stickney, the daughter of A. B. Stickney. They lived in St. Louis. Source:
1,27,34,40,58

> C292 Frederick Banning
> C293 Jane Banning

C102 WILLIAM LOWBER BANNING born Feb. 2, 1869 in St. Paul, Minn. He married
Evangeline Ruth Gauthier on Aug. 20, 18?? in St. Paul. They lived in Chicago.
Source: 1,27,34,40,58

> C294 Evangeline Ruth Banning
> C295 Beatrice Banning
> C296 William Lowber Banning

C103 KATHERINE STEWART BANNING born Feb. 4, 1866 in St. Paul, Minn. She
married her cousin, Joseph Brent Banning (C124) of Los Angeles, Calif. on May 23,
1888 in St. Paul. She was one of the founders of Children's Hospital. Source:
1,27,34,57,58

> C297 Joseph Brent Banning
> C298 Katherine Mary Banning
> C299 William Phineas Banning

C104 through C107 unknown children of C21.

C108 ELIZA ELLIOTT no information. Source: 1

C109 FANNY BANNING ELLIOTT no information. Source: 1

C110 ISAAC C. ELLIOTT no information. Source: 1

C111 RICHARD BANNING ARMSTRONG no information. Source: 1

C112 ANNIE B. ARMSTRONG no information. Source: 1

C113 WILLIAM JOHN ARMSTRONG no information. Source: 1

C114 ARTHUR CALVIN BANNING born May 22, 1866 in Delphia, Ind. He married
    Malinda Jane Fletcher on Dec. 20, 1887 in Willowbrook, Buchannan Co., Mo. She
    was born Feb. 27, 1870 in St. Joseph, Mo. They lived in Chicago. Source: 1,13

> C300 Edna Leona Banning
> C301 Cora Ethel Banning
> C302 Arthur Lowber Banning
> C303 Emily Kathryn Banning
> C304 Andrew Calvin Banning

C115 EFFIE VIOLA BANNING born Sept. 4, 1868 in Delphia, Ind. She married James
    H. Gillispie on June 12, 1889 in St. Joseph, Mo. They lived in Chicago. Source: 1

> C305 James Arthur Gillispie
> C306 Frederick Banning Gillispie
> C307 Emily Gladys Gillispie

C116 WALTER F. BANNING he lived in Chicago for a time. Source: 1

> C308 through C313 for children

C117 through C122 unknown children of C26

C123 WILLIAM BANNING born 1858 in Los Angeles, Calif. and lived unmarried in
    Wilmington, Calif. One of his passions was driving a stage coach, which he did until
    he was well into his 70's. He and his brothers purchased Santa Catalina Island off
    the coast of Southern Calif. in 1892 for $200,000 and ran the resort like a feudal
    kingdom. They had constables who deported anyone that misbehaved. The island
    was sold in 1919 to the chewing gum king, William Wrigley. He died Jan. 27, 1946.
    Source: 1,27,51,57,58

C124 JOSEPH BRENT BANNING born Aug. 12, 1861 in Los Angeles, Calif. He
    married his cousin, Katherine Stewart Banning of St. Paul, Minn. in 1888. See
    C103. Along with his brother, Hancock, he ran the immense Banning interest in
    Calif. She was a founder of Children's Hospital. He died in 1920. Source: 1,27,
    30,34,51,57,58

> C297 Joseph Brent Banning Jr.
> C298 Katherine Mary Banning
> C299 William Phineas Banning

C125 HANCOCK BANNING born May 12, 1865 in Wilmington, Calif. and married
    Anna Ophelia Smith on Nov. 12, 1890 in Los Angeles, Calif. She was born Feb. 25,
    1871 in Calif. and was the daughter of George Hugh Smith and Susan Glassell
    Patton. They lived in Los Angeles, Calif. Along with his brother, Joseph, he ran the
    Banning business created by his father. She was the founder of the Assistance
    League of Southern Calif. Hancock installed a solar water heating system in the
    Banning family home in 1921. He died Aug. 7, 1925 in Los Angeles and she passed
    away Dec. 19, 1951/57 in San Marino, Calif. Source: 1,27,30,51,57,58

C126 FRANCENIA {Fanny} ALLIBONE BANNING born Dec. 1855 and died Sept. 21, 1857. Source: 1,27,51,57,58

C127 VINCENT EDGAR GRIFFITH BANNING born Jan. 4, 1868 and died in May 1868. Source: 1,27,51,57,58

C128 JOHN GRIFFIN BANNING born 1856 and died Oct. 17, 1859/60. Source: 1,27,51,57,58

C129 ELIZABETH {Bessie} BANNING born July 1865 and died 1866. Source: 1,27,51,57,58

C130 -----? BANNING born and died 1863. Source: 1,27,51,58

C131 MARY HOLLISTER BANNING born Jan. 13, 1871 in Wilmington, Calif. She married Wilt Watseman Norris on Nov. 18, 1897 in Los Angeles, Calif. They lived in New York City and had no children. He died in 1905. She died in 1953. Source: 1,27,57,58

C132 ELLEN MERRMAN BANNING born July 26, 1874 in Wilmington, Calif., where she died March 27, 1875. Source: 1,27,57,58

C133 LUCY TICHENOR {Ginger} BANNING born Feb. 11, 1876 in Wilmington, Calif. She married John Bradbury on Dec. 4, 1896 in Oakland, Calif. They lived in Los Angeles. She married 2nd, Mace Eustace Greenleaf on Sept. 20, 1906 in Los Angeles, where they lived. She married 3rd Robert E. Ross in 1912, and 4th Setsuya Ota. She died about 1929. She had no children. Source: 1,27,57,58

C134 JOHN H. HORN died an infant. Source: 1

C135 MARY B. HORN died an infant. Source: 1

C136 WILLIAM BANNING HORN died an infant. Source: 1

C137 HENRY JOHN HORN married Josephine Robinson. They had 4 children. Source: 1

C138 ALEXANDER E. HORN married Margaret Hall and had one child. Source: 1

C139 PRISCILLA F. HORN married John W. Adams in 1888 and had 4 children. Source: 1

C140 LAURA B. HORN married McNeil V. Seymour in 1895 and had 4 children. Source: 1

C14I MABLE B. HORN she was unmarried in 1908. Source: 1

C142 HENRY BANNING born July 28, 1856 in Platt Co., Mo. where he died April 16, 1874. Source: 1

C143 NICHOLAS LOWBER BANNING born Aug. 2, 1860 in Platt Co., Mo. He married Ella Jones. They lived in Farley, Platt. Co., Mo. Source: 1

C323 Maud Banning
C324 Helen Banning

C144 ALICE BANNING born July 22, 1865 in Platt Co., Mo. She married Charles H. Fariss in 1884 in Leavenworth, Ks. They lived in Kansas City, Mo. Source: 1

C325 John Fariss
C326 Edna W. Fariss

C145 MAMMIE BANNING she married Mr. Oliver. Source: 1

C327 Charles Oliver
C328 Albert Oliver
C329 Ollie Oliver
C330 Walter Oliver
C331 Wallace Oliver

C146 JESSIE FREEMONT BANNING born July 22, 1879 in Platt Co., Mo. She married Samuel Lafayette Couts in 1903 in Kansas City. They lived at 1916 Cypress St. in Kansas City. She died Sept. 6, 19??. Source: 1,30

C332 Samuel Lloyd Couts
C333 Clarence Kenneth Couts
C334 through C337 for children

C147 HARRY BANNING born May 1, 1881 in Platt Co., Mo. Source: 1

C338 through C343 for children

C148 KATHERINE WALLACE BANNING born March 18, 1883 in Platt Co., Mo. She married -----? on April 27, 1907 in Leavenworth, Ks. Source: 1

C344 through C349 for children

C149 through C225 unknown children of C30 through C59

C350 through C550 for children

C226 ELIZANNE BANNING born Sept. 4, 1841 in Cochocton Co., Ohio and died April 21, 1843. Source: 24

C227 JOHN WILLIAM BANNING born March 21, 1843 in Coshocton Co., Oh. and married Catherine Mahala Oxley Dec. 25, 1866 in Coshocton Co. She was the daughter of George Washington Oxley and Eliza Jane Blue born April 19, 1849 in Coshocton Co., Ohio. He died April 4, 1925 and she died Jan, 20, 1915, both in Ossian, Winneshiek Co., Iowa. They are buried in the Centennial Cemetery in Winneshiek Co. Source: 22,24

C551 Addie G. Banning
C552 Alma Jane Banning
C553 Charles Herbert Banning

C554 Grace Banning
C554A Infant
C555 Lula May Banning
CS56 Calla Almeda Banning
C557 Neva Pearl Banning
C558 Vernon Laval Banning

C228 ABRAHAM BANNING born Jan. 5, 1845 in Cochocton Co., Oh. and married
Mary Ellen Harvey Jan. 1, 1867 in Iowa. She was the daughter of John B. Harvey
and Sarah Wheeler, born March 31, 1849 in West Mansfield, Ohio. He died Oct.
12, 1930 and is buried in the National Cemetery in N.D. She died March 14, 1926 in
N.D. Source: 24

C559 Ira Alton Banning
C560 Etta Luella Banning
C561 Bertha Mae Banning
C562 David Alfred Banning
C563 Charles Henry Banning
C564 Edith Lillian Banning
C565 John Phineas Banning
C566 Sadie Mahala Banning
C567 Verna Rue Banning

C229 NATHANIEL BANNING born March 4, 1847 in Green Co. , Wisc. and married
1st Deborah Cary on Nov. 14, 1871. She died Aug. 2, 1872. He married 2nd Julia
M. White on Dec. 25, 1875. She was the daughter of Henry Winters White and
Lydia C. Baumwait, born July 7, 1857 in Norfolk Co., Ontario, Canada. He died
Sept. 25, 1937 in Canestata, S.D. She died March 16, 1933 in Canestata. Both are
buried in the Centennial Cemetery in Ossian, Iowa. Source: 24

C568 Millie Mabel Banning
C569 Florence May Banning

C230 ELIZABETH JANE BANNING born Feb. 24, 1844 in Green Co., Wisc. She
married Joseph Weitgenant Dec. 25, 1867 and died Feb. 15, 1871. Source: 24

C570 through C574 for children

C231 DAVID BANNING born NOV. 18, 1850 in Ossian, Winneshiek Co., Iowa. He
married Emma Elizabeth White Jan. 1, 1881 in Canistota, S.D. She was the
daughter of Henry White and Lydia C. Baumwat born Dec. 22, 1862 in Wood
House, Ontario, Canada. He died March 15, 1905 and is buried in the Riverside
Cemetery. She died in Feb. 1943 in Canestata, S.D. Source: 22,24

C575 Nellie Mahala Banning
C576 Julia Estella Banning
C577 Myrtle Mae Banning
C578 Ray Ernest Banning

C232 PETER S. BANNING born Jan. 15, 1852 in Ossian, Winneshiek Co., Iowa. He
married Mary Elizabeth Cole Sept. 8, 1875 and died Aug. 27, 1921. Source: 24

C579 through C583 for children

C233 SUSANA BANNING born Feb. 22, 1855 in Ossian, Winneshiek Co., Iowa. She married Frank Allen Jan. 21, 1877 and died Jan. 25, 1927. Source: 24

C584 through C588 for children

C234 RICHARD BANNING born June 15, 1857 in Ossian, Winneshiek Co., Iowa. He married Bertha Hannah Hokenson Nov. 1, 1886 and died Feb. 10, 1906. Source: 24

C589 Albert Phineas Banning
C590 Charles Banning

C235 NANCY ASBURY BANNING born April 15, 1859 in Ossian, Winneshiek Co., Iowa. She married Thomas Perry Logsdon March 24, 1878 and died May 14, 1929. Source: 24

C591 through C595 for children

C236 MARY FRANCES BANNING born July 23, 1861 in Ossian, Winneshiek Co., Iowa. She married Christian Jacob Vance Aug. 21, 1881 and died June 5, 1932. Source: 24

C596 through C600 for children

C237 PHINEAS MICHAEL BANNING born April 7, 1864 in Ossian, Winneshiek Co., Iowa. He married Cora Ada Vance Sept. 28, 1885 and died Jan. 25, 1940. Source: 24

C601 through C605 unknown children

C238 through C255 unknown children of C76 through C78

C606 through C646 for children

C256 LYDIA ANN BANNING born Sept. 25, 1841 in Ohio(?) and married Louis Proschling Oct. 6, 1859. She died in 1879. Source: 24

C647 through C651 for children

C257 ELIZABETH BANNING born Aug. 2, 1843 in Ohio(?) and married Edward Morgan in 1857. She died in 1860. Source: 24

C652 through C655 for children

C258 REBECCA BANNING born Sept. 22, 1847 in Ohio(?) and died Jan. 1848. Source: 24

C259 JONATHAN BANNING born April 25, 1849 in Ill. (or Ohio) and married Mary Ann Porter July 24, 1869. She was born in 1853 and died in 1949. He was living in Marshall CO., Ks. in 1860. He died in 1917 in Baxter Springs, Cherokee Co., Ks. Source: 6,24

C656 through C659 for children

C260 PHINEAS BANNING born Jan. 31, 1852 in Winneshiek Co., Iowa (or Ohio) and married 1st Hannah Stebbins in July 1875. She died in 1881. He was living in Marshall Co., Ks. in 1860. He married 2nd, Sarah Jane Rossman on June 1, 1886 in Baxter Springs, Cherokee Co., Ks. She was the daughter of Jacob Adolph Rossman and Lydia Ann Horn born Dec. 22, 1866 in Findlay, Hancock Co. Oh. He served in Co. K of the 19th U.S. Infty. from Mar. 1881 to March 1886. He died May 23, 1913 in Petrolia, Clay Co., Tex. She died July 11, 1962 in Wichita Falls, TX. and is buried in the Highland Park Cemetery in Iowa Park, Tx. Source: 6,13,16,24

C660 Blanche Inez Banning
C660A William Jacob Banning
C660B Hubert W. Banning
C661 Jonathan Franklin Banning
C662 Earl Bryan Banning
C663 Winifred Banning
C664 Albert Otto Dewey Banning
C665 Josephine Banning

C261 SOPHIA MISOURIA BANNING born Jan. 12, 1856 and died Nov. 12, 1858. Source: 24

C262 NANCY HELEN BANNING born March 7, 1859 in Minn. She died July 28, 1882. Source: 24

C263 MARY ELLEN BANNING born Jan. 3, 1862 in Iowa and married Erasmus Boles in Jan. 1892. Source: 24

C666 Josephine Boles
C667 through C670 for children

C264 SARAH JANE BANNING born Nov. 11, 1864 in Iowa and died April 28, 1898. Source: 24

C671 through C675 for children

C265 RUTH LORETTA BANNING born May 5, 1868 in Iowa and married James Robelaillo Dec. 9, 1886. She died Dec. 23, 1889 in Baxter Springs, Cherokee Co., Ks. Source: 24

C676 through C679 for children

C266 through C279 unknown children of C80 & C80d

C680 through C704 for children

C280 through C289 unknown children of C94 through C96

C705 through C729 for children

C290 BERTRICE BANNING AYER married George Smith Patton III (1885-1945). He was a well known Army Commander in WW II. They had at least 1 daughter, Ruth, born in 1913. They lived in South Hamilton, Mass. Source: 1,30,32,57

C291 FREDERICK BANNING AYER no information. Source: 1,57

C292 FREDERICK BANNING no information Source: 1

C730 through C734 for children

C293 JANE BANNING no information Source: 1

C735 through C739 for Children

C294 EVANGELINE RUTH BANNING born in St. Paul, Minn. Source: 1

C740 through C744 for children

C295 BERTRICE BANNING no information Source: 1

C745 through C749 for children

C296 WILLIAM LOWBER BANNING no information. Source: 1

C750 through C754 for children

C297 JOSEPH BRENT BANNING born April 3, 1889 in Calif. He married Alice M. Morse and died in 1969. Source: 1,27,34,57,58

C755 through C759 for children

C298 KATHERINE MARY BANNING born July 3, 1890/91 in Calif. She married Francis Porter Groves\Graves, who was the son of Jackson A. Groves. She died in 1965. Source: 1,27,34,57,58

C760 through C764 for children

C299 WILLIAM PHINEAS BANNING born May 2, 1899 in Calif. He married 1st, Evangeline Grier and 2nd, Janet Kirby Post. He died in 1981. Source: 1,27,34,57,58

C765 through C769 for Children

C300 EDNA LEONA BANNING born Oct. 1, 1888 in Chicago. Source: 1

C770 through C774 for children

C301 CORA ETHEL BANNING born Nov. 28, 1891 in St. Joseph, Buchannan Co., Mo. She married William August Phillips on Aug. 2, 1911 in Wathena, Doniphan Co., Ks. Source: 1

C775 through C779 for children

C302 ARTHUR LOWBER BANNING born Jan. 21, 1895 in Chicago. Source: 1

C780 through C784 for children

C303 EMILY KATHRYN BANNING born Sept. 25, 1898 in Chicago. Source: 1

C785 through C789 for children

C304 ANDREW CALVIN BANNING born June 19, 1907 in Chicago. Source: 1

C790 through 794 for children

C305 JAMES ARTHUR GILLESPIE born Sept 2, 1890 in St. Joseph, Mo. Source: 1

C306 FREDERICK BANNING GILLESPIE born June 30, 1892 in St. Joseph, Mo. Source: 1

C307 EMILY GLADYS GILLESPIE born March 16, 1895 in Chicago. Source: 1

C308 through C313 unknown children of C116

C314 HANCOCK BANNING born Feb. 3, 1892 in Calif. He attended Cornell University and received his degree in electrical engineering in 1914. He married Florence Lewers Johnston on Oct. 8, 1919 in Los Angeles, Calif. She was born July 13, 1895 in Louisville, Ky. and died Jan. 11, 1989 in San Marino, Calif. He died Nov. 25, 1982 in San Marino. Source: 1,27,51,57,58,61

C795 Hancock Banning
C796 Robert J. Banning
C797 Elizabeth A. Banning

C315 ELEANOR ANNE BANNING born June 1893 and married John McFarland. She became a Regent of the University of Calif. and died July 27, 1940. Source: 1,27,30,51,58

C798 through C802 for children

C316 GEORGE HUGH BANNING born March 17, 1895 and married 1st, Gladys Armstrong, 2nd Helen Barnes and 3rd Ruth Lockett. He died Oct. 15, 1989. Source: 1,27,51,57,58

C803 through C809 for children

C317 through C322 unused

C323 MAUD BANNING no information Source: 1

C810 through C814 for children

C324 HELEN BANNING no information Source: 1

C815 through C819 for children

C325 JOHN FARISS born Oct. 23, 1885. Source: 1

C326 EDNA W. FARISS born Sept 18, 1889. Source: 1

C327 CHARLES OLIVER born July 28, 1894. Source: 1

C328 ALBERT OLIVER born Sept. 6, 1896. Source: 1

C329 OLLIE OLIVER born Aug. 11, 1898. Source: 1

C330 WALTER OLIVER born June 6, 1901. Source: 1

C331 WALLACE OLIVER born Sept. 15, 1902. Source: 1

C332 SAMUEL LLOYD COUTS born Sept. 9, 1904. Source: 1,30

C333 CLARENCE KENNETH COUTS born May 12, 1907. Source: 1,30

C334 through C343 children of C146 & C147

C820 through C870 for children

C344 through C349 children of C148

C350 through C550 children of C149 through C225

C871 through C1824 for children

C551 ADDIE G. BANNING born 1870 in Castalia, Winneshiek Co., Iowa and died in 1873. Source: 24

C552 ALMA JANE BANNING born May 23, 1872 in Castalia, Winneshiek Co. , Iowa and married Fred. C. Winn on Oct. 25, 1891. She died April 25, 1949. They had no children. Source: 22,24

C553 CHARLES HERBERT BANNING born Nov. 16, 1877 in Ossian, Winneshiek Co., Iowa and married 1st Grace Anna Weiland on Dec. 14, 1904 in Canistota, McCook Co., S.D. She was the daughter of Benjamin Rolf Weiland and Mary Jane Silence, born April l5, 1883 in Canistota, S.D. They lived on 35th St. in Anacortes, Wa. She died Jan. 19, 1944 in Anacortes, Wa. He married 2nd Pearl B. Hartman on Jan. 10, 1946 and died May 26, 1952 in Anacortes, Skagit Co., Wa. Source: 16,24,61

C1825 Lila Marie Banning
C1826 Lloyd Harold Banning
C1827 Orval Ladell Banning
C1828 Verda Irene Banning
C1829 Lois Rosemond Banning

C554 GRACE BANNING born July 30, 1879 in Castalia, Winneshiek Co., Iowa and married 1st Henry Webster on March 23, 1898. She married 2nd, C.M. Elliot on April 1, 1916 in New Hamton, Iowa. She died Oct. 14, 1944 in Waterloo, Iowa and is buried in the Methodist Park Cemetery. Source: 22,24

C1830 Donald Elliot
C1831 through C1834 unused

C554A INFANT BANNING born and died Jan. 9, 1882. Source: 24

C555 LULA MAY BANNING born Oct. 3, 1883 in Castalia, Winneshiek Co., Iowa and married Andrew J. Baker in 1915. He was born in 1872 in Springfield, Ill. and died July 23, 1935 in Blackfoot, Idaho. She died Jan. 1, 1967 in Decorah, Iowa. Source:

C1835 Norma Leone Baker
C1836 Minnie Viola Baker
C1837 Arthur Jackson Baker

C556 CALLA ALMEDA BANNING born July 29, 1889 in Castalia, Winneshiek Co.,
Iowa and married George Andrew Wiltgen on Sept. 9, 1908 in Ossian, Winneshiek
Co., Iowa. He was born Dec. 29, 1886 in Ossian and died July 1, 1948 in
Rochester, Minn. She died March 29, 1980 in Mason City, Iowa and is buried in
Memorial Park Cemetery in Mason City. Source: 22,24

C1838 Jack Wiltgen
C1839 Katherine Rosemond "Billy" Wiltgen

C557 NEVA PEARL BANNING born Feb. 19, 1885 in Castalia, Winneshiek Co., Iowa
and married 1st, William H. Draves on Mar. 23, 1903 in Ossian, Winneshiek Co.,
Iowa. She married 2nd, Charles Solomn Dewey on Aug. 30, 1916 and died Oct. 12,
1974. Source: 16,22,24

C1840 Wayne "Sparky" Draves
C1841 Kathleen Dewey

C558 VERNON LAVAL BANNING born June 5, 1891 in Castalia, Winneshiek Co.,
Iowa and married Hannah Wilhemena Appel on Nov. 20, 1913. She was born Nov.
20, 1895 in Frolick, Iowa. He died Feb. 9, 1969 in Mason City Iowa and is buried in
the Elmwood Cemetery. Source: 16,22,24

C1842 Milan Kenneth Banning
C1843 through C1852 unused

C559 IRA ALTON BANNING born 1868 and married May McLoud. He died in 1943
and is buried in the National Cemetery in N.D. Source: 24

C1853 through C1857 for children

C560 ETTA LUELLA BANNING born Dec. 6, 1869 in Iowa and married Stephen Riley
Sams on Nov. 10, 1885 in Minnehaha, S.D. He was the son of John Sams and
Perlina Dowers, born Sept. 15, 1858 in Ripley, In. She died May 19, 1897 in Ia. and
is buried in Centennial Cemetery. in Ia. He married 2nd, Bertha Mae Banning, see
C561. Source: 16,24

C1858 Inez Sams
C1859 Walter Abraham Sams
C1859 Cora Sams
C1861 Pearl Sams
C1862 Mary Etta Sams
C1863 Verna Mae Sams

C561 BERTHA MAE BANNING born May 1872 in Iowa, and married 1st William
Lowsing. After the death of her sister, C560, she married Stephen Riley Sams. She
died in 1952 and he died May 10, 1956 in Snohomish Co., Wa. He is buried in the
Evergreen Cemetery. in Seattle, Wa. Source: 16,24

C1864 Myrtle Estella Sams
C1865 Perry Frances Sams
C1866 Kenneth Webb Sams

C562 DAVID ALFRED BANNING born 1874 and married Maggie ???. Source: 24

C1867 through C1871 for children

C563 CHARLES HENRY BANNING born 1876 and married Christina Chadon. Source: 24

C1872 through C1876 for children

C564 EDITH LILLIAN BANNING born 1880 and married Charles Webb. Source: 24

C1866 Kenneth Webb

C565 JOHN PHINEAS BANNING born June 6, 1883 in Sioux Falls, S.D. and married Gertrude West on Jan. 18, 1916. She was the daughter of Frank West & Edith W??? born March 1, 1896 in Wisc. He died Sept. 13, 1970 in S.D. Source: 16,24,61

C1877 Doris Ellen Banning
C1878 Duane Edison Banning
C1879 Mary Louise Banning
C1880 John Richard Banning
CI88l Lowell Robert Banning
C1882 LaVern Calvin Banning
C1883 Gladys Pauline Banning
C1884 Barbara Jean Banning
C1885 Wesley Gene Banning

C566 SADIE MAHALA BANNING born 1886 and married 1st, William Sloan 2nd, Walter McMahon. Source: 24

C1886 through C1890 for children

C567 VERNA RUE BANNING born 1890 and married Alvin Bohn. Source: 24

C1891 through C1895 for children

C568 MILLIE MABEL BANNING born June 24, 1880 in Ossian, Iowa and married William Spencer Aug. 18, 1898. Source: 24

C1896 through C1901 for children

C569 FLORENCE MAY BANNING born Aug. 26, 1886 in Ossian, Iowa and married Frederick Charles Ondrozeck On June 22, 1910 in Canistota, S.D. He was the son of Karl and Anna Ondrozeck, born Jan. 16, 1873 in Germany. He died Jan. 13, 1934 in Canistota, where she died Nov. 8, 1966. Source: 16,24

C1902 Jerry Nathan Ondrozeck
C1903 Joy Julia Ondrozeck
C1904 Waldo Russell Ondrozeck

C570 through C574 children of C230

C575 NELLIE MAHALR BANNING born Aug. 22, 1882 and married Roelf Johnson
Weiland Feb. 18, 1903. He was the son of Benjamin R. Weiland (1849-1929) and
Mary Jane Silence (1856-1919) born Jan. 1, 1879 and died June 17, 1939. She
died Sept. 27, 1956. Source: 24

> C1905 Ray Edmond Weiland
> C1906 Charles Merl Weiland
> C1907 Robert Lyle Weiland
> C1907A Earl Kenneth Weiland
> C1907B Benjamin Roelf Weiland
> C1907C Russell Lloyd Weiland
> C1907D Stanley Arthur Weiland

C576 JULIA ESTELLA BANNING born May 23, 1884 in East Sioux Falls, S.D. She
married Willmer A. Gordon on Nov. 24, 1909 in McCook Co. , S.D. He was the son
of Nelson James Gordon and Nellie Cook, born July 22, 1883 in Kankakee, Ill. She
died in Aug. 1957. He died Feb. 1957 and both are buried in Riverside Cemetery. in
McCook Co. Source: 16,24

> C1908 Velma Gordon
> C1909 Ralph Gordon
> C1910 Viola Gordon
> Cl911 Ray Gordon

C577 MYRTLE MAE BANNING born Jan. 30, 1885 and married Edmond Silence
Weiland Nov. 16, 1910. He was the son of Benjamin Roelf Weiland and Mary Jane
Silence (C575) born June 6, 1881. She died Feb. 3, 1964 and he died Nov. 9,
1937. Source: 24

> C1912 Lyle Edmond Weiland
> C1913 Kenneth LeRoy Weiland
> C1914 Lester William Weiland
> C1915 Lela Mae Weiland

C578 ERNEST RAY BANNING born Jan. 22, 1889 and married Emma Lena Weiland
Oct. 12, 1910. She was the daughter of Benjamin Roelf Weiland and Mary Jane
Silence (see C575) born March 23, 1889. He died Aug. 6, 1960 and she died Oct.
12, 1977. Source: 24

> C1916 David Benjamin Banning
> C1917 Harold Lavern Banning
> C1918 Glen Dale Banning

C579 through C588 unknown children of C232 & C233

> C1919 through C1939 for children

C589 ALBERT PHINEAS BANNING born July 23, 1887 and married Mamie Louise
Johnson on Feb. 13, 1911. He died July 24, 1951 and she died Feb. 4, 1966. Both
are buried in the Mt. Pleasant Cemetery. Source: 16,24

C1940 Virginia Alberta Banning

C590 CHARLES BANNING born Jan. 4, 1891 and married Mae E. Fish on Dec. 29, 1916. He died Jan. 1976. Source: 16,24

C1941 Richard Franklin Banning
C1942 Madeline Evon Banning
C1943 Mavis Lorraine Banning

C591 through C659 unknown children of C235 through C259

C1944 through C2023 for children

C660 BLANCHE INEZ BANNING born Sept. 6, 1888 in Baxter Springs, Cherokee Co., Ks. She married James Levigie Owensby Feb. 12, 1908 in Anadarko, Caddo Co., Ok. Source: 16,24

C2024 through C2026 for children

C660A WILLIAM JACOB BANNING born April 8, 1890 and died Nov. 2, 1891 both in Cherokee Co., Ks. Source: 16,24

C660B HUBERT W. BANNING born Aug. 8, 1892 and died Oct. 19, 1892 both in Cherokee Co., Ks. Source: 16,24

C661 JONATHAN FRANKLIN BANNING born Aug. 16, 1894 near Ingalls, Payne Co., Ok. He married Ruby Thorpe Aug. 31, 1924 in Shamrock, Creek Co., Ok. He served in Co. E, 81st Field Art. Btln. from 1917 through 1919. He died Nov. 21, 1963 in Wichita Falls, Tx. and was buried in Highland Cemetery. in Iowa Park, Tx. Source: 16,24

C2027 through C2030 for children

C662 EARL BRYAN BANNING born Oct. 29, 1896 near Ingalls, Payne Co., Ok. He married Ruth Thorpe Oct. 20, 1927 in Wichita Falls, Tx. He died Oct. 12, 1972 in Wichita Falls and is buried in the Highland Cemetery. in Iowa Park, Tx. Source: 13,16,24

C2031 through C2034 for children

C663 WINIFRED BANNING born Aug. 31, 1899 near Ingalls, Payne Co., Ok. She married Earl P. Harber July 31, 1927 in Wichita Falls, Tx. Source: 16,24

C2035 through C2038 for children

C664 ALBERT OTTO DEWEY BANNING born July 14, 1903 in Caddo Co., Ok. and married Adeline Kirk on March 1, 1930 in Wichita Falls, Tx. He died Feb. 25, 1967 in Wichita Falls and was buried in Highland Cemetery. in Iowa Park, Tx. Source: 16,24

C2039 through C2042 for children

C665 JOSEPHINE BANNING born April 8, 1906 in Caddo Co., Ok. She married Raymond R. Brewer Dec. 10, 1929 in Walters, Cotton Co., Ok. Source: 16,24

141

C2043 through C2046 for children

C666 JOSEPHINE BOLES she married a Mr. Bond.

C667 through C679 children of C263 through C265

C680 through C729 children of C266 through C289

C2047 through C2087 for children

C730 through C794 children of C292 through C304

C2088 through C2188 for children

C795 HANCOCK BANNING 3rd born May 12, 1921. Source: 27,51,61

C2189 through C2195 for children

C796 ROBERT JOHNSTON BANNING born July 27, 1924 in Los Angeles, Calif. and married Joan Spain Bridge. She was the daughter of Herman Spain and Doris Bridge, born July 24, 1925. He is retired was living in Pasadena, Calif. in 1992. Source: 27,51,61

        C2196 Robert Johnston Banning Jr.
        C2197 Winthrop Hancock Banning

C797 ELIZABETH A. BANNING born Jan. 20, 1932. She married a Mr. Ames. Source: 27,51,61

C2198 through C2205 for children

C798 through C819 children of C315 through C324

C2206 through C2289 for children

C820 through C870 children of C334 through C343

C2290 through C2329 for children

C871 through C1824 children of C350 through C550

C2330 through C3330 for children

C1825 LILA MARIE BANNING born June 1, 1906 in Ossian, Winnishiek Co., Ia. She married Charles Hamlin King June 15, 1926 in Pukwana, Brule Co. , S.D. He was the son of John M. King, born Oct. 18, 1901 in St. Lawrence, Hand Co., S.D. He was a Teacher and Accountant, served in the National Guard and lived on 35th St. in Anacortes, Wa. He died May 9, 1983 in Anacortes, Skagit Co. Wa. Source: 16,24,61

        C3331 Charles Herbert King
        C3332 Duane Eugene King

C1826 LLOYD HAROLD BANNING born Feb. 21, 1909 on a farm in Hand Co., S.D. and married 1st Sadie Helen Smith on April 30, 1935. She was born Nov. 3, 1903 and died Aug. 29, 1983 in Albany, Linn Co., Or. He married 2nd, Louise Nelson. She died March 12, 1989 in Albany, Or. He married 3rd, Erika Louise Hoyler. He graduated from the South Dakota School of Mines in 1931 and retired in 1974 after 30 years as a metallurgist with the U.S. Berea of mines. They are living in Bradenton, Fla in 1992. Source: 16,24,61

C3333 Maurice Ray Banning

C1827 ORVAL LADELL BANNING born March 1, 1911 in St. Lawrence, Hand Co. , S.D. and married Estella Maria Harris Aug. 25, 1932. She was the daughter of William C. Harris and Mary Hirz, born Jan. 9, 1907 in Meade Co. , S.D. She died Sept. 18, 1983 in Rapid City, S.D. and is buried in the Rosehill Cemetery. in Spearfish, S.D. He was a farmer and died July 26, 1975 in Spearfish. Source: 16,24

C3334 Robert Orval Banning
C3335 Shirley Ann Banning
C3336 Jerry Eugene Banning

C1828 VERDA IRENE BANNING born Nov. 29, 1913 in Canistota, McCook Co., S.D. She married Warner Merton Evenson May 18, 1933 in Rapid City, S.D. He was the son of Elmer Evenson & Tilda Gurina Tolrud, born Aug. 5, 1913. She is employed by the Bureau of Mines and he is an accountant. They live in Denver, Col. Source: 16,24,61

C3337 Dennis Warner Evenson
C3338 Vernon Harold Evenson

C1829 LOIS ROSEMOND BANNING born Sept. 12, 1922 in St. Lawrence, Hand Co., S.D. She married Robert Eugene Herth Jan. l5, 1943 in Tacoma, Wa. He is the son of Jacob George Herth and Helena Fusch, born July 8, 1923 in Endicott, Whitman Co., Wa. He served in the U.S. Army and is now a manager. She is an officer in Tacoma Savings & Loan Assoc. and supplied much of the information on this line. They live in Tacoma, Wa. Source: 16,24,61

C3339 Robert Eugene Herth Jr
C3340 Lynnette Lee Herth
C3341 Lorayne Kae "Lori" Hearth

C1830 DONALD ELLIOT born in Iowa. He died Oct. 28, 1944 in the Palau Islands. Source: 22

C1831 through C1834 unused

C1835 NORMA LEONE BAKER born Aug. 2, 1917 in Clarksdale, Mo. and married Frederick Lloyd Schafer on Sept. 28, 1940. He is the son of William R. Schafer and Christine Ann Knip, born Sept. 21, 1915 in Minot, N.D. He died March 15, 1985 in Blackfoot, Idaho and she died in 1987, in Madison, Wisc. They had 6 children, Celeste Sue, born Dec. 6, 1942 in Waterloo, Iowa; Frederick Lloyd, born Nov. 13, 1943 in Minot, N.D.; Dominic Gregory, born Oct. 7, 1946 in Minot; Bruce Layne, born March 15, 1949 in Minot; Christine Ann, born Aug. 5, 1952 in Minot and Vincent Lee, born Jan 31, 1954 in Minot. Source: 16,22,24

C1836 MINNIE VIOLA BAKER born July 7, 1920 in Clarksdale, Mo. She died Nov. 21, 1937. Source: 16,24

C1837 ARTHUR JACKSON BAKER born Aug. 27, 1922 in Clarksdale, Mo. Source: 16,24

C1838 JACK WILTGEN born July 15, 1914 in Mason City, Iowa. He married Doris Lenora Mickelson on April 4, 1935 in Northwood, Iowa. She was born Jan. 5, 1912 in Albert Lee, Minn. Their children are, Geraldine Louise, born June 14, 1944; Judy Louise, born in Mason City and George Michael, born May 8, 1950. Source: 16,22

C1839 KATHERINE ROSEMOND "Billy" WILTGEN born Nov. 24, 1912 in Mason City, Iowa. She married Carl Lewis Scharlau on May 9, 1937 in Mason City. He was born Aug. 5, 1912 in Elkhart, Ind. Their children are, Lynn Carl, born July 12, 1939 in Mason City and Jay Dean, born March 31, 1940 in Mason City. Source: 16,22

C1840 WAYNE "Sparky" DRAVES born 1908 in Charles City, Iowa and died unmarried on Feb. 24, 1964 in Waterloo, Iowa. Source: 22

C1841 KATHLEEN DEWEY born April 18, 1916 in West Union, Iowa. She married Harry J. Mohs on Nov. 29, 1934 in Iowa. He was born Jan. 7, 1908 in Lime Springs, Iowa. Their children are, Karen Kay, born Nov. 26, 1939 in Waterloo and Donna, born March 15, 1951 in Waterloo. Source: 16,22

C1842 MILAN KENNETH BANNING born July 22, 1918 in Castalia, Winnishiek Co., Iowa. He married Maxine Miller on May 2, 1942 in Santa Monica, Calif. He died Oct. 30, 1978 in Chico, Ca. They had no children. Source: 22

C1843 through C1852 unused

C1853 through C1857 children of C559

C3342 through C3362 for children

C1858 INEZ SAMS born Dec. 13, 1886 in Canton, Lincoln Co., S.D. and died Oct. 31, 1918. Source: 16,24

C1859 WALTER ABRAHAM SAMS born July 30, 1888/9 in Canton, Lincoln Co. , S.D. He married Lillian Dunn. He died July 24, 1935 in Bismarck, N.D. and was buried in Sangor, N.D. Source: 16,24

C1860 CORA SAMS born Sept. 12, 1890 in Canton, Lincoln Co., S.D. She married 1st Otto Batschi and 2nd, Curt Hansen. Source: 16,24

C1861 PEARL SAMS born June 14, 1892 in Seneca, Newton Co., Mo. and died June 17, 1892. Source: 16,24

C1862 MARY ETTA SAMS born Dec. 18, 1893/4 in Canton, Lincoln Co., S.D. and married Rolland McGwin on Dec. 24, 1913. She died June 5, 1916. Source: 16,24

C1863 VERNA MAE SAMS born Aug. 19, 1896 and married 1st, Howard Biddleman in 1918. She married 2nd, Oscar Gullicks. She died in 1968 in Monroe, Wa. Source:

16,24

C1864 MYRTLE ESTELLA SAMS born May 5, 1899 in Canton, Lincoln Co., S.D. She married 1st, Leslie Robinson and 2nd, Cecil Gant. She died June 3, 1919. Source: 16,24

C1865 PERRY FRANCIS SAMS born Mar. 18, 1901 in Worthing, Lincoln Co., S.D. He married Grace Day and died in 1938. Source: 16,24

C1866 KENNETH WEBB SAMS born June 29, 1918 in Mott, N.D. He was the son of Edith (Banning) Webb (C564) see C1876. He married Helen Doyle. Source: 16,24

C1867 through C1876 children of C562 & C563

C3363 through C3393 for children

C1877 DORIS ELLEN BANNING born Oct. 15, 1916 and married Kenneth Thoreen. Source: 16,24,61

C3394 through C3396 for children

C1878 DUANE EDISON BANNING born April 20, 1918. Source: 16,24,61

C3397 through C3399 for children

C1879 MARY LOUISE BANNING born April 20, 1920 and married a Mr. Reno. She died in 1971. Source: 16,24,61

C3400 through C3402 for children

C1880 JOHN RICHARD BANNING born Aug. 21, 1922 in Mott, N.D. He married Kathryn E. Beers. She was the daughter of William & Bertha Natte Beers, born Oct. 2, 1922. In 1992 they were both retired and living in Port Townsend, Wa. Source: 16,24,61

C3403 Norma Jean Banning
C3404 James Richard Banning
C3405 Rita Kay Banning
C3406 Sandra Lee Banning

C1881 LOWELL ROBERT BANNING born July 2, 1925. He married Hilda (???). Source: 16,24,61

C3407 Patricia Ann Banning
C3408 Cynthia Kaye Banning

C1882 LaVERN CALVIN BANNING born Sept. 7, 1927 in Hettinger Co., N.D. He married Arlene Ann Knutson. She was the daughter of Melvin Benheart and Laura Fannie (Wallace) Knutson, born Jan. 25, 1931. They are both retired and living in Rapid City, S.D. in 1992. Source: 16,24,61

C3409 Susan Kay Banning
C3410 Russell Lee Banning
C3411 Ronald Ray Banning

C1883 GLADYS PAULINE BANNING born Feb. 6, 1930. She married a Mr. Jorgenson. Source: 16,24,61

C3412 through C3416 for children

C1884 BARBARA JEAN BANNING born Feb. 11, 1931 and died in Aug. 1942. Source: 16,24,61

C1885 WESLEY GENE BANNING born May 29, 1935. Source: 16,24,61

C3417 through C3420 for children

C1886 through C1901 children of C566 through C568.

C1902 JERRY NATHANIEL ONDROZECK born March 9, 1911 and married Maxine McKillap on Sept. 8, 1943. He died Sept. 23, 1958. Source: 16,24

C1903 JOY JULIA ONDROZECK born Feb. 4, 1914 and married Louis H. Briedenbach on Dec. 27, 1941. Source: 16,24

C1904 WALDO RUSSELL ONDROZECK born June 22, 1919 and married Anna Mae Beisel June 3, 1941. Source: 16,24

C1905 RAY EDMOND WEILAND born Jan. 21, 1904 and married Vivian Ethel Starkey Dec. 22, 1924. She was born Sept. 22, 1903. They had 7 children. He died June 3, 1932. Source: 24

C1906 CHARLES MERL WEILAND born Sept. 25, 1905 and died Sept. 29, 1805. Source: 24

C1907 ROBERT LYLE WEILAND born Oct. 29, 1908. He married 1st, Mildred Spicer on Dec. 24, 1934. They divorced Sept. 23, 1949 and he married 2nd, Mrs. Ann (Schwams) Erickson on Feb. 20, 1952. She was born April 30, 1902. He died March 6, 1979. Source: 24

C1907A EARL KENNETH WEILAND born March 13, 1911 and married Lois L. Tarrell July 6, 1932. She was born June 1, 1917. They had 5 children. Source: 24

C1907B BENJAMIN ROELF WEILAND born Jan. 13, 1916 and married Rose Marie Krumvieda Feb. 25, 1947. She was born Aug. 28, 1925. They had 4 children. Source: 24

C1907C RUSSELL LLOYD WEILAND born Oct. 9, 1918 and married 1st, Opal Krantz and 2nd, Inola Grace Krumvieda on Feb. 8, 1943. Inola was born June 7, 1921. Source: 24

C1907D STANLEY ARTHUR WEILAND born Jan. 29, 1922 and married Irene Bernice Ortman on Dec. 15, 1945. She was born April 6, 1925. They had 3 children. Source: 24

C1908 VELMA GORDON died as an infant. Source: 16,24

C1909 RALPH GORDON married Evelyn Jennings. Source: 16,24

146

C1910 VIOLA GORDON married 1st, Glen Johnson and 2nd, Louie Larson Jr. Source: 16,24

C19l1 ROY GORDON married Darlene Parker. Source: 16,24

C1912 LYLE EDMOND WEILAND born Dec. 30, 1911 and married Gladys Garder Oct. 3, 1931. She was born July 30, 1912. They had a son Garold Lee born 1932. He died Oct. 23, 1981. Source: 24

C1913 KENNETH LeRoy WEILAND born Dec. 24, 1915 and married Ione Amanda Schafer June 11, 1939. She was born June 11, 1918. They had a daughter Julianne born Feb. 8, 1952. Source: 24

C1914 LESTER WILLIAM WEILAND born April 8, 1919 and married Dolores Wilcox on March 1, 1946. She was born May 21, 1926. Their children were, Gloria Jean born 1946, Jacqueline Rose born 1950 and Edmond Lloyd born in 1953. He died Jan. 4, 1956. Source: 24

C1915 LELA MAE WEILAND born Nov. 29, 1928 and married Robert Charles Uecker Dec. 27, 1947. He was born May 31, 1933. Their children are Ronald Charles born 1949, Karon Sue born 1951, Barbara Jane born 1953, Gregg Robert born 1961, Barry John born 1963 and Douglas Dale born in 1965. Source: 24

C1916 DAVID BENJAMIN BANNING born Jan. 3, 1914 and married Thelma Leona Scovil Feb. 26, 1938. She was born April 26, 1915. Source: 24

> C3421 Vicky Rae Banning
> C3422 Davey Lee Banning
> C3423 Dennis Gene Banning

C1917 HAROLD LAVERN BANNING born Aug. 14, 1917 and died Aug. 9, 1938. Source: 24

> C3424 through C3426 for children

C1918 GLEN DALE BANNING born July 4, 1925 and married Betty Lou Lobdell Nov. 13, 1948. She was born Nov. 2, 1929. Source: 24

> C3427 Dale Edward Banning
> C3428 Joyce Ann Banning
> C3429 Audrey Banning
> C3430 Brian Ray Banning

C1919 through C1939 children of C579 through C588

> C3431 through C3451 for children

C1940 VIRGINIA ALBERTA BANNING born April 30, 1912 and died Dec. 2, 1923. Source: 16,24

> C3452 through C3454 for children

C1941 RICHARD FRANKLIN BANNING born May 11, 1918 and died unmarried Aug.

147

10, 1943 in the Solomon Islands. Source: 16,24

C1942 MADELINE EVON BANNING born May 26, 1920 and married Berger Anderson June 26, 1939. Source: 16,24

C3455 through C3457 for children

C1943 MAVIS LORRAINE BANNING born Jan. 2, 1926 and married Doyle Nelson April 18, 1947. Source: 16,24

C3458 through C3460 for children

C1944 through C2026 children of C591 through C660

C3461 through C3660 for children

C2027 through C2195 children of C661 through C795

C3661 through C3990 for children

C2196 ROBERT JOHNSTON BANNING born Jan. 4, 1963. Source: 61

C3991 through C3994 for children

C2197 WINTHROP HANCOCK BANNING born March 8, 1965. Source: 61

C3995 through C3999 for children

C2198 through C3330 children of C797 through C1824

C4000 through C5660 for children

C3331 CHARLES HERBERT KING born Nov. 9, 1935 in Wasta, S.D. and married Margaret Mary Moore June 15, 1957 in Clear Lake, Skagit Co. , Wa. She was born May 4, 1935. Their children were, John Thomas born May 10, 1959, David Charles born 1961, Joseph Edward born 1963 and Timothy born 1968. Source: 16,22,24

C3332 DUANE EUGENE KING born Jan. 9, 1949 in Anacortes, Skagit Co., Wa. He married Mrs. Patricia (Clayton) Jones on Nov. 7, 1977. She was born Dec. 17, 1947. Source: 24

C3333 MAURICE RAY BANNING born April 1, 1940 in Deadwood, Lawrence Co., S.D. and married Joann Marilyn Mabry June 4, 1962 in Albany, Linn Co. , Or. She was born Oct. 14, 1940. Source: 24,61

C5661 Kevin Ross Banning
C5662 Jeffery Scott Banning

C3334 ROBERT ORVAL BANNING born March 25, 1933 in Rapid City, S.D. and married Donna Rose Walker July 6, 1951 in Spearfish, Lawrence Co., S.D. She was born July 2, 1934. Source: 16,24

C5663 Dale Bruce Banning
C5664 Connie Lea Banning

C5665 Orval Bernard Banning
C5666 Callie Rosemarie Banning

C3335 SHIRLEY ANN BANNING born May 28, 1937 in Deadwood, Lawrence Co., S.D. and married Donald Dewey Sipe June 3, 1955 in Spearfish, S.D. He was born Nov. 19, 1931. Source: 24

C5667 Darrel Donald Sipe
C5668 Cheryl Sue Sipe

C3336 JERRY EUGENE BANNING born July 24, 1940 in Deadwood, Lawrence Co., S.D. and married Catherine Mable Maria Larson Jan. 23, 1960 in Spearfish, S.D. She was born Oct. 1, 1941. Source: 24

C5669 Diana Rae Banning
C5670 Cory Eugene Banning
C5671 Brett Alan Banning

C3337 DENNIS WARNER EVENSON born March 28, 1943 in San Diego, Calif. Source: 24

C3338 VERNON HAROLD EVENSON born Sept. 4, 1945 in Rapid City, S.D. He married Ramona Louise Gasser Nov. 25, 1967 in Denver, Col. She was born Dec. 26, 1945. Source: 24

C3339 ROBERT EUGENE HERTH JR. born Dec. 19, 1943 in Anacortes, Skagit Co., Wa. He married 1st, Janet Marie Nordi in 1965 and 2nd, Yvonne Marie Clements on March 21, 1975 in Tacoma, Wa. She was born July 10, 1947 and he served in the U.S. Marines. His children are Tracy Marie, born 1967 and Brian Robert born 1978. Source: 16,22,24

C3340 LYNNETTE LEE HERTH born April 19, 1947 in Tacoma, Wa. She married 1st, John Earl Dammeier (born 1946) on April 29, 1967, in Tacoma, and 2nd, Michael Terry Morris on April 4, 1980. He was born May 9, 1948. The children of the 1st marriage are John Earl born 1970 and Jodie Lynn born 1973. Source: 16,22,24

C3341 LORAYNE KAE (LORI) HERTH born April 17, 1955 in Tacoma, Wa. and married Richard Johan Andre Zanders. He was born Feb. 28, 1951 in Amsterdam, Holland. They had a child, Andre Nicholas Herth Zanders born Dec. 8, 1985. Source: 16,24

C3342 through C3362 Children of C1853 through C1857

C5672 through C5700 for children

C3363 through C3393 children of C1867 through C1876

C5701 through C5750 for children

C3394 through C3402 children of C1877 through C1879

C5751 through C5759 for children

C3403 NORMA JEAN BANNING born Aug. 3, 1944. Source: 61

> C5760 through C5762 for children

C3404 JAMES RICHARD BANNING born July 16, 1947. Source: 61

> C5763 through C5765 for children

C3405 RITA KAY BANNING born April 6, 1949. Source: 61

> C5766 through C5768 for children

C3406 SANDRA LEE BANNING born June 7, 1950. Source: 61

> C5769 through C5771 for children

C3407 PATRICIA ANN BANNING born April 24, 1956 and married John Miles Buck on Oct. 17, 1992. He is the son of Irvin Eugene and Jean Mable Buck, born July 24, 1961. She is a receptionist and they are living in Williston, N.D. Source: 61

> C5772 through C5774 for children

C3408 CYNTHIA KAYE BANNING born June 30, 1958 in Williston, N.D. She was a day care center operator in Williston in 1992. Source: 61

> C5775 through C5777 for children

C3409 SUSAN KAY BANNING born Dec. 6, 1952 and married a Mr. Clark. Source: 61

> C5779 through C5781 for children

C3410 RUSSELL LEE BANNING born May 2, 1956. Source: 61

> C5782 through C5784 for children

C34411 RONALD RAY BANNING born May 6, 1960. Source: 61

> C5785 through C5787 for children

C3412 through C3420 children of C1883 through C1885

> C5788 through C5800 for children

C3421 VICKY RAE BANNING born Dec. 20, 1940 and married Daniel Charles Timmins Aug. 8, 1959. He was born Dec. 29, 1937. Source: 24

> C5801 Stephen Faron Timmins
> C5802 Eddie Daniel Timmins
> C5803 Laurie Danette Timmins

C3422 DRVEY LEE BANNING born May 23, 1943 and married Laurel Lee Howard Aug. 14, 1965. She was born June 11, 1946. Source: 24

C5804 through C5806 for children

C3423 DENNIS GENE BANNING born July 25, 1945. Source: 24

C5807 through C5809 for children

C3427 DALE EDWARD BANNING born Feb. 27, 1950. Source: 24

C5810 through C5812 for children

C3428 JOYCE ANN BANNING born Feb. 25, 1952. Source: 24

C5813 through C5815 for children

C3429 AUDREY JOAN BANNING born Feb. 2, 1954. Source: 24

C5816 through C5818 for children

C3430 BRIAN RAY BANNING born July 31, 1960. Source: 24

C5819 through C5821 for children

C3431 through C5660 children of C1919 through C3330

C5822 through C8599 for children

C5661 KEVIN ROSS BANNING born Feb. 20, 1963 in Pensacola, Fla. He married Pamela Denise Durham on May 26, 1985. She is the daughter of William Bryan and Annette Coker Durham, born Aug. 13, 1963. In 1992 they were living in Glen Allen, Va. Source: 16,22,24,61

C8600 Elizabeth Brydin Banning

C5662 JEFFERY SCOTT BANNING born Feb. 25, 1964. Source: 24

C5663 DALE BRUCE BANNING born Feb. 19, 1954. Source: 24

C5664 CONNIE LEA BANNING born Feb. 14, 1955 in Deadwood, Lawrence Co., S.D. She married Michael Patrick Christopher May 15, 1975 in Orange, Ca. He is the son of Robert Christopher and Joan Marie Dagherty, born June 1952 in Hollywood, Ca. She married 2nd, Constantine Dean Poundris on Dec. 24, 1982. He was born May 24, 1943 in New York City, N.Y. Source: 22,24

C8603 Carrie Michalle Christopher

C5665 ORVAL BERNARD BANNING born March 29, 1956. Source: 24

C5666 CALLIE ROSEMARIE BANNING born April 20, 1960 in Tacoma, Wash. She married Ricky Edward Sanders Dec. 18, 1976 in Orange. He is the son of Richard Ernest Sanders and Barbara Buck, born April 4, 1957 in Long Beach, Ca. She married 2nd, Peter Hollander on April 5, 1986 in Palm Desert, Calif. Source: 16,22,24

C8609 Breia Rosemarie Sanders

C5667 DARREL DONALD SIPE born May 1, 1956. Source: 24

C5668 CHERYL SUE SIPE born July 2, 1960. Source: 24

C5669 DIANA RAE BANNING born Aug. 13, 1960 and married Kirby Naota on March 9, 1983. Source: 24

C5670 CORY EUGENE BANNING born April 20, 1962. Source: 24

C5671 BRETT ALAN BANNING born Feb. 19, 1974. Source: 24

C5801 STEPHEN FARON TIMMINS born May 19, 1960. Source: 24

C5802 EDDIE DANIEL TIMMINS born Feb. 6, 1962. Source: 24

C5803 LAURIE DANETTE TIMMINS born June 11, 1964. Source: 24

C8600 ELIZABETH BRYDIN BANNING born May 20, 1988 in Penn. Source: 22,24,61

C8603 CARRIE MICHALLE CHRISTOPHER born Sept 13, 1977 Santa Anna, Orange Ca. Source: 24

C8609 BREIA ROSEMARIE SANDERS born Jan. 15, 1978 Orange, Ca. Source: 24

JOHN C. BANNING of DELAWARE

DI JEREMIAH BANNING no other information. Source: 1,40

        D2 John C. Banning
        D3 through D8 for children

D2 JOHN C. BANNING born 1800-1810 in Succex County, Delaware. Married
    Sarah Sparks and lived in Del. Source: 1,40

        D9   James L. Banning
        D10 Samuel Banning
        D11 William Station Banning
        D12 John Banning
        D13 Alfred Banning
        D14 Mary Banning
        D15 Annie Banning
        D16 Emma Banning
        D17 Hester Banning
        D18 Louise "Sallie" Banning

D3 through D8 unknown children of D1

        D19 through D49 for children

D9 JAMES L. BANNING born Sept. 28, 1825 in Delaware. Married Maria ----? in
    1852. She was born in Aug. 1825. He died March 6, 1904 in Del. Source: 1,40

        D50 Clair C. Banning
        D51 John Wesley Banning
        D52 Mary Ann Banning
        D53 William Banning
        D54 Samuel L. Banning

D1O SAMUEL BANNING born in Del. Source: 1,40

        D55 through D62 for children

D11 WILLIAM STATION BANNING born Feb. 10, 1840 in Kent Co., Del. He married
    ----? Tucker in Jan. 1865. They lived in the Dover Del. area. He died in Del.
    Source: 1,40

        D63 Florence Banning
        D64 Annie Banning
        D65 William Banning
        D66 Samuel Banning
        D67 Johnnie Banning
        D68 Vira Banning
        D69 Julia Banning

D12 JOHN BANNING born 1842 in Kent Co., Del. Source: 1

        D70 through D76 for children

D13 ALFRED BANNING born near Millford, Del. He left home during the Civil War and never married. Source: 1

D14 MARY BANNING born near Millford, Del. She married Mr. Pierce. Source: 1

D77 through D83 for children

D15 ANNIE BANNING no information Source: 1

D84 through D90 for children

D16 EMMA BANNING born at Millford, Del. Source: 1

D91 through D97 for children

D17 HESTER BANNING born at Millford, Del. She married Mr. Glad and moved "out west". Source: 1

D98 Katie Glad

D18 LOUISE "SALLIE" BANNING born near Millford, Del. and lived in Lockhaven. Source: 1

D99 through D105 for children

D19 through D49 unknown children of D3 through D8

D106 through D166 for children

D50 CLAIR C. BANNING born Oct. 2, 1864 in Philadelphia, Pa. She married Joseph Lowry in 1886 in Philadelphia, where they lived. Source: 1

D167 Joseph Lowry
D168 Annie Lowry

D51 JOHN WESLEY BANNING born Oct. 5, 1866 in Philadelphia, Pa. He married Mary Frangler in 1903 in Philadelphia, where they lived. Source: 1

D169 Joseph Banning
D170 Henry Banning

D52 MARY ANN BANNING born Feb. 5, 1869. She married Joseph Martin of Jersey in 1885. They lived in Philadelphia, Pa. Source: 1

D171 James Martin
D172 Mamie Martin
D173 Lizzie Martin

D53 WILLIAM BANNING born Sept. 8, 1872 near Millford, Del. He married Bessie Smith and they lived in Philadelphia, Pa. Source: 1

D174 William Banning

D54 SAMUEL L. BANNING born Jan. 25, 1875 in Philadelphia, Pa. He married Mary Jordan and they lived in Philadelphia. Source: 1

D175 Minnie Banning

D55 through D62 unknown children of D10

D176 through D216 for children

D63 FLORENCE BANNING born Sept. 19, 1870 in Kent Co., Del. She married Watson Marvel on April 19, 1905. They lived near Magnolia, Del. Source: 1

D217 through D222 for children

D64 ANNIE BANNING born May 25, 1875 in Kent Co., Del. She married Joseph Minner in March 1897. She died March 14, 1906. Source: 1

D223 Laura Minner
D224 Helen Minner
D225 Lawrence Minner
D226 William Minner

D65 WILLIAM BANNING born 1875 in Kent Co., Del. He married Annie Hepnor on April 21, 1905. They lived in Elmer, New Jersey. Source: 1

D227 through D232 for children

D66 SAMUEL BANNING born 1879 and died 1884. Source: 1

D67 JOHNNIE BANNING born Sept. 19, 1882 in Kent Co., Del. and died April 9, 1898. Source: 1

D68 VIRA BANNING born April 7, 1885 in Kent Co., Del. She married Emerson Saxon on Nov. 30, 1905. They lived in Dover, Del. Source: 1

D233 through D238 for children

D69 JULIA BANNING born March 14, 1888 in Kent Co., Del. Source: 1

D239 through D245 for children

D70 through D76 unknown children of D12

D246 through D276 for children

D77 through D97 unknown children of D14 through D16

D98 KATIE GLAD no information Source: 1

D99 through D105 unknown children of D18

D106 through D166 unknown children of D19 through D49

D277 through D427 for children

D167 JOSEPH LOWRY no information Source: 1

D168 ANNIE LOWRY no information Source: 1

D169 JOSEPH BANNING born 1905 in Philadelphia, Pa. Source: 1

D170 HENRY BANNING born 1906 in Philadelphia, Pa. Source: 1

D171 JAMES MARTIN no information Source: 1

D172 MAMIE MARTIN no information Source: 1

D173 LIZZIE MARTIN no information Source: 1

D174 WILLIAM BANNING born Philadelphia, Pa. Source: 1

D175 MINNIE BANNING born Philadelphia, Pa. Source: 1

D176 through D216 unknown children of D55 through D62

D217 through D222 unknown children of D63

D223 LAURA MINNER no information Source: 1

D224 HELEN MINNER no information Source: 1

D225 LAWRENCE MINNER no information Source: 1

D226 WILLIAM MINNER no information Source: 1

JOHN BANNING of LYME, CONN.

This arrangement of the origins of the "E" and "F" line is different than in Source 1. After much research by Mary Friedlander, Source 64, locating copies of wills, deeds and other primary records, the following arrangement has been proven. The error in Source 1 can be traced to a letter written in 1866 by Amelia Vinning Eels (or Bells as indicated in some sources). Much of the information in Mrs. Eels letter is accurate, but this error was picked up by source 1 and publications that followed, including the first edition of this book.

E1, F1 JOHN BANNING was born about 1652 and first appears in 1683 in the records of New Shoreham, on Block Island near the coast of Rhode Island. At this time he had a son, John (E2) about 4 years old and may have been accompanied by a wife, but she does not appear in the records, and remains nameless. In 1689 he was given 3 acres of land on Block Island by Peter George for "good will and respect". He was a tailor, and almost always referred to by the title of "Mr.", which was usually reserved for teachers, gentlemen or Officials. Sometime before 1701, perhaps as early as 1689, he married for the second time, Abigail Niles, the widow of John Niles. She had two sons, John and Ambrose Niles, and perhaps also had 2 girls, Penelope and Abigail Niles. On June 11, 1701, John Banning and partners, Consider Tiffany (husband of Abigail Niles) and and Ephraim Tiffany/ Edward Mott (husband of Penelope Niles) purchased a large tract of land, about 1000 acres, in Joshuas Town, Lyme Conn. John and his family moved to this property in 1702. He and his son John (E2) were both in New London Co, Conn. in Aug. 1702 signing papers on property they owned on Block Island. John (E1) died in in Lyme in 1717.
 Source: 12,33,64,70,72,73

E2 F2 John Banning Jr.

E2, F2 JOHN BANNING born about 1678. His 1st wife was possibly Sarah Tiffany, born June 6, 1683, the daughter of Humphrey and Elizabeth Tiffany. He married 2nd, in 1751, Mary Daniels Roland, who was born 1690. She was the widow of Daniel Daniels and also the widow of Henry Roland. John became an "admitted inhabitant" of Lyme Conn. on Jan. 17, 1714, which means he was a Freeman and could vote. He became the pound keeper at Joshua town on Dec. 31, 1718 and was chosen a "grandjurey man" Dec. 19, 1727. He died 1759. Source: 12,55,64,70

> E3, F3 Elizabeth Banning (See E3)
> E4, F4 Girl Banning   (See E4)
> E5, F5 John Banning Jr.   (See E5
> E6, F6 Samuel Banning (See F6)
> E7, F7 Mary Banning   (See F7)
> E8, F8 Hannah Banning (See F8)

E3 ELIZABETH BANNING She was born 1705. She married Lieut. John Brockway, on March 1, 1727, at New London, Lyme, Conn. John was the son of William (1666-1755) and Elizabeth Brockway, born May 10, 1697. She died April 26, 1738 in childbirth at Brockway's Ferry. John married 2nd, Sarah Scovil on March 22, 1739. Source: 12,13,14,55,64,65

> E25 Elizabeth Brockway
> E26 John Brockway

E27 Ebenezer Brockway
E28 Sarah Brockway
E29 Mary Brockway

E4 GIRL BANNING born 1707 and married a Mr. Dibble. Source: 12,64

E33 Thomas Dibble

E5 JOHN BANNING JR. born about 1711 and married 1st, Margaret DeWolf of
Killingworth, Conn. on July 15, 1734 in Lyme, New London County Conn. She was
the daughter of Benjamin DeWolf (died 1766) and Margaret Smith (1696-1742) and
was born in 1717. After Margaret's death on March 31, 1744, he married 2nd,
Jemima Marvin Peck, the widow of William Peck, on May 22, 1744. Jemima was
born July 20, 1711 in Lyme, Conn. and was the daughter of John Marvin (1665-
1711) and Sarah Graham (1670-1760). He died about June 3, 1755. Source:
12,13,33,55,64,65,72,83

E14 John Banning
E15 Benjamin Banning
E16 Irena "Phreaney" Banning
E17 Ebenezer Banning
E18 William Banning
E19 Joseph Banning
E20 Margaret "Peggy" Banning
E21 Sarah Banning

E6 thru E8, see F6 thru F8

E9 thru E13 unused numbers

E14 JOHN BANNING born April 8, 1735 in Lyme, New London County Conn. and
married Deborah Reed June 2, 1757 in the 2nd Congreagational Church in Lyme,
Middlesex Co. Conn. Source: 1,3,12,13,40,55,64,65,71,83

E85 Abigail Banning
E86 Margaret Banning
E87 Irene Banning
E88 thru E99 for children

E15 BENJAMIN BANNING born Jan. 1, 1740 in Lyme, New London County Conn. on
Jan. 1, 1740. Fought in the Colonial Wars of 1758-60, 61 & 62. He was in the 1st
Co. of a detachment from the 7th regiment for 16 days and went to the relief of Ft.
William Henry under Maj. Aaron Elliot. Benjamin was a Sargent in the 8th Co of the
1st Regiment for the campaign of 1762, under Capt. Zebulon Butler. He died in
1762. Source: 1,12,13,17,40,55,64,65,83

E16 IRENA "PHREANEAY" "LURANA" BANNING born in Lyme, New London County
Conn. on May 20, 1742 and married "Deacon" Joseph Willey Jr. at Hadlyme, Conn.
on March 3, 1764. He was the son of Joseph & Lucretia (Holms) Willey, born
March 22, 1734 in East Haddam, Ct. He died Oct. 5, 1793 at the age of 60.
Source: 1,12,13,55,64,65,83

E100 Temperance Willey

E17 EBENEZER BANNING born Feb. 6, 1745 at Lyme, New London County, Conn. and married Sarah Harvey in 1774. She was the daughter of Joshua and Joanna (Sill) Harvey of Lyme, born in 1752. He died in Lyme on Sept. 20, 1793. Source: 3,12,13,14,55,64,83

      E51 Sarah Banning
      E52 John Banning
      E53 Joshua Banning
      E54 Sill Banning
      E55 Ebenezer Banning
      E56 Sally Banning
      E57 Fanny "Betsy" Banning
      E58 Clarissa Banning
      E59 Jemima Banning

E18 WILLIAM BANNING born Nov. 5, 1747 in Lyme, New London County, Conn. and married Lucy Tiffany, the daughter of Lieut. Nathan Tiffany "a well known indian fighter", in Lyme, where they lived. They bought land in Lyme on Sept. 22, 1772. He was living with his son William in 1810 in N.Y. Source: 1,2,3,12,13, 18,33,40,55,64,83

      E60 Lucy Banning
      E61 Azubah Banning
      E62 William Banning
      E63 Benjamin B. Banning
      E64 Temperance Banning
      E65 Elisha Banning
      E66 Amasa Banning
      E67 Calvin Banning
      E68 Clarissa Banning

E19 JOSEPH BANNING born Aug. 6, 1748 in Lyme, New London Co., Conn. and married Susanna Warner in Dec. 1773 in East Haddam, Conn. They lived in East Haddam, where he owned a large farm. After his death, his son, Seldon, occupied the farm. His wife was the daughter of Jabez and Hanna Brainard Warner and was born on April 9, 1753, and died April 3, 1829. He died in Hadlyme, Conn. on April 16, 1834. Source: 1,12,13,40,55,64,83

      E76 Marvin "Bondod" Banning
      E77 Brainard Banning
      E78 Philemon Fuller Banning
      E79 Lucinda Banning
      E80 Joseph Banning
      E81 Selden Warner Banning
      E82 Nancy Banning
      E83 Susannah Banning
      E84 Benjamin Banning

E20 MARGARET "PEGGY" BANNING born Aug. 6, 1750 in Lyme, New London County Conn. and married a Brockway about 1770. Source: 1,12,13,55,64,65,83

      E69 thru E75 for children.

E21 SARAH BANNING born April 20, 1753 in Lyme, New London County Conn. She married David Beebe Pratt about 1775. He was the son of Azarian Pratt. Source: 1,12,13,55,64,83,96

> E108 Elisabeth Pratt
> E109 Mary Pratt
> E110 Noah Pratt
> E111 David Pratt
> E112 Sarah Pratt
> E113 Benjamin Pratt

E22 thru E24 unsued

E25 ELIZABETH BROCKWAY born April 1 or 2, 1728. Source: 14,55,64

E26 JOHN BROCKWAY born July 28, 1729. He married Caroline Reed. Source: 14,55,64,90

E27 EBENEZER BROCKWAY born Oct. 15, 1731 and married Mary Butler, the daughter of John Butler. Ebenezer was a sea captain and owned the sloop "Polly". Source: 14,55,64,90

E28 SARAH BROCKWAY born March 15, 1734 and married Nathan Beckwith. Source: 14,55,64,90

E29 MARY BROCKWAY born April 26, 1738. She married Capt. Elijah Bingham who died in New London Ct, on Aug. 26, 1798 of yellow fever. Mary died of the same illness on Sept. 15, 1798. Source: 14,55,64,90

E30 thru E32 unused

E33 THOMAS DIBBLE born 1727. Source: 12,64

E34 thru E50 Unused numbers

E51 SARAH BANNING born in 1775 in Conn.

> E201 thru E208 for children.

E52 JOHN BANNING born in 1777 (1781?) in Conn. Probably the twin brother of Joshua. He was alive in 1850. He married Salma (???) who was born 1790 and died 1862. The 1807 census of Leyden, Lewis Co., N.Y. lists John as having the right to vote. He died in 1861. Both are buried in the Wilcox Cemetery in N.Y. Source: 1,3,4,15,40,93

> E209 Joseph Banning
> E210 John Banning
> E211 George Banning
> E212 Lysander Banning
> E213 Caroline Banning
> E214 Leander Banning
> E215 thru E219 for children.

E53 JOSHUA BANNING born in 1777 in Conn. Source: 1,40

E220 thru E227 for children

E54 SILL BANNING born about 1780 in Conn. Source: 1,40

E228 thru E235 for children

E55 EBENEZER BANNING born in Conn. Source: 1,40

E236 thru E242 for children.

E56 SALLY BANNING born in Conn. Source: 1

E243 thru E251 for children.

E57 FANNY "BETSY" BANNING born 1786 in Conn. and married Josiah Post Jr. He was the son of Josiah and Lydia Platts Post, born April 13, 1784 in Saybrook, Conn. The 1810 Census places him in Rodman, Jefferson Co., N.Y. and by 1825 he is in Leyden, Lewis Co., N.Y., where he has 18 acres of improved land. He died Feb. 26, 1827 in Leyden, Lewis Co., N.Y. and is buried in the Lord (Leyden Hill) Cemetery. She died Sept. 8, 1833 in Lewis Co. and was buried in the Lord Cemetery. Source: 1,15,93

> E252 Josaiah Post
> E253 William H. Post
> E254 Lorenzo Post
> E255 Fanny Ann Post
> E256 Philo Post
> E257 Alonzo Post
> E258 Lydia Post
> E259 Eliza Post
> E260 Charles Post
> E260a Nathan Post

E58 CLARISSA BANNING born in Conn. Source: 1

E261 thru E268 for children.

E59 JEMIMA BANNING born in Conn. in 1785 and married 1st Isaac Bartlett. He was born in Mass. in 1778 and died Oct. 4, 1816 in Ohio. She married 2nd Oliver Clark. He is buried in McArthur, Oh. She moved to Belendon, Ohio in 1807 and died July 17, 1840. She is buried in Blendon West Pioneer Cemetery in Franklin Co. Source: 1

E269 thru E277 for children.

E60 LUCY BANNING born May 8, 1770 in Lyme, New London County Conn. She married Josiah Benjamin. He was the son of William and Sarah Benjamin, born June 19, 1769. He died in 1836 in Berlin. Source: 2,12,13,18,55

E278 thru E286 for children

E61 AZUBAH BANNING She was born Nov. 28, 1771 in Lyme, New London County

Conn. Source: 12,13,18,55

E287 thru E295 for children.

E62 WILLIAM BANNING born Aug. 26, 1773 in Lyme, New London County Conn.
Married Lydia Church, on April 9, 1798 in East Haddam, Middlesex County Conn.
She was the daughter of Samuel Church Jr. and his wife Sarah. Lydia was born
Sept. 24, 1776. They moved to Monroe County N.Y. before 1810. He died in N.Y.
Source: 3,4,12, 13,14,18,35,38,55

> E296 Male Banning (Selden C. ?) born 1798 to 1800.
> E297 Female Banning born 1798 to 1800.
> E298 Female Banning born 1798 to 1800.
> E299 Female Banning born 1800 to 1810.
> E300 Female Banning born 1800 to 1810
> E301 Female Banning born 1800 to 1810
> E302 Nelson Banning
> E303 Male Banning born 1810 to 1820 (William ?)
> E304 Female Banning born 1810 to 1820.

E63 BENJAMIN B. BANNING born Feb. 26, 1775 in Lyme, Conn. He married Clarissa
Corwin, the daughter of Theophilus and Mary (Lord) Corwin, in Lyme, Conn. She
was born about 1780. He joined the 1st Congregational Church on April 27, 1794.
He died Oct. 31, 1859 and she died June 20, 1864 in Lyme, Joshuatown Society,
now called Brockway. They are both buried in Joshuatown Cem., New London
County, Ct. The 1850 census indicates he is a"mechanic".   Source:
1,2,3,5,12,13,14,18,40,55

> E305 Benjamin F. Banning
> E306 Edwin Hall Banning
> E307 William Hall Banning
> E308 Marie E. Banning
> E309 Caroline L. Banning
> E310 Elisha W. Banning
> E311 William Theophilus Banning
> E312 Orin A. Banning
> E313 George W. Banning
> E314 Catherine C. Banning
> E315 Newel E. Banning
> E316 Ephraim Henry Banning.

E64 TEMPERANCE BANNING born June 14, 1776 in Lyme, New London County
Conn. Source: 12,13,18,55

E317 thru E325 for children

E65 ELISHA BANNING born Jan. 29, 1778 in Lyme, New London County Conn.
Source: 12,13,18,55

E326 thru E334 for children.

E66 AMASA BANNING born in Lyme, New London County Conn. on Oct. 4, 1779.
Source: 1,3,12,13,18,40,55

E335 thru E343 for children

E67 CALVIN BANNING born June 2, 1785 in Lyme Conn. He married Eunice
Beckwith in Lyme. She was the daughter of Josiah & Mehitable (Pearson) Beckwith,
and was born Feb. 26, 1786. They lived in Lyme, Conn. He died Oct. 1, 1856 and
she died April 23, 1835 in Lyme. Source: 1,3,5,12,13,18,33,40,55

E344 Melinda (Lynda) M. Banning
E345 Mehitable P. Banning
E346 William Josiah Banning
E347 Calvin Banning
E348 Albert Tiffany Banning
E349 Eunice Beckwith Banning
E350 Mathilda L. Banning

E68 CLARISSA BANNING born in Lyme, New London County Conn. on June 2, 1781.
Source: 1,12,13,18,55

E351 thru E359 for children

E69 thru E75 unknown PRATT children.

E76 MARVIN "BANDO" BANNING born Nov. 1, 1774 in East Haddam, Middlesex
County Ct. and died July 21, 1848. He married Alice Peck. Source: 1,3,13,40,64

E360 David Banning
E361 Joseph Banning
E362 Marvin Banning
E363 Nancy Banning
E364 Emily Banning

E77 BRAINARD BANNING born on May 6, 1785 in East Haddam, Middlesex County
Ct. He married Mary Pratt, the daughter of David B. and Sarah Banning Pratt. She
was born in May 1779. (See E109) They lived in Hadlyme. He drowned in Essex,
Ct. when he fell into the water and struck his head while repairing his vessel. This
may have occurred between 1820 and 1830. Source: 1,3,13,40,64,83,96

E365 Charles Banning
E366 Sarah Banning
E367 James Banning
E368 Henry Banning
E369 Henry Banning, 2nd
E370 Elisa Banning
E371 Emily Banning

E78 PHILEMON FULLER BANNING born April 10, 1787 in East Haddam, Middlesex
County Ct. and married Mary Millard. He was a minister and farmer. Enlisted in the
Conn. Militia from Aug. 15 to Aug. 25, 1814. The 1850 census indicates he was
living alone in the city of Hartford with 4 children. He died 1870 in Winchester.
Source: 1,5,13,40

E372 Erastus Millard Banning
E373 Mary Ann Banning
E374 Elizabeth R. Banning

E375 Augustus Banning
E376 Carlos Banning
E377 Horace Banning
E378 Theodore Banning
E379 Laura R. Banning
E380 Julia Etta Banning
E301 Carrie A. Banning
E382 Ellen E. Banning

E79 LUCINDA BANNING born 1795 in Hadlyme, Ct. and married Capt. Ebenezer
Brockway Warner on April 24, 1814. They lived in Hadlyme, Ct. She died Dec. 14,
1867 and is buried in the church cemetery in Hadlyme. Source: 1,64

E383 Joseph Warner
E384 Harriet (Susan) Warner

E80 JOSEPH BANNING born March 2, 1780 in East Haddam, Middlesex County Ct.
and married Asubah (Azubah) Clark, who was born about 1784. He was a captain
on a large ocean going ship engaged in shipping flour to England at the time of the
famine. Both were living in Saybrook, Middlesex Co. in 1850. Source: 1,3,5,13,40

E385 Joseph Lewis Banning
E386 Henry Seabury Banning
E387 Arba Hanson Banning

E81 SELDEN WARNER BANNING born Sept. 27, 1782 in East Haddam, Middlesex
County Conn. and married Alice Ransome. They lived in Hadlyme. She died and he
married a Miss Fanny Keeny. She was born about 1800. They had one child. He
was a farmer and ship's carpenter. He enlisted in the Conn. Militia in 1814. They
were living in East Haddam in 1850. Source: 1,5,13,40

E388 George Banning
E389 Mary Banning
E390 Sophia Banning
E390A Susan Banning

E82 NANCY BANNING born 1790 in Hadlyme, Ct. and married Erastus Lay of
Saybrook on July 20, 1809. They lived in Hadlyme. He died and she married her
late sister's husband, Capt. Brockway Warner. They lived and died in Hadlyme.
She died May 14, 1866 and he died Feb. 27, 1839. Both are buried in Joshuatown
Cemetery. Source: 1

E391 Lemira Lay
E392 Julius A. Lay
E393 Erastus L. Lay
E394 Mary Lay
E395 Nancy Lay
E396 George Lay

E83 SUSANNAH BANNING born Oct. 28, 1776 in East Haddam, Middlesex County
Conn. She died unmarried on April 23, 1820. Source: 1,13

E84 BENJAMIN BANNING born about 1794 in Hadlyme, Ct. and married Theadocia
(Dotice) Bramble of Lyme on March 23, 1821. She was born about 1803. They had

20 children, of which 17 lived. He was a farmer. She was the daughter of Silas Bramble, a minister, and a Rev. War pensioner. They were living in East Haddam, Middlesex County Conn. in 1850. Source: 1,5,12,40,55

> E397 Benjamin Banning
> E398 Joseph Banning
> E399 Rosetta Banning
> E400 Charlotte Banning
> E401 William Warner Banning
> E402 Jabez Warner Banning
> E403 Samuel Banning
> E404 Clarissa Banning
> E405 Betsy Elizabeth Banning
> E406 Calvin Banning
> E407 Matilda Banning
> E408 Simon Banning
> E409 Laura Banning
> E410 Mary Banning
> E411 Rachel Banning
> E412 Almira Banning
> E413 Clarissa Banning

E85 ABIGAIL BANNING born about 1760 and married Capt. Zebulon Brockway of Lyme, Ct. He was the son of Ebenzer and Mary Butler Brockway (E27). He died March 16, 1837 and she died April 10, 1838. They both are buried in Joshuatown, Lyme, Ct. Source: 64

> E414 John Cotton Mather Brockway
> E414a Zebulon Brockway
> E414b Mary Brockway
> E414c Betsey Brockway

E86 MARGARET BANNING Born about 1762 and married Ezra Brockway about 1790. He was the son of John and Caroline Reed Brockway (E26), born 1764 and died Oct. 20, 1844. She died Oct. 20, 1853. Source: 64,83

> E415 Deborah Reed Brockway
> E416 Caroline Brockway
> E417 Lucina Brockway
> E418 Ezra Brockway
> E419 Niles Brockway
> E420 Margaret Brockway

E87 IRENE BANNING married Francis E. Beckwith of Saybrook, Ct. They lived in Utica, N.Y. where they were among the early settlers. They died in Utica. Source: 2,64,83

> E421 Benjamin Beckwith
> E422 Reed Beckwith
> E423 Lucinda Beckwith
> E424 Debora Beckwith
> E425 Francis Beckwith
> E426 George Beckwith
> E427 Caroline Irene Beckwith

E428 John E. Beckwith

E88 thru E99 for unknown children of E14

E429 thru E499 for children

E100 TEMPERANCE WILLEY born Dec. 15, 1768 in East Haddam, Ct. She married David Phelps on Feb. 12, 1784 in East Haddam. He was born March 22, 1762/3 in E. Haddam and served in the Revolutionary war. He enlisted at Lyme, Ct. as a fifer in Feb. 1777 at the age of 14. They moved to Middlesex, Vt. about 1795. They had a daughter, Betsey Phelps (Dow) with whom David was living in 1850 in Duxbury, Vt. Their children were Irena, Beulah, Joseph, David, Temperance, Benjamin, Parnal, Betsey and Hannah. Source: 83

E101 thru E107 unused

E108 ELISABETH PRATT born April 19, 1777. Source: 83

E109 MARY PRATT born in May 1779 and married Brainerd Banning (E77). Source: 64,83,96

E110 NOAH PRATT born Aug. 12, 1781 and married Nancy Mack about 1802. They lived in Waterford, Pa. Source: 64,83,96

> E500 Noah Pratt
> E501 Nancy Pratt
> E502 Noah Pratt
> E503 Josiah Pratt
> E504 George Partt
> E505 Alfred Pratt
> E506 Albert Pratt
> E507 Gilbert Pratt
> E508 Julia Pratt
> E509 Betsey Pratt
> E510 Almira Pratt
> E511 Maria Pratt
> E512 William Pratt
> E513 Lafayette Pratt
> E514 Phebe Pratt
> E515 Amanda Pratt
> E516 Eli Pratt
> E517 Sally Pratt

E111 DAVID PRATT born June 6, 1784 and married Submit Pratt in July 1808. She died Dec. 1, 1835 and David died Aug. 14, 1851. Source: 64,83,96

> E518 Phineas Pratt
> E519 Philo Pratt
> E520 Alpheus Pratt
> E521 Hepsibah Pratt
> E522 Alva Pratt

E112 SARAH PRATT born Feb. 11, 1789 and married Lawrence Johnson on March 28, 1813. Source: 64,83,96

E523 Sarah P. Johnson
E524 Asa H. Johnson
E525 Benjamin L. Johnson
E526 William P. Johnson
E527 Elizabeth H. Johnson
E528 George W. Johnson

E113 BENJAMIN PRATT born & died at Amboy, N.J. Source: 83

E114 thru E200 unsued

E201 thru E208 for unknown children of E50 and E51.

E529 thru E1000 for children

E209 JOSEPH E. BANNING born June 12, 1810 in Lyden, Lewis County N.Y. Married
Sally M. Foster on Nov. 24, 1832 in Turin, Lewis County N.Y. She died in Jan. 1885
in Mendota, Ill. He died Jan. 29, 1882 in Lewis Co. Source: 1,30,40

E1001 Walter Edgar Banning
E1002 Emelin Harriet Banning
E1003 Orson Benjamin Banning
E1004 Chauncey Henry Banning
E1005 Mattie Banning
E1006 Ellen Banning
E1007 Helen Banning
E1008 Lydia Ann Banning
E1009 Jay Foster Banning

E210 JOHN BANNING born in Leyden, Lewis Co., N.Y. 1781 and died 1861 in
Leyden. He married Salma (???) who was born 1790 and died 1862. Both are
buried in the Wilcox Cemetery. Source: 1,15,40

E1010 thru E1016 for children

E211 GEORGE BANNING born 1823 in Leyden, Lewis, Co., N.Y. Married Anna
Atkins on May 3, 1854 in Boonville, N.Y. She was born 1829 and died in 1907.
They lived in Leyden. Both are buried in the Wilcox Cemetry. Source:
1,15,30,40,93

E1017 John F. Banning

E212 LYSANDER BANNING born in Leyden, Lewis Co., N.Y. His wife died in Feb.
1892 at their home in Locust Grove. He died a few days later. Source: 1,30,40,93

E1018 Wallace Banning
E1019 Nellie Banning

E213 CAROLINE BANNING no information. Source: 1

E1020 thru E1024 for children.

E214 LEANDER BANNING born about 1815 and married twice. During the Civil War, he served in the 5th N.Y. H.A. He died Nov. 10, 1890 and is buried in Talcotville Cemetery, Leyden, Lewis Co., N.Y. Source: 1,15,30,40,93

E1025 Mary Banning
E1026 Charles Banning
E1027 Henrietta Banning
E1028 Selinda Banning

E215 thru E251 unknown children of E52 thru E56

E1029 thru E1129 for children

E252 JOSAIAH POST born 1814 and married Catherine Windsor. She was born about 1820 and died 1889. He died in 1902. Both are buried in the Wilcox Cemetery. Source: 15,93

E1130 Juane M. Post
E1131 Mary E. Post
E1132 & E1133 for children

E253 WILLIAM H. POST born 1815. He married 1st, Eliza Douglass. She was born about 1812 and died Sept. 13, 1842 and is buried in the Locust Grove, Lord, Cemetery. William married 2nd, Ann (???) and 3rd Achsah Douglass. He died Nov. 8, 1867. Source: 15,93

E1134 thru E1138 for children

E254 LORENZO POST born Sept. 28, 1817 and married 1st, Eliza (???) and 2nd, Hannah T. Newsom. Hannah was born about 1823 and died Feb. 13, 1874. He died Dec. 4, 1902. Both are buried in the Port Leyden Cemetery. Source: 15,93

E1139 thru E1143 for children

E255 FANNY ANN POST born 1818 and married Andrew Jackson. He was born in 1811 and ide Oct. 29, 1879. She died in 1895. Both are buried in the Wilcox Cemcetery, 1 mile S. of Collinsville, N.Y. Source: 15,93

E1144 Anson G. Jackson
E1145 Charles E. Jackson
E1146 William A. Jackson
E1147 Nancy Ann Jackson
E1148 & E1149 for children

E256 PHILO POST born May 31, 1819 and married Nancy E. Douglass on Nov. 30 1855. He died Nov. 24, 1894 and is buried in the Wilcox Cemetery. Source: 15,93

E1150 Ida Post
E1151 thru E1153 for children

E257 ALONZO POST He, was alive in 1827. Source: 93

E1154 thru E1159 for children

E258 LYDIA POST born 1821 and married Amasa Walters. She died in Oct. 1861 and is buried in the Wilcox Cemetery. Source: 15,93

E1160 thru E1164 for children

E259 ELIZA POST born Feb. 29, 1824 and married Nathan Douglass on May 3, 1846.
He was born May 16, 1817 and died in Nov. 1879. She died Feb. 13, 1887.
Source: 93

E1165 thru E1169 for children

E260 CHARLES POST he was alive in 1827 and under the age of 21. Source: 93

E1170 thru E1174 for children

E260a NATHAN POST No information. Source: 93

E1175 thru E1179 for children

E261 thru E295 unknown children of E58 thru E61.

E1180 thru E1299 for children of E261-E295.

E296 Male Banning (Selden C. Banning ?) born between 1798-1800 census. Married
and living in N.Y. in 1830 & 40. Source: 4

E1300 Male born 1825-30
E1301 Male born 1830
E1302 thru E1308 for children.

E297 Female Banning born between 1798 and 1800 census. Source: 3

E1309 thru E1317 for children.

E298 Female Banning born between 1798 and 1800 census. Source: 3

E1318 thru E1326 for children.

E299 Female Banning born between 1800 and 1810 census. Source: 3

E1327 thru E1335 for children

E300 Female Banning born between 1800 and 1810 census. Source: 3

E1336 thru E1344 for children.

E301 Female Banning born between 1800 and 1810 census. Source: 3

E1345 thru E1353 for children.

E302 NELSON BANNING born Oct. 4, 1818 in Ogden, Monroe County N.Y. Married
Susan Malora Murray who was born July 25, 1820, in Pike, Allegheny County N.Y.,
and was the daughter of Noah and Mercy (Doty) Murray, on Jan. 13, 1841. They
moved to Iowa sometime prior to 1850. The 1850 census shows he was a
goldminer in El Dorado County Calif. He died in Preston, Jackson County Iowa on

April 6, 1907. She died in 1908 in Preston. Both are buried in the Buckeye Cem. in Preston. Source: 4,5,6,7,8,12,14,19,35,38

E1354 Ellen E. Banning
E1355 Clarence Nelson Banning
E1356 Malora B. Banning
E1357 Florence Isabel Banning
E1358 Laura Pamelia Banning
E1359 Lydia Philura Banning
E1360 Agnes Violet Banning
E1361 Walter Edwin Banning

E303 Male Banning born between 1810 and 1820 census. Source: 4

E1362 thru E1370 for children.

E304 Female Banning born between 1810 and 1820 census. Source: 4

E1371 thru E1379 for children.

E305 BENJAMIN F. BANNING born May 7, 1800 in Lyme, Conn. Married Annie Shaler or Ursula Marie Shailer (born about 1813 in Ct.) of Hadlyme, Conn. on Jan. 7, 1835 in Haddam, Middlesex County Ct. He died in Hadlyme in 1843. She was living with her parents in Haddam in 1850. Source: 1,5,13,40

E1380 George Banning
E1381 Ursula Banning

E306 EDWIN HALL BANNING born May 19, 1802 in Lyme, Conn. Married Emily M. Wells of Colchester, Conn. in Aug. 1828 in Hadlyme Society in Lyme. Lived in North Lyme Society, where he died March 1, 1875. She died Oct. 30, 1880. Source: 1,12,40,55

E1382 Leander Edwin Banning
E1383 George Wilson Banning
E1384 Emily Maria Banning
E1385 George Wilson Banning
E1386 Frances Wells Banning
E1387 Albert Brainard Banning

E307 WILLIAM HALL BANNING born Jan. 19, 1804 in Lyme, Conn. He died Jan. 28, 1806. Source: 1

E308 MARY E. BANNING born Jan. 19, 1806 in Lyme. Died June 9, 1808. Source: 1

E309 CAROLINE L. BANNING born Jan. 18, 1808 in Lyme. Married Horace S. Chapel on March 23, 1835 in Lyme where they lived. She died June 12, 1854 in Boston and is buried in New London, Conn. Source: 1,14,55

E1388 Francis Chapel
E1389 Levia Chapel
E1390 Marrion Chapel
E1391 Victoria S. Chapel

E1392 unknown child.

E310 ELISHA W. BANNING born Feb. 2, 1810 in Lyme. Died March 29, 1817.
Source: 1

E311 WILLIAM THEOPHILUS BANNING born Dec. 6, 1811 in Lyme. Married Mary
Ann Ransom the daughter of Richard Ely (1773-1848) and Betsy (Chadwick)
Ransom {1782-1820}, on April 30, 1839 in Lyme, New London Co. Ct. The lived in
Fon Du Lac, Wisc. where he died Jan. 28, 1901. She was born Aug. 3, 1816 and
died April 17, 1905. He was a farmer. Source: 1,5,12,13,14,40,55

> E1393 Newell Bartlett Banning
> E1394 Emerett Turner Banning
> E1395 Ellen Amelia Banning
> E1396 Ester Ely Banning
> E1397 Mary E. Banning

E312 ORIN A. BANNING born April 2, 1814 in Lyme, Ct. Married Charlotte Davis of
Riverhead, Conn. in Joshuatown, Conn. She
was born about 1829 in Ct. They lived in Lyme and then moved to Long Island, N.Y. He
died April 6, 1886. Source: 1,5,40

> E1398 Cora Banning
> E1399 Willis Scott Banning
> E1400 Frederick Banning
> E1401 Herbert Banning
> E1402 Carrie Banning
> E1403 Benjamin Banning

E313 GEORGE W. BANNING born Sept. 15, 1815 in Lyme. Married Frances Bull.
He was a Justice of the Peace in Essex. For many years he was a officer on the
"S.S. Granite State" sailing between Hartford and New York City. Source: 1,40

> E1404 Mattie Banning
> E1405 Clara Banning

E314 CATHERINE C. BANNING born Feb. 20, 1820 in Lyme. Married Monroe (Orin
?) Luther, on (Oct. 11, 1846 ?). They lived in Lyme. He died and she married a
Capt. Waterman. Source: 1,14,55

> E1406 Albert Luther
> E1407 Leora Luther
> E1408 Dell Luther
> E1409 Mittie Luther
> E1410 Ellen Luther

E315 NEWEL E. BANNING born Nov. 20, 1817 and died in 1835, both in
Lyme. Source: 1,40

E316 EPHRAIM HENRY BANNING (or Henry Ephraim) born Oct. 17, 1823 in Lyme.
Lived in Lyme and died unmarried. The 1860 census indicates he was a mechanic
and was living with his parents in New London Co. Source: 1,5,6

E317 thru E334 unknown children of E64 and E65

E335 thru E343 unknown children of E66

E1411 thru E1462 for children.

E344 MELINDA (LINDA) BANNING born Feb. 11, 1806 in Old Lyme, Conn. She
married Prentice Comstock of Lyme, on Dec. 13, 1825 in Lyme, New London
County, Ct. where they lived. She died Oct. 26, 1896. He was born Sept. 5, 1795
and died July 5, 1890 in Old Lyme. Source: 1,13,14,55

E1463 Alexander Comstock
E1464 James A. Comstock
E1465 Mary E. Comstock
E1466 Albert M. Comstock
E1467 Ellen M. Comstock
E1468 Angeline Comstock
E1469 Warren F. Comstock
E1470 Harriet M. Comstock
E1471 Julia T. Comstock
E1472 Eugene S. comstock

E345 MEHITABLE P. BANNING born Feb. 12, 1808 in Old Lyme, Conn. Married Eli
Rogers. They had no issue. Source: 1

E346 WILLIAM JOSIAH BANNING born Aug. 30, 1810 in Lyme, Conn. Married Lucy
Lay of Lyme, on June 4, 1835 at Lyme. She was born about 1816 in Ct. and was the
daughter of David and Lucy (Ingraham) Lay. He was an artist and portrait painter,
as well as a singing master and poet. He listed himself as a farmer in 1850 and died
in Lyme on Dec. 21, 1856. She died in Lyme Feb. 20, 1899. Source:
1,5,12,14,33,40,55,64

E1473 Frances Sill Banning
E1474 William Banning
E1475 David Lay Banning
E1476 Samuel Waldo Banning
E1477 Laura Lay Banning
E1478 Hubbard Sill Banning
E1479 Lucy Jane Banning
E1480 William Calvin Banning
E1481 Emma Banning
E1482 Adeline Louise Banning
E1483 Harriet Butler Banning

E347 CALVIN NODATE BANNING born May 15, 1814 in Lyme. Source: 1,40

E1484 thru E1492 for children.

E348 ALBERT TIFFANY BANNING born Jan. 24, 1816 in Lyme, Conn. Married
Charlotte Perry in Pavilion, Genesee Co. New York. They lived in Rochester New
York, where he was a painter and decorator. He died April 9, 1872. She was born
April 20, 1820 and died March 22, 1893 in Rochester. Source: 1,40

E1493 William Augustus Banning
E1494 Albert Roland Banning

E349 EUNICE BECKWITH BANNING born March 18, 1818 at Lyme, Conn. Married Martin Doty of Ypsilanti, Mich. on Dec. 9, 1845 at Lyme Conn. They had no issue. After he died she married 2nd, either Mr. Vorhees or Willis Goodwin of Hartford in Oct. 1837, again no issue. Source: 1,14,55

E350 MATHILDA L. BANNING born May 7, 1820 in Lyme, Conn. Married Mr. George Thomas of Norwich on Nov. 3, 1839 in Lyme, New London County Ct. at the home of Prentice Comstock (E344) Source: 1,13,14,55

        E1495 George Thomas
        E1496 Martha Thomas

E351 thru E359 for children of E68.

E360 DAVID BANNING born July 9, 1800 in East Hadlyme, Conn. Source: 1,13

        E1497 thru E1505 for children.

E361 JOSEPH BANNING born Sept. 1, 1802 in East Haddam, Middlesex County Conn. Married Lucetta Riddell on June 1, 1825 in Hamilton, New York. They lived in Poolville, New York and had 4 children. She died and he married 2nd, the sister of his first wife, Almira Isham on Aug. 31, 1873 in Poolville. He died on Sept. 8, 1887. Source: 1,13,40

        E1506 Joseph Dwight Banning
        E1507 Ozro Demott Banning
        E1508 Helen Lucetta Banning
        E1509 John Malcoam Banning

E362 MARVIN BANNING born Oct. 20, 1804 in Hadlyme, Conn. and lived at home in Hadlyme. He was a farmer and died unmarried June 12, 1879. Source: 1,5

E363 NANCY BANNING born Jan. 28, 1807 in Hadlyme, Conn. She disappeared for many years, finally returned home where she died unmarried about 1898. She was in a retreat at Poughkeepsie, New York for many years, and after leaving there she fell heir to a good size fortune. Source: 1

E364 EMILY A. BANNING born May 20, 1810 in Hadlyme, Conn. and married Alanson Wright of East Haddam on July 23, 1828 in Hadlyme. Source: 1,14,55

        E1510 thru E1518 for children.

E365 CHARLES BANNING no information. Source: 1,40,64,96

        E1519 thru E1527 for children.

E366 SARAH M. BANNING born about 1813-15 in Lyme, Conn. and married Daniel Southmayd Miner on Dec. 9, 1834 in Lyme, Conn. He was the son of Jared Spencer and Caroline Brockway Miner (See E414). Source: 1,14,55,64,83,96

        E1528 Caroline Miner
        E1529 Orrin Southmayd Miner

E1530 Charles Carroll Miner
E1531 Janette Miner
E1532 Laura F. Miner
E1533 Sarah E. Miner
E1534 Harriet Miner
E1535 Annah L. Miner

E367 JAMES BANNING died as an infant. Source: 1,64,96

E368 HENRY BANNING died as an infant. Source: 1,64,96

E369 HENRY BANNING 2nd born in Millington, Conn. He was married five times and
   had several children by each wife. He lived and died in Millington. Source:
   1,40,64,96

          E1536 thru E1545 for children.

E370 ELISA BANNING no information. Source: 1,64,96

          E1546 thru E1554 for children.

E371 EMILY BANNING no information. Source: 1,64,96

          E1555 thru E1563 for children.

E372 ERASTUS MILLARD BANNING born Nov. 25, 1812 in East Haddam, Conn. He
   married Almena Hall and lived in Worcester, Mass. She was born Jan. 17, 1819.
   He died in 1883 in, Oakdale, Worcester Co, Mass. Source: 1,13,40

          E1564 Mary Ann Banning
          E1565 Levi Wilber Banning
          E1566 Celestine Banning
          E1566A Albertine Banning
          E1567 Erastus Millard Banning
          E1568 Janette Banning
          E1569 Adeline Banning
          E1570 Emeline Banning
          E1571 Charles Banning
          E1572 Edward Banning
          E1573 Alfred Banning
          E1574 Albert Banning
          E1575 George Banning

E373 MARY ANN BANNING born in 1817 in Hadlyme, Conn. She married Manly
   Palmiter. They lived in Unionville, Conn. and had no children. She died in 1882 in
   New Britain, Conn. and he died about 1875. Source: 1

E374 ELIZABETH A. BANNING born Aug. 5, 1819 at Hadlyme, Conn. She married
   Royal G. Ackley on Nov. 1, 1836 in the 1st Presbyterian Church in New Hamburg,
   Dutchess County N.Y. They had 2 children. After his death she married 2nd, James
   Bryant. They lived in Hartford Conn. where she died. Source: 1,13

          E1576 Helen Ackley
          E1577 Jane M. Ackley

E1578 Maria Bryant
E1579 Mary Bryant

E375 AUGUSTUS BANNING born in 1821 in Hadlyme, Conn. He married Elizabeth
------? They lived in Taunton, Mass, where he died. Source: 1,40

E1580 Ellen Banning
E1581 Elon Banning
E1582 Elizabeth Banning
E1583 Edgar (Edward) Banning

E376 CARLOS BANNING, Rev. born Nov. 10, 1823 or 1814 in Hadlyme, Conn. He
married Harriet Elizabeth Oitman on April 6, 1852 at New Bedford, Mass. They lived
in Newport, Rhode Island where he died Aug. 7, 1898. Source: 1,13,40

E1584 Matilda Thurston Banning
E1585 Willie Carlos Banning
E1586 Arthur Staples Banning
E1587 Edwin Thomas Banning
E1588 Mary Elizabeth Banning
E1589 Alice Crocker Banning

E377 HORACE BANNING born 1825 in Hadlyme, Conn. He was killed in a railway
accident in Springfield, Mass. Source: 1,40

E1590 thru E1598 for children.

E378 THEODORE BANNING born in 1827 in Hadlyme, Conn. He was living in
Hartford County Ct. in 1850 and died unmarried. Source: 1,5,40

E379 LAURA A. BANNING born Aug. 30, 1829 in Hadlyme, Conn. Married Charles L.
Hill, the fire chief of New York City. They lived in Omega, New York, where she
died. She was living with her Dad in Hartford County Ct. in 1850. Source: 1,5

E1599 Stella Hill
E1600 Carrie Hill
E1601 Angeline Hill
E1602 Lulu Hill
E1603 William Hill
E1604 Charles Hill
E1605 Unknown child

E380 JULIA ETTA BANNING born Feb. 4, 1832 in Hadlyme, Conn. She married
Timothy Colvin on Dec. 23, 1851 in Hartford, Conn. He was born Oct. 19, 1827 in
Wetherfield, Conn. and died July 13, 1874 (1894?) at Meriden, Conn. He was in the
Mexican War and a New Jersey State Trooper in the Civil War. Source: 1,5

E1606 Irene A. Colvin

E381 CARRIE A. BANNING born Oct. 10, 1834 at Hartford, Conn. She was living in
Hartford Co. , Ct. in 1850. She died unmarried. Source: 1,5

E382 ELLEN E. BANNING born Sept. 14, 1837. She died an infant. Source: 1

E383 JOSEPH WARNER lived in Hadlyme, Conn. and had children by 2 wives.
Source: 1

E384 HARRIET (SUSAN) WARNER married a Mr. Francis. They had no children.
Source: 1

E385 JOSEPH LEWIS BANNING He was born about 1808 in Essex County, Conn.
and married Sylvia Minerva Post of Saybrook, on Aug. 16, 1835 in Saybrook,
Middlesex County Ct. She was the daughter of Adin Post and was born about 1808.
In 1840 they moved to Georgia. They lived in Greenville, Georgia, and in 1850 they
were living in Meriweather Co., Ga. He was a merchant and died in 1870. Source:
1,5,13,14,40

    E1607 James Wootin Banning
    E1608 Mystes Asuba Banning
    E1609 Joseph Aden Banning
    E1610 Ellen Minerva Banning
    E1611 George Osborn Banning
    E1612 Frank Banning

E386 HENRY SEABURY BANNING born Jan. 27, 1810 in Essex, Middlesex County,
Conn. He married Nancy M. Robinson on Sept. 23, 1833 at Coventry, Conn. They
lived in New Haven Ct. where he died Sept. 2, 1891. He was a tavern keeper. She
was born about 1813 in Conn. and died May 18, 1900 in Boston. Source: 1,5,13,40

    E1613 Henry clay Banning
    E1614 George Wilmarth Banning
    E1615 Charles Lewis Banning
    E1616 Joseph Olney Banning
    E1617 Ellen Clarissa Banning

E387 ARBA HANSON BANNING born about 1817 in Essex County Conn. Married
Hannah Moore of Chesterfield, Conn. on Nov. 10, 1839. She was born about 1817.
They lived in Deep River, Conn., where he was a Probate Judge for 16 years. He
owned the oldest shoe store in the area. They were living in Saybrook, Middlesex
County Ct. in 1850. He died in 1880 in Deep River. Source: 1,5,40

    E1618 Joseph Beaumont Banning
    E1619 Louise Camilla Banning
    E1620 Hannah Moore Banning
    E1621 Mary Pritchard Banning

E388 GEORGE BANNING born 1824 in Hadlyme, Conn. He married Selinda C.
Keeney of Colchester, Conn. at Hadlyme. They lived in Hadlyme where he died in
1899. She was born in 1834 and died in 1900. Source: 1,5,40

    E1622 Emma Banning
    E1623 Ida Banning
    E1624 Mary Jane Banning
    E1625 William Seldon Banning
    E1626 Minnie Banning
    E1627 Jennie Pansy Banning
    E1628 Frederick Ellsworth Banning
    E1629 Della Banning

E1630 Ernest Banning

E389 MARY A. BANNING born about 1815 in Hadlyme, Conn. and married William
Abbie of Hadlyme. She was living with her parents in 1850. Source: 1,5

> E1631 William Abbie
> E1632 Ellen Abbie
> E1633 Jane Abbie

E390 SOPHIA BANNING born about 1817 in Ct. and was living with her parents in
1850. Source: 1,5

E390A SUSAN BANNING born about 1820 and was listed as an "idiot" in the 1850
census. Source: 5

E391 LEMIRA LAY born 1819 and died May 16, 1831. Source: 1

E392 JULIUS R. LAY born 1827 and died Oct. 31, 1844 at Joshuatown, Conn.
Source: 1

E393 ERASTUS L. LAY died Jan. 1, 1884 in Joshuatown, Conn. Source: 1

E394 MARY LAY no information. Source: 1

E395 NANCY LAY no information. Source: 1

E396 GEORGE LAY no information. Source: 1

E397 BENJAMIN BANNING born Nov. 6, 1819 and married Mary Green of Montville,
Conn. They lived in Montville. He was killed returning from an evangelistic meeting
at New London, Conn. in a railroad accident. Source: 1,40

> E1634 Mary Banning
> E1635 Jennie Banning

E398 JOSEPH BANNING born Oct. 1, 1821 and died unmarried. Source: 1,40

E399 ROSETTA BANNING born Dec. 16, 1822 and married Jonathan Stevens.
Source: 1

> E1636 Addie Stevens
> E1637 Rowland Stevens

E400 CHARLOTTA BANNING born March 13, 1824. She married 1st, Phineas Doud.
It is said he starved to death in Libby prison during the Civil War. She married 2nd,
Charles Button of East Haddam, Conn. Source: 1

> E1638 Emory Doud
> E1639 Elizabeth Doud
> E1640 Frank Doud
> E1641 Adeline Doud
> E1642 Emma Doud

E401 WILLIAM WARNER BANNING born Sept. 1, 1825 at Millington, Conn. He married Mary Annette Hayden Flood in 1847 in East Hampton, Conn., where they lived. He died July 5, 1907. She was born Aug. 4, 1830 and was the daughter of Richard and Phoebe Ann Johnson Flood. The 1850 census indicates he was a laborer and living in Chatham, Middlesex County Ct. She died May 9, 1889. Source: 1,5,40

E1643 Phoebe Adocia Banning
E1644 William Samuel Banning
E1645 Joseph Brainard Banning
E1646 Mary EliZabeth Banning
E1647 Nellie Maria Banning

E402 JABEZ WARNER BANNING born March 15, 1828 in Ct. He married Mary Emily Brown of Yantic, Conn. and died in 1870. Jabez is listed twice in the 1850 census. Mary was born in 1832 and died Feb. 15, 1902. Source: 1,5,40

E1648 Louise Rogers Banning
E1649 Morton Hale Banning
E1650 Fannie Loulla Banning
E1651 Lillian Augusta Banning

E403 SAMUEL BANNING born Jan. 15, 1829 in Ct. He married Katherine Banta of Lyme, Conn. They had three children. After her death, he married, 2nd, Eliza Fox of Pleasant Valley, Lyme. They lived in Groton, Conn. and had several children. Samuel is listed twice in the 1850 census. Source: 1,5,40

E1652 thru E1659 for children.

E404 CLARISSA BANNING born April 21, 1831 and died as an infant. Source: 1

E405 BETSY ELIZABETH BANNING born Nov. 11, 1832. She married Nathan Stark of East Haddam, Conn. Betsy is listed twice in the 1850 census. Source: 1,5

E1660 Lewis Stark
E1661 Ella Stark

E406 CALVIN BANNING born April 4, 1834. Source: 1,40

E1662 thru E1670 for children.

E407 MATILDA BANNING born Oct. 28, 1835 in Ct. She married a Mr. Brown and lived in Ill. Source: 1,5

E1671 thru E1679 for children.

E408 SIMON BANNING born Jan. 1, 1837-38 in East Haddam, Ct. He married Lydia Ann Knight on Dec. 12, 1864 in Norwich, Ct. She was born March 8, 1845 in Waterford, New London County, Ct. They lived in Westerly, Rhode Island, where he died. Source: 1,5,40

E1680 Ella Pelina Banning
E1681 William Otis Banning
E1682 Benjamin Simon Banning
E1683 Clara May Banning

E1684 Frederick Leroy Banning

E409 LAURA BANNING born Feb. 11, 1838 in Ct. She married her first cousin,
Nelson Bramble. They lived in Moosup, Ct. where she died. Source: 1,5

> E1685 Rose Bramble
> E1686 George Bramble
> E1687 Willis Bramble
> E1688 Mary Bramble
> E1689 Louise Bramble
> E1690 Lorian Henry Bramble
> E1691 Frederick Bramble
> E1692 Robert Bramble
> E1693 Burton Bramble
> E1694 Grace Bramble

E410 MARY BANNING born April 10, 1839 in Ct. She married Henry Derby and they
lived in Middletown, Ct. He starved to death in Libby Prison during the Civil War.
Source: 1,5

> E1695 Arthur Derby
> E1696 Lilla Derby
> E1697 thru E1702 for children.

E411 RACHEL BANNING born Dec. 13, 1840 in Ct. She married Elichor Brown of
Moodus, Ct. They lived in Moodus, where she died. Source: 1,5

> E1703 Albert Brown
> E1704 Leanor Brown
> E1705 thru E1709 for children.

E412 ALMIRA BANNING born April 5, 1842 in Ct. She married Theron Markham and
they lived in Hartford, Ct. Source: 1,5

> E1710 Alice Markham
> E1711 Flora Markham
> E1712 John Markham
> E1713 thru E1715 for children

E413 CLARISSA BANNING 2nd born Nov. 31, 1845 in Ct. She married Lorin Lewis
and they lived in Meriden, Ct. Source: 1,5

> E1716 Elmer Lewis
> E1717 thru E1720 for children.

E414 JOHN COTTON MATHER BROCKWAY born 1784 and married Elizabeth
Beckwith, the daughter of George and Penelop Beckwith. He was a physician.
Source: 64

E414a ZEBULON BROCKWAY born March 10, 1791 and married Caroline Brockway.
He was a member of the Methodist Church and an Out-spoken anit-slavery man.
He was an Associate Justice on the County Cort and became boath a representative
and a senator in the Conn. legislature. Source: 64

E414b MARY BROCKWAY born in 1794 in Lyme, Ct. and married Selden Jewett Warner of Hadlyme. Source: 64

E414c BETSEY BROCKWAY married Semillius Brockway Ely. Source: 64

E415 DEBORAH REED BROCKWAY born 1788 and married Barak Beckwith Willey in 1810. They then moved to New York state. Source: 64

E416 CAROLINE BROCKWAY born 1790 and married Jared Spencer Miner of Millington, Ct. in East Haddam, Ct. Their children were, Daniel Southmayd Miner, twins Harriet & Caroline and Charles Miner. See E366. Source: 5,55,64,83

E417 LUCINA BROCKWAY born 1795 and married Nathan Damon of Ellington, Ct. They lived in North Lyme, Ct. Source: 64

E418 EZRA BROCKWAY born 1796 and married Leonora Brockway of Lyme, Ct. in 1821. Source: 64

E419 NILES BROCKWAY born 1798 and died unmarried in 1853. He is buried in Joshuatown, Ct. Source: 64

E420 MARGARET BROCKWAY born 1805 and married Jabez Comstock. They had 12 children and lived in Hadlyme, Ct. Source: 64

E421 BENJAMIN BECKWITH born Feb. 15, 1791. Source: 1,64

E422 REED BECKWITH married twice. Source: 64

E423 F76 LUCINDA BECKWITH no information. Source: 64

E424 F77 DEBORA BECKWITH no information. Source: 64

E425 F78 FRANCIS BECKWITH no information. Source: 64

E426 F79 GEORGE BECKWITH no information. Source: 64

E427 F80 CAROLINE IRENE BECKWITH no information. Source: 64

E428 F81 JOHN E. BECKWITH no information. Source: 64

E429 thru E499 for children of E88 thru E99

E1721 thru E3000 for children

E500 NOAH PRATT born June 29, 1804 at Lyme, and died young. Source: 64,96

E501 NANCY PRATT born June 25, 1805 at Lyme. Source: 64,96

E502 NOAH PRATT born March 24, 1807 at Lyme. Source: 64,96

E503 JOSIAH PRATT born Nov. 25, 1808 at Lyme. Source: 64,96

E504 GEORGE PRATT born Nov. 21, 1810 at Lyme. Source: 64,96

E505 ALFRED PRATT born March 10, 1812 at Lyme. Source: 64,96

E506 ALBERT PRATT born March 10, 1812 at Lyme. Source: 64,96

E507 GILBERT PRATT born Sept. 4, 1813 at Waterford, Pa. and died March 19, 1815. Source: 64,96

E508 JULIA PRATT born June 13, 1815 at Waterford, Pa. Source: 64,96

E509 BETSEY PRATT born March 9, 1817 at Waterford, Pa. Source: 64,96

E510 ALMIRA PRATT born Oct. 30, 1818 at Waterford, Pa. Source: 64,96

E511 MARIA PRATT born July 8, 1820 at Waterford, Pa. Source: 64,96

E512 WILLIAM PRATT born May 15, 1822 at Waterford, Pa. Source: 64,96

E513 LAFAYETTE PRATT born Aug. 6, 1824 at Waterford, Pa. Source: 64,96

E514 PHEBE PRATT born Aug, 19, 1826 at Waterford, Pa. Source: 64,96

E515 AMANDA PRATT born April 18, 1828 at Waterford, Pa. Source: 64,96

E516 ELI PRATT born April 19, 1830. Source: 64,96

E517 SALLY PRATT born April 14, 1833. Source: 64,96

E518 PHINEAS PRATT born about 1812. Source: 64,96

E519 PHILO PRATT born about 1814. Source: 64,96

E520 ALPHEUS PRATT born April, 12, 1816. Source: 64,96

E521 HEPSIBAH PRATT born 1820. Source: 64,96

E522 ALVA PRATT born about 1822 and drowned in Meriden. Source: 64,96

E523 SARAH P. JOHNSON born Dec. 5, 1814 and married Philo Parmelee on March 30, 1834. Source: 64,96

E524 ASA H. JOHNSON born Sept. 4, 1816 and died the next day. Source: 64,96

E525 BENJAMIN L. JOHNSON born Sept. 5, 1818 and married Nancy M. Mack on Oct. 2, 1842. Source: 64,96

E526 WILLIAM P. JOHNSON born Jan. 28, 1823 and married Catherine C. Wright on Feb. 4, 1845. Source: 64,96

E527 ELIZABETH H. JOHNSON born Feb. 13, 1826 and married Richard E. Ransom on March 9, 1851. Source: 64,96

E528 GEORGE W. JOHNSON born May 26, 1829. Source: 64,96

E529 thru E1000 for unknown children of E201 thru E208.

E3001 thru E4200 for children.

E1001 WALTER EDGAR BANNING born March 18, 1833 in Leyden, N.Y. He
married Mary J. Sanford in Delta, Oneida County, N.Y. They lived in Syracuse, N.Y.
where he was living in 1901. Source: 1,30,40,93

E4201 Ella May Banning

E1002 EMELIN HARRIET BANNING born Oct. 22, 1835 in Leyden, N.Y. She
married Harvey Teller on Oct. 21, 1855 and they lived in Leyden. He died about
1898. She died in Sept. 1901 and was buried in Talcottville. Source: 1,30,93

E4202 William Joseph Teller
E4203 Minnie Mary Teller

E1003 ORSON BENJAMIN BANNING born Sept. 5, 1838 in Leyden, N.Y. He
married Louise E. Phelps in 1864 in Turin, N.Y. They lived in Jefferson, Iowa. He
was reported as living in Ohio in 1901. Source: 1,30,40,93

E4204 William Jay Banning
E4205 Minnie Banning
E4206 Mary Banning

E1004 CHAUNCEY HENRY BANNING born Aug. 13, 1840 in Leyden, N.Y. He
married Elizabeth Sanford in Delta, N.Y. and they lived in Taberg, N.Y. He was
living in 1901. Source: 1,30,40,93

E4207 Lilly Banning
E4208 Frank Banning

E1005 MATTIE BANNING born Jan. 7, 1841 in Leyden, N.Y. She married George
Merry on Jan. 31, 1854 in Leyden and they lived in Carthage, N.Y. where she was
living in 1901. Source: 1,30,93

E4209 Clara Merry
E4210 Jessie Merry
E4211 Ida Merry
E4212 Albert Merry
E4213 Minnie Merry
E4214 Bertha Merry
E4215 Florence Merry
E4216 George Merry
E4217 Jennie Merry

E1006 ELLEN MARIA BANNING born May 25, 1848 in Leyden, Lewis Co., N.Y. She
died Jan. 12, 1854 of "Croup" and is buried in the Talcotville Cemetery in Leyden.
Source: 1,15,30,93

E4220 thru E4239 unused

E1007 HELEN SOPHIA BANNING born May 25, 1848 in Leyden, Lewis Co., N.Y. and
died Dec. 30, 1853 of "Croup" and is buried in the Talcotville Cemetery in Leyden.
Source: 1,15,30,93

E1008 LYDIA ANN BANNING born Dec. 18, 1850 in Leyden, N.Y. and died Jan. 9, 1954 of "Croup". Source: 1,30,93

E1009 JAY FOSTER BANNING born Sept. 17, 1855 in Leyden, N.Y. He married Lizzie Lewis in 1882 at Peoria, Ill. They lived in Ottawa, Ill. He was alive in 1901. Source: 1,30,93

          E4240 Bessie May L. Banning
          E4241 Myrtle Del Banning
          E4242 thru E4246 for children.

E1010 thru E1016 unknown children of E210.

          E4247 thru E4289 for children.

E1017 JOHN F. BANNING born 1856 and died 1919. He is buried in the Wilcox Cemetery, 1 mile S. of Collinsville, N.Y. Source: 1,15,40,93

          E4290 thru E4299 for children.

E1018 WALLACE BANNING born in Leyden, Lewis Co., N.Y. about 1854. He died Sept. 9, 1884 and is buried in Talcotville Cemetery in Leyden. Source: 1,15,40,93

          E4300 thru E4307 for children.

E1019 NELLIE E. BANNING Married Thomas E. Parkhurst on Oct. 28, 1884 at the home of her parents in Locust Grove, N.Y. She was alive in 1892. Source: 1,30,93

          E4308 thru E4314 for children.

E1020 thru E1024 unknown children of E213.

E1025 MARY BANNING no information. Source: 1

          E4315 thru E4323 for children

E1026 CHARLES BANNING no information. Source: 1,40

          E4324 thru E4332 for children

E1027 HENRIETTA BANNING no information. Source: 1

          E4333 thru E4341 for children.

E1028 SELINDA BANNING no information. Source: 1

          E4342 thru E4350 for children.

E1029 thru E1129 for unknown children of E215 thru E242

          E4351 thru E4800 for children

E1130 JUANE M. POST No information. Source: 93

E1131 MARY E. POST No information. Source: 93

E1132 thru E1l43 for unknown children of E252 thru E254

E1144 ANSON G. JACKSON Born 1836 and died in 1909. He is buried in the Wilcox Cemetery, 1 mile South of Collinsville, N.Y. Source: 15,93

E1145 CHARLES E. JACKSON Born 1845 and died 1870. He is buried in the Wilcox Cemetery, 1 mile South of Collinsville, N.Y. Source: 15,93

E1146 WILLIAM A. JACKSON Born 1847 and died 1909. He is buried in the Wilcox Cemetery, 1 mile South of Collinsville, N.Y. Source: 15,93

E1147 NANCY ANN JACKSON born Sept. 30, 1856 in West Turin, N.Y. and married Milton George Ford on July 16, 1879 in Port Leyden, Lewis Co., N.Y. He was the son of George and Marion Ford, born Sept. 30, 1849 in Boonville, N.Y. Their children are, Fanny Ann, born Feb. 3, 1883; Violet Virginia, married Nov. 30, 1929; Louis Milton, born 1890 and Pearl Etta, born 1894. Nancy died Jan. 21, 1915 and He died May 6, 1915. Both are buried in the Beach Bridge Cemetery in Lewis Co., N.Y. Source: 16,93

E1148 & E1149 for unknown children of E255

E1150 ADA POST No information. Source: 93

E1151 thru E1179 for unknown children of E256 thruE260a

E1180 thru E1299 for unknown children of E261 thru E295

E4801 thru E5500 for children.

E1300 thru E1353 for unknown children of E296 thru E301. E296 had 2 son's born 1825 to 1830.

E5501 thru E5550 for children

E1354 ELLEN E. BANNING born either Dec. 14, 1846 or Dec. 25, 1842. She married George E. Webb. They were living in Preston Iowa in 1897. Source: 12,35,38

E5551 thru E5559 for children.

E1355 CLARENCE NELSON BANNING born either Dec. 14 or 18, 1846 or 48, in Iowa. Source: 6,14,35,38

E5560 thru E5568 for children.

E1356 MALORA B. BANNING born July 23, 1849 in Iowa. She married a Mr. Moore. Thet were living in Preston Iowa in 1897. Source: 6,7,12,35,38

E5569 thru E5577 for children.

E1357 FLORENCE ISABEL BANNING born March 21, 1852 in Iowa. She married a Mr. Hawk. They were living in Scranton, Iowa in 1897. Source: 6,7,35,38

E5578 thru E5586 for children.

E1358 LAURA PAMELIA BANNING born May 2, 1856 in Preston, Jackson County, Iowa. She married Charles Alfred Moore on Jan. 7 or 13, 1874 in Preston. They were living in Bagley Iowa in 1897. She died Sept. 15, 1950 in Kearney, Buffalo County, Neb. Source: 6,12,35,38

E5587 thru E5595 for children.

E1359 LYDIA PHILURA BANNING born Jan. 20, 1858 in Iowa. She married a Mr. Purinton. They were living in Bagley Iowa in 1897. Source: 6,7,12,35,38

E5596 thru E5604 for children.

E1360 AGNES VIOLET BANNING born Aug. 26, 1860 in Iowa. She married Edwin M. Fowler. They were living in Churden Iowa in 1897. Source: 7,12,35,38

E5605 thru E5613 for children.

E1361 WALTER EDWIN BANNING born Sept. 23 or 28, 1861-63, in Jackson County Iowa. He married Anetta Hawk on Dec. 28, 1882 in Green Co., Iowa. She was born in Jan. 1861 in Iowa. They left Hugo, Okla. in 1888 and moved into the Indian Terr. south of Okla. City. He died July 11, 1906 in Okla. and is buried in the Morris Hill Cemetery, near Pink, Okla. She died in 1936 and is buried in Santa Monica, Calif. Source: 7,8,12, 15,20,26,35,38,94

    E5614 Cloid Francis Banning
    E5615 Rasco Jay Banning
    E5616 Vernon Casuas Banning
    E5617 Leon Walter Banning
    E5618 Frank Wesley Banning
    E5619 Ray Nelson Banning

E1362 thru E1379 for unknown children of E303 and E304

E5620 thru E5670 for children

E1380 GEORGE BANNING born 183?, no other information. Source: 1,40

E5671 thru E5679 for children.

E1381 URSULA ANN BANNING born about 183?, no other information. Source: 1

E5680 thru E5687 for children.

E1382 LEANDER EDWIN BANNING born Oct. 20, 1830 in North Lyme, Ct. He married Isabel McVain. They lived for a time in Wisconsin and then moved to Memphis, Tenn., where he died on Aug. 15, 1895. She was born Feb. 11, 1836 in N.Y. Source: 1,40

    E5688 Alberto Lyman Banning
    E5689 Clarence Edwin Banning
    E5690 Cora Bell Banning

E5691 James Bryon Banning
E5692 Fannie Banning
E5693 Grace Banning
E5694 Lottie Eva Banning
E5695 Ida May Banning

E1383 GEORGE WILSON BANNING born May 2, 1833 in North Lyme, Ct.
He died in Lyme in April 1836. Source: 1

E1384 EMILY MARIE BANNING born Jan. 14, 1837 in North Lyme, Ct. Married
Charles E. Bailey of Groton, Ct. on Dec. 7, 1865 in Norwich, Ct. He was born June
4, 1837 and died at sea on Nov. 22, 1877. She married 2nd, Erastus H. Gardner on
Jan. 2, 1893 in Bozrak, Ct. They lived in Norwich Town, Ct. Source: 1

E5696 Lyman Wells Bailey

E1385 GEORGE WILSON BANNING born Dec. 7, 1840 in North Lyme, Ct. He died
there on Feb. 2, 1842. Source: 1

E1386 FRANCES (FANNY) WELLS BANNING born Aug. 14, 1844 in North Lyme, Ct.
Married Simon Abell of Bozrak, Ct. on Oct. 8, 1867 in North Lyme. He was the son
of William C. (born July 24, 1829) and Lucy H.L. Abell. They lived in Bozrak.
Source: 1,42

E5697 Charles Jared Abell
E5698 Lucy Leffingwell Abell

E1387 ALBERT BAINARD BANNING born Aug. 17, 1849 in Lyme, Ct. He lived in
North Lyme and died Oct. 22, 1871 in Norwich, Ct. Source: 1,12,55

E5699 thru E5703 for children.
E5704 thru E5802 numbers not used

E1388 FRANCIS CHAPEL born Aug. 13, 1836 in Lyme, Ct. Died March 21, 1844.
Source: 1

E1389 LIVIA CHAPEL born June 5, 1840 in Lyme, Ct. She married John Comstock on
Oct. 14, 1862 in Norwich, Ct. Source: 1

E1390 MARRION CHAPEL born Oct. 11, 1844 in New London, Ct. She married
Henry F. Rogers on Nov. 9, 1858 in Norwich, Ct. They had two children. Source:
1

E1391 VICTORIA G. CHAPEL born Aug. 31, 1846 and married Gordon L. Munger in
1872. Source: 1,55

E1392 -------- CHAPEL no information. Source: 1

E1393 NEWELL BARLETT BANNING born Feb. 8, 1841 in Laysville, Ct. He married
Elizabeth McKean on June 28, 1868 in Forest, Wisc. Source: 1,5

E5803 Garnette Ely Banning
E5804 William Theophilous Banning
E5805 Emerett Turner Banning

E5806 Leora Eugenia Banning
E5807 Mary Ora Banning

E1394 EMERETT TURNER BANNING born Oct. 18, 1842 in Laysville, Ct. He married
Alanson P. Lyons on Dec. 27, 1863. Source: 1,5

E5808 Milton Alberto Banning
E5809 Herbert Ernest Banning
E5810 Edward Sherman Banning
E5811 Gertrude Ula Banning

E1395 ELLEN AMELIA BANNING born April 7, 1845 in Laysville, Ct.
She lived unmarried in Fon du Lac, Wisc. Source: 1,5

E1396 ESTER ELY BANNING born May 20, 1849 in Hamburg, Lyme Town, Ct. She
was not married. Source: 1

E1397 MARY E. BANNING born May 13, 1849 in Lyme, Ct. Source: 5,12,14,55

E5812 thru E5818 for children

E1398 CORA BANNING she married a Mr. Miller of Middletown, Ct. He died and she
married 2nd, Charles Churchill of Hartford, Ct. They lived in Hartford and had one
child. Source: 1

E5819 Lottie Churchill
E5820 thru E5825 for children.

E1399 WILLIS SCOTT BANNING born April 24, 1854 in Lyme, Ct. He married
Elizabeth Brockway of Joshuatown, Ct. on Nov. 24, 1881 in Old Lyme, Ct. They
lived on a farm at Joshuatown, Ct. She was born June 28, 1841 and was the
daughter of "Deacon" William Brockway of Lyme. Source: 1

E5826 Son ----? Banning
E5827 Son ----? Banning

E1400 FREDERICK BANNING married Angee Clark. Source: 1

E5828 thru E5835 for unknown children.

E1401 HERBERT BANNING married Linda Stone. Source: 1

E5836 Frank Banning

E1402 CARRIE BANNING no information. Source: 1

E5837 thru E5843 for children.

E1403 BENJAMIN BANNING married Agatha "Aggie" Daniels and had 3 children.
They Lived in Flanders, Ct. Source: 1,30,90

E5844 Cecil B. Banning
E5845 Ellen Banning
E5846 Orrin Banning

E5847 Beatrice Banning

E1404 MATTIE BANNING no information. Source: 1

E5848 thru E5855 for children

E1405 CLARA BANNING no information. Source: 1

E5856 thru E5862 for children.

E1406 ALBERT LUTHER no information. Source: 1

E1407 LEORA LUTHER no information. Source: 1

E1408 DELL LUTHER no information. Source: 1

E1409 MITTIE LUTHER no information. Source: 1

E1410 ELLEN LUTHER no information. Source: 1

E1411 thru E1462 unknown children of E335 thru E343

E5863 thru E6299 for Children

E1463 ALEXANDER COMSTOCK born Oct. 6, 1826. Source: 1

E1464 JAMES COMSTOCK born 1827 and died June 21, 1836. Source: 1

E1465 MARY E. COMSTOCK born March 30, 1828. Source: 1

E1466 ALBERT M. COMSTOCK born April 16, 1830. Source: 1

E1467 ELLEN M. COMSTOCK born March 6, 1832. Source: 1

E1468 ANGELINE COMSTOCK born May 13, 1834. Source: 1

E1469 WARREN P. COMSTOCK born Aug. 23, 1836. Source: 1

E1470 HARRIET M. COMSTOCK born Nov. 4, 1838 and died June 5, 1853. Source: 1

E1471 JULIA T. COMSTOCK born July 16, 1843. Source: 1

E1472 EUGENE S. COMSTOCK born Sept. 11, 1845. Source: 1

E1473 FRANCES SILL BANNING born May 31, 1836 in Lyme, Ct. She married Wales R. Hayward on May 19, 1857. They lived in Wabashaw, Minn. for a time and then moved to Boston, Mass. Source: 1,5

E6300 Frances Stella Hayward
E6301 Waldo Banning Hayward
E6302 Ernest Wales Hayward
E6303 Harry Bradbury Hayward

E1474 WILLIAM BANNING born Nov. 6, 1837 in Lyme, Ct. and died an infant. Source: 1

E1475 DAVID LAY BANNING born Sept. 19, 1838 in Ct. and married Carrie M. Lane on Nov. 17, 1869. He died Sept. 9, 1892 and she died April 19, 1886. Source: 1,5,40

        E6304 Murry Banning
        E6305 Maud Banning

E1476 SAMUEL WALDO BANNING born May 9, 1840 in Ct. He married Kate DeWitt Scofield on Oct. 9, 1872. He died June 27, 1887. She was living in Lyme in 1907. Source: 1,5,40

        E6306 Scofield Banning
        E6307 Mable Banning
        E6308 Waldo Banning

E1477 LAURA LAY BANNING born June 19, 1841 in Lyme, Ct. She married Enoch Noyes of Lyme on June 12, 1861. He was a direct descent of Rev. James Hayes. They lived in Blackhall, Ct. He died June 13, 1897. Source: 1,5

        E6309 William Curtis Noyes
        E6310 Enoch Noyes
        E6311 Clarissa Dutton Noyes
        E6312 Jennie Banning Noyes
        E6313 Harry Dutton Noyes
        E6314 Martha Noyes
        E6315 Frances Banning Noyes
        E6316 Laura Banning Noyes
        E6317 Charles Reginald Noyes

E1478 HUBBARD SILL BANNING born June 9, 1843 in Lyme, Ct. and died Nov. 13, 1857. Source: 1,5

E1479 LUCY JANE BANNING born Nov. 3, 1845 in Lyme, Ct. She married George C. Thomas (E1495) on June 9, 1885. They lived in Lyme. He was born July 8, 1842 and died Nov. 22, 1897. Source: 1,5

        E6318 Martha Thomas

E1480 WILLIAM CALVIN BANNING born Aug. 28, 1848 in Lyme, Ct. He married Helen Josephine Mellen on Nov. 14, 1877. She was the daughter of Abner and Helen Louise (Caldwell) Mellen, born in 1850 and died in 1922. They had 3 children and lived in New York City. He was a partner in the Mfg. company of Banning & Bissell. He died Aug. 20, 1904 in N.Y.C. Source: 1,5,14,40,55

        E6319 Kendall Banning
        E6320 Helen Banning
        E6321 Dorothy Banning

E1481 EMMA MARVIN BANNING born Dec. 5, 1850 in Lyme, Ct. Married Edward Payson Bancroft on May 23, 1882. She died June 9, 1887. Source: 1

E6322 Pearly Hubbard Bancroft
E6323 Lucy Lay Bancroft
E6324 Emma Banning Bancroft

E1482 ADELINE LOUISE BANNING born Nov. 4, 1852 in Lyme, Ct. Died Jan. 21, 1891, unmarried. Source: 1

E1483 HARRIET BUTLER BANNING born Jan. 28, 1855 in Lyme, Ct. Married Charles G. Bartlett on July 6, 1897. They had no children (as of 1908). They lived at Black Hall, Ct. Source: 1

E1484 thru E1492 unknown children of E347.

E6325 thru E6359 for children

E1493 WILLIAM AUGUSTUS BANNING born May 24, 1844 in Rochester, N.Y. Married Mary S. Low of Ogdenburg, N.Y. in July 1867 in Ogdenburg. She was born Jan. 1, 1844 and died Dec. 23, 1875. Source: 1

E6360 Frank Low Banning
E6361 Sarah Charlotte Banning

E1494 ALBERT ROLAND BANNING born Oct. 15, 1852 in Rochester, N.Y. He married Adra Adelaide Welch on June 15, 1876. They lived in Rochester. Source: 1

E6362 Paul Welch Banning
E6363 Pansy Banning
E6364 Windsor Morgan Banning
E6365 George Albert Banning

E1495 GEORGE C. THOMAS born July 8, 1842. He married his cousin, Lucy Jane Banning (E1479). He died Nov. 22, 1897. Source: 1

E1496 MARTHA THOMAS no information. Source: 1

E1497 thru E1505 for children of E360

E6366 thru E6399 for children

E1506 JOSEPH DWIGHT BANNING born April 1826 near Poolville, N.Y. He married Mary Brainard on Oct. 10, 1850. They lived near Poolville where he died Oct. 20, 1890. Source: 1,40

E6400 Elodia Adela Banning
E6401 Nellie Lucetta Banning

E1507 OZRO DEMOTT BANNING born Feb. 3, 1830 near Poolville, N.Y. He married Sarah Williams on June 26, 1861. They lived near Poolville where he died on Oct. 20, 1895. Source: 1,40

E6402 Frank Banning

E1508 HELEN LUCETTA BANNING born Aug. 11, 1833 near Poolville, N.Y. She married Rexford R. Hall on Dec. 3, 1856. They lived near Poolville, and he died March 16, 1903 at Sherburne, N.Y. Source: 1

E6403 Georgia Mary Hall

E1509 JOHN MALCOM BANNING born Aug. 3, 1839 in Poolville, N.Y. He married Mary J. Harmon on Jan. 7, 1862. They lived in Hamilton, N.Y. where he died on Feb. 1, 1886. Source: 1,40

E6404 Walter John Banning

E1510 thru E1527   for children of E364 & 365

E6405 thru E6424 for children

E1528 CAROLINE MINER born about 1836 in Lyme, Conn. Source: 83

E1529 ORRIN SOUTHMAYD MINER born about 1837 in Lyme, Conn. and married Janette Frances Brockway. He died Sept. 10, 1879 at Esses, Conn. Source: 83

E1530 CHARLES CARROLL MINER born about 1844 in Lyme, Conn. and died in 1929. He may have married Emerette Brockway. Source: 83

E1531 JANETTE MINER born about 1846 in Lyme, Conn. Source: 83.

E1532 LAURA F. MINER born about 1846 in Lyme, Conn. Source: 83

E1533 SARAH E. MINER born Feb. 28, 1848 in Lyme, Conn. Source: 83

E1534 HARRIET P. MINER born about 1851 in Lyme, Conn. Source: 83

E1535 ANNAH L. MINER born about 1856 in Lyme, Conn. Source: 83

E1536 thru E1563 for children of E364 thru E371

E6425 thru E6489 for children

E1564 MARY ANN BANNING born Oct. 19, 1838 at Glostenburry, Ct. She married Levi Moore of Worcester, Ct. They lived and she died in Worcester. Source: 1

E6490 thru E6497 for children.

E1565 LEVI WILBUR BANNING born Oct. 2, 1839 in Glostenburry, Ct. He married Sarah Burnette of Amherst, Mass. on May 29, 1884 in Amherst. They lived and he died in Amherst on May 29, 1903. Source: 1,40

E6498 Loma Almina Banning
E6499 Nelson Wilbur Banning
E6500 Charles Hubert Banning

E1566 CELESTINE BANNING born Dec. 11, 1841 in Southampton, Mass. She married Jesse Taft of Worcester, Mass. Source: 1

E6501 Alma Taft

E1566A ALBERTINE BANNING born Dec. 1, 1842 in Southampton, Hampshire County Mass. Source: 13

E6501A thru E6501C for children

E1567 ERASTUS MILLARD BANNING born Oct. 27, 1843 in Southampton, Mass. He married Lucy Clapp of Worcester, where they lived. Source: 1,13

E6502 Warren Banning

E1568 JANETTE BANNING born July 24, 1845 in Ellington, Ct. She married Henry Jensen of Vermont. They lived in Worcester, Mass. Source: 1

E6503 Alma Jensen
E6504 Sarah Jensen
E6505 thru E6510 for children.

E1569 ADELINE BANNING born Sept. 27, 1847 at Hartford, Ct. She married George Hapgood of Worcester. Source: 1

E6511 thru E6519 for children

E1570 EMELINE BANNING born in 1849 in East Hartford, Ct. She married Lemuel Bolles of Newport, Vermont. They lived in Amherst, Mass. where she died. Source: 1

E6520 Ernest Bolles
E6521 Grace Bolles

E1571 CHARLES BANNING born Sept. 7, 1857 in Worcester, Mass. He married Jennie Rice of Worcester. Source: 1

E6522 thru E6529 for children

E1572 EDWARD BANNING born in 1857 in Worcester, Mass. He married and moved out west. Source: 1

E6530 thru E6537 for children

E1573 ALFRED BANNING born in 1860 in Worcester, Mass. and died as an infant. He was the twin to Albert. Source: 1

E1574 ALBERT BANNING same as above. Source: 1

E1575 GEORGE BANNING born June 30, 1862 in Worcester, Mass. He died unmarried.

E1576 HELEN ACKLEY born June 18, 1839 in Chicopee, Mass. She married Albert W. Roberts of Hartford, Ct. on March 12, 1877. Source: 1

E1577 JANE M. ACKLEY born Mar. 14, 1841 in Springfield, Mass. She married William G. Waterman. Source: 1

E1578 MARIA BRYANT married Perry L. Edgerton in Hartford, Ct. Source: 1

E1579 MARY BRYANT died in childhood. Source: 1

E1580 ELLEN BANNING no information. Source: 1

E6538 thru E6545 for children

E1581 ELON AGUSTUS BANNING married Ellen Augusta Burnham in Newburyport, Mass. on Sept. 21, 1875. She was born in Vergennes, Vt. on Dec. 9, 1850. They lived in Providence, R.I. Source: 1

E6546 Ida May Banning
E6547 Hattie Estelle Banning
E6548 thru E6551 not used

E1582 ELIZABETH BANNING no information. Source: 1

E6552 thru E6558 for children

E1583 EDGAR (EDWARD) BANNING no information. Source: 1

E6559 thru E6566 for children

E1584 MATILDA THURSTON BANNING born June 30, 1854 in North Dighton, Mass. She married Thomas Weaver Freeborn of Newport, R.I. on Nov. 15, 1877 in Newport. They lived in Newport, where she was well known for her organ recitals. Source: 1,13,30

E6567 Jane Thurston Freeborn
E6568 Thomas Laurence Freeborn
E6569 Marguerite Freeborn

E1585 WILLIE CHARLES BANNING born May 17, 1860 in Phoenix (Harrisonville) R.I. (or Coventry, Kent Co.) He died Oct. 8, 1864 in Danielson, Ct. Source: 1,13

E1586 ARTHUR STAPLES BANNING born June 9, 1862 in Norwich, Ct. and died Jan. 31, 1865 in Danielson, Ct. Source: 1

E1587 EDWIN THOMAS BANNING born May 11, 1864 in Danielson, Ct. He married Isabel Thornton of Providence, R.I. on June 13, 1883 at Tounton, Mass. They lived in Providence where he became a prominent architect. Source: 1

E6570 Bernice Thornton Banning

E1588 MARY ELIZABETH BANNING born Feb. 28, 1867 in Newport, R.I. She married Benjamin Franklin Thurston of Newport on March 6, 1884 in Rhode Island. They lived in Newport and she died in N.Y. City on Jan. 24, 1902. Source: 1,13

E6571 Donald Pitman Thurston

E1589 ALICE CROCKER BANNING born Oct. 8, 1858 in Providence, R.I. She lived in Newport and never married. Source: 1

E1590 thru E1598 unknown children of E377

E6572 thru E6640 for children

E1599 ESTELLA HILL no information. Source: 1

E1600 CARRIE HILL no information. Source: 1

E1601 ANGELINE HILL no information. Source: 1

E1602 LULU HILL no information. Source: 1

E1603 WILLIAM P. HILL no information. Source: 1

E1604 CHARLES HILL no information. Source: 1

E1605 Unknown HILL child. Source: 1

E1606 IRENE A. COLVIN born May 2, 1835 in Hartford, Ct. Married Eugene P. Goldman on Oct. 2, 1872 in Meriden, Ct. Source: 1

E1607 JAMES WOOTIN BANNING born Greenville, Ga. 1834-1839. He was a Major in the 28th Ga. Reg. C.S.A. He was visiting his uncle (E387) in Conn. in 1850. Source: 1,5,40

E6641 thru E6646 for children.

E1608 MYSTES AZUBA BANNING born about 1939 in Ga. Source: 1,5

E6647 thru E6652 for children

E1609 JOSEPH ADEN BANNING born in Ga. Source: 1,40

E6653 thru E6659 for children

E1610 ELLEN MINERVA BANNING born about 1845 in Ga. Source: 1,5

E6660 thru E6665 for children

E1611 GEORGE OSBORN BANNING born about 1848 in Ga. Source: 1,5

E6666 thru E6671 for children

E1612 FRANK BANNING born 185? in Deep River, Ct. He lived unmarried. Source: 1

E1613 HENRY CLAY BANNING born 1837 or 1839 in Meriden, Ct. He lived unmarried in New Haven, Ct. He was a member of the 7th Ct. Vols. and enlisted on Sept. 7, 1861. He died June 2, 1862 at Ft. Paluski, Ga. and was "buried outside of the mote". Source: 1,5

E1614 GEORGE WILMARTH BANNING born in Nov. 1840 in New Haven, Ct. He married Helen Wheelock in 1864 in Jewet City, Ct. They had one child and lived in New Britain, Ct. where he died in 1895. He was a member of the 7th Reg. of Ct.

Vols. Source: 1,5,40

E6672 George Wheelock Banning

E1615 CHARLES LEWIS BANNING born in 1850 in New Haven, Ct. and died there on Jan. 2, 1862. Source: 1

E1616 JOSEPH OLNEY BANNING born Jan. 29, 1843 in New Haven, Ct. He married Anna Hudson Stover in 1867 in Providence, R.I. They had 3 children and lived in New York City where he was a physician. He enlisted in the 7th Ct. Vols. on Sept. 7, 1861, and was wounded on May 14, 1864 near Pittsburgh. He was alive in 1910. Source: 1,5,30

E6673 Charles Henry Banning
E6674 Willard Gardner Banning
E6675 Earl Hudson Banning

E1617 ELLEN CLARISSA BANNING born in 1836 at Meriden, Ct. She married George Sherman Thomas of Fair Haven, Ct. in 1858. They lived in West Haven, Ct. where she died in 1898. She is buried at the Oak Grove Cemetery. Source: 1,5

E6676 Edwin Plant Thomas
E6677 Charlotte Warner Thomas

E1618 JOSEPH BEAUMONT BANNING born Dec. 16, 1840 in Deep River, Ct. He married Ansolette A. Smith on Dec. 31, 1862 in Deep River. They had no children. They lived in Deep River where he became a Representative, was Clerk of the Court, on the Prison Committee and a Probate Judge for more than 20 years, for which he had an enviable reputation. He was also Secretary of the Ct. Probate Assembly. Source: 1,5

E1619 LOUISE CAMILLA BANNING born Oct. 2, 1842 in Deep River, Ct. She married Jabez Southworth on Jan. 12, 1860. They had one adopted daughter. Source: 1,5

E1620 HANNAH MOORE BANNING born July 12, 1845 in Deep River, Ct. She married J. Ely Beebe of Lyme, Ct. on Dec. 11, 1866. Source: 1,5

E6678 Louise Beebe
E6679 Marian Beebe
E6680 Elsie Beebe
E6681 Clyde M. Beebe
E6682 Victor Lloyd Beebe

E1621 MARY PRITCHARD BANNING born Oct. 29, 1847 in Deep River, Ct. She married Charles E. Alling of Waterbury, Ct. They had no children. Source: 1,5

E1622 EMMA BANNING she married William Day and had 2 children. He died and she married 2nd, Monroe Church. They had one child. She married 3rd, Peter F. Davis and had one child. Source: 1

E6683 Ansell Day
E6684 Burt Day
E6685 Addie Church

E6686 Henry Davis

E1623 IDA BANNING she married Edgar Warner Brockway Ferry in Lyme, Ct. Source: 1

E6687 thru E6693 for children

E1624 MARY JANE BANNING born in 1847 and died Dec. 13, 1860. Source: 1

E1625 WILLIAM SELDEN BANNING born Sept. 6, 1859 and married Sady Sage. They lived in Hartford, Ct. Source: 1

E6694 Lola Banning
E6695 thru E6699 for children

E1626 MINNIE BANNING born 186? and married George Bingham. He died and she married 2nd, Oscar Perine. They lived in Brooklyn, N.Y. Source: 1

E6700 thru E6705 for children

E1627 JENNIE PANSY BANNING no information. Source: 1

E6706 thru E6711 for children

E1628 FREDERICK ELLSWORTH BANNING born Nov. 20, 1862. He married Lucy S. Huntley on Nov. 27, 1887. They lived in Hadlyme, Ct. She was the daughter of Henry and Martha E. (Fox) Huntley, born May 25, 1868. Source: 1,90

E6712 Lillias Josephine Banning
E6713 Keeney Ellsworth Banning
E6714 Leona Martha Banning

E1629 DELLA BANNING she married a Mr. Tiffany. Source: 1

E6715 Harrison Tiffany

E1630 ERNEST BANNING he lived unmarried in Brockway Ferry, Lyme, Ct. Source: 1

E1631 WILLIAM ABBIE born about 1845 in Ind. He was Captain of a schooner coasting the Ct., Hudson and Long Island Sound. Source: 1,5

E1632 ELLEN ABBIE born about 1842 in Ind. Source: 1,5

E1633 JANE ABBIE born about 1838 in Ct. Source: 1,5

E1634 MARY BANNING she married a Mr. King. He was a sea Captainand drowned. She married 2nd, Burton Hebern of New London, Ct. Source: 1

E6716 thru E6721 for children

E1635 JENNIE BANNING she lived unmarried. Source: 1

E1636 ADDIE STEVENS no information. Source: 1

E1637 ROWLAND STEVENS no information. Source: 1

E1638 EMORY DOUD married Jane Lewis and had 2 children. Source: 1

E1639 ELIZABETH DOUD married a Mr. Goff of East Hampton and had one child. Source: 1

E1640 FRANK DOUD he never married. Source: 1

E1641 ADLAIDE DOUD she married Arthur Spencer of Moodus, Ct. and had 3 children. Source: 1

E1642 EMMA DOUD married George Martin of Millington, Ct. Source: 1

E1643 PHOEBE ADOCIA BANNING born Dec. 13, 1848 in East Hampton, Ct. She married Marshall Daniel Wright of East Hampton on Oct. 14, 1869. They lived in East Hampton. Source: 1,5

> E6722 Fred Warren Wright
> E6723 Grace Annett Wright
> E6724 Ethel Mary Wright
> E6725 Franklin Benjamin Wright
> E6726 Clara Cone Wright
> E6727 Hiram Child Wright
> E6728 Daniel Newton Wright

E1644 WILLIAM SAMUEL BANNING born Feb. 13, 1851 in East Hampton, Ct. He married Ella Evelyn King of Thompsonville, Ct. on Oct. 14, 1875. They lived in Springfield, Mass. from 1872, where he was a contractor and builder. She was born April 19, 1856 in Hartford County, Ct. and was the daughter of William Andrus King and Sarah R. Ferry. Source: 1,30

> E6729 Son (?) Banning
> E6730 Susie Geneva Banning

E1645 JOSEPH BRAINARD BANNING born Feb. 28, 1853 in East Hampton, Ct. He married Almeda M. Rich of East Hampton, in East Hampton, where they made their home. Source: 1

> E6731 Joseph Brainard Banning
> E6732 Alminey C. Banning
> E6733 Alfred J. Banning
> E6734 Minnie L. Banning
> E6735 Ada Banning
> E6736 Sophia A. Banning

E1646 MARY ELIZABETH BANNING born in 1855 in East Hampton, Ct. She married Benjamin B. Huntley of East Hampton on Feb. 4, 18??. She died in East Hampton on June 27, 1907 on Chestnut Hill. Source: 1

> E6737 Fred Adriel Huntley
> E6738 Nellie Georgia Huntley
> E6739 Gertrude Lillian Huntley

E1647 NELLIE MARIA BANNING born Aug. 1, 1863. She lived unmarried on the old homestead. Source: 1

E1648 LOUIS ROGERS BANNING born 1856 and married Ludia Dominee. He may have died at the age of 27. Source: 1

E6740 Ida May Banning
E6741 Lloyd Harry Banning

E1649 MORTON HALE BANNING born 1862 and died as an infant. Source: 1

E1650 FANNIE LOULLA BANNING born July 13, 1863 and married Edward D. Collins on Oct. 29, 1888. They lived in Yantic, Ct. Source: 1

E6742 Mary Elizabeth Collins
E6743 Bessie Luella Collins
E6744 Laurence Edward Collins

E1651 LILLIAN AUGUSTA BANNING born Nov. 16, 1867 and married Charles Stough in April 1891. They lived in Yantic, Ct. Source: 1

E6745 Charles Lester Stough

E1652 thru E1659 for unknown children of E403

E6746 thru E6810 for children

E1660 LEWIS STARK no information. Source: 1

E1661 ELLA STARK married Walter Smith. Source: 1

E1662 thru E1679 for unknown children of E406 & E407.

E6811 thru E6889 for children

E1680 ELLA PELINA BANNING born Feb. 21, 1867 in New London, Ct. She married George Taylor on Sept. 6, 1881 in Fall River, Mass. They lived in Blackstone, Mass. Source: 1

E6890 George Taylor
E6891 Florence Taylor

E1681 WILLIAM OTIS BANNING born May 10, 1869 in New London, Ct.
He married Hepsy Estella Manwarring of Essex on Feb. 7, 1894 in Essex. No children. She died April 15, 1896 in Essex and he married 2nd, Ida May Platt of Westbrook, Ct. on Sept. 5, 1899 in New London, Ct. They lived in Ivorytown, Ct. Source: 1

E6892 Nellie Banning
E6893 Everett Banning
E6894 Alice May Banning

E1682 BENJAMIN SIMON BANNING born Feb. 26, 1872 in Norwich City, Ct. and married Caroline Elizabeth Pickett of Essex on July 2, 1896 in Essex. They lived in

Westerly, R.I. Source: 1

E6895 Clara Elizabeth Banning

E1683 CLARA MAY BANNING born Aug. 23, 1880 in Scituate, R.I., and died Aug. 23, 1884 in Moodus, Ct. Source: 1

E1684 FREDERICK LEROY BANNING born Sept. 23, 1881 in Scituate, R.I. He married Alice M. Lane of Brooklyn, N.Y. on March 24, 1903 in Stonington, Ct. They lived in Westerly, R.I. Source: 1

E6896 Esther May Banning
E6897 Ruth Estella Banning
E6898 William Otis Banning

E1685 ROSE BRAMBLE no information. Source: 1

E1686 GEORGE BRAMBLE died prior to 1908. Source: 1

E1687 WILLIS BRAMBLE married 3 times and lived in Yantic, Ct. Source: 1

E1688 MARY BRAMBLE she married 2 times and lived in Norwichtown, Ct. She had one son. Source: 1

E1689 LOUIS BRAMBLE married Melissa Green of Norwich, Ct. Source: 1

E1690 LORIAN HENRY BRAMBLE married ? Source: 1

E1691 FREDERICH BRAMBLE married ? Source: 1

E1692 ROBERT BRAMBLE died prior to 1908. Source: 1

E1693 BURTON BRAMBLE unmarried in 1908. Source: 1

E1694 GRACE BRAMBLE died prior to 1908. Source: 1

E1695 ARTHUR DERBY lived in Middletown, Ct. Source: 1

E1696 LILA DERBY lived in Middletown, Ct. Source: 1

E1697 thru E1702 for unknown Derby children of E410

E1703 ALBERT BROWN married Ella Skinner of Westchester, Ct. and lived at Moodus, Ct. Source: 1

E1704 LEANOR BROWN married Arthur Chandler of Hartford, Ct. and lived in Hartford. They had one son. Source: 1

E1705 thru E1709 for unknown Brown children of E411

E1710 ALICE MARKHAM married Fred Work of Middletown, Ct. Source: 1

E1711 FLORA MARKHAM she was married by 1908. Source: 1

E1712 JOHN MARKHAM died prior to 1908. Source: 1

E1713 thru E1715 for unknown Markham children of E412

E1716 ELMER LEWIS he was married by 1908. Source: 1

E1717 thru E1719 for unknown Lewis children of E413

E1721 thru E1731 for unknown children of E414 thru E417

E6899 thru E6920 for children

E1732 thru E4200 for unknown children of E418 thru E1000

E6921 thru E9899 for children

E4201 ELLA MAY BANNING born April 13, 1855 in Delta, N.Y. She married Frank
Darby Chollar of Syracuse, N.Y. on June 24, 1875 in Syracuse, where they lived.
Source: 1

E9900 Bessie Chollar
E9901 Walter Edward Chollar
E9902 Anne Lucinette Chollar
E9903 Mary Sanford Chollar

E4202 WILLIAM JOSEPH TELLER lived in Leyden, N.Y. He was alive in 1901.
Source: 1,30,93

E4203 MINNIE MARY TELLER lived in Boonville, N.Y. She married Edward S. Clark.
She was alive in 1901. Source: 1,30,93

E4204 WILLIAM JAY BANNING born Oct. 21, 1866 in Mendota, Ill. Married Jessie
Source: 1 Fowler on April 10, 1890 in Grand Junction, Iowa. They lived in Farlin,
Iowa. Source: 1

E9904 Nina Banning
E9905 Alice Banning
E9906 Dorothy Banning

E4205 MINNIE BANNING born June 23, 1870 in Mendota, Ill. Married M.L. Phillips in
1888 at Jefferson, Iowa. They lived in Jefferson. Source: 1

E9907 Alma E. Phillips
E9908 Roy Phillips

E4206 MARY (or MAY) BANNING born April 2, 1878 in Jefferson, Iowa. Married Harry
Wise at Jefferson and lived in Jefferson. Source: 1

E9909 and E9910 for children.

E4207 LILLY BANNING born in Leyden, N.Y. She married Edgar Ballard on May 9,
1895. Source: 1,30,93

E9911 Mable Ballard

E9912 Hazel Ballard
E9913 Marian Ballard

E4208 FRANK BANNING no information Source: 1

E9914 thru E9919 for children

E4209 CLARA MERRY married Frank Stafford of Little Falls, N.Y. Source: 1

E4210 JESSIE MERRY married Fred Smith of Utica, N.Y. Source: 1

E4211 IDA MERRY she died young. Source: 1

E4212 ALBERT MERRY he was unmarried in 1908. Source: 1

E4213 MINNIE MERRY married Tom Longon. Source: 1

E4214 BERTHA MERRY she married and had one child by 1908. Source: 1

E4215 FLORENCE MERRY she married and had one child by 1908. Source: 1

E4216 GEORGE MERRY no information Source: 1

E4217 JENNIE MERRY no information Source: 1

E4218 HELEN ------? died at age 5 in Lyeden, N.Y. Source: 1

E4219 LYDIA ANN ------? died at age 8 in Lyeden, N.Y. Source: 1

E4220 thru E4223 for unknown children of E1006

E4224 thru E4239 for unknown children of E1007 & E1008

E4240 BESSIE MARY L. BANNING born 188? in Ottawa, Ill. Married in 1908.
Source: 1

E9920 thru E9925 for children

E4241 MYRTLE DEL BANNING born in Ottawa, Ill. Source: 1

E9926 thru E9930 for children

E4242 thru E5613 for unknown children of E1009 thru E1360

E9931 thru E10800 for children

E5614 CLOID FRANCIS BANNING born Oct. 21, 1883 in Iowa. Married Mary Alice
Bohannon on Dec. 25, 1904 in Norman, Okla. She was the daughter of John L. and
Mary (Owens) Bohannon, and was born Dec. 25, 1887 in Hugo, Okla. He was a
carpenter, farmer and rancher. Moved to Calif. in 1923 and to LaSalle County,
Texas about 1934. While in Okla., she became a Pastor. He died on July 24,
1963 and is buried in the Dilley, Texas cemetery. She died March 2, 1975 and is
buried in Dilley. Source: 12,15,16

E10801 Gladys Zenora Banning
E10802 John L. Banning
E10803 Anetta Pearl (Nettie) Banning
E10804 Leroy Francis Banning
E10805 Charles Wesley Banning
E10806 Ruby Irene Banning
E10807 Mary Fay Banning
E10808 Martha May Banning
E10809 Paul Richard Banning
E10810 Earl James Banning

E5615 RASCO JAY BANNING born 1886. Married Maud Bohannon. She was the daughter of John L. and Mary (Owens) Bohannon. They moved to Calif. about 1925. Source: 16

E10811 Walter Edwin Banning
E10812 Jewel Banning
E10813 Velma Mildred Banning

E5616 VERNON CASUAS BANNING no information. Source: 16

E10814 thru E10820 for children

E5617 LEON WALTER BANNING born Aug. 18, 1893 in Kearny, Buffalo Co., Neb. and married Jessie Lee Henry on Jan. 15, 1914. She was the daughter of Willie and Laura Anna Henry, born Aug. 18, 1897 in Little Rock, Ark. He was a farmer and lived out of Norman, Cleveland Co., Okla. They moved to Okla. City. They are both buried in the Resthaven Cemetery in Okla. City. Source: 16,20

E10821 Unmarned Banning Daughter
E10822 Orvel Lee Banning
E10823 Lorene June Banning
E10824 Anna Glendene Banning
E10825 Helen Marlene Banning

E5618 FRANK WESLEY BANNING born Dec. 28, 1896 in Kearny, Buffalo Co., Neb. He married Myrtle Bartholomew in 1918 in Norman, Cleveland Co., Okla. She was the daughter of Oliver and Jenny (Kirkendall) Bartholomew, born Jan. 24, 1898 in Norman. He was a farmer, served in the U.S. Army in WWI and died in Sept. 1966 in Okla. City. She died April 10, 1971 in Okla. City. Both are buried in Sunnyland Cemetery in Okla. City. Source: 16,20

E10826 Harvey Lee Banning
E10827 Lester Olicer Banning
E10828 Leo Melvin Banning
E10829 Dora Mae Banning

E5619 RAY NELSON BANNING born Sept. 22, 1899 in Moore, Okla. and married Nellie Frances Soloman on Sept. 21, 1919 in Norman, Cleveland Co., Okla. She was the daughter of John T. and Matilda Jane (Barnett) Soloman, born Jan. 16, 1900 in Joplin, Mo. He was a farmer and they lived near Norman Okla., then Calif., Col. and then in Mo. He died Dec. 27, 1987 in Phillipsburg, Mo. and was buried in the City Cemetery in Lebanon, Mo. She died Sept. 10, 1985 in Lebanon, Mo. where she is buried. Source: 16,20,94

E10830 Unmamed Banning daughter
E10831 Ruth Isabel Banning
E10831A Unnamed Banning son
E10832 Naomi Elizabeth Banning
E10833 Hazel Joyce Banning
E10834 Ralph Nelson Banning
E10835 Basil Ray Banning

E5620 thru E5687 for unknown children of E1362 thru E1381

E10836 thru E11019 for children

E5688 ALBERTO LYMAN BANNING born Sept. 6, 1857 in East Orange, Wisc.
Married Eva Ralston on March 14, 1881 in Memphis, Tenn. They lived in Memphis.
Source: 1

E11020 Alberto Lyman Banning
E11021 Addie Eva Banning
E11022 Clarence Edgar Banning

E5689 CLARENCE EDWIN BANNING born Feb. 2, 1859 in Watoma, Wisc. Married
Addie Haener on March 5, 1883 in Memphis, Tenn. They lived in Memphis and had
no children. Source: 1

E5690 CORA BELL BANNING born May 10, 1861 in Oconowoc, Wisc. Married
Richard M. Hilton on Jan. 23, 1882 in Memphis, Tenn. They lived in Memphis.
Source: 1

E11023 Ethel Alberta Hilton
E11024 Addie Frances Hilton
E11025 Ruth Bell Hilton
E11026 Eva Hilton
E11027 Mable Hilton

E5691 JAMES BYRON BANNING born in Memphis and died as an infant. Source: 1

E5692 FANNIE BANNING born in Memphis and died as an infant. Source: 1

E5693 GRACE BANNING born in Memphis and died as an infant. Source: 1

E5694 LOTTIE EVA BANNING born in Memphis and died as an infant. Source: 1

E5695 IDA MAY BANNING born Nov. 5, 1878 in Memphis, Tenn. Married William B.
East on Dec. 24, 1905 in Memphis. Source: 1

E11028 thru E11033 for children

E5696 LYMAN WELLS BAILEY born May 18, 1874 in Memphis, Tenn. and died Sept.
21, 1891. Source: 1

E5697 CHARLES JARED ABELL born Oct. 9, 1869. married Alice Dickey of Norwich
Town, Conn. on Oct. 8, 1903. Source: 1,42

E5698 LUCY LEFFINGWELL ABELL born Nov. 8, 1871 and died Jan. 19, 1883. Source: 1,42

E5699 thru E5703 for unknown Banning children of E1387

E11034 thru E11049 for children

E5704 thru E5802 numbers not used

E5803 GARNETTE ELY BANNING born July 29, 1869 in Empire, Wisc. Married Joseph Hall on May 2, 1894 in Empire. They lived in Mitchell, Neb. Source: 1

E11050 thru E11055 for children

E5804 WILLIAM THEOPHILUS BANNING born Feb. 26, 1871 in Empire, Wisc. He died June 15, 1887 in Empire. Source: 1

E11056 thru E11060 for children

E5805 EMERETT TURNER BANNING born Nov. 30, 1875 in Empire, Wisc. Married ----? Curtis on Jan. 24, 1903 in Empire. They lived in Mitchell, Neb. Source: 1

E11061 thru E11065 for children

E5806 LEORA EUGENIA BANNING born Oct. 20, 1877 in Empire, Wisc. Died in 1883 in Empire. Source: 1

E5807 MARY ORA BANNING born Dec. 31, 1885 in Empire, Wisc. Married Charles Nathan Law on June 18, 1907 in Neb. They lived in Neb. Source: 1

E11066 thru E11070 for children

E5808 MILTON ALBERT BANNING no information. Source: 1

E11071 thru E11075 for children

E5809 HERBERT ERNEST BANNING no information. Source: 1

E11076 thru E11080 for children

E5810 EDWARD SHERMAN BANNING no information. Source: 1

E11081 thru E11085 for children

E5811 GERTRUDE ULA BANNING no information. Source: 1

E11086 thru E11090 for children

E5812 thru E5818 for unknown children of E1397

E5819 LOTTIE CHURCHILL no information. Source: 1

E5820 thru E5825 for unknown Churchill children

E5826 SON-----? BANNING no information. Source: 1

> E11091 thru E11095 for children

E5827 SON-----? BANNING no information. Source: 1

> E11096 thru E11100 for children

E5828 thru E5835 for unknown children of E1400

> E11101 thru E11125 for children

E5836 FRANK BANNING no information. Source: 1

> E11126 thru E11130 for children

E5837 thru E5843 for unknown children of E1402

> E11131 thru E11134 for children

E5844 CECIL B. BANNING born Aug. 12, 1899 in East Lyme, Ct. He married Helen Elizabeth Richmond on Oct. 1, 1927 in New London, Ct. She died Feb. 2, 1963. Cecil spent his whole life in East Lyme, was a member of the Flanders Baptist Church and a cicil engineer and surveyor for the Ct. Light & Power Co. He died April 18, 1996 and was buried in the East Lyme Cemetery. Source: 30,90

> E11135 Joan banning
> E11136 Kent B. Banning

E5845 ELLEN BANNING She married a Mr. Congdon. Source: 30,90

> E11137 thru E11141 for children

E5846 ORRIN BANNING no information. Source: 30,90

> E11142 Raymond Banning
> E11143 thru E11145 for children

E5847 BEATRICE BANNING she married a Mr. Beebe. Source: 30,90

> E11146 thru E11149 for children

E5848 thru E6299 for unknown children of E1404 thru E1462

> E11150 thru E11880 for children

E6300 FRANCES STELLA HAYWARD born Nov. 11, 1861 and died Dec. 28, 1867. Source: 1

E6301 WALDO BANNING HAYWARD born Nov. 22, 1861 and lived in Somerville, Mass. Source: 1

E6302 ERNEST WALER HAYWARD born July 1, 1865 and died Jan. 6, 1866.

Source: 1

E6303 HARRY BRADBURY HAYWARD born July 21, 1871. Married Grace M. Freeman in 1889. They had 4 children. Source: 1

E6304 MURRY BANNING no information. Source: 1

E11881 thru E11B85 for children

E6305 MAUD BANNING married Robert A. Peet and they lived in Highwood, N.J. Source: 1

E11886 thru E11890 for children

E6306 SCOFIELD BANNING no information. Source: 1

E11891 thru E11895 for children

E6307 MABLE BANNING no information. Source: 1

E11896 thru E11900 for children

E6308 WALDO BANNING no information. Source: 1

E11901 thru E11905 for children

E6309 WILLIAM CURTIS NOYES born Nov. 16, 1862. Married Josephine Sylvester on March 28, 1896, and died July 12, 1904. Source: 1

E6310 ENOCH NOYES born July 17, 1864 and died May 28, 1902. Source: 1

E6311 CLARISSA DUTTON NOYES born Oct. 3, 1866. Source: 1

E6312 JOHNNIE BANNING NOYES born Dec. 27, 1867. Died April 1, 1872. Source: 1

E6313 HARRY DUTTON NOYES born Dec. 1, 1871. Died Nov. 2, 1898. Source: 1

E6314 MARTHA NOYES born Jan. 28, 187? and lived in Lyme, Conn. Source: 1

E6315 FRANCIS (FRANK) BANNING NOYES born July 17, 1874. Source: 1

E6316 LAURA BANNING NOYES born Sept. 6, 1875. Married Robert C. Davidson on Nov. 14, 1905. They lived in New York City. Source: 1

E6317 CHARLES REGINALD NOYES born Oct. 10, 1883. Married his cousin, Lucy Lay Bancroft (E6323) on Oct. 11, 1906. Source: 1

E6318 MARTHA THOMAS born April 24, 1888 and lived in Lyme, Conn. Source: 1

E6319 KENDALL BANNING born Sept. 20, 1879 in New York City. Married Hedwig V. Briesen of N.Y.C. on May 19, 1906 in N.Y.C., where they lived. She was born Nov. 28, 1883, died July 7, 1912 and was the daughter of Arthur V. Briesen. They had 1 child. Kendall married 2nd, Dorothy Carter Sanders on Nov. 15, 1915. She was the daughter of Lewis Sanders, a Lawyer, of New York, and was born Aug. 17, 1891 in Mendham, N.J. Kendall graduated from Dartmouth in 1902, was editor and manager of "System" from 1904 thru 1917, editor of "Cosmopolitan" from 1919 to 1921. In WWI he was a Capt. in the 1st Aero Squadron and rose to the rank of Maj. He was on the Comm. of Public Information in Washington and on the General Staff 1918-1919. He returned to publishing in 1922. Source: 1,40

E11906 Barbara Banning
E11907 Calvin Banning

E6320 HELEN BANNING born Oct. 22, 1881 in New York City. She lived in Walpole, N.H. and married Rev. Alfred James Wilson. Source: 1,40

E11908 thru E11914 for children

E6321 DOROTHY BANNING born Oct. 22, 1881 (twin to Helen) in New York City. Married Francis Ewing Repplier in Oct., 1906 in N.Y.C., where they lived. Source: 1,40

E11915 thru E11920 for children

E6322 PEARLY HUBBARD BANCROFT born Feb. 25, 1883 in New York City. Married Louise Jussen on June 12, 1907 in N.Y.C., where they lived. Source: 1

E6323 LUCY LAY BANCROFT born July 24, 1884. Married her cousin (E6317) Charles Reginald Noyes on Oct. 11, 1906. They had 1 son by 1908. Source: 1

E6324 EMMA BANNING BANCROFT born May 18, 1889 and lived in Nahaut, Mass. Source: 1

E6325 thru E6359 for unknown children of E1484 thru E1492

E11921 thru E11990 for children

E6360 FRANK LOW BANNING born Dec. 15, 1869 and died Feb. 15, 1878. Source: 1

E6361 SARAH CHARLOTTE BANNING born Dec. 16, 1871 and married P. C. Broadman. They lived in Brooklyn, Flatbush, N.Y. Source: 1

E11991 thru E11995 for children

E6362 PAUL WELCH BANNING born Dec. 26, 1880 in Rochester, N.Y. Married Mary Cook on March 1, 1900. They lived in Rochester. Source: 1

E11996 Arthur Roland Banning
E11997 thru E12000 for children

E6363 PANSY BANNING born Sept. 5, 1884 in Rochester, N.Y. and lived in Rochester. Source: 1

E12001 thru E12005 for children

E6364 WINDSOR MORGAN BANNING born Aug. 8, 1894 in Windsor Beach, N.Y.

Married Leah Spalsbury on Aug. 10, 1908 in Clayton, N.Y. They lived in Rochester, N.Y. Source: 1

E12006 thru E12010 for children

E6365 GEORGE ALBERT BANNING born Aug. 8, 1894 in Windsor Beach, N.Y. and lived in Rochester, N.Y. Source: 1

E12011 thru E12015 for children

E6366 thru E6399 for unknown children of E1497 thru E1505

E12016 thru E12090 for children

E6400 ELODIA ADELLA BANNING born March 20, 1852 in Poolville, N.Y. Married Gates Samuel Comstock on Oct. 6, 1873 or Oct. 10, 1900 in Milton, Madison County N.Y. They lived in Grover Pennsylvania. Source: 1,13

     E12091 Dwight Ray Comstock
     E12092 Clarence Burnap Comstock
     E12093 Claud Lynn Comstock

E6401 NELLIE LUCETTA BANNING born March 1, 1857 near Poolville, N.Y. Married Fred L. Dunham on Dec. 18, 1879 at Poolville. They lived near Poolville. Source: 1

E12094 Mary Ester Dunham

E6402 FRANK BANNING born March 23, 1863 near Poolville, N.Y. Died Nov. 11, 1863 near Poolville. Source: 1

E6403 GEORGIA MARY HALL born May 9, 1858 near Poolville, N.Y. Married Edgar Westcott on Dec. 21, 1881 near Poolville. They had 2 girls. Source: 1

E6404 WALTER JOHN BANNING born May 4, 1864 near Poolville, N.Y. Married Lida H. Gates on Jan. 28, 1885 in Hamilton, N.Y. They had no children. They lived in Hamilton for a time and then moved west to ------? Source: 1

E12095 thru E12100 for children

E6405 thru E6489 for unknown children of E1510 thru E1563

E12101 thru E12340 for children

E6490 thru E6497 for unknown children of E1564

E6498 LONA ALMINA BANNING born Nov. 10, 1866 at Amhurst, Mass. Source: 1

E12341 thru E12346 for children

E6499 NELSON WILBUR BANNING born Oct. 11, 1868 in Amhurst, Mass. Source: 1

E12347 thru E12352 for children

E6500 CHARLES HURBERT BANNING born April 30, 1873 in Amhurst, Mass. and died July 22, 1873 at Amhurst. Source: 1

E6501 ALMA TAFT no information. Source: 1

E6502 WARREN BANNING no information. Source: 1

E12353 thru E12358 for children

E6503 ALMA JENSEN no information. Source: 1

E6504 SARAH JENSEN no information. Source: 1

E6505 thru E6510 for unknown Jensen children of E1568

E6511 thru E6519 for unknown children of E1569

E6520 ERNEST BOLLES no information. Source: 1

E6521 GRACE BOLLES no information. Source: 1

E6522 thru E6537 for unknown Banning children of E1571 & E1572

E12359 thru E12395 for children

E6538 thru E6545 unknown children of E1580

E6546 IDA MAY BANNING born about 1878 and lived in Dogeville, N.Y.

E6547 HATTIE ESTELLE BANNING born about 1881 and lived in Dogeville, N.Y.

E6548 thru E6551 unused

E6552 thru E6558 unknown children of E1582

E6559 thru E6566 for unknown children of E1583

E12396 thru E12416 for children

E6567 JANE THURSTON FREEBORN born July 15, 1878. She married John Gladding Jr. of Newport, Rhode Island. They had 4 children. Source: 1

E6568 THOMAS LAURENCE FREEBORN born July 8, 1879 in Newport, R.I. He married Katherine Lansing Biselow of Plattsburg, N.Y. on April 25, 1907. They had one child. Source: 1

E6569 MARGURITE FREEBORN born April 30, 1888 in Bellview, Fla. and died as an infant. Source: 1

E6570 BERNICE THORNTON BANNING she lived in Providence, R.I. Source: 1

E12417 thru E12422 for children

E6571 DONALD PITMAN THURSTON no information. Source: 1

E6572 thru E6640 for unknown children of E1590 thru E1598

E12423 thru E12523 for children

E6641 thru E6671 for unknown children of E1607 thru E1611

E12524 thru E12584 for children

E6672 GEORGE WHEELOCK BANNING born Oct. 25, 1869 in Rockville, Ct. He
married Mary Louise Caldwell on March 17, 1898 in Syracuse, N.Y. She was the
daughter of Leslie & Harriet Caldwell. They lived in Davenport, Iowa where he was a
Physician. He was a member of the class of 1895, College of Physicians &
Surgeons, Columbia University, N.Y.C. In his early days, he lived in New Britain, Ct.
Source: 1

E12585 George Caldwell Banning

E6673 CHARLES HENRY BANNING born May 1, 1867 in New Haven, Ct. He
married Charlotte Bartley, who was the daughter of Joshua Bartley of Wisahicken,
Philadelphia, Pa., in 1892. They lived in N.Y.C. where she died in 1907. Source: 1

E12586 Earl Hudson Banning
E12587 Susan Bartley Banning
E12588 Charles Henry Banning

E6674 WILLARD GARDNER BANNING born 1873 in Chicago, Ill. He married Emma
Willard of N.Y.C. in 1895 in N.Y. They lived in New York, where he was a stock &
bond broker, and they had no children. Source: 1

E6675 EARL HUDSON BANNING born Aug. 20, 1880 in New Haven, Ct. He died
Dec. 17, 1891 in Philadelphia. Source: 1

E6676 EDWIN PLANT THOMAS (Edwin Thomas Plant ?) born in 1860 in West
Haven, Ct. He was a Professor. Source: 1

E6677 CHARLOTTE WARNER THOMAS (Charlotte Warner Plant) born 1866. She
married W. Howard Smith. They lived in Atlanta, Ga. Source: 1

E6678 LOUISE BEEBE no information. Source: 1

E6679 MARIAN BEEBE no information. Source: 1

E6680 ELSIE BEEBE no information. Source: 1

E6681 CLYDE M. BEEBE no information. Source: 1

E6682 VICTOR LLOYD BEEBE no information. Source: 1

E6683 ANSELL DAY no information. Source: 1

E6684 BURT DRY no information. Source: 1

E6685 ADDIE CHURCH married Lewellen Brockway. They lived in Hadlyme, Ct.

Source: 1

E6686 HENRY DAVIS no information. Source: 1

E6687 thru E6693 for unknown children of E1623

E6694 LOLA BANNING no information. Source: 1

E12589 thru E12594 for children

E6695 thru E6711 for unknown children of E1625 thru E1627

E12595 thru E12610 for children

E6712 LILLIAS JOSEPHINE BANNING born April 25, 1894. She married Albert H. Hammond. They lived in Yantic, Ct. She died in 1931 Source: 1,90

E12611 thru E12616 for children

E6713 KEENEY ELLSWORTH BANNING born Nov. 5, 1898(or 1896) in Hadlyme, Ct. He died in 1941. Source: 1,90

E12617 thru E12622 for children

E6714 LEONA (Levia ?) MARTHA BANNING born Jan. 8, 1906 in Hadlyme, Ct. She married Edward T. Augustine in 1937. They lived in Springfield, Ma. Source: 1,90

E12623 thru E12628 for children

E6715 HARRISON TIFFANY no information. Source: 1

E6716 thru E6721 for unknown children of E1634

E6722 FRED WARREN WRIGHT born May 14, 1871 in East Hampton, Ct. He married Ada Banning (E6735). Source: 1

E6723 GRACE ANNETT WRIGHT born Jan. 22, 1873 in East Hampton, Ct. Source: 1

E6724 ETHEL MARY WRIGHT born March 13, 1875 in East Hampton, Ct. Source: 1

E6725 FRANK BENJAMIN WRIGHT born April 18, 1B77 in East Hampton, Ct. Source: 1

E6726 CLARA CONE WRIGHT born Oct. 11, 1880 in East Hampton, Ct. Source: 1

E6727 HIRAM CHILDS WRIGHT born March 16, 1882 in East Hampton, Ct. Source: 1

E6728 DANIEL NEWTON WRIGHT born Jan. 10, 1887 in East Hampton, Ct. Source: 1

E6729 SON (?) BANNING unnamed, died as an infant. Source: 1

E6730 SUSIE GENEVA BANNING born Aug. 8, 1875 in Springfield, Mass. She married Harrison Hall Buxton of Washington, D.C. on Dec. 21, 1899. They lived in Lynn, Mass. Source: 1

> E12629 Eleanor Jewel Buxton
> E12630 William Banning Buxton

E6731 JOSEPH BRAINARD BANNING born June 17, 1877 in East Hampton, Ct. He married and lived in East Hampton. He was in the Spanish War in Cuba and Manilla. Source: 1

> E12631 Joseph Brainard Banning
> E12632 Minnie L. Banning

E6732 ALMINEY C. BANNING born March 21, 1882 in East Hampton, Ct. Source: 1

> E12633 thru E12638 for children

E6733 ALFRED J. BANNING born March 21, 1882 in East Hampton, Ct. where he lived. Source: 1

> E12639 thru E12644 for children

E6734 MINNIE L. BANNING born Feb. 3, 1879 in East Hampton, Ct. She married ----? Walden and lived in N.Y.C. Source: 1

> E12645 thru E12650 for children

E6735 ADA BANNING born Sept. 2, 1880 in East Hampton, Ct. She married Frederick Warren Wright (E6722). Source: 1

> E12651 thru E12656 for children

E6736 SOPHIA A. BANNING born April 23, 1886 in East Hampton, Ct. and died as an infant. Source: 1

E6737 FREDERICK ADRIEL HUNTLEY born Feb 23, 1888 and married Edith Nellie Chase. Source: 1,90

E6738 NELLIE GEORGIA HUNTLEY born May 10, 1879 and married Ellery Flood. Their children are, Gertrude and Harley. She died in 1966. Source: 1,90

E6739 GERTRUDE LILLIAN HUNTLEY born May 5, 1877 and married Haynes Hollister. Source: 1,90

E6740 IDA MAY BANNING born in 1876 and married Irving Franklin. They had 3 children. Source: 1

> E12657 thru E12662 for children

E6741 LLOYD HENRY BANNING born 1878. Source: 1

> E12663 thru E12668 for children

E6742 MARY ELIZABETH COLLINS born Sept. 1890 and died Sept. 14, 1890.
Source: 1

E6743 BESSIE LUELLA COLLINS born July 1, 1893 and died May 1, 1894. Source: 1

E6744 LAURENCE EDWARD COLLINS born June 27, 1897. Source: 1

E6745 CHARLES LESTER STROUGH born Dec. 26, 1092. Source: 1

E6746 thru E6810 unknown children of E1652 thru E1659

                E12669 thru E12819 for children

E6811 thru E6B89 unknown children of E1662 thru E1619

                E12820 thru E12970 for children

E6890 GEORGE TAYLOR born Feb. 12, 1883. Source: 1

E6891 FLORENCE TAYLOR born April 15, 1892. Source: 1

E6892 NELLIE BANNING born July 23, 1900 in Ivorytown, Ct. where she lived.
Source: 1

                E12971 thru E12976 for children

E6893 EVERETT BANNING born April 23, 1902 in Ivorytown, Ct. Source: 1

                E12977 thru E12982 for children

E6894 ALICE MAY BANNING born May 20, 1908 in Ivorytown, Ct. Source: 1

                E12983 thru E12988 for children

E6895 CLARA ELIZABETH BANNING born Sept. 4, 1900 in Stonington, Ct. Source:
1

                E129B9 thru E12996 for children

E6896 ESTER MAY BANNING born Feb. 13, 1904 in Stonington, Ct. Source: 1

                E12997 thru E13004 for children

E6897 RUTH ESTELLA BANNING born June 16, 1905 in Stonington, Ct. Source: 1

                E13005 thru E13010 for children

E6898 WILLIAM OTIS BANNING born Sept. 28, 1907 in Stonington, Ct. Source: 1

                E13011 thru E13016 for children

E6899 thru E9899 for unknown children of E1721 thru E4200

                E13017 thru E17000 for children

E9900 BESSIE CHOLLAR born Aug. 2, 1877 in Syracuse, N.Y. She married Harvy L. King in 1900 and had 2 children. Source: 1

E9901 WALTER EDWARD CHOLLAR born Aug 28, 1879 in Syracuse, N.Y. He married Estell ----? in 1908. Source: 1

E9902 ANNE LUCINETT CHOLLAR born Dec. 14, 1886 in Syracuse, N.Y. She was unmarried in 1908. Source: 1

E9903 MARY SANFORD CHOLLAR born Aug. 12, 1898 in Sherwood, Tenn. Source: 1

E9904 NINA BANNING no information. Source: 1

E17001 thru E17006 for children

E9905 ALICE BANNING no information. Source: 1

E17007 thru E17012 for children

E9906 DOROTHY BANNING no information. Source: 1

E17013 thru E17018 for children

E9907 ALMA E. PHILLIPS no information. Source: 1

E9908 ROY PHILLIPS no information. Source: 1

E9909 and E9910 for unknown children of E4206

E9911 MABLE BALLARD no information. Source: 1

E9912 HAZEL BALLARD no information. Source: 1

E9913 MARIAN BALLARD no information. Source: 1

E9914 thru E9919 for unknown Banning children of E4208

E17019 thru E17039 for children

E9920 thru E9930 for unknown children of E4240 & E4241

E9931 thru E10800 for unknown children of E4242 thru E5613

E17040 thru E19040 for children

E10801 GLADYS ZENORA BANNING born May 23, 1906 near Norman, Okla. Married Duncan Eve Bess on June 14, 1924 in Los Angles, Calif. He served in the U.S. Army in W.W. One. They moved to Dilley Texas in the mid 1930's. He was a farmer. He was born Feb. 1, 1900, and died Feb. 10, 1982 in Dilley, Texas. She died Jan. 17, 1983 and is buried in the Dilley Cem. Source: 15,16

E19041 Mary Alice Bess

E19042 Alfia Mae Bess
E19043 Leroy Bess
E19044 Sheron Bess

E10802 JOHN L. BANNING born Feb. 15, 1910 near Norman, Cleveland County Ok.
Married Eltha Lennis Ridge in West Los Angles, Calif. She was the daughter of
William Jacob Ridge (born Dec.16, 1878 died Feb. 11, 1948) and Sarah Melissa
Castle (born Feb. 1, 1874 and died July 21, 1959), born June 21, 1913 in
Washington, Ok. She died May 22, 1981 in San Antonio, Texas and is buried in the
Dilley, Texas Cemetery. They had four children. He married 2nd, Annie D.
(Willeford) Beshears on Jan. 10, 1982 in Dilley, Texas She was a widow born June
1, 1916 in Gonzales County Texas John had a farm near Millett, Texas in the mid
1930's and 40's and then became a building contractor. Source: 15,16,61

E19045 Ronald David Banning
E19046 Raymond John Banning
E19047 Bobby Harland Banning
E19048 Brenda Irene Banning

E10803 ANETTA PEARL BANNING born Jan. 20, 1908 near Norman, Okla. Married
Isaac Henry Ridge on Oct. 12, 1925 in Los Angles, Calif. He was the son of William
Jacob Ridge and Sarah Melissa Castle, born March 22, 1906 in Komawa, Seminole
County Ok. They moved to Millett, Texas in the mid 1930's and then to Dilley, Texas
about 1949. He was an Assembly of God minister. He died Jan. 3, 1986 and is
buried in the Dilley Cem. Source: 15,16

E19049 Charles William Ridge
E19050 Chester LeRoy Ridge
E19051 Richard Lee Ridge

E10804 LEROY FRANCIS BANNING born April 28, 1916 in Cleveland County, Okla.
Married Hattie Roberta Sharp on Jan. 12, 1935 on the Banning farm near Millett,
Texas. She was the daughter of Russell Kelly Sharp and Sarah Margaret Yandell,
and was born Aug. 7, 1910 near Norman, Okla. He worked for Douglas Aircraft
from 1934 thru 1945. During the war he helped open aircraft plants in Calif. and
Okla. They returned to Texas after the war and opened a grocery store. The last
store was in Lytle, Texas. He died Feb. 15, 1983 and is buried in the Dilley, Texas
Cem. Source: 15,16

E19052 Leroy Francis Banning

E10805 CHARLES WESLEY BANNING born Aug. 19, 1918 near Little Axe, Ok. and
died Dec. 1, 1918. He is buried in the Morris Hill Cem. 11 miles south of Pink, Ok.
Source: 15

E10806 RUBY IRENE BANNING born Feb. 7, 1920 near Little Axe, Ok. She married
Marvin Lonnie Mathews in Millett, LaSalle County Texas, on Sept. 30, 1939. He was
a born March 27, 1912 in Millett and is the son of Joseph Mathews and Florence
Sossaman. Marvin was a farmer and worked for a butane Co. They moved to
Dilley, Texas about 1960. Source: 16

E19053 Patricia Ann Mathews
E19054 Joe Marvin Mathews
E19055 Jerry Lee Mathews

E19056 Linda Joy Mathews
E19057 James Earl Mathews

E10807 MARY FAYE BANNING born Sept. 23, 1922 near Little Axe, Okla. She married Simeon (Dick) Reese Stephenson on July 24, 1941 near Millett, Texas. He was born June 1, 1913. They lived in Cotulla, Texas and moved to Dilley. He was a farmer and then drove a butane truck in South Texas. He died Oct. 10, 1985, and is buried in the Dilley Cem. Source: 15,16

E19058 Jack Reese Stephenson
E19059 Larry Stephenson

E10808 MARTHA MAY BANNING born Sept. 23, 1922 in Norman, Okla. (twin of E10807). She married Herman Smith on July 24, 1941 near Millett, Texas. He is the son of Nay W. Smith and Ethel Mathews and was born Oct. 13, 1919 in Center, Shelby County Texas. They lived in Los Angles, Calif., San Augustine, Cleveland and Dilley Texas. He was a carpenter and school teacher. She was a bank teller. They are retired and living in Seguin, Texas. Source: 16

E19060 Sandra Lee Smith
E19061 Kenny Ray Smith

E10809 PAUL RICHARD BANNING born July 23, 1926. He married Lucy Belle Dudley in Pearsall, Texas. He was in the Army during WW II. They lived in Dilley, Texas where he worked for CP&L, then transferred to Victoria, Texas.

E19062 Beverly Banning
E19063 James Paul Banning
E19064 Gary Banning
E19065 Ricky Banning

E10810 EARL JAMES BANNING born Aug. 4, 1930 in Santa Monica, Los Angles County Calif. He married Joyce Darlene Fisher in Bonesteel S.D. on June 27, 1952. She was the daughter of Merton Lyle Fisher and Vivian Joyce Flisram, born June 11, 1931 in Bonesteel. He served in the U.S. Army as a X-ray tech. He then became an Assembly of God Pastor. They moved to Houston, Texas about 1970 where he built the largest Assembly church in the city. Source: 16,61

E19066 Stephen Earl Banning
E19067 Susan Rae Banning
E19068 Lori Lee Banning

E10811 WALTER EDWIN BANNING born April 5, 1908 in Okla. Married Jewel Ridge. She was born April 1, 1910 and was the daughter of Jacob William Ridge and Sarah Cassell, (See E10802). After her death he married 2nd, Pearl Strickland. He was a Farmer in Dilley, Texas and moved to Arkadelphia, Ark. in 1949, where he worked for an Alum. Co. Source: 16

E19069 Walter Lee Banning
E19070 Delores Banning

E10812 JEWEL BANNING born about 1910 and married Harold Shepard. She died at age 26 in Ark.

E19071 thru E19074 for children

E10813 VELMA MILDRED BANNING born about 1914 and married Pat Gentry.

E19075 thru E19079 for children

E10814 thru E10820 unknown children of E5616

E19080 thru E19100 for children

E10821 Unnamed BANNING daughter born and died March 4, 1918 and is buried in the Morris Hill Cemetery, 11 miles south of Pink, Ok. Source: 15

E10822 ORVEL LEE BANNING born Dec. 15, 1921 in Pottawatomie Co., Okla. and married Helen Irene Todd on May 25, 1941 in Norman Cleveland Co., Okla. She was born Nov. 21, 1924 in Norman. They lived in Okla. City. Source: 16,20

E19101 Norma Lee Banning
E19102 Michael Larry Banning

E10823 LORENE JUNE BANNING born June 11, 1924 in Norman, Cleveland Co., Okla. and married Lester Charles McGahey on Sept. 16, 1939 in Norman. He is the son of Henry and Viola (Osborn) McGahey, born Oct. 26, 1917 in Pottawatomie Co., Okla. They lived in Okla. and Calif. and had two children. She married 2nd, D.R. Clinkenbeard on March 2, 1983. He was born Sept. 6, 1917 in Norman. Source: 16,20

E19103 Bonnie McGahey
E19104 Marieta McGahey

E10824 ANNA GLENDENE BANNING born April 19, 1931 in Los Angeles, Calif. and married Leslie Earl Louderback on Aug. 6, 1955 in Newalla, Okla. He is the son of George Will and Virginia Emma (White) Louderback, born Feb. 25, 1925 in Inola, Rogers Co., Okla. They lived in Okla. and Odessa, Texas, where he worked for Phillips Pet. Co. Source: 16,20

E19105 Reba Ann Louderback

E10825 HELEN MARLENE BANNING born Dec. 25, 1940 in Norman, Cleveland Co., Okla. and married Russell Eugene Krohmer on March 15, 1958 in Okla. City. He is the son of William F. and Louis M. (Hall) Krohmer, born March 17, 1936 in Norman. He is a Plumbing contractor and she works in data processing. Source: 16,20

E19106 Marla Ann Krohmer

E10826 HARVY LEE BANNING born Jan. 25, 1919 in Norman, Cleveland Co., Okla. and married Hazel Louise Gossage on Jan. 19, 1947 in Chickasha, Okla. She is the daughter of Lite and Julia (Sanders) Gossage, born Jan. 30, 1927 in Chickasha. He served in the U.S. Army in WW2 and did aircraft maintaince. She was a Nurse. He died May 1, 1972 in Tecumseh, Pottowatomie Co., Okla. and is buried in the Brown Cemetery in that city. Source: 16,20

E19107 Roger Lee Banning
E19108 Karen Beth Banning

E19109 Bruce Gregory Banning
E19110 Glen David Banning
E19111 Teresa Delores Banning

E10827 LESTER OLIVER BANNING born June 7, 1920 East of Norman, Cleveland Co., Okla. He married Juanita Jewel Shelton on Jan. 29, 1941 near Tecumseh, Pottowatomie Co., Okla. She was the daughter of John A. and Clara (Melcalf) Shelton, born March 26, 1923 in Tecumseh, Okla. He is Pastor of the Dell Haven Tabernacle in Dell City, Okla. Source: 16,20

E19112 Betty Maye Banning
E19113 Thomas Lester Banning
E19114 John Wesley Banning

E10828 LEO MELVIN BANNING born Oct. 7, 1921 in Cleveland Co., Okla. and married Thelma Irene Einsenhower on March 15, 1943 in Sand Springs, Okla. She was born March 19, 1926 in Tecumseh, Okla. They had one child. He married 2nd, Louise Anna McClain on Sept. 2, 1967 in St. Charles, Mo. She was the daughter of Jessie and Beth (McGraw) McClain, born Nov. 1, 1932 in St. Louis, Mo. He served in the Army Air Force, was employed in the Aerospace industry and has lived in Okla., Calif., Ala., and Mo. Source: 16,20

E19115 Keith Douglas Banning

E10829 DORA MAE BANNING born Dec. 24, 1925 in Norman, Cleveland Co., Okla. and married Carter James Tacker Jr. on May 22, 1946 in Shawnee, Pottowatomie Co., Okla. He is the son of Carter James and Letha (Melott) Tacker, born Aug. 25, 1924 in Shawnee. He served in the army Air Force in WW2. They both are Teachers in Tecumseh, Okla. Source: 16,20

E19116 Tamara Kay Tacker
E19117 James Philip Tacker

E10830 Unnamed BANNING Daughter born and died June 23, 1920 and buried in the Morris Hill Cemetery, 11 miles South of Pink, Ok. Source: 15

E10831 RUTH ISABEL BANNING born July 26, 1921 in Norman, Cleveland Co., Okla. and married (Ted) Lowell (NMI) Schleicher on July 6, 1947 in Grand Junction, Col. He is the son of Carl John and Lois Vashti (French) Schleicher, born Dec. 9, 1925 in Glenwood Springs, Col. He served in the U.S. Army in WW2 and was a Research Chemist. He retired in 1990 and is now a Consultant. She is a Secretary. They lived in Col., Mich., Ohio and now live in Appleton, Wisc. She is source 94. Source: 16,20,94

E19118 Katherine Lynn Schleicher
E19119 Chris Lee Schleicher

E10831A Unmamed BANNING Son born and died Aug. 20, 1923 and buried in the Morris Hill Cemetery, 11 miles South of Pink, Okla. Source: 15

E10832 NAOMI ELIZABETH BANNING born Sept. 13, 1925 in West Los Angeles, Calif. and married John George Underwood on July 6, 1946 in Grand Junction, Mesa Co., Col. He was the son of George and Anna Mae (Griffith) Underwood, born March 16, 1925 in New Castle, Garfield Co., Col. He was in the U.S. Army and then in sales. She died May 5, 1987 in Westminster, Adams Co., Col. John died May 23, 1996 in Westminster, and both are buried in the Fort Logan Cemetery in Denver. Source: 16,20,94

E19120 Darr Ann Underwood
E19121 John Nelson Underwood
E19122 and E19123 unused

E10833 HAZEL JOYCE BANNING born Oct. 21, 1928 near Norman, Cleveland Co., Okla. on the Little River. She married Murl Edward Porter on Oct. 21, 1954 in Lebanon, Mo. He was the son of John and Minnie (Radar) Porter, born May 5, 1922 in Conway, Laclede Co., Mo. He is retired and they live in Conway. Source: 16,20,94

E19124 Sampson Wayne Porter
E19125 Delilah Ann Porter
E19126 Earl Edward Porter
E19127 Patricia Lynn Porter
E19128 Marie Abigail Porter
E19129 Mary Frances Porter

E10834 RALPH NELSON BANNING born Dec. 13, 1930 in South Los Angeles, Calif. and married Minnie Ann Crismon on Oct. 18, 1952 in Mountain View, Calif. She was born Aug. 2, 1931 in Waynesville, Mo. He served 20 years in the U.S. Navy and then worked in the Aerospace industry and lived in Lanham, Md. As of 1996, they were retired and live in Nixa, Mo. Source: 16,20,94

E19130 Jack Dewayne Banning

E10835 BASIL RAY BANNING born Oct. 10, 1938 in Fruita, Col. and died Jan. 29, 1955 in Springfield, Mo. He is buried in the City Cemetery in Lebanon, Mo. Source: 16,20,94

E10836 thru E11019 for unknown children of E5620 thru E5687

E19131 thru E19460 for children

E11020 ALBERTO LYMAN BANNING born Aug. 1, 1882 in Memphis, Tenn. He married Louise Carlson on Dec. 10, 1907 in Memphis, where they lived. Source: 1

E19461 thru E19466 for children

E11021 ADDIE EVA BANNING born March 10, 1886 in Memphis, Tenn. and died Aug. 14, 1886 in Memphis. Source: 1

E11022 CLARENCE EDGAR BANNING born April 25, 1889 in Memphis, Tenn. Source: 1

E19467 thru E19472 for children

E11023 ETHEL ALBERTA HILTON born Dec. 11, 1882 in Memphis, Tenn. She married Charles H. Ziermann on Aug. 16, 1904 in Memphis. They had a daughter, Irma, born May 10, 1906. Source: 1

E11024 ADDIE FRANCES HILTON born Nov. 5, 1894 in Memphis. Source: 1

E11025 RUTH BELL HILTON born 189? in Memphis, Tenn. and died as an infant. Source: 1

E11026 EVA HILTON born Aug. 6, 1896 in Memphis, Tenn. Source: 1

E11027 MABLE HILTON born Aug. 2, 1899 in Memphis, Tenn. Source: 1

E11028 thru E11033 for unknown children of E5695

E11034 thru E11065 for unknown children of E5699 thru E5805

E19473 thru E19550 for children

E11066 thru E11090 for unknown children Of E5807 thru E5811

E19551 thru E19590 for children

E11091 thru E11134 unknown children of E5826 thru E5843

E19591 thru E19649 for children

E11135 JOAN BANNING she married a Mr. Cassel. Source: 30,90

E19650 thru E19654 for children

E11136 KENT B. BANNING living in Scottsdale, Az. in 1996. Source: 30,90

E19655 thru E19659 for children

E11137 thru E11141 unknown children of E5845

E11142 RAYMOND BANNING born April 29, 1910 in Lebanon, New London Co. Ct. Source: 13

E19660 thru E19603 for children

E11143 thru E11880 unknown children of E5846 thru E6299

E19603 thru E21600 for children

E11881 thru EI1905 unknown children of E6304 thru E6308

E21601 thru E21641 for children

E11906 BARBARA BANNING born March 8, 1908 in New York City. Source: 1,40

E21642 thru E21647 for children

E11907 CALVIN BANNING born May 23, 1917 in New York. Source: 40

E21648 thru E21653 for children

E11908 thru E11920 unknown children of E6320 & E6321

E11921 thru E11990 unknown children of E6325 thru E6359

E21654 thru E21830 for children

E11991 thru E11995 unknown children of E6361

E11996 ARTHUR ROLAND BANNING born Jan. 1, 1901 in Rochester, N.Y. Source: 1

E21831 thru E21836 for children

E11997 thru E12OOO for unknown children of E6362

E21837 thru E21847 for children

E12001 thru E12005 unknown children of E6363

E12006 thru E12015 unknown children of E6364 & E6365

E21848 thru E21875 for children

E12016 thru E12090 unknown children of E6366 thru E6399

E21876 thru E22076 for children

E12091 DWIGHT RAY COMSTOCK no information. Source: 1

E12092 CLARENCE BURNAP COMSTOCK no information. Source: 1

E12093 CLAUD LINN COMSTOCK no information. Source: 1

E12094 MARY ESTHER DUNHAM no information. Source: 1

E12095 thru E12100 unknown children of E6404

E22077 thru E22087 for children

E12101 thru E12340 for unknown children of E6405 thru E6489

E22088 thru E22688 for children

E12341 thru E12346 unknown children of E6498

E12347 thru E12358 unknown children of E6499 & E6502

E22689 thru E22719 for children

E12359 thru E12416 unknown children of E6522 thru E6566

E22720 thru E22870 for children

E12417 thru E12422 unknown children of E6570

E12423 thru E12584 unknown children of E6572 thru E6671

E22871 thru E23271 for children

E12585 GEORGE CALDWELL BANNING born Aug. 26, 1904 in Davenport, Iowa.
Source: 1

E23272 thru E23277 for children

E12586 EARL HUDSON BANNING born 1893 in New York City. Source: 1

E23278 thru E23283 for children

E12587 SUSAN BARTLEY BANNING born 1895 in New York City. Source: 1

E23284 thru E23289 for children

E12588 CHARLES HENRY BANNING born 1896 in New York City. Source: 1

E23290 thru E23295 for children

E12589 thru E12594 unknown children of E6694

E12595 thru E12610 unknown children of E6695 thru E6711

E23296 thru E23336 for children

E12611 thru E12628 unknown children of E6712 thru E6714

E12629 ELEANOR JEWEL BUXTON born Dec. 11, 1900 in East Orange, N.J.
Source: 1

E12630 WILLIAM BANNING BUXTON born Nov. 25, 1902 in Cincinnati, Ohio.
Source: 1

E12631 JOSEPH BRAINARD BANNING no information. Source: 1

E23337 thru E23342 for children

E12632 MINNIE L. BANNING no information. Source: 1

E23343 thru E23348 for children

E12633 thru E12656 unknown children of E6732 thru E6735

E23349 thru E23375 for children

E12657 thru E12668 unknown children of E6740 & E6741

E23376 thru E23391 for children

E12669 thru E12970 unknown children of E6746 thru E6889

222

E23392 thru E24150 for children

E12971 thru E13016 unknown children of E6892 thru E6898

E24150 thru E24180 for children

E13017 thru E17000 unknown children of E6899 thru E9899

E24180 thru E34000 for children

E17001 thru E17018 unknown children of E9904 thru E9906

E17019 thru E17039 unknown children of E9914 thru E9919

E34001 thru E34051 for children

E17040 thru E19040 unknown children of E9931 thru E10800

E34052 thru E38975 for children

E19041 MARY ALICE BESS born July 21, 1926 and married 1st. Mr. Gillispie. After
his death, she married 2nd, Leroy Ray Smith. Source: 16

        E38976 Lynn D. Gillispie
        E38977 Donnie R. Smith
        E38978 Rickey D. Smith

E19042 ALPHE MAE BESS born May 21, 1929 and married Billy Reese Zahn. He
was born Sept 1, 1927. Source: 16

        E38979 Virginia Mae Zahn
        E38980 Billy Michael Zahn

E19043 LEROY BESS born May 17, 1937 and died Jan. 11, 1951 of a brain tumor.
Buried in the Dilley, Texas Cemetery. Source: 15,16

E19044 SHARON ELAINE BESS born Sept 12, 1947 and married Mr. Griagar.
Source: 16

        E38981 Stephanie Machael Griagar
        E38982 thru E39000 unused

E19045 RONALD DAVID BANNING born Feb. 29, 1932 in Los Angeles, Calif.   He
died of leukemia while in the Navy on Oct. 6, 1953 at the Corpus Christi Naval
Hospital and is buried in the Dilley, Texas Cemetery.
Source: 15,16,61

E19046 RAYMOND JOHN BANNING born Nov. 14, 1934 in Los Angeles, Calif. He
married Judy Cosby in 1955 in Dilley, Texas. Source: 16,61

        E39001 Ronald Dean Banning
        E39002 Kathy Banning
        E39003 Lisa Banning

E19047 BOBBY HARLAND BANNING born June 26, 1937 in Woodward, LaSalle County Texas and married Dorris Vanetta Laster on March 21, 1959. She is the daughter of Orie and Erzula Mae Laster and was born March 7, 1940 in Millett, LaSalle County Texas. He served in the U.S. Navy and is Manager of the telephone system in Dilley, Texas. She is a bookkeeper for a church in Dilley. Source: 16,61

> E39004 John Earl Banning
> E39005 Mark Steven Banning

E19048 BRENDA IRENE BANNING born Sept. 11, 1941 in Pearsall, Frio County Texas. She married Benny Harlan in Dilley Texas. Source: 16,61

> E39006 Bryson Harlan
> E39007 Brandon Harlan
> E39008 Bennyce Harlan

E19049 CHARLES WILLIAM RIDGE born July 22, 1926 in Sawtell, Los Angeles County Calif. He married Mary Louise Jones on March 17, 1947 in Millett, LaSalle County Texas She was the daughter of William Alton Jones and Lila E. Fulmer, born June 26, 1930 in Houston, Texas He served 2 years in the U.S. Army and works for the Ethel Corp. She is a school teacher. They live in Baytown, Texas. Source: 16

> E39009 Sheila Jean Ridge
> E39010 Sherry Lynette Ridge
> E39011 Marilyn Sue Ridge
> E39012 Charles Russell Ridge

E19050 CHESTER LEROY RIDGE born Feb. 29, 1932 in Sawtell, Los Angeles County Calif. He married Wilma Leona Harr on April 13, 1951 in Dilley, Texas She was the daughter of Emanule Harr and Nettie Hall and was born Jan. 6, 1932 in Dilley. They had 4 children. He married 2nd, Martha Elizabeth Nobles on June 2, 1971 in Carrizo Springs, Dimmit County Texas She was the daughter of Woodie Parr Nobles and Pauline Frances Skinner, born May 2, 1949 in Carrizo Springs. He served in the U.S. Navy and is an electrical service man for the power co. in Carrizo Springs. Source: 16

> E39013 Randall Dean Ridge
> E39014 Rhonda Lea Ridge
> E39015 Chestina Louise Ridge
> E39016 Clifford Alan Ridge
> E39017 Sandra Lee Ridge
> E39018 Roy Dean Ridge

E19051 RICHARD LEE RIDGE born Nov. 12, 1934 in Sawtell, Los Angeles County Calif. Married Mary Ann Brake on Sept 30, 1952 in Dilley, Frio County Texas She was the daughter of Melburn Brake and Dorothy Norton, born Sept. 10, 1936 in San Antonio, Texas He was an electrician, lived in Dilley and Baytown, Texas They had 4 children. He married 2nd Eva Nita Moore on March 4, 1977 in Baytown. She was the daughter of Millord Moore and Lillian Juanite Hicks, born Nov. 24, 1943 in Dallas, Texas She is a loan officer. He died of a heart attack July 30, 1986 and is buried in Baytown.
Source: 16

E39019 Richard Scott Ridge
E39020 Jeffrey Lee Ridge
E39021 Susan Gail Ridge
E39022 Kevin Tracy Ridge

E19052 LEROY FRANCIS BANNING born Sept. 27, 1937 in Santa Monica, Calif. Married 1st, Betty Lou Forester in Dilley, Frio Co. Texas. She is the daughter of Heman W. and Leona (Miman) Forester, born Sept. 1, 1938 in Pearsall, Texas. They had two children. He married 2nd, Patricia L. Downs on June 2, 1973. She is the daughter of Charles P. and Martha I. Downs, born July 13, 1940 at Ft. Sam Houston, Bexar County Texas. He is a salesman and they have lived in Houston and Dallas, Texas, Chicago, Ill. and Birmingham, Ala. They Moved to San Antonio, Texas in 1984. Source: 16,61

E39023 Michael Forester Banning
E39024 Craig Francis Banning

E19053 PATRICIA ANN MATHEWS born Aug. 22, 1940 in Pearsall, Frio County Texas. Married Berman Dwight Brown on Dec. 26, 1959 in Dilley, Frio County Texas. He was born June 10, 1938 in Monticello, Drew County Ark. and was the son of Lamar Anguish Brown and Lois Hoover. He served in the U.S. Army and served in Viet Nam. He is an Elect. Eng. and they live in Portland, Nueces County Texas. Source: 16

E39025 Michael Lane Brown
E39026 Steven Dwight Brown
E39027 Pamela Ann Brown

E19054 JOE MARVIN MATHEWS born July 27, 1944 in Pearsall, Frio County Texas Married Patsy Nadine Roberson on Jan. 11, 1963 in Sinton, San Patricio County Texas She was born March 12, 1945 in Pearsall, Texas and is the daughter of Howard G. Roberson and Lela Nadine Outlaw. Joe is a farmer and rancher and they live in Dilley, Texas. Source: 16

E39028 Sheryl Nadine Mathews
E39029 Todd Marvin Mathews

E19055 JERRY LEE MATHEWS born July 14, 1948 in Pearsall, Frio County Texas Married Sharla Crowell on Aug. 22, 1970 in Kingsville, Kleberg County Texas She was born Dec. 28, 195? in Freer, Duval Co. Texas and is the daughter of James and Barbara Crowell. He is a carpenter and they live in Kingsville, Texas. Source: 16

E39030 Jason James Mathews
E39031 Justin Rutherford Mathews
E39032 Joey Mathews

E19056 LINDA JOY MATHEWS born Dec. 31, 1951 in Dilley, Frio County Texas She married Johnnie Daniel Showalter on April 21, 1973 in Dilley. He was born Dec. 1, 1949 in Long Beach, Calif. and is the son of Milton John and Monnie Mae Showalter. She is a teacher and he is in the U.S. Air Force. They lived in Anchorage, Alaska and now live in San Antonio, Texas. Source: 16

E39033 Heather Sidon Showalter
E39034 Matthew Scott Showalter

E19057 JAMES EARL MATHEWS born Aug. 24, 1954 in Cotulla, LaSalle County Texas He married Virginia Carter on May 7, 1976 in Corpus Christi, Texas. She was born April 22, 1958 in Corpus Christi and is the daughter of Jack and Kathy Carter. They live in Corpus Christi. Source: 16

> E39035 James Buckley Mathews
> E39036 Melanie Jane Mathews
> E39037 Marie Alice Mathews

E19058 JACK REESE STEPHENSON born April 19, 1942 and married Marjorie Williams on April 24, 1962. She was born June 11, 1943 in Freeport, Brazoria County Texas. He is a rancher, horse trainer and rodeo cowboy. Source: 16

> E39038 Jack Reese Stephenson Jr.
> E39039 Lori Ann Stephenson
> E39040 Robb Stephenson

E19059 LARRY STEPHENSON born Feb. 12, 1944 and married Patsy Youngblood on May 8, 1965. She was born Nov. 19, 1941. He is a pilot. Source: 16

> E39041 Kimberly Ann Stephenson
> E39042 Scott Stephenson

E19060 SANDRA LEE SMITH born Aug. 6, 1942 in Pearsall, Frio County Texas. Married Paul James Smith on Dec. 22, 1962 in Dilley, Frio County Texas. He was the son of Elmer Lafayett Smith and Irene Reeves, born Nov. 18, 1942 in Rosenberg, Texas. She is a school teacher and he is Vice Pres. of Seguin Fabricators. They live in Seguin, Texas. Source: 16

> E39043 Rodney Brent Smith
> E39044 Shannon Lynne Smith

E19061 KENNY RAY SMITH born Nov. 19, 1946 in Alhambra, Los Angeles County Calif. He married Henrietta Beshears (See E10802). He married 2nd, Dawn Hooper on July 14, 1986. Source: 16

> E39045 Justin Richard Smith
> E39046 Tonya Laynette Smith
> E39047 Justin
> E39048 Ashley

E19062 BEVERLY BANNING no information

> E39049 thru E39052 for children

E19063 JAMES PAUL BANNING no information

> E39053 thru E39056 for children

E19064 GARY BANNING no information

> E39057 thru E39060 for children

E19065 RICKY BANNING no information

E39061 thru E39064 for children

E19066 STEPHEN EARL BANNING born Feb. 10, 1955 in Yankton, S.D. He married
Donna Gayle Montgomery Oct. 18, 1974 in Houston, Tx. They live in Stafford, Tx.
Source: 16,61

E39065 James Mark Banning

E19067 SUSAN RAE BANNING born April 14, 1959 in San Francisco, Ca. She
married David Clay Webster Aug. 25, 1978 in Houston, Tx. They live in Kingswood,
Tx. Source: 16,61

E39066 Tiffany Webster
E39067 Jessica Webster

E19068 LORI LEE BANNING born June 28, 1961 in San Francisco, Ca. She married
John Henry Moon June 20, 1980 in Houston, Tx. They live in Pasadena, Tx.
Source: 16,61

E39068 John Moon 3rd
E39069 Dovavan Moon

E19069 WALTER LEE BANNING born March 13, 1936 in Los Angeles, Calif. He
married 1st, Rose Juanita Rerich on Oct. 19, 1963 in Carson City, Navada. She
was born Nov. 19, 1942 in Oakland, Calif. and was the daughter of Anton and Mable
Irene (Cook) Rerich. He married 2nd, Frances Herald, and is living in Provo, Utah.
Source: 16

E39070 Elizabeth Ann Banning
E39071 David Jacob Banning
E39072 Andrew Walter Banning
E39073 Sarah Rose Banning
E39074 Michael Adam Banning

E19070 DELORES BANNING born Sept. 19, 1932 in Los Angeles, Calif. Source: 16

E19071 thru E19079 unknown children of E10812 & E10813

E19080 thru E19100 unknown children of E10814 thru E10820

E19101 NORMA LEE BANNING born Aug. 4, 1942 in Norman, Cleveland Co., Okla.
and married David Ray Summers in Feb 1963 in Okla. City. He is the son of Ray
Summers, born Jan. 1941. He works at Tinker Field in Midwest City, Okla.
Source: 16,20

E41001 David Tay Summers Jr.
E41002 Shawn Lee Summers

E19102 MICHAEL LARRY BANNING born July 8, 1944 in Norman, Cleveland Co.,
Okla. and married Cheri L. Johnson on Jan. 27, 1968 in Okla. City. She is the
daughter of Junior R. and Jo Ellen Johnson, Born March 17, 1949 in Okla. City. He
is a mechanic and served 8 years in the U.S. Army Reserves. Source: 16,20

E41003 Kelly Banning
E41004 Michael Banning

E19103 BONNIE McGAHEY born June 11, 1943 in Okla. She married Paul Ralph Kisselberg on Jan. 1, 1958. He was born July 10, 1938 in Frisco, Tex. They had three children, Gwendolyn S. (born 10-26-58, married William Arthur Pond), Rayma Lynn (born 3-10-61 Okla. City, married Daniel Wesley Whitten) and Renetta Kaye (born 7-17-62 Okla. City, married Floyd Bryan Melrien). She married 2nd, Michael Lee Billotte, who was born June 22, 1938 in Okla. City. Source: 16,20

E119104 MARIETA McGAHEY born Feb. 28, 1946 in Okla. and married Ronald F. Burnett on July 23, 1962. He is the son of Forest and Naomi Burnett, born Nov. 2, 1942 in Ada, Okla. They had one child, Daphne J. who was born Nov. 11, 1963 in Ikla. City, and married Steven T. Renolds in 1982. Marieta married 2nd, Robert Duane Tucker on Aug. 2, 1980. He was born July 30, 1941. Source: 16,20

E19105 REBA ANN LOUDERBACK born Jan. 11, 1953 in Okla. City and married Allen Carl Wallar on June 20, 1970 in Okla. City. He is the son of A.C. and Lois Wallar, born Sept. 28, 1949 in Okla. City. They lived in Okla. City and Dallas, Texas. Their children are, Mark Allen (born June 23, 1973, Okla. City) and Lesli Shantel (born July 21, 1976, Okla. City). Source: 16,20

E19106 MARLA ANN KROHMER born nov. 28, 1964 in Okla. City and married David Wayne Shook on Aug. 11, 1984 in Okla. City. He is the son of Harry A. and Peggy Jean (Hutchpath) Shook, born July 1, 1964 in Albuquerque, N.M. They live in Okla. City, where he is a typewriter tech and she is a college student. Source: 16,20

E19107 ROGER LEE BANNING born May 14, 1948 in Okla. City and married Beverly Yvonne Carter on July 10, 1970. She is the daughter of Joseph Elmer and Lillian Belle (Corgill) Carter, born Nov. 15, 1949 in Shawnee, Pottawatomie Co., Okla. He served in Viet-Nam, in the U.S. Army 1967-69. They live in Shawnee. Source: 16,20

E41101 Teri Michelle Banning
E41102 Randy Lance Banning

E19108 KAREN BETH BANNING born Dec. 19, 1949 in Okla. City and married William E. Vallandingham on March 30, 1968. He is the son of Edward H. and Anna Belle (Edwards) Vallandingham, born Aug. 30, 1946 in Oskaloosa, Mahaska Co., Iowa. They have lived in Iowa, Alaska and Okla. He served in the U.S. Army 1968-70, and is now a contractor. Source: 16,20

E41103 Clint Allen Vallandingham
E41104 Kristy Lea Vallandingham

E19109 BRUCE GREGORY BANNING born Sept. 14, 1953 in Midwest City, Okla. and married Deborah Ann Tipton Littleton on Aug. 31, 1984 in Tecumseh, Pottawatomie Co., Okla. She is the daughter of Jerry and Saundra Kay Tipton, born March 9, 1962 in Turlock, Calif. Source: 16,20

E19110 GLEN DAVID BANNING born March 25, 1959 in Okla. City and married Tammy Lachell Richardson on Nov. 27, 1987 in Tecumseh, Pottawatomie Co., Okla It was the second marriage for both. She was the daughter of Freddie and Jeanne

(Prichard) Richardson, born March 8, 1964 in Tecumseh. He is a machinest and she is a student. Source: 16,20

E19111 TERESA DELORES BANNING born May 3, 1960 in Okla. City. Source: 16,20

E19112 BETTY MAE BANNING born Jan. 25, 1942 East of Norman in Pottawatomie Co., Okla. She married Thomas Sherman Rogers Jr. on April 3, 1976 in Gainsville, Tex. He is the son of Thomas S. and Ruth (Wantland) Rogers, born Sept. 30, 1930 in Mountain View, Kiowa Co., Okla. They live in Okla. City and both are in sales or marketing. Source: 16,20

E41201 Thomas Sherman Rogers III

E19113 THOMAS LESTER BANNING born Dec. 1, 1944 in Shawnee, Pottawatomie Co., Okla. and married Carol Marie Bradley on June 21, 1963 in Del City, Okla. She is the daughter of Carl and Dolly Netty (Hicks) Bradley, born Nov. 20, 1947 in Okla. City. They live Choctaw, Okla where he works for AT&T and she sells real estate. Source: 16,20

E41202 Mark Anthony Banning
E41203 Misty Dianne Banning

E19114 JOHN WESLEY BANNING born Aug. 12, 1949 in Shawnee, Pottawatomie Co., Okla. Source: 16,20

E19115 KEITH DOUGLAS BANNING born Jan. 6, 1951 in Tulsa, Okla. and married Morgan Rose on June 26, 1976 in Tallahassee, Fla. She was born Dec. 30, 1953 in Reno, Nev. Source: 16,20

E19116 TAMARA KAY TACKER born Dec. 11, 1954 in Colorado Springs, Col. and married Gary Wayne McGuire on Nov. 3, 1979 in Miss. He was born April 8, 1952 in Okla. City, and served in the U.S. Army. They live in Del City, Okla. where he is a machine operator and she is a computer analyst. They have one child, Merrick Keaton Tacker McGuire, born Jan. 22, 1987 in Okla. City. Source: 16,20

E19117 JAMES PHILLIP TACKER born Nov. 17, 1959 in Okla. City. Source: 16,20

E19118 KATHERINE LYNN SCHLEICHER born Jan. 25, 1953 in Dayton, Montgomery Co., Ohio and married Donald Bayard Oakland Jr. on July 14, 1979. He is the son of Donald Bayard and Helen (Herrmann) Oakland, born Oct. 7, 1950 in Chicago, Ill. He is in public relations and she works for Mary Kay. They live in Wausau, Wisc. and have two daughters, Sarah Katherine (born Oct. 13, 1983) and Melissa Maxine (born Nov. 24, 1985). Source: 16,20,94

E19119 CHRIS LEE SCHLEICHER born Nov. 7, 1955 in Dayton, Montgomery Co., Ohio and married 1st, Mary Ann O'Connell. She is the daughter of John D. and Larae A. (Gebheim) O'Connell, born March 27, 1957 in Appleton, Outagamie Co., Wisc. He is a machinist and she is a teacher. they had a daughter, Tera Lee, born July 31, 1974. He married 2nd, Sylvia Gabriel Spielmann on Aug. 4, 1994. Sylvia is the daughter of Manfred Gustav and Elsa (Gottl) Spielmann Winters, born July 9, 1957. They live in Appleton, Wisc. Source: 16,20,94

E19120 DARR ANN UNDERWOOD born Nov. 12, 1951 in Hillsdale, Mich. and married 1st, Kurt Alan Wallace on Dec. 25, 1971. He is the son of Austin and Mildred Maxine (Lande) Wallace, born Sept. 17, 1948 in Burley, Cassia Co., Idaho. They live in Westminster, Col. and have a daughter, Leigh Ann, born April 27, 1973. She married 2nd, Bruce Edward Jablonski on Nov. 18, 1993. Bruce is the son of Chester & Mary Jablonski of Torrington, Conn. He was born May 25, 1952, is a West Point graduate and a mechanical engineer. Darr is a receptionist for an auditing company. They live in Arvada, Col. Source: 16,20,94

E19121 JOHN NELSON UNDERWOOD born Aug. 16, 1959 in Montrose, Col. He married Diana Lynn Martindale on Oct. 18, 1980 in Westminster, Adams Co., Col. She is the daughter of Bill Eugene and Vivian Virginia (Keein) Martindale, born June 6, 1960 in Denver, Col. They live in Thornton, Col. and have a daughter, Amanda Nicole, born June 11, 1985 and a son, Johnathan Eugene, born Oct. 24, 1988. Source: 16,20

E19122 and E19123 unused

E19124 SAMPSON WAYNE PORTER born Nov. 23, 1955 in Lebanon, Laclede Co., Mo. He married Debra Kay Donica and had 2 children, Matthew Wayne (born Dec. 1, 1976) and Gary Allen (born March 12, 1978). He married 2nd, Sandra Kay Walston on Sept. 30, 1981 in Lebanon, Mo. She is the daughter of Arthur Richard Roy and Amy Agnes (Garrett) Walston, born Aug. 17, 1954 in Redmond, Oregon. Their children are Amy Suzanne (born Nov. 28, 1980) and Aaron Marie (born Nov. 24, 1981). They live in Springfield, Mo. Source: 16,20,94

E19125 DELILAH ANN PORTER born Aug. 1, 1958 in Muskatine, Iowa and married Dean Edward Oliver, on Jan. 18, 1976. He is the son of Otis and Esther (Hill) Oliver, born Nov. 19, 1957 in Buffalo, Dallas Co., Mo. They live in Lebanon, Mo. and have a daughter, Elizabeth Ann who was born Nov. 16, 1976. Source: 16,20

E19126 EARL EDWARD PORTER born June 16, 1959 in Conway, Laclede Co., Mo. and married Jeanne Clara Jackson on March 28, 1987 in Niangua, Webster Co. Mo. She is the daughter of Daniel and Velma (Norris) Jackson, born Dec. 14, 1962 in Swell Springs, Mo. They live in Conway and have a daughter, Shanna Marie born Nov. 4, 1987 and a son, Timmy Ray born July 28, 1989. Source: 16,20,94

E19127 PATRICIA LYNN PORTER born Aug. 21, 1960 in Marshfield, Webster Co., Mo. and died Nov. 15, 1960. Source: 16,20

E19128 MARIA ABIGAIL PORTER born Sept. 28, 1962 in Conway, Laclede Co., Mo. and married Daniel Lawrence Oliver on Nov. 25, 1983. He is the son of Otis Oren and Esther (Hill) Oliver, born May 14, 1965 in Columbia, Boone Co., Mo. They live in Lebanon, Mo. and have two sons, Joshua Lawrence, born Nov. 21, 1986 and Justin Edward, born Aug. 24, 1989. Source: 16,20,94

E19129 MARY FRANCES PORTER born March 17, 1965 in Conway, Laclede Co., Mo. and married Kevin Robert Wallace on Jan. 16, 1987 in Lebanon, Mo. He is the son of Paul Kenneth and Alice Carole (Koge) Wallace of Lebanon, Mo., born Nov. 27, 1963 in Alton, Madison Co., Ill. He is a driller and they live in Lebanon, Mo. They have a daughter, Jamie Frances, born Oct. 6, 1990. Source: 16,20,94

E19130 JACK DEWAYNE BANNING born Feb. 20, 1949 in St. Louis, Mo. He served two years in the U.S. Navy and for 17 years was employed by Hall's Security Analysts, Inc. at Goddard Space Flight Center in Greenbelt, Md. He died March 4,

1996 and was buried at Chelteham Veterans Cemetery with full military hornors on March 11. Source: 16,20,94

E38976 LYNN D. GILLISPIE married Judy (???). They have 3 children, Kim, Kelly and Kassey. Source: 16,20

E38977 DONNIE R. SMITH married Lou (???). They have two children, Heather and Calvin.

E38978 RICKEY D. SMITH married Tammie (???). They have two children, Sam and Lea Ann.

E38979 VIRGINIA MAE ZAHN born Aug 24, 1950 in Texas.

E38980 BILLY MICHAEL ZAHN born Oct. 5, 1953 in Texas.

E38981 STEPHANIE MACHAEL GRIAGAR born Oct. 3, 1971.

E38982 thru E39000 not used

E39001 RONALD DEAN BANNING

E39002 KATHY BANNING

E39003 LISA BANNING

E39004 JOHN EARL BANNING born Nov. 9, 1959 in Cotulla, LaSalle County Texas. He is a fireman for the City of Austin, Tx. and was living in San Marcos in 1992. Source: 16,61

E39005 MARK STEVEN BANNING born Dec. 30, 1962 in Cotulla, LaSalle County Texas. Source: 16,61

E39006 BRYSON HARLAN

E39007 BRANDON HARLAN

E39008 BENAYCE HARLAN

E39009 SHEILA JEAN RIDGE born Jan. 20, 1948 in Cotulla, LaSalle County Texas She married John Bennie Churchill on Sept. 17, 1966 in Baytown, Texas He was the son of Joseph Benjamin Churchill and Edith Clairy, born Jan. 31, 1948 in Poteet, Atascosa County Texas He owns a trucking co. and they live in Baytown. Source: 16

        E50001 John Britton Churchill
        E50002 Janci Leshay Churchill

E39010 SHERRY LYMETTE RIDGE born July 15, 1949 in Pearsall, Frio County Texas She married David Donald Lefler on July 28, 1973 in Baytown, Texas He was the son of Leonard Doak Lefler and Hedwig Elizabeth Kornandosky, born March 8, 1946 in Pearsall. She is a teacher and he is a draftsman. Source: 16

        E50003 Jamie Lynn Lefler

E50004 Jacob Alan Lefler

E39011 MARILYN SUE RIDGE born Sept. 8, 1951 in Dilley, Frio County Texas She married Arthur Ray Starnes in Baytown, Texas on Sept. 11, 1971. He was the son of William Walter Starnes and Nora Louise Shull, born Dec. 31, 1950 in Dilley. She is a teacher and he is a chemical operator. They live in Baytown. Source: 16

E50005 Anthony Ryan Starnes
E50006 Autumn Rae Starnes
E50007 Adam Ross Starnes

E39012 CHARLES RUSSELL RIDGE born Dec. 14, 1955 in Baytown, Texas He married Kari Elliott on June 25, 1975 in Baytown. She was the daughter of James Kelly and Bobbie Nell Elliott, born Jan. 15, 1956. He is an Auditor and she is a Sec. They live in Baytown. Source: 16

E50008 Keli Diane Ridge
E50009 Kaelyn Nichole Ridge

E39013 RANDALL DEAN RIDGE born Feb. 27, 1952 in Dilley, Frio County Texas He died of polio on Aug. 16, 1955 in San Antonio, Texas He is buried in Dilley Cem. Source: 15,16

E39014 RHONDA LEA RIDGE born Dec. 29, 1959 in Bryan, Texas She married Clay Justin Hamlyn in Corpus Christi, Texas on Nov. 20, 1982. He was the son of John Harold Hamlyn and Marjorie Jacaquelin Burney, born Aug. 12, 1959 in Pampa, Texas She is a Sec. and he is a diesel mech. They live in Corpus Christi. Source: 16

E50010 Michelle Leigh Hamlyn

E39015 CHESTINA LOUISE RIDGE born Feb. 20, 1962 in Austin, Texas She married Douglas Simpson in Tanglewood, Williamson County Texas on Sept. 1, 1984. He was the son of Harold Eugene Simpson and Ruby Lorena Newman, born Feb. 2, 1962 in Rockdale, Milam County Texas She is a court reporter and he is an electrician. Source: 16

E39016 CLIFFORD ALAN RIDGE born June 30, 1965 in Pleasenton, Texas. Source: 16

E39017 SANDRA LEE RIDGE born June 15, 1971 in Casterville, Medina County Texas. Source: 16

E39018 ROY DEAN RIDGE born Aug. 21, 1974 in Dilley, Texas. Source: 16

E39019 RICHARD SCOTT RIDGE born April 4, 1953 in Dilley, Texas Married Remau Painter in Baytown, Texas on April 4, 1973. She was the daughter of Jr. and Jeanetta Painter, born in Baytown in Feb. 1956. They had 1 son. He married 2nd, Katrina Ann Smith on March 5, 1979 in Houston, Texas She was the daughter of Joe & Mary Smith, born Oct. 3, 1952 in Waco, Texas He is a computer tech. and lives in Scottsdale, Az. Source: 16

E50021 Richard Kirk Ridge
E50022 Angela Marie Ridge

E50023 Amanda Michelle Ridge

E39020 JEFFREY LEE RIDGE born Sept. 22, 1954 in Dilley, Texas. Source: 16

E39021 SUSAN GAIL RIDGE born July 2, 1957 in Dilley, Texas She married Robert
Charles Killian on Jan. 10, 1983 in Dilley, Texas He was the son of Walter Lawrence
Killian and Victoria Frances Jarzabek, born Jan. i6, 1952 in Newport New, W. Va.
She is a sect. and he is mgr. for a car rental co. Source: 16

E39022 KEVIN TRACY RIDGE born Sept 10, 1960 in Dilley, Texas. Source: 16

E39023 MICHAEL FORESTER BANNING born Aug. 10, 1959 in Dallas, Texas.
Married Rhonda Nonast of Bessie, Okla. in Bessie on June 24, 1978. She is the
daughter of Floyd E. Nonast. He works for the Alief School Dist. in Houston, Texas
where they live. Source: 16,61

E50031 Ashley Nicole Banning
E50032 Tyler Daniel Banning

E39024 CRAIG FRANCIS BANNING born Feb. 24, 1966 in Dallas, Texas. He
married Nancy U. Mendoza on Jan. 16, 1988 in San Marcos, Hays Co., Tex. She is
the daughter of Pauline Mendoza. He works for Delta Airlines and they were living in
Arlington, Tx. in 1993. Source: 16,61

E39025 MICHAEL LANE BROWN born Oct. 1, 1962 in Kingsville, Kleberg County
Texas Married Brenda Gay Roach on July 14, 1984 in Corpus Christi, Texas.
Source: 16

E39026 STEVEN DWIGHT BROWN born Sept. 27, 1964 in Dilley, Frio County Texas.
Source: 16

E39027 PAMELA ANN BROWN born Oct. 7, 1970 in Sinton, San Patricio County
Texas. Source: 16

E39028 SHERYL NADINE MATHEWS born March 14, 1964 in Sinton, San Patricio
County Texas. She married Mr. Foster on Aug. 13, 1983 in Dilley, Frio County
Texas. Source: 16

E39029 TODD MARVIN MATHEWS born Nov. 2, 1967 in Dilley, Frio County Texas.
Source: 16

E39030 JASON JAMES MATHEWS born Dec. 15, 1973 in Corpus Christi, Texas.
Source: 16

E39031 JUSTIN RUTHERFORD MATHEWS born Feb. 22, 1975 in Corpus Christi,
Texas. Source: 16

E39032 JOEY MATHEWS born July 25, 1980 in Corpus Christi, Texas. Source: 16

E39033 HEATHER SIDON SHOWALTER born Oct. 25, 1977 in San Antonio, Texas.
Source: 16

E39034 MATTHEW SCOTT SHOWALTER born Oct. 23, 1979 in Anchorage, Alaska.
Source: 16

E39035 JAMES BUCKLEY MATHEWS born March 25, 1977 in Corpus Christi, Texas. Source: 16

E39036 MELANIE JANE MATHEWS born March 20, 1979 in Corpus Christi, Texas. Source: 16

E39037 MAMIE ALICE MATHEWS born Oct. 16, 1980 in Corpus Christi, Texas. Source: 16

E39038 JACK REESE STEPHENSON JR. born Dec. 31, 1962 in Pearsall, Frio County Texas. Source: 16

E39039 LORI ANN STEPHENSON born Feb. 24, 1965 in Cotulla, LaSalle County Tx. She married Rickey Joe Lee on May 11, 1985. He was born Jan. 5, 1965. Source: 16

E39040 ROBB STEPHENSON born Sept. 21, 1969 in Cotulla, LaSalle County Texas. Source: 16

E39041 KIMBERLY MESCHELL STEPHENSON born July 22, 1976 in San Antonio, Texas. Source: 16

E39042 SCOTT STEPHENSON born Feb. 14, 1971 in Kingsville, Texas. Source: 16

E39043 RODNEY BRENT SMITH born Nov. 5, 1969 in Seguin, Guadalupe County Texas. Source: 16

E39044 SHANNON LYNNE SMITH born Aug. 20, 1975 in Seguin, Guadalupe County Texas. Source: 16

E39045 JUSTIN RICHARD SMITH born Feb. 13, 1968 in Dilley, Frio County Texas. Source: 16

E39046 TONYA LNYNETTE SMITH born May 14, 1972 in Dilley, Frio County Texas. Source: 16

E39047 JUSTIN   Source: 16

E39048 ASHLEY   Source: 16

E39049 thru E39064

E39065 JAMES MARK BANNING born April 10, 1980. Source: 16

E39066 TIFFANY WEBSTER born Nov. 9, 1982. Source: 16

E39067 JESSICA WEBSTER born Dec. 16, 1986. Source: 16

E39068 JOHN MOON 3rd born Oct. 19, 1983. Source: 16

E39069 DOVAVAN MOON born Feb. 2, 1987. Source: 16

E39070 ELIZABETH ANN BANNING born Oct. 13, 1966 in Jackson Miss. Source:

E39071 DAVID JACOB BANNING born Jan. 27, 1971 in Concord, Calif. Source: 16

E39072 ANDREW WALTER BANNING born July 18, 1972 in Concord, Calif.
Source: 16

E39073 SARAH ROSE BANNING born Jan. 16, 1976 in Tulsa, Okla. Source: 16

E39074 MICHAEL ADAM BANNING born May 27, 1977 in Bristow, Okla. Source: 16

E41001 DAVID RAY SUMMERS born Nov. 23, 1963 in Okla. City. Source: 16,20

E41002 SHAWN RAY SUMMERS born Sept. 9, 1967 in Okla. City. Source: 16,20

E41003 KELLY BANNING born Dec. 10, 1966 in Okla. City. Source: 16,20

E41004 MICHAEL BANNING born April 25, 1969 in Okla. City. Source: 16,20

E41101 TERI MICHELLE BANNING born April 13, 1974 in Shawnee, Pottawatomie
Co., Okla. Source: 16,20

E41102 RANDY LANCE BANNING born March 10, 1978 in Shawnee, Pottawatomie
Co., Okla. Source: 16,20

E41103 CLINT ALLEN VALLANDINGHAM born Aug. 26, 1975 in Anchorage, Alaska.
Source: 16,20

E41104 KRISTY LEA VALLANDINGHAM born Feb. 20, 1979 in McAlaster, Pittsburg
Co., Okla. Source: 16,20

E41201 THOMAS SHERMAN ROGERS III born July 24, 1978 in Okla. City. Source:
16,20

E41202 MARK ANTHONY BANNING born March 31, 1964 in Okla. City. Source:
16,20

E41203 MISTY DIANNE BANNING born Oct. 8, 1969 in Okla. City. Source: 16,20

E50001 JOHN BRITTON CHURCHILL born April 22, 1973 in Houston, Texas.
Source: 16

E50002 JANCI LESHAY CHURCHILL born July 19, 1974 in Dallas, Texas. Source:
16

E50003 JAMIE LYNN LEFLER born May 30, 1976 in Whorton, Whorton County
Texas. Source: 16

E50004 JACOB ALAN LEFLER born Feb. 22, 1980 in Whorton, Whorton
County Texas. Source: 16

E50005 ANTHONY RYAN STARNES born June 20, 1977 in San Antonio, Texas.
Source: 16

E50006 AUTUMN RAE STARNES born Sept. 8, 1978 in Baytown, Texas. Source: 16

E50007 ADAM ROSS STARNES born March 30, 1980 in Baytown, Texas. Source: 16

E50008 KELI DIANE RIDGE born April 30, 1981 in Bryan, Brazos County Texas. Source: 16

E50009 KAELYN NICHOLE RIDGE born Jan. 19, 1984 in Houston, Texas. Source: 16

E50010 MICHELLE LEIGH HAMLYN born April 11, 1984 in Corpus Christi, Texas. Source: 16

E50021 RICHARD KIRK RIDGE born Nov. 12, 1973 in Baytown, Texas. Source: 16

E50022 ANGELA MARIE RIDGE born June 4, 1984 in Corpus Christi, Texas. Source: 16

E50023 AMANDA MICHELLE RIDGE born Oct. 25, 1985 in Corpus Christi, Texas. Source: 16

E50031 ASHLEY NICOLE BANNING born Oct. 11, 1985 in Houston, Texas. Source: 16

E50032 TYLER DANIEL BANNING born March 30, 1990 in Houston, Tx. Source: 16

SAMUEL BANNING of LYME, CONN.

This arrangement of the origins of the "E" and "F" line is different than in Source 1. After much research by Mary Friedlander, Source 64, locating copies of wills, deeds and other primary records, the following arrangement has been proven. The error in Source 1 can be traced to a letter written in 1866 by Amelia Vinning Bells (or Eells), Source 41. Much of the information in Mrs. Bells letter is accurate, but this error was picked up by source 1 and publications that followed, including the first edition of this book.

F1 E1 JOHN BANNING born about 1652 and first appears in the records of New Shoreham, now Block Island, near the coast of Rhode Island in 1683 with his son John, mother unknown. He was made a freeman of that Colony on May 5, 1696. He was given 3 acres of land on Block Island by Peter George in 1689. He married Abigail Niles some time before June 11, 1701, perhaps 1689. She may have been John's 2nd wife and was the widow of John Niles, who died in 1685. They lived in New Shoreham, R.I. where he became Constable in 1704. John Banning and partners, Consider Tiffany and Ephraim Tiffany/ Edward Mott, of Block Island purchased a large tract of land at Joshuatown in Lyme Conn. on June 11, 1701. He and his son John (E2, F2) were both in New London Co, Conn. in Aug. 1702 signing papers on property they owned on Block Island. John, Abigail and her two sons, John & Ambrose Niles, moved to Lyme. He died in 1717. Source: 12,33,64, 70,72,73

F2 E2 John Banning Jr.

F2 E2 JOHN BANNING born 1678. His 1st wife was possibly Sarah Tiffany, born about 1678, the daughter of Humphrey and Elizabeth Tiffany. He married 2nd, in 1751, Mary Daniels Roland, who was born 1690. She was the widow of Daniel Daniels and also the widow of Henry Roland. He became an "admitted inhabitant" of Lyme Conn. on Jan. 17, 1714. John became the pound keeper at Joshua town on Dec. 31, 1718 and was chosen a "grandjurey man" Dec. 19, 1727. He died 1759. Source: 12,55,64,70

F3, E3 Elizabeth Banning (See E3)
F4, E4 Girl Banning   (See E4)
F5, E5 John Banning Jr. (See E5)
F6, E6 Samuel Banning (See F6)
F7, E7 Mary Banning   (See F7)
F8, E8 Hannah Banning (See F8)

F6 SAMUEL BANNING born about 1714, in Lyme, Conn. He married 1st, about 1738, Hannah (surname unknown) who was born about 1721. They had 3 sons and 5 daughters. Samuel sold his farm of 90 acres in Lyme and moved North about 50 miles to East Hartland, Conn. about 1765. Hannah died the 2nd night in Hartland. She is buried in the East Hartland Cemetery. Her Tombstone indicates she died in 1765 at age 45. Samuel married 2nd, Eleanor Barnes about 1768. She was an original member of the Hartland First Church to which she had transferred fron the Third Church in Lyme. Eleanor was the daughter of Thomas and Rebecca (Cone) Barnes of East Haddam, born 1724. They had 2 daughters. Samuel died on his son David's farm April 22, 1803. He is buried in East Hartland. Eleanor died a few months later on Sept. 29, 1803 in East Hartland. Source: 1,2,3,12,14, 15,40,41,45,64,83

F15 Samuel Banning Jr.
F16 Lucy Banning
F17 Sarah Banning
F18 Mary Banning
F19 Hannah Banning
F20 Abner Banning
F21 David Banning
F22 Rhoda Banning
F23 Rebecca Banning
F24 Lucretia Banning

F7 MARY BANNING born 1718 & married 1st, George Reed of Lyme, Ct. on March 4, 1743. Her father gave them 7 acres of land, probably as a wedding present. They had at least one son before George died in 1750. She married 2nd, John Wood of Lyme sometime between 1752 & 1755. George Reed (Jr.?) of Lyme, In June 1785, gave to John Wood (Jr.?) all rights he inherited to the 7 acres. Oct. of that year, Mary Wood gave her rights in the same 7 acres to her son, John Wood. Source: 12,64

F25 George Reed
F26 John Wood
F27 & F28 for children

F8 HANNAH BANNING born 1720 and married Joseph Wilder of East Haddam about 1747. He was a Deacon. Both were alive in 1757. Source: 12,64

F29 Elijah Wilder
F30 Thomas Wilder
F31 Hannah Wilder
F32 Sarah Wilder
F33 for children

F9 thru F14 unused

F15 SAMUEL BANNING Jr. born about 1739 in Lyme, Ct. Married 1st, Lydia Scovill {Scovel} on Sept. 13, 1764 in the 1st Congregational Church in East Haddam, Middlesex Co., Conn. She was the daughter of Edward and Deborah (Ackley) Scovel, born 1735 and died 1767. He married 2nd, Abigail Sterling, who was born May 12, 1742, and was the daughter of John and Jane (Ransom) Sterling of Lyme. His father bought him a new farm in West Hartland, and a yoke of cattle. Abigail was probably the mother of all of Samuel's children. Samuel died Feb. 26, 1815 in West Hartland, Conn. His will was dated May 10, 1813. He was an Ensign in the l5th Co. of the 18th Regiment, Conn. Militia. Abigail died April 12, 1818. Source: 1,2,3,12,13,14,17,40,41,64,71,83

F53 Abigail Banning
F54 Hannah Banning
F55 Samuel Banning
F56 Seba Banning
F57 John Banning
F58 Lucy Banning
F59 Ruth Banning
F60 Sterling Banning

F16 LUCY BANNING born about 1743 and married William Rathbone about 1764. He was born Jan. 1, 1740 to Daniel and Thankful (Higgins) Rathbone in Lyme, Conn. They lived in Hartland and Granby, Conn. where he died on Oct. 17, 1804. Source: 12,64

> F74 Diorama (Jedidah) Rathbone
> F75 Daniel Rathbone
> F76 Frances Rathbone
> F77 William Rathbone
> F78 Hannah Rathbone
> F79 Didy Rathbone
> F80 Johnathan Rathbone
> F81 Elijah Rathbone

F17 SARAH BANNING born about 1745 in Lyme, Conn. and married 1st Jonathan Mack in East Hartland. He was born in 1731 to Jonathan and Sarah (Bennet) Mack of Lyme. They had two daughters before he died in Hartland on Feb. 12, 1776. She married 2nd, Daniel Adams of East Hartland in Aug. 1783. They may have moved to N.Y. state. Source: 12,64

> F95 Hannah Mack
> F96 Sarah Mack
> F97 Elihu Adams
> F98 Guy Fitch Adams
> F99 Sophronia Adams

F18 MARY BANNING born about 1747 and married William Chapman in Hartland, Ct. about 1768. Source: 12,14,64

> F89 William Chapman
> F90 Mary Chapman
> F91 Jemima Chapman
> F92 David Chapman
> F93 Amasa Chapman
> F94 Ebenezer Chapman
> F94a Rhoda Chapman

F19 HANNAH BANNING born about 1750 and married Elijah Clark. He was born Sept 12, 1741 and was the son of Samuel and Hannah Champion Clark. Elijah died in 1790. Source: 12,64

> F82 Walter Clark
> F83 Abner Clark
> F84 Eber Clark
> F85 Charles Clark
> F86 Elijah Clark
> F87 Wilson Clark
> F88 Rhoda Clark

F20 ABNER BANNING born 1755 in East Hartland, Ct. He was over 6' tall with a strong muscular frame. He married Annah Sparrow, who was the daughter of John and Anna (Atwood) Sparrow of East Haddam, Mass. at the 1st Church of Christ, in

East Haddam, on April 3, 1777. She was born in 1752 and died in June 1820 in East Hartland. His father gave him 15 acres of land "about 3/4 miles N.W. of the center of East Hartland." He worked by day and by night he built the house they would live in the rest of their life. At one point he owned 600 acres, 1/2 of which he sold to purchase land in Ohio for his sons. He was in Pvt. in Captain Benjamin Hutchen's Co. of the 18th Reg. of the Conn. Militia, arriving in N.Y. on Aug. 18 and staying until Sept. 14, 1776. Abner and Annah transferred their church membership from Hartland Conn. to Windsor on Oct. 3, 1779. He died Aug. 28, 1829 of "Dropsy" and is buried in the East Hartland Cemetery. Source: 1,2,3,12,13,14,15,17,32,40,41,64,71,72,83

> F61 Malinda Banning
> F62 Benjamin Banning
> F63 Asahel Banning
> F64 Morgan Banning
> F65 Calvin Banning
> F66 Samuel Banning

F21 DAVID BANNING born July 12, 1756 in East Hartland, Ct. Married 3 times. 1st to Mary Rathbone of East Hartland on Feb. 3, 1779 in the Congregational Church in East Hartland, Hartford Co., Conn. She was born 1760 and died March 21, 1792. No issue. He married 2nd, on Nov. 10, 1794, Hannah Coe who was born May 7, 1766. She died April 15, 1808 in childbirth and is buried in the East Hartland Cemetery. They had 7 children. David married 3rd, Climena (???) He died Jan. 20, 1820 in East Hartland. His will indicates he had more than $16,000. in property, which was a large sum for the time. Source: 1,2,3,12,13,14,15,40,64,71,83

> F67 Josiah C. Banning
> F68 Schuyler Banning
> F69 James Banning
> F70 Benjamin Hector Banning
> F71 Polly Banning
> F72 Nancy Banning
> F73 Elmina Banning

F22 RHODA BANNING born about 1761 in Conn. and married Phineas Coe of Durham Conn. on Aug. {Oct.} 15, 1780 in the Congregational Church in East Hartland, Middlesex Co., Conn. on Oct. 15, 1780. He was born 1753 and died 1832. They lived on a farm adjoining that of Abner and David Banning. Source: 1,2,12,13,14,64,71

> F102 Miles Coe
> F103 Anson Coe
> F104 Polly Coe
> F105 Sallie Coe
> F106 thru F109 for children

F23 REBECCA BANNING Born about 1767 and married Daniel Bushnell on March 1, 1786 in the Congregational Church in East Hartland, Hartford Co., Ct. He was a contractor and builder. His name appears on the threshold of the church at Hartland Ct. "Built by Daniel Bushnell, raised June 10, 1801". He was born Dec. 18, 1763 in Lyme, Ct. and was the son of Capt. Alexander Bushnell (1739-1818) and his wife Chloe (Waite), (1738-1832). He served for a time in the Rev. war, at the age of 16.

The family moved to Trumbull Co., Ohio in 1803. She died in 1809 and was the 2nd adult buried in the cemetery in the middle of Hartford T/S. Source: 1,2,12,13,14,64,71

> F110 Lewis Bushnell
> F111 George W. Bushnell
> F112 Alexander Bushnell
> F113 & F114 for children

F24 LUCRETIA BANNING born about 1769 and died unmarried in East Hartland, Ct. on Dec. 11, 1851. Source: 12,64

F25 GEORGE REED about 1744. Source: 64

F26 JOHN WOOD born about 1752. Source: 64

F27 & F28 unknown children of F7

F29 ELIJAH WILDER born Sept. 10, 1752. Source: 64

F30 THOMAS WILDER born Feb. 26, 1756. Source: 64

F31 HANNAH WILDER born May 25, 1759. Source: 64

F32 SARAH WILDER born Oct. 19, 1762. Source: 64

F33 unknown children of F8

F34 thru F52 unused

F53 ABIGAIL BANNING She was born about 1766, married, had children and was dead by May 1813. Source: 12,64

> F180 thru F186 for children

F54 HANNAH BANNING born about 1767 and married Joseph Wilcox of Barkhamsted on Dec. 16, 1784 in Hartland, Conn. They had children. Source: 12,64

> F187 thru F194 for children

F55 SAMUEL BANNING born about 1768 and died July 31, 1788 at Hartland Conn. He died July 31, 1788 at Hartland. Source: 12,64

> F195 thru F201 for children

F56 SEBA BANNING baptized June 4, 1769 in East Hartland, Ct. She married Truman Holcomb of Barkhamsted on Jan. 2, 1794, and had children. Source: 12,14,64,72

> F219 thru F223 for children

F57 JOHN BANNING born March 14, 1773 and married Lydia Reede in Jan. 1801 in Hartland, Ct. She was born Aug. 23, 1782. Moved to Hartford, Trumbull Co., Ohio in the spring of 1817, where he was living in 1820 & 30. Lydia died Dec. 26, 1828. He was living with his son Nelson (F208) in Trumbull Co., Oh. in 1850. He died in

Hartford, Oh. on May 30, 1858. Source: 1,4,5,12,14,18,40,41,64

> F206 Harriet Banning
> F207 Orrill Banning
> F207A Charles Banning
> F208 Nelson Banning
> F209 John Banning
> F210 Useba M. Banning
> F211 Electa L. Banning
> F212 Lucy Banning
> F213 Dexter Banning
> F214 Abner Banning
> F215 Charles Banning
> F215A Lydia Banning
> F216 Gaylord Banning
> F217 Abigail Banning
> F218 Margaret Banning

F58 LUCY BANNING She married Norton Wright of Colebrook, Ct. on July 7, 1791 and had children. She was dead by May 1813. Source: 12,64

> F224 thru F229 for children

F59 RUTH BANNING baptised July 5, 1778 in East Hartland, Ct. She married Nathan Kent of Colebrook, Ct. They had no children. Source: 12,14,64,83

F60 STIRLING BANNING born Oct. 15, 1783 in West Hartland, Ct. where he lived and died on May 4, 1855. He married Eunice Nichols on March 1, 1805 in the West Hartland Congregational Church. She was born about 1778. She died some time after 1850. Source: 1,5,12,14,40,41,64,83,84

> F202 George Banning
> F203 Samuel Banning
> F204 Eunice Banning
> F205 for children.

F60a LYDIA BANNING born 176? and married Sylvester Stevens of Hartland, Conn. on Feb. 24, 1799 in Hartland. They had children. She was dead by 1813. Source: 12,64

> F230 thru F235 for children

F61 MALINDA BANNING married Richard Vinning Jr. of Grandby Ct. They were "both of tall and slender form." They had two children and lived in Johnstown, Ohio. He died about 1810 of "consumption" after 7 years of marriage. Four years later she married John Robins. About a year later, she died leaving Robins with a 2 week old girl. He left the children to be raised by their grandfather, Abner Banning. Source: 1,2,41,64

> F236 Amelia Vinning
> F237 Abner Vinning
> F238 Malinda Robins
> F239 Number not used

F62 BENJAMIN BANNING born 1780 in Ct. and married Mary Coe, the daughter of Elijah Coe of Hartland, Ct. Nov. 25, 1802 in East Hartland, Ct. She was born about 1781. They had one child. Mary died Feb. 22, 1804. Shortly there after, he joined a group of 20 families that left East Hartland for Ohio. He married Peggy Tanner of Canfield, Ohio on Nov. 20, 1804 in Trumbull Co., Oh. She was the daughter of Trial Tanner. They had 3 sons and upon her death of "consumption" about 1910, he married Mary Munger of Litchfield, Ct. in 1813. She was born in 1791 and died in 1868. They had 2 sons and 4 daughters and lived in Trumbull Co., Ohio. He enlisted as a private in the Conn. Militia on June 14, 1813 and remained until Aug. 25, 1814. He died in 1827 in Ohio of heart disease. His will is on file in Lorain Co., Ohio, where he owned land. Source: 1,2,14,32,40,41,49,64,83,88

> F240 Mary Coe Banning
> F241 Elisha Banning
> F242 Edmund Prior Banning
> F243 Elijah Banning
> F244 Laura Banning
> F245 Cornelia Ann Banning
> F246 Sylvester Vandalian Banning
> F247 Granville Banning
> F248 Maryette Banning
> F249 Amy Jane Banning

F63 ASAHEL BANNING born Aug. 4, 1782 and married Amelia Wilcox on Sept. 22, 1803 in East Hartland, Ct. They had 3 children. She was the daughter of Dr. Jeremiah Wilcox. She died of "consumption" after 11 years of marriage. He then married Denney (Dorcy ?) Crosby on Sept. 30, 1817 in Trumbull Co., Oh. She was born 1790 in Conn. They had 7 children and lived in Vernon, Ohio. He died May 7, 1837 in Gustavus, Ohio, after being struck on the head by a falling timber. She was living in Trumbull Co., Oh in 1850 and was alive in 1866. His estate papers are on file in Trumbull Co., Ohio. Source: 1,2,4,5,12,14,40,41,64,83,88

> F250 Abner Wilcox Banning
> F251 Amelia Banning
> F252 Melinda Banning
> F253 David Banning
> F254 Jeremiah Wilcox Banning
> F255 Timothy Banning
> F256 Mary Ann Banning
> F257 Mary Ann Banning
> F258 Converse Banning
> F259 Stoddard Banning
> F260 Melinda Banning

F64 MORGAN BANNING born Sept. 26, 1784 and married Laura Tanner on Jan. 15, 1805 in Trumbull Co., Oh. They had no children. Moved to Oh. in 1804. The 1820 census has him in Trumbull Co., Oh. He died Nov. 31, 1821, and is buried in the Giddings-Brown Cemetery in Vernon Township, Ohio. His estate papers were filed in Trumbull Co in 1821. Source: 1,2,4,5,12,14,15,40,41,49,64,83,88

F65 CALVIN BANNING born Dec. 28, 1786 in East Hartland, Hartford Co., Ct. Married Lucy Case of Grandby, Ct. He was a professor of religion. Enlisted in the Ct. Militia at New London from June 21 thru June 25, 1813. He was a very tall man and died April 2, 1864. She then lived with her son Almon. She died Jan. 24, 1881.

Both are buried in the East Hartland Cemetery. Source: 1,2,3,12,13,14,
15,40,41,64,83

F261 Edwin Rutherford Banning
F262 Jerome Banning
F263 Almon C. Banning
F264 Calvin Hudson Banning
F265 Lucy Lovina Banning
F266 Lavinia Lucelia Banning

F66 SAMUEL BANNING born Oct. 18, 1789 and married Betsy Jones the youngest
daughter of Samuel Jones of East Hartland, Ct. on Sept. 14, 1809 in Hartland,
Hartford Co., Ct. They moved to Vernon, Ohio in 1810 and lived on the East side of
Vernon Creek where 4 of the 5 sons of Abner had farms. He died in 1819 near
Vernon, Ohio. She was born April 22, 1789 in Ct. and was living with her son
James in Hartland in 1850. She died March 12, 1862 and is buried in East Hartland
Cemetery. His estate papers were filed in Trumbull Co., Ohio in 1821. Source:
1,2,5,12,13,14,15,40,41,64,83

F267 Ruth A. Banning
F268 James M. Banning
F269 Nancy Banning
F270 Samuel W. Banning
F271 Abbie E. Banning

F67 JOSIAH C. BANNING born Sept. 9, 1796 in Hartland, Conn. Married Affiah
Giddings (Gideon), daughter of Benjamin Giddings (Gideon), on May 30, 1820 in
East Hartland. They had one child. She died after 1829, he married 2nd, Edith
Cowdery (Cowdry) of East Hartland on July 21, 1833. Edith was born 1810 in Conn.
Josiah moved to New Hartford, Ct. where he died Nov. 8, 1848. He was a
physician. As a young man, his father bought him the "ride", of the physician of E.
Hartland, along with a house and lot in the center of the "ride"'. Source: 1,5,12,13,
14,40,64,83

F271a Roswell H. Banning
F271b Affiah Climena Banning
F271c Zeruiah Emily Banning
F271d Benjamin Oscar Banning
F272   Josiah Banning
F272a Edith Banning
F272b Martha Banning
F273   David Banning
F274   Mary Banning

F68 SCHUYLER BANNING born Feb. 2, 1800 in Ct. He married Rhoda Miller on Nov.
28, 1822 in Hartland Hollow, Ct. She was born Oct. 26, 1801 in Ct. He died in June
30, 1844 of "consumption". She died Sept. 5, 1855. Both are buried in the East
Hartland Cemetery. Source: 1,5,14,15,40,64,83

F275 Talcot T. Banning
F276 Silas B. Banning
F277 for children

F69 JAMES BANNING born May 4, 1801 in Conn. and married Emily (Amerilla)

(Aurilla) (Amrilla) Miller on March 20, 1822 in East Hartland, Ct. She was the sister of George Miller. See F71. She was born about 1806 in Ct. James was a farmer and died 1888. His wife died Sept. 9, 1894. Source: 1,5,12,14,40,64,83

> F278 Philura Banning
> F279 Lester Miller Banning
> F280 Albert J. Banning
> F281 Josephine Banning
> F282 & F283 for children

F70 BENJAMIN HECTOR BANNING born Aug. 15, 1808 and married Martha B. Cowdry, sister of the wife of Dr. Josiah Banning, F67, on Oct. 22, 1829 in East Hartland, Ct. She was born about 1811 in Ct. They lived in East Hartland, Ct. close to his brother Schuyler on part of his dad's farm. He died Feb. 8, 1845 of "consumption". She died Nov. 9, 1870 and both are buried in the East Hartland Cemetery. Source: 1,5,14,15,40,64,83

> F284 Ambrose C. Banning
> F285 John Banning
> F285A Lucy Banning
> F286 Edith Elmina Banning
> F287 Jane Banning
> F287A Emily Lucretia Banning
> F288 Cowdry Banning
> F288A Nancy Banning

F71 POLLY BANNING born March 11, 1798 married George Miller of Hartland on Jan. 8, 1816 in East Hartland. She died March 21, 1822. See F69. Source: 1,14,64,83

> F289 thru F297 for children

F72 NANCY BANNING born Oct. 21, 1804 in Hartland, Ct. She married John Church on Aug. 29, 1821 in East Hartland. Source: 1,14,64,83

> F298 thru F305 for children

F73 ELMINA BANNING born Nov. 1, 1806 and baptized March 15, 1807 in Hartland, Ct. She married Edward Miller of Northington on April 13, 1825 in East Hartland and died in Sept. 1827. Source: 1,14,64,83

> F306 thru F313 for children

F74 DIORAMA (JEDIDAH) RATHBONE born July 28, 1765 in Hartford Conn. Source: 64

F75 DANIEL RATHBONE born Feb. 24, 1767 at Granby, Ct. and married Deziah Rice on Sept. 15, 1784. She was born in Granby on June 21, 1764 and died April 24, 1863. He died in 1854. Source: 12,64

F76 FRANCES RATHBONE born Oct. 7, 1768 in Hartford, Ct. She married a Mr. Rice. Source: 12,64

F77 WILLIAM RATHBONE born Aug. 10, 1770 in Hartford, Ct. and married Dorotha Rockwell. Source: 12,64

F78 HANNAH RATHBONE born April 7, 1773 in Granby and married A. Rockwell. Source: 12,64

F79 DIDY RATHBONE no inforamation. (May be the same as F74.) Source: 64

F80 JONATHAN RATHBONE born Nov. 6, 1780 in Granby, Ct. Source: 12,64

F81 ELIJAH RATHBONE born July 14, 1783 in Granby, Ct. and married Cynthia Messenger on Nov. 11, 1802. Source: 12,64

F82 WALTER CLARK no information. Source: 1

F83 ABNER CLARK no information. Source: 1

F84 EBER CLARK no information. Source: 1

F85 CHARLES CLARK no information. Source: 1

F86 ELIJAH CLARK no information. Source: 1

F87 WILSON CLARK no information. Source: 1

F88 RHODA CLARK died as an infant. Source: 1

F89 WILLIAM CHAPMAN baptized June 11, 1779 and married Sylvia (???) befor 1796. Source: 1,14,64

F90 MARY CHAPMAN born 1771 and married Elijah Spelman in 1788. She died Aug. 18, 1814. Source: 1,14,64

F91 JEMIMA CHAPMAN baptized June 11, 1779 and married Aaron Cowles of Hartland on Nov. 27, 1794. Source: 14,64

F92 DAVID CHAPMAN baptized June 11, 1779. Source: 1,14,64

F93 AMASA CHAPMAN baptized Jan. 2, 1780 and married Polly Exeter of Hartland, Ct. on Aug. 27, 1807. Source: 14,64

F94 EBENEZER CHAPMAN baptized Sept. 12, 1784. Source: 1,14,64

F94a RHODA CHAPMAN baptized March 3, 1782 and married Willis Wright of Hartland on June 30, 1802. Source: 1,14,64

F95 HANNAH MACK no information. Source: 64

F96 SARAH MACK no information. Source: 64

F97 ELIHU ADAMS born May 20, 1784 in Preston, Ct. Source: 12,64

F98 GUY FITCH ADAMS born July 13, 1786 in Preston, Ct. Source: 12,64

F99 SOPHRONIA ADAMS born March 7, 1790 in Preston, Ct. Source: 12,64

F100 thru F101 unused

F102 MILES COE married Lucy Boran of East Hartland, Conn. Source: 1,64

F103 ANSON COE married Anna Haines of Granby, Ct. on May 12, 1807. Source: 1,64

F104 POLLY COE no information. Source: 1

F105 SALLIE COE no information. Source: 1

F106 thru F109 unknown COE children

F110 LEWIS BUSHNELL no information. Source: 1

F111 GEORGE W. BUSHNELL born Aug. 11, 1800 in Hartland, Conn. Source: 1,2

F112 ALEXANDER BUSHNELL he married his 2nd cousin, (F212) the daughter of John Banning. Source: 1

F113 & F114 unknown children of F23

F115 thru F120 unknown children of F24

F121 thru F179 unused

F180 thru F201 unknown children of F53 thru F55

F314 thru F487 for children

F202 GEORGE BANNING born about 1804 in Ct. The 1860 & 1870 census has him living with his brother, F203, in Trumbull Co. Ohio. He was listed as a farm laborer. Source: 5,6,7,84

F488 thru F494 for children

F203 SAMUEL BANNING born about 1806 in Hartland, Conn. and married Harriet French on Sept. 14, 1828. She was born in Hartland to William & Rachel French about 1806 and died Jan. 20, 1881. Samuel and some of his family mover to Ohio in 1856. He was living with his brother, F202, in Trumbull Co. Ohio in the 1860 & 1870 census. The census makes no mention of Harriet and in 1870 is listed as "insane". Samuel died Oct. 1, 1876 in New Haven Ct. and is buried in Westville Cemetery. Source: 5,6,7,84,86

> F495 Julia M. Banning
> F496 Nicholas Banning
> F497 Abigail Banning
> F498 Andrew J. Banning
> F499 Eunice "Jennie" Banning

F204 EUNICE BANNING She married Wyllys Goodwin Marsh on Oct. 17, 1837 in Hartland, Conn. He was born in 1814 and was from Cleveland, Ohio. He died on March 22, 1838. Source: 5,84 See F499

F500 thru F505 for children

F205 unknown child of F56

F506 thru F524 for children

F206 HARRIET BANNING born Nov. 29, 1801 and married Nelson Andrews on March 1, 1823. They then "went west". She died March 20, 1874. Source: 1,18,41,64

F525 thru F531 for children.

F207 ORRILL BANNING born Feb. 25, 1803 and married Orris Mason on Oct. 16, 1823. She died Sept. 21, 1885. Source: 18,64

F532 thru F538 for children

F207A CHARLES BANNING born July 19, 1804 and died Jan. 29, 1813. He did not marry. Source: 18,64

F208 NELSON BANNING born March 2, 1806 in Conn. He married Florilla Lane on Feb. 25, 1836 in Trumbull Co., Oh. She was the sister of Sarah, see F209. They had no children. He died May 7, 1889. Source: 1,5,18,41,64,88

F209 JOHN BANNING born March 1, 1808 and married Sarah Lane on March 14, 1833 in Trumbull Co., Oh. She was the sister of Florilla, see F208. He died on Dec. 30, 1897 in Hartford, Ohio. Source: 1,18,40,41,64,88

F539 & F540 Two Banning sons

F210 USEBA M. BANNING born Jan. 3, 1810 and married Ransom Johnson on Oct. 2, 1835. She died Jan. 8, 1896. Source: 18,64

F541 thru F545 for children

F211 ELECTA L. BANNING born Feb. 14, 1812 and married Edward B. Cartright on March 5, 1844. She died June 15, 1860. Source: 13,18,64

F546 thru F550 for children

F212 LUCY BANNING born May 9, 1814 and married her 2nd cousin, Alexander Bushnell (F112) on Aug. 19, 1833. She died Jan. 2, 1893 Source: 1,18,41,64

F551 thru F555 for children.

F213 DEXTER BANNING born Dec. 1, 1816 and died Jan. 14, 1846. Source: 18,64

F556 thru F560 for children

F214 ABNER BANNING born March 11, 1819 in Ohio and married Harriet Marie Borden on May 27, 1841 in Trumbull Co., Oh. She was born bout 1824 in Ohio. They had no children. He died April 11, 1902. Source: 1,5,18,41,64,88

F215 CHARLES BANNING born May 13, 1822 in Ohio and married Amelia A. (Catharine?) Kepner on Feb. 2, 1843 in Trumbull Co., Oh. She was born about 1821 in

Ohio. They lived in Hartford, Trumbull Co., Ohio. He died there on Dec. 24, 1903.
Source: 1,5,18,40,41,64,88

F561 Wright H. Banning
F562 Banning Daughter

F215A LYDIA BANNING born Sept. 13, 1824 and died April 1, 1834. Source: 18,64

F216 GAYLORD BANNING born Nov. 11, 1828 in Ohio and married Maria Sophronia
Jones on March 29, 1849 in Trumbull Co., Oh. She was the daughter of John R.
and Sophronia Bowen Jones, born April 1, 1831 in Ohio. They had 2 sons and 3
daughters. She died Sept. 12, 1903 and he passed away Jan. 11, 1904. Source:
1,5,13,18,40,41,64,88

F563 Dexter Banning
F564 Alda Banning
F565 Flora Banning
F566 J. Grant Banning
F567 Lucy Banning

F217 thru F235 unknown children of F58 thru F60.

F236 AMELIA VINNING born about 1804. Her father died when she was 6 years old.
She married Rev. Osiah Sheldon Bells (or Eells) of Johnstown, Ohio (born about
1795) and had 3 children, Samuel, Jerome and Henry, all of whom died in the Civil
War. She provided much of the information on this branch. Source: 1,41,83

F237 ABNER VINNING born about 1806 and married Ellen Benton of Clinesburg, Ct.
They moved to Quincy, Ill. and had one son, John. He served in the Civil War, was
captured at Pittsburgh Landing and was a POW for 6 months. Source: 1,41

F238 MALINDA ROBINS born about 1815. After the death of her father, she lived with
her grandfather, Abner Banning. He died when she was 14. She then lived with
F236. She taught school from age 15 to 22 and married Lorenzo Bushnell of
Wawakeom, Iowa when she was 22. They had 2 boys & 3 girls. Source: 1,41

F239 Number not used

F240 MARY COE BANNING born about 1803 and married Mr. Granger. They lived in
Ohio and then moved to Conn. where she died. Source: 1,41

F578 Henry Granger
F579 Mary Granger

F241 ELISHA BANNING died an infant. Source: 1

F242 EDMUND PRIOR BANNING born June 3, 1810 in Canfield, Ohio. He was
brought up by his mothers parents, Trial Tanner in Canfield. He married Lydia
Humiston Peck of Centerville, on May 7, 1834. She was the daughter of Charles
and Elizabeth (Crowley) Peck. They lived in Ohio, and then moved to New York
City. She was born Dec. 30, 1811 in Harpersfield, Delaware Co., N.Y., where her
family had moved from Wellingford, Ct. He was a surgeon of advanced ideas, and
founded the field of Orthopedics. In 1838 he was the first Physician to open the
abdominal cavity to correct an intestinal obstruction. In 1839 he invented the first

mechanical device for the permanent cure of Enteroptosis. He was a writer and lecturer of great power. He died Jan. 8, 1892 in Mt. Vernon, N.Y. She died there April 30, 1888. Source: 1,40,41,64,85

> F580 "Walter" Archibald Tanner Banning
> F581 Emma Elmira Banning
> F582 Wells Tanner Banning
> F583 Elizabeth Emma Banning
> F584 Emily Laura Banning
> F585 Edmund Prior Banning
> F586 William Peck Banning
> F587 Georgiana Mary Banning
> F588 Caroline Louise Banning
> F589 Archibald Tanner Banning

F243 ELIJAH T. BANNING born about 1807 and married Patience Hart. She was born about 1809/10 in Vermont. He lived in Conn. and was in Lorain Co. Ohio by 1827. They lived in Rochester, Oh., where he was place in an "insane retreat". The 1850 census places him in Lorain Co., Oh. as a farmer. He had a large family and died in Ohio. Source: 1,5,40,41,49,64

> F590 Ann Banning
> F591 Archibald Banning
> F592 Cornelia Banning
> F593 thru F595 for children

F244 LAURA BANNING married Mr. Robins. She was left a widow with 1 child. Source: 1,41

> F596 -------? Robins

F245 CORNELIA ANN BANNING born May 4, 1815 in Litchfield, Ct. Married William Wasson on June 30, 1836 in Richland, Oh. She probably married Franklin peck Sept. 4, 1860 in Ashland Co., Oh. She died Nov. 25, 1897 in Harrisburg, Pa. Source: 1,13,41

> F597 Warren Hastings Wasson
> F598 Mary Jane Wasson
> F599 Robella Bell Wasson
> F600 unknown child

F246 SYLVESTER VANDALIAN BANNING born in Ct. (or N.Y. in 1815). Married Laura Tinker of Mass. Feb. 22, 1835 in Lorain Co., Oh. They lived in Colorado, where she died at Pikes Peak in 1860. He was a tailor by trade & died in Lincoln, Neb. in 1886. (The 1850 census lists his as a farmer, born in N.Y., living with Sarah and children in Lorain Co., Oh.) Source: 1,5,13,40,41

> F601 George Sylvester Banning
> F602 Edmund Prior Banning
> F603 William Wasson Banning
> F604 Benjamin Franklin Banning
> F605 Silas Robin Banning
> F606 Granville Banning

F247 GRANVILLE BANNING died an infant. Source: 1,41

F248 MARYETTE BANNING died an infant. Source: 1,41

F249 AMY JANE BANNING born in 1821 in Oh. and married William E.G. Caldwell on
Oct. 11, 1840 in Richland Co., Oh. He was born in 1817 and died in 1890. They
lived in Iowa City, Iowa. She died in 1909. Source: 1,13,32

> F607 Laura Caldwell
> F6O8 Charles CaldWell
> F609 Myra N. Caldwell

F250 ABNER WILCOX BANNING born Dec. 30, 1804 in Vernon, Ohio. He married
Juliete Melissa Brockway of Hartford, Oh. on Oct. 22, 1829 in Hartford, Trumbull
Co., Oh. They lived in Richfield, Oh. where he died Nov. 20, 1844. She was born in
1809 and died May 10, 1880. His will was filled in Summit Co., Ohio. She married
2nd, Samuel Button and was living in Summit Co., Oh in 1850. Source:
1,4,5,12,40,41,88

> F610 Dudley Wells Banning
> F611 George Edward Banning
> F612 Mary Amelia Banning
> F613 Malinda Stevens Banning
> F614 Jerusha Adelaide Banning
> F615 Martha Ellen Banning

F251 AMELIA BANNING born 1804-10 and married Stoddard C. Stevens. See F252.
Source: 1,41

> F616 Seth Banning Stevens

F252 MELINDA BANNING born 1810-20. After the death of her sister, she married
her sister's husband Stoddard C. Stevens. See F251. She died in Covington, Ky.
Source: 1,41

> F617 Amelia C. Stevens

F253 DAVID BANNING born April 11, 1819 in Vernon, Trumbull Co., Ohio. He
married Asenath C. Bradley of Waterford, Pa. on April 28, 1848. They lived in
Cincinnati, Oh. She was born June 16, 1824. David and his brother, Jeremiah,
entered the commission business in 1847 in Cincinnati. They had the business for
25 years and both became wealthy. He died March 8, 1901 in Cincinnati. Source:
1,40,41

> F618 Charles Banning
> F619 Blanche Banning
> F620 Kate Banning
> F621 Star Banning
> F622 William Banning
> F623 Harry Banning

F254 JEREMIAH WILCOX BANNING born Aug. 17, 1820 in Vernon, Oh. He married
Ruth Adelia Gates on Oct. 11, 1843 in Trumbull Co., Ohio. She was born March 5,
1823 and died Nov. 27, 1875. They moved to Cincinnati, Oh. in 1847 and went into

the commission business with his brother David. They were instrumental in getting the first bridge across the Ohio River in that area. Source: 1,13,40,41,88

> F624 Myron Banning
> F625 Hannah Luella Banning
> F626 Leland Gates Banning

F255 TIMOTHY BANNING born March 5, 1822 in Vernon, Oh. He married Sarah Peabody on May 10, 1855 in Gustavus, Oh. (Source 88 indicates marriage on Nov. 11, 1844 in Trumbull Co., Oh. She was born Jan. 24, 1824 in Gustavus. He was a farmer and living in Trumbull Co., Oh. in 1850, with real estate valued at $1000. He died April 24, 1882 in Geneva, Oh. Source: 1,5,40.41,88

> F627 Asenath Banning
> F628 Amelia Banning
> F629 Ella C. Banning

F256 MARY ANN BANNING died as an infant. Source: 1

F257 MARY ANN BANNING born Sept. 30, 1826 in Vernon, Oh. She married Dr. Benjamin H. Peabody on May 25, 1849 in Gustavus, Trumbull Co., Oh. They lived in Pittsburgh, Pa. He was born in 1825. Source: 1,13,41

> F630 George Lee Peabody
> F631 Mary A. Peabody

F258 CONVERSE BANNING born April 10, 1830 in Vernon, Oh. He died unmarried on July 12, 18?? in Covington, Ky. Source: 1,40

F259 STODDARD BANNING born June 15, 1832 in Vernon, Oh. He married Alma M. Clisby on June 4, 1856 in Gustavus, Oh. She was born March 21, 1833 and died Jan. 4, 1867 in Gustavus. He was farming in Trumbull CO., Oh. in 1850. Source: 1,5,40,41,88

> F632 Frank Banning
> F633 Estella Banning
> F634 Alma Banning

F260 MELINDA BANNING born Oct. 22, 1834 in Vernon, Oh. She married Newton Robins on April 18, 1855 in Gustavus, Oh. He was born Nov. 19, 1832 and died May 30, 1900 in Kinsman, Oh. They lived in Kinsman where she died the same time he did. Source: 1,5,41

> F635 Mary Robins
> F636 Burt Robins
> F637 Lee C. Robins

F261 EDWIN RUTHERFORD BANNING born 1815 in Hartland, Conn. He married Orphania Hall. She was born in 1813 in Tolbard, Mass. They lived in Hartland where he was a farmer and died Sept. 23, 1854. He is buried in East Hartland Cemetery. Source: 1,5,15,40,41,64,83

> F638 Richmond Hall Banning
> F639 Charles Banning

F640 Lamira Banning
F641 Charles Banning (2nd)

F262 JEROME BANNING born Nov. 16, 1818 in Hartford, Ct. He married Sarah Maria
Hall, the daughter of Nathan and Elizabeth Wolcott Hall in 1840. She was born in
1821 in Robinson, Ill. They had 4 children and lived in Robinson, where she died
Sept. 3, 1851. He was farming in Licking Co., Oh in 1850. He married 2nd, Jane
Noris in 1857 in Robinson. They had 3 children and he died May 30, 1898 in
Robinson. Source: 1,5,40,41,68

F642 Edwin Rutherford Banning
F643 Gordon Hall Banning
F644 Hiram B. Banning
F645 Franklin Banning
F646 James C. Banning
F647 Almon Hall Banning
F648 Minta Banning

F263 ALMON CASE BANNING born about 1827 and baptized April 29, 1835 in East
Hartland, Ct. He married his cousin, Lucy A. Banning (F285A). He was a carpenter
and lived on the old homestead of his grandfather (F16). He served as a 1st Lieut.
in Co. E, 25th C.V.I. during the Civil War and was wounded near New Orleans in
1865. She died June 11, 1865. He married 2nd, Emily L. (???) (see F287a), who
was born about 1823 and died Feb. 10, 1905. He died Sept. 1, 1896 and both all
three are buried in the East Hartland Cemetery. Source: 1,14,12, 15,40,41,64,83

F649 Orcencia Banning
F650 Pearl Banning
F651 Frank Almon Banning
F652 Lucy Banning

F264 CALVIN HUDSON BANNING born about 1832 and baptized April 29, 1835 in
East Hartland, Ct. He died Oct. 25, 1852 and is buried in the East Hartland
Cemetery. Source: 1,12,14,15,40,64,83

F653 thru F658 for children

F265 LUCY LOVINA (LARINA) BANNING born about 1830 in East Hartland, Ct. and
baptized April 29, 1835 in East Hartland. Source: 1,5,12,14,64,83

F659 thru F663 for children

F266 LAVINIA LUCELIA (LARINY) BANNING baptized April 29, 1835 in East
Hartland, Ct. Source: 1,12,14,64,83

F664 thru F669 for children

F267 RUTH A. BANNING born Feb. 21, 1813. She married Bryant Marks of West
Hartland, Ct. on May 5, 1835 in Hartland, Hartford Co., Ct. Source: 1,13,14,41,83

F670 Cornelius Marks
F671 Maria Marks
F672 Bryant Marks
F673 thru F675 for children

F268 JAMES M. BANNING born Nov. 29, 1815. He died unmarried on May 29, 1851 and is buried in the East Hartland Cemetery. Source: 1,5,12,15,41,64,83

F269 NANCY BANNING born Nov. 6, 1817. She married Elijah Chapman Spelman on Sept. 25, 1868. He was the son of Deacon Elijah and Mary (Chapman) Spelman born Jan. 6, 1802 in Granville, Mass. Nancy was his 3rd wife. He was 1st a shoemaker and then a farmer. He died Oct.8, 1889 and she died April 1904, both in Granville, Mass. Source: 1,5,37,41

F676 thru F681 for children

F270 SAMUEL W. BANNING born March 20, 1820 in Ct. He married Albina Case on July 13, 1842 in Hartland, Hartford Co., Ct. She died and he married again. He died March 15, 1850 of typhoid fever. He was a farmer. Source: 1,5,13,40

F682 Dora Banning
F683 Samuel Banning
F684 Addie "Noyes" Banning

F271 ABBIE E. BANNING born 1825 in Hartland, Ct. She married Edwin Ozias Goodwin. They lived in East Hartland, Ct. and had one child. He was a Justice of the Peace for 10 years and a representative to the General Assembly of 1886, as well as a director of the Dime Savings Bank of Hartford, Ct. Source: 1

F685 ------? Goodwin

F271a ROSWELL H. BANNING born May 21, 1821 in Hartland, Hartford Co., Ct. He died Nov. 23, 1833 of "consumption" and is buried in the East Hartland Cemetery. Source: 13,15,83

F271b AFFIAH CLIMENA BANNING born April 7, 1824 in Hartland, Hartford Co., Conn. Source: 13

F686 thru F691 for children

F271c ZERUIAH EMILY BANNING born Feb. 24, 1827 in Hartland, Hartford Co., Conn. Source: 13

F692 and F695 for children

F271d BENJAMIN OSCAR BANNING born Aug. 1, 1829 in Hartland, Hartford Co., Ct. He died June 28, 1833. Source: 13,14,83

F272 JOSIAH BANNING born 1834 in Conn. He was a Clockmaker in 1850. Source: 5

F696 thru F701 for children

F272a EDITH BANNING born 1836 in Ct. Source: 5

F702 and F703 for children

F272b MARTHA BANNING born 1838 in New York. Source: 5

F704 and F705 for children

F273 DAVID BANNING born 1847 in Conn. Source: 1,5,40

F706 thru F709 for children

F274 MARY BANNING she was born 1839 in New York and married George Miller of Hartland Hollow, Ct. After her marriage, her father deeded her a piece of land and furnished a house for them. Source: 1,5

F710 thru F713 for children

F275 TALCOT T. BANNING he was born Sept. 24, 1823 in Ct. and lived on the old homestead. He died in Conn. Source: 1,5,40

F714 thru F717 for children

F276 SILAS B. BANNING he was born April 10, 1825 in Ct. and lived at the old homestead with his brother Talcot. He died in Conn. Source: 1,5,40

F718 thru F721 for children

F277 unknown children of F68

F724 thru F727 for children

F278 PHILURA BANNING born about 1825 in Ct. She married Moses C. Gates on Sept. 1, 1846 in East Hartland, Ct. Source: 12,14,64,83

F728 thru F730 for children

F279 LESTER MILLER BANNING born about 1833 in Ct. Source: 1,5,40

F731 thru F734 for children

F280 ALBERT J. BANNING born about 1840 in Ct. Source: 1,5,40

F735 thru F738 for children

F281 JOSEPHINE BANNING born about 1835 in Ct. Source: 5

F739 thru F742 for children

F282 & F283 unknown children of F69

F743 thru F750 for children

F284 AMBROSE COWDREY BANNING baptized June 30, 1831 in East Hartland, Ct. Source: 1,14,40,83

F751 William Banning
F752 thru F755 for children

F285 JOHN BANNING died as an infant. Source: 1

F285A LUCY BANNING born about 1822 in Ct. She married her cousin, Almon
Banning. See F263. She died June 11, 1865 and is buried in the East Hartland
Cemetery. Source: 5,15,64,83

F286 EDITH ELMINA (ALMIRA) BANNING born about 1833 in Ct. Counted twice in
1850 census, listed with an aunt (F67). She married Ashbel J. Selby of Hartland on
March 4 or Dec. 16, 1856. Source: 5,12,14,64,83

F756 thru F757 for children

F287 JANE BANNING born about 1836 in Ct. Source: 1,5

F758 thru F759 for children

F287A EMILY LUCRETIA BANNING baptized Sept. 3, 1843 in East Hartland, Ct. I
think she married Almon C. Banning (F263) and died Feb. 10, 1905. Source:
5,12,14,15,64,83

F760 for children

F288 COWDRY A. BANNING born Oct. 29, 1837. He married Martha Bowers on May
8, 1862. She was the daughter of William Bowers (B 13 Aug. 1806, D 2 Dec. 1866)
and Lavinia R. Northway (B 3 June 1808, D 17 Jan. 1892) born June 11, 1841. He
died Sept. 23, 1918 and is buried in the East Hartland Cemetery. Source:
1,5,15,40,64,83

F761 William Bowers Banning
F762 Clara Jane Banning

F288A NANCY BANNING baptized in 1843 in East Hartland, Ct. Source: 14,83

F763 for children

F290 thru F305 Unknown children of F71 & F72

F306 thru F313 unknown children of F73

F764 thru F793 for children

F314 thru F487 unknown children of F180 thru F201

F794 thru F1159 for children

F488 thru F494 unknown children of F202

F1160 thru F1199 for children

F495 JULIA M. BANNING born Aug. 5, 1829 in Barkhamsted, Litchfield Co., Ct., and
married Philemon R. Allen on Sept 16, 1850 in Hartland, Hartford Co., Ct. He was
the son of Joel and Rhosanna (Case) Allen, born June 10, 1829 in Barkhamsted.
The 1850 census has her living with her father and grandparents (F56) in Hartford.
Philemon was died April 18, 1852 in Panama, Central America. She married 2nd,

Edwin H. Abbott, to whom she was married at the time of the 1860 census. Edwin was born about 1829 and died in Beaufort, S.C. in the Civil War on Aug. 7, 1862. He was a member of the 6th Ct. Infantry Band. She married 3rd, Lucius C. Utley, whom she divorced. Lucius was born about 1809. She married 4th, Dr. Cyrus F. Edison to whom she was married and living in New Haven, Ct. at the time of the 1880 and 1900 census. It was the 2nd marriage for Cyrus. Dr. Edison was a cancer specialist in New Haven, Ct. and died in Hartford about 1909. Julia died Sept. 7, 1910 in New Haven Ct. Source: 5,13,16,84

> F1200 Hermon Adelbert Allen
> F1201 Julia A. Allen
> F1202 George Franklin Abbott

F496 NICHOLAS BANNING born 1831 in Hartland, Conn., and married Antoinette "Annett" Rice on April 24, 1854. She was born about 1839. He married 2nd Mary Ward on Feb. 28, 1876 in Woodbury, Conn. She was born about 1838 in Ireland. The 1850 census has him living with his father and grandparents (F56) in Hartford, Conn. Nicholas died on Oct. 8, 1894 in Woodbury. He was a farmer. Mary was living with her sister-in-law (F495) in New Haven in 1910. Source: 5,84

> F1203 Estella Banning
> F1204 Howard E. Banning
> F1205 Artemesia Banning
> F1206 Josephene Banning
> F1207 Sevator Banning

F497 ABIGAIL "ABBIE" BANNING born about 1833 in Hartland, Conn. The 1850 census has her living with her father and grandparents (F56) in Hartford, Conn. She married Edward Ozias Goodwin on May 10, 1865. She divorced him. She was listed as a "Clairvoyant" in the 1895 New Haven Directory. Abigail died on May 8, 1896 in New Haven. (Something wrong, see F271) Source: 5,84

> F1208 Child Goodwin

F498 ANDREW J. BANNING born March 14, 1835 in Hartland Ct. The 1850 census has him living with his father and grandparents (F56) in Hartford. He did not get along with his father, so at age 16, with his mothers help, he got a job on a whaling ship. He eventually ecame a harpooner. It appears that he left his ship in New Zealand and about 1861 he arrived in Queensland, Australia. He married Margaret Lee on July 6, 1865 at St. John's Church, Brisbane, Queensland, Australia. She was the eldest daughter of Patrick and Ellen (O'Keefe) Lee of Labamalogga, County Cork, Ireland, born Dec. 26, 1840 in Labamalogga county. They went to Cairns, Queensland where they had a small hotel. They sold the hotel and purchased 400 acres of land on Freshwater Creek, three miles from Redlynch and called it "Glen Retreat". They left the farm in the care of Wilfred (Bill), and moved to the Perth, Australia area about 1895 and started a road building supply company. He became a wealthy man & lived in Victoria Park. Andrew was listed as a farmer in 1898 and as a contractor at the time of his death. He smoked a pipe and had a good handwriting. Andrew & Margaret lived at the corner of Hamilton St. and Fremantle Road. She died on March 17, 1919 in Canning, Western Australia. He died on December 16, 1916 of cancer in Canning, Western Australia. Both are buried in the Roman Catholic Cemetery, Karakatta, in Perth. Source: 5,17,20,84,86

> F1209 Andrew J. Banning Jr.

                    F1210 Ellen Maria Banning
                    F1211 Wilfred (Bill) Banning
                    F1212 Maurice Banning
                    F1213 Harriet (Hattie) Banning
                    F1214 Samuel Banning
                    F1215 Lucia Anne Banning
                    F1216 Alvin Seth Banning

F499 EUNICE "JENNIE" BANNING born 1837 in Ct. The 1850 census has her living
    with her father and grandparents (F56) in Hartford. She married (2nd?), Samuel W.
    Ralph on Sept. 5, 1857 in Trumbull Co., Ohio. He was born in Vernon, Ohio in
    1858(?) and died on April 27, 1897 in New Haven, Ct. She died on Aug. 31, 1897 in
    New Haven and is buried in Blake Street Cemetery. They were living in Vernon,
    Trumbull Co. Ohio in 1860, living one dwelling away from F202 & F203. He was a
    carpenter/wagon maker. The 1870 & 80 census places them in Mecca, Trumbull
    Co. Ohio. She was listed as a "Clairvoyant" in the 1895 New Haven Directory.
    (Something maybe wrong here. See F204) Source: 5,6,7,8,84,88

                    F1217 thru F1219 for children

F500 thru F538 unknown children of F204 thru F207

                    F1220 thru F1309 for children

F539 thru F560 unknown children of F209 thru F213

                    F1310 thru F1390 for children

F561 WRIGHT H. BANNING married Selma A. McFarland on April 4, 1879. She Was
    born June 22, 1859. Source: 1,40

                    F1391 Charles G. Banning
                    F1392 Alice P. Banning
                    F1393 Marshall Banning

F562 Daughter of F215

                    F1394 for children

F563 DEXTER BANNING born March 17, 1850 and married Luella Bacon. Source:
    18,64

                    F1395 & F1396 for children

F564 ALDA BANNING born May 1, 1854 and married Charles H. Turner. Source:
    18,64

                    F1397 & F1398 for children

F565 FLORA BANNING born July 5, 1856 and married William Ott. Source: 18,64

                    F1399 for children

F566 J. GRANT BANNING born April 7, 1864 in Hartford, Ohio and married Minnie

Brown on July 17 1886. They liven in Hartford until 1913, when they moved to Kinsman, Oh. Both of them were living in Kinsman in July 1934. Source: 18,30,64,84

> F1400a Grace Banning
> F1400b Blanch Banning
> F1400c Edna Banning
> F1400d Gail Banning
> F1400e Ruby Banning
> F1400f Cora Banning
> F1400g Frank Banning
> F1400h Ralph Banning
> F1400i Selms Banning
> F1400j Leon Banning
> F1400k Harry Banning
> F1400l Arthur Banning
> F1400m Ward Banning
> F1400n Jay Banning

F567 LUCY BANNING born July 29, 1866 and died Aug. 15, 1867. Source: 18,64

F568 thru F577 unknown children of F217 & F218

F578 HENRY GRANGER he died at age 17 of heart disease. Source: 1,41

F579 MARY GRANGER no information. Source: 1

F580 "WALTER" ARCHIBALD TANNER BANNING born March 20, 1835 in Titusville, Pa. and died as an infant. Source: 1

F581 EMMA ELMIRA BANNING born Sept. 16, 1836 in Titusville, Pa. She died Nov. 9, 1840 in Titusville. Source: 1

F582 WELLS TANNER BANNING born Oct.10, 1838 in Titusville, Pa. Graduated with a B.A. degree from New York Free Academy (later known as College of New York) at the age of 19. He married Flora Hutchens on March 28, 1862 in Providence, R.I. They lived in New York. He was a brilliant musician and had a marvelous mind. He had a strong literary ability and was a man of lofty ideals. He could play 7 games of Chess at one time, blindfolded. He died July 28, 1862 in Providence. There were no children. Source: 1

F583 ELIZABETH EMMA BANNING born Dec. 9, 1840 in Titusville, Pa. She died unmarried on July 11, 1876 in Washington, D.C. Source: 1

F584 EMILY LAURA BANNING born Dec. 8, 1842 in Titusville, Pa. She married Tompkins Mann on May 2, 1881 in New York City. They had no children. Source: 1

F585 EDMUND PRIOR BANNING born Jan. 1, 1845 in Titusville, Pa. He was educated in the public schools of New York City and the Irving Institute at Tarrytown-on-the-Hudson. At the outbreak of the Civil War, he enlisted in the U.S. Marine Corp in 1861 and served in the fleets of Admiral Porter, Foot, Dahlgren, Farragut, Goldsboro and Wilks. At the request of all his commanding officers, on July 2, 1864 President Lincoln commissioned him a Lieutenant in the Marine Corp.

He married Florida Morrell on July 10, 1866 in Pensacola, Fla. They had no children and she died in New Orleans on June 16, 1869. In Oct. of 1869, he resigned his commission. He married 2nd, Mary E. Ordway on July 20, 1871 at Milton, on the Hudson. They lived in New York City and had no children. For many years he was a partner with his father in the practice of medicine and surgery in New York city. Mary died in Brooklyn, N.Y. He married 3rd, Carina B. Carpenter on Feb. 11, 1879 in Geneva, N.Y. They lived in Ft. Wayne, Ind. and Chicago, Ill. this marriage ended in divorce. He then married Anna Mae Taylor. She was the daughter of William David and Ida Elvira (Clark) Taylor, born Feb. 24/25 1887 in Jefferson Co. Pa. She died in 1965. For many years, Edmund lectured at the Herring Medical College on Orthopedics, which science his father was the originator. The 1908 graduating class gave him a special award. He was a Physician of considerable note. Source: 1,64,85

          F1401 Lydia Jennette Banning
          F1402 Carina Carpenter Banning
          F1403 Florida Jennette Banning
          F1404 Dahlgren Banning
          F1404a Maesimund Banning

F586 WILLIAM PECK BANNING born May 23, 1847 in New York City and died as an infant. Source: 1

F587 GEORGIANA MARY BANNING born April 17, 1849 in Titusville, Pa. She died unmarried on July 24, 1876 at Catskill, on the Hudson. Source: 1

F588 CAROLINE LOUISE BANNING born March 20, 1852 in New York City. She married Dr. Gilbert Clark of Centerville, Pa. on Jan. 12, 1880 in N.Y.C. He was born Feb. 15, 1849 in Centerville and died in Parkersburg, W. Va. at the home of his daughter, Grace. They lived in Centerville, where she died Aug. 6, 1934. Source: 1

          F1405 Ralph Clark
          F1406 Inez Clark
          F1407 Grace Clark
          F1408 Archie Clark
          F1409 Carina Clark

F589 ARCHIBALD TANNER BANNING born May 15, 1854 in New York City. He married Jessie Ionia Helena Lockwood on July 23, 1879 in Mount Vernon, N.Y. She was born in 1860 and died in 1945. They lived in Mount Vernon where he was a physician. He held the office of Coroner for many years and was often elected by a larger majority than any other candidate for any other office, in that election. He died in 1924. Source: 1,64,81

          F1410 William Peck Banning
          F1411 Elizabeth Georgiana Banning
          F1412 Archibald Tanner Banning Jr.
          F1413 Laura Banning
          F1414 Benjamin Blain Banning
          F1415 George Wright Banning
          F1416 Lydia Esther Banning
          F1417 Jessie Octavia Banning
          F1418 Theodore Roosevelt Banning
          F1419 John Peck Banning

F590 ANN BANNING born 1832 in Ohio. Source: 5

F1420 thru F1425 for children

F591 ARCHIBALD BANNING born 1836 in Ohio and married Eliza A. Smith on Nov. 11, 1860 in Ashland Co., Oh. Source: 5,13

F1425 thru F1429 for children

F592 CORNELIA BANNING born 1843 in Ohio. Source: 5

F1430 thru F1434 for children

F592 thru F595 unknown children of F243

F1435 thru F1449 for children

F596 -----? ROBINS no information Source: 1

F597 WARREN HASTINGS WASSON born April 27, 1842 and died Nov. 2, 1903. Source: 1

F598 MARY JANE WASSON born Feb. 8, 1844. She married, had 4 children and lived in Mansfield, Oh. Source: 1

F599 ROBELLA BELL WASSON born in 1851 and had one child. Source: 1

F600 Unknown WASSON child no information

F601 GEORGE SYLVSTER BANNING born July 1836 in Lorine Co., Oh. He married Melethia Rose. She was born 1840 in Ill. (or N.Y.). They lived in Glenwood Springs, Col. and were living in Carbondale, Col. in 1900. Source: 1,5,10,40

        F1450 Herbert Banning
        F1451 Edward Banning
        F1452 Albert Banning

F602 EDMUND PRIOR BANNING born 1838 in Pa. (or Ohio). He married Frances VanDrillar from Germany. They had no children. He died in 1885 in Death (?) Nevada. Source: 1,5

F603 WILLIAM WASSON BANNING born July 30, 1840 in Larine Co., Ohio (or Pa.). He married Martha Elitha Markham in 1877 in Colusa Co., Calif. They lived in Colusa Co. where she was born Dec. 19, 1857. He died there Nov. 17, 1903. Source: 1,5,40

        F1453 Alice Armelda Banning
        F1454 Edmund Wasson Banning
        F1455 Nellie Victoria Banning
        F1456 David Fletcher Banning
        F1457 Emma Gertrude Banning
        F1458 Francis Merrian Banning
        F1459 Annie Pearl Banning

F1460 Martha Williams Banning
F1461 Jasper James Banning
F1462 Myrtle Viola Banning

F604 BENJAMIN FRANKLIN BANNING born 1842 in Lorine Co., Ohio (or Pa.). He married ----? Thomas in 1866 in Ill. They had 9 children and lived in Carbondale, Col. Source: 1,5

F1463 thru F1471 for children

F605 SILAS ROBIN BANNING born 1843-44 in Lorine Co., Ohio (or Pa.). He died unmarried about 1874 in Red River Co., Calif. Source: 1,5

F606 GRANVILLE BANNING born 1846-48 in Lorine Co., Ohio. He was a miner in Chaffee Co., Col. in 1880. He lived in Calif. and died unmarried in Oct. 1895 in Colusa Co., Calif. Source: 1,5,8

F607 LAURA CALDWELL born 1843 and married William Ashton in 1861. He was born in 1834 and died in 1896. They lived in Iowa City, Iowa and had at least one girl, Jessie. Source: 1,32

F608 CHARLES CALDWELL no information. Source: 1

F609 MYRA N. CALDWELL born 1854 in Ashland, Ohio. She married Daniel Burns Crapsey in 1873. He was born in 1848. Source: 1,32

F610 DUDLEY WILLS BANNING born July 50, 1630 in Richfield, Ohio, and died as an infant. Source: 1

F611 GEORGE EDWARD BANNING born Nov. 13, 1831 in Summit Co., Richfield, Oh. He married Melinda Walker on Nov. 15, 1865 in Newberg, Cuyahoga Co., Oh. They lived in Cleveland, Oh. where he died Oct. 27, 1895. He was well known locally for his ability on the violin. Source: 1,5,13,40,41

F1472 Ida May Banning
F1473 Eva Louise Banning
F1474 Edna Maria Banning
F1475 Georgiana Blanch Banning

F612 MARY AMELIA BANNING born Nov. 12, 1833 in Summit Co., Richfield, Oh. She married Joseph A. Spencer on July 2, 1862 in Princeton, Ill. and Lincoln, Neb. They lived in Brooklyn, Iowa and had no children. She died April 18, 1900. Source: 1,5,41

F613 MELINDA STEVENS BANNING born Nov. 21, 1835 in Summit Co., Richfield, Oh. She married Leverett Clark on Jan. 2, 1859 in Twinsburg, Summit Co., Oh. They lived in Syracuse and Lincoln, Neb. She died about 1910. Source: 1,5,13

F1476 Charles Elmore Clark
F1477 Jennie Clark

F614 JERUSHA ADELAIDE BANNING born July 17, 1839 in Summit Co., Richfield, Oh. She married Peter H. Krum (or Rumer) on Aug. 29, 1857 in Cuyahoga Co., Oh. They lived in Indianapolis and North Manchester, Ind. and had no children. He was connected with the National Press Assoc. in Indianapolis. Source: 1,5,13

F615 MARTHA ELLEN BANNING born Sept. 5, 1843 in Summit Co., Richfield, Oh. She married Dezell E. Hollister on Sept. 5, 1861 in Bedford, CuyahOga Co., Oh. They lived in Rensalear, Ind. Source: 1,5,13

F1478 George E. Hollister
F1479 J. Spencer Hollister
F1480 Pearl Louise Hollister

F616 SETH BANNING STEVENS he died soon after he married. Source: 1,41

F617 AMELIA C. STEVENS she married Benjamin Stanhope, an Army Officer, and had Benjamin and Phillip. Source: 1

F618 CHARLES BANNING born Sept. 15, 1850 in Covington, Ky. He drowned in the Ohio River on Sept. 18, 1855. Source: 1,41

F619 BLANCHE BANNING born Nov. 11, 1853 in Covington, Ky. and died Sept. 18, 1861. Source: 1

F620 KATE BANNING born March 26, 1857 in Covington, Ky. She lived in Cincinnati, Oh., where she died unmarried. Source: 1

F621 STAR BANNING born May 13, 1860 in Covington, Ky. and died Oct. 20, 1865. Source: 1

F622 WILLIAM BANNING born July 1, 1863 in Covington, Ky. and died July 3, 1863. Source: 1

F623 HARRY BANNING born July 1, 1863 in Covington, Ky. and died April 29, 1874. He was the twin of William, F622. Source: 1

F624 MYRON BANNING born April 24, 1845 in Gustavus, Oh. He died unmarried on Oct.16, 1907 in Cincinnati, Oh. Source: 1

F625 HANNA LUELLA BANNING born Oct. 10, 1852 in Covington, Ky. She lived in Cincinnati, Oh., and died unmarried. Source: 1

F626 LELAND GATES BANNING born Sept. 27, 1860 in Covington, Ky. He married Jessie Paul Clinton of Avondale, Cincinnati, Oh. on Nov. 27, 1890. She was born July 19, 1863 and the daughter of Charles Clinton and Harriet P. Stanteme. She died March 27, 1903 in Cincinnati. He was in the lumber business in Cincinnati. They had no children. Source: 1

F627 ASENATH (SENNA) BANNING born 1846 in Trumbull Co., Oh. and married Frank A. Giddings on May 11, 1869 in Ashtabula Co., Oh. They lived in Cleveland, Oh. and had no children. Source: 1,5

F628 AMELIA BANNING born 1848 in Trumbull Co., Oh. and married Dennis Warren. They lived in Los Angeles, Calif. and had no children. Source: 1,5

F629 ELLA C. BANNING born March 26, 1852. She married Thomas McKinnie of Cleveland, Oh. on Aug. 5, 1888. They lived in Los Angeles, Calif. Source: 1

F630 GEORGE LEE PEABODY born July 21, 1851 in Parkman, Oh. He married Marion Griswold on Dec. 31, 1875 and had 3 children. Source: 1

F631 MARY R. PEABODY born Sept. 15, 1857 in Covington, Ky. She married Edward Bigelow on Sept. 15, 1880. Source: 1

F632 FRANK BANNING born July 27, 1857 in Gustavus, Oh. He married Linda Gillett in 1886 in Kinsman, Oh. They lived in Kinsman and had no children. Source: 1

F633 ESTELLA BANNING born Sept. 10, 1860 in Gustavus, Oh. Source: 1

F1482 thru F1487 for children

F634 ALMA BANNING born May 6, 1863 in Gustavus, Oh. She died Feb. 13, 1889 in Cleveland, Oh. Source: 1

F1488 thru F1493 for children.

F635 MARY ROBINS born Dec. 23, 1860 in Gustavus, Oh. She married Robert Cochran on May 27, 1880 in Gustavus and lived in Salem, Oh.

F636 BURT ROBINS born Aug. 12, 1863 in Gustavus, Oh. He married Nettie Kindleside on Feb. 16, 1888 in Gustavus. They lived in Cleveland, Oh. Source: 1

F637 LEE C. ROBINS born Jan. 7, 1869 in Gusavus, Oh. He married Carrie Starrett on Jan. 14, 1897 in Pittsburgh, Pa., where they lived. Source: 1

F638 RICHMOND HALL BANNING born March 9, 1841 in Hartland, Ct. He married Mary Philena Wilcoxson of North Canton, Ct. on June 18, 1863 in East Hartland, Hartford Co., Ct. She was born in 1842. They lived in South Windsor, Ct. where he was a large tobacco grower. He enlisted in the 10th Ct. Reg. in 1864 and became a Col. Source: 1,5,13,41

F1494 Nellie Orphania Banning
F1495 Fannie Mira Banning

F639 CHARLES BANNING born in 1845 and died April 22 1856. Source: 1,15,64

F640 LAMIRA BANNING born in 1848 in Hartland, Ct. She married Campbell P. Case of Simsbury, Ct. on Dec. 7, 1877. in Hartland. He was born about 1844. Source: 1,5,12,64

F1496 Charles P. Case
F1497 Jessie L. Case
F1498 Ida Mae Case

F641 CHARLES BANNING (2nd) born 1850 and died April 22, 1856. he is buried in the East Hartland Cemetery. Source: 1,15,83

F642 EDWIN RUTHERFORD BANNING born Sept. 19, 1842 in Hartford, Ct. He was in Licking Co., Oh. in 1850. He married Anna W. Lilly on April 4, 1872 in

Greencastle, Ind. They lived in Hughdell, Cumberland Co., Ill. where he was a Physician. He died on March 8, 1874 in Greencastle. Source: 1,5

F1499 Lilly Rutherford Banning

F643 GORDON HALL BANNING born in 1845 and died April 25, 1865 in Robinson, Ill. He was in Licking Co., Oh in 1850. Source: 1,5

F1500 thru F1503 for children

F644 HIRAM B. BANNING born in 1848 in Ct. (or Ohio). He was in Licking Co., Oh in 1850. As a child the family moved to Crawford Co., Ill. He married Emma Barlow of Robinson, Ill. in 1865 in Robinson. In 1872 Hiram and his brother moved to Union Co., Iowa. He and his family then moved to Neosha, Mo. Source: 1,5,30,68

    F1504 Hudson Almon Banning
    F1505 Dora Banning
    F1506 Henry Banning
    F1507 Selma Banning
    F1508 Laura Banning

F645 FRANKLIN B. BANNING born March 17, 1850 in Licking Co., Ohio. As a small child the family moved to Crawford Co., Ill. and in 1872 he and his brother moved to Union Co., Iowa. He married Matilda (Tillie) Jane Botleman of Creston, Iowa on March 6, 1878 in Creston. She was the daughter of Newton M. and Minerva (Swearingen)(Nov. 11, 1834 - April 14, 1924) Botleman, born Nov. 13, 1858 in Adams Co., Ohio. They lived in Shannon City, Union Co., Iowa, where he owned the Red Cedar Stock Farm. He died March 16, 1918 in Des Moines, Iowa of pneumonia and was buried in Shannon City. She died July 1, 1939 in Union Co., Iowa. Source: 1,5,12,30,68

F1509 Burton Alva Banning

F646 JAMES C. BANNING born 1858 in Ill. He married ----? Manhart. He died in Ill. in 1898. Source: 1

    F1510 Platha Banning
    F1511 Emma Banning
    F1512 Cleopatra Banning
    F1513 Milo H. Banning

F647 ALMON HALL BANNING born 1860 in Ill. He married Rilla Star in 1885 in Ill. They lived in Ill. where he died in 1898. Source: 1

    F1514 Bessie Banning
    F1515 Myra Banning
    F1516 Guy Banning
    F1517 Lola Banning
    F1518 Maud Banning
    F1519 Almon Banning

F648 MINTA BANNING born 186? in Ill. and married -----? Patterson of Garden City, Ks. Source: 1

F1520 thru F1525 for children

F649 ORCENCIA BANNING born Hartland, Ct. She married Stephen Bates, and they lived in Hartland, Ct. Source: 1

F1526 thru F1531 for children.

F650 PEARL BANNING born Hartland, Ct. and married Berth Wright. They had 2 children and lived and died in Hartland. Source: 1

F1532 & F1533 for children

F651 FRANK ALMON BANNING born in Simsbury, Ct. where he lived. Source: 1

F1534 Pearl Banning
F1535 Ellert Banning
F1536 Junie Banning
F1537 & F1538 for children

F652 LUCY BANNING no information. Source: 1

F1539 thru F1544 for children

F653 thru F658 unknown children of F264

F1545 thru Fl550 for children

F659 thru F669 for unknown children of F265 & F266

F670 CORNELIUS MARKS no information. Source: 1

F671 MARIA MARKS no information. Source: 1

F672 BRYANT MARKS no information. Source: 1

F673 thru F675 for unknown Marks children

F676 thru F681 for unknown Spellman children

F682 DORA BANNING born about 1860 in Old Lyme, Ct. At age 15, her father left her and the other children, who were taken care of by others. Source: 1

F1551 thru F1556 for children

F683 SAMUEL BANNING born 186? in Old Lyme, Ct. He lived in Chicago for a time. Source: 1

F1557 thru F1562 for children.

F684 ADDIE "NOYES" BANNING born 186? in Old Lyme, Ct. She married Cortland A. Stanton of Wethersfield, Ct. They lived in Wethersfield. Source: 1

F1563 Grace N. Stanton
F1564 Ralph Winthrop Stanton

F1565 Harry Albert Stanton
F1566 Edith Stanton
F1567 Winthrop Stanton
F1568 Maud Stanton
F1569 Ruth Noyes Stanton

F685 ------? GOODWIN born Oct. 2, 1866 and died an infant.

F686 thru F709 for unknown children of F271a thru F273

F1581 thru F1631 for children

F710 thru F713 unknown Miller children

F714 thru F723 unknown children of F275 & F276

F1632 thru F1672 for children

F724 thru F730 unknown children of F277 & F278

F1673 thru F1703 for children

F731 thru F738 unknown children of F279 & F280

F1704 thru F1734 for children

F739 thru F750 unknown children of F281 thru F283

F1735 thru F1765 for children

F751 WILLIAM BANNING no information. Source: 1

F1766 thru F1771 for children

F752 thru F755 unknown Banning children of F284

F1772 thru F1792 for children

F756 thru F760 unknown children of F286

F761 WILLIAM BOWERS BANNING born July 26, 1867 and died Sept. 7, 1888. He
is buried in the East Hartland Cemetery. Source: 1,15,64,83

F1793 & F1794 for children

F762 CLARA JANE BANNING born April 17, 1873. She married Charles S. Leonard
on March 8, 1893. Source: 1

F1795 Deforest Leonard
F1796 Lloyd Earl Leonard

F763 thru F1199 unknown children of F306 thru F494

F1797 thru F2600 for children

F1200 HERMON ADELBERT ALLEN born June 8, 1851 in New Hartford, Litchfield Co., Ct. and died Nov. 21, 1917 in Hampton, Windham Co. Ct. He married Catherine "Kate" Dorrance Greenslit Sept. 13, 1881 in Brooklyn, Windham Co. Ct. She was born May 26, 1853 in Hampton, Windham Co., Ct. and died June 25, 1940 in Llanerch, Delaware Co., Pa. The 1880 census has them living in New Haven, Ct. They had a child, Grace Dorrance Allen, (1883-1965) that married Frank Joseph Moran (1881-1948). Source: 16,84

F1201 JULIA A. ALLEN born 1852 in New Hartford, Litchfield Co., Ct. and died in 1924 in West Haven, New Haven Co., Ct. She married Stiles T. Platt On Dec. 23, 1891 in New Haven, Ct. Stiles was born in 1844 and died in 1928. Both are buried in Oakgrove Cemetery in West Haven, Ct. Source: 16,84

F1202 GEORGE FRANKLIN ABBOTT born Aug. 8, 1858 in New Hartford, Ct. and died Dec. 11, 1922. He married 1st, Dora W. Beach, who was dead by 1900. He married 2nd, Josephine Richie. By 1920 he was living in Orange, Ct. They had a son and a daughter. Source: 16,84

F1203 ESTELLA BANNING born about 1856 and married a Mr. Bassett. Source: 84

F2601 thru F2604 for children

F1204 HOWARD E. BANNING born Oct. 12, 1859. Source: 84

F2605 thru F2608 for children

F1205 ARTEMESIA BANNING born about 1867. Source: 84

F2609 thru F2612 for children

F1206 JOSEPHENE BANNING born about 1877. She and her mother were living with F495 in New Haven, Conn in 1910. Source: 84

F2613 thru F2616 for children

F1207 SEVATOR BANNING born about 1878. Source: 84

F2617 thru F2620 for children

F1208 CHILD GOODWIN born and died on Oct. 2, 1866 in East Hartford, Ct. Source: 84

F1209 ANDREW (Andy) JACKSON BANNING JR. born April 10, 1866 in South Brisbane, Australia. He left home at age 14, due to disagreement with his father. His mother gave him the money she had saved from selling eggs. He married Louisa Ryan on Dec. 6, 1894 in Winton, Queensland. She was born May 18, 1876 and died July 21, 1974. He died Dec. 15, 1941 at his home, "Woodstock" in Winton. Woodstock at that time covered 2000 square miles. He was a well known and respected "Grazier" in Western Queensland. He enjoyed horse racing and was an amateur rider and owner of some note. He was on the Winton Shire Council for many years. He was buried near the station homestead. "Woodstock" was sold by the family in 1975. Source: 17,30,84,86

F2621 Alvin Logan Banning
F2621a Frank Banning
F2622 Andrew Jackson Banning
F2622a Samuel Banning
F2622b Rowland Banning
F2623 Sylvia Banning
F2623a Louise Banning
F2623b Margaret Banning
F2624 Ellen (Nell) Banning
F2624a Stella Banning
F2624b Mary Banning

F1210 ELLEN MARIA BANNING born June 3, 1867 in Queensland, Australia, and died Sept. 9, 1953. She married Charles Burslem (or Burstein) Harris on Dec. 31, 1898 in Perth, Australia. He was the son of Joseph and Mary Ann Elizabeth (Churchyard) Harris, born Aug. 29, 1873 and died July 17, 1953 in Como, Western Australia. Both are buried in Kenwick Cemetery. The election rolls of 1920 has him as a farmer. Source: 17,30,84,86

F2625 Evelyn Harris
F2626 Elsie Margaret Harris
F2627 Irene (RENLE) Ellen Harris
F2628 Charles A. Harris
F2629 Daisy Harris
F2630 Leonard Samuel Harris
F2631 Donald Burslem Harris
F2632 Grace Lillian Harris

F1211 WILFRED (Bill) BANNING born Jan. 13, 1869 in Queensland, Australia. He married a widow, Mrs. Beddick. She was a school teacher at the Mareeba Goldfield. They lived near Freshwater creek where he had a farm. Bill also cut and hauled timber into Redlynch, where it was loaded onto the railway. He provided shelter on his land for a small tribe of Aborigines that survived a massacre at Speewah during a re-settlement attempt. The tribe adopted the Banning name. Bill died about 1962 in Herberton at the age of 91. Source: 17,30,84,86

F2633 Lucy Banning
F2634 thru F2636 for children

F1212 MAURICE BANNING born Aug. 6, 1870 in Queensland, Australia. He married and had at least 1 daughter. He worked on stations and managed properties around Burktown & Mt. Surprise. Later in life he ran a hotel at Mt. Milligan. He died in Innisfail at the home of his daughter. Source: 17,84,86

F2637 Banning Daughter
F2638 and F2639 for children

F1213 HARRIET (HATTIE) BANNING born Sept. 15, 1873 in Queensland, Australia and married Charles Wallace Lawrence on Oct. 25, 1897 in Fremantle, Western Australia. He was born March 3, 1870 and died Jan. 2, 1948. She died September 27, 1952. Source: 17,30,84,86

F2640 Daisy Irene Lawrence
F2641 Willford Wallace Lawrence

F2642 Charles Banning Lawrence
F2643 Alan Andrew Lawrence
F2644 Nancye Jean Lawrence

F1214 SAMUEL BANNING born April 21, 1875 in Queensland, Australia. He was listed as a farmer in 1910 on the voter rolls of Cannington, Fremantle, Australia. On these same rolls, he was listed as a contractor in 1912, 14 & 16. He never married and died sitting in a chair at a hotel in Cloncurry. Source: 17,84,86

F1215 LUCIA ANNE BANNING born Nov. 17, 1877 in Queensland, Australia and died July 30, 1929 at her sisters home in Kenwick, Western Australia. She was listed as a "domestic" in 1901 and a spinster in 1910 on the voter rolls of Cannington, Freemantle, Australia. She never married. Source: 17,30,84,86

F1216 ALVIN SETH BANNING born April 19, 1880 in Queensland, Australia. He was listed as a laborer in 1901 and a "carter" in 1910 on the voter rolls of Cannington, Freemantle, Australia. On these same rolls, he was listed as a contractor in 1912, 14, 16, 18 & 20. He never owned any property and died July 5, 1964. He is buried in Olinda Cemetry in Victoria. He never married. Source: 17,30,84,86

F1217 thru F1365 unknown children of F499 thru F546

F2645 thru F2990 for children

F1366 thru F1380 unknown children of F547 thru F549

F1381 thru F1390 unknown children of F550 & F551

F2991 thru F3015 for children

F1391 CHARLES G. BANNING born April 14, 1882. Source: 1

F3016 thru F3019 for children

F1392 ALICE P. BANNING born Oct. 16, 1887. Source: 1

F3020 thru F3023 for children

F1393 MARSHALL BANNING born July 22, 1889. Source: 1

F3024 thru F3027 for children

F1394 & F1395 unknown children of F563

F3028 thru F3034 for children

F1396 thru F1399 unknown children of F564 & F565

F1400a GRACE BANNING born about 1887 in Hartford, Oh. She was alive and married in 1934. Source: 30,84

F3035 thru F3037 for children

F1400b BLANCH BANNING born about 1888 in Hartford, Oh. She was alive and married in 1934. Source: 30,84

F3038 and F3039 for children

F1400c EDNA BANNING born about 1889 in Hartford, Oh. She was alive and married in 1934. Source: 30,84

F3040 and F3041 for children

F1400d GAIL BANNING born about 1890 in Hartford, Oh. He was a teacher and alive and married in 1934. Source: 30,84

F3042 thru F3044 for children

F1400e RUBY BANNING born about 1891 in Hartford, Oh. She was alive and married in 1934. Source: 30,84

F3045 and F3046 for children

F1400f CORA BANNING born about 1892 in Hartford, Oh. She was alive and married in 1934. Source: 30,84

F3047 and F3048 for children

F1400g FRANK BANNING born about 189? in Hartford, Oh. He was a school superintendent, was alive and married in 1934. Source: 30,84

F3049 thru F3051 for children

F1400h RALPH BANNING born about 189? in Hartford, Oh. He was alive and married in 1934. Source: 30,84

F3052 thru F3054 for children

F1400i SELMS BANNING born about 189? in Hartford, Oh. She was alive and married in 1934. Source: 30,84

F3055 and F3056 for children

F1400j LEON BANNING born about 189? in Hartford, Oh. He was alive and married in 1934. Source: 30,84

F3057 thru F3059 for children

F1400k HARRY BANNING born about 190? in Hartford, Oh. He was alive in 1934. Source: 30,84

F3060 and F3061 for children

F1400l ARTHUR BANNING born about 190? in Hartford, Oh. He was alive in 1934. Source: 30,84

F3062 and F3063 for children

F1400m WARD BANNING born about 190? in Hartford, Oh. He was a teacher and alive in 1934. Source: 30,84

F3064 thru F3066 for children

F1400n JAY BANNING born about 199? in Hartford, Oh. He was a teacher and alive in 1934. Source: 30,84

F3067 thru F3069 for children

F1401 LYDIA JENNETTE BANNING born Feb. 1880 in Boston, Ma. and died an infant. Source: 1

F1402 CARINA CARPENTER BANNING born Dec. 25, 1881 in Boston, Ma. She lived in Ft. Wayne, Ind. Source: 1

F3070 and F3071 for children

F1403 FLORIDA JENNETTE BANNING born Nov. 11, 1883 in Boston, Ma. She lived in Ft Wayne, Ind. Source: 1

F3072 and F3073 for children

F1404 DAHLGREN BANNING born Nov. 30, 1888 in Dayton, Oh. He lived in Ft. Wayne, Ind. Source: 1

F3074 thru F3076 for children

F1404A MAESIMUND BANNING born in New York City. She is a medical doctor and married a Mr. Panos. They were living in Tipp City, Ohio in 1995. Source: 85

F3077 thru F3079 for children

F1405 RALPH CLARK born Nov. 11, 1880. He attended Allegheny College, married Blanche Stockton and had 2 children, Elizabeth Stockton and Louise Banning. Source: 1

F1406 INEZ CLARK born Nov. 2, 1882. She married Dr. Horace Hall. Source: 1

F1407 GRACE CLARK born Feb. 7, 1884. She married Webster H. Sillon Dec. 24, 1910 and had 3 children, Elaine Banning, Webster H. and Mauncie L.. Source: 1

F1408 ARCHIE CLARK born Nov. 2 1886, and drowned April 26, 1905. Source: 1

F1409 CARINA CLARK born March 29, 1896 and married Claude Stockwell in May 1918. They had 5 children, Carolyn, Viola, Gilbert, Josephine and Wells. She died March 30, 1930. Source: 1

F1410 WILLIAM PECK BANNING born May 25, 1880 in New York City and married Helen Cameron Vroom in 1916. She was born March 12, 1890. He received his A.B. degree from New York University in 1902. After several yeary writing for several national magazines, he went to China in 1911 as one of the founders of the newspaper "China Press". In 1920 he joined AT&T and ended his career with then in 1944 as Asst. Vice President of public relations. 1946 saw the publication of his book "Commercial Broadcasting Pioneer". He was also an excellent pianist. He died June 18, 1962 and she passed away April 12, 1982. Source: 1,64,80

F3080 Helen Cameron Banning
F3081 George V. Banning
F3082 William P. Banning

F1411 ELIZABETH GEORGIANA BANNING born Nov. 1, 1881 in New York City and lived in Mount Vernon, N.Y. Source: 1,64

F3083 thru F3088 for children

F1412 ARCHIBALD TANNER BANNING born May 10, 1884 in New York City and married Margaret Frances Culkin in 1914 and divorced in 1929. She was born in 1891, attended Vassar College and died in 1982. She was a writer by profession. He lived in Washington, D.C., Duluth, Mn. and Mount Vernon, N.Y. He received his A.B. degree at Cornell University in 1904 and his LL. B. from George Washington University in 1908. He worked as a private Sect. at the Gallatin National Bank in New York City, then for the President of Cornell University. Later he worked for the Bureau of the Census as a Lawyer. He died in 1965. Source: 1,64

F3089 Mary Margaret Banning
F3090 Archibald Tanner Banning 3rd
F3091 William Culkin Banning
F3092 Margaret Bridgit Banning

F1413 LAURA BANNING born Dec. 4, 1886 at Mount Vernon, N.Y. and married Harrison Foska of Montana on June 8, 1928. She received her A.B. degree from Syracuse University in 1908. She taught biology. Source: 1,64,81

F3093 June ???

F1414 BENJAMIN BLAIN BANNING born July 11, 1889 in Mount Vernon, N.Y. He attended New York University as a member of the class of 1912. Source: 1,64

F3094 Benjamin Banning
F3095 Fred Banning

F1415 GEORGE WRIGHT BANNING born Oct.29, 1891 in Mount Vernon, N.Y. His wife's first name was Amy. Source: 1,64

F3096 Sybyl Banning
F3097 Shirley Banning
F3098 Suzanne Banning

F1416 LYDIA ESTHER BANNING born Dec. 27, 1893 in Mount Vernon, N.Y. and married Richard Holmes. Source: 1,64

F3099 thru F3104 for children

F1417 JESSIE OCTAVIA BANNING born March 15, 1896 in Mount Vernon, N.Y. and married Clinton Farrington. Source: 1,64,81

F3105 Jessie Lockwood Farrington
F3106 Lydia Banning Farrington

F1418 THEODORE ROOSEVELT BANNING born Jan. 12, 1899 in Mount Vernon, N.Y. and married Evelyn. He died in 1985. Source: 1,64

F3107 Bruce Banning

F1419 JOHN PECK BANNING born Feb. 18, 1901 in Mount Vernon, N.Y. and married Irene Emma Finer on July 16, 1922. She was from London England. Source: 1,64,81

F3108 Constance Irene Banning
F3109 Theodora Joan Banning
F3109 John Peck Banning, Jr

F1420 thru F1449 unknown children of F590 thru F595

F3111 thru F3198 for children

F1450 HERBERT BANNING born 1868 in Idaho. He was living in Carbondale, Col. in 1900. Source: 10

F3199 thru F3203 for children

F1451 EDWARD BANNING no information. Source: 1

F3204 thru F3207 for children

F1452 ALBERT BANNING no information. Source: 1

F3208 thru F3212 for children

F1453 ALICE AMELIA BANNING born Oct. 15, 1879 in Calusa Co., Calif. She married George Robbins on Feb. 20, 1904 in Calif. Source: 1

F3213 thru F3217 for children

F1454 EDMUND WASSON BANNING born March 28, 1881 in Calusa Co., Calif. Source: 1

F3218 thru F3223 for children

F1455 NELLIE VICTORIA BANNING born March 14, 1883 in Calusa Co. Calif. She married C. Coleman on Aug. 2, 1906 in Calif. They lived in Calusa, Calif. Source: 1

F3224 thru F3229 for children

F1456 DAVID FLETCHER BANNING born Feb. 28, 1885 in Calusa Co., Calif. He lived in San Francisco. Source: 1

F3230 thru F3235 for children

F1457 EMMA GERTRUDE BANNING born Aug. 24, 1887 in Calusa Co., Calif. and lived in Uba City, Calif. Source: 1

F3236 thru F3241 for children

F1458 FRANCIS MERRIAN BANNING born Feb. 10, 1892 in Calusa Co., Calif. Source: 1

F3242 thru F3247 for children

F1459 ANNIE PEARL BANNING born Aug. 17, 1892 in Calusa Co., Calif. Source: 1

F3248 thru F3253 for children

F1460 MARTHA WILLIAMS BANNING born Oct.8, 1894 in Calusa Co., Calif. Source: 1

F3254 thru F3259 for children

F1461 JASPER JAMES BANNING born Dec. 30, 1896 in Calusa Co., Calif. Source: 1

F3260 thru F3265 for children

F1462 MYRTLE VIOLA BANNING born Oct. 15, 1900 in Calusa Co., Calif. Source: 1

F3266 thru F3271 for children

F1463 thru F1471 unknown children of F604

F3272 thru F3312 for children

F1472 IDA MAY BANNING born Aug. 29, 1866 in Newberg, Cleveland, Ohio. She lived in Cleveland and died unmarried. Source: 1

F1473 EVA LOUISE BANNING born Dec. 26, 1867 in Newberg, Cleveland, Ohio. She was the assistant principal of Broadway School in Cleveland. She lived and died unmarried in Cleveland. Source: 1

F1474 EDNA MARIE BANNING born May 10, 1870 in Newberg, Cleveland, Ohio. She lived in Cleveland and was a traveling Evangelist of considerable ability. She was an excellent speaker, singer and had a strong personality. She died unmarried. Source: 1

F1475 GEORGIANA BLANCH BANNING born Sept. 15, 1875 in Newberg, Cleveland, Ohio. She married Frank Flick on July 25, 1894 in Cleveland. They lived in Bedford, Oh. Source: 1

F3313 Elvira Maude Flick
F3314 Cora Marie Flick
F3315 Clarence Flick
F3316 Eva Flick

F1476 CHARLES ELMORE CLARK born June 6, 1860 in Bureau Co., Ill. He married Hattie C. Williams on March 31, 1885 in Oberlin, Ohio. They had 4 children. Source: 1

F1477 JENNIE CLARK born April 20, 1862 in Bureau Co., Ill. and died as an infant. Source: 1

F1478 GEORGE E. HOLLISTER born Oct. 1, 1862 in Newberg, Ohio. He married Maud Carnack in April 1, 1891 in Hillsburg, Ind. Source: 1

F1479 J. SPENCER HOLLISTER born July 11, 1868 in Newberg, Ohio. He married and had 2 children. Source: 1

F1480 PEARL LOUISE HOLLISTER born June 26, 1877 in Newberg, Ohio. She married, had 1 child and lived in Rensselear, Ind. Source: 1

F1481 WILLOW McKINNIE no information. Source: 1

F1482 thru F1493 unknown children of F633 and F634

F1494 NELLIE ORPHRNIA BANNING born March 18, 1864 in Hartland, Ct. She married H. Bennett Case of New Hartford, Ct. in 1885 in West Hartford. They lived in New Hartford. Source: 1

> F3317 Hazel Fannie Case
> F3318 Gladys Elizabeth Case
> F3319 Kathryn Lucinda Case

F1495 FANNIE MIRA BANNING born Oct. 23, 1868 in Westfield, Hampden Co., Mass. She married Frank E. Bidwell of Hartford, Ct. on April 14, 1892 in West Hartford. They lived in Hartford and South Windsor, Ct. Source: 1,13

> F3320 Waldo Trundy Bidwell
> F3321 Marshall Frank Bidwell

F1496 CHARLES P. CASE born Sept. 18, 1879 and married Jane Brown of Simsbury, Ct. They had at least one child. Source: 1

F1497 BESSIE L. CASE born Sept. 22, 1886. Source: 1

F1498 IDA MAE CASE born Feb. 11, 1888. Source: 1

F1499 LILLY RUTHERFORD BANNING she married 1st, George M. Silver and had children. She married 2nd, Alfred A. Barnes and had children. They lived in Indianapolis, Ind. Source: 1

> F3322 thru F3329 for children

F1500 thru F1503 unknown children of F643

> F3330 thru F3350 for children

F1504 HUDSON ALMON BANNING born Dec. 8, 1869 and married Mina Kester in 1898 in Shannon City, Taylor Co., Iowa. They lived in Shannon City where he died of tuberculosis on Oct. 12, 1909. He was listied as a "Hotel Keeper" and is buried in the Shannon City Cemetery. Source: 1,15,68

> F3351 Golda Grace Banning
> F3352 thru F3354 for children

F1505 DORA BANNING no information. Source: 1

> F3355 thru F3359 for children

F1506 HENRY BANNING no information. Source: 1

> F3360 thru F3364 for children

F1507 SELMA BANNING no information. Source: 1

> F3365 thru F3369 for children

F1508 LAURA BANNING no information. Source: 1

> F3370 thru F3374 for children

F1509 BERTON ALVA BANNING born May 14, 1879 in Shannon City, Union Co., Iowa and married Alta Jean Baxter on April 4, 1900 in Gravity, Taylor Co., Iowa. She was the daughter of Charles W. and Mary F. (Shellabarger) Baxter, born Aug. 21, 1879 in Muscatine, Muscatine Co., Iowa. They were living in Des Moines, Iowa in 1918. Alta died Sept. 7, 1949 in Creston, Union Co., Iowa. Burton died Oct. 19, 1953 in Kimberly, Twins Falls Co., Idaho in a fire. Both are buried in Graceland Cemetery in Creston, Iowa. He was a retired farmer. Source: 1,12,13,15,16,30,68

> F3375 Harold Edwin Banning
> F3376 Ralph Baxter Banning
> F3376a Infant Daughter

F1510 PLATHA BANNING no information. Source: 1

> F3377 thru F3379 for children

F1511 EMMA BANNING no information. Source: 1

> F3380 thru F3382 for children

F1512 CLEOPATRA BANNING no information. Source: 1

> F3383 thru F3385 for children

F1513 MILO H. BANNING no information . Source: 1

> F3386 thru F3388 for children

F1514 BESSIE BANNING no information. Source: 1

> F3389 thru F3391 for children

F1515 MYRA BANNING no information. Source: 1

                    F3392 thru F3394 for children

F1516 GUY BANNING no information. Source: 1

                    F3395 thru F3397 for children

F1517 LOLA BANNING no information. Source: 1

                    F3398 thru F3400 for children

F1518 MAUD BANNING no information. Source: 1

                    F3401 thru F3403 for children

F1519 ALMON BANNING no information. Source: 1

                    F3404 thru F3406 for children

F1520 thru F1533 unknown children of F648 thru F650

F1534 PEARL BANNING lived in Simsbury, Ct. Source: 1

                    F3407 thru F3409 for children

F1535 ELLERT BANNING no information. Source: 1

                    F3410 thru F3412 for children

F1536 JUNNIE BANNING lived in Hartland, Ct. Source: 1

                    F3413 thru F3415 for children

F1537 & F1538 unknown children of F651

F1539 thru F1544 unknown children of F652

F1545 thru F1550 unknown children of F653 thru F658

                    F3416 thru F3436 for children

F1551 thru F1556 unknown children of F682

F1557 thru F1562 unknown children of F683

                    F3437 thru F3457 for children

F1563 GRACE N. STANTON born in Ct. Source: 1

F1564 RALPH WINTHROP STANTON born in Ct. Source: 1

F1565 HARRY ALBERT STANTON born in Ct. Source: 1

F1566 EDITH STANTON born in Ct. Source: 1

F1567 WINTHROP STANTON no information. Source: 1

F1568 MAUD STANTON no information. Source: 1

F1569 RUTH NOYES STANTON no information. Source: 1

F1570 thru F1794 unknown children of F685 thru F761

F1795 DEFOREST LEONARD born Jan. 24, 1897. Source: 1

F1796 LLOYD EARL LEONARD born Jan. 15, 1901 and died July 28, 1904. Source: 1

F1797 thru F2620 unknown children of F763 thru F1207

F3458 thru F5259

F2621 ALVIN LOGAN BANNING born Sept. 13, 1895 and was living at "Tulmur", Winton, Australia in 1941. He died May 18, 1985. Source: 84,86

F5260 thru 5263 for children

F2621a FRANK BANNING born Nov. 25, 1915. He died of a burst appendix on July 7, 1935 due to floods that kept the family from getting him to a doctor. He is buried in Winton Cemetery. Source: 84,86

F2622 ANDREW JACKSON {TEA} BANNING born Dec. 20, 1897 and was living at "Cannington", McKinlay, Australia in 1941. He died Sept. 7, 1982. Source: 84,86

F5264 thru F5267 for children

F2622a SAMUEL BANNING born Oct. 7, 1908 and was living at "Woodstock", Winton, Australia in 1941. Source: 84,86

F5268 thru F5271 for children

F2622b ROWLAND BANNING born Aug. 8, 1910 and was living at "Woodstock", Winton, Australia in 1941. Source: 84,86

F5272 thru F5275 for children

F2623 SYLVIA BANNING born April 6, 1899. She married a Mr. Jefferies and was living at "Elrose", Oorindi, Australia in 1941. Sylvia died March 15, 1977. Source: 84.86

F5276 thru F5279 for children

F2623a LOUISE BANNING born Oct. 19, 1902. She married a Mr. Young and lived at "Yandaburra", Springsure, Australia in 1941. Source: 84,86

F5280 thru F5284 for children

F2623b MARGARET BANNING born Oct. 17, 1904. She married a Mr. McKerrow and lived at "Moorooka", McKinlay, Australia in 1941. Source: 84,86

F5285 thru F5289 for children

F2624 ELLEN (NELL) BANNING born Oct.8, 1906 in Winton, Queensland, Australia. She married Frederick Geoffry Arnold on April 10, 1932 in Townsville, Queensland. He was born March 31, 1902 in Sydney, Australia and died Nov. 15, 1972 in Brisbane. They were living in Sydney in 1941. She died Sept. 12, 1976 in Brisbane. Source: 84,86

F5290 Roland James Arnold
F5291 Cecily Edith Arnold

F2624a STELLA BANNING born Sept. 19, 1913. She was married to Mr. Barnes and lived at "Chatsworth", Selwyn, Australia in 1941. Stella died June 14, 1976. Source: 84,86

F5292 thru F5295 for children

F2624b MARY BANNING born Nov. 17, 1917 and was living at "Woodstock, Winton, Australia in 1941. Mary married Tom Triplett on Sept. 11, 1943. Source: 84,86

F5296 Peter Triplett
F5297 Tom Triplett

F2625 EVELYN HARRIS born 1899 and died 1982. She was living in Melbourne in 1953. Source: 30,84,86

F2626 ELSIE MARGARET HARRIS born 1900. She is a nurse and was living in Como in 1953. Source: 30,84,86

F2627 IRENE ELLEN (RENLE) HARRIS born in 1901 and married Clarance White. They were living in Como in 1953. She is a nurse. Source: 30,84,86

F2628 CHARLES ALVIN HARRIS born in 1903 and married Helen "Nellie" ---? Their children are, Maureen, Shirley, Alva, Judith, Charles and Tom. Source: 30,84,86

F2629 DAISY HARRIS born 1905. She was living in Sydney in 1953. Source: 30,84,86

F2630 LEONARD SAMUEL HARRIS born 1907 and married Dolly ---?. Their children are, Eileen, Leonard, Doreen, Alvin, Evelyn, Marrianne and Fay. Source: 30,84,86

F2631 DONALD BURSLEM HARRIS born Jan. 12, 1909 and married Clairice ---?. Their children are, Robert, Joan, Neil and Frank, who was born Jan. 24, 1944. Source: 30,84,86

F2632 GRACE LILLIAN HARRIS born 1911 and married Lewis Jackson. Their children are, Ronnie, Todd and Browynne. Source: 30,84,86

F2633 LUCY BANNING Married Ned Harte and was living in Denbeigh St., Cairns in 1969. Source: 86

F2634 thru F 2636 unknown children of F1211

F2637 BANNING DAUGHTER she married Mr. T. Ryan. Source: 86

F2638 and F2639 unknown children of F1212

F2640 DAISY IRENE LAWRENCE born Sept. 28, 1898 and married James Reginald Cox on Dec. 15, 1920. She died June 6, 1983. Their children are Norma, James, Kerry, Pam and Regina. Source: 86

F2641 WILLFORD WALLACE (WALLY) LAWRENCE born April 2, 1904 and married Allison (???). He died May 26, 1950. Their children are Rita and Dawn. Source: 86

F2642 CHARLES BANNING LAWRENCE born Nov. 25, 1902 and married Amy (???). Their children are Glenda, Leigh, Nancy, Reg, Marjorie and Alan. Source: 86

F2643 ALLAN ANDREW (STUMPY) LAWRENCE born April, 27, 1905 and married Beryl Jean Kerrisk on June 12, 1940. He died June 12, 1991. Their children are Laurie, Kay and Denise. Source: 86

F2644 NANCYE JEAN LAWRENCE born July 12, 1914 and married Gray McKenzie on July 8, 1937. They had a daughter, Jennifer Rae. Source: 86

F2645 thru F3079 unknown children of F1217 thru F1404

F5316 thru F6005 for children

F3080 HELEN CAMERON BANNING born Jan. 1, 1919 and died about July 24, 1928. Source: 16,64,80

F3081 GEORGE VROOM BANNING born April 22, 1917 in Hackensack, N.J. and married Jean Juliet Ely on Jan. 18, 1945 in San Francisco, Ca. She was born April 29, 1919 in Washington, D.C. and graduated fron the University of Calif. at Berkeley in 1940. He received his AB degree from Princeton University in 1939 and his Master of Architecture from Harvard in 1942. He joined the U.S. Navy and served from 1942 to 1945. He practised Architecture in San Francisco and San Rafael, Ca. until he retired in 1984. He and his family have lived in Belvedere, Ca, since 1955. Source: 16,64,80

F6006 Juliet Helen Banning
F6007 Peter Vroom Banning

F3082 WILLIAM PECK BANNING born March 10, 1923 in Hackensack, N.J. and married Rita C. Conger on Nov. 7, 1947. He served in the U.S. Marine Corps fron 1942 to 1945. Source: 16,64,80

F6008 Barbara R. Banning
F6009 Karen L. Banning

F3083 thru F3088 unknown children of F1411

F3089 MARY MARGARET BANNING born 1915 and married Gardner Louis Friedlander. He was born in 1919. He attended Dartmouth and was a business manager. She attended Vassar College and Johns Hopkins University. She was a Physicist. Source: 64

F6010 Margaret Louise Friedlander
F6011 Gardner LeRoy Friedlander
F6012 Thomas William Friedlander

F3090 ARCHIBALD TANNER BANNING born 1918 and married Virginia O'Neil. She was born in 1922 and attended Smith College. He was a graduate of Harvard, was a chemical engineer and died in 1994. Source: 64

F6013 William Tanner Banning
F6014 Sally Banning
F6015 Michael Banning
F6016 Mark Banning

F3091 WILLIAM CULKIN BANNING born 1920 and died 1922. Source: 64

F3092 MARGARET BRIDGIT BANNING born 1922 and died 1925. Source: 64

F3093 JUNE ???? no information Source: 64

F3094 BENJAMIN BANNING no information. Source: 64

F6017 thru F6019 for children

F3095 FRED BANNING no information. Source: 64

F6020 thru F6022 for children

F3096 SYBYL BANNING no Information. Source: 64

F6023 thru F6025 for children

F3097 SHIRLEY BANNING no information. Source: 64

F6026 thru F6028 for children

F3098 SUZANNE BANNING no information. Source: 64

F6029 thru F6031 for children

F3099 thru F3104 unknown children of F1417

F3105 JESSIE LOCKWOOD FARRINGTON no information. Source:64,81

F3106 LYDIA BANNING FARRINGTON no information. Source: 64,81

F3107 BRUCE BANNING no information. Source: 64

F6032 thru F6034 for children

F3108 CONSTANCE IRENE BANNING born Oct. 23, 1923. "Connie married James Moore Gatling on Feb. 28, 1947. He was from Raleigh, N.C. Source: 64,81

> F6035 James Moore Gatling Jr
> F6036 Irene Banning Gatling

F3109 THEODORA JOAN BANNING born July 7, 1933. "Teddy" married Henry Taylor Gibson on May 2, 1953. They were divorced and she married 2nd, Peter VanDyk Berg on Dec. 16, 1972. Source: 64,81

> F6037 Edith Gay Gibson
> F6038 Henry Taylor Gibson Jr
> F6039 Joy Banning Gibson
> F6040 Theodore Banning Gibson

F3110 JOHN PECK BANNING, Jr. Born June 12, 1939 and married Nancy Otto. "Jack" was in the state Department. He and Nancy divorded. Source: 64,81

> F6041 John Peck Banning, III

F3111 thru F3198 unknown children of F1420 thru F1449

F3199 thru F3271 unknown children of F1450 thru F1462

F3272 thru F3312 unknown children of F1463 thru F1471

F3313 ELVIRA MAUD FLICK born Jan. 31, 1896 and died an infant. Source: 1

F3314 CORA MARIE FLICK born Sept. 5, 1898 in Auburn, Ohio. Source: 1

F3315 CLARENCE FLICK born June 25, 1900 in Bedford, Ohio. Source: 1

F3316 EVA MILDRED FLICK born June 25, 1905 in Bedford, Ohio. Source: 1

F3317 HAZEL FANNIE CASE born Feb. 23, 1890 in New Hartford, Ct. Source: 1

F3318 GLADYS ELIZABETH CASE born Dec. 31, 1892 in New Hartford, Ct. Source: 1

F3319 KATHRYN LUCINDA CASE born Dec. 3, 1893 in New Haven, Ct. Source: 1

F3320 WALDO TRUNDY BIDWELL born April 30, 1893 in Hartford, Ct. Source: 1

F3321 MARSHALL FRANKLIN BIDWELL born Dec. 9, 1895 in Hartford, Ct. Source: 1

F3322 thru F3350 unknown children of F1499 thru F1503

F3351 GOLDA GRACE BANNING no information. Source: 1

F3352 thru F3354 unknown children of F1504

F3355 thru F3359 unknown children of F1505

F3360 thru F3364 unknown children of F1506

F3365 thru F3374 unknown children of F1507 & F1508

F3375 HAROLD EDWIN BANNING born Jan. 18, 1901 in Shannon City, Union Co.,
Iowa and married Velma Lucille Fell on Nov. 22, 1920 in Des Moines, Polk Co.,
Iowa. She was the daughter of Jesse Benjamin and Sarah Elizabeth (Parsons) Fell,
born June 26, 1900 in Jefferson Township, Ringgold Co., Iowa. The family moved
to Kimberly, Idaho in 1935 where he was a farmer and rancher in the Rock Creek
area. They were living in Hansen, Idaho in 1949. He died April 12, 1972 in Jerome,
Jerome Co., Idaho. She died Jan 20, 1978 in Jerome. Both are buried in Sunset
Memorial Park in Twin Falls, Idaho. Source: 1,13,16,30,68

> F7003 Robert Clair Banning
> F7004 James Franklin Banning
> F7005 Shirley Banning

F3376 RALPH BAXTER BANNING born Aug. 16, 1908 in Shannon City, Union Co.,
Iowa and moved to Idaho in 1929. He married Loretta Lucile Pace on May 7, 1932 in
Odgen, Weber Co., Utah. She was born Jan. 15, 1906 in Welch, Craig Co, Okla.
and was the daughter of William H. (1867-1953) and Annie L. (1870-1962)
(Downing) Pace. Lucile was a teacher. Ralph was living in Kimberly, Twin Falls
Co., Idaho in 1949 and 1953. He died May 7, 1985 in Mountain Home, Elmore Co.,
Idaho and was buried in Sunset Memorial park in Twin Falls, Idaho. He was a
farmer and motel owner. Source: 1,12,16,30,68

> F7006 Ardis Lucile Banning
> F7007 Richard Baxter Banning

F3376a INFANT BANNING DAUGHTER born and died of premature birth on June 17,
1916 in Clearfield, Taylor Co, Iowa. She is buried in the Clearfield Cemetery.
Source: 16,68

F3377 thru F3385 unknown children of F1510 thru F1512

F3386 thru F3388 unknown children of F1513

> F7008 thru F7016 for children

F3389 thru F3394 unknown children of F1514 & F1515

F3395 thru F3397 unknown children of F1516

> F7017 thru F7025 for children

F3398 thru F3403 unknown children of F1517 & F1518

F3404 thru F3406 unknown children of F1519

> F7026 thru F7034 for children

F3407 thru F3409 unknown children of F1534

F3410 thru F3412 unknown children of F1535

F7035 thru F7043 for children

F3413 thru F3415 unknown children of F1536

F3416 thru F3457 unknown children of F1545 thru F1550 & F1557 thru F1562

F7044 thru F7120 for children

F3458 thru F5289 unknown children of F1797 thru F2624

F7121 thru F9000 for children

F5290 ROLAND JAMES (JIM) ARNOLD born June 6, 1933 in Yass, NSW, Astralia. He married Lorraine Stevens. Source: 86

F5291 CECILY EDITH ARNOLD born Aug. 17, 1934 in Yass, NSW, Australia. She married Ken O'Dowell. Source: 86

F5292 thru F5295 unknown children of F2624a

F5296 PETER TRIPLETT no information. Source: 86

F5297 TOM TRIPLETT no information. Source: 86

F5298 thry F6005 unknown children of F2633 thru F3079

F9001 thru F9959 for children

F6006 JULIET HELEN BANNING born Nov. 9, 1945 in San Francisco, Ca. and married James M. Allen in 1977. She received her AB degree in 1967 and her Master of City Planing in 1969, both from the University of Calif. at Berkeley. She is currently Chief Planner of Sequoia National Forest. They live in Springville, Ca. Source: 16,80

F9960 & F9961 for children

F6007 PETER VROOM BANNING Born Oct. 26, 1949 in San Francisco, Ca. and married Elizabeth Krause in 1994. He received his AB degree from the University of Calif. at Berkeley in 1972 as well as a Certificate in City & Regional Planning in 1980. He is currently Executive Officer, San Mateo Co. Local Agency Formation Commission. They live in Mill Valley, Ca. Source: 16,80

F9962 & F9963 for children

F6008 BARBARA R. BANNING No information. Source: 80

F9964 & F9965 for children

F6009 KAREN L. BANNING No information. Source: 80

F9966 & F9967 for children

F6010 MARGARET LOUISE FRIEDLANDER born 1949 and married Joseph F. Brinig. He attended Georgetown & George Mason University and is a lawyer. She is a graduate of Duke University and Seaton Hall and is a Professor of Law at George Mason University. Their children are; Mary Margaret, born 1978; Wendy Christine, born 1980; Kathleen Ann, born 1982; Jill Elizabeth, born 1985 and Brian Joseph, born 1991. Source: 64

F6011 GARDNER LeROY FRIEDLANDER born 1951, attended Princeton and married Karen Hoffman. She was born in 1951 and graduated from Wheaton College. They are both teachers. Their children are David Gardner, born 1982 and Elizabeth Banning Hoffman, born 1984. Source: 64

F6012 THOMAS WILLIAM FRIEDLANDER born 1954 and married Catherine Ann Olszowy in 1977. She was born in 1953. Their children are: Rebecca Ann, born 1980; Caleb Gardner, born 1982 and Peter Mark, born 1983. They were divorced in 1992. Source: 64

F6013 WILLIAM TANNER BANNING He married Martha Pauli. Source: 64

> F9968 William Banning
> F9969 Laura Banning
> F9970 Gretchen Banning

F6014 SALLY BANNING married Michael Beaumont. He was born in 1942. Source: 64

F6015 MICHAEL BANNING no information. Source: 64

F6016 MARK BANNING He died in 1980. Source: 64

F6035 JAMES MOORE GATLING, Jr. Born July 8, 1951. Source: 81

F6036 IRENE BANNING GATLING born March 27, 1956. Source: 81

F6037 EDITH GAY GIBSON born Sept. 28, 1954 and died Feb. 13, 1992. She had one son. Source: 81

F6038 HENRY TAYLOR GIBSON, Jr. Born on Jan 27, 1956 and married Sarah Marshall. They had two daughters and were divorced. Source: 81

F6039 JOY BANNING GIBSON born May 27, 1957 and married David Palmer. They have 5 children. Source: 81

F6040 THEODORE BANNING GIBSON born Jan. 25, 1962. Source: 81

F6041 JOHN PECK BANNING, III born Dec. 24, 1964 in Buenos Aires. After his parents were divorced, he was adopted by his mothers 2nd husband. He has changed his name back to Banning. Source: 81

F7003 ROBERT CLAIR BANNING born July 21, 1921 in Creston, Union Co., Iowa and married Ethel Mae Compton April 16, 1944 in Kimberly, Idaho. She was the daughter of Earl Charles and Nora Mae (Edmondson) Compton, born March 12, 1921 in Nampa, Canyon Co., Idaho. He died April 15, 1982 in Pocatello, Bannock Co., Idaho and is buried in Sunset Memorial Gardens in Twin Falls, Idaho. Source: 16,68,69

> F11988 Michael Robert Banning
> F11989 Scott C. Banning
> F11990 Ricky J. Banning

F7004 JAMES FRANKLIN BANNING born July 11, 1932 in Creston, Union Co., Iowa and married 1st, Leona Patsy Smith on June 5, 1955. They were divorced. He joined the U.S. Air Force in 1952 and was stationed at Edwards Air Force Base where he was a crew chief for test helicopters. He became a funeral director and in 1978 an insurance agent. He married 2nd, Barbara Thompson Miller (Persons ?) in 1968. James died Sept 21, 1995 in the V.A. Nursing Home in Boise, Idaho and is buried in the Rock Creek Cemetery. Source: 16,30,68

> F11991 Jess Banning
> F11992 Matt Banning
> F11993 Stacey Banning

F7005 SHIRLEY MAY BANNING born Nov. 20, 1928 in Creston, Union Co., Iowa and married William Hill of Gooding, Idaho in 1951 in Elko, Nevada. She earned her Masters degree in Education from Idaho State Univ. She was a teacher in Idaho Falls. The family moved to Meridian, Ada Co, Idaho in 1978. Shirley died in her sleep at her Meridian home on Nov. 6, 1995. She was cremated and interned at Clover Dale Cemetery in Boise. Source: 16,30,68

> F11994 Debra Hill
> F11995 Linda Sue Hill
> F11996 Sandra Jo Hill
> F11997 Pamela Lynn Hill

F7006 ARDIS LUCILE (BILLIE) BANNING born Nov. 12, 1934 in Twin Falls, Twin Falls, Co., Idaho and married William Clem Holstine on June 3, 1956 in Kimberly, Twin Falls Co., Idaho. He was born March 11, 1932 in Mountain Home, Baxter Co. Ark. and was the son of Hugh Washington Holstine (1901 - 1973) and Lydia Myrtle Haley (1905 - 1980). In November 1956 Bill and Billie moved to Seattle, Wa to work for the Boeing Co. Source: 16,30,68

> F11998 Kirk Michael Holstine
> F11999 Carolyn Kay Holstine

F7007 RICHARD BAXTER (DICK) BANNING born Jan. 29, 1939 in Twin Falls, Twin Falls Co., Idaho and married Paula Nelle Gable on Dec. 4, 1966 in Kimberly, Twin Falls Co., Idaho. She is the daughter of Arthur M. (1906-1954) and Beulah B. (Wales)(1909-1985) Gable, born June 13, 1940 in Long Pine, Brown Co., Neb. Dick attended the University of Idaho and then joined the U.S. Army in 1962. He was a helicopter pilot in Germany and Vietnam. In 1969 Dick was a test pilot for Southern Airways. By 1979 he was aviation manager for the Bonneville Power Administration. Source: 16,17,30,68

> F12000 Christina Louise Banning

F12001 Timothy Baxter Banning

F9968 WILLIAM BANNING no information. Source: 64

F9969 LAURA BANNING no information. Source: 64

F9970 GRETCHEN BANNING no information. Source: 64

F11988 MICHAEL ROBERT BANNING born July 22, 1945 in San Bernardino, Calif.
He married Martha Jean Rudeseal Dec. 13, 1975 in McCall, Idaho. She was the
daughter of Herman and Clydelle (Cook) Rudeseal, born Nov. 12, 1944. Source:
16,69

F 15001 Scott Michael Banning
F 15002 Steven Robert Banning

F11989 SCOTT C. BANNING born Dec. 12, 1946 in Pocatello, Idaho. He died Sept. 2,
1963 in Rupert, Idaho. Source: 16,69

F11990 RICKY J. BANNING born Jan. 14, 1958 in Twin falls, Idaho and married 1st.
Wendy Star Wilson in Sun Valley, Idaho. Source: 16,69

F11991 JESS BANNING living in Price, Utah in 1995. Source: 30,68

F11992 MATT BANNING living in Pocatello, Idaho in 1995. Source: 30,68

F11993 STACEY BANNING living in Twin Falls, Idaho in 1995. Source: 30,68

F11994 DEBRA (DEBBIE) HILL she married a Mr. Fondren and was living in Boise,
Idaho in 1995. Source: 30,68

F11995 LINDA SUE (SUSIE) HILL she married a Mr. Ulacky and was living in Boise,
Idaho in 1995. Source: 30,68

F11996 SANDRA JO (SANDY) HILL she married a Mr. Vogel and was living in Boise,
Idaho in 1995. Source: 30,68

F11997 PAMELA LYNN HILL she married a Mr. Hansen and was living in Idaho Falls,
Idaho in 1995. Source: 30,68

F11998 KIRK MICHAEL HOLSTINE born Sept. 10, 1960 in Seattle, Wa. He attended
the University of Washington, University of Puget Sound Law School and Seattle
University. He married Deborah Lynn Weis on April 15, 1987. Source: 68

F11999 CAROLYN KAY HOLSTINE born Seot. 9, 1963 in Seattle, Wa. and married
Richard Roy Marlow on Aug. 16, 1987. She attended the University of Washington.
Carolyn and Richard had twins, Kelly Kay and Taylor Ray, born Feb. 11, 1993.
Source: 68

F12000 CHRISTINA LOUISE BANNING born Dec. 12, 1967 in Nuernberg, Bavaria,
Germany. She attended Pacific Lutheran University in tacoma, Wa. and married
Geoffery Dana Richardson on June 9, 1990 in Vancouver, Clark Co., Wash.
Source: 16,17,68

F12001 TIMOTHY BAXTER BANNING born Oct. 2, 1969 in Mineral Wells, Palo Pinto Co., Tx. He attended Linfield College in McMinnville, Or. Source: 16,17,68

F15001 SCOTT MICHAEL BANNING born June 30, 1980 in Hailey, Idaho. Source: 16,69

F15002 STEVEN ROBERT BANNING born June 23, 1987 in Sun Valley, Idaho. Source: 16,69

JAMES BANNING of CANADA

Tradition carries this branch from Orange County, New York, back to Northern Ireland on both sides of the family, but as to exact location or proof, nothing is known.

The Banning's in Ireland likely came from Scotland or England, but nothing is known about just when they migrated. From Orange County, N.Y., the progenitor of this branch moved to Wardsville, Ontario. Descendants moved on to Detroit, Nevada, California, Winnipeg, Honolulu and elsewhere.

It is also just possible that they belong to the lines coming out of Conn.

G1 UNKNOWN BANNING said to have come to N.Y. State from Ireland. Source: 1

> G2 James Banning
> G3 Isabel Banning
> G4 Daughter Banning
> G5 thru G9 for children

G2 JAMES BANNING born Dec. 17, 1794 (supposedly in Albany, Orange Co., N.Y.) Married Mary Ann Ward, the only daughter of Sir George Ward of Ireland, about 1820, near Wardsville, Ontario. He died May 3, 1860 in Wardsville. She died in April 1896. Source: 1

> G10 John Banning
> G11 James Banning
> G12 Alexander A. Banning
> G13 Margaret Banning
> G14 Lorinda Adella Banning
> G15 Alfred Douglas Banning
> G16 Angelina Banning
> G17 William Ward Banning
> G18 George Edward Banning
> G19 Mary Jane Banning
> G20 Sheldon Arthur Banning
> G21 Elizabeth Alexandria Banning

G3 ISABEL BANNING no information. Source: 1

> G22 thru G28 for children

G4 BANNING DAUGHTER no information

> G29 thru G35 for children

G5 thru G9 for unknown children of G1

> G36 thru G61 for children

G10 JOHN BANNING born about 1823 near Wardsville, Ontario. Married Arminda Keys at Royal Oaks, Mich. She died, no issue. Married 2nd, Frances R. Lynch of Canton, Ohio in 1867 in San Francisco, Calif. where he died on Feb. 26, 1883.

Source: 1

G62 Katherine F. Banning
G63 Margary Banning
G64 Edward James Banning
G65 John William Banning
G66 Eliza Mary Banning

G11 JAMES BANNING born June 11, 1825 near Wardsville, Ontario. Married Mary Fleming in 1852 near Wardsville. They had one son. She died about 1884 in Chatham, Ontario. He married 2nd, Bell Rutherford of Wardsville on Feb. 11, 1885. They lived in Chatham where he died May 2, 1897. She died in 1904. Source: 1

G67 James Banning
G68 Andrew Banning
G69 Maud Banning
G70 Stanley Banning
G71 Blanch Banning

G12 ALEXANDER A. BANNING born Feb. 21, 1828 near Wardsville, Ontario. He married in Virginia City, Nevada, and lived in Vanderbilt and Needles, Calif. He died in Calif. Source: 1

G72 William Banning

G13 MARGARET BANNING born in 1830 near Wardsville, Ontario. Married James Thompson of Newbury, Ontario in 1854. They lived in Windsor, Ontario. Source: 1

G73 Albert Edward Thompson
G74 John Bell Thompson
G75 Addie Thompson

G14 LORINDA ADELLA BANNING born Sept. 1832 near Wardsville, Ontario. She lived unmarried in Honolulu, Hi. Source: 1

G15 ALFRED DOUGLAS BANNING born Sept. 4, 1834 near Wardsville, Ontario. Married Lusannah Susan Gibbs of Aldborough, Ontario in 1862. They lived in Chicago. Source: 1

G76 John Alexander Banning
G77 Charles Banning
G78 Alta Banning

G16 ANGELINA BANNING born 1838 near Wardsville, Ontario. Married Peter High of Beamsville, Ontario. They lived in Honolulu, HI. Source: 1

G79 Clifford Bell High

G17 WILLIAM WARD BANNING born Nov. 16, 1842 near Wardsville, Ontario. Married Mary Dick of Springfield, Winnipeg. They lived in Winnipeg where he died in 1888. Source: 1

G80 Clarence Banning
G81 William Ward Banning
G82 Claud Percival Banning
G83 Elmer Banning

G18 GEORGE EDWARD BANNING born June 13, 1846 near Wardsville, Ontario.
Married Cynthia Priscilla Cuisak of Newbury, Ontario, in 1872. They lived in
Winnipeg, where he died on Sept. 19, 1904. Source: 1

G85 Courtland Banning
G86 Mable Florence Banning

G19 MARY JANE BANNING born 1850 at Wardsville, Ontario. She died while young.
Source: 1

G20 SHELDON ARTHUR BANNING born Aug. 12, 1848 near Wardsville, Ontario.
Married Sarah M. Campbell of Strathroy, Ontario on April 19, 1869 in Strathroy.
They lived in Detroit, Mich. and had 2 children. She died and he married 2nd,
Jennie Roberts of Detroit on Aug. 12, 1896. They had no children. Source: 1

G87 Alexander Bruce Banning
G88 Ella May Banning

G21 ELIZABETH ALEXANDRIA BANNING born 1853 near Wardsville, Ontario.
Married Charles A. Bagwell of Hamilton, Ontario on Feb. 23, 1881 at Chatham,
Ontario. They had no children. When he died, she moved to Honolulu, Hi. Source:
1

G22 thru G35 unknown children of G3 & G4

G36 thru G61 unknown children of G5 thru G9

G89 thru G149 for children

G62 KATHERINE F. BANNING she married and lived in San Francisco. Source: 1

G150 thru G155 for unknown children

G63 MARGARY BANNING born in San Francisco, Calif. Married Mr. Kelly of
Chicago,in 1898, in San Francisco, Calif. They lived in Chicago.

G156 thru G161 for children

G64 EDWARD JAMES BANNING born June 6, 1873 in San Francisco, Calif. He was
the 1st Assistant U.S. District Att. for the Northern Dist. of Calif. He died Feb. 4,
1906 in San Francisco. Source: 1

G65 JOHN WILLIAM BANNING born Aug. 15, 1876 and died June 26, 1884, both in
San Francisco, Calif. Source: 1

G66 ELIZA MARY BANNING born Aug. 23, 1880 and died Feb. 6, 1891, both in San
Francisco, Calif. Source: 1

G67 JAMES BANNING no information. Source: 1

G162 thru G167 for children

G68 ANDREW BANNING born Jan. 1864 near Wardsville, Ontario. He married Edna
Mae (???) in 1889 in Red Bluff, Calif. They lived in Oakland, Calif. Source: 1,61

G168 Wanda Banning
G169 Clifford Banning
G170 Gertrude Banning

G69 MAUD BANNING born Nov. 19, 1888 in Chatham, Ontario. Source: 1

G171 thru G176 for children

G70 STANLEY BANNING born Nov. 30, 1890 and died as an infant. Source: 1

G71 BLANCH BANNING born 1886 and died as an infant. Source: 1

G72 WILLIAM BANNING born Sept. 30, 1872 in Virginia City, Nevada. He lived in
Vanderbilt, Calif. Source: 1

G177 thru G182 for children

G73 ALBERT EDWARD THOMPSON born April 18, 1858 in Newbury, Ontario. He
married Helen Valenda Glendenning of Newbury on Dec. 17, 1879. They lived in
Winnipeg, Manitoba and had 3 children. Source: 1

G74 JOHN BELL THOMPSON born Oct. 12, 1863 in Newbury, Ontario. He married
Emily Atherton of Windsor, Ontario on Dec. 2, 1905 in Windsor. They lived in
Windsor and had at least one child. Source: 1

G75 ADDIE THOMPSON died an infant. Source: 1

G76 JOHN ALEXANDER BANNING born March 29, 1864 near Chatham, Ontario. He
married Helen Ford from Jersey, England in 1887 in Detroit, Mi. They lived in
Chicago. Source: 1

G183 Frances Mary Banning
G184 Alta Florence Banning
G185 Olive Alberta Banning

G77 CHARLES BANNING born Aug. 17, 1867 in Aldborough, Ontario. He married
Emeline Reno on Nov. 8, 1886 in Chatham, Ontario. They lived in Detroit, Mi.
Source: 1

G186 Ethel May Banning
G187 Harry Banning

G78 ALTA BANNING born March 4, 1869 in Aldborough, Ontario. She married
George Smith of Chatham, Ontario in 1901 in Chatham. They lived in Chicago.
Source: 1

G188 Ruby Lillian Smith
G189 George Smith

G79 CLIFFORD BELL HIGH born 1868 near Wardsville, Ontario. He lived in
Honolulu, Hi. where he was a physician. Source: 1

G80 CLARENCE BANNING born in Winnipeg, Manitoba. He lived in Los Angeles,
Calif., with his mother. Source: 1

G190 thru G195 for children

G81 WILLIAM WARD BANNING born in Winnipeg, Manitoba. Source: 1

G196 thru G201 for children

G82 CLAUD PERCIVAL BANNING born in Winnipeg, Manitoba. He married
Florence Ashdown of Winnipeg in June 1907. They lived in Winnipeg where he was
a physician. Source: 1

G202 thru G207 for children

G83 ELMER BANNING born in Winnipeg, Manitoba. Source: 1

G208 thru G213 for children

G84 ETHEL ISABEL BANNING born Jan. 1882 in Winnipeg, Manitoba. She married
John H. Dunsheath of Winnipeg, where they lived. Source: 1

G214 thru G219 for children

G85 COURTLAND BANNING born Aug. 1879 in Newbury, Ontario. He married in
1906, lived in Winnipeg, Manitoba where he died in 1807. Source: 1

G220 & G221 for children

G86 MABLE FLORENCE BANNING born in 188? and died as an infant. Source: 1

G87 ALEXANDER BRUCE BANNING born April 15, 1878 in Chatham, Ontario. He
married Kate Catlin on July 18, 1900 in Detroit, Mi. where they lived. Source: 1

G222 Katherine Margaret Banning
G223 Alexander Bruce Banning

G88 ELLA MAY BANNING born Jan. 14, 1881 in Detroit, Mi. She married Arthur
Cunningham on April 9, 1901 in Detroit, where they lived. Source: 1

G224 Arthur Cameron Cunningham
G225 Donald Shelton Cunningham

G89 thru G149 unknown children of G36 thru G61

G226 thru G376 for children

G150 thru G161 unknown children of G62 & G63

G162 thru G167 unknown children of G67

G377 thru G382 for children

G168 WANDA BANNING no information. Source: 1

G169 CLIFFORD OWEN BANNING born Oct. 7, 1907 and married Effie Kathryn
Ginder. She is the daughter of Seth & Barbara Ellen (Gish) Ginder, born March 2,
1910 in Solamon, Ks. He was a railroad engineer, retired from the Southern Pacific
R.R. and died prior to 1992. Effie was living in Alameda Calif in 1992. They had no

children. Source: 1,61

G170 GERTRUDE BANNING no information. Source: 1

G171 thru G176 unknown children of G69

G177 thru G182 unknown children of G72

G383 thru G433 for children

G183 FRANCES MARY BANNING born Aug. 1, 1888 in Chatham, Ontario. She lived in Chicago. Source: 1

G184 ALTA FLORENCE BANNING born Oct. 28, 1889 in Chatham, Ontario. Source: 1

G185 OLIVE ALBERTA BANNING born Dec. 24, 1902 in Chicago, Ill. Source: 1

G186 ETHEL MAY BANNING born Oct. 30, 1888 in Detroit, Mi. Source: 1

G187 HARRY BANNING born Nov. 25, 1889 in Detroit, Mi. Source: 1

G188 RUBY LILLIAN SMITH born 1892 in Chicago, Ill. Source: 1

G189 GEORGE SMITH born 1906 in Chicago. Source: 1

G190 thru G213 unknown children of G80 thru G83

G214 thru G219 unknown children of G84

G220 & G221 unknown children of G85

G222 KATHERINE MARGARET BANNING no information. Source: 1

G223 ALEXANDER BRUCE BANNING no information. Source: 1

G224 ARTHUR CAMERON CUNNINGHAM no information. Source: 1

G225 DONALD SHELTON CUNNINGHAM no information. Source: 1

G226 thru G376 unknown children of G89 thru G149

G377 thru G382 unknown children of G162 thru G167

G383 thru G433 unknown children of G177 thru G182

THOMAS C. BANNING OF DELAWARE

H1 THOMAS C. BANNING born about 1807 in Del. He married Sarah Webb on Nov. 10, 1830. She was born about 1814 in Del. He was a farmer. He married Pinkey M. Clendaniel on June 3, 1856. (He may have been married 3 times. In 1850 he was living in Sussex Co., Nanticoke Hundred, wife is Sarah. In 1860 he is in Sussex Co. Cedar Creek Hundred, wife is Pinkney.) He died Jan. 15, 1877. Source: 4,6,22,50

> H2 Jeremiah Banning
> H3 James Banning
> H4 Thomas 0. Banning
> H5 Sally Banning
> H6 Nancy Banning
> H7 Mary Banning
> H8 John Banning
> H8a Daniel G. Banning
> H8b Catherine Banning
> H8c Mark Lofland Banning
> H8d William Banning
> H8e Elizabeth Banning
> H8f Pinkey Banning

H2 JEREMIAH BANNING born about 1835 in Del. Source: 50

> H9 Marietta Banning
> H10 William Banning
> H11 Jefferson J. Banning
> H12 thru H15 for children

H3 JAMES BANNING born about 1836 in Del. Source: 5

> H16 thru H22 for children

H4 THOMAS 0. BANNING born May 16, 1840 in Del. He married Mary Elizabeth Isaacs, the daughter of Minos Isaacs in Greenwood Del. He died Feb. 15, 1908 in Greenwood and is buried in the Oakley Church Cementery. She died about 1879. Source: 5,6,12,22,50

> H23 Minos B. Banning
> H24 Charles P. Banning
> H25 Charles T. Banning
> H26 George H. Banning
> H27 Mary Elizabeth Banning
> H28 William Carlton Banning
> H29 John L. Banning
> H30 Alice Banning
> H31 Sally Banning

H5 SALLY BANNING born about 1842 in Del. and married Samuel Passwaters. Source: 5,6,12,50

> H32 thru H36 for children

H6 NANCY ANN BANNING born about 1844 in Del. and married J.W. Collins.
Source: 5,12,50

H37 thru H41 for children

H7 MARY BANNING born about 1846 in Del. and married Alexander Hellens. Source:
5,6,12,50

H42 thru H46 for children

H8 JOHN T. BANNING born about 1848 in Del. Source: 5,6,50

H47 thru H52 for children

H8a DANIEL G. BANNING born July 20, 1859 and died Aug. 20, 1938. He never
married and is buried in the Oakley Church Cemetery in Greenwood Del. Source:
6,50

H8b CATHERINE BANNING she married George F. Webb. They had 9 children.
Source: 6,50

H53 thru H57 for children

H8c MARK LOFLAND BANNING born March 16, 1857 in Cedar Creek Hundred, Del.
and married Frances Emily Truitt July 4, 1877 in Lincoln, Del. She was born Oct.
11, 1856 in Cedar Creek, Sussex Co. Del. She was the daughter of Nemiah Truitt
and died March 29, 1937. He was a farmer and died March 29, 1953. Both are
buried in the Oakley Church Cemetery in Greenwood Del. Source: 6,16,49,50

H58a Harry Elmer Banning
H58b Roy Benjamin Banning
H58c Lenora Catherine Banning
H58d Lester Earl Banning

H8d WILLIAM BANNING born Nov. 6, 1837 and died March 8, 1904. He is buried in
the Oakley Church Cemetery in Greenwood Del. Source: 6,12,22,50

H59 thru H63 for children

H8e ELIZABETH BANNING born about 1852 and married William Wharton. Source:
6,12,22,50

H64 thru H67 for children

H8f PINKEY BANNING born about 1861 and married Samuel Clendaniel on Nov. 30,
1878. He was born in 1860 and died in 1931. They had several children. She died
in 1953. Source: 50

H68 thru H70 for children

H9 MARIETTA BANNING. no information. Source: 50

H71 thru H74 for children

H10 WILLIAM BANNING no information. Source: 50

H75 thru H78 for children

H11 JEFFERSON J. BANNING no information. Source: 50

H79 thru H82 for children

H12 thru H22 unknown children of H2 & H3

H83 thru H113 for children

H23 MINORS B. BANNING born Oct. 29, 1865 and married Mary Emma Kneas. Source: 22

H114 Edna May Banning
H115 Elwood Irving Banning
H116 Oakley Minos Banning
H117 Osborn Emerson Banning

H24 CHARLES P. BANNING born July 25 1867 and died July 27, 1869. Source: 22

H25 CHARLES T. BANNING born March 21, 1869 and married Bessie D. Lord. She was born in 1883 and died in 1968. He died in 1947. Both are buried in the Oakley Church Cemetery om Greenwood, Del. Source: 22

H118 Meneolia Banning
H119 Homer Banning
H120 Vinal Banning
H121 Charles Banning
H122 Mildred Banning
H123 Mae Banning
H124 Myrtle Banning
H125 Edna Banning
H125a Norman Banning
H125b Walter Banning

H26 GEORGE H. BANNING born Nov. 18, 1870 and died Dec. 30, 1884. Source: 22

H27 MARY ELIZABETH BANNING born May 29, 1872. She married a Mr. Roland Bokar. She died Jan. 6, 1909 in Camden, N.J. Source: 22

H126 Floyd Bokar
H127 thru H132 for children

H28 WILLIAM CARLTON BANNING born Sept. 23, 1873 in Greenwood, Del. He married Lydia Elizabeth Miles in New Haven, Conn. on May 6, 1903. She was the daughter of Daniel L. Miles and Rose Ann Kelly and was born in New Haven on Sept. 17, 1877. He was an Inspector for the Winchester Repeating Arms Co. They purchase a home a 202 Fitch Street in New Haven in 1911. This home is still in the family. He died April 12, 1931 in New Haven where he is buried. She died Feb. 29, 1976 in Milford. Conn. and is buried in New Haven. Source: 16,22

H133 Evelyn Dorothy Banning
H134 William Miles Banning
H135 Miles Banning
H136 George Oakley Banning
H137 Lydia Elizabeth Banning
HI38 Anna May Banning

H29 JOHN L. BANNING born Feb. 25, 1875 and married Mina Anna Hemmonds. She was born in 1882 and died in 1950. He died in 1946. They both are buried in the Oakley Church Cemetery in Greenwood Del. Source: 22

H139 Ethel Banning
H140 Alice Banning
H141 Melvin Banning
H142 Lynwood Banning
H143 Daniel Banning
H144 Thomas Melvin Banning

H30 ALICE BANNING born Sept. 21, 1876 and died Dec. 27, 1884. Source: 22

H31 SALLY BANNING born Jan. 7, 1878 and died July 23, 1878. Source: 22

H32 thru H46 unknown children of H5 thru H7

H47 thru H52 unknown children of H8

H145 thru H173 for children

H53 thru H57 unknown children of H8b

H58a HARRY ELMER BANNING born Sept. 11, 1879 in Sussex Co., Del. and married 1st.Ida Hitchens on March 12, 1899. She died about 1900. They had no children. He married 2nd Lizza McCauley on May 21, 1902 in Sussex Co. She was born Jan 22, 1883 in Sussex Co. and was the daughter of Charles H. and Mary Ann (Issacs) McCauley. She was a teacher and died Dec. 28, 1972. He was a chicken farmer and died Dec. 6, 1957 in Greenwood, Del. They are buried in the Oakley Church Cemetery. Source: 16,22,50,61

H174 Harry Cannon Banning
H175 Geneva Emily Banning
H175a Leona C. Banning
H175b Alma Elizabeth Banning
H175c Thurman Charles Banning
H175d Leon Edwin Banning

H58b ROY BENJAMIN BANNING born Aug. 22, 1885 in Sussex Co., Del. and married Bertha Alice Johnson on Aug. 10, 1910. She was born Nov. 13, 1866 in Milford, Sussex Co., Del. and died Jan. 12, 1969 in Florence, S.C. He owned a music store, died Nov. 22, 1973 in Milford, Sussex, Co. Del. and is buried in Florence, S.C. Source: 16,50

H176 Aimee (Amy) Banning
H176a Orville Fisher Banning

H58c LENORA CATHERINE BANNING born Feb. 9, 1890 in Sussex Co., Del. and married Harry Edward Deatrick Nov. 24, 1912 in Houston, Kent Co., Del. He was born Dec. 15, 1888 and was the son of Edward and Aldema (Laucks) Deatrick. He was a painter and died March 13, 1965 in Lancaster, Pa. She died June 22, 1980 in Lancaster, where they are both buried. Source: 16,50

> H177   Emily Aldema Deatrick
> H177a   Gladys Isabel Deatrick
> H177b   Harry Mark Deatrick
> H177c   Frances Romaine Deatrick
> H177d   Verna Jane Deatrick
> H177E   Charles William Deatrick

H58d LESTER EARL BANNING born July 29, 1897 in Sussex Co., Del. and married 1st, Nora Casandra Morris on Aug. 29, 1922 in Rock Hall, Md. He served in the U.S. Army. He married 2nd, Cora Jester Brown on Sept. 8, 1962 in New Castle Del. It was her second marriage. She was born Sept. 23, 1900 and was the daughter of Samuel Jester. Cora died June 30, 1975 in Midway, Del. He died March 27, 1976 in Midway, Del. and is buried in Centerville, Md. Source: 50

> H178   Lester Earl Banning Jr.

H59 thru H113 unknown children of H9 thru H22

> H179 thru H299 for children

H114 EDNA BANNING married a L. Baynard Marvel. Source: 22

> H300   Anita Marvel

H115 ELWOOD IRVING BANNING married Mary E. Richards. Source: 22

> H301 thru H307 for children

H116 OAKLEY MINOS BANNING married Mary Etta Skeggs. Source: 22

> H308 thru H314 for children

H117 OSBORN EMERSON BANNING married Myra Brian. He died in Ft. Lauderdale, Fla. in 1964. Source: 22

> H315 thru H323 for children

H118 MENOLIA BANNING born Sept. 17, 1900 and married Robert Workman of Ellendale, Del. They were divorced in 1946. She married 2nd, Samuel Downey of Chester, Pa. in 1951. He died in 1958. She had no children and died April 9, 1971. She is buried in the Oakley Church Cemetery in Greenwood, Del. Source: 16,22,48

H119 HOMER BANNING born July 6, 1902. He married Huldah Ann Moore on Dec. 24, 1923. She was born Sept. 10, 1906. He died Dec. 31, 1966. She died Aug. 9, 1985. Source: 16,22,48

> H324   Doris Aileen Banning

H325 Frances Ann Banning
H326 Elizabeth Jane (Betty) Banning
H327 Jeanette Dolores Banning
H328 Richard Homer Banning

H120 VINAL BANNING born Oct. 18, 1907 in Greenwood, Del. He married Pauline
Carroll in 1926. He died Jan. 12, 1967 and she died March 17, 1977. Source:
16,22,48

H329 Delema Mae Banning
H330 William Thomas Banning
H331 Nancy Banning

H121 CHARLES HENRY BANNING born Sept 13, 1905. He married Ethel Kate
Moore June 25, 1926. She was born April 20, 1909 and died May 8, 1953. He died
March 30, 1984. Source: 16,22,48

H332 Norma Elizabeth Banning
H333 Ronald Charles Banning

H122 MILDRED BANNING born July 18, 1911 and married Roger E. Adams on Dec.
7, 1930 Source: 16,22,48

H334 Roger E. Adams Jr.

H123 MAY RUTH BANNING born May 23, 1914 and married William A. Chandler on
Aug. 25, 1935. Source: 16,22,48

H335 William A. Chandler Jr.
H336 Edna Ann Chandler
H337 Gloria Lynn Chandler

H124 MYRTLE BANNING born Aug. 25, 1916 and married 1st, Harry Waishes in
1934. He died in 1938. She married 2nd, George M. McNeal of Wayne, Pa. She
died July 19, 1977. Source: 16,22,48

H338 Niki C. McNeal

H125 EDNA M. BANNING born Sept. 12, 1918 and married Paul Wilkinson on Aug.
22, 1942. They divorced in 1951. They had no children. She is the source for
much information on this line. Source: 16,22,48

H125a NORMAN BANNING born 1909 and died 1910. He is buried in the Oakley
Cemetery in Greenwood Del.

H125b WALTER BANNING born and died in 1914. He is buried in the Oakley Church
Cemetery in Greenwood, Del.

H126 FLOYD BOKAR no information

H127 thru H132 unknown children of H27

H133 EVELYN DOROTHY BANNING born Aug. 12, 1905 in New Haven, Conn. and
married Robert Earle Bamberg in New Haven on Sept. 4, 1926. He was the son of

302

George Andrew and Mary K. (Earle) Bamberg, born May 14, 1901 in New Haven. Retired as Pres. of C.S. Leete and died Sept. 29, 1984 in Stratford, Conn. He was buried in Sunapee, Merrimac Co., N.H. They lived at 533 Carriage Dr. in Oeange, Conn. Source: 16,22

H372 Arleen Carol Bamberg
H373 Robert Wesley Bamberg

H134 WILLIAM MILES BANNING born March 19, 1907 in New Haven, Conn. and married Alice Murphy Nov. 28, 1928 in Port Chester, Westchester Co., N.Y. She was the daughter of Michael and Elizabeth C. (McCormick) Murphy born Dec. 15, 1906 in New Haven. They had 3 children. She died July 14, 1959 in Stamford, Conn. where she is buried. He married 2nd, Grace Michelson on Oct. 8, 1960. He retired from the SNET Co. and lived at 104 Dogwood Trail, Leesburg, Lake Co., Fla. where he died Nov. 18, 1979. He is buried in St. John's Cemetery in Stamford, Conn. Grace died April 2, 1989 at Hilton Head Island, S.C. and was buried in Samford, Fairfield Co., Ct. Source: 16,22

H374 William Raymond Banning
H375 George C. Banning
H376 Richard Charles Banning

H135 MILES BANNING born July 13, 1908 in New Haven, Conn. and married Margaret VanDer Maelen on Feb. 2, 1932 in Port Chester, Westchester Co., N.Y. She was the daughter of Benoit and Marie Louise (Herregodst) VanDer Maelen born March 3, 1910 in New Haven. He was a splicer for American Steel Co. They lived at 202 Fitch St. in New Haven, and died Sept. 10, 1973 in Killingworth, Middlesex Co., Conn. He was buried in New Haven. Source: 16,22

H377 Joan Louise Banning
H378 Miles Carlton Banning

H136 GEORGE OAKLEY BANNING born Jan. 13, 1910 in New Haven, Conn. and married Alice Mara in Stamford, Fairfield Co., Conn. She was born June 22, 1909. He was an installer for SNET Co. and died July 22, 1961 in Stamford, where he is buried. They lived in Springdale, Conn. Source: 16,22

H379 Barbara Banning
H380 Oakley George Banning
H381 Claire Marie Banning

H137 LYDIA ELIZABETH BANNING born June 19, 1913 in New Haven, Conn. and married Raymond Renth Hudson on June 17, 1939 in New Haven. He was the son of Charles Raymond and Edith Evelyn (Renth) Hudson born May 11, 1913. He retired as purchasing supervisor of United Illuminating Co. They lived in Woodbridge, New Haven Co. Conn. Lydia furnished much of the information on this line. Source: 16,22

H382 Richard Banning Hudson
H383 Roberta Sue Hudson

H138 ANNA MAY BANNING born Sept. 2, 1917 in New Haven, Conn. and died July 3, 1920. Source: 22

H139 ETHEL BANNING married Leonard Wisseman. She died July 20, 1977. Source: 22

H384 thru H388 for children

H140 ALICE BANNING married Gideon Wisseman. She died March 22, 1985. Source: 22

H389 thru H393 for children

H141 MELVIN BANNING died prior to 1987. Source: 22

H394 thru H398 for children

H142 LYNWOOD BANNING died prior to 1987. Source: 22

H399 thru H403 for children

H143 DANIEL BANNING born Oct. 6, 1916. He was a Sgt. in Co. C, 104 Infty. Reg. Died Jan. 19, 1961. Source: 22

H144 THOMAS MELVIN BANNING married Mary Bowman of Virginia. He died June 10, 1982. Source: 22

H404 Virginia A. Banning
H405 Melva A. Banning

H145 thru H173 unknown children of H47 thru H52

H406 thru H490 for children

H174 HARRY CANNON BANNING born March 11, 1915 in Bridgeville, Susses Co., Del. and married Hildred Jessie Spence on Feb. 9, 1935 in Denton, Md. She was born May 22, 1915 in Greenwood, Sussex Co., Del and was the daughter of Oscar Wiley and Jessie Deborah (Murphy) Spence. They lived at 107 Walnut St. Bridgeville, Del. She died Oct. 22, 1982 in Bridgeville and is buried in St. Johnstown Cemetery in Greenwood. He married 2nd, Dorothy Rust Dearman on Feb. 5, 1986 in Denton, Md. This was her 2nd marriage. She was born July 6, 1911. Source: 16,50

H491 Alma Jean Banning
H492 Kathryn Hildred Banning

H175 GENEVA EMILY BANNING born April 12, 1913 in Bridgeville, Sussex Co. Del. and married Walter Franklin Spence on March 20, 1942 in Denton, Caroline Co., Md. He was born Sept. 6, 1916 in Greenwood, Sussex Co., Del. and was the son of Oscar Willey and Jessie Deborah (Murphy) Spence. He worked 39 years for the Del. Elect. Co-op and died Nov. 4, 1977. He is buried in St. Johnstown Cemetery in Greenwood. She was the source of much information on this line. Source: 16,50

H493 Larry Wayne Spence
H494 Franklin Merle Spence

H175a LEONA CATHERINE BANNING born Dec. 23, 1903 in Oakley, Sussex Co.,

304

Del. She married Ralph Lofton (or Lufkin) Wheatley on Dec. 23, 1922 in Greenwood, Susses Co. He was born Feb. 24, 1900 in Frederalsburg, Md. and was the son of Joseph and Clattie (O'Day) Wheatley. He was a chicken farmer. They liced in Bridgeville, Del. where he died Feb.22, 1980. She died Jan. 7, 1989 and both are buried in Bridgeville Cemetery. Source: 16,50

H495 Joseph Ralph Wheatley

H175b ALMA ELIZABETH BANNING born July 15, 1907 in Oakley, Sussex Co., Del. She married John Nathaniel Johnson on June 23, 1928 in Chester, Pa. He was born April 4, 1906 in Kennedyville, Md. and was the son of Nathaniel and Maggie (Sylvester) Johnson. He owned a laundry in Clarksville, Tenn. where he died and was buried Oct. 11, 1955. She married 2nd Durward Smith Tarpley on Jan 28, 1962 in Clarksville, Montgomery Co., Tenn. He was born April 11, 1907 in Clarksville and was the son of Branch and Mabel (Smith) Tarpley. They lived at 157 Liberty Pkwy in Clarksville. He died Oct. 17, 1979 and is buried in Greenwood Cemetery in Clarksville. Source: 16,50

H496 Wanda Lee Johnson

H175c THURMAN CHARLES BANNING born June 13, 1918 in Bridgeville, Sussex Co., Del. and married Leatha Elizabeth Morgan June 16, 1939 in Seaford, Sussex Co., Del. She was born Oct. 13, 1919 in Redden, Sussex Co., Del and was the daughter of George Elmer and June Elizabeth (Caldwell) Morgan. He was a truck driver. They were living in Milford, Del. in 1992. They had no children. Source: 16,50,61

H175d LEON EDWIN BANNING born Jan. 10, 1922 in bridgeville, Sussex Co., Del. and died March 7, 1923. He is buried in the Oakley Cemetery in Oakley, Del. Source: 50

H176 AIMEE (AMY) BANNING born Sept. 10, 1911 in Milford, Del. and married Samuel James Powell on Dec. 23, 1931. He was born June 4, 1901 in Frederica, Del. and was the son of James Thomae and Mae (Miner) Powell. She worked for the Telephone Co. and died Oct. 13, 1980 in Milford. She is buried in Florence, S.C. He was a farmer, died Jan. 1, 1983 and is buried in Fritztown, Pa. Source: 16,50

H497 Joyce Louise Powell

H176a ORVILLE FISHER BANNING born June 14, 1917 in Milford, Del. and married Ruby Bell. She was the daughter of Samuel Hendricks and Emma (Stroud) Bell. He worked in a piano store and died April 28, 1971 in Florence, S.C. where they lived. Source: 16,50

H498 Alice Elaine Banning
H499 Betty Jane Banning
H500 Barbara Jean Banning
H501 William Benjamin Banning
H502 Rosie Marie Banning

H177 EMILY ALDEMA DEATRICK born Sept. 3, 1913 in Bridgeville, Del. and married James David Saturno. He was born Nov. 19, 1911 and was the son of Samuel and Therisa (Pisani) Saturno. They liced in Lancaster, Pa. where she died Oct. 15,

305

1969. Their children are Gloria Theresa (1932), Gladys Elizabeth (1932) and James Louis (1937). Source: 16,50

H177a GLADYS ISABEL DEATRICK born Aug. 20, 1916 in Bridgeville, Sussex Co., Del. and married William Franklin Kissinger on Nov. 1, 1938 in Elkton, Md. He was born April 5, 1913 in Lancaster, Pa. and was the son of George Washington and Carolyn Regina (Hammel) Kissinger. She died Jan. 15, 1987 in Lancaster. They had one child Kathy Regina, born 1959. Source: 16,50

H177b HARRY MARK DEATRICK born Dec. 11, 1919 in Lancaster, Pa. and married Grace Christine Offner on June 14, 1943 in Lancaster. She was born Oct. 17, 1919 in Lancaster and was the daughter of Arthur Andrew and Katie Jane (Haring) Offner. He served in the U.S. Army and worked for the City Warer Dept. Their children are Michael James (1947) and Joyce Ann (1951). Source: 16,50

H177c FRANCES ROMAINE DEATRICK born July 19, 1922 in Lancaster, Pa. and married Theodore Gifford Burtnett on Feb. 10, 1942 in Elkton, Md. He is the son of Charles Ambrose and Nora (Straub) Burtnett born Feb. 16, 1923 in Harrisburg, Pa. He served in the U.S. Navy. Their children are Verna Jane (1943), Marilyn Jean (1945), Debra June (1954) and Theodore Gifford Jr. (1955). Source: 16,50

H177d VERNA JANE DEATRICK born Dec. 18, 1924 in Lancaster, Pa. and married Clyde Robert Cover, Jr. on April 6, 1946 in Middletown, Pa. He is the son of Clyde Robert and Margaret (Ierley) Cover born May 25, 1922 in Middletown. He served in the Sea Bees in The U.S. Navy. Their children are Clyde Robert 3rd (1947) and Melissa Rae (1952). Source: 16,50

H177e CHARLES WILLIAM DEATRICK born Dec. 31, 1928 in Lancaster, Pa. He married Marie Keller in Pa. Source: 50

H178 LESTER EARL BANNING, JR. born Sept 12, 1923 in Pa. and married Marjorie Ann Seymour. He is in auto sales. Source: 16,50

> H503 Michael Terry Banning
> H504 Mark Trowbridge Banning
> H505 Lester Earl Banning, III

H179 thru H299 unknown children of H59 thru H113

> H506 thru H700 for children

H300 ANITA MARVEL married Joseph Hutchison. they are living in Townsend, Del.

H301 thru H323 for children of H115 thru H117

> H701 thru H759 for children

H324 DORIS AILEEN BANNING born Jan. 24, 1925 and died at birth. Source: 16,48

H325 FRANCES ANN BANNING born Oct. 26, 1927 and married George Hall Betts II on July 3, 1948. They were divorced Jan. 27, 1969. She married 2nd, Walter Francis Smith on April 1, 1969. Source: 16,48

> H760 Darlene Ethel Betts

H761 Debra Naioma Betts

H326 ELIZABETH JANE (Betty)   BANNING born Nov. 25, 1929 and married
Clarence James Reed on March 31, 1945. Source: 16,48

> H762 Kenneth Lee Reed
> H763 Beverly Ann Reed
> H764 Clarence James Reed
> H765 Richard Allan Reed

H327 JEANETTE DOLORES BANNING, born July 31, 1932 and married Robert
Eugene Furroughs on March 31, 1949. He was born in 1926 and died July 6, 1988,
She died March 1, 1972. Source: 16,48

> H766 James Eugene Furroughs
> H767 David Wayne Furroughs
> H768 Penny Diane Furroughs
> H769 Bonnie Kay Furroughs
> H770 Richard Allen Furroughs

H328 RICHARD HOMER BANNING born Jan. 26, 1940 and died at birth. Source:
16,48

H329 DELMEA MAE BANNING born Jan. 23, 1927 in Milford, Del. and married
William P. Jester of Milford in 1944. Source: 16,48

> H771 William P. Jester, Jr.
> H772 Donald W. Jester
> H773 Ronald E. Jester
> H774 Donna L. Jester

H330 WILLIAM THOMAS BANNING born March 10, 1929 in Milton, Del. and married
Vietta M. West of Georgetown, Del. in 1947. Source: 16,48

> H775 William C. Banning
> H776 Linda M. Banning

H331 NANCY BANNING born Feb. 19, 1944 in Milford, Del. and married Roy Farens
Jan. 28, 1962. They divorced May 13, 1976. She married 2nd, Jack Burress on
Dec. 20, 1978. Source: 16,48

> H777 Tonya F. Farens
> H778 Shannon Renee Farens
> H779 Jason A. Burress

H332 NORMA ELIZABETH BANNING born May 10, 1932 and married Lew F. White,
Jr. in June 1949. They were divorced in 1960. She married 2nd, Charles Darlington
in 1973. There were no children from this union. She died Feb. 9, 1977. Source:
16,48

> H780 Charles Lawrence (Larry) White
> H781 Gary Lee White
> H782 Keith Lew White

H333 RONALD CHARLES BANNING born Aug. 18, 1941 and married Jane Ingram. They had 2 children and divorced. He married 2nd, Cissy T. Agler. They had 1 child and divorced. He was single as of Mar. 1989. Source: 16,48

H783 Charles Richard Banning
H784 Cherry Lynn Banning
H785 Kimberly Kate Banning

H334 ROGER E. ADAMS Jr. born Sept. 30, 1932 and married Carolyn J. Nelte in 1954. Their children are; Deborah Gwen (1954), Gregory W. (1956), Brian K. (1957) and Kevin C. (1960). Source: 16,48

H335 WILLIAM A. CHANDLER, Jr. born Sept. 8, 1937 and married Frances A. Robbins on Jan. 31, 1959. Their children are; Robin L. (1960), Shelly Mae (1963) and William K. (1967). Source: 16,48

H336 EDNA ANN CHANDLER born June 30, 1942 and married Theodore M. Newhouse on June 3, 1961. Their children are; Theodore M. Jr. (1962) and Scott C. (1964). Source: 16,48

H337 GLORIA LYNN CHANDLER born Nov. 27, 1944 and married Benjamin R. Bridgers Jr. on April 12, 1964. Their children are; Darren Benjamin (1967) and Narc David (1970). Source: 16,48

H338 NIKI C. McNEAL born Nov. 10, 1950 in Boston, Mass. She married Robert Fowler of Rochester, N.Y. on March 10, 1989. Source: 16,48

H339 thru H371 unused numbers

H372 ARLEEN CAROL BAMBERG born April 30, 1928 in New Haven, Conn. She married Richard Webster Arnold Jr. on Dec. 2, 1950 in Woodbridge, New Haven Co., Conn. He was the son of Richard W.and Madaline (Ver Steeg) Arnold, born Sept. 18, 1928 in New Haven. He was a Lt. in the U.S. Navy (1950-53) and retired as a Sr. V.P. at the A.T.& T. Foundation. She is the Director of Branch Libraries at Stamford, Conn., where they live. Source: 16,22

H817 Katheryn Webster Arnold
H818 David Richard Arnold

H373 ROBERT WESLEY BAMBERG born June 30, 1929 in New Haven, Conn. He married Margaret Ann Howgate May 8, 1954 in Greenwich, Fairfield Co., Conn. She is the daughter of Dr. Henry Otis and Mary (Wallace) Howgate, born Aug. 17, 1931 in Greenwich. He served in the U.S. Army 1951-53 and retired as Pres./Treas. of C.S. Leete, Inc. They live in Woodbury, Conn. Source: 16,22

H819 Claire Wallace Bamberg
H820 Robert Otis Bamberg
H821 John Carlton Bamberg
H822 Paul Henry Bamberg

H374 WILLIAM RAYMOND BANNING born Oct. 17, 1929 in Stamford, Fairfield Co., Conn. He married Dorothy Ann McMahon on Sept. 29, 1951 in Stamford. She is the daughter of William E. McMahon Jr. and Anna (Hostos) McMahon, born March

15, 1928 in Stamford. He served in the Korean War and in Germany 1952-54 and is now retired from SNET Co. They live in West Redding, Conn. Source: 16,22

H823 Mary Ellen Banning
H824 William G. Banning
H825 Alison Marie Banning
H826 John McMahon Banning
H827 Thomas Joseph Banning
H829 Mark Banning

H375 GEORGE C. BANNING born May 18, 1931 in Stamford, Fairfield Co., Conn. He was a PFC in Co. B of the U.S. 5th Inf. and died May 11, 1953 in Korea. He is buried in Stamford Conn. Source: 22

H376 RICHARD CHARLES BANNING born Jan. 19, 1940 in Stamford, Fairfield Co., Conn. He married Carol Ann Beland Oct. 8, 1962 in Stamford. She is the daughter of Oliver and Evelyn Ralma (Tourigny) Beland born March 14, 1941 in Stamford. He was in the U.S. Army in 1963, and was a computer analyst. They lived in New Fairfield, Conn. They had 3 children. He died March 4, 1982 in Boston, Mass. and is buried in New Fairfield. She is now married to Robert Dugan. Source: 16,22

H830 Heather Anne Banning
H831 Scott Richard Banning
H832 Glenn Oliver Banning

H377 JOAN LOUISE BANNING born Sept 30, 1932 in New Haven, Conn. She married Francis H. Cove April 11, 1953 in New Haven. He is the son of Leo A. and Helen Mary (Stratton) Cove, born Feb. 5, 1930 in New Haven. He was a Staff Sgt. in the U.S. Air force and in now a V.P. at Security Insurance Co. They live in Northford, Conn. Source: 16,22

H833 Karen Lynn Cove
H834 Valerie Ann Cove
H835 David Francis Cove
H836 Brian Michael Cove
H837 Kevin Peter Cove
H838 Jay Scott Cove

H378 MILES CARLTON BANNING born Dec. 26, 1941 in New Haven, Conn. He married Sharon Joy Raccio on Aug. 7, 1965 in New Haven. She is the daughter of Peter W. and Betty (Waldorf) Raccio, born Oct. 19, 1943 in New Haven. He was in the U.S. Army in Thailand 1963-66. They live in Gainesville, Fla. where she is a Secretary and he owns a Trucking Co. Source: 16,22

H839 Troy William Banning
H840 Cindy Lane Banning

H379 BARBARA BANNING born Sept. 28, 1935 in Stamford, Conn. Source: 22

H380 OAKLEY GEORGE BANNING born May 17, 1939 in Stamford, Conn. He married Mary Evans Nov. 19, 1960 in Stamford. She is the daughter of Paul and Marie (Moore) Evans, born Sept. 27, 1940 in Norfolk, Vir. They live in Norwalk, Conn. Source: 16,22

        H841 Kathryn Alice Banning
        H842 Susan Margaret Banning
        H843 Cynthia Maria Banning

H381 CLAIRE MARIE BANNING born June 29, 1941 in Stamford. She married
    Robert Piscitelli. He was born May 29, 1942 in Springfield, Mass. They now live in
    Calif. Source: 16,22

        H844 Robert T. Piscitelli
        H845 Marie Piscitelli
        H846 Dawn Piscitelli
        H847 Pamela Piscitelli

H382 RICHARD BANNING HUDSON born May 19, 1944 in New Haven. He married
    Nancy Ann Lindstrom Dec. 18, 1965 in Oakland, Calif. She is the daughter of Elmer
    Emanuel and Bernice (Warren) Lindstrom, born July 8, 1945 in Oakland. He served
    in the U.S. Navy 1962-66 and is now a goldsmith. They lived in Oakland where they
    had one child, Christine E. Hudson. He married 2nd, Jann Lynn Smallwood Sept.
    15, 1974 in Lake Tahoe, Calif. She is the daughter of Thomas Edward and Mildred
    Anne (Campbell) Smallwood, born Aug. 23, 1946. They live in Orangevale,
    Sacramento Co., Calif. Source: 16,22

H383 ROBERTA SUE HUDSON born June 7, 1946 in New Haven, Conn. She
    married Kenneth Sawyer Aug. 2, 1976 in Marion, Flathead Co., Mont. They
    divorced, no children. Source: 22

H384 thru H393 unknown children of H139 & H140

H394 thru H403 unknown children of H141 & H142.

        H848 thru H878 for children

H404 VIRGINIA A. BANNING she married a Mr. Mitchell and lives in Newark, Del.
    Source: 22

        H879 thru H883 for children

H405 MELVA A. BANNING she married a Mr. Anthony and lives in Bear, Del. Source:
    22

        H884 thru H887 for children

H406 thru H490 unknown children of H145 thru H173

        H888 thru H1000 for children

H491 ALMA JEAN BANNING born Oct. 26, 1943 in Clarksville, Tenn. and married
    Wilmer Tull Wilson Oct. 29, 1961 in Bridgeville, Sussex Co., Del. He is the son of
    Wilmer Tull Wilson Sr. born Oct. 31, 1941 in Lewes, Del. He is in Farming and
    construction work and she is a teacher's aide. They live in Bridgeville, Del. Source:
    16,50

        H1001 Melissa Dale Wilson

H492 KATHRYN HILDRED BANNING born Jan. 31, 1948 in Milford, Del. and married Richard Farber Carlisle on Nov. 21, 1970 in Greenwood, Sussex Co., Del. He was born Sept. 10, 1944 in Milford. They live in Bridgeville, Del. He is an instructor at the University of Del. She is a Teacher's Aide. Source: 16,50.

H1002 Richard Banning Carlisle
H1003 Cameron Scott Carlisle
H1004 Jessica Carlisle

H493 LARRY WAYNE SPENCE born Jan. 17, 1946 in Milford, Sussex Co., Del. and married 1st, Cynthia Sue Snyder on May 30, 1967 in Perry, Okla. She is the daughter of Olin and Ruby (Kelly) Snyder, born June 21, 1947 in Perry, Okla. He served in the U.S. Army 1968-71, including a year in Viet-Nam. They had one child, Lane Kelly Spence, born 1971 in Perry. He married 2nd, Patricia Ann Snyder on Jan. 10, 1981 in Albert Lee, Minn. She was born Feb. 7, 1954 in Perry, Okla. They have 2 sons, Gale Dean (1978) and Seth Ryan (1980). Source: 16,50

H494 FRANKLIN MERLE SPENCE born Oct. 18, 1950 in Milford, Del. and married Karen Mary Outten Dec. 21, 1968 in Lincoln, Sussex Co., Del. She is the daughter of Tilghman and Delema (Paskey) Outten, born Sept. 11, 1950 in Milford. He spent 3 years in the U.S. Army including 1 in Viet-Nam. He now ownes a Hardware store in Greenwood, Del. where they live. She is a Post Mistress. Their children are Lisa Beth (1974) and Michele Lynn (1977). Source: 16,50

H495 JOSEPH RALPH WHEATLEY born Sept. 12, 1923 in Bridgeville, Sussex Co., Del. and married Marilda Hazel West on Oct. 23, 1943 in Bridgeville. She was the daughter of Paul Washington and Olive (burton) West, born Feb. 18, 1923. They have a furniture store and live on Jacob,s Ave in Bridgeville. Their children are Sharon Kaye (1946), Joanne (1949) and Joseph Ralph (1954). Source: 16,50

H496 WANDA LEE JOHNSON born Oct. 10, 1931 in Chester, Pa. and married Henry Beltram Bonecutter on March 11, 1951 in Clarksville, Tenn. He is the son of Beltram Lee and Fannie (Greer) Bonecutter, born April 28, 1928. He served 5 years in the U.S. Army and he was a director of the Red Cross. He died Dec. 31, 1980 and is buried in Clarksville. Their children are Henry Beltram (1953) and John Steven (1955). Source: 16,50

H497 JOYCE LOUISE POWELL born Aug. 24, 1933 in Milford, Del. and married Charles D. Ennis. They had a daughter, Susan Pamela, born 1966. She married 2nd, Joseph W. Poe on June 28, 1986. Source: 16,50

H498 ALICE ELAINE BANNING born Aug. 21, 1948 in Orangeburg, S.C. and married Gene Langston Hatchell on April 14, 1968. He is the son of Clyde William and Eunice (Langston) Hatchell, born Sept. 16, 1945 in Timmonsville, S.C. He worked for Sears Roebuck and died June 1, 1972 in Florence, S.C. where he is buried. She married 2nd, Dr. James Arthur Jones on Jan. 4, 1980 in Florence. He is the son of Edward Floyd and Bessie Ruth (Ward) Jones, born June 6, 1943 in Atlanta, Ga. James is a Dentist and they live in Florence. Source: 16,50

H1005 Gena DaLaine Hatchell
H1006 Jason Ward Jones

H499 BETTY JANE BANNING born Nov. 30, 1949 in Florence, S.C. and married Thomas Allen Dowling on Dec. 30, 1967 in Florence. He was the son of Laurin

Pinkney and Orillo Margarite (Truluck) Dowling, born Feb. 27, 1944 in Darlington, S.C. He served 6 years in the U.S. Navy and now ownes an Automotive parts rebuilding co. They live in Timmpnsville, S.C. Source: 16,50

> H1007 Natalie Yvonne Dowling
> H1008 Thomas Allen Dowling
> H1009 Adam Timothy Dowling

H500 BARBARA JEAN BANNING born Jan. 26, 1951 in Florence S.C. and married Kenneth Laran Shirley on Dec. 3, 1972. He is the son of Harold J. and Minnie N. (Hatcher) Shirley, born April 13, 1952 in Seneca, S.C. They live in Oswego, N.Y. Source: 16,50

> H1010 Lance Kenneth Shirley
> H1011 Trent Justin Shirley
> H1012 Chad Matthew Shirley

H501 WILLIAM BENJAMIN BANNING born March 9, 1953 in Florence, S.C. and married Wanda Ann Gore on March 29, 1975 in Florence. She was the daughter of William Leon Gore, born June 28, 1950. Source: 16,50

> H1013 William Benjamin Banning
> H1014 Angela Michelle Banning

H502 ROSE MARIE BANNING born Jan. 26, 1955 in Florence, S.C. and married Jefferson Waldo Peeples on July 1, 1978. He is the son of Jefferson Waldo and Lillian (Moore) Peeples, born Dec. 1, 1954 in Jacksonville, Fla. He is a computer programer and she is in banking. They live in Fla. Source: 16,50

> H1015 & H1016 for children

H503 MICHAEL TERRY BANNING born Oct. 13, 1952 in Lewes, Sussex Co., Del. and married Edith Lucille Morris on Oct. 27, 1979 in Denton, Md. She is the daughter of Raymond and Amanda Doris (Melvin) Morris. He served in the U.S. Marines. Source: 16,50

> H1017 & H1018 for children

H504 MARK TROWBRIDGE BANNING born July 9, 1955 in Lewes, Sussex Co., Del and married Okemah Jenkins. She is the daughter of William Jenkins Jr. He is a construction worker and she is a beautician. Source: 16,50

> H1019 Shawn Patrick Banning
> H1020 Justin Trowbridge Banning

H505 LESTER EARL BANNING, III born April 14, 1957 in Milford, Sussex Co., Del. and married Donna Sue Webb on April 4, 1976 in Milford. She is the daughter of Cyril D. and Cathering F. (Stevenson) Webb. born Dec. 18, 1956 in Milford. He is a building contractor and she is a bookkeeper. They live in Milford. Source: 16,50

> H1021 Robie Ian Banning
> H1022 Rachel Anne Banning
> H1023 Emily Ann Banning

H760 DARLENE ETHEL BETTS born Feb. 16, 1954 and married Robert Blackston
Dorman on March 29, 1968. They had 2 children and were divorced April 16, 1973.
She married 2nd, Douglas George Bryant Aug. 24, 1973. They had 2 children and
he adopted her 2 Dorman Sons. Her children are; (Daryl Anderson (1969), Douglas
Aldon (1971), Danielle Grace (1974) and Deanna Marie (1975). Source: 16,48

H761 DEBRA NAIOMA BETTS born Sept 15, 1956 and married Randy Elious
Parsons April 14, 1974. They had 2 children and were divorced in 1979. Their
children are; Nicole Renee (1975) and Jaime Rae (born & died 1977). Source:
16,48

H762 KENNETH LEE REED born 1945. He had no children and was single in 1989.
Source: 16,48

H763 BEVERLY ANN REED born Feb. 20, 1947 and married Robert Allen White in
Jan. 1965. They had 2 children, Robert Allan Jr. (1966) and Brian Lee (1970).
They also adopted Denise Lynn Furroughs (1968) from her cousin, Bonnie Kay
(H769). Source: 16,48

H764 CLARENCE JAMES (Jim) REED 2nd. born July 20, 1960 and married Catherine
Orendorf July 14, 1978. Their children are Clarence James (1979) and Carlyn
Danielle (Carly, born 1982). Source: 16,48

H765 RICHARD ALLEN REED born Sept. 27, 1963 and married Karen Cousins on
Nov. 28, 1981. Their children are Brandi Elizabeth (1983) and Ryan Dennis (1986).
Source: 16,48

H766 JAMES EUGENE FURROUGHS born & died Jan. 22, 1950. Source: 16, 48

H767 DAVID WANE FURROUGHS born July 21, 1952 and married Linda Dorrell on
June 19, 1982. Their children are David Jr. (1980) and Cherry Lynn (1982).
Source: 16,48

H768 PENNY DIANE FURROUGHS born July 21, 1953 and married Dennis Ellis on
Jan. 12, 1972. They had 2 children and divorced in 1979. She was single in 1989.
The children are Jessica (1974) and Erica (1978). Source: 16,48

H769 BONNIE KAY FURROUGHS born Nov. 27, 1955 and married Carlton Rust in
1971. They had 3 children and divorced in 1986. She married 2nd, Carl Zellman.
There were no children of this union as of March 1989. Her children are Nikki
(1972), Beth (1980) and Mark (1981). Source: 16,48

H770 RICHARD ALLAN FURROUGHS born Oct. 17, 1956 and married Shirley
Meredith on April 19, 1977. They had 2 children and divorced in 1982. He has
remarried and is living in Fla. His children are Richard Allen Jr. (1978) and
Christopher (1980). Source: 16,48

H771 WILLIAM P. JESTER Jr. born June 9, 1945 and married 1st. Rose Sehn on
June 24, 1967. They had a child, Ryan M. born 1977(?). He married 2nd, Barbara
Parkhurst on Sept. 20, 1975 and had 2 children, Kimberly M. (1976) and Rachael

Joy (1983). Source: 16,48

H772 DONALD W. JESTER born Mar. 4, 1949 and married Bernadette Sehn in 1969. They had one child, Stephanie M. (born & died 1969) and divorced in 1972. Source: 16,48

H773 RONALD E. JESTER born Mar. 19, 1955 and married Lee Ann Welch on Aug. 26, 1978. They had Christopher Donovan (1981) and Katherine Ann (1986). Source: 16,48

H774 DONNA L. JESTER born Mar. 19, 1955 and married Michael Rivera on May 17, 1975. They have one child, Michael L. Jr. born 1980. Source: 16,48

H775 WILLIAM C. BANNING born Nov. 14, 1947 and married Jackie L. Brown on May 22, 1963. Source: 16,48

> H1301 William C. Banning Jr.
> H1302 Robin Banning
> H1303 Kelly R. Banning
> H1304 Adam T. Banning

H776 LINDA M. BANNING born in Nov. 1949 and married 2nd. Gary Longshaw. Source: 16,48

> H1305 Jennifer P. Mahoney
> H1306 Sean M. Mahoney

H777 TONYA F. FARENS born Nov. 14, 1962. Source: 16,48

H778 SHANNON RENEE FARENS born April 7, 1964. Source: 16,48

H779 JASON A. BURRESS born Oct. 4, 1979. Source: 16,48

H780 CHARLES LAWRENCE (Larry) WHITE born Sept. 17, 1952 and married Cherry Turnahand in 1974. Their children are Larry Jr. (1977), Regina (1984) and Carey (1986). Source: 16,48

H781 GARY LEE WHITE born July 27, 1955 and married Cynthia Keller in 1977. Their children are Travis Lee (1984 and Cody James (1986). Source: 16,48

H782 KEITH LEW WHITE, born Aug. 20, 1957 and married Barbara (???) in 1983. They had a child, Melissa Marie, born July 1987. Source: 16,48

H783 CHARLES RICHARD BANNING born Oct. 4, 1963. He is married and has no children as of March 1989. Source: 16,48

> H1307 thru H1310 for children

H784 CHERRY LYNN BANNING born Oct. 11, 1961 and is married. She has no children as of March 1989. Source: 16,48

> H1311 thru H1314 for children

H785 KIMBERLY KATE BANNING born Dec. 23, 1971. Source: 16,48

H1315 thru H1318 for children

H786 thru H816 not used

H817 KATHERYN WEBSTER ARNOLD born May 27, 1953 in New Haven, New Haven Co. Conn. She married Michael George Pugh June 21, 1980 in Greenwich, Fairfield Co., Conn. He is the son of Arthur Whitson Pugh, Jr. and Josephine (Ruckes) Pugh, born July 24, 1946 in Jacksonville, Duval Co., Florida. They live in New York City where is a Data Processing Consultant and she is and Advertising Acct. Supervisor. Source: 16,22

H1471 & H1472 for children

H818 DAVIS RICHARD ARNOLD born June 8, 1955 in New Haven, Conn. He married Susan Diane Rojos June 17, 1978 in Morris Plains, Morris Co., N.J. She is the daughter of Luis Joseph and Audrey ElFreida (Tonts) Rojos, born Oct. 16, 1956 in Brooklyn, Kings Co., N.Y. They live in Jefferson Co., N.J. Source: 16,22

H1473 Lia May Arnold
H1474 for children

H819 CLAIRE WALLACE BAMBERG {Reverend} born April 14, 1956 in New Haven, Conn. She married Rev. Bruce John Johnson Dec. 22, 1979 in Orange, New Haven Co., Conn. He is the son of William Edward and Lola M. J. (Toleen) Johnson, born April 23, 1953 in Deluth, Saint Louis Co., Minn. They live in Bethel, Vermont. Source: 16,22

H1475 Matthew G. Banberg Johnson
H1476 Nathaniel Ross Bamberg Johnson

H820 ROBERT OTIS BAMBERG born April 20, 1957 in New Haven, Conn. He married Barbara Malifronte May 8, 1987 in Derby, New Haven Co., Conn. She is the daughter of Anthony E. and Jean (Rourke) born Nov. 22, 1955 in Derby. Source: 16,22

H1477 Nina Jean Bamberg
H1478 thru H1480 for children

H821 JOHN CALRTON BAMBERG born May 23, 1959 in New Haven, New Haven Co., Conn. He married Kimberlee Lewis Fisher June 26, 1982 in Orange, New Haven Co., Conn. She is the daughter of Robert Alvin and Martha (Lewis) Fisher, born Dec. 8, 1962 in Bridgeport, Fairfielkd Co., Conn. They live in West Haven, New Haven Co., Conn. Source: 16,22

H1481 Lindsay E. Bamberg
H1482 thru H1484 for children

H822 PAUL HENRY BAMBERG born April 3, 1963 in New Haven, New Haven Co., Conn. Source: 22

H1485 thru H1488 for children

H823 MARY ELLEN BANNING born Sept. 27, 1952 in Stamford, Conn. She married

William Francis Eagen III on Aug. 6, 1977 in Georgetown, Conn. He is the son of William F. Eagen Jr. and Doris (Foster) Eagen, born March 26, 1952 in Stamford. He is a salesman and she is a reg. nurse. They live in Waterbury, Conn. Source: 16,22

> H1489 Christopher M. Eagen
> H1490 Brian Patrick Eagen
> H1491 Elizabeth Ann Eagen
> H1492 Mary Courtney Eagen

H824 WILLIAM G. BANNING born March 12, 1954 in Stamford, Conn. Source: 22

> H1493 thru H1495 for children

H825 ALISON MARIE BANNING born April 13, 1955 in Stamford, Conn. She married Michael W. Heibeck Nov. 3, 1979 in Georgetown, Conn. He is the son of George and Barbara (Haajanen) Heibeck, born April 8, 1951 in Norwalk, Conn. They live in Redding, Conn. where he is a mechanic. Source: 16,22

> H1496 Jason Michael Heibeck
> H1497 Matthew William Heibeck
> H1498 Sean Patrick Heibeck

H826 JOHN McMAHON BANNING born Aug. 27, 1956 in Stamford, Conn. He married Maha Abdel-Hamied Zayed Feb. 18, 1985 in Greenville, N.C. She is the daughter of Abdel-Hamied Mahmoud and Nadra Fathie (Elsharkawi) Zayed, born Nov. 5, 1962 in Detroit, Mich. Her parents were both born in Egypt. He served in the U.S. Air Force and is now a air conditioning tech. and she is a medical sect. They live in Greenville, N. C. Source: 16,22

> H1499 Erica Marie Bannin
> H1500 thru H1503 for children

H827 THOMAS JOSEPH BANNING born Aug. 6, 1958 in Stamford, Conn. He married Lori Seaverns Aug. 11, 1984 in Hingham, Plymouth Co., Mass. She is the daughter of Dana and Gladys (Saunders) Seaverns, born Dec. 18, 1958 in Brockton, Mass. He is a college Prof. and she is a reg. nurse. They live in Monument Beach, Bourne Co. , Mass. Source: 16,22

> H1504 Jenna Saunders Banning
> H1505 thru H1507 for children

H829 MARK BANNING born in 1960 in Stamford, Conn. and died that same year. Source: 22

H830 HEATHER ANNE BANNING born March 30, 1966 in Stamford, Conn. Source: 22

H831 SCOTT RICHARD BANNING born Aug. 1, 1969 in Stamford, Conn. Source: 22

H832 GLENN OLIVER BANNING born Feb. 10, 1972 in Stamford, Conn. Source: 22

H833 KAREN LYNN COVE born April 26, 1955 in New Haven, Conn. She married

Warren W. Worster Aug. 26, 1976 in Northforth, New Haven Co., Conn. He is the son of Fred Sawyer and Mona Mae (Andrews) Worster, born April 11, 1953 in Greenville, Piscataquis Co., Maine. He is a salesman and they live in Tampa, Fla. They have 2 children, Sara Beth and Amanda Marie. Source: 16,22

H834 VALERIE ANN COVE born June 25, 1956 in New Haven, Conn. She married Ronald A. Caturano Sept. 19, 1980 in Northford, Conn. He is the son of John Arthur and Elizabeth Catania Caturano, born Sept. 24, 1956 in New Haven, Conn. He owns a beauty salon, and they live in Clinton, Middlesex Co,, Conn. They have 2 children Michael A. and Christopher J. Source: 16,22

H835 DAVID FRANCIS COVE born Sept. 5, 1957 in New Haven, Conn. He married Patty Ann Bloomer Aug. 27, 1983 in Scotia, Schnectady Co., N.Y. She is the daughter of Milton Dayton and Barbara Ann (Saltford) Bloomer, born April 26, 1958. He is an electronic engr. and she is a software engr. They live in Glendale, Maricopa Co., Az. Their children are, Jennifer Lynn , Michael David and Teresa Marie who was born in 1988. Source: 16,22

H836 BRIAN MICHAEL COVE born Feb. 20, 1960 in New Haven, Conn. Source: 22

H837 KEVIN PETER COVE born Jan. 31, 1963 in Northford, Conn. and married Lee Ann Michaud on Nov. 8, 1986 in Durhham, Middlesex Co., Conn. She is the daughter of Louis & Lillian (Ruszczyk) Michaud. He is a truck driver, they have 1 child, Ryan Thomas, and live in Durham, Conn. Source: 22

H838 JAY SCOTT COVE born Oct. 11, 1967 in Northford, Conn. Source: 22

H839 TROY WILLIAM BANNING born Sept. 26, 1966 in Tacoma, Washington. Source: 22

H840 CINDY LANE BANNING born June 17, 1971 in Hew Haven, Conn. Source: 22

H841 KATHRYN ALICE BANNING born Aug. 6, 1962 in Norwalk, Conn. She married Steve Mayor Sept. 28, 1985 in Norwalk, Conn. Source: 22

H842 SUSAN MARGARET BANNING born Aug. 31, 1963 in Norwalk, Conn. Source: 22

H843 CYNTHIA MARIE BANNING born Aug. 23, 1966 in Norwalk, Conn. Source: 22

H844 ROBERT T. PISCITELLI born Dec. 7, 1959 and married Mary Serene Hughes on May 24, 1980 in Calif. They have a daughter, Meghan Serene, born Sept. 10 1983, and a son Robert G. born July 30, 1987 in Mission Viejo, Calif. Source: 22

H845 MARIE PISCITELLI born May 27, 1961. Source: 22

H846 DAWN PISCITELLI born Dec. 9, 1970. Source: 22

H847 PAMELA PISCITELLI born June 29, 1972. Source: 22

H848 thru H878 unknown children of H394 thru H403

H879 thru H887 unknown children of H404 and H405

H888 thru H1000 unknown children of H406 thru H490

H1001 MELISSA DALE WILSON born Dec. 3, 1968 in Milford, Del. Attended University of Del. Source: 16,50

H1002 RICHARD BANNING CARLISLE born July 8, 1974 in Milford, Del. Source: 16,50

H1003 CAMERON SCOTT CARLISLE born May 31, 1977 in Milford, Del. Source: 16,50

H1004 JESSICA CARLISLE born April 25, 1980 in Milford, Del. Source: 16,50

H1005 GENA DaLAINE HATCHELL born Oct. 13, 1969 in Florence, S.C. Source: 16,50

H1006 JASON WARD JONES born May 12, 1982 in Florence, S.C. Source: 16,50

H1007 NATALIE YVONNE DOWLING born Jan. 1, 1969 and married Dana Patrick Epting on Aug. 13, 1988. Source: 16,50

H1008 THOMAS ALLEN DOWLING born Oct. 17, 1972. Source: 16,50

H1009 ADAM TIMOTHY DOWLING born Oct. 28, 1983. Source: 16,50

H1010 LANCE KENNETH SHIRLEY born March 4, 1977 in Florence, S.C. Source: 16,50

H1011 TRENT JUSTIN SHIRLEY born Sept. 28, 1978 in Florence, S.C. Source: 16,50

H1012 CHAD MATTHEW SHIRLEY born Dec. 20, 1984 in Falls Church, Va. Source: 16,50

H1013 WILLIAM BENJAMIN BANNING born Feb. 22, 1977 in Florence, S.C. Source: 16,50

H1014 ANGELA MICHELLE BANNING born Jan, 24, 1981. Source: 16,50

H1015 thru H1018 unknown children of H502 and H503

H1019 SHAWN PATRICK BANNING born March 24, 1983. Source: 16,50

H1020 JUSTIN TROWBRIDGE BANNING born March 24, 1983. Source: 16,50

H1021 ROBBIE IAN BANNING born May 17, 1980 in Milford, Del. Source: 16,50

H1022 RACHEL ANNE BANNING born July 16, 1983 in Milford, Del. Source: 16,50

H1023 EMILY ANN BANNING born Jan. 9, 1987 in Milford, Del. Source: 16,50

H1024 thru H1300 for children of H506 thru H759

H1301 WILLIAM C. BANNING born March 20, 1969. Source: 16,48

H1302 ROBIN BANNING born June 19, 1967 and married a Mr. Kemper. Source: 16,48

H1303 KELLY R. BANNING born Aug. 3, 1971. Source: 16,48

H1304 ADAM T. BANNING born Oct. 31, 1976. Source: 16,48

H1305 JENNIFER P. MAHONEY born July 11, 1970. Source: 16,48

H1306 SEAN M. MAHONEY born Feb. 27, 1973. Source: 16,48

H1307 thru H1318 unknown children of H783 thru H785

H1319 thru H1470 unused

H1471 & H1472 unknown children of H817

H1473 LIA MAY ARNOLD born June 6, 1980 in Stamford, Fairfield Co., Conn. Source: 16,22

H1475 MATTHEW G. BAMBERG JOHNSON born April 1, 1984 in Hanover, Grafton Co., N.H. Source: 22

H1476 NATHANIEL ROSS BAMBERG-JOHNSON born July 10, 1990 in Bloomington, Monroe Co., Ind. Source: 22

H1477 NINA JEAN BAMBERG born Aug. 22, 1990 in Meriden, New Haven Co., Ct. Source: 22

H1481 LINDSAY E. BAMBERG born March 30, 1985 in Milford, New Haven Co., Conn. Source: 22

H1489 CHRISTOPHER M. EAGEN born May 3, 1979 in Waterbury, Conn. Source: 22

H1490 BRIAN PATRICK EAGEN born Dec. 1, 1980 in Waterbury, Conn. Source: 22

H1491 ELIZABETH ANN EAGEN born Jan. 28, 1985 in Waterbury, Conn. Source: 22

H1492 MARY COURTNEY EAGEN born Aug. 22, 1989 in Hartford, Hartford Co., Ct. Source: 22

H1493 thru H1495 unknown children of H824

H1496 JASON MICHAEL HEIBECK born Jan. 24, 1982 in Danbury, Fairfield Co., Conn. Source: 22

H1497 MATTHEW WILLIAM HEIBECK born Sept. 6, 1983 in Danbury, Fairfield Co., Conn. Source: 22

H1498 SEAN PATRICK HEIBECK born March 30, 1986 in Danbury, Fairfield Co., Conn. Source: 22

H1499 ERICA MARIA BANNING born Jan. 17, 1988 in Greenville, Pitt Co., N. Carolina. Source: 22

H1504 JENNA SAUNDERS BANNING born Nov. 25, 1987 in Weymouth, Plymouth Co., Mass. Source: 22

JACOB G. BANNING of INDIANA

Where Jacob G. Banning, the founder of this line, came from is unknown. As of 1908, most of his descendants were still in and around Indianapolis. This line no doubt belongs to one of the larger lines in this country, but nothing is known.

I1 UNKNOWN BANNING

> I2 Jacob Greenberg Banning
> I3 thru I8 for children.

I2 JACOB GREENBERG BANNING married Ellen What. They had four children and lived in Troy, Miami County, Ohio. After her death, he married 2nd, Mary Rhodeheimn. They lived in Troy, Ohio, where he died. Source: 1

> I9 Jacob J. Banning
> I10 Elizabeth Watson Banning
> I11 Greenberg Randolph Banning
> I12 Nancy Banning
> I13 Sarah Banning
> I14 Rebecca Banning
> I15 Margaret Banning
> I16 Mary Banning
> I17 Frederick Banning
> I18 Emma Banning
> I19 Richard Banning
> I20 Henry Banning
> I21 Alexander Banning
> I22 George Banning
> I23 John Banning
> I24 Benjamin Banning
> I25 Twin Banning's

I3 thru I8 for unknown children of I1

> I26 thru I65 for children

I9 JACOB J. BANNING born (about 1812 ?) near Troy, Ohio and lived in Indianapolis, Indiana. (He married Barbara ???. She was born in Pa. ?) Source: 1,6

> I66 Ellen E. Banning
> I67 Sarah Banning

I10 ELIZABETH WATSON BANNING born in Wayne County, Indiana, and lived in Wayne County most of her life. Source: 1

> I68 William Watson -------?
> I69 Daughter -------?

I11 GREENBERG RANDOLPH BANNING born July 4, 1826 (or 1821) in Miami County, Ohio. Married Rachel Eline on April 12, 1848. She was born about 1822 in Pa. He was a shoemaker in Butler Co., Oh. in 1850. Source: 1,5,6

I70 Josephine Banning
I71 Edwin F. Banning
I72 George P. Banning
I73 Lizzie P. Banning

I12 NANCY BANNING no information. Source: 1

I74 thru I80 for children.

I13 SARAH BANNING no information. Source: 1

I81 thru I87 for children.

I14 REBECCA BANNING no information. Source: 1

I88 thru I94 for children.

I15 MARGARET BANNING no information. Source: 1

I95 thru I101 for children.

I16 MARY BANNING no information. Source: 1

I102 thru I108 for children.

I17 FREDERICK BANNING no information. Source: 1

I109 thru I115 for children.

I18 EMMA BANNING no information. Source: 1

I116 thru I122 for children.

I19 RICHARD BANNING no information. Source: 1

I123 thru I129 for children.

I20 HENRY BANNING no information. Source: 1

I130 thru I136 for children.

I21 ALEXANDER BANNING no information. Source: 1

I137 thru I143 for children.

I22 GEORGE BANNING no information. Source: 1

I144 thru I150 for children.

I23 JOHN BANNING no information. Source: 1

I151 thru I157 for children.

I24 BENJAMIN BANNING no information. Source: 1

I158 thru I164 for children.

I25 TWIN BANNING'S died as infants. Source: 1

I26 thru I65 unknown children of I3 thru I8

I165 thru I364 for children

I66 ELLEN E. BANNING born (about 1845 ?) in Indianapolis, Ind. (or Ohio ?) and married Mr.Allen. They lived in Indianapolis and had no children. Source: 1,6

I67 SARAH BANNING born in Indianapolis, Ind. and married Mr. Brooks. They lived in Indianapolis. Source: 1,6

I365 Daughter ? Brooks

I68 WILLIAM WATSON --------? he was a carpenter in Indianapolis, Ind. Source: 1

I69 DAUGHTER --------? no information. Source: 1

I70 JOSEPHINE BANNING she was born 1844-49 (in Pa. ?) and married Mr. Kirby. Source: 1,5,6

I366 O. T. Kirby
I367 Benjamin Kirby
I368 Maud Kirby
I369 Harriet Kirby
I370 Lizzie Kirby
I371 Myrtle Kirby
I372 Evlyn Kirby

I71 EDWIN F. BANNING (born about 1850 in Ohio. ?) He lived in Indianapolis, Ind. Source: 1,6

I373 thru I380 for children

I72 GEORGE P. BANNING (born about 1854 in Ohio.?) He lived in Muncie, Ind. Source: 1,6

I381 thru I387 for children

I73 LIZZIE P. BANNING (born about 1856 in Ind.?) and she married Mr. Davis. They lived in Chilocco, Okla. Source: 1,6

I388 George B. Davis
I389 thru I395 for children

I74 thru I108 unknown children of I12 thru I16

I109 thru I115 unknown children of I17

I396 thru I411 for children

I116 thru I122 unknown children of I18

I123 thru I164 unknown children of I19 thru I24

I412 thru I512 for children

I165 thru I364 unknown children of I26 thru I65

I513 thru I913 for children

I365 DAUGHTER ? BROOKS lived in Indianapolis, Ind. Source: 1

I366 0. T. KIRBY lived in Indianapolis, Ind. Source: 1

I367 BENJAMIN K. KIRBY lived in Indianapolis, Ind. Source: 1

I368 MAUD KIRBY lived in indianapolis, Ind. Source: 1

I369 HARRIET KIRBY she married a Mr. Millie and they lived in Yorktown, Ind.
    Source: 1

I370 LIZZIE KIRBY no information. Source: 1

I371 MYRTLE KIRBY no information. Source: 1

I372 EVLYN KIRBY no information. Source: 1

I373 thru I387 unknown children of I71 & I72

I388 GEORGE B. DAVIS he was a Physician in Chicago, Ill. Source: 1

HENRY BANNING of IOWA

J0 UNKNOWN BANNING (J.P. Banning ???)

> J1 Henry Bousley Banning
> J2 Josiah Ellis Banning

~J1 HENRY BOUSLEY BANNING born about 1824 in Md. He married 1st, Sarah Thomas on March 7, 1833 in Ross Co., Oh. and had 4 children but only Henry P. lived. He married 2nd, Eliza Nichols on Oct. 7, 1841 in Pickaway Co., Oh. and had 2 children, Charles & Thomas Henry. He married 3rd, Mary Borne who was born 1846 in Germany. She died Nov. 15, 1897 and was buried in Exira, Iowa. The 1850 census has them in Vigo Co. Indiana. He died in Audubon Co., Hamlin T/S, Iowa Oct. 15, 1889 of a heart attack. Source: 5,13,26

> J3 Henry P. Banning
> J3A Lavina Banning
> J4 Charles Banning
> J5 Thomas Henry Banning
> J6 Julie Ann Banning
> J7 Jacob Ellis Banning
> J8 ??? (Twin to Jacob)
> J9 David Lincoln Banning
> J10 William Anthony Banning
> J11 Elisa Jane (Lizzie) Banning
> J12 Lydia Ellen Banning
> J13 James T. Banning
> J14 Benjamin Franklin Banning
> J15 Martha Alice Banning
> J16 Christine Banning
> J17 Andrew J. Banning
> J18 Sarah Bell Banning

J2 JOSIAH ELLIS BANNING born in Pickaway Co., Ohio on Aug. 28, 1827. He married Mary Catherine Monnick on December 13, 1853 in Des Moines, Iowa. She was born April 30, 1836 in Munich, Germany and came to America at age 5. During the Civil war he enlisted in Co. A of the 23nd Iowa Infantry of the Union Army on July 28, 1862 and fought at Vicksburgh, Miss. He was a corporal and was discharged at Vicksburgh Aug. 9, 1863. He built the first all brick building at Ames Agricultural College, which was called Banning Hall, and was living in Washington T/S, Ames, Iowa in 1885. He died Dec. 8, 1890 after being hit by a train Dec. 4 at Audubon, Iowa and is buried in Exira, Audubon Co., Iowa. She died March 5, 1906 at the home of her daughter Maggie in St. Joe, Mo. and is buried in Exira, Iowa. Source: 26

> J19 Sarah Jane (Mattie) Banning
> J20 Mary Ellen Banning
> J21 John Phillip Banning
> J22 Martha Ann Banning
> J23 Eliza Alice (Liz) Banning

J24 Charles Thomas Banning
J25 Ada Elizabeth (Lizzie) Banning
J26 Carrie Rachel Banning
J27 Hattie Marie Banning
J28 William Arthur Banning
J29 Margaret Florence (Maggie) Banning
J30 Jessie Blanche Banning

J3 HENRY P. BANNING born Sept. 29,1836 in Chillcothe, Ohio. He married Malinda (???) who was born in Germany on Oct. 11, 1838. They were living in Nebraska in 1880. Henry died Jan. 17, 1910 and she died Nov. 30, 1924, both in Mound City, Holt Co., Mo. Source: 5,8,16,62,99

J31 Sara Jane Banning
J31a John Henry Banning
J31b Lavina Banning
J31c Elizabeth Banning
J31d George Banning
J32 Emma Banning
J32a Charles Banning
J33 Thomas Banning
J33a Alfred Banning
J34 Ada Banning
J34a Nettie (Frances?) Banning
J35 Mattie Alice Banning

J3a LAVINA BANNING born 1834 in Ohio. Source: 5

J36 thru J40 for children

J4 CHARLES BANNING born 1845 in Ohio. Source: 5

J41 thru J44 for children

J5 THOMAS HENRY BANNING born 1847 in Ohio. Source: 5

J45 thru J48 for children

J6 JULIE ANN BANNING born Sept. 22, 1857 and married Alexander Tillford Buford on Dec. 16, 1886. He was born July 10, 1846 and died Jan. 13, 1921. She died Feb. 16, 1929. Source: 26

J49 Effie Sarah Buford
J50 William Thomas Buford
J51 Mary Elizabeth Buford
J52 James E. Buford
J53 Robert Franklin Buford
J54 Charlie Buford
J55 Alice Birtha Buford
J56 Zula Rose Buford
J57 Beulah May Buford

J7 JACOB ELLIS BANNING born May 19, 1858 in Ames, Iowa and died Feb. 24, 1943 in Arnolds Park, Iowa. He married Rebecca Ann Cheever Dec. 16, 1882 in Brayton,

Ia. She was the daughter of R. B. Cheever & Amanda Lower born in Crawford Co., Wi. Source: 26

J58 Mable Banning
J59 Willie Banning
J60 Amanda Banning
J61 Walter Banning
J62 Myrle Cave Banning
J63 Jacob Banning Jr
J64 Dewey Banning
J65 Charles H. Banning
J66 Mattie Lambi Banning
J67 Frank Banning
J68 John Banning

J8 ??? (Twin Brother to Jacob) died stillborn.

J9 DAVID LINCOLN BANNING born July 12, 1861 in Iowa. He was a Blacksmith until 1916 and then became a carpenter at Ottawa, Ks. He married Olive Salome Linder. She was born May 29, 1868 in Ia. and died July 9, 1951 in Hutchinson, Ks. He died in Enid, Okla. Source: 26

J69 Pearl Banning
J70 James Leroy Banning
J71 Charles Floyd Banning
J72 Alfred Henry Banning
J73 Clara Irene Banning
J74 Grace Violet Banning

J10 WILLIAM ANTHONY BANNING born Sept 17, 1863. Married Maude J. Emery. He died April 12, 1939 and is buried in the Belmont Cemetery in Doniphen Co., Ks. Source: 26

J75 thru J80 for children

J11 ELIZABETH JANE (Lizzie) BANNING born July 21, 1866 in Iowa. She married John Phillip Banning on Dec. 24, 1884 in Iowa. (See J21) She died March 15, 1927 and is buried in Highland Park Cemetery, Pawnee, Okla. Source: 16,25,26,30

J12 LYDIA ELLEN BANNING born Oct. 6, 1865 and married Charles L. Morris. He was born 1863 and died 1917. Source: 26

J81 thru J86 for children

J13 JAMES T. BANNING born Feb. 17, 1869

J87 thru J93 for children

J14 BENJAMIN FRANKLIN BANNING born June 24, 1870

J94 thru J100 for children

J15 MATILDA ALICE BANNING born Jan. 3, 1872 in Story Co., Iowa and married

327

Arthur Wellington Carmichal on Oct. 25, 1895. He was the son of Isaac Newton and Mary Ann (Wolf) Carmichal, born Jan. 11, 1867 in Keokuk, Iowa. She died Jan. 18, 1906 and he died Nov. 13, 1947 in Waurika, Jefferson Co. Okla. Source: 26

J101 thru J104 for children

J16 CHRISTINE BANNING born Aug 7, 1873. Source: 26

J105 thru J108 for children

J17 ANDREW J. BANNING born Jan. 11, 1876. Source: 26

J109 thru J112 for children

J18 SARAH BELL BANNING born Jan. 21, 1877. She married Charles Henry Wells who was the son of Henry & Mary Jane Wells, born in 1868 and died Feb. 21 or 22, 1941 in Exira or Audubon, Ia. She died 1964 in Exira or Audubon, Ia. Source: 26

    J113 Edna Wells
    J114 Henry Clay Wells
    J115 Mary Emma Wells
    J116 Flossie May Wells
    J117 Eva Rose Wells
    J118 George (Sonny) Wells
    J119 Arlo Arthur (Bill) Wells
    J120 Harriet Opal Wells
    J121 Loraine R. Wells
    J122 Charles Henry Wells
    J123 Royal H. Wells

J19 SARAH JANE (Mattie) BANNING born Jan. 1855 and married a Mr. McCraken. Source: 26

J124 thru J129 for children

J20 MARY ELLEN BANNING born April 1856 and married a Mr. Billings. Source: 26

J130 thru J133 for children

J21 JOHN PHILLIP BANNING born May 22 or 27, 1857-8 in Ames, Iowa and married Elizabeth Jane Banning, (see J11) on Dec. 24, 1884 in Iowa. He died April 23, 1935 in Stillwater, Ok. and is buried in Highland Park Cemetery in Pawnee, Ok. Source: 13,16,25,26,30

    J134 Ida Bell Banning
    J135 Henry Banning
    J136 Sherman Ellis Banning
    J137 Harley Ceres Banning
    J138 Hulda Jane Banning
    J139 Hazel Alice Banning
    J140 Hattie Banning
    J140a Jennie Lou (Lucille) Banning
    J140b Roy Austin Banning

J22 MARTHA ANN BANNING born 1858 in Iowa and married a Mr. McCracken and moved to Seattle, Wa. Source: 26

J141 thru J145 for children

J23 ELIZA ALICE (LIZ) BANNING born July 1860 in Iowa and married Wilbur Smith. Source: 26

        J146 Lee Smith
        J147 Earl Smith
        J148 Claude Smith

J24 CHARLES THOMAS BANNING born Aug. 29, 1866 in Iowa and married Elizabeth ???. He moved to Okla. and in 1898, went to Chesterville, Tx. By 1926 they were living in Eagle Lake, Tx. Source: 26,30

        J149 Eva Banning
        J150 May Banning

J25 ADA ELIZABETH (LIZZIE) BANNING born Oct. 7, 1867 in Iowa. She married 1st, George Henry Morey on Oct. 26, 1881. He was born Dec. 15, 1856 and died June 7, 1909. They were living in Audubon, Ia. in 1926. She married 2nd, Marshal Orlando Smith, who died May 12, 1944 in Exira, Ia. She died Sept. 29, 1936 and is buried in the Exira Cemetery in Exira, Ia. Source: 26,30

        J151 William Arthur Morey
        J152 Theo Pearl Morey
        J153 Edith Morey
        J154 Clara Morey
        J155 Ellis Morey
        J156 Georgie Morey
        J157 Mildred Morey
        J158 Vernon E. Morey

J26 CARRIE RACHEL BANNING born June 7, 1869 in Ames, Iowa and married Wilson Nathaniel Hopkins in the spring of 1885. He was the son of Benjamin Franklin Hopkins (1835-1910) and Caroline   Cloud (1841-i920) born Jan. 15, 1863 in Johnson Co., Ia. He was a farmer and died Feb. 11, 1946 in Exira, Ia. She died Dec. 29, 1925 at her home in Guthrie Center, Ia. Source: 26,30

        J159 Mary Agnes Hopkins
        J16O Viola Caroline Hopkins
        J161 Lulu Minerva Hopkins
        J162 Margaret Blanche Hopkins
        J163 Vera Elizabeth Hopkins
        J164 George Arthur Hopkins
        J165 Nellie May Hopkins

J27 HATTIE MARIE BANNING born Dec. 25, 1871 in Audubon Co., Iowa or Clark Co., Mo. She married Asa Sanders Johnson on Nov. 2, 1888 in Exira, Ia. He was the son of Horace F. Johnson (1832-1911) and Celestina Fuller (1838-1865) born Nov. 12, 1866 (?) in Story Co., Ia. He was a farmer, raised horses, and died Aug. 4, 1922 at their farm near Massena, Ia. She died Jan. 21, 1951 in Denver, Col. and is buried in Massena, Ia. Source: 26,30

                    J166 Dora May Johnson
                    J167 Mary Myrtle Johnson
                    J168 James Lloyd Johnson
                    J169 Harold Albert Johnson
                    J170 Frances Marie Johnson
                    J171 Asa Earl (Jack) Johnson
                    J172 Edith Bessie Johnson
                    J173 George Merrill Johnson
                    J174 Ida Olivene Johnson
                    J175 Gladys Ethel (Babe) Johnson
                    J176 Glenn Everett Johnson
                    J177 Merle Ervin Johnson

J28 WILLIAM ARTHUR BANNING born Oct. 30, 1872 in Clark Co., Mo. and died Nov.
     1875. Source: 26

J29 MARGARET FLORENCE (MAGGIE) BANNING born June 7, 1877 in Ames,
     Iowa. She married Archibald Loren Abbey on Oct. 12, 1896 in Wathena, Doniphan
     Co., Ks. He was born 1876 and died 1920 in Wathena, Ks. She was a Nurse, died
     Aug. 10, 1944 and is buried in Denver, Col. Source: 26,30

                    J178 Florence Zephry Abbey
                    J179 Vernice Lucille Abbey

J30 JESSIE BLANCHE BANNING born Oct. 22, 1878/9 in Ames, Iowa. She married
     Clarence Ogden DeHart on June 5, 1898 in Wathena, Ks. He was the son of John
     Wesley DeHart (School teacher) and Mary Elizabeth Rankin (1854-1946) born April
     19, 1875 in Trenton, Mo. He was a carpenter and died 1956 in Troy, Ks. She died
     Jan. 31, 1953 and is buried in Belmont Cemetery, Wathena, Ks. Source: 26,30

                    J180 Clarence DeHart
                    J181 Betty Ethel DeHart
                    J182 Zora Irene DeHart
                    J183 Gaylord Ogden DeHart
                    J184 Muriel Patrice DeHart
                    J185 Ruby Lucille DeHart

J31 SARA JANE BANNING born June 15, 1857 and married Charles Henry Wells.
     He was born in 1868 and died Feb. 21, 1941 in Axira, Iowa. Source: 16,99

                    J186 to J187 for children

J31a JOHN HENRY BANNING born March 15, 1859. Source: 16,99

                    J188 to J190 for children

J31b LAVINA BANNING born Aug. 27, 1861. Source: 16,99

                    J191 to J192 for children

J31c ELIZABETH BANNING born June 3, 1866 in Iowa. Source: 8,16,62,99

                    J193 to J194 for children
                              330

J31d GEORGE BANNING born June 3, 1866 in Iowa. Source: 8,16,62,99

J195 to J197 for children

J32 EMMA BANNING born Nov. 18, 1868 in Iowa. Source: 8,16,62,99

J198 to J199 for children

J32a CHARLES BANNING born Feb. 28, 1870 in Story City, Iowa. He married Lora G. Harrison, who was born in 1880. She died in 1944 and he died June 6, 1947 in Mound City, Holt Co., Mo. Source: 8,16,62,99

J200 to J202 for children

J33 THOMAS BANNING born June 18, 1872 in Iowa. He married Mary Ellen Lindsay on Nov. 26, 1902. She was born May 5, 1883 and died in Sept. 1958. Thomas died Aug. 30, 1951. Source: 8,16,62,99

J203 Hazel Pearl Banning
J203a Ruby Mae Banning
J204 William Henry Banning
J204a Howard Thomas Banning
J205 Edna Belle Banning

J33a ALFRED BANNING born March 4, 1875 in Iowa. He remained single and died in 1944 in Mound City, Holt Co., Mo. Source 8,16,62,99

J34 ADA BANNING born Jan. 5, 1878 in Loomis, Neb. She married Oscar A. Vandeventer, who was born May 4, 1877. They had 2 sons. Ada died May 5, 1956 and Oscar died Feb. 29, 1951. Source: 8,16,62,99

J206 to J207 for children

J34a NETTIE (FRANCES?) BANNING born March 27, 1880 in Neb. Source: 8,16,62,99

J208 to J209 for children

J35 MATTIE ALICE BANNING born in York Co., Neb. On Dec. 17, 1883. Moved to Mound City, Mo. where she married Charles Vandeventer on Jan. 20, 1902. He was born Feb. 1, 1878. She died March 27, 1909 at Gracemont, Caddo Co, Okla. He died Dec. 5, 1972 in Anadarko, Caddo Co, Okla. Source: 16,62,99

J210 Vernie Valdo Vandeventer
J211 Elsie Leona Vandeventer
J212 Mattie Katrine Vandeventer

J36 thru J48 unknown children of J3a thru J5

J213 to J250 for children

J49 EFFIE SARAH BUFORD no information Source: 26

J50 WILLIAM THOMAS BUFORD no information Source: 26

J51 MARY ELIZABETH BUFORD no information Source: 26

J52 JAMES E. BUFORD no information Source: 26

J53 ROBERT FRANKLIN BUFORD no information Source: 26

J54 CHARLIE BUFORD no information Source: 26

J55 ALICE BIRTHA BUFORD no information Source: 26

J56 ZULA ROSE BUFORD the twin of Beulah May. Source: 26

J57 BEULAH MAY BUFORD the twin Of Zula Rose. Source: 26

J58 MABEL BANNING born April 26, 1885 died May 18, 1892 of Diphtheria. Source: 26

J59 WILLIE BANNING died of Diphtheria. Source: 26

J60 AMANDA BANNING died of Diphtheria. Source: 26

J61 WALTER BANNING died prior to 1943. Source: 26

J251 thru J255 for children

J62 MYRLE CAVE BANNING living in Arnolds Park, Ia. in 1943. Source: 26

J256 thru J260 for children

J63 JACOB BANNING JR. living in Arnolds Park, Ia. in 1943. Source: 26

J261 thru J265 for children

J64 DEWEY BANNING was in the Armed Forces in Tex. in 1943. Source: 26

J266 thru J270 for children

J65 CHARLES H. BANNING was in the Army in Callan, Ca. in 1943. Source: 26

J271 thru J275 for children

J66 MATTIE LAMBI BANNING living in Des Moines, Ia. in 1943. Source: 26

J276 thru J280 for children

J67 FRANK BANNING living in Spirit Lake, Ia. in 1943. Source: 26

J281 thru J285 for children

J68 JOHN BANNING living in Arnolds Park, Ia. in 1943. Source: 26

J286 thru J290 for children

332

J69 PEARL BANNING born 1885 and died May 1, 1901 of T.B. in Wathena, Ks. Source: 26

J70 JAMES LEROY BANNING born 1889 in Wathena, Ks. He died March 1930 and is buried in Omaha, Neb. Source: 26

J291 thru J295 for children

J71 CHARLES FLOYD BANNING born Nov. 2, 1892 and died 1974. He is buried in Fresno, Ca. Source: 26

J296 thru J300 for children

J72 ALFRED HENRY BANNING born Oct. 1899 and died Aug. 19, 1900 in Wathena, Ks. Source: 26

J73 CLARA IRENE BANNING born July 8, 1901 at Wathena, KS. Living in 1984. Source: 26

J301 thru J305 for children

J74 GRACE VIOLET BANNING born Mar. 28, 1904 at Horton, Ks. Living in Newton, Ks. in 1984. Source: 26

J306 thru J310 for children

J75 thru J112 unknown children of J10 thru J17

J311 thru J398 for children

J113 EDNA WELLS no information Source: 26

J114 HENRY CLAY WELLS no information Source: 26

J115 MARY EMMA WELLS no information Source: 26

J116 FLOSSIE MAY WELLS no information Source: 26

J117 EVA ROSE WELLS no information Source: 26

J118 GEORGE (Sonny) WELLS born Marion, KS. Aug 29, 1908 and married Rosa Hulda Andersen on Sept. 11, 1930. Had 7 daughters, Linda, Frances, Mary, Jeanette, Gwen, Joyce & Betty. He died Jan. 12, 1968 in Des Moines, Ia. Source: 26,30

J119 ARLO ARTHUR (Bill) WELLS alive in 1968. Source: 26

J120 HARRIET OPAL WELLS born May 14, 1912 and married Mr. Clouse. She died Oct. 26, 1984. Source: 26

J121 LORAINE A. WELLS born Dec. 16, 1917 and married Mr. Duke. She died April 10, 1980. Source: 26

J122 CHARLES HENRY WELLS alive in 1968. Source: 26

J123 ROYAL H. WELLS alive in 1968. Source: 26

J124 thru J133 unknown children of J19 and J20

J134 IDA BELL BANNING born Sept. 5, 1885 in Brown Co., Neb. She came to Payne Co., Ok in Aug. 1899. She married Mr. A. W. Wright in 1909 in Perry, Ok. He died in 1940. She died March 16, 1957 in Pawnee, Ok. Source: 16,25,30

> J399 Argul Wright
> J400 Ruby Wright
> J401 Cecil Wright
> J402 Ray Wright
> J403 Owen Wright
> J404 Dick Wright
> J405 Marie Wright

J135 HENRY BANNING born Feb. 10, 1888 in Iowa. He was living in Lavaca, Ark in 1935 and in Button Willow, Calif. in 1957. Source: 16,25,30

> J406 thru J410 for children

J136 SHERMAN ELLIS BANNING born Feb. 14, 1890 in Des Moines, Iowa. He married Celia Ann Hamner in Topeka, Ks. She was born April 4, 1894 in Morris Co., Ks. He died Jan. 25, 1966 in Stillwater, Okla. and is buried in Pawnee, Ok. They divorced. She died Dec. 4, 1977 in Okla. City and is buried in the Sunnyland Cemetery in Okla. City. He married 2nd Etta Evelyn Crain on March 19, 1935 in Pawnee, Ok. She was the daughter of Edward W. and Rebecca Crain, born June 9, 1911 in Turkey Ford, Ok. She died March 24, 1982 in Marietta, Ga. Source: 16,25,30

> J411 Bertha Ellen Banning
> J412 Jack Phillip Banning
> J413 Grace Bell Banning
> J414 Beaulah Mae Banning
> J415 Henry Ellis Banning
> J416 Dorothy M. Banning
> J417 Raymond D. Banning
> J418 Roy D. Banning
> J419 Dale Banning
> J420 George L. Banning
> J421 Charles B. Banning
> J422 Gene Banning

J137 HARLEY CERES BANNING born Jan. 12, 1892 in Iowa. He married Zella Smith. He was alive in 1935. When Harley died, she married his brother J140b. Source: 16,25,30

> J423 Clarence Elton Banning
> J424 Harold Laverne Banning
> J425 John Franklin Banning
> J426 Delores Jane Banning
> J427 Dorothy Jean Banning

334

J138 HULDA JANE BANNING born June 3, 1894 in Audubon, Iowa. She married 1st, Todd A. Van Brunt on March 10, 1909 in Perry, Ok. He was born 1894 and died Aug. 11, 1928. She married 2nd, Joe Johnson on Nov. 6, 1944. Joe died in May 1952. She died Aug. 12, 1968 and is buried in Highland Park Cemetery in Pawnee, Ok. Source: 16,25,30

> J428 Jane Van Brunt
> J429 Mae Van Brunt
> J430 John Van Brunt
> J431 Robert Van Brunt
> J432 Charlie Van Brunt

J139 HAZEL ALICE BANNING born Aug. 3, 1897 in Wathena, Doniphan Co., Ks. She married William Edward Carmichael on May 17, 1912 in Burrton, Harvey Co., Ks. They were living in Stillwater, Ok. in 1935. She was living in Yakima, Wa. in 1957. Source: 13,16,25,30

> J433 thru J438 for children

J140 HATTIE BANNING born Nov. 7, 1899 in Okla. She married Bert Adams. He was born 1881 and died 1949. They were living in Morrison, Ok. in 1935. Source: 16,25,30

> J439 thru J444 for children

J140a JENNIE LOU (LUCILLE) BANNING born Jan. 1, 1903 in Ok. She married 1st. John Schooley and 2nd, Leo Dawson. They were living in Stillwater, Ok. in 1957. Source: 16,25,30

> J445 thru J449 for children

J140b ROY AUSTIN BANNING born Sept. 5, 1904 in Coyle, Ok. He married Zella Smith Banning on May 10, 1941. She was the widow of his brother. See J137. Roy died Aug. 14, 1949 and is buried in the Highland Park Cemetery in Pawnee, Ok. Source: 16,25,30

> J450 thru J454 for children.

J141 thru J145 unknown children of J22

J146 LEE SMITH no information

J147 EARL SMITH no information

J148 CLAUDE SMITH no information

J149 EVA BANNING married Bryant Skeeters. Source: 26

> J455 thru J459 for children

J150 MAY BANNING married Mr. Mozan. Source: 26

> J460 thru J464 for children

J151 WILLIAM ARTHUR MOREY born Oct. 30, 1882 in Exira, Audubon Co., Ia.
Source: 26

J152 THEO PEARL MOREY born March 28, 1884 Exira, Greeley T/S, Audubon Co.,
Ia. Source: 26

J153 EDITH MOREY born April 8, 1888 in Exira, Greeley T/S, Audubon Co., Ia.
Source: 26

J154 CLARA MOREY born June 29, 1890 in Exira, Greeley T/S, Audubon Co., Ia.
Source: 26

J155 ELLIS MOREY born March 7, 1893 in Exira, Greeley T/S, Audubon Co., Ia.
Source: 26

J156 GEORGIE MOREY born April 7, and died June 7, 1898 in Exira, Greeley T/S,
Audubon Co., Ia. Source: 26

J157 MILDRED MOREY born May 7, 1900 in Exira, Greeley T/S, Audubon Co., Ia.
Source: 26

J158 VERNON E. MOREY born June 25, 1902 in Exira, Greeley T/S, Audubon Co., Ia.
Source: 26

J159 MARY AGNES HOPKINS born March 14, 1886 and died April 22, 1905 in Exira,
Ia. Source: 26,30

J160 VIOLA CAROLINE HOPKINS born Nov. 7, 1888 and died March 9, 1891 in Exira,
Iowa. Source: 26,30

J161 LULU MINERVA HOPKINS born May 16, 1892 and married Arden H. Shelley on
May 20, 1908. He was born July 25, 1883 at Ross, Ia. died Aug. 10, 1973 and is
buried in Guthrie Center, Ia. She died March 2, 1954 in Guthrie Center. They had 2
boys and 1 girl, Max, Lowell & Ruth. Source: 26

J162 MARGARET BLANCHE HOPKINS born July 31, 1895 and married Carl
McCluen. They had no children. She married 2nd, Vern Gustin and had 2 boys & 2
girls, Margaret Ilene, Leslie Vernon, Verle Wilson & Donna Maxine. She died Sept.
30, 1981 in Guthrie Center, Ia. Source: 26

J163 VERA ELIZABETH HOPKINS born March 10, 1899 and died April 30, 1899 in
Exira, Ia. Source: 26,30

J164 GEORGE ARTHUR HOPKINS born Oct. 16, 1902. He married 1st, Bertha
Scoverner and had a son, George Jr. He married 2nd, Florence ??? and had a son,
Donald. He died Oct. 27, 1984 in Mt. Dora, Fla. Source: 26

J165 NELLIE MAY HOPKINS born Jan. 30, 1905 and died June 22, 1905 in Exira, Ia.
Source: 26,30

J166 DORA MAE JOHNSON born Oct. 18, 1889 Exira, Audubon Co., Ia. Source: 26

J167 MARY MYRTLE JOHNSON born July 19, 1891 Exira, Audubon Co., Ia. Source:

26

J168 JAMES LLOYD JOHNSON born Aug. 31, 1893 Exira, Audubon Co., Ia. Source: 26

J169 HAROLD ALBERT JOHNSON born Nov. 16, 1895 Exira, Audubon Co., Ia. Source: 26

J170 FRANCES MARIE JOHNSON born Oct. 25, 1897 Exira, Audubon Co., Ia. Source: 26

J171 ASA EARL (Jack) JOHNSON born March 27, 1901 Exira, Audubon Co., Ia. Source: 26

J172 EDITH BESSIE JOHNSON born Aug. 15, 1903 Exira, Audubon Co., Ia. Source: 26

J173 GEORGE MERRILL JOHNSON born Sept. 27, 1905 Exira, Audubon Co., Ia. Source: 26

J174 UDA OLIVENE JOHNSON born March 31, 1908 Exira, Audubon Co., Ia. Source: 26

J175 GLADYS ETHEL (Babe) JOHNSON born July 28, 1910 Exira, Audubon Co., Ia. Source: 26

J176 GLENN EVERETT JOHNSON born Oct. 22, 1912 Exira, Audubon Co., Ia. Source: 26

J177 MERLE ERVIN JOHNSON born May 5, 1916 Exira, Audubon Co., Ia. Source: 26

J178 FLORENCE ZEPHRY ABBEY born Aug. 13, 1897 and died Oct. 6,1888. Source: 26

J179 VERNICE LUCILIE ABBEY born July 19, 1900 in St. Joseph, Mo. Source: 26

J180 CLARENCE DeHART born and died March 3, 1899. Source: 26

J181 BETTY ETHEL DeHART born Jan. 7, 1901 Wathena, Ks. Source: 26

J182 ZORA IRENE DeHART born Jan. 15, 1903 Wathena, Ks. Source: 26

J183 GAYLORD OGDEN DeHART born 1905 Wathena, Ks. Source: 26

J184 MURIEL PATRICE DeHART born Aug. 16, 1907 Wathena, Ks. Source: 26

J185 RUBY LUCILLE DeHART born Sept. 9, 1909 Blair, Ks. Source: 26

J186 to J202 for children of J31 to J32a

J465 to J495 for children

J203 HAZEL PEARL BANNING born Dec. 12, 1903 and married Roy Hill. She died in

July 1983 and is buried in Horton, Ks. Source: 16,99

J496 Nancy Hill

J203A RUBY MAE BANNING born Oct. 21, 1906 and married Claude Jones. He was born Aug. 21, 1903, and died May 22, 1981. Ruby died Jan. 23, 1969. Source: 16,99

J497 Margaret Jones
J498 Robert Paul Jones

J204 WILLIAM HENRY BANNING born Feb. 9, 1909 and married Lucille Baumgartenner. William died in 1966 in Wycliffe, Ohio. Source: 16,99

J499 Larry Banning
J500 Tommy Banning

J204A HOWARD THOMAS BANNING born March 6, 1914 and married Minnie Carter. Source: 16,99

J501 Tommy Banning
J502 James Banning
J503 Joanne Banning

J205 EDNA BELLE BANNING born Dec. 31, 1919 and married Lawrence Ohlsen on Oct. 3, 1942. He died in Horton, Ks. Source: 16.99

J504 Ronald Lee Ohlsen
J505 Gerald Wayne Ohlsen
J506 David Lee Ohlsen
J507 Vicki Jean Ohlsen

J206 to J209 for children of J33a to J34a

J210 VERNIE VALDO VANDEVENTER born Aug. 11, 1902 in Gracemont, Okla. and married Mable Elizabeth Manning in Dec. 1927 in Riverside, Calif. She was born May 27, 1877. Vern died April 15, 1966 in Pasadena, Calif. And she died April 16, 1977 in Anaheim, Calif. Source: 16,99

J508 Shirley Joyce Vandeventer

J211 ELSIE LEONA VANDEVENTER born Oct. 21, 1906 in Gracemont, Caddo Co. Okla. She married Carl Melvin Allen on Nov. 19, 1933 in Gracemont. Carl was born Sept. 14, 1908 in Corsicana, Navarro Co. Tx and died April 13, 1992 in Chickasha, Grady Co, Okla. Source: 16,99

J509 William Dale Allen
J510 Buster Valdo Allen
J511 Melba Jean Allen
J512 Earl Wayne Allen

J212 MATTIE KATRINE VANDEVENTER born March 26, 1909 in Gracemont, Caddo Co. Okla. She married Robert Earl Blakesly on Sept. 1, 1931 in Guthrie, Logan Co. Okla. He was born Feb. 25, 1901 in Mulhall, Logan Co., Okla. And died April 3,

338

1956 in Mulhall. They had no children. Source: 16,99

J213 to J250 children of J36 thru J48

J513 thru J1000 for children

J251 thru J398 children of J61 thru J112

J1001 thru J2075 for children

J399 ARGUL WRIGHT living in Bokchito, Ok. in 1957.

J400 RUBY WRIGHT married a Mr. Cavett and was living in Morrison, Ok. in 1957.
Source: 30

J401 CECIL WRIGHT living in Ga. in 1957.

J402 RAY WRIGHT living in Stillwater, Ok. in 1957. Source: 30

J403 OWEN WRIGHT living in Guthrie, Ok. in 1957. Source: 30

J404 DICK WRIGHT living in Raymond, Wa. in 1957. Source: 30

J405 MARIE WRIGHT married a Mr. Elliott. They were living in Pawnee, Ok. in 1957.
Source: 30

J406 thru J410 children of J135

J2076 thru J2108 for children

J411 BERTHA ELLEN BANNING born April 4, 1912 in Coyle, Payne Co., Ok. She
married LeRoy Person July 4, 1930. Source: 16,25

J2109 Dorothy Ann Person

J412 JACK PHILLIP BANNING born Jan. 1, 1914 in Stillwater, Payne Co., Okla. He
never married and died Aug. 22, 1960 in Okla. City, where he was buried in Sunny
Land Cemetery. Source: 16,25

J413 GRACE BELL BANNING born Jan. 26, 1917 in Pawnee, Ok. She
married Daniel Webster Carter on Oct. 10, 1933 in Okla. City, Ok. He was the son
of Thomas Henry LaFette and May Berdie (Gatlin) Carter, born March 15, 1913 in
Eupora, Webster Co., Miss. He died May 26, 1968 in Okla. City and is buried in
Sunny Land Cemetery. She married 2nd, George Lewis Hendrix. Source: 16,25

J2110 Richard Marion Carter
J2111 Betty Lucill Carter
J2112 Loretta Mae Carter
J2113 Bonnie Jean Carter
J2114 Franciel Eyvon Carter
J2115 James Carl Carter
J2116 Wanda Lee Carter
J2117 Peggy Louise Carter

J414 BEAULAH MAE BANNING born Nov. 1, 1922 in Pawnee, Ok. She married James Carl Pinkley on July 22, 1939 in Okla. City, Ok. He was the son of William Elbert and Vera (Haven) Pinkley, born June 4, 1917 in Rossville, Okla. He died April 30, 1979 on Cherokee, Ok. and is buried in Sunny Land Cemetery in Okla. City. Source: 16,25

J2118 James Warren Pinkley
J2119 Jackie Dewayne Pinkley

J415 HENRY ELLIS BANNING born Nov. 26, 1918 in Pawnee, Okla. Source: 16,25

J416 DOROTHY M. BANNING born in Okla. and married Mr. Bradford. Living in Somerset, Ky in 1982. Source: 25,30

J417 RAYMOND D. BANNING born in Okla. Living in Marietta, Ga. in 1982. Source: 25,30

J418 ROY DON BANNING born in Okla. and married Linda C. (???). He is employed in the nuclear ndustry and was living in Murphy, N.C. in 1992. Source: 25,30

J419 DALE BANNING born in Okla. Living in Broken Arrow, Okla. in 1982. Source: 25,30

J420 GEORGE L. BANNING born in Okla. Living in Stillwater, Okla. in 1982. Source: 25,30

J421 CHARLES B. BANNING born in Okla. Living in Stilleater, Okla. in 1982. Source: 25,30

J422 GENE BANNING born in Okla. Living in Stillwater, Okla. in 1982. Source: 25,30

J423 CLARENCE ELTON BANNING Source: 30

J424 HAROLD LAVERNE BANNING Source: 30

J425 JOHN FRANKLIN BANNING Source: 30

J426 DELORES JANE BANNING Source: 30

J427 DOROTHY JEAN BANNING Source: 30

J428 JANE VAN BRUNT married Chester Johnson and was living in Tulsa, Ok. in 1952. Source: 30

J429 MAE VAN BRUNT married Pete Bruner and was living in Thibodeau. La. in 1952. Source: 30

J430 JOHN VAN BRUNT living in garber, Ok. in 1952. Source: 30

J431 ROBERT VAN BRUNT living in Pawnee in 1952. Source: 30

J432 CHARLIE VAN BRUNT living in Paden, Ok. in 1952. Source: 30

J496 NANCY HILL born Jan. 11, 1945 and married John McClain. Their children are,

Sherri, John Mark, Scott, Travis and Shelley. Source: 16,99

J497 MARGARET JONES born March 27, 1932 and married Tom Gaskell. Their children are Gwendolyn, Tim, Kirk, Lisa, Jill, Bruce, Mark, Paul, Trudy and Sally. Source: 16,99

J498 ROBERT PAUL JONES born March 17, 1934. He married and their children are Allen, born 1958, died 1978; Ben, Beth and Sarah. Source: 16,99

J499 LARRY BANNING no information. Source: 16,99

J500 TOMMY BANNING no information. Source: 16,99

J501 TOMMY BANNING born 1936 and died 1937 in Horton, Ks. Source: 16,99

J502 JAMES BANNING No information. Source: 16,99

J503 JOANNE BANNING she married Bill Edmond and had two sons, Von and Don. Source: 16,99

J504 RONALD LEE OHLSEN born April 1, 1944 and married Diane Ace. Their children are Kimberly, Michael and Robin. Source: 16,99

J505 GERALD WAYNE OHLSEN born Aug. 24, 1947 and married Shelli Douglas. Their children are Carri Beth and Shawn. Source: 16,99

J506 DAVID LEE OHLSEN born Nov. 10, 1949 and married Marian Stovall. Their children are Kyle Thonas and Sarah Nichell. Source: 16,99

J507 VICKI JEAN OHLSEN born June 22, 1957 and married Thomas Drechsler. They had one child, Heidi, born April 16, 1991. Source: 16,99

J508 SHIRLEY JOYCE VANDEVENTER born May 1, 1931 in Hollywood, Calif. and married Arthur Seibel on June 30, 1950 in Glendale, Calif. Arthur was born July 20, 1931 in Los Angles, Calif. Their children are Michael, born Feb. 26, 1951; Curtis, Dec. 18, 1953; Steve, Oct. 3, 1955 and Vernon, July 27, 1959. She married 2nd, Lee Morgan, on May 2, 1976. Lee was born Oct. 25, 1931 in Orange, Calif. They have had on children. Source: 16,99

J509 WILLIAM DALE ALLEN born Jan. 11, 1935 in Gracemont, Caddo Co. Okla. He married Mary Catherine Galloway on Nov. 12, 1957 in Anadarko, Caddo Co. Okla. She was born Sept. 4, 1938 in Anadarko. They had one child, Christopher Leon, born Oct. 21, 1968. Source: 16,99

J510 BUSTER VALDO ALLEN born April 24, 1937 in Gracemont, Caddo Co. Okla. He married Hazel Marie Williams on May 24, 1957 in Gracemont. Hazel died in 1958. There were no children. Buster married 2nd Virginia Mitchner on April 5, 1963 in New Castle, McClain Co. Okla. Virginia was born May 2, 1937 in Blanchard, Okla. Buster died June 12, 1984 in Boulder City, Nevada. Their children are Shonda Kay, born Nov. 12, 1967 and died the next day; Kristi Ann, Nov. 21, 1968 and Shannon Gay, Feb. 8, 1971. Source: 16,99

J511 MELBA JEAN ALLEN born Nov. 22, 1939 in Gracemont, Caddo Co. Okla. Melba married Carl (Babe) Edwards Jr. On June 7, 1957 in Gracemont. Carl was born

Feb. 14, 1938 in Gracemont.. Their children are Debra, born may 15, 1960; Janet Lee, Jan. 12, 1962 and Jimmy Earl, Sept. 1, 1967. Melba is source 99. Source: 16,99

J512 EARL WAYNE ALLEN born Oct. 31, 1944 in Gracemont, Okla. And married Juanita Pitts on Jan. 26, 1963 in Oklahoma City. She was born July 10, 1944. Their Children are Kenneth James, born Aug. 1, 1966; David Dewayne, June 4, 1968 and Ricky Don, May 1, 1970. Source: 16,99

J2109 DOROTHY ANN PERSON born March 19, 1936 in Okla. City, Ok. Source: 16,25

J2110 RICHARD MARION CARTER born April 4, 1934 in Okla. City, Ok. He married Dorothy Ruth Thompson on March 31, 1953 in Okla. City. Source: 16,25

J2111 BETTY LUCILL CARTER born March 15, 1935 in Okla. City, Ok. and married Billy Wayne Eugene Coggins on May 22, 1952 in Okla. City. He is the son of Floyd and Lorean Rae (Huggins) Coggins, born May 22, 1932 in Okla. City. Their children are Floyd Wayne (born and died Feb. 2, 1962), LaDonna Lynn (Feb. 5, 1964) and Brenda Lee (Sept. 23, 1965). They live in Ratliff City, Okla. Source: 16,25

J2112 LORETTA MAE CARTER born April 30, 1936 in Okla. City, Ok. and died June 3, 1936. Source: 16,25

J2113 BONNIE JEAN CARTER born Aug. 23, 1937 in Okla. City, Ok. and married Bud Thomas in Nov. 1951. She married 2nd, Sherman Andrew Thompson Feb. 18, 1954 in Chickasha, Ok. Sherman died Sept. 12, 1973. Source: 16,25

J2114 FRANCIEL EYVON CARTER born Feb. 11, 1940 in Okla. City, Ok. She married 1st, Jonny Daniels. Source: 16,25

J2115 JAMES CARL CARTER born May 27, 1942 in Okla. City, Ok. and married Patricia Baumgardner. He married 2nd, Deborah Erling. Source: 16,25

J2116 WANDA LEE CARTER born May 23, 1944 in Okla. City, Ok. and married Jerry Don Henderson. She married 2nd, Tommy Speak. Source: 16,25

J2117 PEGGY LOUISE CARTER born Aug. 8, 1946 in Okla. City, Ok. and married Vernon Malloy. She married 2nd, Edward Jacob Schwartz. Edward died Jan. 16, 1987. Source: 16,25

J2118 JAMES WARREN PINKLEY born Feb. 7, 1943 in Okla. City, Ok. and married Karen McCune on Oct. 16, 1964. He married 2nd, Maxine Joy Battles. He died Oct. 13, 1983 and is buried in Sunny Land Cemetery in Okla. City. Source: 16,25

J2119 JACKIE DEWAYNE PINKLEY born Sept. 1, 1944 in Okla. City, Ok. and married Lilla Ruth Arnold on May 16, 1964. He married 2nd, Carolyn Gossey. Source: 16,25

ENGLISH BANNINGS

K, L & M branches

The date that the first Banning came to England is not definite, but it is believed that they came from Holland. The Banning name is found as early as 1438, the spelling may differ sometime, but it is clearly traceable from 1694 forward.

The probability is that the first Bannings settled near the present site of Banningham in Norfolk, but today little trace is left. Sir Paul Bayning, Lord Mayor of London, had his estate, Little Bently, in County Essex. When he was elevated to the Peerage and created the first Baron and then Viscount Banning in 1611, he changed the spelling of the name in the patent of nobility, to it's present form, Banning. The Peerage became extinct and only exists in the female line in the peerage of Pembroke and Leigh. A coat of Arms was granted in London in 1588 for services rendered in the Crusades by Bannings.

Records of some branches are traceable to 1438, but further back than 1694, little is certain. Additional research may well bring to light missing and valuable facts that would connect the English and American lines. At this point, all that is known is that in 1790 a family of Bannings came to Philadelphia, however all but one, John, returned to England.

The number of Bannings in England today is limited, with most living in London, Wiltshire, Worcestershire and Lancashire. Bannings are said to be in Scotland also.

Dr. Robert Joseph Banning of Sheeburyness, Essex, whose grandfather lived in Philadelphia from 1793 to 1799 is the authority for most of the facts on the Bannings in England.

ROBERT BANNING of WILTSHIRE

K1 ROBERT BANNING born about 1490 during the reign of Tudor King Henry VII. He lived at Burbage, Wiltshire in 1539 and was an old man in 1565. Source: 1,28,29,35

> K2 John Banning
> K3 Robert Banning

K2 JOHN BANNING lived at Burbage, Wiltshire in 1565. He married Elizabeth (???) and was a "Yoman". He signed his will in 1579 and was dead by April 30, 1580. Source: 1,2,28,29,35

> K4 John Banning
> K5 Johanna Banning
> K6 Elizabeth Banning
> K7 Agnes Banning
> K8 Mary Banning

K3 ROBERT BANNING He was alive in 1579. Source: 28

K9 thru K14 for children

K4 JOHN BANNING was alive in 1613. Source: 1,28,29,35

K15 John Banning
K16 thru K20 for children

K5 JOHANNA BANNING no information Source: 12

K21 thru K25 for children

K6 ELIZABETH BANNING no information Source: 12

K26 thru K30 for children

K7 AGNES BANNING no information Source: 12

K31 thru K35 for children

K8 MARY BANNING no information Source: 12

K36 thru K40 for children

K15 JOHN BANNING attended Burbage & Magdalena College and received his B.A. in
1630 and his M.A. in 1634, as per the Oxford Register. His name is on the
Subsidiary Roll in 1642 also. Source: 1,2,14 24,28,29,35

K41 Stephen Banning
K42 thru K45 for children

K16 thru K40 children of K4 thru K8

K46 thru K70 for children

K41 STEPHEN BANNING married Mary _____? and died in 1688. Source:
1,14,24,28,29,35

K71 Stephen Banning
K72 thru K75 for children

K42 thru K70 children of K15 thru K20

K76 thru K125 for children

K71 STEPHEN BANNING he was alive in 1714. See A1 Source: 1,24, 28,29,35

K126 John Banning
K127 Edward Banning
K128 Unknown Banning
K129 & K130 for children

K72 thru K125 children of K41 thru K70

K131 thru K230 for children

344

K126 JOHN BANNING (See A2) Lived in Milton Wilts and married Elizabeth Noyes of Wooton Rivers, Wilts in 1694. She was the heiress of Noyes. She died in 1719 and he died in 1716. Source: 1,14,24,27,28,29,35

> K231 Elizabeth Banning
> K232 Mary (Maria ?) Banning
> K233 Frances Banning
> K234 John Banning
> K235 Martha Banning
> K236 Susannah Banning

K127 EDWARD BANNING (See A3) He moved to Talbot Co., Md about 1650 and died about 1710. Source: 24,28,35,45,49

K128 UNKNOWN BANNING (See B1) He was the brother of John and his grandfather was Stephen. Source: 24,28,35

K129 thru K230 children ofK71 thru K125

> K237 thru K350 for children

K231 ELIZABETH BANNING born in Sept. 1695 in Milton, Wilts and died unmarried. Source: 1,24,27,28,29,35

K232 MARY (MARIA ?) BANNING born in 1698 in Milton, Wilts and died unmarried. Source:1,14,24,28,29 ,35

K233 FRANCES BANNING born in 1702 in Milton, Wilts and died unmarried. Source: 1,14,29,35

K234 JOHN BANNING born in 1705 in Milton, Wilts. He married Mary Ayers (Eyers) the widow of Henry Ayers in 1744. She was the sole heiress of John Griffin and descended as follows: Rev. John White, wife Mary, the Vicar of Avebury, had a daughter, Mary White, who married John Griffin. They had a daughter Mary, who married 1st, H. Ayers and 2nd, John Banning in 1745. She died in 1805 and John died in 1772 in Milton, Wilts. Both are buried in Milton. Source: 1,14,24,27,28,29,35

> K351 John Banning
> K352 Thomas Banning
> K353 Elizabeth Banning
> K354 and K355 for children

K235 MARTHA BANNING born March 1707 and married Simon Alexander of Milton Wilts in Sept. 1737. Source: 1,14,14,28,29,35

> K356 Thomas Alexander
> K357 Mary Alexander
> K358 thru K360 for children

K236 SUSANNAH BANNING born March 1712 and married Jasper Easter of Wooten Wilts in Dec. 1736. They had one Son. Source: 1,14,24, 28,29,35

K361 -----? Easter
K362 thru K365 for children

K237 thru K350 children of K129 thru K230

K366 thru K600 for children

K351 JOHN BANNING born 1746 in Milton, Wilts and married Frances Neal of
    Wooten Rivers in March 1774. They lived in Wooten Rivers. She was born about
    1752 and died in Nov. 1817. He died in July 1825 at Wooten Rivers where both are
    buried. Source: 1,14,28,35

> K601 John Banning
> K602 Thomas Banning
> K603 Philip Banning
> K604 thru K605 for children

K352 THOMAS BANNING born in 1748 and married Esther Westley at St. Johns
    Hersledown in 1773. He died in 1829 and is buried at Fetchan Surrey. Source:
    1,28,35

> K606 Thomas Banning
> K607 Elizabeth Banning
> K608 Mary Banning
> K609 Mary Ann Banning
> K610 John Banning
> K611 Elizabeth Banning
> K612 Martha Banning
> K613 Edward Banning
> K614 Hetty Banning

K353 ELIZABETH BANNING born March 1751 and died in 1758. Source: 1,28,35

K354 and K355 children of K234

K615 thru K624 for children

K356 THOMAS ALEXANDER he died unmarried. Source: 1

K357 MARY ALEXANDER died unmarried Source: 1

K358 thru K360 children of K235

K361 ------? Son EASTER born 1738. Source: 1

K362 thru K600 children of K236 thru K350

K625 thru K1250 for children

K601 JOHN BANNING born 1775 in Wooten and married Rebecca Somerset in
    Marlborough in Jan. 1802. He died in Aug. 1836 and is buried in Wooton Rivers.
    Source: 1

> K1251 Thomas Banning

K1252 Philippina Banning
K1253 thru K1255 for children

K602 THOMAS BANNING born 1776 in Wooton and died unmarried in 1844. He is buried in Wooton. Source: 1

K603 PHILIP BANNING born July 1781 at Burbage. He died with no children in Jan. 1835. Source: 1

K604 and K605 children of K351

K1256 thru K1265 for children

K606 THOMAS BANNING born 1775 and married Mary Barras in 1802. They had no children. She died in 1804 and is buried at North Dunstans, London. He then married Ann Caroline Lyon Stuart of London in St. Margaret Pattens in 1815. She was born 1785 at Clerkenwell and died in 1856. He died in 1859. Source: 1

K1266 Emma Banning
K1267 John Stephen Banning
K1268 Mary Banning
K1269 Ann Caroline Banning

K607 ELIZABETH BANNING born in 1776 and died an infant. Source: 1

K608 MARY BANNING born in 1777 and died an infant. Source: 1

K609 MARY ANN BANNING born in 1778 and died an infant. Source: 1

K610 JOHN BANNING born in 1779 at Horsledown and married Elizabeth Martha Northcust in 1807 at Tedworth Wilts. Source: 1

K1270 Thomas Banning
K1271 Elizabeth Martha Banning
K1272 thru K1274 for children

K611 ELIZABETH BANNING born 1781 and married William Pugh in 1803 at Fetcham Surrey. She died in 1810 and is buried at Laubeth. Source: 1

K1275 Charles Pugh
K1276 William Pugh
K1277 Charles Pugh
K1278 Edward Pugh

K612 MARTHA BANNING born 1784 and died unmarried in 1854. Source: 1

K613 EDWARD BANNING died as an infant. Source: 1

K614 HETTY BANNING died as an infant. Source: 1

K615 thru K1250 children of K362 thru K600

K1279 thru K2900 for children

K1251 THOMAS BANNING born 1804 in Burbage and died unmarried in Oct. 1832. Buried at Wooton. Source: 1

K1252 PHILIPPINA BANNING born at Wooton and married M.E.A. Carrington in 1833. They had no children. She died in 1858 and is buried in Wooton. Source: 1

K1253 thru K1265 children of K601 thru K605

K2901 thru K2930 for children

K1266 EMMA BANNING born Sept. 1818 and died July 1820. She is buried at St. Margaret Pattens, London. Source: 1

K1267 JOHN STEPHEN BANNING born 1823 in Great Tower Street and married Elizabeth Jane Carpenter in 1858. She was born in 1832. They lived in London where he was a wine merchant and a common Councillor of the city of London. He died in 1877. Source: 1

> K2931 Stephen Thomas Banning
> K2932 Edith Spencer Banning
> K2933 thru K2935 for children

K1268 MARY BANNING born 1825. She lived unmarried in London in 1908. Source: 1

K1269 ANN CAROLINE BANNING born 1827 and married Edward Pugh (see K1278) in 1850. This was her 2nd husband. She died in 1870. Source: 1

> K2936 Mary Banning Pugh
> K2937 Edward Stuart Pugh
> K2938 Caroline Elizabeth Pugh
> K2939 Alice Jane Pugh
> K2940 Walter Thomas Pugh
> K2941 Elizabeth Annie Pugh
> K2942 Arthur Lyon Pugh
> K2943 Elinor Stuart Pugh

K1270 THOMAS BANNING born 1816 and married Emma Waters of Stratford Wilts in 1844. He died in 1844 and is buried at Tedwort. See K1276. Source: 1

> K2944 Martha Northcust Banning

K1271 ELIZABETH MARTHA BANNING born 1820 and died 1844. She is buried at St. Dunstans in East London. Source: 1

K1272 thru K1274 children of K610

K2945 thru K2964 for children

K1275 CHARLES PUGH born 1804 and died the same year. Source: 1

K1276 WILLIAM PUGH born 1805 and married Emma Banning, the widow of Thomas Banning (K1270) in 1844. Source: 1

K2965 William Carrington Pugh
K2966 Emma Pugh
K2967 Florence Martha Pugh

K1277 CHARLES PUGH born 1805 and died unmarried at Blackheath. Source: 1

K1278 EDWARD PUGH born 1809 and married Ann Caroline Banning (K1269) in 1850. He died in 1873. Source: 1

K1279 thru K2930 children of 615 thru K1265

K2968 thru K6900 for children

K2931 STEPHEN THOMAS BANNING born 1859 at 21 Great Tower Street. He married Isabel Margaret Moriarty on April 28, 1886. She was born in 1862 in Duncistin, County Kerry. He was a Lieut. Col. in the Royal Munster Fusiliers, J.P. Co., Dublin, and a barrister at law, middle temple. B.A. from the Royal University of Ireland. Source: 1

K6901 Percy Stuart Banning
K6902 thru K6905 for children

K2932 EDITH SPENCER BANNING born 1860 and married Frederick George Ambrose Povah in 1885. He was born 1855. Source: 1

K6906 Alfred Povah
K6907 Mary Spencer Povah

K2933 thru K2935 children of K2167

K???

K2936 MARY BANNING PUGH married Arthur W. Drake. Source: 1

K2937 EDWARD STUART PUGH he married. Source: 1

K2938 CAROLINE ELIZABETH PUGH married Alfred Stevens and was a widow in 1908. Source: 1

K2939 ALICE JANE PUGH married Walter Stevens. Source: 1

K2940 WALTER THOMAS PUGH no information Source: 1

K2941 ELIZABETH ANNIE PUGH born 1853 and married Allen Booth. They had one daughter. Source: 1

K2942 ARTHUR LYON PUGH no information Source: 1

K2943 ELINOR STUART PUGH no information. Source: 1

K2944 MARTHA NORTHCUST BANNING born 1845 and married J. Chapman. Source: 1

K2945 WILLIAM CARRINGTON PUGH died in Canada. Source: 1

K2946 EMMA PUGH born 1851 and married in 1894. Source: 1

K2947 FLORENCE MARTHA PUGH no information Source: 1

K6901 PERCY STUART BANNING born 1887. Source: 1

K6906 ALFRED POVAH born 1886. Source: 1

K6907 MARTHA SPENCER POVAH born 1886. Source: 1

WILLIAM BANNING of WORCHESTERSHIRE

L1 WILLIAM BANNING born about 1710 and was a miller at Worchestershire. Source: 1

> L2 John Banning
> L3 William Banning

L2 JOHN BANNING born about 1730 in Worchester and lived in Glovstershire where he was a farrier (blacksmith). Source: 1

> L4 John Banning
> L5 Joseph Banning

L3 WILLIAM BANNING born about 1732 in Worchester. He married Hannah Clowes about 1755 at Uttexter. They lived at Stafford where he was an innkeeper and property owner. Source: 1

> L6 William Banning
> L7 Thomas Banning
> L8 John Banning
> L9 Joseph Banning
> L10 Annie Banning
> L11 Sarah Banning
> L12 James Banning

L4 JOHN BANNING lived in London where he was a groom to King George II. Source: 1

> L13 thru L19 for children

L5 JOSEPH BANNING lived in London where he was a groom to King George II. Source: 1

> L20 thru L26 for children

L6 WILLIAM BANNING born July 26, 1756 at Stone in Staffordshire. He married Mary -----?. They lived at Reach, Lancashire where he died Aug. 3, 1846. Source: 1

> L27 John Banning
> L28 Elizabeth Banning

L7 THOMAS BANNING born Jan. 22, 1759 in Stafford and married 4 times. 1st, Miss. Haines. They had two children. He married 4th, Mary Driver and they had 5 children. He lived in Liverpool where he was Postmaster from 1798 thru 1819. He died on March 10, 1833. Source: 1

> L29 Thomas Haines Banning
> L30 William Banning
> L31 John Johnson Banning
> L32 Benjamin Banning
> L33 Charles Barber Greaves Banning

L34 Mary Banning
L35 Eliza Patterson Banning

L8 JOHN BANNING born Aug. 15, 1760 in Stafford and married twice. He had a son by his first wife and moved to Philadelphia, Pa. U.S.A. about 1790. He also had children by his 2nd wife, who lived in the U.S.A. Source: 1,45

L36 Daniel Banning
L37 thru L42 for children

L9 JOSEPH BANNING born Nov. 15, 1761 in Stafford and married Margaret Wrenshall of Preston, Lancashire on March 14, 1791. She was born in 1761 and died in 1857. They moved to Philadelphia, Pa. U.S.A. and opened a store on North 3rd St., 1 door down from Brewert Alley. He was in this business from 1793 thru 1799 with his brother-in-law, John Wrenshall, who died in Pittsburgh in 1823. 1799 saw Joseph and his family return to England due to a Yellow Fever plague in which 2 of their children died. They settled in Meller, near Blackburn, where he died on Jan. 25, 1829. He was a prominent Wesleyan Methodist. Source: 1

L43 Joseph Banning
L44 James Banning
L45 Hannah Banning
L46 Esther Banning
L37 William Banning
L48 Thomas Banning
L49 Nathaniel Banning
L50 Elisa Banning
L51 Jesse Banning

L10 ANNIE BANNING born Oct. 11, 1764 in Stafford and died unmarried. Source: 1

L11 SARAH BANNING born Sept. 15, 1757 in Stafford and married Thomas Salt of Liverpool. They lived in Liverpool where she died. Source: 1

L52 Joseph Salt
L53 Emma Salt
L54 Sarah Salt

L12 JAMES BANNING born March 29, 1767 in Stafford and died an infant. Source: 1

L13 thru L26 unknown children of L4 & L5.

L55 thru L115 for children

L27 JOHN BANNING born May 21, 1787 at Blackburn, Lancashire. He married Ellen Anderson in 1810. They lived in Manchester where he died July 29, 1854. Source: 1

L116 Eliza Banning
L117 William Banning
L118 Mary Banning
L119 John Banning
L120 Emma Banning
L121 James Banning

                    L122 Ann Banning
                    L123 Thomas Banning
                    L124 Elinor Banning
                    L125 Henry Banning
                    L126 Josiah Banning

L28 ELIZABETH BANNING born in 1792 in Blackburn and married John Wesley Dall.
     They lived in Roach, Lancashire where he owned a Cotton Mill. He was related to
     Lord Wolverhampton. She died in Nov. 1872. Source: 1

                    L127 Charles Dall
                    L128 Robert Dall
                    L129 William Dall
                    L130 Joseph Dall
                    L131 Mary Ann Dall
                    L132 Elizabeth Dall
                    L133 John Dall
                    L134 James Hartley Dall
                    L135 Margaret Dall
                    L136 George Dall
                    L137 Maria Dall

L29 THOMAS HAINES BANNING born 1784 and was a Physician to the Royal
     Infirmary and a graduate of Edinburgh. He died unmarried Jan. 1, 1861. Source: 1

L30 WILLIAM BANNING born Jan. 7, 1785 and was Postmaster of Liverpool from
     1819 thru 1847. He died unmarried Feb. 7, 1857 in Liverpool. Source: 1

L31 JOHN JOHNSON BANNING born 1807 and married Harriet Dudley of
     Staffordshire. She was born about 1807 and died in 1890 at age 83. They had no
     children. They lived in Liverpool where he was a Solicitor. He died in 1886 in
     Southport, Lancashire. Source: 1

L32 BENJAMIN BANNING (Rev.) married Helen Maria Lacy. She was the daughter of
     H.L. Lacy and the sister of Lady Baggallay. He was the Vicar of Wellington and
     Rector of Eyton Solon. He died in 1899. Source: 1

                    L138 Henry Thomas Banning
                    L139 Helen Banning

L33 CHARLES BARBER GREAVES BANNING born 1813 and married Louisa Sophia
     Whitlow. She was the daughter of Richard Whitlow. They lived in Liverpool where
     he was postmaster from 1847 to 1875. Upon succeeding to the property of Mr.
     Greaves of Manchester, through his wife, he assumed the name of
     Greaves-Banning and obtained Arms, described as follows; "Greaves-Banning
     impaled and great-ostrich differencated by a circlet, Or." Source: 1

                    L140 Ada Sarah Georgiana Banning
                    L141 Madaline Banning
                    L142 Arthur Charles Banning

L34 MARY BANNING born 1811 and married John Richardson in 1837. She died in
     1906. Source: 1

L143 John William Richardson
L144 Thomas Banning Richardson
L145 James Aitken Richardson
L146 Charles Banning Richardson
L147 Alfred Gordon Richardson

L35 ELIZA PATTERSON BANNING married Edward Banks. They had no children and she died Dec. 10, 1857. Source: 1

L36 DANIEL BANNING born 1785 and lived in Philadelphia or Pittsburgh, Pa. U.S.A. Source: 1,45

L148 thru L154 for children

L37 thru L42 unknown children of L8

L155 thru L180 for children

L43 JOSEPH BANNING born Jan. 27, 1792 at Bolton Lemoor, Lancashire and married Nancy Talbot of Blackburn on May 1, 1815. She was born in 1793 and died in 1826 in Liverpool. They had 5 children. He married 2nd, Anna Burton Pidcock in Jan. 1827. She was born in 1801 in Kirk Ireton, Derbyshire and died in 1857. They had 4 children. He lived in Liverpool where he was apprenticed as a violin maker, but shortly after became a school master. While he was still quite young, he joined his uncle, Thomas Banning, as his sole clerk in the Liverpool Postoffice. Joseph later became Deputy Postmaster and Surveyor of Liverpool where he remained about 50 years. When he retired in 1865, he had over 1000 men under him. He died Dec. 10, 1874 in Liverpool. Source: 1

L181 Julia Banning
L182 Joshua Banning
L183 Thomas Wrenshall Banning
L184 William Banning
L185 Izetta Banning
L186 Robert Joseph Banning
L187 Charles Henry Banning
L188 Emma Banning
L189 Edwin Banning

L44 JAMES BANNING born April 1, 1793 in Bolton. He died of Yellow Fever on July 15, 1796 in Philadelphia, Pa. U.S.A. Source: 1

L45 HANNAH BANNING born Jan. 24, 1796 in Philadelphia, Pa. She returned to England with her parents and married Thomas Hayes of Blackburn. She died in Lancashire April 23, 1843. Source: 1

L190 Francis Hayes
L191 Margaret Hayes

L46 ESTHER BANNING born 1798 in Philadelphia, U.S.A. where she died of Yellow Fever the same year. Source: 1

L47 WILLIAM BANNING born 1799 in Houghton and died in 1800. Source: 1

L48 THOMAS BANNING born March 11, 1801 in Liverpool and died June 27, 1802.
Source: 1

L49 NATHANIEL BANNING born April 7, 1803 and died May 2, 1803. Source: 1

L50 ELIZA BANNING born Jan. 18, 1806 in Mellor, Lancashire. She married George
Stones in Liverpool. He was the principal clerk in the Postoffice in Liverpool. She
died May 3, 1848 in Liverpool. Source: 1

L192 Margaret Ann Stones
L193 Thomas Joseph Stones
L194 William Henry Stones
L195 Mary Beaumont Stones
L196 Eliza Banning Stones

L51 JESSE BANNING born Feb. 24, 1808 in Mellor, Lancashire and married Anne Holt
in 1834 in Liverpool. They lived in Liverpool where he was Professor of Music and a
composer. He died in 1893 in Birkenhend. Source: 1

L197 Frederick Joseph Banning
L198 William James Banning
L199 Jessie Banning
L200 Stanley Banning
L201 Emily Banning
L202 Mary Ellen Banning
L203 Harriet Banning

L52 JOSEPH SALT no information. Source: 1

L53 EMMA SALT married a Mr. Earp of Uttexter, Staffordshire. They had children.
Source: 1

L54 SARAH SALT no information. Source: 1

L55 thru L115 unknown children of L13 thru L26

L204 thru L304 for children

L116 ELIZA BANNING married Mr. Neilson. Source: 1

L305 thru L310 for children

L117 WILLIAM BANNING no information. Source: 1

L311 thru L315 for children

L118 MARY BANNING no information. Source: 1

L316 thru L320 for children

L119 JOHN BANNING no information. Source: 1

L321 thru L325 for children

L120 EMMA BANNING no information. Source: 1

L326 thru L330 for children

L121 JAMES BANNING no information. Source: 1

L331 thru L335 for children

L122 ANN BANNING no information. Source: 1

L336 thru L340 for children

L123 THOMAS BANNING no information. Source: 1

L341 thru L345 for children

L124 ELINOR BANNING no information. Source: 1

L346 thru L350 for children

L125 HENRY BANNING no information. Source: 1

L351 thru L355 for children

L126 JOSIAH BANNING no information. Source: 1

L356 thru L360 for children

L127 CHARLES DALL no information. Source: 1

L128 ROBERT DALL no information. Source: 1

L129 WILLIAM DALL no information. Source: 1

L130 JOSEPH DALL no information. Source: 1

L131 MARY ANN DALL no information. Source: 1

L132 ELIZABETH DALL no information. Source: 1

L133 JOHN DALL no information. Source: 1

L134 JAMES HARTLEY DALL received his M.A. from Dublin. Source: 1

L135 MARGARET DALL no information. Source: 1

L136 GEORGE DALL no information. Source: 1

L137 MARIA DALL married Mr. Smallpace. Source: 1

L138 HENRY THOMAS BANNING born 1844 and married Annie Laura Druce. They
lived in Blackheath, London where he died in 1899. He received his M.A. at
Blackheath, London where he was a Barrister. Source: 1

L361 Henry Druce Banning
L362 Helen Laura Banning

L139 HELEN BANNING born 184?. She lived unmarried in London. Source: 1

L140 ADA SARAH GEORGIANA BANNING married Joseph Keating Pollock, the son of Arch-Deacon Pollock. Source: 1

L363 Douglas William Pollock
L364 Charles Stewart Pollock
L365 Hilda Louise Pollock
L366 Hubert Charles Pollock

L141 MADALINE BANNING she lived unmarried. Source: 1

L142 ARTHUR CHARLES BANNING married Annie Evelyn Hutton of Edgebarton, Birmingham. She died June 28, 1892. Source: 1

L367 Irene Greaves Banning

L143 JOHN WILLIAM RICHARDSON born in 1838 and married Anna S. M. Carinthen, the daughter of Rev. W. H. Carinthen, the Vicar of Ayleseare, Devonshire. They had 6 children. Source: 1

L144 THOMAS BANNING RICHARDSON died in 1841 as an infant. Source: 1

L145 JAMES AITKEN RICHARDSON died in 1845 as an infant. Source: 1

L146 CHARLES BANNING RICHARDSON no information. Source: 1

L147 ALFRED GORDON RICHARDSON died in 1871 unmarried. Source: 1

L148 thru L180 unknown children of L36 thru L42

L368 thru L448 for children

L181 JULIA BANNING born March 16, 1816 in Mellor, near Blackburn Lane. Married Edward Widdows of Liverpool in 1835 in Liverpool. They lived in Liverpool where he was the principal clerk in the post office and a property owner. She died Nov. 8, 1896. He died in 1851, both in Liverpool. Source: 1

L449 Elizabeth Julia Widdows
L450 Frances Izetta Widdows
L451 Richard Widdows
L452 Joseph Banning Widdows
L453 Ada Bromley Widdows
L454 Richard Widdows
L455 Edward Widdows
L456 Mary Ellen Widdows

L182 JOSHUA BANNING born Jan. 27, 1817 in Mellor, near Blackburn Lane. Married Ann Molyneau in 1840 in Upton, Cheshire. They lived in Whitmore, Cheshire. He was a station master for the London & Northwestern Railway. He died in 1850. Source: 1

L457 William Albert Banning
L458 Annie Mona Banning
L459 Frances Theidosa Banning
L460 Jesse Wrenshall Banning

L183 THOMAS WRENSHALL BANNING born March 17, 1819 in Mellor and educated at Blackburn. He died unmarried in 1855 in New York City, U.S.A. and is buried in the Greenwood Cemetery. He was a sailor in the Royal Navy. Source: 1

L184 WILLIAM BANNING born Jan. 24, 1821 in Liverpool and married Charlotte Waters in 1854 in London. They lived in Liverpool, Isle of Man and Birmingham. She died in 1905 and he died in 1898, both in Liverpool. They had no children. Source: 1

L185 IZETTA BANNING born Dec. 31, 1825 in Liverpool and married Alfred Pickup of Liverpool in 1848. They lived in Liverpool where she died Sept. 9, 1856. Source: 1

L461 Thomas Hartley Pickup
L462 James Pickup
L463 Alfred Edwin Pickup
L464 Margaret Ann Pickup

L186 ROBERT JOSEPH BANNING born June 17, 1832 in Liverpool and married Mary Ann Travis of Liverpool in 1860 in that city. They lived in Liverpool and had one child. She died and he then married Alice Cooper in 1869. They had one child. During the Crimean War, 1854-55, he was a Civil Surgeon and later was Justice of the Peace. He lived in Shoeburyness, Essex as a retire physician and was alive in 1908. Source: 1

L465 John Travis Banning
L466 Alice Maud Banning

L187 CHARLES HENRY bANNING (Rev.) born Oct. 7, 1833 in Liverpool and married Eliza Amelia Smeed of Gore Court, Sittinbourn. He received his M.A. at Dublin and was Vicar successively of Strood, Highbury, London and Vicar of Spring Grove, Middlesex. He died Nov. 7, 1906. Source: 1

L467 Henry Burton Smeed Banning

L188 EMMA BANNING born Nov. 27, 1839 in Liverpool and married Daniel Rea of Liverpool in 1868. They lived in Liverpool. Source: 1

L468 Josephine Banning Rea
L469 Daniel Arthur Rea
L470 Mary Beatrice Rea
L471 William Lawrence Rea
L472 Muriel Amy Rea

L189 EDWIN BANNING born Nov. 27, 1839 (twin to Emma) and died an infant. Source: 1

L190 FRANCIS HAYES he married the sister of Monseingor Nugent of Liverpool and died June 29, 1877. Source: 1

L191 MARGARET HAYES died unmarried on Jan. 22, 1862 at the age of 40. Source: 1

L192 MARGARET ANN STONES born in 1837 and lived unmarried in Ireland. Source: 1

L193 THOMAS JOSEPH STONES born 1840 and died in 1851. Source: 1

L194 WILLIAM HENRY STONES born 1842 and died in 1851. Source: 1

L195 MARY BEAUMONT STONES born 1845 and married Capt. David A. Cook in 1869. They had three girls. She died in 1896. Source: 1

L196 ELIZA BANNING STONES born 1848 and married Thomas Worrall in 1873. They had one girl. Source: 1

L197 FREDERICK JOSEPH BANNING born 1843 and married Hannah Poctiers. They had no children and he died in 1879. Source: 1

L198 WILLIAM JAMES BANNING born in 1837 and died unmarried in 1872. He was a sailor. Source: 1

L199 JESSIE BANNING born in 1840 and died an infant. Source: 1

L200 STANLEY BANNING born in 1841 and married Nina Brewer. They lived in London where he was a financier. He died in 1908. They had no children. Source: 1

L201 EMILY BANNING born in 1845, she lived unmarried at Golden Green, London. Source: 1

L202 MARY ELLEN BANNING born in 1847 and lived unmarried in Southport. Source: 1

L203 HARRIET BANNING born in 1849. She married Edward Sherman Wardley. They moved to Australia and had 4 children. Source: 1

L473 thru L476 for children

L204 thru L360 unknown children of L55 thru L126

L477 thru L877 for children

L361 HENRY DURCE BANNING no information. Source: 1

L878 thru L883 for children

L362 HELEN LAURA BANNING no information. Source: 1

L884 thru L889 for children

L363 DOUGLAS WILLIAM POLLOCK born July 24, 1872. He was an officer in the British Army. Source: 1

L364 CHARLES STEWART POLLOCK born April 21, 1875. He lived in South Africa.
Source: 1

L365 HILDA LOUISE POLLOCK born Dec. 3, 1876. She married Edward Edgerton
Todd. They had 1 girl. Source: 1

L366 HUBERT CHARLES POLLOCK born April 29, 1878 and died July 30, 1883.
Source: 1

L367 IRENE GREAVES BANNING born Aug. 5, 1886. Source: 1

L890 thru L895 for children

L368 thru L448 unknown children of L148 thru L180

L896 thru L1096 for children

L449 ELIZABETH JULIA WIDDOWS born 1836 and died unmarried in 1881. Source:
1

L450 FRANCES IZETTA WIDDOWS born 1837. She married Robert Scott. She died
in 1867, after having 4 children. Source: 1

L451 RICHARD WIDDOWS born 1839 and died as an infant. Source: 1

L452 JOSEPH BANNING WIDDOWS born 1840. He married Amelia Empson in
1882 and had 2 children. Source: 1

L453 ADA BROMLEY WIDDOWS born in 1842. She married Henry Bayford of
Liverpool in 1875 and had 5 children. Source: 1

L454 RICHARD WIDDOWS born in 1846 and married Florence Ford in 1881. They
had 1 child. Source: 1

L455 EDWARD WIDDOWS born in 1846 and married Elizabeth Houghton in 1878.
They had 3 children. Source: 1

L456 MARY ELLEN WIDDOWS born 1848 and married Henry George Stafford in
1872. They had 4 children. Source: 1

L457 WILLIAM ALBERT BANNING born in 1841 and married Anna Williams. They
lived in Cheshire. Source: 1

L1097 Albert Williams Banning
L1098 thru L1101 for children.

L458 ANNIE MONA BANNING born in 1839 (?) and married Henry Rowland. They
had no children. She married 2nd, Thomas Brassey and lived in Cheshire. There
were no children and she died in 1891. Source: 1

L459 FRANCES THEIDOSA BANNING born in 1844 and married George Brassey,
the brother of Thomas Brassey. They lived in Cheshire and had no children.
Source: 1

L460 JESSE WRENSHALL BANNING born in 1846 and died in 1850. Source: 1

L461 THOMAS HARTLEY PICKUP born in 1849 and died as an infant. Source: 1

L462 JAMES PICKUP born in 1850. He received his M.A. at Cambridge and was a Barrister at Law. He married Louise Richardson in 1882 and had 4 children. Source: 1

L463 ALFRED EDWIN PICKUP died as an infant. Source: 1

L464 MARGARET ANN PICKUP born in 1854 and died in 1857. Source: 1

L465 JOHN TRAVIS BANNING born in 1861 in Gateshead on Tyne, and died in 1862. Source: 1

L466 ALICE MAUD BANNING born Dec. 3, 1869 in Gateshead, and lived unmarried at Shoeburyness, Essex. Source: 1

L467 HENRY BURTON SMEED BANNING born in 1877 in Strood, Kent. He married Constance Daisy Holt on Nov. 1, 1905. They lived in Claygate, Surrey. He received his M.A. at Cambridge and was a Barrister in London. Source: 1

L1102 thru L1107 for children

L468 JOSEPHINE BANNING REA born in 1870 and married Andrew William Duncan, a Publisher in Liverpool, in 1896. They had 1 child. Source: 1

L469 DANIEL ARTHUR REA born in 1871 and married Frances Emily Hardy in 1897. They lived in Liverpool and had 3 children. Source: 1

L470 MARY BEATRICE REA born in 1873 and married Rev. Samuel Barrow in 1906. He was the Vicar of St. Athanasias Church in Liverpool. Source: 1

L471 WILLIAM LAWRENCE REA born in 1876. Source: 1

L472 MURIEL AMY REA born in 1879. Source: 1

L473 thru L1096 unknown children of L203 thru L448

L1097 ALBERT WILLIAM BANNING he married in 1896 and had at least 1 son. Source: 1

JAMES BANNING of EVERLEIGH

M1 JAMES BANNING born about 1795 in Bristol. He lived for many years in Everleigh where he was a farrier. Later in life he moved to Workingham where he died.
Source: 1

> M2 Frank Banning
> M3 Jake Banning
> M4 John Banning
> M5 Charles Banning
> M6 Frederick Banning
> M7 Harry Banning

M2 FRANK BANNING no information. Source: 1

> M8 William Banning
> M9 thru M15 for children

M3 JAKE BANNING no information. Source: 1

> M16 thru M23 for children

M4 JOHN BANNING no information. Source: 1

> M24 thru M31 for children

M5 CHARLES BANNING no information. Source: 1

> M32 thru M39 for children

M6 FREDERICK BANNING no information. Source: 1

> M40 thru M47 for children

M7 HARRY BANNING no information. Source: 1

> M48 thru M55 for children

M8 WILLIAM BANNING he married and had children. He lived at 30 Melton St., Euston Sq. N.W. London. Source: 1

> M56 thru M63 for children

The BANNINGS (Benningh) of Holland and Germany.

The Bannings are traceable thru history to an earlier definite date in Holland than in any other country. Their activities in Holland span a period of about 300 years from 1500. During that time they were among the most influential families in the land. The records are many, the name often mentioned and their position both social and political were of the highest.

Their migration started in the 17th century to Germany and probably elsewhere, although prior to that time no doubt individual families or persons migrated to other countries.

As of 1908, many descendants of the original families still live in Holland and their vocations cover many fields. As of yet, no one has found a record of the family history in Holland, but sufficient search will no doubt bring to light several such valuable histories.

As a result of the migrations from Holland, Germany has several families of Bannings, who in the main, have held positions of influence and power (prior to 1910) in government, as well as in social affairs.

Hermann Banning of Berlin held the highly prized position of Legal Advisor in the government service. Felix H. Banning of Duren, Reinland, was a very successful paper machinery manufacturer. Almost without exception German Bannings were comfortably well off.

It is through the searches made by Felix H. Banning that much of the valuable early history of the Holland Bannings is presented, as well as all that is set forth about the German Bannings, which represents his line only.

Belgium has had a few Bannings. Emil Banning was probably the most well known. He was the confidential legal advisor to the King for years, and was a lawyer of international repute, as well as an author of high standing in several lines. He was decorated by Kaiser Wilhelm. His brother, Alphonse Banning, in 1908 held a highly coveted office in the government in Brussels.

Denmark has many Bannings living to this day, no doubt descendants of the 1st known Banning, but facts about them are lacking.

ADOLPH BANNING of GERMANY

N1 ADOLPH FRIEDREICH BANNING he married Anna Elisabeth Detmeyers, the widow of Herr Foges, on May 11, 1686. They lived in Tecklenburg, Westfalen, Germany. Source: 1

        N2 Johann Marcus Banning
        N3 thru N8 for children

N2 JOHANN MARCUS BANNING born May 24, 1688 in Tecklenburg, Westfalen. He married Maria Focke on June 1, 1720 in Ladbergen, Westfalen. They lived in

Ladbergen where he was a minister from 1719 on. He died April 11, 1754 in Ladbergen. Source: 1

N9   Ernst Johann Adolph Banning
N10 Moritz Hildebrand Banning
N11 Ernestine Margaret Elizabeth Banning
N12 Ernst Bernhard Banning
N13 Friedreich Banning
N14 Lornhard Hermann Banning
N15 Christine Wilhelmine Margarethe Banning
N16 Alexander Banning
N17 Maria Magdalena Banning

N3 thru N8 unknown children of N1

N18 thru N47 for children

N9 ERNST JOHANN ADOLPH BANNING born Aug. 28, 1721 in Ladbergen, where he became a minister. He was succeeded by his son John Johann, who was succeeded in turn by his younger brother Ernest Ludwig Banning. Source: 1

N48 John Johann Mathias Marcus Adolph Banning
N49 Ernest Ludwig Banning
N50 thru N54 for children

N10 MORITZ HILDEBRAND BANNING born Dec. 17, 1722 in Ladbergen. He lived in Lungerich, Westfalen where he was a merchant. Source: 1

N55 Johann Bernard Banning
N56 Maria Elisabeth Banning
N57 Johann Adolph Banning
N58 Christine Maria Banning
N59 Friedreich Mauritz Banning
N60 Ernst Moritz Banning

N11 ERNESTINE MARGARET ELIZABETH BANNING born Nov. 1, 1724 in Ladbergen. Source: 1

N61 thru N66 for children

N12 ERNST BERNHARD BANNING born April 29, 1726 in Ladbergen. Source: 1

N67 thru N72 for children

N13 FRIEDREICH BANNING born April 20, 1729 in Ladbergen. Source: 1

N73 thru N78 for children

N14 LORNHARD HERMANN BANNING born Feb. 15, 1731 in Ladbergen. Source: 1

N79 thru N84 for children

N15 CHRISTINE WILHELMINE MARGARETHE BANNING born Jan. 7, 1733 in Ladbergen. Source: 1

366

N85 thru N90 for children

N16 ALEXANDER BANNING born July 15, 1734 in Ladbergen. Source: 1

N91 thru N96 for children

N17 MARIA MAGDALENA BANNING born June 24, 1736 in Ladbergen. Source: 1

N97 thru N102 for children

N18 thru N47 unknown children of N3 thru N8

N103 thru N202 for children

N48 JOHN JOHANN MATHIAS MARCUS ADOLPH BANNING born in Ladbergen where he became a minister and succeeded his father. Source: 1

N203 thru N208 for children

N49 ERNEST LUDWIG BANNING born in Ladbergen where he became a minister and succeeded his brother. Source: 1

N209 thru N214 for children

N50 thru N54 unknown children of N9

N215 thru N235 for children

N55 JOHANN BERNARD BANNING born 1748 in Ladbergen, Westfalen. He was baptized Nov. 1, 1748. Source: 1

N236 thru N241 for children

N56 MARIA ELIZABEIN BANNING born Oct. 13, 1751 in Ladbergen, Westfalen. Source: 1

N242 thru N247 for children

N57 JOHANN ADOLPH BANNING born June 12, 1754 in Lengerich. Source: 1

N248 thru N253 for children

N58 CHRISTINE MARIA BANNING born April 20, 1757 in Lengerich. Source: 1

N254 thru N259 children

N59 FRIEDREICH MAURITZ BANNING born Oct. 8, 1760 in Lengerich. Source: 1

N260 thru N265 for children

N60 ERNST MURITZ BANNING born May 6, 1767 in Lengerich. Married Friederike Louise Smend in Lengerich where they lived. He was an apothaker, and died May 16, 1811 in Lengerich. Source: 1

N266 Ernst Bernhard Banning
N267 Florens Ludwig Banning
N268 thru N271 for children

N61 thru N265 unknown children of N11 thru N59

N272 thru N672 for children

N266 ERNST BERNHARD BANNING born 1796 in Lengerich. He married
   Wilhelmeine Kreige. There were no children. He married 2nd, Elizabeth Henriette
   Kandelhardt in Lengerich and had 1 child. He married 3rd, Sophia Elizabeth
   Kandelhardt in Lengerich. No issue from that marriage. He was an apotheker and
   died June 21, 1834. Source: 1

N673 Henrich Ernst Banning

N267 FLORENS LUDWIG BANNING born in Lengerich and married Augusta
   Wilehemine Grote of Bremem in Lengerich. They lived in Lengerich where he was a
   Physician. Source: 1

N674 Johann Ernst Gustav Banning

N268 thru N672 unknown children of N60 thru N265

N675 thru N1675 for children

N673 HENRICH ERNST BANNING born April 29, 1833 in Lengerich. He married
   Antonie Schull. They lived in Duren, Rheinland, where he was an apotheke. He
   died Sept. 12, 1872 in Duren. Source: 1

N1676 Felix Heinrich Wilhelm Banning
N1677 Elli Banning

N674 JOHANN ERNST GUSTAV BANNING born Jan. 19, 1833 in Lengerich. He
   married his cousin, Elisabeth --------? in Hanm, Westfallia. They lived in Hanm
   where he was a manufacture of machinery. He died there Feb. 7, 1895. Source: 1

N1678 Lizzie Banning
N1679 Heinrich Banning

N675 thru N1675 unknown children of N268 thru N672

N1680 thru N3680 for children

N1676 FELIX HEINRICH WILHELM BANNING born Aug. 3, 1861 in Duren,
   Rheinland. He married his cousin Lizzie Banning of Hanm on July 10, 1888 in
   Hanm. (N1678) They lived in Duren where he was a manufacturer of paper
   machinery. (He furnished the facts on this line.) Source: 1

N3681 Margarite Banning
N3682 Elli Banning
N3683 Hans Banning
N3684 Felix Banning

N3685 Hellmuth Banning
N3686 Wolfgang Banning

N1677 ELLI BANNING born July 8, 1864 in Duren, Rheinland. She married Wilhelm Peters on April 15, 1885 in Duren. They lived in Duren where he was a manufacturer of cloth. Source: 1

N3687 Elisabeth Peters
N3688 Lathen Peters
N3689 Friderich Peters

N1678 LIZZIE BANNING born Jan. 4, 1864 in Hanm. She married her cousin Felix Henrich Wilhelm Banning of Duren. (N1676) Source: 1

N1679 HEINRICH BANNING born June 16, 1868 in Hanm. He married Clare Witte in Aug. 1899. They lived in Hanm where he was a machinery manufacturer. Source: 1

N3690 Werner Banning
N3691 Hermine Banning

N1680 thru N3680 unknown children of N675 thru N1675

N3692 thru N6692 for children

N3681 MARGURITE BANNING born May 15, 1889 in Duren. Source: 1

N3682 ELLI BANNING born Oct. 2, 1890 in Duren, where he lived. Source: 1

N3683 HANS BANNING born Aug. 6, 1893 in Duren, where he died Feb. 1894. Source: 1

N3684 FELIX BANNING born Jan. 19, 1895 in Duren. Source: 1

N3685 HELLMUTH BANNING born Jan. 19, 1898 in Duren. Source: 1

N3686 WOLFGANG BANNING born Oct. 19, 1902 in Duren. Source: 1

N3687 ELISABETH PETERS born March 19, 1886 and married Oscar Lyman. Source: 1

N3688 LATHEN PETERS born Oct. 1891. Source: 1

N3689 FRIDERICH PETERS born Oct. 1894. Source: 1

N3690 WERNER BANNING born March 2, 1903 in Hanm. Source: 1

N3691 HERMINE BANNING born Dec. 7, 1900 in Hanm. Source: 1

P 0 ELISHA BANNING married Ann ???. They lived in either LaChute, Quebec or ByTown (now Ottawa), Ontario, Canada. He may have come from Scotland to Canada. Source: 23

> P1 William Banning
> P2 Ozias Banning
> P3 Benjamin Banning
> P4 Elisha Banning
> P5 Sarah Banning
> P6 Lucinda Banning
> P7 Annie Banning
> P8 Laura Banning

P1 WILLIAM BANNING no information. Source: 23

> P9 thru P15 for children

P2 OZIAS BANNING no information. Source: 23

> P16 thru P22 for children

P3 BENJAMIN BANNING born March 17, 1816 in the Province of Quebec, Canada and married Margaret Jane Stevens (or Stephens) on Sept. 8, 1842 in LaChute, Quebec, Canada. She was born Feb. 8, 1825, probably at LaChute, Argenteuil Co., Quebec and was of Scotch-English decent. Her parents were Robert Stevens (1806-1882) and Lydia S. Allen (1806-1856). Benjamin served as a private in Capt. Linus Waldron's 3rd Co. in 1838. He was a farmer and head sawyer in a large saw mill in the LaChute, Quebec, Canada area and lived on a farm one mile east of LaChute until about 1849 when they moved to Bytown (now Ottawa). By 1857 the family was in Ogle Co., Ill. and moved to Hand Co., Dakota Terr. in 1884. He died July 15, 1891 in Hand Co., S.D. as the result of injuries sustained in a horse and wagon runaway. He was buried in Hand Co. and four years later the body was moved to Rock Rapids, Lyon Co., Iowa. She died March 22, 1902 in Rock Rapids Iowa, of a paralytic stroke and is buried in Rock Rapids next to her husband. Source: 23

> P23 Robert E. Banning
> P24 Benjamin E. Banning
> P25 Susannah Ann Banning
> P26 Lydia Banning
> P27 David B. Banning
> P28 Clark A. Banning
> P29 George W. Banning
> P30 Martha Banning
> P31 Leonard Jeffries Banning
> P32 Ida Jane (Jennie) Banning

P4 ELISHA BANNING no information. Source: 23

> P33 thru P39 for children

P5 SARAH BANNING married ??? Stearns. Source: 23

> P40 thru P45 for children

P6 LUCINDA BANNING no information. Source: 23

> P46 thru P50 for children

P7 ANNIE BANNING no information. Source: 23

> P51 thru P55 for children

P8 LAURA BANNING no information. Source: 23

> P56 thru P60 for children

P9 thru P22 children of P1 & P2

> P61 thru P110 for children

P23 ROBERT E. BANNING born April 8, 1843 and married Mary ??? Source: 23

> P111 thru P115 for children

P24 BENJAMIN E. BANNING born July 2, 1845 and married Roxy ??? Source: 23

> P116 thru P120 for children

P25 SUSANNAH ANN BANNING born June 6, 1848 and married George Sylvester Briggs. She died Nov. 1931. Source: 23

> P121 Walter E. Briggs
> P122 thru P125 for children

P26 LYDIA BANNING born March 29, 1851 and married Robert Moore Peile. He was born May 31, 1853. They lived in S. D. prior to 1900 when they moved to Rock Rapids, Iowa. She died in 1939. Source: 23

> P126 Minnie E. Peile
> P127 Lydia J. Peile
> P128 Robert Moore Peile Jr.
> P129 Myrtle Peile

P27 DAVID B. BANNING born Feb. 22, 1853 and married Hattie ??? He died Oct. 21, 1910. Source: 23

> P130 thru P134 for children

P28 CLARK A. BANNING born Oct. 14, 1856. He never married and died in 1911 during an emergency operation for appendicitis performed in the kitchen of his home in Rock Rapids, Iowa. He was 6' 2" tall and weighed 225 pounds. Source: 23

P29 GEORGE W. BANNING born April 4, 1861. He lived with his family on a farm near Greene, Butler Co., Iowa, and married Ella Butler Fisher on Dec. 10, 1893. He died July 6, 1937 at Greene, where he is buried. She then married Omer Hubbard and moved to Eldora, Iowa. Source: 23

> P135 Susan D. Banning
> P136 Ruth Banning
> P137 Unknown daughter

P30 MARTHA BANNING born March 21, 1863 and died about 1873. Source: 23

P31 LEONARD "LEN" JEFFRIES BANNING born March 3, 1865 and married Irene ???. They lived in Rock Rapids, Iowa. He died July 4, 1954. Source: 23

> P138 Edna Banning
> P139 Zuneita Banning

P32 IDA JANE "JENNIE" BANNING born June 30, 1869 on a farm southwest of Rochelle, Ogle Co., Ill., and married Henry Herman Determan in 1886 at Huron, S.D. He was born July 15, 1852 at Potosi, Grant Co., Wisc. and was the son of Herman Bernard Determan (1823-1897) and Maria Margaretha Elskamp (1824-1901). They moved to Carroll Co., Iowa about 1900 and Cerro Gordo Co., Iowa in 1911. He was a farmer and died Sept. 10, 1923 in Mason City, Iowa. She died April 25, 1939 in Mason City, Cerro Gordo Co., Iowa. They are both buried in Elmwood Cemetery in Mason City. Source: 23

> P140 Benjamin Determan
> P141 Lewis T. Determan
> P142 Margaret Theresa Determan
> P143 Henry Clem Determan
> P144 Sarah Theresa Determan
> P145 Raymond Bernard Determan
> P146 Leland George Determan
> P147 Grace Determan

P33 thru P39 for children of P4

> P148 thru P175 for children

P40 thru P60 for children of P5 thru P8

P61 thru P120 children of P9 thru P24

> P176 thru P300 for children

P121 WALTER E. BRIGGS He lived and died in Fla. where he was in the real estate business following WW1. Source: 23

P126 MINNIE E. PEILE no information. Source: 23

P127 LYDIA J. PEILE no information. Source: 23

P128 ROBERT MOORE PEILE JR. no information. Source: 23

P129 MYRTLE PEILE no information. Source: 23

P135 SUSAN D. BANNING married Mr. Horace C. Lepley on Feb. 19, 1916 in Eldora, Hardin Co., Iowa. Source: 13,23

P301 thru P305 for children

P136 RUTH BANNING married a Mr. Wilkins. Source: 23

P306 thru P310 for children

P137 UNKNOWN DAUGHTER died as a teenager. Source: 23

P138 EDNA BANNING no information. Source: 23

P311 thru P315 for children

P139 ZUNEITA BANNING married a Mr. Underwisch. Source: 23

P316 thru P320 for children

P140 BENJAMIN DETERMAN born in 1888 and died about 1891 as the result of falling into a cistern while visiting relatives in Breda, Carroll Co., Iowa. Source: 23

P141 LEWIS T. DETERMAN born Aug. 24, 1891 and married Tennie Anderson. He was a farmer on the family farm near Rockwell in Cerro Gordo Co., Iowa. They had a daughter, Marcille, who died at three years of age. They adopted a daughter who went to Calif. as a teenager. He died about 1948. Source: 23

P142 MARGARET THERESA DETERMAN born May 28, 1894 in Carroll Co., Iowa. She married Joseph August Lemker on May 28, 1912 at St. Joseph's Catholic Church in Mason City, Iowa. He was born Aug. 26, 1891 in Carroll Co., Iowa and was the son of John Bernard Lemker (1844-1928) and Mary Ann Kuhl (1850-1930). His father was born in Germany in 1844 and came to America in 1860. Joseph was a farmer then was employed in the Mason City, Iowa post Office for 25 years. He died March 3, 1980 in Mason City. She died May 7, 1988 in Mason City. Both are buried in Elmwood Cemetery in Mason City. Source: 23

P321 Leona Mary Lemker
P322 Viola Jennie Lemker

P143 HENRY CLEM DETERMAN he was born in 1897 and was the founder of H.C. Determan Electric Co. in Mason City, Iowa. He and his wife, Josephine Lynch, had 3 children, Jack, Jean and Patsy. Source: 23

P144 SARAH THERESA "PAT" DETERMAN born June 24, 1900 and married 1st, Jack Maloney. She was employed for many years by the City of Chicago as a payroll clerk. She married 2nd, James L. Peck, who was in the real estate business, and is buried in the Queen of Angels Mausoleum in Hillside, Ill. She had no children. She died Aug. 8, 1982 and is buried in the Elmwood Cemetery in Mason City, Iowa. Source: 23

P145 RAYMOND BERNARD DETERMAN born Dec. 30, 1906 and married Bonita Shire. He was an electrician employed by H.C. Determan Electric Co. in Mason City. They had 4 daughters, 3 of whom became Catholic nuns. The other daughter,

Donna Lou, married Robert Umbarger who is a banker in Mason City and Northwood, Iowa. Raymond died March 14, 1988. Source: 23

P146 LELAND GEORGE DETERMAN born Jan. 14, 1912 and is the twin of Grace (P147). He died from injuries in an automobile accident 2 miles west of Mason City, Iowa on Nov. 1, 1928. Source: 23

P147 GRACE DETERMAN born Jan. 14, 1912 and died at six months of age. Source: 23

P321 LEONA MARY LEMKER born March 29, 1913. She married 1st, Lloyd R. Johnson and had 2 daughters, Joan and Patsy. They divorced and she married 2nd, Carl Knutson. They had no children. Source: 23

P322 VIOLA JENNIE LEMKER born July 14, 1915 on a farm 5 miles north of Mason City, Cerro Gordo Co., Iowa and married James L. Pauley Jr. at St. Joseph's Church in Mason City. (He developed much of the information on this line.) He was born Dec. 6, 1916 in Mason City and is the son of Dr. James Leroy Pauley (1889-1962) and Clara May Lampson (1887-1963). He graduated from the University of Iowa College of Law and practiced law in Scranton and Jefferson, Greene Co., Iowa from 1940 to 1982 except for 3 years during World War II when he was a Special Agent of the Federal Bureau of Investigation. They had two children, James Donald (born 11-15-1941 and married Martha Mary Lammers) and Richard Joseph (born 3-16-1946 and married Shirley Anne Stringer). They are currently living in Jefferson, Iowa. Her hobbies are that of a seamstress and artist. Source: 23

WILLIAM BANNING of CANADA

Most of the below information on this line is from a book entitled "The Roy Family Tree From The British Isles, United Empire Loyalists Europe and Pioneers" printed privately in 1968 and written by Elspeth Margaret Roy. The copy I have was given to me by Ken Banning, (Source 60) listed as person Q150 below.

Where William Banning, the founder of this line, came from is unknown.

Q1 WILLIAM BANNING born 1817 in Granville, Quebec. He married Sarahann Howard on Aug. 6, 1839. She was born in 1825 and died June 10, 1874. He died May 13, 1866. Source: 60

> Q2 Lucinda Banning
> Q3 Rial Banning
> Q4 Charles H. Banning
> Q5 William Banning Jr.
> Q6 David E. Banning
> Q7 Esther Abigal Banning
> Q8 Lucy Maria Banning

Q2 LUCINDA BANNING born May 3, 1840 in Mayo, Quebec. She married Francis Xavier Roy on June 11, 1862. He was the son of Francis Xavier Roy and Mary Landreville, born Jan. 4, 1835 in Monte Bello, Quebec. She inherited ome "Farm-Crown Land" from her father. Francis died Jan. 20, 1920 in Mayo, Quebec. She died June 30, 1925 in Mayo. They are both buried in Baptist Cemetery, Thurso, Quebec. Source: 18, 60

> Q9   William Frank Roy
> Q10 Emma Lavina Roy
> Q11 Charles Albert Roy
> Q12 Sarah Louise Roy
> Q13 Joseph Roy
> Q14 Malissa Roy
> Q15 Esther Roy
> Q16 David Joseph Roy
> Q17 Howard Roy
> Q18 Ethel Minnie Maud Rose Roy

Q3 RIAL BANNING born June 17, 1842 and married Bridget Agnes McCoy. She was born Dec. 10, 1842 in Ireland and died Nov. 6, 1923. He died March 11, 1930 at Lockarbor Bay, Quebec. Source: 60

> Q19 William Frank Banning
> Q20 Benjamin Banning
> Q21 Sarah Ellen Banning
> Q22 Thomas Banning
> Q23 David Banning
> Q24 Henry Banning
> Q25 James Banning
> Q26 Sandy Allen Banning

Q4 CHARLES H. BANNING born April 9, 1845 and married Julia Sweezie of Scranton, Pa. He died in 1910 with his hand on the throttle of of a Lackawanna Rail Road locomotive. Source: 60

Q27 Arthur Banning
Q28 Minnie Banning
Q29 Bertram Banning
Q30 Stella Banning

Q5 WILLIAM BANNING JR. born Feb. 20, 1848 and married Margaret Wait. Source: 60

Q31 thru Q35 for children

Q6 DAVID E. BANNING born Nov. 25, 1851 and married Mary Jane Ryan on Nov. 3, 1874. She was born Jan. 1, 1858 and died Dec. 2, 1946. He died Nov. 11, 1923. Source: 60

Q36 Edgar Banning

Q7 ESTHER ABIGAL BANNING born Sept. 27, 1859 and married William McDermid on Oct. 10, 1876. He was born Jan. 26, 1852 and died March 3, 1935. She died in Boston, Mass. on Feb. 13, 1937. Source: 60

Q37 Ida Grace McDermid
Q38 Peter Albinas McDermid
Q39 Violet May McDermid
Q40 Effie Genevive McDermid
Q41 James Earl McDermid
Q42 Myrtle Dean McDermid
Q43 Lilah Claire McDermid
Q44 William McDermid Jr.
Q45 Cletta Esther McDermid

Q8 LUCY MARIA BANNING born July 5, 1863 in Lochabar Township and married Thomas Humphery Moors on Nov. 17, 1882 in Thurso, Quebec. He was born Oct. 26, 1857 and died Jan. 5, 1930 in Arnprior, Ontario. She died May 17, 1937 in Arnprior. Source: 60

Q46 Arthur Rial Moors
Q47 Thomas William Moors
Q48 Della Moors
Q49 Lucy Moors
Q50 Bessie Mary Elizabeth Moors
Q51 Charles Henry Moors
Q52 Hubert Moors
Q53 Sarah Jane Moors
Q54 Ida Ethel Moors

Q9 WILLIAM FRANK ROY born May 14 1863 in North Nation Mills, Quebec. He married Mary Josephine Lowe on Aug. 23, 1888. She was born Feb. 16, 1869 in Buckingham, Quebec and died Dec. 8, 1951 in Ottawa, Ontario. He died March 13, 1955 in Ottawa, Ontario. Their children are; Birtha C., born May 17, 1890 in Chicago, Ill. and died Feb. 3,1896; Eve Blanch, born Jan. 25, 1893 in Chicago, Ill.; Mable Sarah, born Jan 3, 1897 in Chicago, Ill.; Beulah Winnifred, born July 12, 1899 in Chicago, Ill.; and Frank Henry, born Jan. 19, 1905 in Chicago, Ill. Source: 60

Q10 EMMA LAVINA ROY born March 18, 1865 in North Nation Mills, Quebec. She married Jobe Smith on Dec. 4, 1883. He was born May 27, 1854 and died June 9, 1940. She died Jan. 24, 1944. Their children are; Edith, born March 14, 1885 at Silver Creek, Quebec.; Lewis Levi, born April 12, 1887 at Silver CreekQuebec.; Celina Elizabeth, born Feb. 14, 1887 at Silver CreekQuebec.; Victor Boyd, born Aug. 1, 1893 at Silver CreekQuebec.; Urban Earl, born Dec. 30, 1894 at Silver CreekQuebec.; and Howard, born March 31, 1909 at Silver CreekQuebec. Source: 60

Q11 CHARLES ALBERT ROY born Jan. 12, 1867 in North Nation Mills, Quebec. He married Mary Jane Ross on July 11, 1892. She was born April 23, 1866 and died July 4, 1933 of cancer. He died Aug. 27, 1949 of a stroke. Their children are; Gladys Estelle, born Oct. 8, 1893 in Ottawa, Ontario; Elspeth Margaret, born Aug. 21, 1896 in Chicago, Ill.; Isa Collins, born June 8, 1898 in Ottawa, Ontario; Earle Picken, born Jan. 28, 1900 in Peterborough, Ontario; and Clayton Albert, born Oct. 17, 1903 in Ottawa, Ontario. Source: 60

Q12 SARAH LOUISE ROY born Feb. 1, 1869 in Chelsea, Quebec. She married 1st, Robert Ferdinand Ralph on June 10, 1891. He was born in 1867 and died Nov. 11, 1897. She married 2nd, Hiram Walter Ralph on Dec. 5, 1900. Hiram was born Oct. 8, 1869 and died Jan. 9, 1933. She died Jan. 23, 1950. Her children are; Gordon Francis, born Dec. 5, 1894 and killed in WW1 on Oct. 4, 1916; Ethel Lucinda, born Jan. 1, 1896; Elbert Elam, born Feb. 17, 1902; and Victor Denzil, born July 5, 1904. Source: 60

Q13 JOSEPH ROY born 1870 in North Nation Mills, Quebec and died about age 3 of diptheria. Source: 60

Q14 MALISSA ROY born March 29, 1871 in North Nation Mills, Quebec. She married Frederick J. Harding on June 5, 1900. He was born Nov. 3, 1869 and died Nov. 17, 1947. She died June 27, 1923 of cancer. Their children are; Elsie Edna born April 15, 1901; Roy Channings, born Nov. 15, 1903; Lilda, born Jan. 25, 1906; Arthur, born March 22, 1912. Source: 60

Q15 ESTHER ROY born 1874 and died in 1876 of diptheria in North Nation Mills, Quebec. Source: 60

Q16 DAVID JOSEPH ROY born Aug. 24, 1878 in North Nation Mills, Quebec. He married Lulu Belle Roberts of Logan Port, Indiana on Nov. 19, 1902. She was born Nov. 26, 1883 and died Feb. 2, 1963 of heart failure. He died Jan. 31, 1964. Their children are; Bertram Stanley, born Oct. 30, 1905; George David, born Nov. 23, 1908; Iva Pearl, born Nov. 21, 1912; Milfred Margaret, born Aug. 30, 1917; and William Milton, born Jan. 11, 1918. Source: 60

Q17 HOWARD ROY born Sept. 13, 1880 in North Nation Mills, Quebec. He married Alice Millar on Jan. 7, 1903. She was born Feb. 14, 1878. He died March 20, 1914. Their children are; Clinton, born Dec. 8, 1903; Fred, born Nov. 29, 1906; Ernest, born Sept. 4, 1913. Source: 60

Q18 ETHEL MINNIE MAUD ROSE ROY born March 9, 1881 in North Nation Mills, Quebec. She married 1st, Robert Albert Waterston on June 3, 1908. He was born Sept. 24, 1877 and was killed in WW1 on March 4, 1918. Their children are; Robert, born Feb. 26, 1909 and died by drowning at Buckingham, Quebec on Dec.

28, 1931; William, born May 21, 1910; Inez Julia, born Nov. 22, 1911; Norris Everett, born Dec. 10, 1912; Irene Ann, born June 24, 1914; and Lloyd Orville, born Oct. 14, 1916. She married 2nd, Earl Schingo on May 6, 1931. Earl was born May 6, 1904. Source: 60

Q19 WILLIAM FRANK BANNING born Aug. 17, 1865. He married Martha Purdy on Jan. 27, 1891. She was born Dec. 19, 1872 and died May 28, 1945. He died Jan. 25, 1938. Source: 60

> Q55 Stella Banning
> Q56 Earl Banning
> Q57 Hilda Banning
> Q58 Harold Banning
> Q59 Hubert Banning
> Q60 Edna Banning
> Q60a Arthur Boyd Banning

Q20 BENJAMIN BANNING born Aug. 18, 1867 and married Nellie (???) of Buffalo, N.Y. Source: 60

> Q61 Maria Banning
> Q62 Kenneth Banning
> Q63 Andres Banning

Q21 SARAH ELLEN BANNING born May 14, 1870 and died at an early age. Source: 60

Q22 THOMAS BANNING born May 10, (or Feb. 11) 1872. He married Addie MacDonald on Nov. 15, 1898. She was born Jan. 6, 1879 and died Jan. 12, 1944. He died Jan. 28, 1968. Source: 60

> Q64 Marvin Rial Banning

Q23 DAVID BANNING born Feb. 11, 1874 and married Jessie Watterson. Source: 60

> Q65 Effie Banning
> Q66 Peter Banning

Q24 HENRY BANNING born April 28, 1876 and married Maggie Blackburn. They had no children. Source: 60

Q25 JAMES (Jim) BANNING born July 2, 1878. He married Lena McCullough on April 14, 1909. She was born Aug. 22, 1886. He died Dec. 19, 1942. Source: 60

> Q67 Mildred Kathleen Banning
> Q68 Robert James Banning
> Q69 Verna Ethel Banning
> Q70 Lorne Murry Banning
> Q71 Jean Lois Banning

Q26 SANDY ALLEN BANNING born April 12, 1880 and died July 16, 1911. Source: 60

Q72 thru Q76 for children

Q27 ARTHUR BANNING He married Martha Davis. When she died she was buried in her wedding dress. Source: 60

Q77 Maud Banning

Q28 MINNIE BANNING she married John H. Reed. Source: 60

Q78 Charles Reed

Q29 BERTRAM (Bart) BANNING Born Sept. 22, 1874 and died Sept. 11, 1956. He was a bachelor. Source: 60

Q30 STELLA BANNING she married D. F. Mayo. Source: 60

Q79 Elsie Mayo

Q36 EDGAR BANNING born Nov. 5, 1875 and Married Mary Dunnigan. She was born May 8, 1882 and died Feb. 3, 1967. He died Oct. 9, 1959. Source: 60

Q80 Gerald Banning
Q81 Leo Banning
Q82 Mary Banning
Q83 Mark Banning
Q84 David Banning
Q85 Victor Banning

Q37 IDA GRACE McDERMID born April 21, 1878 and married 1st, William I. Jackson. They had no children and were divorced. She married 2nd George A. McNeil. He died Feb. 25, 1939. They had a child, Ralph, born April 30, 1910. Source: 60

Q38 PETER ALBINAS McDERMID born Oct. 7, 1883 and married Jean Campbell in 1904. Their children are; Florence, born Jan. 19, 1905; Esther; and twins Murray and J. Sturart McDermid. Peter died July 1, 1952. Source: 60

Q39 VIOLET MAY McDERMID born Dec. 9, 1885 and married Ralph G. Ester of Boston, Ma. on Sept. 11, 1912. He was born July 8, 1887 and died in 1960. They had one child, Marion, born Sept. 1, 1914. Source: 60

Q40 EFFIE GENEVIVE McDERMID born Oct. 14, 1887 and married William Howard Lummis on Sept. 8, 1914. He was born July 14, 1889 and died Jan. 15, 1967. They had two children, William Wallace, born May 8, 1921 and Betty Esther, born Nov. 23, 1921 (?). Source: 60

Q41 JAMES EARL (Jim) McDERMID born Feb. 28, 1892 and married Mamie Stewart in Oct. 1912. Their children are; Doris; Douglas, born May 2, 1917; Beryle, born Dec. 7, 1918; Pauline; Esther; James Jr.; David and Arthur. Source: 60

Q42 MYRTLE DEAN McDERMID born May 19, 1895 and married James E. Davies on July 3, 1914. He died Nov. 19, 1959 of cancer. She died July 17, 1953 of heart problems. They had a child, Lyla Jean, born June 19, 1915. Source: 60

Q43 LILLAH CLAIRE McDERMID born Aug. 26, 1897 and married Walter Ester on

June 21, 1922. He was born May 27, 1897 and died Oct. 11, 1967 of heart problems. They had two children, Walter Kenneth born Oct. 9, 1923 and Gail Claire, born Jan. 21, 1937. Source: 60

Q44 WILLIAM McDERMID Jr. born Oct. 9, 1899 and married Birdie Bidgood on June 28, 1931. He was on duty and was killed when he was thrown from a fire truck on May 26, 1941. They had one child, Colin. Source: 60

Q45 CLETTA ESTHER McDERMID born July 2, 1904 and died Jan. 12, 1928 of pneumonia. Source: 60

Q46 ARTHUR RIAL MOORS born Aug. 26, 1883 and died Dec. 8, 1884. Source: 60

Q47 THOMAS WILLIAM MOORS born Jan. 4, 1885 and married Jane Mary Hall of Perkins, Ontario on June 30, 1919. She was born Feb. 7, 1891. They had two children, William Herbert, born July 9, 1922 and Marguerite Della, born Feb. 7, 1926. Source: 60

Q48 DELLA MOORS born March 25, 1887. She was a Registered Nurse and died April 6, 1954. Source: 60

Q49 LUCH (Dollie) MOORS born March 21, 1889 and married Alphonso Bertram Silman on June 17, 1922. He was born in 1888 in Charleston, W. Virginia and died in 1940. They had a child, Jack Forrest Banning Silman, born Aug. 22, 1923. She married 2nd, Thomas Herbert O'Brien on Dec. 5, 1942. Thomas was born in 1879 and died Oct. 31, 1955 in Pembroke, Ontario. Source: 60

Q50 BESSIE MARY ELIZABETH MOORS born June 8, 1892 in Arnprio, Ontario. She married John Stewart Scullion on June 6, 1918. He was born March 8, 1890 and died July 24, 1964 in Bracebridge, Ontario. She died Jan. 5, 1963 in Brockville, Ontario. Their children are; Lucy Elizabeth, born March 8, 1919; Grace Kathleen, born Feb. 24, 1925 and John Sterwart Jr., born July 30, 1927. Source: 60

Q51 CHARLES HENRY MOORS born April 21, 1895. He was a member of the 94th Battalion and was killed Dec. 22, 1916 in the First World War. He is buried in the Villers Au Bois Military Cemetery near Bethune, France. Source: 60

Q52 HUBERT MOORS born Nov. 29, 1896. Source: 60

Q53 SARAH JANE (Sadie) MOORS born July 15, 1900 and married Leonard Cracraft Steele in Sept. 1923. He died in 1958. She died Feb. 21, 1934 of heart problems. They had two children, Dorcas, born Dec. 7, 1928 and Samuel, born May 15, 1925. Source: 60

Q54 IDA ETHEL MOORS born June 7, 1903 and married Archibald Knight on Aug. 29, 1921. He was born July 5, 1896 in Renfrew, Ontario. She died May 12, 1967. They had a child, Charles Archibald born May 12, 1922. Source: 60

Q55 STELLA MAY BANNING born May 30, 1892 in Thurso, Quebec and married Eldon McKenzie in 1908. He was born in 1888 and died in 1908. They had one child. Stella married 2nd, Donald Campbell in 1910. He was born June 12, 1882 and died July 21, 1931 in a fire. Stella married 3rd, Holland McKenzie who was born in 1892, died on Dec. 28, 1963 and is buried in Gore Cemetery. Stella died Dec. 29, 1963. There were no children of the 3rd marriage. Source: 60

Q86 Henrietta (Etta) Grace McKenzie
Q87 Gurtrude May Campbell
Q88 Merle Muriel Martha Campbell
Q89 Gordon Edward Campbell
Q90 Arthur William Campbell

Q56 EARL BANNING born March 5, 1898 and married Ida Delorme in 1916. She was born in 1896. Earl died Feb. 16, 1966 in Thurso, Quebec. Source: 60

Q91 Bertha Banning
Q92 Russell Banning
Q93 Herbert Banning

Q57 HILDA JANE BANNING born Oct. 20, 1900 and married Robert Ivall on June 16, 1916. He was born Jan. 28, 1895. Source: 60

Q94 Cecil Robert Ivall
Q95 Norman Ivall
Q96 Lloyd Ivall
Q97 Grace Ivall

Q58 HAROLD BANNING born Feb. 26, 1904 and married Irene McCartney on June 22, 1926. Source: 60

Q98 Basil Banning
Q99 Lyla Banning
Q100 David Banning
Q101 Helen Banning

Q59 HUBERT BANNING born June 9, 1906 and married Eleen Hardy. She was born in Thurso, Quebec. He died Dec. 16, 1954. Source: 60

Q102 Elgin Banning
Q103 Ina Banning

Q60 EDNA BANNING born April 5, 1909 and married William Deslaurier. He was born Nov. 15, 1904. She died in 1956. Source: 60

Q104 Irene Deslaurier
Q105 Melvin Deslaurier
Q106 Kenneth Deslaurier
Q107 Shirley Deslaurier
Q108 Hilma Deslaurier
Q109 Marlyn Deslaurier

Q60a ARTHUR BOYD BANNING no information Source: 60

Q110 thru Q112

Q61 MARIA BANNING no information Source: 60

Q113 thru Q115 for children

Q62 KENNETH BANNING died 1963. Source: 60

Q116 thru Q118 for children

Q63 ANDRES BANNING no information   Source: 60

Q119 thru Q121 for children

Q64 MARVIN RIAL BANNING born Jan. 24, 1904 and died Sept. 30, 1904 at Tupper Lake, New York and is buried at Gore Church in Lochabar Bay, Quebec. Source: 60

Q122 thru Q125 for children

Q65 EFFIE BANNING no information   Source: 60

Q126 thru Q129 for children

Q66 PETER BANNING born in Vancouver, B.C.   Source: 60

Q130 thru Q133 for children

Q67 MILDRED KATHLEEN BANNING born April 20, 1910 and married Donald C. McIWatters on Dec. 22, 1934. He was born July 18, 1905. Source: 60

Q134 thru Q137 for children

Q68 ROBERT JAMES BANNING born Aug. 20, 1912 and married Yvette Aube on Oct. 20, 1938. She was born July 5, 1919. Source: 60

Q138 thru Q141 for children

Q69 VERNA ETHEL BANNING born Jan. 29, 1919 in Thurso, Qubec and married Ernest E. Lippiatt on Feb. 14, 1937 in Thurso. He was born Sept. 9, 1914 in Montreal, Quebec. His father was David Lippiatt. She married 2nd, Harold Herbert McGregor on April 19, 1945. Harold was born July 17, 1914 in Almonts, Ontario and died Feb. 19, 1988. He was the son of William A. and Rebecca Thompson McGregor. Verna was living in Carleton Place, Ontario in 1993. Source: 16,60

Q142 Harvey Ernest Lippiatt
Q143 Gerald Edward Lippiatt
Q144 June Shirley Lippiatt
Q145 William (Billie) James McGregor
Q146 Ronald Leslie McGregor
Q147 Marjorie Lois McGregor
Q148 Robert Alan McGregor

Q70 LORNE MURRAY BANNING born Aug. 28, 1924 in Thurso, Quebec and married Muriel Emma McCuaig on June 28, 1947 in St. Anedee, Quebec. She was born Jan. 7, 1924 in St Anedee and was the daughter of Leslie James and Mary Wigney McCuaig. Source: 16,60

Q149 Murray James Banning
Q150 Kenneth Robert Banning
Q151 Eleanor Muriel Banning

Q152 Angus Stewart Banning

Q71 JEAN LOIS BANNING born Dec. 29, 1930 in Thurso, Quebec and married Donald William John Lay on July 13, 1950. He was born March 18, 1929 in Carleton Place, Ontario and was the son of Albert John and Dorthy Irene Huckstep Lay. They were living in Carleton Place in 1993. Source: 16,60

      Q153 Donald Roy Lay
      Q154 Dorothy Lena Ann Lay
      Q155 Kin Albert Lay

Q72 thru Q76 for children of Q26

Q156 thru Q176 for children of Q72 thru Q76

Q77 MAUD BANNING married 1st, Everett Allahen and 2nd, Charles Bertram. Source: 60

Q177 thru Q180 for children

Q78 CHARLES REED married Maud Pritchard. Their children are Ralph, Lawrence and Kenneth. Source: 60

Q79 ELSIE MAYO born March 29, 1895. Source: 60

Q80 GERALD BANNING born June 17, 1907 and married Anne Belec on Aug. 12, 1937. She was born Jan. 24, 1912. Source: 60

      Q181 Lorraine Banning
      Q182 Dennis Banning
      Q183 Gerard Banning
      Q184 Margaret Anne Banning

Q81 LEO BANNING born March 23, 1909 and married Helen Paolini on June 29, 1935. She was born Feb. 26, 1908. Source: 60

      Q186 Patrick Banning
      Q187 Maureen Banning
      Q188 Victor Banning

Q82 MARY BANNING born May 16, 1911 and married Maurice Thompson on June 9, 1938. He was born July 10, 1907. Source: 60

      Q189 Karen Thompson
      Q190 Neil Thompson
      Q191 Mark Thompson
      Q192 Nora Thompson
      Q193 Joseph Thompson
      Q194 Mary Thompson

Q83 MARK BANNING born Oct. 29, 1916 and married Margaret Smith on Sept. 28, 1943. She was born in 1917. Source: 60

      Q195 Sharon Banning

Q196 Patricia Banning
Q197 Danny Banning
Q198 Michael Banning
Q199 Callum Banning

Q84 DAVID BANNING born March 4, 1921 and married Mary Robson on July 7, 1945. She was born March 31, 1923. Source: 60

Q200 Colleen Banning
Q201 Elizabeth Banning
Q202 Paul Banning
Q203 Brian Banning

Q85 VICTOR BANNING born in 1923. He was in the Royal Canadian Air Force and died in 1944 when he was shot down over Iceland. Source: 60

Q86 HENRIETTA GRACE (Etta) McKENZIE born Dec. 18, 1908 in Thurso, Quebec and married Clifford Johnstone on June 17, 1933. He was born April 16, 1909 (?). They had a child, Donald Hugh, born Dec. 18, 1938. Source: 60

Q87 GERTRUDE MAY CAMPBELL bornm Jan. 28, 1911 and married Fred Ward on April 27, 1935. He was born Nov. 20, 1911. Their children are Elizabeth Ada, born Sept. 12, 1936; Freda Henrietta, born Aug. 14, 1940 and Heather Jean Adelaide, born July 13, 1946. Source: 60

Q88 MERLE MURIEL MARTHA CAMPBELL born Feb. 3, 1912 and married Gordon Arthurs on July 31, 1932. He was born March 8, 1904. Their children are; Marvyn Gordon, born July 1, 1933; Ethel Esther, born Feb. 1, 1935; Stella, born Jan. 3, 1944 and Clifford, born Aug. 9, 1948. Source: 60

Q89 GORDON EDWARD CAMPBELL born May 30, 1913 and married Florence King. Their children are Edward Donald, Verda Florence and Verna. Source: 60

Q90 ARTHUR WILLIAM CAMPBELL born Feb. 3, 1922 and married Eileen Teske on July 16, 1955. She was born Nov. 28, 1923. Their children are; Donna Angela, born June 27, 1956; Lyall Arthur, born June 12, 1958; Leslie Ann, born June 12, 1958 and Hugh John, born July 27, 1959. Source: 60

Q91 BERTHA BANNING married Herman Purdy. Source: 60

Q204 thru Q207 for children

Q92 RUSSELL BANNING married E. Ivall. Source: 60

Q208 thru Q211 for children

Q93 HERBERT BANNING married Bessie Arthur of Huntingdon, Quebec in 1948. Source: 60

Q212 thru Q215 for children

Q94 CECIL ROBERT IVALL born Aug. 13, 1917 and married Rhoda Ruth Arthurs on April 9, 1938. She was born May 3, 1918. They had a child, Doreen Ruth born May 20, 1940. Source: 60

Q95 NORMAN IVALL born Sept. 21, 1918 and married Effie Cresswell. Source: 60

Q96 LLOYD IVALL born July 31, 1925 and married Jean Hurd. They had two children, Cathy and David. Source: 60

Q97 GRACE IVALL born July 5, 1930 and married Morris Kemp. They adopted a son, Glynn, who was born June 16, 1955. Source: 60

Q98 BASIL BANNING born May 4, 1928. Source: 60

Q216 thru Q219 for children

Q99 LYLA BANNING born Dec. 28, 1929. Source: 60

Q220 thru Q223 for children

Q100 DAVID BANNING born Dec. 24, 1931. Source: 60

Q224 thru Q227 for children

Q101 HELEN BANNING baorn June 17, 1938. Source: 60

Q228 thru Q231 for children

Q102 ELGIN BANNING born Dec. 23, 1941. Source: 60

Q232 thru Q235 for children

Q103 INA BANNING born July 10, 1943. Source: 60

Q236 thru Q239 for children

Q104 IRENE DESLAURIER born Jan. 11, 1931. Source: 60

Q105 MELVIN DESLAURIER born Aug. 3, 1932. Source: 60

Q106 KENNETH DESLAURIER born Jan. 28, 1934. Source: 60

Q107 SHIRLEY DESLAURIER born May, 19, 1935. Source: 60

Q108 HILMA DESLAURIER born Feb. 8, 1939. Source: 60

Q109 MARLYN DESLAURIER born June 13, 1942. Source: 60

Q110 thru Q141 for children of Q60A thru Q68

Q142 HARVEY ERNEST LIPPIATT born Jan. 27, 1938 in Thurso, Quebec and married Donna Knight Williams April 7, 1973. She was born Aug. 26, 1942 in Kemptville, Ontario and is the daughter of Hubert and Hazel Workman Knight. Their children are Michelle A. born April 7, 1975 and Krista D. born Feb. 7, 1977. He is a farmer and they were living in Prescott, Ontario in 1993. Source: 16,60

Q143 GERALD EDWARD LIPPIATT born Oct. 13, 1939 in Thurso, Quebec and married Margaret M. Moffatt Aug. 20, 1966. She was the daughter of George and Dorthy Patterson Moffatt born Oct. 29, 1944 in Meaford, Ontario. He died Sept. 21, 1986 in Sarnia, Ontario where she was living in 1993. Their children are Stefanie M. born Sept. 8, 1967 and Seth M. born March 29, 1969. Source: 16,60

Q144 JUNE SHIRLEY LIPPIATT born June 29, 1942 in Thurso, Quebec and married Howard Daniel Irvine June 4, 1960. He was born Nov. 26, 1937 in Smith Falls Ontario and was the son of Livingston and Carloine Best Irvine. Their children are, Deborah Ann, born Sept. 17, 1961; Kevin Mark, born April 2, 1963 and Julie Kathleen, born 1966. They were living in Carleton Place, Ontario in 1993. Source: 16,60

Q145 WILLIAM JAMES (Billie) McGREGOR born June 18, 1946 in Carleton Place, Ontario and married Judy Horricks on May 17, 1969. She was born Oct. 17, 1947in Calleton Place, Ontario and was the daughter of Earl and Muriel White Horricks. Their children are Scott Alan, born Sept. 23, 1971 and Michael James, born Nov. 11, 1973. Billie and Judy are living in Carleton Place. Source: 16,60

Q146 RONALD LESLIE McGREGOR born Nov. 2, 1947 in Carleton Place, Ontario and married Patricia Villenuve Oct. 28, 1967. She was born Oct. 1, 1948 in Carleton Place and was the daughter of Bill and Joyce Skinner Villenuve. Their children are Kelly Dean, born April 18, 1969 and Shelley Ann, born May 6, 1972. Ronald and Pat were living in Carleton Place in 1993. Source: 16,60

Q147 MARJORIE LOIS McGREGOR born Feb. 8, 1949 in Carleton Place, Ontario and married David Clyde Nov. 30, 1963. He was born Aug. 27, 1940 in Almonte and was the son of Jhon and Hester McKee Clyde. They were living in Carleton Place in 1993 where he is a painter and she is an accountant. Their children are, Ruth P., born July 2, 1964; Colleen, born June 16, 1965 and Lena, born Dec. 10, 1971. Source: 16,60

Q148 ROBERT ALAN McGREGOR born March 4, 1957 in Carleton Place, Ontario and married Valerie Ferguson Aug. 27, 1977. She was born May 10, 1957 in Carleton Place to Donald and Ruby Reid Ferguson. Robert died March 7, 1980. Valerie was living in Carleton Place in 1993. They had one child, Robert James, born June 16, 1979. Source: 16,60

Q149 MURRAY JAMES BANNING born June 15, 1948 in Thurso, Quebec and married Arlene Hilda Baier May 12, 1972. She was born Sept. 3, 1952 in Compeea, Alberta and was the daughter of George and Rose Baier. Source: 16,60

Q240 Craig Banning
Q241 Colin Banning
Q242 Clinton James Banning
Q243 Cory Banning

Q150 KENNETH ROBERT BANNING born July 29, 1949 in Thurso, Quebec and married Susan Rushton May 11, 1973 in Osgoode, Ontario. She was born Sept. 19, 1947 in Osgoode. He married 2nd, Darlene Mary Knight on May 11, 1984 in Algonquin, Ontario. She was born June 13, 1938 in Cardinal, Ontario and was the daughter of Hubert and Hazel Workman Knight. Source: 16,60

Q244 thru Q246 for children

Q151 ELEANOR MURIEL BANNING born Dec. 24, 1950 in Thurso, Quebec and married Ronald Kerr May 15, 1972 in Osgoode, Ontario. He was born Aug. 17, 1948 in Hallville, Ontario and was the son of Thomas and Nelda Crowder Kerr. Source: 16,60

> Q247 Lynn Tracy Kerr
> Q248 Rhonda Eleanor Kerr

Q152 ANGUS STEWART BANNING born Feb. 19, 1953 in Ottawa, Ontario and married Barbara Louise Heggart July 30, 1977 in Carsonby, Ontario. She was born July 3, 1953 in St. Paul, Alberta and was the daughter of Eric William and Marjorie Agnes Asselstine Heggart. He is a mechanic and she is a systems analyst and were living in Osgoode, Ontario in 1993. Source: 16,60

> Q249 Sheila Marie Banning
> Q250 Rebecca Jane Banning
> Q251 Jennifer Lynn Banning

Q153 DONALD ROY LAY born Jan. 29, 1951 in Carleton Place, Ontario and married Eilleen May Villeneuve on Aug. 1, 1973 in Almonte, Ontario. She was born Nov. 11, 1954. Their children are Kevin Roy Lay, born May 5, 1975 and Cindy Patricia Lay, born July 11, 1978 Source: 16,60

Q154 DOROTHY LENA ANN LAY born Aug. 31, 1953 in Carleton Place, Ontario and married a Mr. Done July 13, 1973 in Carleton Place. Their children are Raymond Alan, born Dec. 6, 1972; Joann Lois, born Feb. 21, 1974 and Jeremy Robert, born Aug. 27, 1976. Source: 16,60

Q155 KIM ALBERT LAY born Oct. 23, 1956 in Carleton Place Ontario. Source: 60

Q156 thru Q180 for children of Q72 thru Q77

Q181 LORRAINE BANNING born May 14, 1938. Source: 60

Q182 DENNIS BANNING born Feb. 18, 1941 and married Donna Jay on May 21, 1966. Source: 60

Q183 GERARD BANNING born Aug. 29, 1945. Source: 60

Q184 MARGARET ANNE BANNING born Aug. 29, 1945. Source: 60

Q185 Omitted

Q186 PATRICK BANNING born July 8, 1936 and married Christina Toranek on Nov. 5, 1960. She was born May 25, 1938. Source: 60

Q187 MAUREEN BANNING born Aug. 30, 1938 and married Leonard Hendricks. He was born Oct. 26, 1936. Source: 60

Q188 VICTOR BANNING born Nov. 29, 1945. Source: 60

Q189 KAREN THOMPSON born Jan. 13, 1940 and married Robert Pate in 1964. Source: 60

Q190 NEIL THOMPSON born July 27, 1941 and married Marlyn Cheap in 1967.
Source: 60

Q191 MARK THOMPSON born Nov. 12, 1942. Source: 60

Q192 NORA THOMPSON born May 28, 1948. Source: 60

Q193 JOSEPH THOMPSON born April 13, 1950. He was adopted. Source: 60

Q194 MARY THOMPSON born Sept. 1, 1951. Source: 60

Q195 SHARON BANNING born Dec. 19, 1946 and married Waren Engdohl in 1964.
Source: 60

Q196 PATRICIA BANNING born Jan. 17, 1947 and married Boris Jelanie in 1965.
Source: 60

Q197 DANNY BANNING born Dec. 14, 1948. Source: 60

Q198 MICHAEL BANNING born Sept. 10, 1952. Source: 60

Q199 CALLUM BANNING born Aug. 21, 1958. Source: 60

Q200 COLLEEN BANNING born March 5, 1947. Source: 60

Q201 ELIZABETH BANNING born July 5, 1952. She was Adopted. Source: 60

Q202 PAUL BANNING born Oct. 4, 1955. He was adopted. Source: 60

Q203 BRIAN BANNING born May 5, 1961. He was adopted. Source: 60

Q240 CRAIG ALLAN BANNING born Feb. 17, 1973 in Blairmore, Alberta. Source:
16,60

Q241 COLIN BANNING born Jan. 29, 1975 in Blairmore, Alberta. Source: 16,60

Q242 CLINTON JAMES BANNING born Nov. 7, 1978 in Coronation, Alberta. Source:
16,60

Q243 CORY BANNING born Oct. 30, 1981 in Coronation, Alberta. Source: 16, 60.

Q247 LYNN TRACY KERR born Nov. 7, 1972 in Hallville, Ontario. Source: 16,60

Q248 RHONDA ELEANOR KERR born Dec. 12, 1974 in Hallville, Ontario. Source:
16,60

Q249 SHEILA MARIE BANNING born Dec. 21, 1981 in Ottawa, Ontario. Source:
16,60

Q250 REBECCA JANE BANNING born Oct. 30, 1984 in Winchester, Ontario.
Source: 16,60

Q251 JENNIFER LYNN BANNING born Feb. 14, 1989 in Winchester, Ontario.
Source: 16,60

GREENBURY BANNING of TALBOT CO., MD.

Greenbury Banning is another branch that must tie into one of the other lines. I have been unable to establish the connection.

R1 GREENBURY BANNING born 1780 to 1785 (?). He may have married the daughter of the William Willoughby who's will was probated Aug. 3, 1790 in Caroline Co. Md. Source: 3,12,66

> R2 Greenbury Banning
> R3 thru R5 for children

R2 GREENBURY BANNING married Mahala (Carmeen) Trice between 1825 and 1828. She was the widow of Silas Trice. She brought with her one son, Willis who was born April 18, 1825, and two daughters, who's names are unknown. They were living in Talbot Co. Md. in Nov. 1831. Greenbury died prior to 1840 and Mahala married William Willoughby on June 28, 1841 in Caroline Co. Source: 4,18,66,98

> R6 Alexander Banning
> R7 Greenbury Banning
> R8 James Alexander Banning
> R9 thru R12 for children

R3 thru R5 children of R1

> R13 thru R29 for children

R6 ALEXANDER BANNING born July 16, 1828 and may have died young as no additional information has been found. Source: 66,98

R7 GREENBURY BANNING born July 10, 1830. On Sept. 14, 1838 his mother indentured him to Zebdial Pratt. By 1850 he was working for and living with the James Shannaha family. He married Ellen Tyler on Aug. 10, 1858 in Talbot Co., Md. She was the daughter of William Tyler and Sarah Burrows, born about 1842 in Md. Some time after 1880 Greenbury moved to Shawnee Co., Ks. where he died prior to 1891. In 1891 the mother and 3 daughters deeded land in Talbot Co. to James. Source: 5,66,98

> R30 Adderine Banning
> R31 Mary V. Banning
> R32 Clara Banning
> R33 James F. Banning
> R34 Anna E. Banning

R8 JAMES ALEXANDER BANNING born Aug. 31, 1832 in Md. and married Mary Ann Tyler on Oct. 30, 1854 in Talbot Co. Md. She was also the daughter of William and Sarah Tyler, born in Feb. 1840 in Md. The 1880 census has them living in Talbot Co., but Mary is a widow in 1900. She died July 1, 1905 in Tunis Mills. Source: 5,8,10,13,66,98

> R35 John Thomas Banning
> R36 Eliza Ellen Banning
> R37 Emma Blanche Banning

R38 James Alvin Banning
R39 William Henry Banning
R40 Alice Mahaly Banning
R41 Charles Francis Banning
R42 Mary Farlen Banning

R9 thru R29 unknown children of R2 thru R5

R43 thru R99 for children

R30 ADDERINE BANNING born Nov. 6, 1862 in Tunis Mills, Md and married Charles
Quant of Troy, N.Y. He was born in 1859 and died in 1940. She died Oct. 15, 1940
in Valley City, N.D. Source: 66

R100 thru R105 for children

R31 MARY V. BANNING born 1868 in Talbot Co., Md. and married William Weigelt.
Source: 66

R106 thru R110 for children

R32 CLARA BANNING Born in April 1870 and died before 1880. Source: 66

R33 JAMES F. BANNING born 1873 and was living in Md. in 1891 when he took title to
some Talbot Co. land from his mother and sisters. Source: 66

R111 thru R115 for children

R34 ANNA E. BANNING born 1875. No other information. Source: 66

R116 thru R120 for children

R35 JOHN THOMAS BANNING born Oct 5, 1855 in Tilghman Island, Talbot Co., Md.
He married Mary Catherine Tufford on Nov. 27, 1878 (1877?) in Tunis Mills, Talbot
Co., Md. She was the daughter of Isaiah Tufford and Annie Skeet, born July 19,
1857 in Cambria, Niagara Co., N.Y. Early in their marriage Thomas and Mary lived
with her parents. They moved with the Tuffords in Sept. 1880 to Custer Co. Neb.
where Tom and Mary homesteaded a farm. Tom retired from the farm in 1908 and
entered the insurance business. They made their home in Mason City where Tom
died on March 17, 1947, followed by Mary on April 14, 1951. They were buried in
Mason City Cemetery. Source: 66,98

R121 Edwin (Winnie) Banning
R122 Mary Bertha Banning
R123 Annie W. Banning
R124 Clara Grace Banning
R125 Isaiah Royden James Banning
R126 Gladys Ida Banning

R36 ELIZA ELLEN BANNING born Oct. 17, 1857 in Tunis Mills, Talbot Co., Md. and
married Thomas Lirty Jones on Dec. 21, 1876 (Dec. 22, 1877?) in Talbot Co.
Thomas died April 19, 1900. Eliza married 2nd, Robert H. Jump. Robert was born
July 26, 1821 and died Dec. 10, 1909. She died Dec. 14, 1940 and is buried in
Springhill Cemetery in Easton, Md. Source: 13,66,98

R127 Louler Virginia Jones
R128 Cora F. Jones
R129 Mary Blanche Jones
R130 James Marion Jones
R131 Sallie May Jones

R37 EMMA BLANCHE BANNING born July 28, 1860 in Tunis Mills, Talbot Co., Md.
and married John Andrew Cook Hissey about 1883. He was born Sept. 14, 1850
and died Jan. 8, 1915. They are both buried in Springhill Cemetery in Easton, Md.
Source: 66,98

R132 Naomi V. Hissey
R133 Ethel M. Hissey
R134 Howard M. Hissey

R38 JAMES ALVIN BANNING born June 18, 1863 in Tunis Mills, Talbot Co., Md and
married Elizabeth F.(???). She was born Dec. 13, 1873 and died Jan. 12, 1955.
James died April 14, 1939. They are both buried in Springhill Cemetery in Easton,
Md. Source: 66,98

R135 thru R140 for children

R39 WILLIAM HENRY BANNING born Oct. 6, 1869 in Tunis Mills, Talbot Co., Md.
He never married and died Sept. 3, 1947 in Easton, Md. He is buried next to his
brother, Charles, in Springhill Cemetery in Easton. Source: 66,98

R40 ALICE MAHALY BANNING born Nov. 5, 1871 in Tunis Mills, Talbot Co., Md. She
moved with her brother, Thomas, to Neb. where she married Edwin William Tufford
on Nov. 30, 1887 in Custer Co. Neb. Edwin was the son of Isaiah Tufford and
Annie Skeet. In LaSalle Co., Ill. On July 9, 1860. He died Oct. 25, 1932 in Mason
City, Neb. See X4035. Source: 66,98

R141 thru R146 for children

R41 CHARLES FRANCIS BANNING born Oct. 6, 1875 in Tunis Mills, Talbot Co., Md.
and married Amelia Louise Warrington on Nov.27, 1902. She was born March 3,
1883 and died July 1, 1939. Charles died Aug. 7, 1968. Both are buried in
Springhill Cemetery, Easton, Md. Source: 66,98

R147 Annie May Banning
R148 James Edward Banning
R149 Charles William Banning

R42 MARY FARLEN BANNING born June 5, 1879 in Tunis Mills, Talbot Co., Md and
married Thomas E. Griffith on Feb. 27, 1901. She died Nov. 28, 1958 and is buried
in Springhill Cemetery in Easton, Md. Source: 66,98

R150 Kenneth Griffith
R151 Meredith Griffith

R43 thru R120 unknown children of R9 thru R34

R152 thru R350 for children

393

R121 EDWIN (Winnie) BANNING born July 29, 1879 in Tunis Mills, Talbot Co., Md. and married Dora Runyan on May 11, 1913 in Mason City, Neb. He died in Mason City on April 20, 1922. They had no children. Source: 66,98

R122 MARY BERTHA BANNING born July 12, 1881 in Mason City, Neb. where she married George Martin Murrish on May 14, 1902. They had 6 children. She died Jan. 30, 1965 in Kearney, Neb. Source: 66,98

R351 thru R355 for children

R123 ANNIE W. BANNING born May 7, 1883 in Mason City, Neb. and died Sept. 12, 1884 of cholera. She is buried near her parents in Mason City. Source: 66,98

R124 CLARA GRACE SKEET BANNING born Sept. 1885 in Mason City, Neb. She married Frederick George Robertson on June 6, 1905 in Broken Bow, Custer Co., Neb. She died Jan. 16, 1906 in Mason City, a few days after giving birth to her son. Source: 66,98

R356 Elwood Robertson

R125 ISAIAH ROYDEN JAMES (ROY) BANNING born March 10, 1892 in a sod house in Custer Co., Neb. and married Ella Frances Reed on March 8, 1923 in Minden, Kearney Co., Neb. Roy served in the 89th Division of the U.S. Army during World War I, in France and Belgium. He was a rural mail carrier for 37 years and died April 29, 1988 in Mason City, Neb. Source: 66,98

R357 Edwin George Banning
R358 Harlene Elizabeth Banning

R126 GLADYS IDA BANNING born Aug. 19, 1900 and married Carey Boyd and moved to LaCross, Wisc. She died after 1988. Source: 66,98

R358 thru R360 for children

R127 LOULER VIRGINIA JONES born April 9, 1879 in St. Michaels, Talbot Co., Md. Source: 66

R128 CORA F. JONES born Oct. 1, 1881 in St. Michaels, Talbot Co., Md. Source: 66

R129 MARY BLANCHE JONES born Sept. 19, 1884 in St. Michaels, Talbot Co., Md. and married a Mr. Faudree.

R130 JAMES MARION JONES born Dec. 14, 1888 in St. Michaels, Talbot Co., Md. Source: 66

R131 SALLIE MAY JONES born Sept 21, 1895 in St. Michaels, Talbot Co., Md. Source: 66

R132 NAOMI V. HISSEY born June 1884 and died in 1977. She is buried with her parents. Source: 66

R133 ETHEL M. HISSEY born Aug. 1887 and died 1983. She is buried near her parents. Source: 66

R134 HOWARD M. HISSEY born July 19, 1890 and married Violet M. (???). He died Nov. 18, 1974. He and his wife are buried near his parents. Source: 66

R135 thru R146 Children of R38 & R40

R147 ANNIE MAY BANNING born Aug. 1, 1904 and married a Mr. Hungerford. Source: 66

R148 JAMES EDWARD BANNING born Jan. 21, 1906 and married Evelyn Winchester. She was born Dec. 27, 1909 and died July 8, 1939. She is buried in Springhill Cemetery, Easton, Md. Source: 66

R149 CHARLES WILLIAM BANNING born May 9, 1908. Source: 66

R150 KENNETH GRIFFITH no information. Source: 66

R151 MEREDITH GRIFFITH no information. Source: 66

R152 thru R350 unknown children of R43 thru R120

R351 thru R355 unknown children of R122

R356 ELWOOD ROBERTSON born Dec. 1905 in Mason City, Neb. and died April 22, 1991 in Portland, Or. Source: 66

R357 EDWIN GEORGE BANNING born Oct. 19, 1923 in Mason City, Neb. And married Helen Henriette Robertson. They are living in Ct. Source: 66,98

> R493 Sheryl Sue Banning
> R494 Lynda Kay Banning

R358 HARLENE ELIZABETH BANNING born Jan. 6, 1926 in Mason City, Neb. She married Homer Evan Cordell on June 22, 1948 in Mason City. Source: 66,98

> R495 Thomas James Cordell
> R496 Michael Joseph Cordell
> R497 Nanci Lynn Cordell

R493 SHERYL SUE BANNING. Born March 21, 1951 in Lincoln, Neb. Source: 98

R494 LYNDA KAY BANNING Born Sept. 25, 1953 in Kansas City, Mo. And married a Mr. Fougere. She is source 98. Source: 98

R495 THOMAS JAMES CORDELL born April 18, 1951 in Mason City, Neb. Source: 66

R496 MICHAEL JOSEPH CORDELL born March 21, 1953 in Mason City, Neb. Source: 66

R497 NANCI LYNN CORDELL born May 23, 1953 in Mason City, Neb. She married James Sherwood. Source: 66

BANNING'S NOT TIED IN WITH OTHER LINES

SYRACUSE NEW YORK BANNING BRANCH

History and tradition is lacking on this line, but it is reasonable to think that they belong to one of the larger lines, probably one of the Connecticut lines. It is also possible they are descendants of Daniel Banning of England. The similarity of some of the names mentioned might connect this line to the John Banning branch.

X1 Unknown

X2 John S. Banning
X3 thru X8 for children.

X2 JOHN S. BANNING married Frances M. Perkins on March 26, 1842. Source: 1

X9 John S. Banning
X10 Anna Eliza Banning
X11 Delos B. Banning
X12 Lewis Banning

X3 thru X8 unknown children of X1

X9 JOHN S. BANNING born Feb. 15, 1848. Married Samantha Andrews in 1867 at Constantina, New York. He was a painter and decorator. He died Sept. 6, 1899 in Cleveland, New York. Source: 1

X13 Carrie Banning
X14 Emma Frances Banning
X15 Florence Elizabeth Banning
X16 George Banning
X17 Newell John Banning

X10 ANNA ELIZA BANNING born Feb. 8, 1849 in Gilberts Mill, New York. Married James M. Taylor on Jan. 21, 1867 in Gilberts Mill. They lived in Oneida, New York, where she died. Source: 1

X18 thru X25 for children.

X11 DELOS B. BANNING born Feb. 4, 1852 and died an infant. Source: 1

X12 LEWIS BANNING born Nov. 26, 1854. He died on Oct. 12, 1864 in a hospital due to amputation of a leg caused by a wound received in a battle in the Shenandoah Valley. Source: 1

X13 CARRIE BANNING she died as an infant. Source: 1

X14 EMMA FRANCES BANNING born 1867 in Constantina, N.Y. She married Edward Marsden in Constantina. They lived in Syracuse, N.Y. where she died June 30, 1892. They had no children. Source: 1

X15 FLORENCE ELIZABETH BANNING born March 31, 1877 in Constantina, N.Y. She married Loyal C. G. Taber on June 14, 1899 in Syracuse, N.Y., where they lived. Source: 1

> X26 Mary Elizabeth Taber
> X27 Clauden Wellington Taber

X16 GEORGE BANNING he died as an infant. Source: 1

X17 NEWELL JOHN BANNING born April 16, 1884 in Constantina, N.Y. and lived in Syracuse, N.Y. Source: 1

X18 thru X25 unknown children of X10

X26 MARY ELIZABETH TABER born June 13, 1900 in Syracuse, N.Y. Source: 1

X27 CLAUDEN WELLINGTON TABER born July 7, 1903 in Syracuse, N.Y. Source: 1

THOMAS C. BANNING of Oregon

X500 THOMAS C. BANNING said to have been born in England. Married Jane Lucinda Gibson on March 8, 1852 in Benton Co. Or. She was born in Mo. They were living in Petaluma Co. Calif. in 1857 and moved to Or. about 1859. The 1860 census indicates she was living with her parents in Lane Co. Or. After his death, she married John B. Hise. Source: 6,20,52

    X501 Laura J. Banning
    X502 Georgina Banning
    X503 Mary Elizabeth Banning
    X504 Thomas Belle Banning

X501 LAURA J. BANNING born in Or. and married Jason Neely May 8, 1868 in Lane Co., Or. Was living in Portland, Or. in 1933. Source: 13,52

    X505 thru X509 for children

X502 GEORGINA BANNING born 185? in Or. and married Henry S. Crow Jan. 9, 1870 in Or. Source: 20,52

    X510 thru X514 for children

X503 MARY ELIZABETH BANNING born Jan. 1, 1857 in Petaluma Co., Calif. and married John Wesley Goodman Nov. 13, 1873 in Lane Co. Or. He died 1924. She died May 10, 1933 in Veneta, Lane Co., Or. of Lobar Pneumonia. She is buried in InMan Cemetery in Elmira, Or. Source: 20,52

    X515 Jim Goodwin
    X516 Frank Goodwin
    X517 Len Goodwin
    X518 Daughter 1
    X519 Daughter 2

X504 THOMAS BELLE BANNING born in Calif. He took the name of his stepfather. Was living in Goldson, Or. in 1933. Source: 52

    X520 thru Z524 for children

X515 JIM GOODWIN living in Noti, Or. in 1933. Source: 52

X516 FRANK GOODWIN living in Alvadore, Or in 1933. Source: 52

X517 LEN GOODWIN living in Stockton, Calif. in 1933. Source: 52

X518 DAUGHTER 1 married W.E. Moore and was living in Veneta, Or. in 1933. Source: 52

X519 DAUGHTER 2 married George Spees and was living in Portland, Or in 1933. Source: 52

FIRST CHICAGO BANNINGS

This Banning line no doubt belongs to one of the larger branches, but all traces have been lost thru a series of circumstances, probably now beyond recovery. Chicago records have been searched but without finding anything of value.

X1001 UNKNOWN

> X1002 Unknown Banning
> X1003 thru X1006 for unknown children.

X1002 UNKNOWN BANNING he lived in Chicago from about 1855 to 1861. After his wife died, he placed his son in an orphan asylum and left for parts unknown. Source: 1

> X1007 Daniel Banning
> X1008 thru X1010 for unknown children.

X1007 DANIEL BANNING born June 24, 1858 in Chicago and married Maryon Paton on Feb. 14, 1883 in Chicago. When he was a child, he was place in the orphan asylum at 22nd St. and Wabash Ave. in Chicago. He was adopted by Mr. Eads, who was in the file business. Daniel worked for the C.M. & St. P. railroad in Chicago. He was killed in a railway accident at Lanark Junction, Ill. in 1888. Source: 1

> X1011 Charles James Banning
> X1012 John Henry Banning

X1011 CHARLES JAMES BANNING born Feb. 19, 1885 in Chicago, Ill. Source: 1

> X1013 thru X1017 for unknown children.

X1012 JOHN HENRY BANNING born June 29, 1887 in Chicago, Ill. Source: 1

> X1018 thru X1021 for unknown children.

"HISTORY OF DELAWARE"
Scharf, J. Thomas, "History of Delaware, 1609-1888", Vol. 2, Page 922 [1888]

X1500 WILLIAM BANNING born 1812 in Sussex Co., Del. and married Nancy Jane
    Meredith.

           X1501 Jeremiah Banning
           X1502 thru X1506 for children

X1501 JEREMIAH BANNING born July 12, 1859 in Kent Co., Del. (Note: Date of
    marriage of X1508 indicates a problem.)

           X1507 Jane Banning
           X1508 Jeremiah Banning Jr.
           X1509 Ann Banning
           X1510 Catherine Banning
           X1511 John H. Banning
           X1512 Jefferson C. Banning
           X1513 George W. Banning

X1502 thru X1506 unknown children of X1500

           X1514 thru X1530 for children

X1507 JANE BANNING married John Banning of Philadelphia, Pa.

           X1531 Rose Banning

X1508 JEREMIAH BANNING JR. married Mary E. Cullen on Dec. 23, 1870.

           X1532 William H. Banning
           X1533 Herman A. Banning
           X1534 Sarah Elizabeth Banning
           X1535 Luther J. Banning
           X1536 John H. Banning
           X1537 Abbie Amanda Banning
           X1538 Daniel Banning
           X1539 George Banning
           X1540 Helen Emily Banning

X1509 ANN BANNING married Charles Emory.

           X1541 Arthur Emory
           X1542 George Emory

X1510 CATHERINE BANNING married Albert Taylor.

           X1543 Gertrude Taylor

X1511 JOHN H. BANNING married Mrs. Emma McCauley.

X1512 JEFFERSON C. BANNING married Matilda Harrington.

X1544 Edward Banning
X1545 Delbert Banning

X1513 GEORGE W. BANNING died at age 12.

From
"The Visitation of Essex, 1612"
Metcalfe, Walter C., "The Visitation of Essex by Raven, 1612", Page 142, 143 [London: Harleian Society, 1870]

X2001 RICHARD BANNING (BAYNING) of Dedham. Married Ann Raven daughter of Robert Raven of Cretinge.

X2002 Richard Banning

X2002 RICHARD BANNING of Dedham married Ann Baker, daughter of John Baker of Ipswich.

X2003 Paul Banning
X2004 Andrew Banning

X2003 PAUL BANNING of London. Made a 36 degree in 1592 of Little Bentley. He was one of the Sheriffs of London. He died Sept. 30, 1616 and was buried in Hartelayne, London. He married 1st. ? Mowse of Nedham, no issue. Married 2nd, Susan Norden of Suffolk. She died April 1623.

X2005 Paul Banning

X2004 ANDREW BANNING of London. He died Dec. 11, 1610 and was buried by his brother in Hartelayne by Marke layne.

X2005 SIR PAUL BANNING of Little Bentley, Essex. Born before 1580. He was created the 1st Baron of Horkesley May 2, 1611 and made Viscount of Sudbery March 8, 1628. He married Ann Glenham. She was the daughter of Sir Henry Glenham of Suffolke, and Lady Ann Sackville. Paul was made a Knight by King James I on July 19, 1614 and High Sheriff of Essex Co. in 1618. He died July 29, 1629 at home in Mark Lane, London.

X2006 Paul Banning
X2007 Cecilia Banning
X2008 Ann Banning
X2009 Susan Banning
X2010 Mary Banning
X2011 Elizabeth Banning

X2006 PAUL BANNING (Son and Heir to titles.) Born 1616 and married Penelope Naunton the daughter of Sir Robert Naunton. He succeeded as 2nd Viscount Bayning of Sudbury and Baron Bayning of Horkesley on July 29, 1629. He was educated at Christ Church College, Oxford and received his B.C.L. of Oxford in April 1633. All Honors expired as he had no son. He died June 11, 1638.

X2012 Ann Banning
X2013 Penelope Banning

X2007 CECILIA BANNING married Henry Viscount Newark, who succeeded his father in 1643.

X2014 Ann Newark
X2515 Grace Newark

X2008 ANN BANNING born after 1628 and married Henry Murray, a Groom of King Charles I. She was created Viscountess Bayning of Foxley, for life, on March 17, 1674. She died 1698.

X2016 Elizabeth Murray

X2009 SUSAN BANNING no information

X2010 MARY BANNING married 1st, Viscount William Grandison and 2nd, Christopher, Earl of Anglesey.

X2011 ELIZABETH BANNING married Francis Leonard, Lord Decre.

X2012 ANN BANNING married Aubrey de Vere, Earl of Oxford.

X2013 PENELOPE BANNING married John Herbert, the son of Phillip.

X2014 ANN NEWARK married John Ros, Earl of Rutland. The marriage was dissolved in 1668.

X2015 GRACE NEWARK died unmarried in 1703

X2016 ELIZABETH MURRAY married Randolph Egerton and had a daughter, Anne.

This Asa Banning should tie in with the "B" line. X3500 may be the son of B12, the same person as B34 or a child of one of the uncles or Brothers of B34. Also note the name Keziah for X3502 and the wife of B12. I have been unable to establish the tie.

X3500 ASA BANNING born 1803-4 in Va. He married 1st, Polly (Mary) Ward in Pike Co., Ohio in 1829. She was alive at the time of the death of her father, William Ward in 1842. Asa married 2nd Elizabeth ? on March 18, 1835. She was born in 1814 and died March 8, 1857. They moved to Colerain T/S, Ohio about 1832. He married 3rd Mahala E. Ogden on Dec. 17, 1857. He owned land in Section 7 of Cold rain T/S. He died June 6, 1859 in Ohio and is buried next to his 2nd wife in the Barnes Family Cemetery, next to the White Oak Christian Church on Blue Rock Road in Colerain T/S, Hamilton Co., Ohio. His will was probated June 23, 1859. Source: 4,5,12,56,76

> X3501 Thomas Banning
> X3502 Keziah Banning
> X3503 Charity Banning
> X3504 Mariana Banning
> X3504A Marvan Banning
> X3505 Jane Banning
> X3506 Stephen Banning
> X3507 George Banning
> X3508 William Banning
> X3509 John Banning
> X3510 Asa Banning

X3501 THOMAS BANNING born 1828 in Ohio and was dead by 1859. He married Elizabeth Crawford in Butler Co., Oh. about 1850. After Thomas died she married Robert M. Hill. She died in 1905. Source: 5,12,56,76,95

> X3511 Olive Elizabeth Banning
> X3512 Mary jane Banning
> X3513 Abraham Banning

X3502 KEZIAH BANNING born March 2, 1832 in Groesbeck, Hamilton Co.,Ohio and married Josiah Strimple on May 11, 1850 in Grosbeck, Clermont Co., Ohio. He was the son of Samuel & Elizabeth Strimple, born July 16, 1822 in Batavia, Clermont Co., Ohio. He died Aug. 16, 1903 in Batavia. She died in Feb. 19, 1907 in Harshmanville, Montgomery Co., Ohio, and is buried in Woodland Cemetery, Dayton, Montgomery Co., Ohio. Source: 12,13,56,76

> X3514 George Strimple
> X3515 Mary Elizabeth Strimple
> X3516 Asa Strimple
> X3517 Harry Strimple
> X3518 Sarah J. Strimple
> X3519 John W. Strimple
> X3520 Amanda Belle Strimple

X3503 CHARITY BANNING born Married Isaac Jessup on Dec. 29, 1845. She died 1859/60. Source: 12,56,76

> X3521 Martha J. Jessup

X3504 MARIANA BANNING born 1834 in Ohio and married Henry Prince. He was born 1830 in England. Source: 5,6,7,12,56,76

X3504a MARVAN BANNING (?) This may have been the son of his 2nd wife. He was farming with Asa in 1850. Source: 5,76

X3505 JANE BANNING born 1838-41 in Ohio. Source: 5,6,12,56

X3506 STEPHEN BANNING born 1843 in Ohio. He married America Barnes on April 3, 1873 in Hamilton Co., Ohio. Source: 5,6,7,12,13,56

X3507 GEORGE BANNING born 1845-46 in Ohio. He married Catherine Ann ? Source: 5,6,12,56 (He married Anna B. Basaker Feb. 25, 1875 in Miami Co., Ohio. ? Source: 13)

X3508 WILLIAM W. BANNING born 1848-50 in Ohio. He married Madora (Dora) Barnes Jan 1, 1873 in Hamilton Co., Ohio. She was the daughter of Martin Barmes and was born 1853. They moved to Dearborn Co., Indiana. He died in 1919 and she died in 1940. They are buried in the Bevis-Cedar Grove Cemetery in Colerain T/S, Ohio. Source: 5,6,7,8,12,13,15,56

> X3545 Annie E. Banning
> X3546 Addie Banning
> X3547 Madora Banning

X3509 JOHN BANNING born Dec. 26, 1851. He married Arabella Jenkins in 1871. They had 12 children. She died 1924 and he died Aug. 30, 1926. Source: 6,7,12,30,56

> X3548 Banning Daughter

X3510 ASA BANNING born 1852-3 in Ohio. He married Lena ?. She was born 1859 in Ky. They were living in Union Co., Liberty T/S, Indiana in 1880. Source: 6,7,8,12,56

> X3560 Estella Banning
> X3561 Maranda Banning

X3511 OLIVE ELIZABETH BANNING born 1851 in Oh. Source: 95

X3512 MARY JANE BANNING born 1853 in Oh. Source: 95

X3513 ABRAHAM BANNING born 1855 in Ohio. he was living in Whipple, Van Buren Co., Ark in 1905. Source: 95

X3514 GEORGE STRIMPLE born Feb. 23, 1851 in Ohio. Source: 76

X3515 MARY ELIZABETH STRIMPLE born July 13, 1853 in Batavia, Clermont Co., Ohio. She married William Edwin Perry on June 6, 1877 in Batavia. He was the son of Samuel and Mary Druscilla Dunham Perry, born May 15, 1856 in Mt. Washington, Hamilton Co., Ohio. Their children are, George Edwin, born May 15, 1878 in Batavia; an unnamed infant, born Dec. 31, 1880 and died the next day; Cora Elizabeth, born Jan. 22, 1882 in Batavia, and died April 25, 1914 in Dayton; Anna

Amanda, born Sept 25, 1885; Edna Mae, born Aug. 22, 1888 in Batavia and died Sept 25, 1969 in Ohio; Kizzie Banning, born May 22, 1889 in Batavia and died Nov. 9, 1983 in Dayton; Albert Alonzo, born Sept 16, 1891 in Batavia and died July 25, 1892 in Batavia; and Charles , born March 24, 1894 in Mungen and died Jan 22, 1895 in Batavia. William died Dec. 22, 1894 in Mungen, Wood Co., Ohio of typhoid while helping during an epidemic. He is buried in Rudolph Cementery in Wood Co., Ohio. Mary died Oct. 2, 1932 in Dayton, Ohio and is buried in Memorial Gardens in Dayton. Source: 76

X3516 ASA STRIMPLE born Oct. 14, 1854 in Ohio. Source: 76

X3517 HARRY STRIMPLE born Oct. 14, 1857 in Batavia, Clermont Co., Ohio. He married Mary Ann Perry on Feb. 18, 1891 in Amelia, Clermont Co., Ohio. She was the daughter of Samuel and Mary Deucilla Durham Perry (See X3515). Their children were, Jesse Elsworth, born Dec. 29, 1891 in Pittsburgh, Crawford Co., Kansas; Samuel William, born Aug 27, 1893 in Hamlet, Ohio; Hilary Perry, born May 22, 1897 in Bird's, Lawrence Co., Ill; Ada Mae, born Aug. 2, 1904 in Hamlet, Ohio. Source: 76

X3518 SARAH J. STRIMPLE born in 1860 in Ohio. Source: 76

X3519 JOHN W. STRIMPLE born june 29, 1865 in Ohio. Source: 76

X3520 AMANDA BELLE STRIMPLE born Mar. 8, 1871 in Ohio. Source: 76

X3521 MARTHA J. JESSUP born 1851. Source: 6,7,56

X3545 ANNIE E. BANNING born 1864 (1873?) in Ohio. (She married Edwin S. Wabnitz). She married John Westen Nov. 4, 1884 in Hamilton Co. Ohio. (Source: 12,13) She died in 1918 and is buried in the Bevis-Cedar Grove Cemetery in Colerain T/S, Ohio. Source: 8,15,56

X3571 Glen M. Wabnitz

X3546 ADDIE BANNING born 1868 in Ohio. Source: 8,56

X3547 MADORA BANNING born 1893 and married a Mr. Perdon. She died 1982 and is buried in the Bevis-Cedar Grove Cemetery in Colerain T/S, Ohio. Source: 15,56

X3581 Doris Perdon

X3548 BANNING DAUGHTER she married Jasper Younts and lived in Fairfield, Ind. Source: 30,56

X3560 ESTELLA BANNING born 1876 in Ohio. Source: 8,56

X3561 MARANDA BANNING born 1878 in Ohio. Source: 8,56

X3571 GLEN M. WABNITZ born 1911 and died 1943. He is buried in the Bevis-Cedar Grove Cemetery in Colerain T/S, Ohio. Source: 15,56

X3581 DORIS PERDON she married a Mr. Pieper and is buried in the Bevis-Cedar Grove Cemetery in Colerain T/S, Ohio. Source: 15,56

Eliphalet G. Banning may tie in with the "E" line. He may be descended from E17, as this in the only area that the name of two of Eliphalet's children occur in this book. It is reasonable to think that Janette and Rosetta were named after relatives.

X3800 ELIPHALET G. BANNING born Sept 1820 in Lyme Ct. and married Louisa Thompson on Oct. 22, 1842 in Hebron, Ct. She was born about 1820 in Millington, Ct. and died in Andover, Ct. July 6, 1862. By 1870 he was married to Cornelia W. (Banning?) (???) born about 1830. Cornelia had divorced her 1st husband, William P. Davison in New London Co., Ct. on Dec. 19, 1863. At various times he was listed as a laborer, farmer and a paper maker. He died in Hebron, Ct. on April 14, 1884 of pneumonia at age 63 years, 8 months, 7 days. Source: 6,7,8,12,13,82

> X3801 Ann Janette Banning
> X3802 Elizabeth Banning
> X3802a   Unnamed Son
> X3803 Albert O. Banning
> X3803a Unnamed Daughter
> X3804 Rosetta Banning
> X3805 Orrin Banning
> X3806 William Banning
> X3806a Fanny Banning

X3801 ANN JANETTE BANNING born Aug. 16, 1847 in Hebron, Ct. She married Diodate G. Wilson on Aug. 9, 1865 in Marlborough, Ct. He was the oldest son of Ogden and Ruth Coleman Wilson, born April 2, 1830 in Chatham, now known as East Hampton, Ct. He was in the Marlborough town Militia in 1851 & 52. In 1870, he was listed as a laborer and she was a "silk dryer". She died June 7, 1890 in Manchester, Ct. of "Consumption". The 1900 census lists Diodate as a "Pauper" at the Manchester almshouse on Porter street. He died in Manchester of Gastritis on Sept. 15, 1905. Source: 6,7,12,13,82

> X3807 Annie Elizabeth Wilson
> X3808 Rose Rebecca Wilson
> X3809 Charles Harvey Wilson

X3802 ELIZABETH BANNING "Lizzie" was born July 7, 1850 and died Feb. 14, 1872 in Hebron, Ct. In 1870 she was living with her sister, X3801, and working in a silk mill. She never married. Source: 6,7,12,82

X3802a UNNAMED SON born and died Sept. 16, 1853. Source: 12,82

X3803 ALBERT O. BANNING born about 1854. Source: 6,7,12,82

> X3810 thru X3815 for children

X3803a UNNAMED DAUGHTER born and died Dec. 26, 1856. Source: 12,82

X3804 ROSETTA BANNING born about 1857. By 1870 she was working in a silk mill and living with her sister, X3801. Source: 6,7,12,82

> X3816 thru X3821 for children

X3805 ORRIN BANNING born about 1865 in Hebron, Ct. Source: 7,8,82

X2822 thru X2827 for children

X3806 WILLIAM BANNING born about 1867 in Hebron, Ct. Source: 7,8,82

X2828 thru X2833 for children

X3806a FANNY BANNING born about 1872 in Hebron, Ct. Source: 8,82

X3807 ANNIE ELIZABETH WILSON born Aug. 11, 1870 in Hebron Ct. and married
John Ellison on Sept. 12, 1890 in Manchester, Ct. John was born in Ireland on Nov.
22, 1871 to John and Eliza Berry Ellison. Their children were, Robert John, born
Sept. 21, 1891, and died July 14, 1909 of tuberculosis and Walter Joseph, born
Sept. 21, 1892 and died about 1960. John and Annie were living at 29 Charter Oak
St in Manchester, Ct. when he died on Jan. 28, 1904. She married 2nd, Carlos
Orlando Walker in Manchester on March 4, 1908. Carlos was born Dec. 27, 1875 in
Coventry, Ct. They had a son, Everett Christopher Walker, born June 24, 1911 in
Manchester, and died April 6, 1992 in Manchester. Annie died on Oct. 2, 1949,
followed by Carlos on Feb. 4, 1963, both in Manchester. Source: 82

X3808 ROSE REBECCA WILSON born Oct. 14, 1875 and died Sept. 22, 1890 of
Typhoid fever in Mamchester, Ct. Source: 82

X3809 CHARLES HARVEY WILSON born Jan. 17, 1873 in Hebron, Ct. The 1910
census places him in Manchester, age 37, single and a boarder with the Campbell
family. Source: 82

SOURCES OF BANNING INFORMATION

1. P.W. Banning, "The First Banning Genealogy", [Chicago, 1908]

2. Boston Evening Transcript, 1909-21

3. 1810 and earlier U.S. census

4. 1820, 30 and 40 U.S. census

5. 1850 U.S. census

6. 1860 U.S. census

7. 1870 U.S. census

8. 1880 U.S. census

9. 1890 U.S. census

10. 1900 U.S. census

11. Re-created census and tax rolls

12. County records, wills, probate records, deeds, marriages, etc.

13. International Genealogical Index (IGI)

14. Church and Parish records

15. Cemetery records and Tombstone inscriptions

16. Family group sheets completed by direct family member

17. State records and files

18. Family bible information

19. Misc. County gazetteers, directories and histories

20. May Tacker, Tecumseh, Okla.

21. Mrs. Virgil Fast, Dodge City, Ks.

22. Mrs. Raymond Hudson, Woodbridge, Ct.

23. James Pauley, Jefferson, Iowa

24. Lois Herth, Tacoma, Wa.

25. Betty Coggin, Ratliff City, Okla.

26. Jo McCamey, Perry, Iowa

27. Garroll Salmons, Lacey, Wa.

28. Barbara Webber, Annandale, Va.

29. Lt. Col. Paul L. Nichols, Yountville, Calif.

30. Misc. Newspapers, Marriages, obit's etc

31. Sheri Talbot

32. DAR & Sons of the American Revolution information

33. Hazel A. Spraker, "The Boone Family" Hazel A. Spraker, [Baltimore: Geno. Pub. Co., 1982]

34. C. H. Browning, "Americans of Royal Descent"

35. Ethan A. Doty, "Doty-Doten Family in America" , [Brooklyn, N.Y., 1897]

36. "The Visitation of Essex, 1612"

37. Fannie C.W. Barbour, "Spelman Genealogy", [New York: Frank Allabey Geno. Co., 1950]

38. Frances Granere, San Marcos, Calif.

39. Charles E. Banks, "History of Martha's Vineyard" Vol.3, [Dukes Co. Historical Society, 1966]

40. Frederick A. Virkus, "Abridged Compendium of American Genealogy", 1926, reprint [Baltimore: Genealogical Pub. Co., 1968]

41. Amelia Vinning Bells (F236), A letter dated Aug. 3, 1866

42. Aaron Tyler Bliss, "The Bliss Family in America", [Midland, Mich. 1982]

43. Gayle Tipsword Norris, Tucson, Az.

44. Donald J. Braffitt, Austin, Tx.

45. Frederick A. Virkus, "Immigrants to America Before 1750", [Baltimore: Genealogical Pub. Co. 1965]

46. "Heritage of Henderson Co., N.C.", 1987

47. Carolyn Malmberg, Dover, Del.

48. Edna M. Banning, Drexel Hill, Pa.

49. Flora Banning Baxter, Rochester, N.Y.

50. Geneva B. Spence, Greenwood, Del.

51. Robert J. Banning, Pasadena, Ca.

52. Dixie Nunn, Sweet Home, Or.

53. Pam Haymes Graham, Houston, Tx.

54. Irene G. Fulton, Los Altos Hills, Ca.

55. Elizabeth B. Plimpton, "Vital Records of Lyme, Conn. to the End of the Year 1850", [Coodus, Conn: Moodus Print Shop, 1976]

56. Ruth Wells, Cincinnati, Ohio.

57. Kilbee Brittain, "The General Phineas Banning Residence Museum", [Wilmington, Ca: Friends of Banning Park, 1984]

58. Family group sheets given to me by Jan Losi, Curator of the Banning Residence Museum, Wilmington, Ca.

59. Cheryle S. Smith Bennett, Wilmington, Ill.

60. Ken Banning, Brockville, Ontario, Canada

61. "Who's Who of America's Bannings", [Scottsdale, Az: Scottsdale Family Treasures, Inc., 1992]

62. Melba Edwards, Gracemont, Okla.

63. Alan M. Streit, Albany, Calif.

64. Mary Friedlander, Milwaukee, Wi.

65. William D. Peck, San Francisco, Calif.

66. Micki Hall, Deer Park, Tex.

67. Jeri Lyon, Toko, Japan

68. Richard B. Banning, Vancouver, Wash.

69. Ethel Banning, Pocatello, Id.

70. "New Shoreham Town Book" (Get add. info.)

71. "Early Connecticut Marriages", Frederic W. Bailey.

72. " New England Historical and Geneological Regester"

73. "Notes on Block Islanders of the 17th Century"

74. "New England Marriages prior to 1700", Clarence A. Torrey

75. Joan Clark, Commerce, Tex.

76. Judy Taylor, Long Beach, Miss.

77. 1910 U.S. Census

78. 1920 U.S. Census

79. Blaine Cooper, Crestview, Fla.

80. George V. Banning, Belvedere, Calif.

81. Constance Banning Gatling, N.Y., N.Y.

82. Herbert C. Walker, Prescot, Az.

83. Albert E. Kirk, Wilbraham, Mass.

84. David J. Riley, New Brunswick, N.J.

85. Maesimund B. Panos, Tipp City, Ohio

86. Laurel Harris, Malaga, Western Australia

87. John Banning, San Antonio, Tx.

88. "Early Marriages of Trumbull Co. Ohio" (Photo copy from Warren-Trumbull Co. Public Library)

89. Rolland F. Tipsword, Taylorville, Il.

90. Virgil W. Huntley, Mistic, Conn.

91. Larry D. Watts, Aloha, Or.

92. Sherri Hilmes, Robins AFB, Ga.

93. James S. Pitcher, Boonville, N.Y.

94. Ruth Banning Schleicher, Appleton, Wi.

95. Debra Morrison, Middletown, Oh.

96. "The Pratt Family" [Marlborough, Mass: Pratt Brothers, Publishers, 1884]

97. Dorothy M. Leeder, Ashville, N.C.

98. Lynda B. Fougere, Duxbury, Ma.

99. Melba Edwards, Gracemount, Ok.

Name	Year	Code	Name	Year	Code
ALLEN, Shannon Gay	1971	J510	ARNOLD, Richard Webster	1928	H372
ALLEN, Shonda Kay	1967 *	J510	ARNOLD, Roland James	1933	F5290
ALLEN, Susana (B=)	1855	C233	ARTHUR, Bessie	192?	Q93
ALLEN, Virginia (Mitchner)	1937	J510	ARTHURS, Clifford	1948	Q88
ALLEN, William Dale	1935	J509	ARTHURS, Ethel Esther	1935	Q88
ALLING, Charles E.	184?	E1621	ARTHURS, Gordon	1904	Q88
ALLING, Mary (B=)	1847	E1621	ARTHURS, Marvyn Gordon	1933	Q88
ALLISON, Alexander T.	1840	B264	ARTHURS, Merle M. (Campb	1912	Q88
ALLISON, Asher	188?	B990	ARTHURS, Rhoda Ruth	1918	Q94
ALLISON, Benjamin	1857	B270	ARTHURS, Stella	1944	Q88
ALLISON, Cassandia (Bir	175?	B17	ASHDOWN, Florence	188?	G82
ALLISON, Elizabeth	1784	B17	ASHTON, Laura (Caldwell)	1843	F607
ALLISON, Ellen	1842	B265	ASHTON, William	1834	F607
ALLISON, George	172?	X2635	ASKINS, John R.	183?	B91
ALLISON, James	1845	B266	ASKINS, Millie	186?	B883
ALLISON, Jemima	1791	B18	ASKINS, Rhody (B=)	183?	B91
ALLISON, Jemima	1851	B268	ASSELSTINE, Marjorie A.	192?	Q152
ALLISON, Mahaila (B=)	1814	B77a	ATHERTON, Emily	187?	G74
ALLISON, Mary D. (B=)	1858	B259	ATTEBERRY, Mr.	181?	B91a
ALLISON, Oliver	188?	B989	ATWOOD, Anna	172?	F20
ALLISON, Oscar	188?	B990a	AUBE, Yvette	1919	Q68
ALLISON, Richard Isaac	1856	B269	AUGDON, Nancy	177?	A17
ALLISON, Sarah (B=)	1722	X2635	AUGUSTINE, Edwart T.	190?	E6714
ALLISON, Sarah (B=)	1857	B280	AUGUSTINE, Leona M. (B=)	1906	E6714
ALLISON, Thomas	175?	B17	AUSELMAN, Ernest	18??	A1582
ALLISON, Thomas	1849	B267	AUSELMAN, Maria (B=)	1860	A656
ALLISON, Thomas	185?	B259	AUSELMAN, Mr.	185?	A656
ALLISON, William	1811	B77a	AUSTIN, Mary	172?	X2634
ALLSTON, Charity	1731	C5	AUSTIN, Sarah (Fullwood)	180?	B61d
ALRICK, Jewel (B=)	190?	B1146	AUSTIN, William T.	180?	B61d
AMES, Elizabeth (B=)	1932	C797	AUSTIN, William Thomas	183?	B61d
AMMERMAN, Sarah	180?	B20	AYERS, Beatrice Banning	188?	C290
ANDERSON, Berger	191?	C1942	AYERS, Ellen (B=)	1853	C97
ANDERSON, Eliza Ann	1815	B32	AYERS, Frederick Jr.	1822	C97
ANDERSON, Ellen	178?	L27	AYERS, Frederick Banni	188?	C291
ANDERSON, Madeline (B=)	1920	C1942	AYERS, Henry	170?	K234
ANDERSON, Tennie	189?	P141	AYERS, Mary	170?	K234
ANDREWS, Harriet (B=)	1801	F206	BAGWELL, Charles A.	185?	G21
ANDREWS, Mona Mae	193?	H833	BAGWELL, Elizabeth (B=)	1853?	G21
ANDREWS, Nelson	179?	F206	BAIER, Arlene H.	1952	Q149
ANDREWS, Samantha	184?	X9	BAIER, George	192?	Q149
ANTHONY, Melva A. (B=)	194?	H405	BAIER, Rose	192?	Q149
ANTHONY, Mr.	194?	H405	BAILEY, Charles E.	1837	E1384
AOSS, Eido F.	190?	B985a	BAILEY, Emily (B=)	1837	E1384
APPEL, Hannah Whilemena	1895	C558	BAILEY, Jane	1800	B53
ARMSTRONG, Annie B.	185?	C112	BAILEY, Lyman Wells	1874 *	E5696
ARMSTRONG, Gladys	189?	C316	BAKER, Andrew J.	1872	C555
ARMSTRONG, Mary (B=)	1820	C23	BAKER, Ann	15??	X2002
ARMSTRONG, Richard Bann	185?	C111	BAKER, Arthur Jackson	1922	C1837
ARMSTRONG, William	182?	C23	BAKER, Catherine (Denny)	180?	A66d
ARMSTRONG, William John	185?	C113	BAKER, Ester (B=)	177?	C15
ARNETT, Mary	183?	A238	BAKER, Hilary	180?	A66d
ARNOLD, Arleen Carol(Bam	1928	H372	BAKER, John	15??	X2002
ARNOLD, Cecily Edith	1934	F5291	BAKER, Lula May (B=)	1883	C555
ARNOLD, David R.	195?	H372	BAKER, Mary E.	181?	B68
ARNOLD, Ellen (B=)	1906	F2624	BAKER, Minnie Viola	1920 *	C1836
ARNOLD, Frederick Geofe	1902	F2624	BAKER, Norma Leone	1917	C1835
ARNOLD, Kathryn W.	195?	H372	BAKER, Thomas	177?	C15
ARNOLD, Lilla Ruth	194?	J2119	BALCH, Jane (B=)	177?	A28
ARNOLD, Lorraine (Stev	193?	F5290	BALCH, Stephen B.	177?	A28
ARNOLD, Madaline	190?	H372	BALDWIN, Ann	1762	A67
ARNOLD, Richard W.	190?	H372	BALES, Dora Elizabeth	1915	B1142

BALES, Ethel D. (Haymes)	1890	B1142	
BALES, George M.	1920	B1142	
BALES, Jasper E.	188?	B1142	
BALLARD, Edgar	187?	E4207	
BALLARD, Hazel	189?	E9912	
BALLARD, Lilly (B=)	187?	E4207	
BALLARD, Mable	189?	E9911	
BALLARD, Marian	189?	E9913	
BALLOU, Florence E.	187?	B589	
BAMBERG, Arleen Carol	1928	H372	
BAMBERG, Clair W.	195?	H373	
BAMBERG, Evelyn D. (B=)	1905	H133	
BAMBERG, George Andrew	187?	H133	
BAMBERG, John Carlton	195?	H373	
BAMBERG, Nina Jean	1990	H1477	
BAMBERG, Margaret Ann(Ho	1931	H373	
BAMBERG, Mary K.	187?	H133	
BAMBERG, Paul Henry	195?	H373	
BAMBERG, Robert E.	1901	H133	
BAMBERG, Robert Wesley	1929	H373	
BAMBERG, Robert Otis	195?	H373	
BANCROFT, Edward Payson	185?	E1481	
BANCROFT, Emma (B=)	1850	E1481	
BANCROFT, Emma Banning	1889	E6324	
BANCROFT, Lucy Lay	1884	E6323	
BANCROFT, Perley Hubbard	1883	E6322	
BANDY, William	16??	A5	
BANKS, Edward	181?	L35	
BANKS, Eliza P. (B=)	181?	L35	
BANNING, Abbie E.	1825	F271	
BANNING, Abbie Amanda	187?	X1537	
BANNING, Abagail	16??	E1	
BANNING, Abigail (Sterl	1742	F15	
BANNING, Abigail (Colbur	175?	X2758	
BANNING, Abigail	1760	E85	
BANNING, Abigail	177?	B11	
BANNING, Abigail	177?	F60a	
BANNING, Abigail (March	1804	B28	
BANNING, Abigail	1833	F497	
BANNING, Abigale	177?	B10j	
BANNING, Abner "Benjamin	1755	F20	
BANNING, Abner Wilcox	1804	F250	
BANNING, Abner	1819	F214	
BANNING, Abnie (Pfister)	186?	B780	
BANNING, Abraham	1845	C228	
BANNING, Abraham Sampson	1848	B118	
BANNING, Abraham	1855	X3513	
BANNING, Ada Sarah	184?	L140	
BANNING, Ada Elizabeth	1867	J25	
BANNING, Ada	1878	J34	
BANNING, Ada	1880	E6735	
BANNING, Adaline (Sprack	184?	B221	
BANNING, Adam T.	1976	H1304	
BANNING, Adderine	1862	R30	
BANNING, Addie "Noyes"	186?	F684	
BANNING, Addie (Heaner)	186?	E5689	
BANNING, Addie	1868	X3546	
BANNING, Addie G.	1870 *	C551	
BANNING, Addie (MacDonal	1879	Q22	
BANNING, Addie Eve	1886 *	E11021	
BANNING, Adelia E.	1879	B749	
BANNING, Adeline	1847	E1569	
BANNING, Adeline Louise	1852	E1482	
BANNING, Adeline (Kirk)	190?	C664	
BANNING, Adolph Friederi	165?	N1	
BANNING, Adolphia (Cox)	187?	B701	
BANNING, Adolphus	See Dolphus		
BANNING, Adolphus A.	1824	B72	
BANNING, Adra A. (Welch)	185?	E1494	
BANNING, Affiah Climena	1824	F271B	
BANNING, Affiah (Gideon)	179?	F67	
BANNING, Aggie (Daniels)	186?	E1403	
BANNING, Agnes	156?	K7	
BANNING, Agnes (Terrill)	183?	B177	
BANNING, Agnes Violet	1860	E1360	
BANNING, Agusta (Grote)	180?	N267	
BANNING, Aimee	1911	H176	
BANNING, Albert Tiffany	1816	E348	
BANNING, Albert J.	1840	F280	
BANNING, Albert Bainard	1849	E1387	
BANNING, Albert Roland	1852	E1494	
BANNING, Albert O.	1854	X3803	
BANNING, Albert	1860 *	E1574	
BANNING, Albert	187?	E1452	
BANNING, Albert William	187?	L1097	
BANNING, Albert Phineas	1887	C589	
BANNING, Albert E.	1893	B967	
BANNING, Albert Otto Dew	1903	C664	
BANNING, Albert	194?	A3595	
BANNING, Albertine	1842	E1566A	
BANNING, Alberto Lyman	1857	E5688	
BANNING, Alberto Lyman	1882	E11020	
BANNING, Albina (Case)	182?	F270	
BANNING, Alda	1854	F564	
BANNING, Aletha Allene	1933	B9602	
BANNING, Alexander	1734	N16	
BANNING, Alexander	1759	A15	
BANNING, Alexander	1785	B19	
BANNING, Alexander	1800	B52	
BANNING, Alexander	1812	A42	
BANNING, Alexander Fraze	1826	B107	
BANNING, Alexander Jr.	1827	B88	
BANNING, Alexander A.	1828	G12	
BANNING, Alexander	1828 *	R6	
BANNING, Alexander	183?	I21	
BANNING, Alexander	1837	B291	
BANNING, Alexander	1841	B171	
BANNING, Alexander	1849	B300	
BANNING, Alexander Bruce	1878	G87	
BANNING, Alexander Bruce	190?	G223	
BANNING, Alfred Douglas	1834	G15	
BANNING, Alfred	184?	D13	
BANNING, Alfred	1860 *	E1573	
BANNING, Alfred	1875	J33A	
BANNING, Alfred J.	1882	E6733	
BANNING, Alfred Henry	1899 *	J72	
BANNING, Alice (???)	174?	X2754	
BANNING, Alice (Peck)	178?	E76	
BANNING, Alice (Ransome)	179?	E81	
BANNING, Alice	183?	C94	
BANNING, Alice (Cooper)	183?	L186	
BANNING, Alice P.	1836	C26	
BANNING, Alice Crocker	1858	E1589	
BANNING, Alice	186? *	B520	

BANNING, Alice	1865	C144		BANNING, Andrew	1726	A9
BANNING, Alice	1866	B272		BANNING, Andrew	177?	A20
BANNING, Alice Maud	1869	L466		BANNING, Andrew	1832	B178
BANNING, Alice Mahaly	1871	R40		BANNING, Andrew J.	1835	F498
BANNING, Alice	1876 *	H30		BANNING, Andrew	1844	B204
BANNING, Alice Armelia	1879	F1453		BANNING, Andrew	1864	G68
BANNING, Alice M. (Lake)	188?	E1684		BANNING, Andrew J.	1866	F1209
BANNING, Alice P.	1887	F1392		BANNING, Andrew J.	1876	J17
BANNING, Alice	189?	E9905		BANNING, Andrew Lorenzo	1877	B942
BANNING, Alice M. (Morse	189?	C297		BANNING, Andrew Jackson	1897	F2622
BANNING, Alice (Murphy)	1906	H134		BANNING, Andrew Calvin	1907	C304
BANNING, Alice May	1908	E6894		BANNING, Andrew Walter	1972	E39072
BANNING, Alice (Mara)	1909	H136		BANNING, Anetta (Hawk)	186?	E1361
BANNING, Alice	191?	H140		BANNING, Anetta Pearl	1908	E10803
BANNING, Alice Elaine	1948	H498		BANNING, Angee (Clark)	186?	E1400
BANNING, Alison Marie	1955	H825		BANNING, Angela Michelle	1981	H1014
BANNING, Allanson (Lyons	184?	E1394		BANNING, Angelica (Frazi	1726	A8
BANNING, Allen	187?	B309a		BANNING, Angelica	1749	B7
BANNING, Alma (Clisby)	1833	F259		BANNING, Angelica	1775	B15
BANNING, Alma	1863	F634		BANNING, Angelica (???)	183?	B89
BANNING, Alma (Smith)	187?	B776		BANNING, Angelina	1838	G16
BANNING, Alma Jane	1872	C552		BANNING, Angus Stewart	1953	Q152
BANNING, Alma Louise	1886	B610		BANNING, Ann (Raven)	15??	X2001
BANNING, Alma Elizabeth	1907	H175b		BANNING, Ann (Baker)	15???	X2002
BANNING, Alma	1919	B998a		BANNING, Ann (Glenham)	15???	X2005
BANNING, Alma Jean	1943	H491		BANNING, Ann	162?	X2008
BANNING, Almeda M. (Rich	185?	E1645		BANNING, Ann	164?	X2012
BANNING, Almena	1807	F73		BANNING, Ann (???)	172?	A36b
BANNING, Almena (Hall)	1819	E372		BANNING, Ann (Clark)	1749	B7
BANNING, Alminda (Keys)	182?	G10		BANNING, Ann	177?	A28a
BANNING, Alminey C.	1882	E6732		BANNING, Ann (Wiley)	177?	B13
BANNING, Almira (Isham)	181?	E361		BANNING, Ann C. (Stuart)	1785	K606
BANNING, Almira	1833	F286		BANNING, Ann (???)	179?	X100
BANNING, Almira	1842	E412		BANNING, Ann	1795	B49
BANNING, Almon	1827	F263		BANNING, Ann (Redmon)	180?	B20
BANNING, Almon Hall	1860	F647		BANNING, Ann	180?	B82
BANNING, Almon	189?	F1519		BANNING, Ann C. (Molyne)	181?	L182
BANNING, Alonzo	184?	B666		BANNING, Ann	182?	L122
BANNING, Alta	1869	G78		BANNING, Ann	1826	B176
BANNING, Alta (Baxter)	1879	F1509		BANNING, Ann E.	1827	B91c
BANNING, Alta Florence	1889	G184		BANNING, Ann Carol (B=)	1827	K1269
BANNING, Alvin Seth	1879	F1216		BANNING, Ann (Adkin)	1829	E211
BANNING, Alvin Logan	1895	F2621		BANNING, Ann	183?	B296
BANNING, Amanda	188? *	J60		BANNING, Ann	1832	F590
BANNING, Amasa	1779	E66		BANNING, Ann	1833	B216
BANNING, Ambrose C.	1831	F284		BANNING, Ann	1837	B224
BANNING, Amelia (Wilcox)	179?	F63		BANNING, Ann	1844	H6
BANNING, Amelia	180?	F251		BANNING, Ann Janette	1847	X3801
BANNING, Amelia	1848	F628		BANNING, Ann	1849	B299
BANNING, Amelia (Kepner)	1821	F215		BANNING, Ann	186?	X1509
BANNING, Amelia (Warring	1883	R41		BANNING, Anna H. (Stover)	184?	E1616
BANNING, America (Barnes	184?	X3506		BANNING, Anna (Detmeyers	16??	N1
BANNING, Amerilla (Mille	1806	F69		BANNING, Anna (Calder)	1748	A12
BANNING, Aminda	1976	A9951		BANNING, Anna (Pidcock)	1801	L43
BANNING, Amos Jacob	1859	A636		BANNING, Anna	1824 *	A245
BANNING, Amy	18??	A1589		BANNING, Anna (Lilly)	184?	F642
BANNING, Amy Jane	1821	F249		BANNING, Anna (Williams)	184?	L457
BANNING, Amy (???)	189?	F1415		BANNING, Anna (Basaker)	184?	X3507
BANNING, Amy	1911	H176		BANNING, Anna (Hurst)	1847	B117
BANNING, Andres	190?	Q63		BANNING, Anna Eliza	1849	X10
BANNING, Andrew	15??	X2004		BANNING, Anna (Smith)	1871	C125
BANNING, Andrew	168?	A5c		BANNING, Anna E.	1875	R34

418

BANNING, Anna Lake	1875	A687	BANNING, Asa	1742	B6
BANNING, Anna (Morris)	1885	B747	BANNING, Asa	1803	X3500
BANNING, Anna May	1917 *	H138	BANNING, Asa	1808	B34
BANNING, Anna Mae (Beis	192?	C1904	BANNING, Asa	1852	X3510
BANNING, Anna Mae	1928	B9601	BANNING, Asa Ephraim	1865	B570
BANNING, Anna Glendene	1931	E10824	BANNING, Asahel {Arbel}	1780	F63
BANNING, Annah (Sparrow)	1752	F20	BANNING, Asenath	1772	X2996
BANNING, Anne (Willeford	1916	E10802	BANNING, Asenath (Bradle	1824	F253
BANNING, Anne (Holt)	180?	L51	BANNING, Asenath	1846	F627
BANNING, Anne (Belec)	1912	Q80	BANNING, Ashley Nicole	1985	E50031
BANNING, Annie	1764	L10	BANNING, Asubah (Clark)	1784	E80
BANNING, Annie	1774 *	A31	BANNING, Audrey Joan	1954	C3429
BANNING, Annie (Shaler)	180?	E305	BANNING, Augusta (McCrea	1855	A259
BANNING, Annie	182?	P7	BANNING, Augusta	1908	A1654
BANNING, Annie M.	1827	A56	BANNING, Augustus	1821	E375
BANNING, Annie E. (Hutto	183?	L142	BANNING, Avis G.	1870 *	A677
BANNING, Annie Mona	1839	L458	BANNING, Avis	1880	A670
BANNING, Annie	184?	D15	BANNING, Azbury	1835	B217
BANNING, Annie L. (Deuce	184?	L138	BANNING, Azubah	1771	E61
BANNING, Annie	1857	B240	BANNING, Azubah (Clark)	1784	E80
BANNING, Annie E.	1864	X3545	BANNING, Bando D. "Marvi	178?	E76
BANNING, Annie	1866	B774	BANNING, Barbara (???)	181?	I9
BANNING, Annie (Hepnor)	187?	D65	BANNING, Barbara	1828	B73
BANNING, Annie	1875	D64	BANNING, Barbara	1858	B229
BANNING, Annie	1883	R123	BANNING, Barbara	1908	E11906
BANNING, Annie Pearl	1892	F1459	BANNING, Barbara	193?	F7004
BANNING, Annie Mae	1904	B986a	BANNING, Barbara Jean	1931 *	C1884
BANNING, Annie May	1904	R147	BANNING, Barbara	1935	H379
BANNING, Annie Lou	1924	B998c	BANNING, Barbara Sue	1941	B9604
BANNING, Ansolette (Smith)	184?	E1618	BANNING, Barbara R.	195?	F6008
BANNING, Anthony	1740	A12	BANNING, Barbara Jean	1951	H500
BANNING, Anthony	176?	A17	BANNING, Barbara (Heggar	1953	Q152
BANNING, Anthony	1768	A25	BANNING, Basil	1928	Q98
BANNING, Anthony	1768	A29	BANNING, Basil Ray	1938 *	E10835
BANNING, Anthony	1809	A74	BANNING, Bea (???)	192?	B9606
BANNING, Anthony	1820	A229	BANNING, Beatrice (Smith	188?	B600
BANNING, Anthony Rogers	1831	A248	BANNING, Beatrice	188?	E5847
BANNING, Antonie (Schull	183?	N673	BANNING, Beatrice	189?	C295
BANNING, Antoinette (Rice)	1839	F496	BANNING, Beaulah Mae	1922	J414
BANNING, Appa (Gideon)	179?	F67	BANNING, Bell (Rutherfor	183?	G11
BANNING, Arabel	1782	F63	BANNING, Ben Franklin	1829	A234
BANNING, Araminta (???)	1751	A11	BANNING, Ben	191?	B2050
BANNING, Arba Hanson	1817	E387	BANNING, Benjamin	1740	E15
BANNING, Arabella (Jenki	185?	X3509	BANNING, Benjamin	1775	E63
BANNING, Arch Tanner	1835 *	F580	BANNING, Benjamin"Abner"	1780	F62
BANNING, Archibald	1836	F591	BANNING, Benjamin	1794	E84
BANNING, Archibald Tanne	1854	F589	BANNING, Benjamin {Rev.}	180?	L32
BANNING, Archibald Tanne	1884	F1412	BANNING, Benjamin F.	1800	E305
BANNING, Archibald Tanne	1918	F3090	BANNING, Benjamin H.	1808	F70
BANNING, Ardis Lucile	1934	F7006	BANNING, Benjamin	1813	B81
BANNING, Arlene (Knuts)	1931	C1882	BANNING, Benjamin	1816	P3
BANNING, Arlene (Baier)	1952	Q149	BANNING, Benjamin	1819	E397
BANNING, Artemsia	1867	F1205	BANNING, Benjamin A.	1820	B71
BANNING, Arthur Charles	184?	L142	BANNING, Benjamin Oscar	1829 *	F271d
BANNING, Arthur Staples	1862 *	E1586	BANNING, Benjamin	183?	I24
BANNING, Arthur Calvin	1866	C114	BANNING, Benjamin Frankl	1842	F604
BANNING, Arthur Lowber	1885	C302	BANNING, Benjamin E.	1845	P24
BANNING, Arthur	188?	Q27	BANNING, Benjamin B.	1850	B222
BANNING, Arthur	190?	F1400L	BANNING, Benjamin	186?	E1403
BANNING, Arthur Roland	1901	E11996	BANNING, Benjamin	1867	Q20
BANNING, Arthur Boyd	191?	Q60a	BANNING, Benjamin Frankl	1870	J14
BANNING, Arwilda (Oller)	187?	B308	BANNING, Benjamin Simon	1872	E1682

419

BANNING, Benjamin Blain	1889	F1414		BANNING, Calvin	1785	E67
BANNING, Benjamin	192?	F3094		BANNING, Calvin	1786	F65
BANNING, Benoni	1744	B7		BANNING, Calvin Nodate	1814	E347
BANNING, Benoni	179?	B51		BANNING, Clavin Hudson	183?	F264
BANNING, Benoni	181?	B85		BANNING, Calvin	1834	E406
BANNING, Bernice T.	188?	E6570		BANNING, Calvin	1917	E11907
BANNING, Bertha H. (Hoke	185?	C234		BANNING, Carina (Carpent	185?	F585
BANNING, Bertha Mae	1872	C561		BANNING, Carina Carpente	1881	F1402
BANNING, Bertha Lucile	1880	B607		BANNING, Carl	1899	B985b
BANNING, Bertha Mary	1881	R122		BANNING, Carl L.	1906	B2505c
BANNING, Bertha (Johnson	1886	H58b		BANNING, Carline M.	1866	B940a
BANNING, Bertha	1892	B2136		BANNING, Carlos	1823	E376
BANNING, Bertha	191?	Q91		BANNING, Carlton	188? *	A706a
BANNING, Bertha Ellen	1912	J411		BANNING, Carol Ann (Bela	1941	H376
BANNING, Bertram	1874	Q29		BANNING, Carol M. (Bradl	1947	E19113
BANNING, Bessie	1865 *	C129		BANNING, Caroline L.	1808	E309
BANNING, Bessie (Robb)	186?	B775		BANNING, Caroline (Cordi	181?	B71
BANNING, Bessie (Smith)	187?	D53		BANNING, Caroline	181?	E213
BANNING, Bessie Maxon	1877	B422		BANNING, Caroline	182?	A57
BANNING, Bessie	188?	F1514		BANNING, Caroline Louise	1852	F588
BANNING, Bessie Mary L.	188?	E4240		BANNING, Caroline	1856	A635
BANNING, Bessie D. (Lord	1883	H25		BANNING, Caroline (Picke	1877	E1682
BANNING, Bessie	1893	B2110		BANNING, Caroline Agnes	1884	B595
BANNING, Bessie (Arthur)	192?	Q93		BANNING, Carrie A.	1834	E381
BANNING, Betsy	178?	E57		BANNING, Carrie M. (Lane	184?	E1475
BANNING, Betsy (Jones)	1789	F66		BANNING, Carrie	185?	E1402
BANNING, Betsy Jane	1827	B154		BANNING, Carrie Rachel	1869	J26
BANNING, Betsy Elizabeth	1832	E405		BANNING, Carrie	187?	X13
BANNING, Betty	192?	B2055		BANNING, Cassandra	1826	B78
BANNING, Betty L. (Lobde	1929	C1918		BANNING, Cassendara	1844	B668
BANNING, Betty (Forester	1938	E19052		BANNING, Catherine C.	1820	E314
BANNING, Betty	194?	B9701		BANNING, Catherine	1823	B153
BANNING, Betty Mae	1942	E19112		BANNING, Catherine (Torr	183?	A248
BANNING, Betty Jane	1949	H499		BANNING, Catherine	1831	B164
BANNING, Beverly B.	194?	B9700		BANNING, Catherine E.	1832	B194
BANNING, Beverly Y. (Car	1949	E19107		BANNING, Catherine	1838	B180
BANNING, Beverly	194?	E19062		BANNING, Catherine Ann(?	184?	X3507
BANNING, Blanch Bayfield	1865	A675		BANNING, Catherine	1844	B668
BANNING, Blanch	188?	F1400b		BANNING, Catherine (Oxle	1849	C227
BANNING, Blanch	1886 *	G71		BANNING, Catherine	185?	H8b
BANNING, Blanch	189?	A1635		BANNING, Catherine	1851	A633
BANNING, Blanche	1853 *	F619		BANNING, Catherine	186?	X1510
BANNING, Blanche Inez	1888	C660		BANNING, Catherine {Kate	1862	B242
BANNING, Blucher	1832	A236		BANNING, Catherine (Lars	1941	C3336
BANNING, Blucher	1868	A673		BANNING, Cecilia	161?	X2007
BANNING, Bobby Harland	1937	E19047		BANNING, Cecil B.	1899	E5844
BANNING, Bodie	1861 *	B770		BANNING, Celestine	1841	E1566
BANNING, Braineard	1785	E77		BANNING, Celia Ann (Hamn	1894	J136
BANNING, Brenda Irene	1941	E19048		BANNING, Charity (Semons	174?	X2752
BANNING, Brett Alan	1975	C5671		BANNING, Charity	1763	X2992
BANNING, Brian Ray	1960	C3430		BANNING, Charity	183?	X3503
BANNING, Brian	1961	Q203		BANNING, Charity	1913	B2506a
BANNING, Bridget (McCoy)	1842	Q3		BANNING, Charles	1700	A12e
BANNING, Brooks	1848	B314d		BANNING, Charles	170?	A5f
BANNING, Bruce	192?	F3107		BANNING, Charles	1730	A34c
BANNING, Bruce Gregory	1953	E19109		BANNING, Charles	176?	C7
BANNING, Burrell	1858	B312g		BANNING, Charles	18??	E365
BANNING, Burton Alva	1879	F1509		BANNING, Charles	18??	E1026
BANNING, Byrd A.	1890	B963a		BANNING, Charles	1804 *	F207a
BANNING, Calla Almeda	1889	C556		BANNING, Charles Barber	1813	L33
BANNING, Callie Rosemari	1960	C5666		BANNING, Charles	182?	M5
BANNING, Callum	1958	Q199		BANNING, Charles	1822	F215

BANNING, Charles L.	1825 *	B106
BANNING, Charles Henry	1833	L187
BANNING, Charles	1845 *	F639
BANNING, Charles	1845	J4
BANNING, Charles H.	1845	Q4
BANNING, Charles	1850 *	F618
BANNING, Charles	1850 *	F641
BANNING, Charles Lewis	1850 *	E1615
BANNING, Charles	1857	E1571
BANNING, Charles Thomas	1866	J24
BANNING, Charles Henry	1867	E6673
BANNING, Charles	1867	G77
BANNING, Charles P.	1867 *	H24
BANNING, Charles Newton	1869	B308
BANNING, Charles T.	1869	H25
BANNING, Charles William	1869	B537
BANNING, Charles Clark	1872	B777
BANNING, Charles	1870	J32A
BANNING, Charles Hubert	1873 *	E6500
BANNING, Charles Francis	1875	R41
BANNING, Charles Henry	1876	C563
BANNING, Charles Herbert	1877	C553
BANNING, Charles	1878	B311b
BANNING, Charles Weaver	1880	B943
BANNING, Charles G.	1882	F1391
BANNING, Charles James	1885	X1011
BANNING, Charles	1891	C590
BANNING, Charles Floyd	1892	J71
BANNING, Charles Henry	1896	E12588
BANNING, Charles H.	190?	J65
BANNING, Charles Henry	1905	H121
BANNING, Charles William	1908	R149
BANNING, Charles	1915	A1644
BANNING, Charles Wesley	1918 *	E10805
BANNING, Charles	193?	A3593
BANNING, Charles B.	194?	J421
BANNING, Charles Richard	1963	H783
BANNING, Charlotta	1824	E400
BANNING, Charlotte (Perr	1820	E348
BANNING, Charlotte	1825	B132
BANNING, Charlotte (Davi	1829	E312
BANNING, Charlotte (Wate	183?	L184
BANNING, Charlotte (Herr	184?	B225
BANNING, Charlotte (Hens	185?	B109
BANNING, Charlotte (Bart	187?	E6673
BANNING, Charlotte	1871	B572
BANNING, Chartery Gertru	177?	C18
BANNING, Chauncy Henry	1840	E1004
BANNING, Cheri L. (Johns	1949	E19102
BANNING, Cherry Lynn	1961	H784
BANNING, Christina (Gree	183?	B156
BANNING, Christina (Chad	187?	C563
BANNING, Christina (Tora	1938	Q186
BANNING, Christina Louis	1967	F12000
BANNING, Christine W.M.	1733	N15
BANNING, Christine Maria	1757	N58
BANNING, Christine	1873	J16
BANNING, Cindy Lane	1971	H840
BANNING, Cissy T. (Agler	194?	H333
BANNING, Clair C.	1864	D50
BANNING, Claire Marie	1941	H381
BANNING, Clara	18??	E1405
BANNING, Clara (Ansleman	186?	A636
BANNING, Clara	1862	B311a
BANNING, Clara M. (Oller	1865	B243
BANNING, Clara	1870 *	R32
BANNING, Clara Jane	1873	F762
BANNING, Clara L. (Wahre	188?	B599
BANNING, Clara May	1880 *	E1683
BANNING, Clara Grace	1885	R124
BANNING, Clara Elizabeth	1900	E6895
BANNING, Clara Irene	1901	J73
BANNING, Clara Louise	1903	B1789
BANNING, Clare (Witte)	187?	N1679
BANNING, Clarence Elton	192?	J423
BANNING, Clarence Nelson	1846	E1355
BANNING, Clarence Edwin	1859	E5689
BANNING, Clarence	187?	G80
BANNING, Clarence Edgar	1889	E11022
BANNING, Clarence Elton	192?	J416
BANNING, Clarissa	178?	E58
BANNING, Clarissa (Corwi	1780	E63
BANNING, Clarissa	1781	E68
BANNING, Clarissa	1831 *	E404
BANNING, Clarissa 2nd	1845	E413
BANNING, Clark	1769	B13
BANNING, Clark	1802	B53
BANNING, Clark	181?	B83
BANNING, Clark	1813	B89a
BANNING, Clark	1821	B70
BANNING, Clark	1840	B202
BANNING, Clark	1843	B227
BANNING, Clark	1850	B238
BANNING, Clark A.	1856	P28
BANNING, Clark	1864	B569
BANNING, Clark	1867 *	B781
BANNING, Claud Percival	187?	G82
BANNING, Clay Ogle	1895	B1748
BANNING, Clementina	177?	A24
BANNING, Cleopatra	188?	F1512
BANNING, Clifford Owen	1907	G169
BANNING, Climena A.	1824	F271b
BANNING, Clinton Kerby	1880	A693
BANNING, Clinton James	197?	Q242
BANNING, Cloid Francis	1883	E5614
BANNING, Clum	1862 *	A658
BANNING, Clyde Eugene	1925	B9607
BANNING, Cole Lowber	1834	C29
BANNING, Colin	197?	Q241
BANNING, Colleen	1947	Q200
BANNING, Connie Lea	1955	C5664
BANNING, Constance (Holt	187?	L467
BANNING, Constance	193?	F3108
BANNING, Converse	1830	F258
BANNING, Cora	185?	E1398
BANNING, Cora Ada (Vance	186?	C237
BANNING, Cora Bell	1861	E5690
BANNING, Cora Bell	1868	B768
BANNING, Cora A. (Presto	1875	B311
BANNING, Cora	189?	F1400f
BANNING, Cora Ethel	1891	C301
BANNING, Cora (Jester)	1900	H58d
BANNING, Cornelia Ann	1815	F245
BANNING, Cornelia (???)	183?	X3800

Name	Year	Code
BANNING, Cornelia	1843	F592
BANNING, Cornelia	1848	B669
BANNING, Cory Eugene	1962	C5670
BANNING, Cory	197?	Q243
BANNING, Courtland	1879	G85
BANNING, Cowdry	1837	F288
BANNING, Craig Francis	1966	E39024
BANNING, Craig Allan	197?	Q240
BANNING, Cynthia (Cuisak	184?	G18
BANNING, Cynthia Ellen	1858	B143
BANNING, Cynthia Kaye	1958	C3408
BANNING, Cynthia Maria	1966	H843
BANNING, Cyrus Walker	1853	B141
BANNING, Cyrus Walker	1888	B611
BANNING, Dahlgren	1888	F1404
BANNING, Dale	194?	B26014
BANNING, Dale	194?	J419
BANNING, Dale Edward	1950	C3427
BANNING, Dale Bruce	1954	C5663
BANNING, Daniel	177?	X1
BANNING, Daniel	1723	X2636
BANNING, Daniel	1747	X2758
BANNING, Daniel	1785	L36
BANNING, Daniel	1858	X1007
BANNING, Daniel G.	1859	H8a
BANNING, Daniel	187?	X1538
BANNING, Daniel	1919 *	H143
BANNING, Danny	1948	Q197
BANNING, Darlene (Knight)	1938	Q150
BANNING, Darrell	1892	A708
BANNING, David	1756	F21
BANNING, David	1800	E360
BANNING, David	1819	F253
BANNING, David Lay	1838	E1475
BANNING, David	1847	F273
BANNING, David	1850	C231
BANNING, David E.	1851	Q6
BANNING, David B.	1853	P27
BANNING, David	1856	B228
BANNING, David Lincoln	1861	J9
BANNING, David Jasper	1870	
BANNING, David	1874	Q23
BANNING, David Alfred	1874	C562
BANNING, David Fletcher	1885	F1456
BANNING, David Benjamin	1914	C1916
BANNING, David	1921	Q84
BANNING, David	1931	Q100
BANNING, David Jacob	1971	E39071
BANNING, Debora (Reed)	173?	E14
BANNING, Deborah (Perry)	172?	A9
BANNING, Deborah	176?	A21
BANNING, Deborah (Cary)	184?	C229
BANNING, Deborah A. (Tip	1962	E19109
BANNING, Delbert	189?	X1545
BANNING, Delema Mae	1927	H329
BANNING, Delila	1841	B297a
BANNING, Delilah (Davison)	184?	F236
BANNING, Della	186?	E1629
BANNING, Delores Jane	192?	J426
BANNING, Delores	1932	E19070
BANNING, Delos B.	1852 *	X11
BANNING, Denney (Crosby)	1790	F63
BANNING, Dennis F.	1851	B314e
BANNING, Dennis	1941	Q182
BANNING, Dennis Gene	1945	C3423
BANNING, Dewey	190?	J64
BANNING, Dexter	1816	F213
BANNING, Dexter	1850	F563
BANNING, Diana Rae	1960	C5669
BANNING, Dice Ann (???)	181?	B81
BANNING, Dola	1892	B963b
BANNING, Dolphus A.	1820	B72
BANNING, Dolphus	1839	B226
BANNING, Dolphus	1840	B234
BANNING, Donald	1875	B573
BANNING, Donna R. (Walke	1934	C3334
BANNING, Donna (Jay)	194?	Q182
BANNING, Donna G. (Montg	1957	C19066
BANNING, Donna S. (Webb)	1956	H505
BANNING, Dora (Barnes)	1853	X3508
BANNING, Dora (Beach)	186?	F1202
BANNING, Dora	1860	F682
BANNING, Dora A. (???)	1864	B237d
BANNING, Dora	187?	F1505
BANNING, Dora	1875	B748
BANNING, Dora (Runyan)	186?	R121
BANNING, Dora Mae	1925	E10829
BANNING, Dorcy (Crosby)	1790	F63
BANNING, Doreen (???)	192?	B9607
BANNING, Doris Ellen	1916	C1877
BANNING, Doris Aileen	1925 *	H324
BANNING, Dorothy (Hale)	172?	X2639
BANNING, Dorothy	1881	E6321
BANNING, Dorothy	189?	E9906
BANNING, Dorothy (Sander	1891	E6319
BANNING, Dorothy (Dalton	191?	B997d
BANNING, Dorothy	191?	B2053
BANNING, Dorothy	191?	B2115
BANNING, Dorothy (Rust)	1911	H174
BANNING, Dorothy Jean	192?	J427
BANNING, Dorothy Ann (Mc	1928	H374
BANNING, Dorothy M.	193?	J416
BANNING, Dorris (Laster)	B263	E19047
BANNING, Dotice (Branble	179?	E84
BANNING, Doty (Aoss)	190?	B985a
BANNING, Dovie A.	1889	B991b
BANNING, Dravey Lee	1943	C3422
BANNING, Duane Edison	1918	C1878
BANNING, Dudley Wills	1830 *	F610
BANNING, E. Lennis (Ridg	1913	E10802
BANNING, Earl Hudson	1880 *	E6675
BANNING, Earl Hudson	1893	E12586
BANNING, Earl Bryan	1896	C662
BANNING, Earl	1898	Q56
BANNING, Earl James	1930	E10810
BANNING, Ebenezer	1745	E17
BANNING, Ebenezer	178?	E55
BANNING, Edgar "Edward"	185?	E1583
BANNING, Edgar	1859 *	A657
BANNING, Edgar	1875	Q36
BANNING, Edith (Cowdry)	1810	F67
BANNING, Edith Elmina	1833	F286
BANNING, Edith	1836	F272a
BANNING, Edith Spencer	1860	K2935

BANNING, Edith Lillian	1880	C564
BANNING, Edith	1881	B602
BANNING, Edith	1906	B997a
BANNING, Edith L. (Morri	195?	H503
BANNING, Edmund Prior	1810	F242
BANNING, Edmund Prior	1838	F602
BANNING, Edmund Prior	1845	F585
BANNING, Edmund Wasson	1881	F1454
BANNING, Edna Marie	1870	F1474
BANNING, Edna May (???)	187?	G68
BANNING, Edna Leona	1888	C300
BANNING, Edna	188?	F1400c
BANNING, Edna	189?	P138
BANNING, Edna	1898	B2508
BANNING, Edna	190?	H114
BANNING, Edna	1909	Q60
BANNING, Edna (Roth)	1909	A1653
BANNING, Edna M.	1918	H125
BANNING, Edna Belle	1919	J205
BANNING, Edward B.	165?	A3,K127
BANNING, Edward Jr.	168?	A5b
BANNING, Edward III	170?	A12g
BANNING, Edward	178? *	K613
BANNING, Edward	1857	E1572
BANNING, Edward	187?	F1451
BANNING, Edward Sherman	187?	E5810
BANNING, Edward James	1873	G24
BANNING, Edward	189?	X1544
BANNING, Edwin Hall	1802	E306
BANNING, Edwin Rutherfor	1815	F261
BANNING, Edwin	1839 *	L189
BANNING, Edwin Rutherfor	1842	F642
BANNING, Edwin F.	185?	I71
BANNING, Edwin Thomas	1864	E1587
BANNING, Edwin {Winnie}	1879	R121
BANNING, Edwin George	1923	R357
BANNING, Edyth (???)	188?	B751
BANNING, Effie Viola	1868	C115
BANNING, Effie (Marrow)	187?	B573
BANNING, Effie	190?	Q65
BANNING, Effie K. (Ginde	1910	G169
BANNING, Eido (Aoss)	190?	B985a
BANNING, Eleanor (???)	1724	F6
BANNING, Eleanor Ann	1893	C315
BANNING, Eleanor Muriel	1950	Q151
BANNING, Electa L.	1812	F211
BANNING, Eleen (Hardy)	190?	Q59
BANNING, Elgin	1941	Q102
BANNING, Elianor Bell	1756	A102b
BANNING, Elias	183?	B294
BANNING, Elijah	1807	F243
BANNING, Elijah	1832	B94
BANNING, Elinor	182?	L124
BANNING, Eliphalet G.	1820	X3800
BANNING, Elisa	18??	E370
BANNING, Elisa Jane	1866	J11
BANNING, Elisha	1778	E65
BANNING, Elisha	179?	P0
BANNING, Elisha	180? *	F241
BANNING, Elisha	181?	P4
BANNING, Elisha W.	1810 *	E310
BANNING, Eliss	1863	306

BANNING, Eliza (???)	1680	E4
BANNING, Eliza (Fox)	183?	E403
BANNING, Eliza (Blacksto	1805	A70
BANNING, Eliza	1806	L50
BANNING, Eliza J. (Barr)	181?	B86
BANNING, Eliza	181?	L116
BANNING, Eliza Patterson	181?	L35
BANNING, Eliza (Bowman)	183?	B129
BANNING, Eliza A. (Smith	183?	F591
BANNING, Eliza (Nickles)	183?	J1
BANNING, Eliza A. (Smeed	183?	L187
BANNING, Eliza Ann (Ande	1832	B32
BANNING, Eliza Ellen	1857	R36
BANNING, Eliza Alice	1860	J23
BANNING, Eliza Jane	1866	J11
BANNING, Eliza	1871	A684
BANNING, Eliza Mary	1880 *	G66
BANNING, Elizabeth (???)	15??	K2
BANNING, Elizabeth	15??	K6
BANNING, Elizabeth (Noye	16??	K126
BANNING, Elizabeth	163?	X2011
BANNING, Elizabeth	169?	A5e
BANNING, Elizabeth	1694	X2545
BANNING, Elizabeth	1695	K231
BANNING, Elizabeth	1705	E3
BANNING, Elizabeth	1731	A34d
BANNING, Elizabeth (Alfo	174?	C5
BANNING, Elizabeth	1751 *	K353
BANNING, Elizabeth (Blac	176?	B9
BANNING, Elizabeth	1772	B14
BANNING, Elizabeth	177?	C14
BANNING, Elizabeth	177?	X2996
BANNING, Elizabeth	1776 *	K607
BANNING, Elizabeth (Nort	178?	K610
BANNING, Elizabeth	1781	K611
BANNING, Elizabeth (Alli	1784	B17
BANNING, Elizabeth	1792	L28
BANNING, Elizabeth (Lowb	1794	C12
BANNING, Elizabeth (Kand	180?	N266
BANNING, Elizabeth	1803	A71
BANNING, Elizabeth (Smith	1805	B52
BANNING, Elizabeth A. (B	1806	B20
BANNING, Elizabeth	181?	C21
BANNING, Elizabeth	181?	B83
BANNING, Elizabeth	1811	B58
BANNING, Elizabeth (???)	1814	X3500
BANNING, Elizabeth (Rigg	1819	B43
BANNING, Elizabeth	1819	E374
BANNING, Elizabeth Watso	182?	I10
BANNING, Elizabeth (Curt	1820	B93
BANNING, Elizabeth Marth	1820	K1271
BANNING, Elizabeth (Mart	1823	B69
BANNING, Elizabeth (???)	183?	N674
BANNING, Elizabeth (Crawf	183?	X3501
BANNING, Elizabeth Griff	1830	B108
BANNING, Elizabeth (Carp	1832	K1267
BANNING, Elizabeth Ann	1833	B216
BANNING, Elizabeth	1834	B289
BANNING, Elizabeth	1835	B199
BANNING, Elizabeth Black	1837	A252
BANNING, Elizabeth Ann	1837	B224
BANNING, Elizabeth (McKe	184?	E1393

423

BANNING, Elizabeth (Sanf	184?	E1004	BANNING, Ellen {Nell}	1906	F2624
BANNING, Elizabeth Emma	1840	F583	BANNING, Ellert	189?	F1535
BANNING, Elizabeth	1841	B297	BANNING, Elli	1864	N1677
BANNING, Elizabeth (Broc	1841	E1399	BANNING, Elli	1890	N3682
BANNING, Elizabeth	1843	B130	BANNING, Elmer	188?	G83
BANNING, Elizabeth Ann	1843	B213	BANNING, Elmina	1807	F73
BANNING, Elizabeth	1843	C257	BANNING, Elmina	1833	F286
BANNING, Elizabeth Jane	1844	C230	BANNING, Elodia Adella	1852	E6400
BANNING, Elizabeth Mary	1847	B138	BANNING, Elon Agustus	185?	E1581
BANNING, Elizabeth (John	185?	B278	BANNING, Elsie	1869	B571
BANNING, Elizabeth	185?	E1582	BANNING, Elvira	1847	B275
BANNING, Elizabeth	1850	X3802	BANNING, Elwood Irving	19??	H115
BANNING, Elizabeth Alexa	1853	G21	BANNING, Emelin Harriet	1835	E1002
BANNING, Elizabeth (???)	186?	J24	BANNING, Emeline	1849	E1570
BANNING, Elizabeth	1860	B237c	BANNING, Emeline (Reno)	186?	G77
BANNING, Elizabeth	1865	B773	BANNING, Emeling	183?	B295
BANNING, Elizabeth	1865 *	C129	BANNING, Emely Kathryn	1898	C303
BANNING, Elizabeth	1866	J31c	BANNING, Emerett Turner	1842	E1394
BANNING, Elizabeth (???)	1873	R38	BANNING, Emerett Turner	1875	E5805
BANNING, Elizabeth (Harp	188?	A688	BANNING, Emilie Jenne	1910	B1791
BANNING, Elizabeth Georg	1881	F1411	BANNING, Emily (Wells)	18??	E371
BANNING, Elizabeth (Bart	189?	A707	BANNING, Emily (Wells)	180?	E306
BANNING, Elizabeth	1927	A1666	BANNING, Emily	1804 *	A49
BANNING, Elizabeth Jane	1929	H326	BANNING, Emily (Miller)	1806	F69
BANNING, Elizabeth	193?	A3594	BANNING, Emily	1810	E364
BANNING, Elizabeth A.	1932	C797	BANNING, Emily L. (???)	1823	F263
BANNING, Elizabeth (Krau	195?	F6007	BANNING, Emily (Eschenbu	1825	A51
BANNING, Elizabeth	1952	Q201	BANNING, Emily Z.	1827	F271c
BANNING, Elizabeth Ann	1966	E39071	BANNING, Emily (Brown)	1832	E402
BANNING, Elizabeth Brydi	1988	C8600	BANNING, Emily Marie	1837	E1384
BANNING, Elizanne	1841 *	C226	BANNING, Emily Laura	1842	F584
BANNING, Ella C.	1852	F629	BANNING, Emily L.	1843	F287a
BANNING, Ella May	1855	E4201	BANNING, Emily	1845	L201
BANNING, Ella E. (King)	1856	E1644	BANNING, Emily (Nash)	1847	C25
BANNING, Ella	1858	B310	BANNING, Emily (Jenne)	185?	B139
BANNING, Ella (Jones)	186?	C143	BANNING, Emily Ann	1987	H1023
BANNING, Ella (Fisher)	186?	P29	BANNING, Emma	1807	A55
BANNING, Ella Pelina	1867	E1680	BANNING, Emma	1818 *	K1266
BANNING, Ella Bell	1869	B586	BANNING, Emma (Waters)	182?	L120
BANNING, Ella Kirby	187?	A692	BANNING, Emma	182?	K1270
BANNING, Ella (Pichforth	188?	B609	BANNING, Emma	183?	I18
BANNING, Ella May	1881	G88	BANNING, Emma Elmira	1836 *	F581
BANNING, Ella F. (Reed)	189?	R125	BANNING, Emma	1839	L188
BANNING, Ella (???)	190?	B986	BANNING, Emma	184? *	B121
BANNING, Ellen (Anderson	178?	L27	BANNING, Emma	184?	E1622
BANNING, Ellen (What)	179?	I2	BANNING, Emma	184?	D16
BANNING, Ellen	183?	C95	BANNING, Emma (Barlow)	184?	F644
BANNING, Ellen Clarissa	1836	E1617	BANNING, Emma (Harris)	185?	A144
BANNING, Ellen E.	1837	E382	BANNING, Emma Marvin	1850	E1481
BANNING, Ellen (Tyler)	1842	R7	BANNING, Emma (McCauley)	186?	X1511
BANNING, Ellen Amelia	1845	E1395	BANNING, Emma Blanch	1860	R37
BANNING, Ellen Minerva	1845	E1610	BANNING, Emma	1868	J32
BANNING, Ellen E.	1845	I66	BANNING, Emma E. (White)	1862	C231
BANNING, Ellen E.	1846	E1354	BANNING, Emma	1867	B536
BANNING, Ellen Maria	1848 *	E1006	BANNING, Emma Frances	1867	X14
BANNING, Ellen	1849	C80d	BANNING, Emma (Willard)	187?	E6674
BANNING, Ellen	185?	E1580	BANNING, Emma	188?	F1511
BANNING, Ellen (Burnham)	1850	E1581	BANNING, Emma Gertrude	1887	F1457
BANNING, Ellen Burrows	1853	C97	BANNING, Emma L. (Weilan	1889	C578
BANNING, Ellen Maria	1867	F1210	BANNING, Emmett Vore	1868	A676
BANNING, Ellen Merrman	1874 *	C132	BANNING, Emmett	1904	A1638
BANNING, Ellen	189?	E5845	BANNING, Emily	1843	F287a

Name	Year	Code
BANNING, Enos F.	1854	B314f
BANNING, Ephraim	1811	B35
BANNING, Ephraim Henry	1823	E316
BANNING, Ephraim	1834	B131
BANNING, Ephraim	1849	B139
BANNING, Ephraim Newton	1864	B584
BANNING, Ephraim Pinkney	1872	B591
BANNING, Ephraim III	1885	B600
BANNING, Ephraim	1898	B1751
BANNING, Ephraim IV	1913	B1792
BANNING, Erastus Millard	1812	E372
BANNING, Erastus Millard	1843	E1567
BANNING, Erica Maria	1988	H1499
BANNING, Erika L. (Hoyle	191?	C1826
BANNING, Ernest Ludwig	175?	N49
BANNING, Ernest	186?	E1630
BANNING, Ernest Ray	1889	C578
BANNING, Ernestine Marga	1724	N11
BANNING, Ernst Johann A.	1721	N9
BANNING, Ernst Bernhard	1726	N12
BANNING, Ernst Muritz	1767	N60
BANNING, Ernst Bernhard	1796	N266
BANNING, Estella	1856	F1203
BANNING, Estella	1860	F633
BANNING, Estella	1876	X3560
BANNING, Estella (Harris	1907	C1827
BANNING, Estelle (Moffit	191?	B997c
BANNING, Estelle (York)	1935	B1792
BANNING, Ester (Wilson)	171?	C3
BANNING, Ester (Westley)	175?	K352
BANNING, Ester	176?	C9
BANNING, Ester	177?	C15
BANNING, Ester Ely	1849	E1396
BANNING, Ester May	1904	E6896
BANNING, Esther (Acton)	175?	B6
BANNING, Esther	1798 *	L46
BANNING, Esther Abigal	1859	Q7
BANNING, Ethel Isabel	1882	G84
BANNING, Ethel May	1888	G186
BANNING, Ethel (Chism)	190?	B985b
BANNING, Ethel K. (Moore	1909	H121
BANNING, Ethel	191?	H139
BANNING, Ethel (Compton)	1921	F7003
BANNING, Etta Luella	1869	C560
BANNING, Etta E. (Crain)	1911	J136
BANNING, Eugene	1863	B780
BANNING, Eunice (Nichols	1778	F56
BANNING, Eunice (Beckwit	1786	E67
BANNING, Eunice	181?	F204
BANNING, Eunice Beckwith	1818	E349
BANNING, Eunice	1837	F499
BANNING, Eva Dora	1857	B310A
BANNING, Eva (Ralston)	186?	E5688
BANNING, Eva Louise	1867	F1473
BANNING, Eva (Pfeiffer)	187?	A666
BANNING, Eva	189?	J149
BANNING, Evangeline (Gau	187?	C102
BANNING, Evangeline Ruth	189?	C294
BANNING, Evangeline (Gri	189?	C299
BANNING, Evans	185? *	C98
BANNING, Evelin Harriet	1835	E1002
BANNING, Evelyn (???)	190?	F1418
BANNING, Evelyn Dorothy	1905	H133
BANNING, Evelyn (Winches	1909	R148
BANNING, Everett	1902	E6893
BANNING, Exa	1904	B997
BANNING, Fannie Loulla	1863	E1650
BANNING, Fannie Mira	1868	F1495
BANNING, Fannie	187? *	E5692
BANNING, Fannie	1900	B1680
BANNING, Fanny {Betsy}	1786	E57
BANNING, Fanny (Kenney)	1800	E81
BANNING, Fanny Alice	1833	C28
BANNING, Fanny	1844	E1386
BANNING, Fanny A.	1855 *	C126
BANNING, Fanny (Raymond)	1861	A263
BANNING, Fanny	1872	X3806a
BANNING, Fay	1874	B782
BANNING, Felix H.W.	1861	N1676
BANNING, Felix H.W.	1895	N3684
BANNING, Flora (Hutchens	184?	F582
BANNING, Flora	1856	F565
BANNING, Flora Corinne	1917	A1655
BANNING, Florilla (Lane)	181?	F208
BANNING, Florence Isabel	1852	E1357
BANNING, Florence (Ballo	187?	B589
BANNING, Florence	1870	D63
BANNING, Florence Elizab	1877	X15
BANNING, Florence (Ashdo	188?	G82
BANNING, Florence May	1886	C569
BANNING, Florence (Johns	1895	C314
BANNING, Florens Ludwig	179?	N267
BANNING, Florida (Morrel	184?	F585
BANNING, Florida Jennett	1883	F1403
BANNING, Francenia A.	1855 *	C126
BANNING, Frances	1702	K233
BANNING, Frances (Neal)	1752	K351
BANNING, Frances (Bull)	181?	E313
BANNING, Frances (Perkin	182?	X2
BANNING, Frances (Lynch)	183?	G10
BANNING, Frances Sill	1836	E1473
BANNING, Frances (VanDri	184?	F602
BANNING, Frances Theidos	1844	L459
BANNING, Frances Wells	1844	E1386
BANNING, Frances M.	1845	B214
BANNING, Frances E.(Trui	1856	H8c
BANNING, Frances	1880	J34A
BANNING, Frances Mary	1888	G183
BANNING, Frances Ann	1927	H325
BANNING, Frances (Herald	194?	E19069
BANNING, Francinia	1833	C28
BANNING, Francis Merrian	1892	F1458
BANNING, Francis	1894	B964
BANNING, Francis R.	1895	A708
BANNING, Francis	193?	B2056
BANNING, Frank	18??	E5836
BANNING, Frank Almon	18??	F651
BANNING, Frank	182?	M2
BANNING, Frank	185?	E1612
BANNING, Frank	1857	F632
BANNING, Frank	1861	A263
BANNING, Frank	1863	E6402
BANNING, Frank Low	1869 *	E6360
BANNING, Frank	187?	E4208

425

BANNING, Frank	1873	A674		BANNING, George Wright	1891	F1415
BANNING, Frank Marchant	1876 *	B421		BANNING, George Albert	1894	E6365
BANNING, Frank	1878	A669		BANNING, George Hugh	1895	C316
BANNING, Frank	189?	F1400g		BANNING, George Caldwell	1904	E12585
BANNING, Frank Wesley	1896	E5618		BANNING, George	191?	F3081
BANNING, Frank	190?	J67		BANNING, George Oakley	1910	H136
BANNING, Frank	1915	F2621a		BANNING, George V.	1917	F3081
BANNING, Franklin	1850	B237		BANNING, George C.	1931	H375
BANNING, Franklin B.	1850	F645		BANNING, George L.	194?	J420
BANNING, Frazier	1781	B17		BANNING, Georgiana Mary	1849	F587
BANNING, Frazier	1786	B26		BANNING, Georgiana Blanc	1875	F1475
BANNING, Frazier	1804	B54		BANNING, Georgina	185?	X502
BANNING, Frazier A.	1835	B217		BANNING, Gerald	1907	Q80
BANNING, Frazier	1840	B235a		BANNING, Gerard	1945	Q183
BANNING, Fred	192?	F3094		BANNING, Gertrude	178?	C18
BANNING, Frederick Mauri	1760	N59		BANNING, Gertrude (Ellis	1867	A673
BANNING, Frederick	182?	M6		BANNING, Gertrude Ula	187?	E5811
BANNING, Frederick	183?	I17		BANNING, Gertrude (West)	1896	C565
BANNING, Frederick Josep	1834	L197		BANNING, Getrude	189?	G170
BANNING, Frederick	185?	E1400		BANNING, Gladys (Armstro	189?	C316
BANNING, Frederick Ellsw	1862	E1628		BANNING, Gladys Ida	1900	R126
BANNING, Frederick Dunle	1865	C101		BANNING, Gladys Zenora	1906	E10801
BANNING, Frederick	188?	C292		BANNING, Gladys Pauline	1930	C1883
BANNING, Frederick Leroy	1881	E1684		BANNING, Glen Dale	1925	C918
BANNING, Freeborn	1777	A23		BANNING, Glen David	1959	E19110
BANNING, Friederike (Sme	176?	N60		BANNING, Glenn Oliver	1972	H832
BANNING, Friedrich	1729	N13		BANNING, Golda Grace	190?	F3351
BANNING, Gail	189?	F1400d		BANNING, Gordon Hall	1845	F643
BANNING, Gardiner	184?	B665		BANNING, Grace	187? *	E5693
BANNING, Garnette Ely	1869	E5803		BANNING, Grace	1879	C554
BANNING, Gartery G.	178?	C18		BANNING, Grace (Edison)	188?	B601
BANNING, Gary	195?	E19064		BANNING, Grace	188?	F1400a
BANNING, Gaylord	1828	F216		BANNING, Grace Ann (Weil	1883	C553
BANNING, Gene	194?	J422		BANNING, Grace Violet	1904	J74
BANNING, Geneva Emily	1913	H175		BANNING, Grace (Michelso	191?	H124
BANNING, George	1804	F202		BANNING, Grace Bell	1917	J413
BANNING, George W.	1815	E313		BANNING, Grant	1864	F566
BANNING, George	1824	E388		BANNING, Granville	181? *	F247
BANNING, George	1823	E211		BANNING, Granville	1848	F606
BANNING, George	1827	A233		BANNING, Greenberg A.	1826	I11
BANNING, George	183?	E1380		BANNING, Greenbury	178?	R1
BANNING, George	183?	I22		BANNING, Greenbury	180?	R2
BANNING, George Edward	1831	F611		BANNING, Greenbury	1830	R7
BANNING, George Wilson	1833 *	E1383		BANNING, Gretchen	197?	F9970
BANNING, George Sylveste	1836	F601		BANNING, Guy	189?	F1516
BANNING, George Wilmarth	1840	E1614		BANNING, Hancock	1866	C125
BANNING, George Wilson	1840 *	E1385		BANNING, Hancock	1892	C314
BANNING, George	1843	A262		BANNING, Hancock 3rd	1921	C795
BANNING, George	1845	X3507		BANNING, Hanna Luella	1852	F625
BANNING, George Edward	1846	G18		BANNING, Hannah (Jones)	169?	A5d
BANNING, George Osborn	1848	E1611		BANNING, Hannah (Broadma	169?	X2543
BANNING, George P.	1854	I72		BANNING, Hannah	1718	X2633
BANNING, George W.	1861	P29		BANNING, Hannah	1720	F8
BANNING, George	1862	E1575		BANNING, Hannah	1721	F6
BANNING, George	1866	J31D		BANNING, Hannah (Clowes)	173?	L3
BANNING, George Wheelock	1869	E6672		BANNING, Hannah	1746 *	X2757
BANNING, George	187?	X16		BANNING, Hannah	1750	F19
BANNING, George W.	187? *	X1513		BANNING, Hannah	1750	X2760
BANNING, George	187?	X1539		BANNING, Hannah	176?	F53
BANNING, George	1870	A666		BANNING, Hannah (Coe)	1766	F21
BANNING, George H.	1870	H26		BANNING, Hannah	177?	B10
BANNING, George	1877	B701		BANNING, Hannah	1796	L45

BANNING, Hannah (Moore)	1817	E387	BANNING, Helen C. (Vroom	1890	F1410
BANNING, Hannah (Poctier	183?	L197	BANNING, Helen (Barnes)	189?	C316
BANNING, Hannah Moore	1845	E1620	BANNING, Helen	189?	C324
BANNING, Hannah (Stebbin	185?	C260	BANNING, Helen (Richmond)	190?	E5844
BANNING, Hannah W. (Appe	1895	C558	BANNING, Helen	191?	B2051
BANNING, Hans	1893 *	N3683	BANNING, Helen Cameron	1919	F3080
BANNING, Harlene Elizabe	1926	R358	BANNING, Helen (Robertso	192?	R357
BANNING, Harley Ceres	1892	J137	BANNING, Helen Irene(Tod	1924	E10822
BANNING, Harold	1889	A700	BANNING, Helen Marlene	1940	E10825
BANNING, Harold Edwin	1901	F3375	BANNING, Helen (Paolini)	1908	Q81
BANNING, Harold	1904	Q58	BANNING, Helen	1938	Q101
BANNING, Harold Lavern	1917	C1917	BANNING, Hellen (Oliver)	184?	C29
BANNING, Harold Laverne	192?	J424	BANNING, Hellen Laura	187?	L362
BANNING, Harriet (Dudley	1807	L31	BANNING, Hellmuth	1898	N3685
BANNING, Harriet (Thomas	177?	A23	BANNING, Henrich Ernst	1833	N673
BANNING, Harriet	1801	F206	BANNING, Henrietta	187?	E1027
BANNING, Harriet (French	1806	F203	BANNING, Henry	172?	A36d
BANNING, Harriet (Oitman	182?	E376	BANNING, Henry	1736	A11
BANNING, Harriet (Borden	1824	F214	BANNING, Henry	175?	A18
BANNING, Harriet (Hubbar	183?	B175	BANNING, Henry	1790	B21
BANNING, Harriet H.(???	183?	B223	BANNING, Henry	1792	B24
BANNING, Harriet	1849	L203	BANNING, Henry	187? *	E368
BANNING, Harriet Butler	1855	E1483	BANNING, Henry 2nd	187?	E369
BANNING, Harriett	1856	B121a	BANNING, Henry	1801	B30
BANNING, Harriet	1873	F1213	BANNING, Henry Seabury	1810	E386
BANNING, Harry	1889	G187	BANNING, Henry	1814	B60
BANNING, Harry	182?	M7	BANNING, Henry Bousley	1814	J1
BANNING, Harry Bryon	1870	A691	BANNING, Henry Geddes	1816	A51
BANNING, Harry Elmer	1879	H58a	BANNING, Henry	182?	L125
BANNING, Harry	1881	C147	BANNING, Henry E.	1823	E316
BANNING, Harry	190?	F1400k	BANNING, Henry	1825	C24
BANNING, Harry Cannon	1915	H174	BANNING, Henry	183?	I20
BANNING, Harry	1863 *	F623	BANNING, Henry	1831	A117
BANNING, Harvy	1852	B312d	BANNING, Henry	1835	B290
BANNING, Hattie (???	185?	P27	BANNING, Henry Blackston	1836	A251
BANNING, Hattie Estella	1881	E6547	BANNING, Henry P.	1836	J3
BANNING, Hattie Marie	1871	J27	BANNING, Henry Clay	1837	E1613
BANNING, Hattie	1873	F1213	BANNING, Henry Thomas	1844	L138
BANNING, Hattie	1899	J140	BANNING, Henry	1849 *	A261
BANNING, Hattie R.(Sharp	1910	E10804	BANNING, Henry	1856 *	C142
BANNING, Hazel	1889	A706	BANNING, Henry	187?	F1506
BANNING, Hazel	1895	B2137	BANNING, Henry Durce	187?	L361
BANNING, Hazel Alice	1897	J139	BANNING, Henry	1876	Q24
BANNING, Hazel Pearl	1903	J203	BANNING, Henry Burton S.	1877	L467
BANNING, Hazel L. (Clint	1927	B9600	BANNING, Henry Geddes	1880	A413
BANNING, Hazel Joyce	1928	E10833	BANNING, Henry	1888	J135
BANNING, Heather Ann	1966	H830	BANNING, Henry	1895	B985
BANNING, Hector	178?	F70	BANNING, Henry	1906	D170
BANNING, Hedwig (Briesse	1883	E6319	BANNING, Henry Ellis	1918	J415
BANNING, Heinrich	1868	N1679	BANNING, Hepsy (Manwarri	187?	E1681
BANNING, Helen	18??	A1571	BANNING, Herbert	185?	E1401
BANNING, Helen (Lacy)	180?	L32	BANNING, Herbert Ernest	186?	E5809
BANNING, Helen Lucetta	1833	E1508	BANNING, Herbert	1868	F1450
BANNING, Helen	184?	L139	BANNING, Herbert	192?	Q93
BANNING, Helen (Wheelock	184?	E1614	BANNING, Herman A.	187?	X1533
BANNING, Helen Sophia	1848 *	E1007	BANNING, Herman E.	1873	B311
BANNING, Helen J. (Melle	1850	E1480	BANNING, Hermine	1900	N3691
BANNING, Helen	186?	A637	BANNING, Hester	184?	D17
BANNING, Helen (Ford)	186?	G76	BANNING, Hettie	1900	B2508a
BANNING, Helen Emily	187?	X1540	BANNING, Hetty	178? *	K614
BANNING, Helen	1881	E6320	BANNING, Hetty J.(Rober	183?	B134
BANNING, Helen Ruth	1883 *	B603	BANNING, Hetty May	1873	B588

BANNING, Hilda Jane	1900	Q57	
BANNING, Hilda (???)	192?	C1881	
BANNING, Hildegard	1913	B1845	
BANNING, Hildred(Spence)	1915	H174	
BANNING, Hiram B.	1848	F644	
BANNING, Homer	1902	H119	
BANNING, Hope	189?	A1636	
BANNING, Horace	1825	E377	
BANNING, Horatio	1834	B114	
BANNING, Howard E.	1859	F1204	
BANNING, Howard Smith	1875	A667	
BANNING, Howard Thomas	1914	J204a	
BANNING, Hubbard Sill	1843 *	E1478	
BANNING, Hubert Ashley	1855	B142	
BANNING, Hubert Temple	1882	B614	
BANNING, Hubert Charles	1890	B612	
BANNING, Hubert W.	1892 *	C660b	
BANNING, Hubert	1906	Q59	
BANNING, Hudson C.	1832	F264	
BANNING, Hudson Almon	1869	F1504	
BANNING, Hugh	1896 *	B1750	
BANNING, Hulda A.(Foulk	183?	C29	
BANNING, Hulda Jane	1894	J138	
BANNING, Huldah A.(Moore	1906	H119	
BANNING, Ida	184?	E1623	
BANNING, Ida	186? *	B521	
BANNING, Ida May	1866	F1472	
BANNING, Ida Jane	1869	P32	
BANNING, Ida May (Platt)	187?	E1681	
BANNING, Ida May	1876	E6740	
BANNING, Ida May	1878	E6546	
BANNING, Ida May	1878	E5695	
BANNING, Ida (Hitchens)	188?	H58a	
BANNING, Ida Bell	1885	J134	
BANNING, Ida (Delorme)	1896	Q56	
BANNING, Ida L.	1897	B964a	
BANNING, Ina B.	1907	B2119	
BANNING, Ina	1922	B998b	
BANNING, Ina	1943	Q103	
BANNING, Inez	1880	A671	
BANNING, Ira Alton	1868	C559	
BANNING, Irena	1742	E16	
BANNING, Irene	1745	F87	
BANNING, Irene (???)	186?	P31	
BANNING, Irene Greaves	1886	L367	
BANNING, Irene E. (Fin	190?	F1419	
BANNING, Irene (McCartne	190?	Q58	
BANNING, Irene (???)	191?	B2050	
BANNING, Irminda (Freder	1846	A235	
BANNING, Isabel	179?	G3	
BANNING, Isabel M. (Camp	1814	B56	
BANNING, Isabel (McVain)	1836	E1382	
BANNING, Isabel (Thornto	186?	K1587	
BANNING, Isabel (Moriart	1862	K44	
BANNING, Isaiah Royden	1892	R125	
BANNING, Iva (Clement)	189?	A708	
BANNING, Iva (Perrin)	1899	A708	
BANNING, Iva Mae	190?	B2048	
BANNING, Izetta	1825	L185	
BANNING, Jabez Warner	1828	E402	
BANNING, Jack Phillip	1914	J412	
BANNING, Jack Dewayne	1949	E19130	
BANNING, Jackie L.(Brown	194?	H775	
BANNING, Jackson	1840	B314b	
BANNING, Jackson	1873	B747	
BANNING, Jacob Greengerg	1790	I2	
BANNING, Jacob Murphy	1794	A68	
BANNING, Jacob	189?	A1592	
BANNING, Jacob J.	1812	I9	
BANNING, Jacob Murphy	1835	A238	
BANNING, Jacob	1842	B236	
BANNING, Jacob Murphy	1855	A653	
BANNING, Jacob Ellis	1858	J7	
BANNING, Jacob Nelson	1866	A663	
BANNING, Jacob Jr.	189?	J63	
BANNING, Jake	182?	M3	
BANNING, Jame Mark	1980	E39065	
BANNING, James	16??	C1	
BANNING, James Anthony	1692	A5	
BANNING, James	171?	A12b	
BANNING, James	1724	A8,B4	
BANNING, James Anthony	1740	A12	
BANNING, James	1742	X2754	
BANNING, James	1746	B8	
BANNING, James	176?	A19	
BANNING, James	176?	C8	
BANNING, James	1767 *	L12	
BANNING, James M. Anthon	1768	A29	
BANNING, James	1776	B23	
BANNING, James	1783	B18	
BANNING, James	1792	B47	
BANNING, James	1793 *	L44	
BANNING, James	1794	G2	
BANNING, James	1795	M1	
BANNING, James	18??	E367	
BANNING, James Smith	1800	A70	
BANNING, James	1801	F69	
BANNING, James	1811	B87	
BANNING, James M.	1815	F268	
BANNING, James	1818	B151	
BANNING, James	182?	L121	
BANNING, James C.	182?	A58	
BANNING, James	1821	B80	
BANNING, James Henry	1824 *	B105	
BANNING, James	1825	G11	
BANNING, James Blackston	1825	A247	
BANNING, James L.	1825	D9	
BANNING, James Alexander	1832	R8	
BANNING, James Henry	1835	B179	
BANNING, James	1836	H3	
BANNING, James Franklin	1836	B182	
BANNING, James D.	1839	B218	
BANNING, James Wootin	1839	E1607	
BANNING, James	184?	B664	
BANNING, James Edgar	1840	B117	
BANNING, James Henry	1840	B135	
BANNING, James	1842	B203	
BANNING, James Henry	1843	B109	
BANNING, James A.	1846	B314c	
BANNING, James Latimer	1848	A144	
BANNING, James	1854	B279	
BANNING, James Henry	1854 *	B321	
BANNING, James	186?	G67	
BANNING, James Edward	186?	B535	

428

BANNING, James Marcus	1861	B260
BANNING, James R.	1863	B233
BANNING, James Alvin	1863	R38
BANNING, James F.	1862	B939a
BANNING, James T.	1869	J13
BANNING, James Byron	187? *	E5691
BANNING, James F.	1873	R33
BANNING, James	1878	Q25
BANNING, James	1879	B539
BANNING, James Latimer	1882	A414
BANNING, James Virgil	1886	B991a
BANNING, James Leroy	1889	J70
BANNING, James Alexander	1907	B1015
BANNING, James Edward	1906	R148
BANNING, James	193?	J502
BANNING, James Franklin	1932	F7004
BANNING, James Paul	194?	E19063
BANNING, James Edward	1945 *	B9605
BANNING, James Richard	1947	C3404
BANNING, Jancy V.	1852	B197
BANNING, Jane (Spencer)	1696	A5
BANNING, Jane	1734	A34e
BANNING, Jane	177?	A21a
BANNING, Jane	177?	A28
BANNING, Jane (Beaty)	1800	B53
BANNING, Jane (???)	181?	B69
BANNING, Jane (Dadley)	1816	A74
BANNING, Jane (Rogers)	1816	B90a
BANNING, Jane (Edgar)	182?	A232
BANNING, Jane (Noris)	182?	F262
BANNING, Jane L. (Gibson	182?	X500
BANNING, Jane (Rogers)	1820	B86
BANNING, Jane	1836	F287
BANNING, Jane (Davis)	1837	B89
BANNING, Jane	1838	B170
BANNING, Jane	1839	X3505
BANNING, Jane	184? *	B120
BANNING, Jane	1846	B227a
BANNING, Jane	185?	A287
BANNING, Jane	1868 *	A661
BANNING, Jane	188?	C293
BANNING, Jane	188?	X1507
BANNING, Jane (Ingram)	194?	H333
BANNING, Jane	195?	A3704
BANNING, Janet K. (Post)	189?	C299
BANNING, Janette	1845	E1568
BANNING, Janette	1847	X3801
BANNING, Jasper James	1896	F1461
BANNING, Jay Foster	1855	E1009
BANNING, Jay	190?	F1400n
BANNING, Jean (???)	191?	F3081
BANNING, Jean J. (Ely)	1919	F3081
BANNING, Jean Lois	1930	Q71
BANNING, Jeanette Dolore	1932	H327
BANNING, Jefferson J.	186?	H11
BANNING, Jefferson C.	186?	X1512
BANNING, Jeffery Scott	1964	C5662
BANNING, Jemima (Marvin)	1711	E5
BANNING, Jemima (Allison	1791	B18
BANNING, Jemima	1785	E59
BANNING, Jemima Florence	1887	B943b
BANNING, Jenna Saunders	1987	H1504

BANNING, Jennie	1837	F499
BANNING, Jennie	184?	E1635
BANNING, Jennie (Rice)	185?	E1571
BANNING, Jennie (Roberts	185?	G20
BANNING, Jennie Pansy	186?	E1627
BANNING, Jennie	1869	P32
BANNING, Jennie Malvern	1882 *	B608
BANNING, Jennie L.	1903	J140a
BANNING, Jennifer L.	1989	Q251
BANNING, Jeremiah	1733	A10
BANNING, Jeremiah	1756	A14
BANNING, Jeremiah	177?	D1
BANNING, Jeremiah	1788	B20
BANNING, Jeremiah	1792	B28
BANNING, Jeremiah	1800	A48
BANNING, Jeremiah	1807	B56
BANNING, Jeremiah Wilcox	1820	F254
BANNING, Jeremiah	1835	H2
BANNING, Jeremiah	184?	X1508
BANNING, Jeremiah Dallas	1853	B198
BANNING, Jeremiah	1854	B312e
BANNING, Jeremiah	1859	X1501
BANNING, Jerome	1818	F262
BANNING, Jerry Eugene	1940	C3336
BANNING, Jerusha Adelaid	1839	F614
BANNING, Jess	195?	F11991
BANNING, Jesse	1808	L51
BANNING, Jesse Wrenshall	1846 *	L460
BANNING, Jessie	1842 *	L199
BANNING, Jessie (Lockwoo	1860	F589
BANNING, Jessie (Fowler)	186?	E4204
BANNING, Jessie (Clinton	1863	F626
BANNING, Jessie (Watters	187?	Q23
BANNING, Jessie Blanche	1878	J30
BANNING, Jessie Freemont	1879	C146
BANNING, Jessie Octava	1896	F1417
BANNING, Jessie (Henry)	1897	E5617
BANNING, Jewel	190?	B1146
BANNING, Jewel (Ridge)	191?	E10811
BANNING, Jewel	1910	E10812
BANNING, Joan	192?	E11135
BANNING, Joan (Bridge)	1925	C796
BANNING, Joan Louise	1932	H377
BANNING, Joann M. (Mabry	1940	C3333
BANNING, Joanne	194?	J503
BANNING, Joel	1846	B205
BANNING, Johann Marcus	1688	N2
BANNING, Johann Bernard	1748	N55
BANNING, Johann Adolph	1754	N57
BANNING, Johann Ernst G.	1833	N674
BANNING, Johanna	157?	K5
BANNING, Johathan B.	1834	B89
BANNING, John	153?	K2
BANNING, John	157?	K4
BANNING, John	16??	C2
BANNING, John	16??	B3, A6
BANNING, John	160?	K15
BANNING, John	1613	X2501
BANNING, John	1639	X2502
BANNING, John	1652	E1
BANNING, John	167?	K126
BANNING, John	167?	A2

BANNING, John	1678	E2	BANNING, John C.	1857 *	B322
BANNING, John	168?	A5a, B2	BANNING, John Phillip	1857	J21
BANNING, John	1692	X2543	BANNING, John Henry	1859	J31a
BANNING, John	1705	K234	BANNING, John H.	186?	X1511
BANNING, John	171? *	X2631	BANNING, John Travis	1861 *	L465
BANNING, John	1712	B5, E5	BANNING, John C.	1862	B237d
BANNING, John	1717	X2632	BANNING, John	1862 *	B771
BANNING, John	172?	A34a	BANNING, John Henry	1863	A145
BANNING, John	1730	L2	BANNING, John Alexander	1864	G76
BANNING, John	1735	E14	BANNING, John Franklin	1865	B243
BANNING, John	1739	X2752	BANNING, John Wesley	1866	D51
BANNING, John	1740	C5	BANNING, John	187?	X1507
BANNING, John	1743	X2755	BANNING, John	187?	X1536
BANNING, John	1746	K351	BANNING, John	1870	B941
BANNING, John	175?	L4	BANNING, John Wesley	1871	B587
BANNING, John J.M.M.A.	175?	N48	BANNING, John L.	1875	H29
BANNING, John	1755 *	A102a	BANNING, John William	1876 *	G25
BANNING, John	1760	L8	BANNING, John Richard	1881	B750
BANNING, John	1764	B9	BANNING, John Phineas	1883	C565
BANNING, John	1765	X2993	BANNING, John	1886	A672
BANNING, John	1768	X2994	BANNING, John Henry	1887	X1012
BANNING, John Wesley	177?	A27	BANNING, John	189?	J68
BANNING, John	1773	F57	BANNING, John	1893	B1747
BANNING, John	1775	K601	BANNING, John	190?	B1147
BANNING, John	1777	E52	BANNING, John Francis	1901	F1419
BANNING, John	1779	K610	BANNING, John Edward	1902	B2036
BANNING, John	1787	L27	BANNING, John L.	1910	E10802
BANNING, John Alford	1790	C12	BANNING, John R.	1916	B2506b
BANNING, John K.	1797 *	B50	BANNING, John Franklin	192?	J425
BANNING, John	18??	E1017	BANNING, John Richard	1922	C1880
BANNING, John C.	180?	D2	BANNING, John Richard	193?	B9600
BANNING, John	1804	B32	BANNING, John Peck	1939	F3110
BANNING, John Johnson	1807	L31	BANNING, John Wesley	1949	E19114
BANNING, John	1808	F209	BANNING, John McMahon	1956	H826
BANNING, John	181?	L119	BANNING, John Earl	1959	E39004
BANNING, John	181?	E210	BANNING, John Peck, III	1964	F6041
BANNING, John	182?	M4	BANNING, Johnathan Cessn	1845	A631
BANNING, John S.	182?	X2	BANNING, Johnnie	1882 *	D67
BANNING, John Alfred	1820	C19	BANNING, Johnnie	1897	B2138
BANNING, John	1823	G10	BANNING, Jonny Bill	191?	B2049
BANNING, John Stephen	1823	K1267	BANNING, Jon Wilroth	1947	A3657
BANNING, John	1825	C76	BANNING, Jonathan	1849	C259
BANNING, John	183? *	F285	BANNING, Jonathan Frankl	1894	C661
BANNING, John	183?	I23	BANNING, Jones	1909	B997b
BANNING, John	1830	B129	BANNING, Joseph	1748	E19
BANNING, John C.	1830	B215	BANNING, Joseph	175?	L5
BANNING, John Anderson	1836	B115	BANNING, Joseph	1761	L9
BANNING, John	1838	B134	BANNING, Joseph	1780	E80
BANNING, John	1838	B201	BANNING, Joseph	1792	L43
BANNING, John Malcom	1839	E1509	BANNING, Joseph	1802	E361
BANNING, John	1841	B312	BANNING, Joseph Lewis	1808	E385
BANNING, John	1842	D12	BANNING, Joseph	1810	E209
BANNING, John	1842	B185	BANNING, Joseph	1821	E398
BANNING, John William	1843	C227	BANNING, Joseph	1822	B93
BANNING, John	1846	B205	BANNING, Joseph Dwight	1826	E1506
BANNING, John T.	1848	H8	BANNING, Joseph Adena	183?	E1609
BANNING, John S.	1848	X9	BANNING, Joseph	1832	B288
BANNING, John	1851	X3509	BANNING, Joseph T.	1839	B225
BANNING, John Sullins	1852	B278	BANNING, Joseph Beaumont	1840	E1618
BANNING, John Thomas	1855	R35	BANNING, Joseph Gilmer	1843	B136
BANNING, John Griffin	1856 *	C128	BANNING, Joseph Olney	1843	E1616
BANNING, John F.	1856	E1017	BANNING, Joseph R.	1849	B276

BANNING, Joseph Brainard	1853	E1645	BANNING, Kathryn Alice	1962	H841
BANNING, Joseph Brent	1861	C124	BANNING, Kathy	195?	E39002
BANNING, Joseph Ivy	1864	B324	BANNING, Kay	194?	B26012
BANNING, Joseph Brainard	1877	E6731	BANNING, Keeny Ellsworth	1898	E6713
BANNING, Joseph Brent	1889	C297	BANNING, Keith Douglas	1951	E19115
BANNING, Joseph Brainard	190?	E12631	BANNING, Kelly R.	1971	H1303
BANNING, Joseph	1905	D169	BANNING, Kendall	1879	E6319
BANNING, Joseph	1911	B2506	BANNING, Kent B.	193?	E11136
BANNING, Josephine	1835	F281	BANNING, Kevin Ross	1963	C5661
BANNING, Josephine	1844	I70	BANNING, Keziah (Gullefe	177?	B12
BANNING, Josephine There	1863	B583	BANNING, Keziah	1832	X3502
BANNING, Josephene	1877	F1206	BANNING, Kimberly Kate	1971	H785
BANNING, Josephine	1906	C665	BANNING, Kenneth	190?	Q62
BANNING, Joshua	1777	E53	BANNING, Kenneth Richard	193?	B2058
BANNING, Joshua	1817	L182	BANNING, Kenneth Robert	1949	Q150
BANNING, Josiah	1796	F67	BANNING, Kenneth Ray	1950	B26001
BANNING, Josiah	182?	L126	BANNING, Kirby	1869	A690
BANNING, Josiah Ellis	1827	J2	BANNING, Lake	1882	A688
BANNING, Josiah	1834	F272	BANNING, Lamira	1848	F640
BANNING, Joyce (Fisher)	1931	E10810	BANNING, Larina	182?	F265
BANNING, Joyce Ann	1952	C3428	BANNING, Lariny	182?	F266
BANNING, Juanita J.(Shel	1923	E10827	BANNING, Larry	193?	J499
BANNING, Juda Elizabeth	1883	B943a	BANNING, LaSatt	1849	B173
BANNING, Judy (Cosby)	193?	E19046	BANNING, Laura (Tanner)	179?	F64
BANNING, Julia	1816	L181	BANNING, Laura	181?	F244
BANNING, Julia M.	1829	F495	BANNING, Laura (Tinker)	181?	F246
BANNING, Julia (Kerby)	183?	A251	BANNING, Laura	182?	P8
BANNING, Julia Etta	1832	E380	BANNING, Laura A.	1829	E379
BANNING, Julia	1836	B200	BANNING, Laura	1838	E409
BANNING, Julia (Sweezie)	184?	Q4	BANNING, Laura Lay	1841	E1477
BANNING, Julia (Gillmore	185?	B279	BANNING, Laura	185?	B557
BANNING, Julia M.(White)	185?	C229	BANNING, Laura J.	185?	X501
BANNING, Julia	1877	B273	BANNING, Laura Amner	1851	B763
BANNING, Julia Elizabeth	1883	B943a	BANNING, Laura Pamelia	1856	E1358
BANNING, Julia Stella	1884	C576	BANNING, Laura	187?	F1508
BANNING, Julia	1888	D69	BANNING, Laura	1886	F1413
BANNING, Julian	1857	B305	BANNING, Laura	197?	F9969
BANNING, Julie Ann	1857	J6	BANNING, Laurel L. (Howa	1946	C3422
BANNING, Juliet Helen	1945	F6006	BANNING, Laurel J. (Barr	1947	B26000
BANNING, Juliete (Brockw	1809	F250	BANNING, Lavern Calvin	1927	C1882
BANNING, Junnie	189?	F1536	BANNING, Lavina	1834	J3a
BANNING, Justin Trowbrid	1983	H504	BANNING, Lavinia Lucelia	183?	F266
BANNING, Kami Jon	1978	A9952	BANNING, Lavina	1861	J31b
BANNING, Karen Beth	1949	E19108	BANNING, Leah (Spalsbury	189?	E6364
BANNING, Karen L.	195?	F6009	BANNING, Leander	1815	E214
BANNING, Karla (Courtwri	194?	A3657	BANNING, Leander Edwin	1830	E1382
BANNING, Kate (Scofield	184?	E1476	BANNING, Leann	1944	B9641
BANNING, Kate	1857	F620	BANNING, Leatha (Morgan)	1919	H175c
BANNING, Kate (Catlin)	188?	G87	BANNING, Leda	1901	B1144
BANNING, Katherine	1770	A30	BANNING, Lena (???)	1859	X3510
BANNING, Katherine	181?	A44	BANNING, Lena (McCulloug	1886	Q25
BANNING, Katherine (???)	182?	B88	BANNING, Lena L.	1895	B967a
BANNING, Katherine (Bant	183?	E403	BANNING, Lenora C.	1890	H58c
BANNING, Katherine Stewa	1866	C103	BANNING, Leland Gates	1860	F626
BANNING, Katherine	187?	G22	BANNING, Leo	1909	Q81
BANNING, Katherine Wooda	1874	B420	BANNING, Leo Melvin	1921	E10828
BANNING, Katherine Walla	1883	C148	BANNING, Leoa E.	1901	B1144
BANNING, Katherine Mary	1891	C298	BANNING, Leon	189?	F1400j
BANNING, Katherine Marga	190?	G222	BANNING, Leon Walter	1893	E5617
BANNING, Kathryn Hildred	1948	H492	BANNING, Leon Edwin	1922 *	H175d
BANNING, Kathryn (Beers)	1922	C1880	BANNING, Leona C.	1903	H175a
BANNING, Kathryn	194?	B26016	BANNING, Leona Martha	1906	E6714

431

BANNING, Leona P. (Smith)	193?	F7004	BANNING, Louisa (Whitlow	181?	L33
BANNING, Leora Eugenia	1877 *	E5806	BANNING, Louisa (Walker)	1817	B35
BANNING, Leonard Jeff	1865	P31	BANNING, Louisa (Thompso	1820	X3800
BANNING, Leroy Francis	1916	E10804	BANNING, Louisa	1836	B314
BANNING, Leroy Francis	1937	E19052	BANNING, Louisa (Ryan)	1876	F1209
BANNING, Lester Miller	1833	F279	BANNING, Louise	18??	A1562
BANNING, Lester Earl	188?	H58d	BANNING, Louise Ann	1817	A227
BANNING, Lester T.	1908	B2116	BANNING, Louise (Cessna)	1823	A229
BANNING, Lester Oliver	1920	E10827	BANNING, Louise "Sallie"	184?	D18
BANNING, Lester Earl Jr.	1923	H178	BANNING, Louise (Phelps)	184?	E1003
BANNING, Lester Earl 3rd	1957	H505	BANNING, Louise Camilla	1842	E1619
BANNING, Letitia (Nillar	1850	B136	BANNING, Louise Ann	1856	A654
BANNING, Letitia Louise	1877 *	B593	BANNING, Louise (Carlson	188?	E11020
BANNING, Levi Wilber	1839	E1565	BANNING, Louise (Frazier	188?	B594
BANNING, Levi W.	1845	B298a	BANNING, Louise	1902	F2623a
BANNING, Lewis	1854 *	X12	BANNING, Louise Anna (Mc	1932	E10828
BANNING, Lewis Wayne	193?	B9622	BANNING, Lowell Robert	1925	C1881
BANNING, Lida (Gates)	186?	E6404	BANNING, Lucetta (Riddel	180?	E361
BANNING, Lila (Watkins)	1878	B598	BANNING, Lucia Anne	1877	F1215
BANNING, Lila Marie	1906	C825	BANNING, Lucile (Pace)	1906	F3376
BANNING, Lilie (Cox)	1882	B263	BANNING, Lucille	1903	J140a
BANNING, Lillian Augusta	1867	E1651	BANNING, Lucille (Baumga	191?	J204
BANNING, Lillias Josephi	1894	E6712	BANNING, Lucinda (???)	179?	B19
BANNING, Lilly	187?	E4207	BANNING, Lucinda	1795	E79
BANNING, Lilly Rutherfor	187?	F1499	BANNING, Lucinda	182?	P6
BANNING, Linda	1806	E344	BANNING, Lucinda (???)	1834	B88
BANNING, Linda (Gillett)	186?	F632	BANNING, Lucinda	1840	Q2
BANNING, Linda (Stone)	186?	E1401	BANNING, Lucretia	1769	F24
BANNING, Linda C. (???)	194?	J418	BANNING, Lucretia	1843	F287a
BANNING, Linda M.	1949	H776	BANNING, Lucretia (Linds	1853	B139
BANNING, Linn (Fletcher	1870	C114	BANNING, Lucy (Tiffany)	174?	E18
BANNING, Lisa	195?	E39003	BANNING, Lucy	1743	F16
BANNING, Liz	1860	J23	BANNING, Lucy	177?	F60
BANNING, Liza Jane	1866	J11	BANNING, Lucy	1770	E60
BANNING, Lizzie (Lewis)	185?	E1009	BANNING, Lucy (Case)	179?	F665
BANNING, Lizzie P.	1856	I73	BANNING, Lucy	187?	F652
BANNING, Lizzie (Wilson)	186?	B569	BANNING, Lucy	1814	F212
BANNING, Lizzie	1864	N1678	BANNING, Lucy (Lay)	1816	E346
BANNING, Lizzie	1867	J25	BANNING, Lucy	1828	F285a
BANNING, Lizzie (McCaule	1883	H58a	BANNING, Lucy Lovina	1830	F265
BANNING, Lloyd Henry	1878	E6741	BANNING, Lucy (Clapp)	184?	E1567
BANNING, Lloyd Harold	1909	C1826	BANNING, Lucy Jane	1845	E1479
BANNING, Lois Rosemond	1922	C1829	BANNING, Lucy (Huntley)	186?	E1628
BANNING, Lola	188?	E6694	BANNING, Lucy (Stickney)	186?	C101
BANNING, Lola	189?	F1517	BANNING, Lucy	1860	B312h
BANNING, Lona Almina	1866	E6498	BANNING, Lucy Maria	1863	Q8
BANNING, Lora (Harrison)	1880	J32a	BANNING, Lucy	1866 *	F567
BANNING, Loree J.	1896	B992b	BANNING, Lucy Tichenor	1876	C133
BANNING, Lorene June	1924	E10823	BANNING, Lucy	190?	F2633
BANNING, Lorenzo	1805	B68	BANNING, Lucy B. (Dudley	192?	E10809
BANNING, Lorenzo B.A.	1838	B233a	BANNING, Ludia (Dominee)	185?	E1648
BANNING, Loretta (Pace)	1906	F3376	BANNING, Luiza	1843	B220
BANNING, Lori (Seaverns)	1958	H827	BANNING, Lula (Vaughn)	1887	A699
BANNING, Lori Lee	1961	E19068	BANNING, Lullius Josephi	1894	E6712
BANNING, Lorinda Adella	1832	G14	BANNING, Lulu May	1883	C555
BANNING, Lorne Murray	1924	Q70	BANNING, Lurana	1742	E16
BANNING, Lornhard Herman	1731	N14	BANNING, Lusannah (Gibbs	183?	G15
BANNING, Lorraine	1938	Q181	BANNING, Luther J.	187?	X1535
BANNING, Lottie Eva	187? *	E5694	BANNING, Lydia (Scovill)	1735	F15
BANNING, Louis P.	1845	B172	BANNING, Lydia	176?	F55
BANNING, Louis Rogers	1856	E1648	BANNING, Lydia (Church)	1776	E62
BANNING, Louis Edward	1883	B751	BANNING, Lydia (Reede)	1782	F57

Name	Year	Code		Name	Year	Code
BANNING, Lydia (Peck)	181?	F242		BANNING, Margaret (Wait)	185?	Q5
BANNING, Lydia	1824 *	F215a		BANNING, Margaret (Carr)	186?	B241
BANNING, Lydia Ann	1841	C256		BANNING, Margaret Ellen	1873	B592
BANNING, Lydia A. (Knigh	1845	E408		BANNING, Margaret Floren	1877	J29
BANNING, Lydia Ann	1850 *	E1008		BANNING, Margaret (Culki	1891	F1412
BANNING, Lydia	1851	P26		BANNING, Margaret	1904	F2623b
BANNING, Lydia Philura	1858	E1359		BANNING, Margaret (VanDe	1910	H135
BANNING, Lydia Jennette	1860 *	F1401		BANNING, Margaret (Smith	1917	Q83
BANNING, Lydia Ellen	1865	J12		BANNING, Margaret Bridgi	1923 *	F3092
BANNING, Lydia E. (Miles	1877	H28		BANNING, Margaret Anne	1945	Q184
BANNING, Lydia Ester	1893	F1416		BANNING, Margary	187?	G23
BANNING, Lydia Elizabeth	1913	H137		BANNING, Marguerite	191?	B2052
BANNING, Lyla	1929	Q99		BANNING, Margurite	1889	N3681
BANNING, Lynda Sue	1953	R494		BANNING, Maria (Focke)	169?	N2
BANNING, Lynwood	191?	H142		BANNING, Maria Magdalena	1736	N17
BANNING, Lysander	181?	E212		BANNING, Maria Elisabein	1751	N56
BANNING, Mabel	187?	E6307		BANNING, Maria (Nicholso	1782	A25
BANNING, Mabel Florence	188? *	G86		BANNING, Maria	180?	A43
BANNING, Mabel	1885 *	J58		BANNING, Maria (Waters)	182?	A117
BANNING, Mable (???)	1886	B750		BANNING, Maria (Birkhead	1821	A42
BANNING, Mable Anna Mar	1906	B2038		BANNING, Maria Coloric	1824	A231
BANNING, Machac	1809	B84		BANNING, Maria (Borden)	1824	F214
BANNING, Madaline	184?	L141		BANNING, Maria	1825	D9
BANNING, Madeline Evon	1920	C1942		BANNING, Maria (Jones)	1831	F216
BANNING, Madora (Barnes)	1853	X3508		BANNING, Maria Luella	1855	B765
BANNING, Madora	1893	X3547		BANNING, Maria Ella	1858	B310
BANNING, Mae (Fish)	189?	C590		BANNING, Maria Inez	1860	A656
BANNING, Maesimund	191?	F1404a		BANNING, Maria	190?	Q61
BANNING, Maggie (???)	187?	C562		BANNING, Mariana	1834	X3504
BANNING, Maggie (Blackbu	187?	Q24		BANNING, Mark Lofland	1857	H8c
BANNING, Maggie Elvira	1872	B518		BANNING, Mark	1916	Q83
BANNING, Maha A. (Hayed)	1962	H826		BANNING, Mark	195?	F6016
BANNING, Mahala Trice	180?	R2		BANNING, Mark Trowbridge	1955	H504
BANNING, Mahala (Ogden)	181?	X3500		BANNING, Mark	1960 *	H829
BANNING, Mahala F. (Blue	182?	C75		BANNING, Mark Steven	1962	E39005
BANNING, Mahalia	1814	B77a		BANNING, Marietta	186?	H9
BANNING, Malenda	1857	B237b		BANNING, Marjorie (Seymo	192?	H178
BANNING, Maletha	1860	B568		BANNING, Mashack	1822	B84
BANNING, Malinda	177?	F61		BANNING, Marshall	1889	F1393
BANNING, Malinda (Sulliv	1827	B72		BANNING, Martha	1707	K235
BANNING, Malinda	1838	J3		BANNING, Martha	1724	X2637
BANNING, Malinda	1849	B283		BANNING, Martha	1784	K612
BANNING, Malinda (Fletch	1870	C114		BANNING, Martha	1806	B33
BANNING, Malora B.	1849	E1356		BANNING, Martha (Cowdry)	1811	F70
BANNING, Mamie L. (Johns	188?	C589		BANNING, Martha (Yountla	1821	B87
BANNING, Mamie	1892	B2505		BANNING, Martha	1838	F272b
BANNING, Mammie	186?	C145		BANNING, Martha A.	1840	B331
BANNING, Marah	1641	X2504		BANNING, Martha (Bowers)	1841	F288
BANNING, Maranda	1878	X3561		BANNING, Martha Louisa	1843	B220
BANNING, Margaret (Bell)	170?	A5a		BANNING, Martha Ellen	1843	F615
BANNING, Margaret	171?	E5		BANNING, Martha Northcus	1845	K2944
BANNING, Margaret (Wrens	1717	L9		BANNING, Martha C.	1849	B186
BANNING, Margaret	1750	E20		BANNING, Martha	1854	B239
BANNING, Margaret	1762	E86		BANNING, Martha Jane	1855	B231
BANNING, Margaret (Clark	180?	B34		BANNING, Martha (Markham	1857	F603
BANNING, Margaret (Hamme	182?	B151		BANNING, Martha Ann	1858	J22
BANNING, Margaret (Steve	1825	P3		BANNING, Martha Bell	1860	B144
BANNING, Margaret	1829	B90		BANNING, Martha J.	1863	B261
BANNING, Margaret	183?	I15		BANNING, Martha	1863 *	P30
BANNING, Margaret	1830	G13		BANNING, Martha Alice	1872	J15
BANNING, Margaret (Lee)	1841	F498		BANNING, Martha (Purdy)	1872	Q19
BANNING, Margaret J.	1841	B219		BANNING, Martha M.	1873	B941a

BANNING, Martha Jane	1874	B778	
BANNING, Martha (Davis)	188?	Q27	
BANNING, Martha Williams	1894	F1460	
BANNING, Martha M.	1899	B964b	
BANNING, Martha Agnes	1903	B2117	
BANNING, Martha May	1922	E10808	
BANNING, Martha (Pauli)	194?	F6013	
BANNING, Martha (Rudesea	1944	F11988	
BANNING, Marvin Bando D.	1774	E76	
BANNING, Marvin	1804	E362	
BANNING, Marvin Rial	1904 *	Q64	
BANNING, Mary	156?	K8	
BANNING, Mary (???)	16??	K41	
BANNING, Mary (Goldsmith	162?	X2501	
BANNING, Mary (Loring)	162?	X2501	
BANNING, Mary	163?	X2010	
BANNING, Mary (Knowlton)	164?	X2503	
BANNING, Mary (???)	169?	A5a	
BANNING, Mary (Pease)	169?	X2541	
BANNING, Mary (Daniels)	1690	E2	
BANNING, Mary (Roland)	1690	E2	
BANNING, Mary	1690 *	X2542	
BANNING, Mary "Maria?"	1698	K232	
BANNING, Mary (Ayers)	170?	K234	
BANNING, Mary (???)	170?	A12j	
BANNING, Mary (Griffin)	170?	K234	
BANNING, Mary	1718	F7	
BANNING, Mary	172?	A36a	
BANNING, Mary (Austin)	172?	X2634	
BANNING, Mary (George)	172?	X2636	
BANNING, Mary	1726	X2638	
BANNING, Mary (Gossage)	173?	A10	
BANNING, Mary (Russell)	173?	C4	
BANNING, Mary (Fairbanks	174?	X2756	
BANNING, Mary	1747	F18	
BANNING, Mary (???)	175?	L6	
BANNING, Mary (Driver)	176?	L7	
BANNING, Mary (Rathbone)	1760	F21	
BANNING, Mary E.	176? *	E308	
BANNING, Mary (Barras)	177?	K606	
BANNING, Mary (Macky)	177?	A22	
BANNING, Mary (Dale)	177?	X2994	
BANNING, Mary	1777 *	K608	
BANNING, Mary Ann	1778 *	K609	
BANNING, Mary (Pratt)	1779	E77	
BANNING, Mary (Coe)	1781	F62	
BANNING, Mary (Millard)	178?	E78	
BANNING, Mary Ann (Ward)	179?	G2	
BANNING, Mary (???)	179?	B51	
BANNING, Mary (Munger)	1791	F62	
BANNING, Mary	18??	E1025	
BANNING, Mary	18??	A1591	
BANNING, Mary (???)	1801	B36	
BANNING, Mary Coe	1803	F240	
BANNING, Mary B.	1805	A72	
BANNING, Mary	1806	B55	
BANNING, Mary	181?	L118	
BANNING, Mary (Potter)	181?	B35	
BANNING, Mary Ann	181? *	F256	
BANNING, Mary E. (Baker)	1811	B68	
BANNING, Mary	1811	L34	
BANNING, Mary	1813	B36	
BANNING, Mary	1815	E389	
BANNING, Mary Ann (Ranso	1816	E311	
BANNING, Mary Ann	1817	E373	
BANNING, Mary (???)	1818	B27	
BANNING, Mary (Curtis)	182?	A247	
BANNING, Mary (Fleming)	182?	G11	
BANNING, Mary (Green)	182?	E397	
BANNING, Mary (Williams)	182?	A247	
BANNING, Mary Lowber	1820	C23	
BANNING, Mary E.	1820	A47	
BANNING, Mary (???)	1822	B60	
BANNING, Mary	1825	K1268	
BANNING, Mary Ann	1826	F257	
BANNING, Mary E.	1829	B90	
BANNING, Mary (Arnett)	183?	A238	
BANNING, Mary (Lake)	183?	A250	
BANNING, Mary (Sanford)	183?	E1001	
BANNING, Mary	183?	I16	
BANNING, Mary Ann (Travi	183?	L186	
BANNING, Mary J. (Murray	183?	B88	
BANNING, Mary P. (Wood)	183?	C80	
BANNING, Mary (Flood)	1830	E401	
BANNING, Mary (Sweeney)	1830	C20	
BANNING, Mary E. (Brown)	1832	E402	
BANNING, Mary Amelia	1833	F612	
BANNING, Mary (Daniel)	1834	B70	
BANNING, Mary C. (Monnic	1836	J2	
BANNING, Mary Ann	1838	E1564	
BANNING, Mary (Ward)	1838	F496	
BANNING, Mary	1839	E410	
BANNING, Mary	1839	F274	
BANNING, Mary (Hardman)	184?	B109	
BANNING, Mary (Mack)	184?	B131	
BANNING, Mary (Bradley)	184?	B185	
BANNING, Mary (Herringto	184?	B225	
BANNING, Mary (Johnson)	184?	B235a	
BANNING, Mary E. (Harvey	184?	C228	
BANNING, Mary	184?	D14	
BANNING, Mary (Harmon)	184?	E1509	
BANNING, Mary	184?	E1634	
BANNING, Mary (Ordway)	184?	F585	
BANNING, Mary (Dick)	184?	G17	
BANNING, Mary (Isaacs)	184?	H4	
BANNING, Mary (???)	184?	P23	
BANNING, Mary C.	1840	B666a	
BANNING, Mary A. (Tyler)	1840	R8	
BANNING, Mary (Wilcoxson	1842	F638	
BANNING, Mary	1843	C96a	
BANNING, Mary Blackstone	1843	A254	
BANNING, Mary	1844	B119	
BANNING, Mary (Low)	1844	E1493	
BANNING, Mary A.	1846	B312a	
BANNING, Mary	1846	H7	
BANNING, Mary (Borne)	1846	J1	
BANNING, Mary (Holister)	1846	C27	
BANNING, Mary Ellen	1847	L202	
BANNING, Mary Jane	1847 *	E1624	
BANNING, Mary Pritchard	1847	E1621	
BANNING, Mary E.	1849	E1397	
BANNING, Mary Ellen (Har	1849	C228	
BANNING, Mary Alice	185?	C100	
BANNING, Mary E. (Cole)	185?	C232	

434

BANNING, Mary E. (Cullen	185?	X1508	BANNING, Mathaila	1867	B262
BANNING, Mary Ann	1850	B206	BANNING, Mathilda L.	1820	E350
BANNING, Mary Jane	1850 *	G19	BANNING, Matilda	181? *	A46
BANNING, Mary M.	1851	B302	BANNING, Matilda	1831	B155
BANNING, Mary Lucinda	1852	B320	BANNING, Matilda	1835	E407
BANNING, Mary Ann (Porte	1853	C259	BANNING, Matilda Thursto	1854	E1584
BANNING, Mary Jane	1853	X3513	BANNING, Matilda (Botlem	1858	F645
BANNING, Mary Elizabeth	1855	E1646	BANNING, Matilda (Harrin	186?	X1512
BANNING, Mary Ellen	1856	J20	BANNING, Matildia Alice	1872	J15
BANNING, Mary Lowry	1856 *	B698	BANNING, Matt	195?	F11992
BANNING, Mary (Tufford)	1857	R35	BANNING, Mattie	18??	E1404
BANNING, Mary Elizabeth	1857	X503	BANNING, Mattie	1841	E10005
BANNING, Mary	1858	A655	BANNING, Mattie Alice	1883	J35
BANNING, Mary D.	1858	B259	BANNING, Mattie Lambi	189?	J66
BANNING, Mary J. (Ryan)	1858	Q6	BANNING, Maud	187?	E6305
BANNING, Mary	186?	B788	BANNING, Maud M. (Dusen	188?	B747
BANNING, Mary (Frangler)	186?	D51	BANNING, Maud (Bohannan)	188?	E5615
BANNING, Mary E. (Kneas)	186?	H23	BANNING, Maud	1888	G69
BANNING, Mary Malisse	1861	B939	BANNING, Maud	189?	F1518
BANNING, Mary Frances	1861	C236	BANNING, Maud	189?	C323
BANNING, Mary Ellen	1862	C263	BANNING, Maud	191?	Q77
BANNING, Mary Matilda	1866	B585	BANNING, Maudee J. (Emer	186?	J10
BANNING, Mary Elizabeth	1867	E1588	BANNING, Maureen	1938	Q187
BANNING, Mary V.	1868	R31	BANNING, Maurice	1870	F1212
BANNING, Mary Ann	1869	D52	BANNING, Maurice Ray	1940	C3333
BANNING, Mary (Caldwell)	187?	E6672	BANNING, Mavis Lorraine	1926	C1943
BANNING, Mary (Jordan)	187?	D54	BANNING, Max	1906	B1752
BANNING, Mary Holister	1871	C131	BANNING, Maxiene (McKill	191?	C1902
BANNING, Mary Maria	1871	A665	BANNING, Maxine (Miller)	191?	C1842
BANNING, Mary Elizabeth	1872	H27	BANNING, May (McLoud)	187?	C559
BANNING, Mary Lake	1875 *	A686	BANNING, May	189?	J150
BANNING, Mary	1878	E4206	BANNING, May Belle (Orr)	191?	B997b
BANNING, Mary Farlen	1879	R42	BANNING, May Ruth	1914	H123
BANNING, Mary (Cook)	188?	E6362	BANNING, Mehitable	1808	E345
BANNING, Mary Bertha	1881	R122	BANNING, Melethia (Rose)	1840	F601
BANNING, Mary (Lindsay)	1883	J33	BANNING, Melinda	1806	E344
BANNING, Mary (Dunningan	1882	Q36	BANNING, Melinda	181?	F252
BANNING, Mary Ora	1885	E5807	BANNING, Melinda (Walker	183?	F611
BANNING, Mary (Bohannan)	1887	E5614	BANNING, Melinda	1834	F260
BANNING, Mary Josephine	1892	B1014a	BANNING, Melinda Stevens	1835	F613
BANNING, Mary E.	1894	B992a	BANNING, Melissa Viola	1837	B184
BANNING, Mary	19??	H144	BANNING, Melissa	1847	B301
BANNING, Mary E. (Richar	19??	H115	BANNING, Melissa E.	1855	B303
BANNING, Mary Etta (Skeg	19??	H116	BANNING, Melissa	195?	B9642
BANNING, Mary (Green)	190?	B2037	BANNING, Melva A.	194?	H405
BANNING, Mary Susan	1905	B2118	BANNING, Melvin	191?	H141
BANNING, Mary Margaret	1906	A1643	BANNING, Mercy (Coffin)	1753	B8
BANNING, Mary	1911	Q82	BANNING, Mercy	1790	B27
BANNING, Mary Margaret	1915	F3089	BANNING, Merleda	1902	A1595
BANNING, Mary	1916	B998	BANNING, Merrill	189?	B1145
BANNING, Mary	1917	F2624b	BANNING, Michael	1842	C80b
BANNING, Mary Ann	192?	B2054	BANNING, Michael	194?	F6015
BANNING, Mary (Bowman)	192?	H144	BANNING, Michael Larry	1944	E19102
BANNING, Mary Louise	1920	C1879	BANNING, Michael Robert	1945	F11988
BANNING, Mary Faye	1922	E10807	BANNING, Michael	195?	A3701
BANNING, Mary (Robson)	1923	Q84	BANNING, Michael Terry	1952	H503
BANNING, Mary (Evans)	1940	H380	BANNING, Michael	1952	Q198
BANNING, Mary	195?	A3702	BANNING, Michael Foreste	1959	E39023
BANNING, Mary Ellen	1952	H823	BANNING, Michael Adam	1977	E39074
BANNING, Maryette	181? *	F248	BANNING, Milan Kenneth	1918	C1842
BANNING, Maryon (Paton)	186?	X1007	BANNING, Mildred Kathlee	1910	Q67
BANNING, Mashack	1822	B84	BANNING, Mildred	1911	H122

BANNING, Miles	1908	H135
BANNING, Miles Carlton	1941	H378
BANNING, Millie Mabel	1880	C568
BANNING, Milo H.	188?	F1513
BANNING, Milton H.	1858 *	B769
BANNING, Milton Albert	186?	E5808
BANNING, Mina (Keester)	187?	F1504
BANNING, Mina A. (Hemmon	1882	H29
BANNING, Minda	1866	A660
BANNING, Minda	190?	A1673
BANNING, Minerva (Waller	181?	B84
BANNING, Minerva (Melvin	183?	A234
BANNING, Minneola	1900	H118
BANNING, Minnie	186?	E1626
BANNING, Minnie (Brown)	186?	F566
BANNING, Minnie	1870	E4205
BANNING, Minnie L.	1879	E6734
BANNING, Minnie	188?	Q28
BANNING, Minnie A.	1884	B962
BANNING, Minnie	190?	D175
BANNING, Minnie L.	190?	E12632
BANNING, Minnie (Carter)	191?	J204a
BANNING, Minnie Ann (Cri	1931	E10834
BANNING, Minors B.	1865	H23
BANNING, Minta	186?	F648
BANNING, Missouri	1835	B181
BANNING, Morgan	1784	F64
BANNING, Morgan	184?	B122
BANNING, Morgan	1894	E6364
BANNING, Morgan (Rose)	1953	E19115
BANNING, Moritz Hildebra	1722	N10
BANNING, Morton Hale	1862 *	E1649
BANNING, Moses C.	1866 *	B767b
BANNING, Muriel (McCuaig	1924	Q70
BANNING, Murray James	1948	Q149
BANNING, Murril	1899	B2505b
BANNING, Murry	187?	E6304
BANNING, Myra	189?	F1515
BANNING, Myra (Brian)	190?	H117
BANNING, Myrle Cave	189?	J62
BANNING, Myron	1845	F624
BANNING, Myrtle Del	188?	E4241
BANNING, Myrtle	1885	C577
BANNING, Myrtle (Barthol	1898	E5618
BANNING, Myrtle Viola	1900	F1462
BANNING, Myrtle	1916	H124
BANNING, Mystes Azuba	1839	E1608
BANNING, N.A. (Nichols)	185?	B198
BANNING, N.C. (Scruggs)	183?	B79
BANNING, Nancy	1754	A103d
BANNING, Nancy (Augdon)	177?	A17
BANNING, Nancy	1774	X2997
BANNING, Nancy	1790	E82
BANNING, Nancy (Talbot)	1793	L43
BANNING, Nancy (Hall)	1796	C16
BANNING, Nancy (Glass)	1798	B20
BANNING, Nancy C.(Petty)	1802	B19
BANNING, Nancy	1804	F72
BANNING, Nancy	1807	E363
BANNING, Nancy (Meredith	181?	X1500
BANNING, Nancy (Johnson)	1813	B57
BANNING, Nancy	1813	B59
BANNING, Nancy (Robinson	1813	E386
BANNING, Nancy	1817	F269
BANNING, Nancy Moore	1819	A228
BANNING, Nancy	182?	I12
BANNING, Nancy	1820	B152
BANNING, Nancy	1829	B163
BANNING, Nancy Melvira	1837	B314a
BANNING, Nancy (Reves)	1839	B235a
BANNING, Nancy J.	1842	B332
BANNING, Nancy	1842	C80c
BANNING, Nancy J. (Thoma	1844	B233a
BANNING, Nancy Ann	1844	H6
BANNING, Nancy (Smith)	1845	A233
BANNING, Nancy Matilda	1847	B318
BANNING, Nancy Seymour	1848	A632
BANNING, Nancy	1856	B312f
BANNING, Nancy Asbury	1859	C135
BANNING, Nancy Helen	1859	C262
BANNING, Nancy (Simpson)	186?	B260
BANNING, Nancy	186?	B952
BANNING, Nancy (Miller)	1861	B141
BANNING, Nancy E. (Rose)	1875	B941
BANNING, Nancy J.	1878	B942b
BANNING, Nancy	1879	B274
BANNING, Nancy (Otto)	194?	F3110
BANNING, Nancy	1944	H331
BANNING, Nancy U. (Mendo	196?	E39024
BANNING, Naomi Elizabeth	1925	E10832
BANNING, Nathniel	1788	C16
BANNING, Nathniel	1803 *	L49
BANNING, Nathniel	1837	C80
BANNING, Nathniel	1847	C229
BANNING, Nell Ellen	1906	F2624
BANNING, Nellie	18??	E1019
BANNING, Nellie Lucetta	1857	E6401
BANNING, Nellie Maria	1863	E1647
BANNING, Nellie Orphania	1864	F1494
BANNING, Nellie (???)	186?	Q20
BANNING, Nellie Mahala	1882	C575
BANNING, Nellie Victoria	1883	F1455
BANNING, Nellie	1900	E6892
BANNING, Nellie (Solo	1900	E5619
BANNING, Nelly (Barton)	189?	B985
BANNING, Nelson	1806	F208
BANNING, Nelson	1818	E302
BANNING, Nelson Wilber	1868	E6499
BANNING, Nettie (Handlin	187?	A674
BANNING, Nettie	1880	J34a
BANNING, Neva Pearl	1885	C557
BANNING, Newel E.	1817	E315
BANNING, Newell Barlett	1841	E1393
BANNING, Newell John	1884	X17
BANNING, Nicholas	1831	F496
BANNING, Nicholas Lowber	1860	C143
BANNING, Nina (Brewer)	184?	L200
BANNING, Nina	189?	E9904
BANNING, Nona	1892	B9638
BANNING, Nora C.(Morris)	188?	H58d
BANNING, Norma Elizabeth	1932	H332
BANNING, Norma Lee	1942	E19101
BANNING, Norma Jean	1944	C3403
BANNING, Norman	1909 *	H125a

BANNING, Norton Sheldon	1830	A235
BANNING, Norton Nathan	1868	A664
BANNING, Oakley Minos	190?	H116
BANNING, Oakley George	1939	H380
BANNING, Obadiah	1648	X2507
BANNING, Okemah (Jenkins	195?	H504
BANNING, Olga (Kurzrock)	188?	B614
BANNING, Olive Elizabeth	1851	X3511
BANNING, Olive L.	1866	B517
BANNING, Olive S. (Linde	1868	J9
BANNING, Olive Alberta	1902	G185
BANNING, Oliver Jackson	1904	B2037
BANNING, Ona A. (Tomlin	1897	B752
BANNING, Orcencia	18??	F649
BANNING, Orin A.	1814	E312
BANNING, Orphania (Hall)	1813	F261
BANNING, Orrill	1803	F207
BANNING, Orrin	1865	X3805
BANNING, Orrin	188?	E5846
BANNING, Orson Benjamin	1838	E1003
BANNING, Orval Ladell	1911	C1827
BANNING, Orval Bernard	1956	C5665
BANNING, Orvel Lee	1921	E10822
BANNING, Orville F.	191?	H176a
BANNING, Osborn Emerson	190?	H117
BANNING, Owen	1914	B997d
BANNING, Ozias	181?	P2
BANNING, Ozro Demott	1830	E1507
BANNING, Pamela D. (Durh	196?	C5661
BANNING, Pamelia (Sprack	184?	B298
BANNING, Pansy	1884	E6363
BANNING, Pareba (McVey?)	1877	B941
BANNING, Parthenia (Elki	1844	B117
BANNING, Patience (Hart)	1809	F243
BANNING, Patricia (Downs	1940	E19052
BANNING, Patricia	1947	Q196
BANNING, Patricia Ann	1956	C3407
BANNING, Patrick	1936	Q186
BANNING, Patty L. (Reisz	1953	B26000
BANNING, Paul	15??	X2003
BANNING, Paul	15??	X2005
BANNING, Paul	1616	X2006
BANNING, Paul Welch	1880	E6362
BANNING, Paul Darrell	1892	A707
BANNING, Paul Richard	1926	E10809
BANNING, Paul	1955	Q202
BANNING, Paula N.(Gable)	1940	F7007
BANNING, Pauline (Willia	184?	B183
BANNING, Pauline (Carrol	190?	H120
BANNING, Pauline (Wood)	191?	A2116
BANNING, Pearl	18??	F650
BANNING, Pearl B. (Hartm	188?	C553
BANNING, Pearl	1885 *	J69
BANNING, Pearl	189?	F1534
BANNING, Pearl (Strickla	191?	E10811
BANNING, Peggy Margaret	1750	E20
BANNING, Peggy (Tanner)	178?	F62
BANNING, Peggy Lee	1937	B9603
BANNING, Penelope (Naunt	161?	X2006
BANNING, Penelope	164?	X2013
BANNING, Percy Stuart	1887	K6901
BANNING, Peter S.	1853	C232

BANNING, Peter	190?	Q66
BANNING, Peter Vroom	1949	F6007
BANNING, Phebe	174?	C6
BANNING, Philadelphia	1794	B22
BANNING, Philadelphia	1833	B92
BANNING, Philenon Fuller	1787	E78
BANNING, Phillip	169?	A12j
BANNING, Phillip	1781	K603
BANNING, Phillippina	180?	K1252
BANNING, Philman	172?	A36
BANNING, Philura	182?	F278
BANNING, Phineas	1740	C6
BANNING, Phineas	1815	C75
BANNING, Phineas	1830	C27
BANNING, Phineas	1852	C260
BANNING, Phineas Michael	1864	C237
BANNING, Phoebe Adocia	1848	E1643
BANNING, Phreaney	1742	E16
BANNING, Pierson Worrall	1879	B598
BANNING, Pinkey (Clendan	181?	H1
BANNING, Pinkey	1858	H8f
BANNING, Pinkney Asa	1845	B137
BANNING, Platha	188?	F1510
BANNING, Pleasant Snow	1840	B180a
BANNING, Plesant Wilson	1824	B175
BANNING, Polly	1798	F71
BANNING, Polly (Ward)	181?	X3500
BANNING, Polly J.	182?	C80a
BANNING, Pricilla	1832	C78
BANNING, Priscilla (Card	174?	C6
BANNING, Priscilla	177?	C17
BANNING, Priscilla	1807	A73
BANNING, Priscilla	1829	A249
BANNING, Priscilla	1873	A685
BANNING, Quilton	172?	A36c
BANNING, Rachael	1830	C77
BANNING, Rachel (Humphre	171?	A12e
BANNING, Rachell	1723	A34
BANNING, Rachel	1796	A69
BANNING, Rachel	1822	A230
BANNING, Rachel (Eline)	1822	I11
BANNING, Rachel	1840	E411
BANNING, Rachel Anne	1983	H1022
BANNING, Ralph	189?	F1400h
BANNING, Ralph Baxter	1908	F3376
BANNING, Ralph	1911	B997c
BANNING, Ralph Nelson	1930	E10834
BANNING, Rasco Jay	1886	E5615
BANNING, Ray	1889	C578
BANNING, Ray Nelson	1899	E5619
BANNING, Raymond	1825	A232
BANNING, Raymond	1910	E11142
BANNING, Raymond D.	193?	J417
BANNING, Raymond John	1934	E19046
BANNING, Raymond	194?	B26015
BANNING, Rebecca	1643	X2505
BANNING, Rebecca	169?	X2541
BANNING, Rebecca (Cheezu	175?	A103
BANNING, Rebecca	1767	F23
BANNING, Rebecca (Somers	177?	K601
BANNING, Rebecca (Griffi	1795	B48
BANNING, Rebecca (Watson	1811	B54

BANNING, Rebecca (Terril	182?	B175	
BANNING, Rebecca (???)	182?	B80	
BANNING, Rebecca	183?	I14	
BANNING, Rebecca (Sanfor	1836	C27	
BANNING, Rebecca	1841	B667	
BANNING, Rebecca	1847 *	C258	
BANNING, Rebecca L. (Bur	185?	B319	
BANNING, Rebecca Jane	1859 *	B767	
BANNING, Rebecca (Cheeve	186?	J7	
BANNING, Rebecca E.	1860	B323	
BANNING, Rebecca Pearl	1889	B1014	
BANNING, Rebecca	195?	A3703	
BANNING, Rebecca J.	1984	Q250	
BANNING, Rhoda	1761	F22	
BANNING, Rhoda (Miller)	1801	F68	
BANNING, Rhoda	1838	B91	
BANNING, Rhoda	1843	B333	
BANNING, Rhoda (Boyingto	186?	B570	
BANNING, Rhoda	1863 *	B767a	
BANNING, Rhoda	1873	B538	
BANNING, Rhody	1838	B91	
BANNING, Rhonda (Nonast)	196?	E39023	
BANNING, Rial	1842	Q3	
BANNING, Richard	15??	X2001	
BANNING, Richard	15??	X2002	
BANNING, Richard	16??	C3	
BANNING, Richard Sr.	171?	C3, A7	
BANNING, Richard	1729	X2640	
BANNING, Richard Jr.	174?	C4	
BANNING, Richard	1745	X2756	
BANNING, Richard	1822	C25	
BANNING, Richard	183?	I19	
BANNING, Richard	1844	B281	
BANNING, Richard	1857	C234	
BANNING, Richard Anthony	1859	A289	
BANNING, Richard Frankli	1918	C1941	
BANNING, Richard Baxter	1939	F7007	
BANNING, Richard H.	1940 *	H328	
BANNING, Richard Charles	1940	H376	
BANNING, Richard Allen	1948	B26000	
BANNING, Richard	195?	B9643	
BANNING, Richmond Hall	1841	F638	
BANNING, Ricky	1952	E19065	
BANNING, Ricky J.	1958	F11990	
BANNING, Rilla (Star)	186?	F647	
BANNING, Rita (Conger)	192?	F3082	
BANNING, Rita Kay	1949	C3405	
BANNING, Robbie Ian	1980	H1021	
BANNING, Robert	153?	K3	
BANNING, Robert {Gossage}	1776	A22	
BANNING, Robert	149?	K1	
BANNING, Robert	1806	A41	
BANNING, Robert Joseph	1832	L186	
BANNING, Robert E.	1843	P23	
BANNING, Robert Freeborn	1847	A120	
BANNING, Robert	1854	B230	
BANNING, Robert Johnson	1854	B314g	
BANNING, Robert Henry	1858	A288	
BANNING, Robert James	1912	Q68	
BANNING, Robert Clair	1921	F7003	
BANNING, Robert Johnston	1924	C796	
BANNING, Robert	1921	A1672	
BANNING, Robert Orval	1933	C3334	
BANNING, Robert Johnston	1963	C2196	
BANNING, Robin	1967	H1302	
BANNING, Roda (Miller)	179?	F68	
BANNING, Rodney	1919	A1671	
BANNING, Roger Lee	1948	E19107	
BANNING, Ronald David	1932	E19045	
BANNING, Ronald Charles	1941	H333	
BANNING, Ronald Dean	195?	E39001	
BANNING, Ronald Ray	1960	C3411	
BANNING, Rosa (McVey)	1877	B941	
BANNING, Rosanne	195?	A3700	
BANNING, Rose	187?	X1531	
BANNING, Rose Edna	1895	B1014b	
BANNING, Rose J. (Rerich	1942	E19069	
BANNING, Rose Marie	1955	H502	
BANNING, Rosemary (Kempt	1923	A1672	
BANNING, Rosetta	1822	E399	
BANNING, Rosetta	1857	X3804	
BANNING, Ross E.	1874	B519	
BANNING, Roswell H.	1821 *	F271a	
BANNING, Rowland	1910	F2622b	
BANNING, Roxalina	1748	X2759	
BANNING, Roxalina	1776	X2998	
BANNING, Roxy (???)	184?	P24	
BANNING, Roy Benjamin	1885	H58b	
BANNING, Roy Austin	1904	J140b	
BANNING, Roy D.	194?	J418	
BANNING, Ruby (Thorpe)	189?	C661	
BANNING, Ruby	189?	F1400e	
BANNING, Ruby Mae	1906	J203a	
BANNING, Ruby (Bell)	191?	H176a	
BANNING, Ruby Irene	1920	E10806	
BANNING, Ruby Kathryn (?	192?	B9606	
BANNING, Rufus	1836	B79	
BANNING, Rureany	1742	E16	
BANNING, Russell	191?	Q92	
BANNING, Russell Lee	1956	C3410	
BANNING, Ruth	1778	F59	
BANNING, Ruth	187?	A1590	
BANNING, Ruth	1813	F267	
BANNING, Ruth (Gates)	1823	F254	
BANNING, Ruth (Reed)	183?	B131	
BANNING, Ruth Loretta	1868	C265	
BANNING, Ruth (Thorpe)	189?	C662	
BANNING, Ruth	189?	P136	
BANNING, Ruth (Lockett)	190?	C316	
BANNING, Ruth Estella	1905	E6897	
BANNING, Ruth Isabel	1921	E10831	
BANNING, Rutha (York)	186?	B324	
BANNING, Sabina (Smith)	1742	B6	
BANNING, Sadie (Fox)	178?	X3000	
BANNING, Sadie (Parker)	184?	A631	
BANNING, Sadie Mahala	1886	C566	
BANNING, Sadie H. (Smith	1903	C1826	
BANNING, Sady (Sage)	186?	E1625	
BANNING, Salina	1803	B31	
BANNING, Sallie	1822	C22	
BANNING, Sally (Bowdel)	177?	A20	
BANNING, Sally	178?	E56	
BANNING, Sally (Foster)	181?	E209	
BANNING, Sally	1815	B150	

BANNING, Sally	1842	H5	
BANNING, Sally	1878 *	H31	
BANNING, Sally	194?	F6014	
BANNING, Salma (???)	1790	E52	
BANNING, Samantha (Andre	184?	X9	
BANNING, Samantha	1858 *	B567	
BANNING, Samuel	1639	X2503	
BANNING, Samuel	1714	F6	
BANNING, Samuel	1738	F15	
BANNING, Samuel	176?	F54	
BANNING, Samuel	1789	F66	
BANNING, Samuel	1806	F203	
BANNING, Samuel S.	181?	A50	
BANNING, Samuel	182?	D10	
BANNING, Samuel W.	1820	F270	
BANNING, Samuel	1829	E403	
BANNING, Samuel C.	1834	B195	
BANNING, Samuel Waldo	1840	E1476	
BANNING, Samuel Terrill	1857 *	B766	
BANNING, Samuel	186?	F683	
BANNING, Samuel L.	1875	D54	
BANNING, Samuel	1875	F1214	
BANNING, Samuel Walker	1878	B601	
BANNING, Samuel	1879 *	D66	
BANNING, Samuel	1908	F2622a	
BANNING, Sandra Lee	1950	C3406	
BANNING, Sandy Allen	1880	Q26	
BANNING, Sanford	176?	C11	
BANNING, Sarah (Hall)	164?	X2502	
BANNING, Sarah	1646	X2506	
BANNING, Sarah (Tibbals)	165?	X2507	
BANNING, Sarah (Needham)	165?	X2508	
BANNING, Sarah (Tiffany)	1683	E2, F2	
BANNING, Sarah	1685	X2540	
BANNING, Sarah (Marshell	170?	A12e	
BANNING, Sarah (Root)	172?	X2632	
BANNING, Sarah	1722	X2635	
BANNING, Sarah	1736	A34f	
BANNING, Sarah (Elwyn)	174?	X2755	
BANNING, Sarah	1741	X2753	
BANNING, Sarah	1743 *	A16	
BANNING, Sarah	1745	F17	
BANNING, Sarah	1748 *	A16a	
BANNING, Sarah	1752	A16b	
BANNING, Sarah (Harvey)	1752	E17	
BANNING, Sarah	1753	E21	
BANNING, Sarah	1757	L11	
BANNING, Sarah (Hall)	176?	X2993	
BANNING, Sarah M. (Pierc	1766	A29	
BANNING, Sarah (Coleman)	177?	A19	
BANNING, Sarah	177?	X2995	
BANNING, Sarah	1775	E51	
BANNING, Sarah	1778	B16	
BANNING, Sarah (Geddes)	1778	A23	
BANNING, Sarah	1787	C13	
BANNING, Sarah (Sparks)	179?	D2	
BANNING, Sarah B.	1792	A67	
BANNING, Sarah M.	18??	E366	
BANNING, Sarah (Simmerma	180?	B20	
BANNING, Sarah (???)	1808	F246	
BANNING, Sarah (Lane)	181?	F209	
BANNING, Sarah (Webb)	1814	H1	
BANNING, Sarah (Bevins)	1820	B71	
BANNING, Sarah	182?	I13	
BANNING, Sarah	182?	P5	
BANNING, Sarah (Hall)	1821	F2622	
BANNING, Sarah (Peabody)	1824	F255	
BANNING, Sarah Ann (Howa	1825	Q1	
BANNING, Sarah Davidson	1826	A246	
BANNING, Sarah (Rickman)	183?	B79	
BANNING, Sarah (Thomas)	183?	J1	
BANNING, Sarah (Williams	183?	E1507	
BANNING, Sarah A. (???)	1830	C19	
BANNING, Sarah A.(Allen)	1830	B77	
BANNING, Sarah (Burnette	184?	E1565	
BANNING, Sarah (Campbell	184?	G20	
BANNING, Sarah	184?	I67	
BANNING, Sarah J. (???)	1843	B114	
BANNING, Sarah	1846	A260	
BANNING, Sarah E.	1846	B334	
BANNING, Sarah J.	1850	B312c	
BANNING, Sarah J. (Hubba	1854	B140	
BANNING, Sarah Jane	1855	J19	
BANNING, Sarah A.E. (Rog	1856	B172	
BANNING, Sarah	1857	B280	
BANNING, Sarah Jane	1857	J31	
BANNING, Sarah Jane	1864	C264	
BANNING, Sarah Jane (Ros	1866	C260	
BANNING, Sarah J.	1867	B953	
BANNING, Sarah Ellen	1868	B940c	
BANNING, Sarah Elizabeth	187?	X1534	
BANNING, Sarah Ellen	1870 *	Q21	
BANNING, Sarah Charlotte	1871	E6361	
BANNING, Sarah (???)	1874	B942	
BANNING, Sarah Bell	1877	J18	
BANNING, Sarah E.(Pitchf	188?	B609	
BANNING, Sarah N.	1886	B962a	
BANNING, Sarah Louise	1888	B605	
BANNING, Sarah Margaret	1963	H842	
BANNING, Sarah Rose	1976	E39073	
BANNING, Sassy Kelly	182?	B74	
BANNING, Schnyler	1800	F68	
BANNING, Scofield	187?	E6306	
BANNING, Scott C.	1946 *	F11989	
BANNING, Scott Richard	1969	H831	
BANNING, Scott Michael	1980	F15001	
BANNING, Seba	1769	F58	
BANNING, Selden Warner	1782	E81	
BANNING, Selden C.	1798	E296	
BANNING, Selinda	17??	E1028	
BANNING, Selinda (Keeney	1834	E388	
BANNING, Selma (McFarlan	1859	F552	
BANNING, Selma	187?	F1507	
BANNING, Selms	189?	F1400i	
BANNING, Senna	1846	F627	
BANNING, Sevator	1878	F1207	
BANNING, Sharon Joy (Rac	1943	H378	
BANNING, Sharon	1946	Q195	
BANNING, Shawn Patrick	1983	H1019	
BANNING, Sheila M.	1981	Q249	
BANNING, Sheldon Arthur	1848	G20	
BANNING, Sherman	1864	B307	
BANNING, Sherman Ellis	1890	J136	
BANNING, Sherman	1896	B2505a	

439

BANNING, Sheryl Sue	1951	R493		BANNING, Susie	1867	B700
BANNING, Shirley	1928	F7005		BANNING, Susie Geneva	1875	E6730
BANNING, Shirley	193?	F3097		BANNING, Suzanne	193?	F3098
BANNING, Shirley Ann	1937	C3335		BANNING, Sybyl	193?	F3096
BANNING, Silas B.	1825	F276		BANNING, Sylvester Vanda	1815	F246
BANNING, Silas Robin	1844	F605		BANNING, Sylvester	187?	B309
BANNING, Sill	1780	E54		BANNING, Sylvia M. (Post	1808	E385
BANNING, Simon	1837	E408		BANNING, Sylvia	1899	F2623
BANNING, Sinda Ann	1868	B940b		BANNING, Tabitha	1693	X2544
BANNING, Solomon	1841	B236		BANNING, Tabitha	1728	X2639
BANNING, Sophia C.(Edmon	1775	A25		BANNING, Tabitha	1751	X2761
BANNING, Sophia (Zimmerm	1798	A68		BANNING, Talcot T.	1823	F275
BANNING, Sophia (Kandelh	180?	N266		BANNING, Tammy L. (Richa	1964	E19110
BANNING, Sophia	1817	E390		BANNING, Temperance	1776	E64
BANNING, Sophia Eva	1834	A237		BANNING, Tempie (Neel)	186?	B237a
BANNING, Sophia Emma	1850	B277		BANNING, Tempy (Harris)	181?	B85
BANNING, Sophia Eva	1855	A634		BANNING, Teresa Delores	1960	E19111
BANNING, Sophia Misouria	1856 *	C261		BANNING, Terry	194?	B26013
BANNING, Sophia	1864	A659		BANNING, Thalia	1916	B1793
BANNING, Sophia A.	1886 *	E6736		BANNING, Theadocia (Bram	1803	E84
BANNING, Sophia E.	1891	B992		BANNING, Thelma L.(Scovi	1915	C1916
BANNING, Stacey	195?	F11993		BANNING, Thelma I.(Einse	1926	E10828
BANNING, Stanley	1841	L200		BANNING, Theodora Joan	1933	F3109
BANNING, Stanley	1890 *	G70		BANNING, Theodore	1827	E378
BANNING, Star	1860 *	F621		BANNING, Theodore Roosev	1899	F1418
BANNING, Stella	187?	Q30		BANNING, Thomas	1650	X2508
BANNING, Stella May	1892	Q55		BANNING, Thomas	1688	X2541
BANNING, Stella	1913	F2624a		BANNING, Thomas	169?	A5d
BANNING, Stephen	163?	K41		BANNING, Thomas	172?	X2634
BANNING, Stephen	166?	K71,A1		BANNING, Thomas	1724	A12a
BANNING, Stephen	1815	B43		BANNING, Thomas	1728	A34b
BANNING, Stephen	1843	X3506		BANNING, Thomas	1748	K352
BANNING, Stephen Thomas	1859	K2931		BANNING, Thomas	175?	A103c
BANNING, Stephen Earl	1955	E19066		BANNING, Thomas	1759	L7
BANNING, Stirling	176?	F56		BANNING, Thomas	177?	B12
BANNING, Stoddard	1832	F259		BANNING, Thomas	1770	A26
BANNING, Susan (Norden)	15??	X2003		BANNING, Thomas	1775	K606
BANNING, Susan	162?	X2009		BANNING, Thomas	1776	K602
BANNING, Susan (Thomas)	178?	A22		BANNING, Thomas Haines	1784	L29
BANNING, Susan	181?	A45		BANNING, Thomas Wiley	1794	B48
BANNING, Susan (Sherwood	181?	A50		BANNING, Thomas	1801 *	L48
BANNING, Susan	1820	E390a		BANNING, Thomas	1804	K1251
BANNING, Susan (Murray)	1820	E302		BANNING, Thomas C.	1807	H1
BANNING, Susan Antonia	1846	A118		BANNING, Thomas A.	1808	B69
BANNING, Susan Jami	1846	B118a		BANNING, Thomas	1816	K1270
BANNING, Susan Andrew	1859	B772		BANNING, Thomas Wrenshal	1819	L183
BANNING, Susan Agnes	1876	B779		BANNING, Thomas	182?	L123
BANNING, Susan D.	189?	P135		BANNING, Thomas C.	182?	X500
BANNING, Susan Bartley	1895	E12587		BANNING, Thomas	1825	B77
BANNING, Susan (Rushton	1947	Q150		BANNING, Thomas	1828	X3501
BANNING, Susan Kay	1952	C3409		BANNING, Thomas Franklin	1834	B156
BANNING, Susan Rae	1959	E19067		BANNING, Thomas Davidson	1840	A253
BANNING, Susan Margaret	1963	H842		BANNING, Thomas O.	1840	H4
BANNING, Susana	1855	C233		BANNING, Thomas M.	1845	B221
BANNING, Susanna (Warner	1753	E19		BANNING, Thomas Henry	1847	J5
BANNING, Susanna H.	1776	E83		BANNING, Thomas Clark	1849	B319
BANNING, Susanna (???)	1804	B68		BANNING, Thomas	185?	A285
BANNING, Susannah (???)	166?	A3		BANNING, Thomas Belle	185?	X504
BANNING, Susannah	170?	A5g		BANNING, Thomas Allen	1851	B140
BANNING, Susannah	1702	A12f		BANNING, Thomas	1858	B232
BANNING, Susannah	1712	K236		BANNING, Thomas Pleasant	1869	B776
BANNING, Susannah Ann	1848	P25		BANNING, Thomas	1872	Q22

440

Name	Year	Code
BANNING, Thomas	1872	J33
BANNING, Thomas Gilmer	1881	B594
BANNING, Thomas Hubert	1882 *	B590
BANNING, Thomas Jasper	1883	B183
BANNING, Thomas Ephraim	1884	B609
BANNING, Thomas D.	1885	B991
BANNING, Thomas Allen	1886	B604
BANNING, Thomas Melvin	191?	H144
BANNING, Thomas Ephraim	1918	B1822
BANNING, Thomas Lester	1944	E19113
BANNING, Thomas Joseph	1958	H827
BANNING, Thurman Charles	1918	H175c
BANNING, Timothy	1777 *	X2999
BANNING, Timothy	1779	X3000
BANNING, Timothy	1822	F255
BANNING, Timothy Baxter	1969	F12001
BANNING, Tommy	193?	J500
BANNING, Tommy	1936 *	J501
BANNING, Troy William	1966	H839
BANNING, Tyler Daniel	1990	E50032
BANNING, Ursula (Sheiler	1813	E305
BANNING, Ursula Ann	183?	E1381
BANNING, Useba M	1810	F210
BANNING, Vanetta (Laster	1940	E19047
BANNING, Velda (Carter)	191?	B2506b
BANNING, Velma L. (Fell)	190?	F3375
BANNING, Velma Mildred	1914	E10813
BANNING, Verda Irene	1913	C1828
BANNING, Verna Rue	1890	C567
BANNING, Verna Ethel	1919	Q69
BANNING, Vernon Laval	1891	C558
BANNING, Vianah R.	1830	B193
BANNING, Vicky Rae	1940	C3421
BANNING, Victor	1923	Q85
BANNING, Victor	1945	Q188
BANNING, Victoria	1847	B282
BANNING, Vietta M.(West)	193?	H330
BANNING, Vincent	1865 *	C127
BANNING, Vinal	1907	H120
BANNING, Viola (Suydam)	185?	B142
BANNING, Vira	1885	D68
BANNING, Virginia Albert	1912 *	C1940
BANNING, Virginia (O'Neil)	1922	F3090
BANNING, Virginia A.	194?	H404
BANNING, Waldo	188?	E6308
BANNING, Walker	1882	B599
BANNING, Walker	1904	B1790
BANNING, Wallace J.	1854	E1018
BANNING, Walter Edgar	1833	E1001
BANNING, Walter F.	186?	C116
BANNING, Walter Edwin	1863	E1361
BANNING, Walter John	1864	E6404
BANNING, Walter	189?	J61
BANNING, Walter Edwin	1908	E10811
BANNING, Walter	1914 *	H125b
BANNING, Walter Lee	1936	E19069
BANNING, Wanda	189?	G168
BANNING, Wanda A.(Gore)	1950	H501
BANNING, Ward	190?	F1400m
BANNING, Warren	187?	E6502
BANNING, Wayne Elson	1893	B613
BANNING, Wells Tanner	1838	F582
BANNING, Wendy (Wilson)	195?	F11990
BANNING, Werner	1903	N3690
BANNING, Wesley	177?	A27
BANNING, Wesley	185?	A286
BANNING, Wesley Gene	1935	C1885
BANNING, White	176?	C10
BANNING, Wilfred	1869	F1211
BANNING, Wilhelmeine (Kr	179?	N266
BANNING, Willard Gradner	1873	E6674
BANNING, William	168?	A5, B1
BANNING, William	169?	A6
BANNING, William	1710	L1
BANNING, William	172?	A36b
BANNING, William	1732	L3
BANNING, William	1747	E18
BANNING, William	1750	A103
BANNING, William	1756	L6
BANNING, William	1773	E62
BANNING, William	1784	B25
BANNING, William	1785	L30
BANNING, William	1799 *	L47
BANNING, William	1799	B29
BANNING, William Hall	1804 *	E307
BANNING, William	1808	A40p
BANNING, William	181?	L117
BANNING, William	181?	X101
BANNING, William Josiah	1810	E346
BANNING, William Theophi	1811	E311
BANNING, William	1812	X1500
BANNING, William Lowber	1814	C20
BANNING, William	1816	B90a
BANNING, William	1817	B86
BANNING, William A.	1817	C79
BANNING, William	1817	Q1
BANNING, William	1821	L184
BANNING, William Warner	1825	E401
BANNING, William Davidso	1830	A250
BANNING, William Bird	1833	B223
BANNING, William	1834	B169
BANNING, William W.	1836	B217a
BANNING, William	1837 *	E1474
BANNING, William	1837	H8d
BANNING, William Frederi	1837	B133
BANNING, William James	1837	L198
BANNING, William Henry	1838	B116
BANNING, William Jackson	1840	B214b
BANNING, William Station	1840	D11
BANNING, William Wasson	1840	F603
BANNING, William	1841	C96
BANNING, William Albert	1841	L457
BANNING, William Ward	1842	G17
BANNING, William J.	1843	B298
BANNING, William Augustu	1844	E1493
BANNING, William Dadley	1844	A259
BANNING, William Birkhea	1845	A119
BANNING, William W.	1847	B196
BANNING, William Peck	1847 *	F586
BANNING, William Calvin	1848	E1480
BANNING, William	1848	Q5
BANNING, William W.	1849	X3508
BANNING, William	185?	M8
BANNING, William Lowber	185? *	C99

Name	Year	Code	Name	Year	Code
BANNING, William Samuel	1851	E1644	BANNING, Willis Scott	1854	E1399
BANNING, William Hicks	1853	B258	BANNING, Willis	1855	B237a
BANNING, William Alonzo	1853 *	B764	BANNING, Willis F.	1888	B963
BANNING, William S.	1856	B304	BANNING, Wilson P.	1848	B312b
BANNING, William	1858	C123	BANNING, Windsor Morgan	1894	E6364
BANNING, William F.	1858	B241	BANNING, Winifred	1899	C663
BANNING, William Selden	1859	E1625	BANNING, Winifred (Willi	190?	B1015
BANNING, William	186?	H10	BANNING, Winnie	186? *	B522
BANNING, William	1863 *	F622	BANNING, Winthrop Hancoc	1965	C2197
BANNING, William Anthony	1863	J10	BANNING, Wolfgang	1902	N3686
BANNING, William Tolman	1863 *	B699	BANNING, Wright H.	185?	F561
BANNING, William R.	1864	B940	BANNING, Yvette (Aube)	1919	Q68
BANNING, William Frank	1865	Q19	BANNING, Zara Jackson	1873	B747
BANNING, William Jay	1866	E4204	BANNING, Zella (Smith)	1897	J137
BANNING, William Bowers	1867	F761	BANNING, Zella (Smith)	189?	J140b
BANNING, William	1867	X3806	BANNING, Zeruiah Emily	1827	F271c
BANNING, William Lowber	1869	C102	BANNING, Zoe Lee (Terr	1906	B2036
BANNING, William Otis	1869	E1681	BANNING, Zuneita	1897	P139
BANNING, William henry	1869	R39	BANTA, Katherine	183?	E403
BANNING, William Ward	187?	G81	BARLETT, Emilie	185?	B139
BANNING, William H.	187?	X1532	BARLOW, Emma	184?	F644
BANNING, William Theophi	1871 *	E5804	BARNARD, Chad Ray	1974	B26038
BANNING, William	1872	G72	BARNARD, Jennifer (Stol	1974	B26038
BANNING, William	1872	D53	BARNES, America	184?	X3506
BANNING, William Arthur	1872 *	J28	BARNES, Alfred A.	187?	F1499
BANNING, William Carlton	1873	H28	BARNES, Eleanor	1724	F6
BANNING, William	1875	D65	BARNES, Helen	189?	C316
BANNING, William Burgess	1876	B589	BARNES, Lilly R. (B=)	187?	F1499
BANNING, William McLain	1876	A668	BARNES, Madora	1853	X3508
BANNING, William {Winnie}	1879	R121	BARNES, Martin	182?	X3508
BANNING, William Peck	1880	F1410	BARNES, Mr.	190?	F2624a
BANNING, William Davidso	1882 *	A689	BARNES, Rebecca (Cone)	169?	F6
BANNING, William C.	1886	B752	BARNES, Stella (B=)	1913	F2624a
BANNING, William Lowber	189?	C269	BARNES, Thomas	169?	F6
BANNING, William Jacob	1890 *	C660a	BARNETT, Matilda Jane	187?	E5619
BANNING, William	1897	B1749	BARR, Eliza Jane	181?	B86
BANNING, William Phineas	1899	C299	BARRAS, Mary	177?	K606
BANNING, William	190?	D174	BARRETT, David M.	192?	B26000
BANNING, William	1901	B986	BARRETT, Jean (Bull)	192?	B26000
BANNING, William Vaughn	1906	A1653	BARRETT, Laurel Jean	1947	B26000
BANNING, William Miles	1907	H134	BARRETT, Sarah Lurinda	182?	A643
BANNING, William Otis	1907	E6898	BARROW, Mary B. (Rea)	1873	L470
BANNING, William Henry	1909	J204	BARROW, Samuel (Rev)	187?	L470
BANNING, William Culkin	1920 *	F3091	BARTHOLOMEW, Jenny(Kirk	187?	E5618
BANNING, William Peck	1923	F3082	BARTHOLOMEW, Myrtle	1898	E5618
BANNING, William Thomas	1929	H330	BARTHOLOMEW, Oliver	187?	E5618
BANNING, William Raymond	1929	H374	BARTLETT, Bessie	189?	A707
BANNING, William C.	193?	B2057	BARTLETT, Charles G.	185?	E1483
BANNING, William	194?	B9702	BARTLETT, Elizabeth	189?	A707
BANNING, William Tanner	194?	F6013	BARTLETT, Harriet (B=)	1855	E1483
BANNING, William C.	1947	H775	BARTLETT, Isaac	1778	E59
BANNING, William	195?	B9644	BARTLETT, Jemima	1785	E59
BANNING, William Benjami	1953	H501	BARTLETT, Otis	18??	B139
BANNING, William G.	1954	H824	BARTLEY, Charlotte	187?	E6673
BANNING, William C.	1966	H1301	BARTLEY, Joshua	184?	E6673
BANNING, William	197?	F9968	BARTON, Nelly	1895	B985
BANNING, William Benjami	1977	H1013	BASAKER, Anna B.	184?	X3507
BANNING, Williamson	1809	B57	BASSETT, Estella (B=)	1856	F1203
BANNING, Williamson	1829	B177	BATES, Orcencia (B=)	18??	F649
BANNING, Williamson	1868	B775	BATES, Stephen	18??	F649
BANNING, Willie Charles	1860 *	E1585	BATSCHELETT, Betty (B=)	194?	B9701
BANNING, Willie	188? *	J59	BATSCHELETT, Mr.	194?	B9701

BATSCHI, Cora (Sams)	1890	C1860
BATSCHI, Otto	188?	C1860
BATTLES, Maxine Joy	194?	J2118
BAUMGARDNER, Patricia	194?	J2115
BAUMGARTENNER, Lucil	191?	J204
BAXTER, Alta Jean	1879	F1509
BAXTER, Charles W.	185?	F1509
BAXTER, Darcy	1981	A3659
BAXTER, Flora (B=)	1917	A1655
BAXTER, Jeffrey	1986	A3659
BAXTER, Lawrence Joel	1949	A3660
BAXTER, Mary (Shellaba	185?	F1509
BAXTER, Matthew	1977	A3659
BAXTER, Robert Clarkson	1916	A1655
BAXTER, Robert Banning	1946	A3659
BAXTER, Sandra (Weber)	194?	A3659
BAXTER, Sandra (Rapkin)	195?	A3660
BAXTER, Victoria	1981	A3660
BAXTER, William Vaughn	1987	A3660
BAYFORD, Ada B. (Widows	1842	L453
BAYFORD, Henry	183?	L453
BEACH, Dora W.	186?	F1202
BEATY, Jane	1800	B53
BEAUMONT, Michael	1942	F6014
BEAUMONT, Sally (B=)	194?	F6014
BECKWITH, Benjamin	1791	E421
BECKWITH, Caroline Irene	179?	E427
BECKWITH, Debora	179?	E424
BECKWITH, Elizabeth	178?	E414
BECKWITH, Eunice	1786	E67
BECKWITH, Francis E.	174?	E87
BECKWITH, Francis	179?	E425
BECKWITH, George	175?	E414
BECKWITH, George	179?	E426
BECKWITH, Irene (B=)	1745	E87
BECKWITH, John E.	179?	E428
BECKWITH, Josiah	175?	E67
BECKWITH, Lucinda	179?	E423
BECKWITH, Mehitable (Pea	176?	E67
BECKWITH, Nathan	172?	E28
BECKWITH, Penelop (??)	175?	E414
BECKWITH, Reed	179?	E422
BECKWITH, Sarah (Brockwa	1734	E28
BEDDICK, Mrs.	187?	F1211
BEEBE, Beatrice (B=)	188?	E5847
BEEBE, Clyde M.	187?	E6681
BEEBE, Elsie	187?	E6680
BEEBE, Hannah (B=)	1845	E1620
BEEBE, J. Ely	184?	E1620
BEEBE, Louise	187?	E6678
BEEBE, Martin	187?	E6679
BEEBE, Victor Lloyd	187?	E6682
BEERS, Kathryn E.	1922	C1880
BELAND, Carol Ann	1941	H376
BELAND, Evelyn R. (Touri	191?	H376
BELAND, Oliver	191?	H376
BELEC, Anne	1912	Q80
BELL, Emma (Stroud)	188?	H176a
BELL, James	170?	A5d
BELL, Margaret (Purnell)	169?	A5a
BELL, Ruby	191?	A176a
BELL, Samuel	188?	A176a
BELL, William	169?	A5a
BELLS, Amelia (Vinning)	176?	F236
BELLS, Henry	179?	F236
BELLS, Jerome	179?	F236
BELLS, Osiah Sheldon	176?	F236
BELLS, Samuel	179?	F236
BENJAMIN, Josiah	1769	E60
BENJAMIN, Lucy (B=)	1770	E60
BENJAMIN, Sarah (???)	174?	E60
BENJAMIN, William	174?	E60
BENNETT, Benjamin	169?	X2545
BENNETT, Elizabeth (B=)	1694	X2545
BENNETT, John A.	184?	A235
BENNINGFIELD, Ben F.	1844	B197
BENNINGFIELD, Charles H.	1878	B808
BENNINGFIELD, james C.	1868	B807
BENNINGFIELD, Jancy (B=)	1852	B197
BENTON, Ellen	178?	F237
BERG, Peter Vandyk	193?	F3109
BERG, Theo Dora (B=)	1933	F3109
BERQUIST, Martha V.	192?	B1783
BERTRAM, Charles	191?	Q77
BERTRAM, Maud (B=)	191?	Q77
BESHEARS, Annie D.	1816	E10802
BESHEARS, Henrietta	194?	E19061
BESS, Alfia Mae	1929	E19042
BESS, Duncan Eve	1900	E10801
BESS, Gladys (B=)	1906	E10801
BESS, Leroy	1937 *	E19043
BESS, Mary Alice	1926	E19041
BESS, Sharon Elaine	1947	E19044
BEST, Carloine	191?	Q144
BETTS, Darlene Ethel	1954	H760
BETTS, Debra Naioma	1956	H761
BETTS, Frances A. (B=)	1927	H325
BETTS, George Hall	192?	H325
BEVINS, Sarah C.	1820	B71
BIDDLEMAN, Howard	189?	C1863
BIDDLEMAN, Verna (Sams)	1896	C1863
BIDGOOD, Birdie	190?	Q44
BIDWELL, Fannie M. (B=)	1869	F1495
BIDWELL, Frank E.	186?	F1495
BIDWELL, Marshall Frankl	1895	F3321
BIDWELL, Waldo Trundy	1893	F3320
BIERSDORFER, Elizabeth	187?	B599
BIESEL, Anna Mae	192?	C1904
BIGELOW, Edward	185?	F631
BIGELOW, Katherine Lansi	188?	E6568
BIGELOW, Mary (Peabody)	1857	F631
BILLINGS, Mary Ellen (B=	1856	J20
BILLINGS, Mr.	185?	J20
BILLOTTE, Bonnie (McGahe	1943	E19103
BILLOTTE, Michael	194?	E19103
BINGHAM, Elijah	173?	E29
BINGHAM, George	186?	E1626
BINGHAM, Mary (Brockway)	1738	E29
BINGHAM, Minnie (B=)	186?	E1626
BIRD, Agusta F.	1849	B64a
BIRD, Angelica (B=)	1775	B15
BIRD, Asbury	1817 *	B64c
BIRD, Ashbury	1823	B62a
BIRD, Benjamin	1745	B15

BIRD, Benjamin	1814	B64a
BIRD, Benjamin Andrew	1846	B62a
BIRD, Benton	1840	B63c
BIRD, Bird	184?	B62a
BIRD, Carmine Sevier	1844	B62a
BIRD, Cassandia	176?	B17
BIRD, Catherine	1850	B63c
BIRD, Ceila Brittain	1832	B62a
BIRD, Charles A.	1859	B64a
BIRD, Clairssia M.(Conle	1823	B64a
BIRD, Clark	1800	B62a
BIRD, Delilah (???)	1817	B63c
BIRD, Eleanor Merinda	1838	B62a
BIRD, Elizabeth (???)	174?	B15
BIRD, Elizabeth	1811	B64
BIRD, Elizabeth Jane	1829	B62a
BIRD, Elizabeth	1844	B63c
BIRD, George W.	1858	B63c
BIRD, Green	1802 *	B62b
BIRD, Harbert	1809	B63c
BIRD, Harriet V.	1844	B64a
BIRD, Hood A.	1856	B64a
BIRD, James Harvey	1821	B62a
BIRD, Jessie Richardson	1840	B62a
BIRD, John Williamson	1824	B62a
BIRD, John W.	1839	B63c
BIRD, Jonathan	1764	B15
BIRD, Jonathan	1826	B62
BIRD, Jonathan Lafayette	1837	B62a
BIRD, Joseph	1852	B63c
BIRD, Joseph L.C.	1854	B64a
BIRD, Joshua Curtis	1828	B62a
BIRD, Lavisa	1802	B62
BIRD, Lemuel	1799	B62
BIRD, Lousia Delilah	1831	B62a
BIRD, Margaret A.	1846	B64a
BIRD, Martha Ovian	1842	B62a
BIRD, Mary Pauline	180?	B62a
BIRD, Mary Ann	1825	B62a
BIRD, Mary R.	1836	B63c
BIRD, Mary C.	1866	B64a
BIRD, Mirnda	1803 *	B63
BIRD, Rebecca (???)	180?	B63b
BIRD, Rebecca Melinda	1835	B62a
BIRD, Rolie A.	1838	B62
BIRD, Sarah Ann	1816 *	B64b
BIRD, Sarah M.	1861	B63c
BIRD, Thomas	1804 *	B63a
BIRD, William	1828	B62
BIRD, Williamson	1806	B63b
BIRKHEAD, Maria S.	181?	A42
BISHOP, Dovie A. (B=)	1889	B991b
BISHOP, Michael	186?	B952
BISHOP, Nancy (B=)	186?	B952
BISHOP, T.	188?	B991b
BLACK, Elizabeth	176?	B9
BLACK, Henry	173?	B9
BLACK, Martha	173?	B9
BLACKBURN, Maggie	187?	Q24
BLACKSTONE, Eliza	1805	A70
BLACKSTONE, James	177?	A70
BLACKSTONE, Sir William	1???	A70

BLAKESLEY, Mattie (Vand	1909	J212
BLAKESLEY, Robert E.	1901	J212
BLANCHARD, Delia (Raymon	1832	A243
BLANCHARD, James	183?	A243
BLEVINS, Bertha A.	190?	B3001
BLOOMER, Barbara Ann	193?	H835
BLOOMER, Milton Dayton	193?	H835
BLOOMER, Patty Ann	1958	H835
BLUE, Abraham	179?	C75
BLUE, Eliza Jane	182?	C227
BLUE, Mahala Frances	1821	C75
BLUE, Susannah (Shinsber	179?	C75
BOATRIGHT, Angela	1984	B26004
BOATRIGHT, Frank	1947	B26004
BOATRIGHT, Frank	1981	B26004
BOATRIGHT, Sherry (Swope	1962	B26004
BOHANNON, John L.	1854	E5614
BOHANNON, Mary (Owen)	1857	E5614
BOHANNON, Mary Alice	1887	E5614
BOHANNON, Maud	188?	E5615
BOHN, Alvin	188?	C567
BOHN, Verna Rue (B=)	1890	C567
BOKAR, Floyd	190?	H126
BOKAR, Mary E. (B=)	1872	H27
BOKAR, Roland	186?	H27
BOLES, Erasmus	186?	C263
BOLES, Mary E. (B=)	1862	C263
BOLLES, Emeline (B=)	1849	E1570
BOLLES, Ernest	187?	E6520
BOLLES, Grace	187?	E6521
BOLLES, Lemuel	184?	E1570
BONECUTTER, Beltran Lee	190?	H496
BONECUTTER, Fannie (Gree	190?	H496
BONECUTTER, Henry B.	1928	H496
BONECUTTER, Henry B.	1953	H496
BONECUTTER, John Steven	1955	H496
BONECUTTER, Wanda (Johns	1931	H496
BOOTH, Allen	185?	K51
BOOTH, Elizabeth (Pugh)	185?	K51
BORDEN, Harriet Marie	1824	F214
BORDEN, Sophronia	180?	F216
BORNE, Mary	1846	J1
BOTLEMAN, Matilda J.	1858	F645
BOTLEMAN, Minerva (Swear	1834	F645
BOTLEMAN, Newton M.	182?	F642
BOULER, Mary (B=)	1844	B119
BOULER, Mr.	184?	B119
BOULTON, Allen	1888	A1569
BOULTON, Caroline (B=)	1856	A635
BOULTON, Edward	185?	A635
BOULTON, Katherine	1880	A1568
BOULTON, Kittie	1880	A1568
BOULTON, Louisa	1892	A1570
BOWDLE, Sally	177?	A20
BOWERS, Lavina A.	1808	F288
BOWERS, Martha	1841	F288
BOWERS, William	1806	F288
BOWMAN, Eliza	183?	B129
BOWMAN, Mary	192?	H144
BOYD, Carey	189?	R126
BOYD, Gladys (B=)	189?	R126
BOYINGTON, Rhoda	186?	B570

BRADBURY, John	187?	C133		BRIGGS, Walter E.	187?	P121
BRADBURY, Lucy (B=)	1876	C133		BRINCKLEE, Elizabeth	180?	C55
BRADFORD, Dorothy (B=)	193?	J416		BRINIG, Brian Joseph	1991	F6010
BRADFORD, Mr.	193?	J416		BRINIG, Jill Elizabeth	1985	F6010
BRADLEY, Asenath C.	1824	F253		BRINIG, Joseph F.	1946	F6010
BRADLEY, Carl	192?	E19113		BRINIG, Kathleen Ann	1982	F6010
BRADLEY, Carol Marie	1947	E19113		BRINIG, Margaret (Friedl	1949	F6010
BRADLEY, Dolly N. (Hicks	192?	E19113		BRINIG, Mary Margaret	1978	F6010
BRADLEY, Ella M.	1874	B317b		BRINIG, Wendy Christine	1980	F6010
BRADLEY, Francis M.	1861	B316		BRITTAIN, Alva Elgon	190?	B2048
BRADLEY, Henry S.	1867	B317		BRITTAIN, Iva May (B=)	190?	B2048
BRADLEY, James	1840	B92		BROADMAN, Hannah	169?	X2543
BRADLEY, James H.	1865	B316b		BROADMAN, P. C.	186?	E6361
BRADLEY, Mary	184?	B185		BROADMAN, Sarah (B=)	1871	E6361
BRADLEY, Nancy E.	1862	B316a		BROCKWAY, Abigail (B=)	1760	E85
BRADLEY, Philadelphia(B=	1833	B92		BROCKWAY, Betsy	179?	E414c
BRADLEY, Prudence B.	1869	B317a		BROCKWAY, Caroline (Reed	173?	E26,E86
BRAINARD, Mary	182?	E1506		BROCKWAY, Caroline	178?	E416
BRAKE, Dorothy	191?	E19051		BROCKWAY, Caroline	179?	E414a
BRAKE, Mary Ann	1936	E19051		BROCKWAY, Deborah Reed	1788	E415
BRAKE, Melburn	191?	E19051		BROCKWAY, Ebenezer	1731	E85
BRAMBLE, Burton	187?	E1693		BROCKWAY, Edgar Warner	183?	E1623
BRAMBLE, Frederick	187?	E1691		BROCKWAY, Elizabeth	167?	E3
BRAMBLE, George	186?	E1686		BROCKWAY, Elizabeth (B=)	1705	E3
BRAMBLE, Grace	187?	E1694		BROCKWAY, Elizabeth	1728	E25
BRAMBLE, Laura (B=)	1838	E409		BROCKWAY, Elizabeth (Beck	178?	E414
BRAMBLE, Lorian Henry	187?	E1690		BROCKWAY, Elizabeth	1841	E1399
BRAMBLE, Louise	186?	E1689		BROCKWAY, Emerette	184?	E1530
BRAMBLE, Mary	186?	E1688		BROCKWAY, Ezra	1764	E86
BRAMBLE, Melissa (Green)	186?	E1689		BROCKWAY, Ezra	1796	E418
BRAMBLE, Nelson	183?	E409		BROCKWAY, Ezra	182?	F218
BRAMBLE, Robert	187?	E1692		BROCKWAY, Janette F.	183?	E1529
BRAMBLE, Rose	186?	E1685		BROCKWAY, John	1697	E3
BRAMBLE, Silas	17??	E84		BROCKWAY, John	1729	E26,E86
BRAMBLE, Theadocia	1803	E84		BROCKWAY, John C.M.	1784	E414
BRAMBLE, Willis	186?	E1687		BROCKWAY, Juliete Maliss	1809	F250
BRAND, Mary Elizabeth	193?	B26007		BROCKWAY, Leonora	180?	E418
BRASSEY, Annie (B=)	1839	L458		BROCKWAY, Lucina	1795	E417
BRASSEY, Frances T. (B=)	1844	L459		BROCKWAY, Margaret (B=)	1762	E86
BRASSEY, George	183?	L459		BROCKWAY, Margaret	1805	E420
BRASSEY, Thomas	183?	L458		BROCKWAY, Margaret (B=)	182?	F218
BRAUN, Hazel L.	1887	B2139		BROCKWAY, Mary (Butler)	173?	E27,E85
BRAUN, Louis	186?	B788		BROCKWAY, Mary	1738	E29
BRAUN, Mary (B=)	18??	B788		BROCKWAY, Mary	1794	E414b
BREUTLINGER, Minnie	18??	A703		BROCKWAY, Niles	1798	E419
BREWER, Josephine (B=)	1906	C665		BROCKWAY, Sarah	169?	E3
BREWER, Nina	184?	L200		BROCKWAY, Sarah	1734	E28
BREWER, Raymond R.	190?	C665		BROCKWAY, William	1666	E3
BRIAN, Myra	190?	H117		BROCKWAY, William	18??	E1399
BRICKHEAD, Maria S.	181?	A42		BROCKWAY, Zebulon	175?	E85
BRIDGE, Doria	190?	C796		BROCKWAY, Zebulon	1791	E414a
BRIDGE, Joan	1925	C796		BRONSON, Alice	183? *	A256
BRIDGERS, Benjamin R.	194?	H337		BRONSON, Charles C. Pink	1800	A71
BRIDGERS, Darren B.	1967	H337		BRONSON, Charles Anthony	1839	A257
BRIDGERS, Gloria (Chandl	1944	H337		BRONSON, Elizabeth (B=)	1803	A71
BRIDGERS, Marc David	1970	H337		BRONSON, Mary Elizabeth	1829	A255
BRIEDENBACH, Joy (Ondroz	1914	C1903		BROOKS, Dillon	178?	B20
BRIEDENBACH, Louis H.	191?	C1903		BROOKS, Elizabeth A.	1806	B20
BRIESEN, Arthur V.	185?	E6319		BROOKS, Sarah (B=)	184?	I67
BRIESEN, Hedwig V.	1883	E6319		BROOKS, William	1747	B20
BRIGGS, George Sylvester	184?	P25		BROWN, Albert	187?	E1703
BRIGGS, Susannah (B=)	1848	P25		BROWN, Barbara	1917	A696

BROWN, Berman Dwight	1938	E19053	BUFORD, Julie Ann (B=)	1857	J6
BROWN, Bessie	1864	A694	BUFORD, Nary Elizabeth	189?	J51
BROWN, Brenda (Roach)	196?	E39025	BUFORD, Robert Franklin	189?	J53
BROWN, Cora (Jester)	1900	H58d	BUFORD, William Thomas	188?	J50
BROWN, Elichor	183?	E411	BUFORD, Zula Rose	189?	J56
BROWN, Eliza	186? *	A697	BULL, Frances	181?	E313
BROWN, Elizabeth Ann	179?	B10a	BULL, Jean D.	192?	B26000
BROWN, Elizabeth (B=)	1837	A252	BURCH, Caroline A. (B=)	1884	B595
BROWN, Ella (Skinner)	187?	E1703	BURCH, John Ernest	188?	B595
BROWN, Ethel (Campbell)	187?	A696	BURCH, John Shirley	1920	B1783
BROWN, Jackie L.	194?	H775	BURCH, John Robert	1947	B1783
BROWN, James	1868	A695	BURCH, Karen Elizabeth	1952	B1783
BROWN, Jane	188?	F1496	BURCH, Linda Kathleen	1951	B1783
BROWN, Lamar Anguish	191?	E19053	BURCH, Martha V. (Berquis	192?	B1783
BROWN, Leanor	187?	E1704	BURCH, Pamela Jean	1949	B1783
BROWN, Lois	191?	E19053	BURGIN, George F.	185?	B323
BROWN, Mary Emily	1832	E402	BURGIN, Rebecca Liticia	185?	B319
BROWN, Matilda (B=)	1835	E407	BURGIN, Rebecca (B=)	1860	B323
BROWN, Michael Lane	1962	E39025	BURKHEAD, Maria S.	1821	A42
BROWN, Minnie	186?	F566	BURNETT, Daphne J.	1963	E19104
BROWN, Mr.	183?	E407	BURNETT, Forest	192?	E19104
BROWN, Pamela Ann	1970	E39027	BURNETT, Marieta (McGahe	1946	E19104
BROWN, Patricia (Mathews	1940	E19053	BURNETT, Naomi	192?	E19104
BROWN, Rachel (B=)	1840	E411	BURNETT, Ronald F.	1942	E19104
BROWN, Steven Dwight	1964	E39026	BURNETTE, Sarah	184?	E1565
BROWN, William Burr	183?	A252	BURNEY, Marjorie Jacaque	193?	E39014
BROWN, William	1868	A696	BURNHAM, Ellen Aughsta	1850	E1581
BROWN, William	1913 *	A696	BURR, Ellen	182?	A222
BRUNER, Mae (Van Brunt)	192?	J429	BURRESS, Jack	194?	H331
BRUNER, Pete	192?	J429	BURRESS, Jason A.	1964	H779
BRYAN, Barbara Sue (B=)	1941	B9604	BURRESS, Nancy (B=)	1944	H331
BRYAN, Charles Andrew	1973	B26011	BURRIS, Carrie	186?	B1194
BRYAN, Clarence Edward	1970	B26010	BURROWS, Sarah	181?	R7
BRYAN, Michael	1946	B9604	BURTNETT, Charles A.	189?	H177c
BRYAN, Shelley R. (Bish	197?	B26011	BURTNETT, Debra June	1954	H177c
BRYAN, William Michael	1994	B26011	BURTNETT, Frances (Deatr	1922	H177c
BRYANT, Danielle Grace	1974	H760	BURTNETT, Marilyn Jean	1945	H177c
BRYANT, Darlene E.(Betts	1954	H760	BURTNETT, Nora (Straub)	190?	H177c
BRYANT, Daryl Anderson	1969	H760	BURTNETT, Theodore G.	1923	H177c
BRYANT, Deanna Marie	1975	H760	BURTNETT, Theodore Giffo	1955	H177c
BRYANT, Douglas George	195?	H760	BURTNETT, Verna Jane	1943	H177c
BRYANT, Douglas Aldon	1971	H760	BURTON, Ambrose	186?	B774
BRYANT, Elizabeth (B=)	1819	E374	BURTON, Annie (B=)	1866	B774
BRYANT, James	181?	E374	BURTON, Olive	190?	H495
BRYANT, Maria	184?	E1578	BUSHNELL, Alexander	1739	F23
BRYANT, Mary	184? *	E1579	BUSHNELL, Alexander	180?	F112
BRYSON, Earl	1898	B1763	BUSHNELL, Chloe (Waite)	1738	F23
BRYSON, Ella (B=)	1869	B586	BUSHNELL, Daniel	1763	F23
BRYSON, J. P.	186?	B586	BUSHNELL, George W.	1800	F111
BRYSON, Raymond A.	1893	B1762	BUSHNELL, Lewis	179?	F110
BRYSON, Susanna	1804	B68	BUSHNELL, Lorenzo	178?	F238
BUCK, Barbara	193?	C5666	BUSHNELL, Malinda (Robin	178?	F238
BUCK, Irvin Eugene	193?	C3407	BUSHNELL, Rebecca (B=)	1767	F23
BUCK, Jean M. (???)	193?	C3407	BUTLER, Abigail	177?	B28
BUCK, John Miles	1961	C3407	BUTLER, Mary	173?	E27,E85
BUCK, Patricia Ann (B=)	1956	C3407	BUTLER, John	169?	E27
BUFORD, Alexander Tillfo	1846	J6	BUTTON, Charles	182?	E400
BUFORD, Alice Bertha	189?	J55	BUTTON, Charlotta (B=)	1824	E400
BUFORD, Beulah May	189?	J57	BUXTON, Eleanor Jewel	1900	E12629
BUFORD, Charlie	189?	J54	BUXTON, Harrison Hall	187?	E6730
BUFORD, Effie Sarah	188?	J49	BUXTON, Susie)B=)	1875	E6730
BUFORD, James E.	189?	J52	BUXTON, William Banning	1902	E12630

BYIRD, Jonathan	177?	B15	CARMICHAEL, Hazel A. (B	1897	J139
CAIRNES, Mary E. (B=)	1894	B992a	CARMICHAEL, William Ed.	1893	J139
CAIRNES, Walter	189?	B992a	CARMICHAL, Arthur W.	1867	J15
CAKENOWELL, Elizabeth(B=	1841	B297	CARMICHAL, Isaac Newton	183?	J15
CAKENOWELL, Michael	183?	B297	CARMICHAL, Martha A. (B=	1872	J15
CALDER, Anna	172?	A12	CARMICHAL, Mary A.(Wolf)	183?	J15
CALDER, Anna	174?	A12	CARNACK, Maud	186?	F1478
CALDER, James	171?	A12	CARNEY, Laura	1870	B560
CALDWELL, Amy JH. (B=)	1821	F249	CARPENTER, Carina B.	185?	F585
CALDWELL, Charles	184?	F607	CARPENTER, Elizabeth Jan	1832	K1267
CALDWELL, Harriet	184?	E6672	CARRINGTON, M.E.A.	180?	K1252
CALDWELL, Helen Louise	182?	E1480	CARROUTHERS, Betty (B=)	192?	B2055
CALDWELL, Jessie	186?	F607	CARROUTHERS, Harvey	192?	B2055
CALDWELL, Laura	1843	F607	CARR, Margaret E.	185?	B241
CALDWELL, Leslie	184?	E6672	CARRINGTON, Philippin(B=	180?	K1252
CALDWELL, Mary Louise	187?	E6672	CARROLL, Pauline	190?	H120
CALDWELL, Myran	1854	F609	CARSON, Maude Mary	188?	B747
CALDWELL, William E.G.	1817	F249	CARTER, Betty Lucill(B=)	1917	J413
CALLAWAY, Emily (Oxford	1859	B794a	CARTER, Beverly Yvonne	1949	E19107
CALLAWAY, J.W.R.	1852	B794a	CARTER, Bonnie Jean	1937	J2113
CAMPBELL, Arthur William	1922	Q90	CARTER, Daniel W.	1913	J413
CAMPBELL, Donald	1882	Q55	CARTER, Deborah (Erling)	194?	J2115
CAMPBELL, Donna Angela	1956	Q90	CARTER, Dorothy R. (Thom	193?	J2110
CAMPBELL, Edward Donald	193?	Q89	CARTER, Franciel Eyvon	1940	J2114
CAMPBELL, Eileen (Teske)	1923	Q90	CARTER, Grace Bell (B=)	1917	J413
CAMPBELL, Ethel	187?	A696	CARTER, Jack	193?	E19057
CAMPBELL, Florence (King	191?	Q89	CARTER, James Carl	1942	J2115
CAMPBELL, Gertrude May	1911	Q87	CARTER, Joseph Elmer	191?	E19107
CAMPBELL, Gordon Edward	1913	Q89	CARTER, Kathy	193?	E19057
CAMPBELL, Hugh John	1959	Q90	CARTER, Lillian B. (Corg	191?	E19107
CAMPBELL, Jean	188?	Q38	CARTER, Loretta Mae	1936 *	J2112
CAMPBELL, Isabell M.	1814	B56	CARTER, May B. (Gatlin)	189?	J413
CAMPBELL, Leslie Ann	1958	Q90	CARTER, Minnie	191?	J204a
CAMPBELL, Lyall Arthur	1958	Q90	CARTER, Patricia(Baumgar	194?	J2115
CAMPBELL, Merle Martha	1912	Q88	CARTER, Peggy Louise	1946	J2117
CAMPBELL, Mildred	192?	H382	CARTER, Richard M.	1934	J2110
CAMPBELL, Sarah M.	185?	G20	CARTER, Thomas H.L.	189?	J413
CAMPBELL, Stella M. (B=)	1892	Q55	CARTER, Velda	191?	B2506b
CAMPBELL, Verda Florence	193?	Q89	CARTER, Virginia	1958	E19057
CAMPBELL, Verna	194?	Q89	CARTER, Wanda Lee	1944	J2116
CARDEEN, Priscilla	174?	C6	CARTHRAN, Hudson	180?	B19
CARDEEN, Rachel (???)	172?	C6	CARTHRAN, Nancy C. (???)	1802	B19
CARDEEN, William	172?	C6	CARTRIGHT, Edward B.	180?	F211
CARINTHEN, Anna S.M.	184?	L143	CARTRIGHT, Electa (B=)	1812	F211
CARINTHEN, W.H. (Rev.)	180?	L143	CARY, Deborah	184?	C229
CARLILE, Benjamin	1853	B794	CASE, Albina	182?	F270
CARLILE, Edgar L.	1881	B794	CASE, Bessie L.	1886	F1497
CARLILE, Ellen	1875	B794	CASE, Campbell P.	1844	F640
CARLILE, Eula M.	1895	B794	CASE, Charles P.	1879	F1496
CARLILE, Laura	1883	B794	CASE, Gladys Elizabeth	1892	F3318
CARLILE, Leonard	1900	B794	CASE, H. Bennett	186?	F1494
CARLILE, Mary (Oxford)	1856	B794	CASE, Hazel Fannie	1890	F3317
CARLILE, Mattie	1893	B794	CASE, Ida Fannie	1888	F1498
CARLILE, Scott	1890	B794	CASE, Jane (Brown)	188?	F1496
CARLISLE, Cameron Scott	1977	H1003	CASE, Kathryn Lucinda	1893	F3319
CARLISLE, Jessica	1980	H1004	CASE, Lamira (B=)	1848	F640
CARLISLE, Kathryn H.(B=)	1948	H492	CASE, Lucy	179?	F65
CARLISLE, Richard Farber	1944	H492	CASE, Nellie O. (B=)	1864	F1494
CARLISLE, Richard Bannin	1974	H1002	CASSEL, Joan (B=)	192?	E11135
CARLSON, Louise	188?		CASSON, Elizabeth	174?	C5
	E11020		CASTLE, Sarah Melissa	1874	E10802
CARLYLE, Frances	1805	B289	CASWELL, Henry	180?	A72

CASWELL, Mary (B=)	1805	A72	CHASE, Edith Nellie	188?	E6737
CASWELL, Unamed child	18?? *	A258	CHEAP, Marlyn	194?	Q190
CATES, Catherine (Swope)	1963	B26005	CHEEVER, A.B.	183?	J7
CATES, Eddie	1986	B26005	CHEEVER, Amanda (Lower)	183?	J7
CATES, James Luther	1981	B26005	CHEEVER, Rebecca Ann	186?	J7
CATES, Jewell	1961	B26005	CHEEZUM, Rebecca	175?	A103
CATES, Mollie	186?	B796	CHENOWETA, Leda (B=)	189?	B1144
CATES, Tawyna	1984	B26005	CHEW, Anna Sophia Penn	180?	A83
CATLIN, Kate	188?	G87	CHEW, Anthony Banning	1809	A85
CATURANO, Christopher J.	198?	H834	CHEW, Benjamin	173?	A30
CATURANO, Elizabeth C.(?	193?	H834	CHEW, Benjamin Jr.	1758	A30
CATURANO, John A.	193?	H834	CHEW, Benjamin	1793	A77
CATURANO, Michael A.	198?	H834	CHEW, Benjamin	183?	A81
CATURANO, Ronald A.	1956	H834	CHEW, Catherine Maria	1811 *	A86
CATURANO, Valerie A.(Cov	1956	H834	CHEW, Charles	183?	A81
CAVETT, Mr.	191?	J400	CHEW, Eliza	1791 *	A76
CAVETT, Ruby (Wright)	1913	J400	CHEW, Eliza Margaret	1798	A80
CESSNA, Louise	1823	A229	CHEW, Elizabeth (Oswald)	1735	A30
CESSNA, William T.	184?	A229	CHEW, Elizabeth (Tilgham	179?	A77
CHADON, Christina	187?	C563	CHEW, Elizabeth (Ralston	180?	A81
CHADWICK, Betsy (Ransom)	17??	E311	CHEW, Harriet (Ridgely)	180?	A81
CHADWICK, Charity (B=)	1913	B2506a	CHEW, Henry	1800	A81
CHADWICK, Earl	191?	B2506a	CHEW, John	1797 *	A79
CHAMBERS, Will	185?	B1027	CHEW, Joseph Turner	1806	A84
CHAMBERS, Mary (Tipsword	1857	B1027	CHEW, Katherine (B=)	177?	A30
CHAMPION, Hannah	171?	F19	CHEW, Oswald	1813 *	A87
CHANDLER, Arthur	187?	E1704	CHEW, Samuel	1789 *	A75
CHANDLER, Edna Ann	1942	H336	CHEW, Samuel	1795	A78
CHANDLER, Frances (Robbi	193?	H335	CHEW, Samuel	183?	A81
CHANDLER, Gloria Lynn	1944	H337	CHEW, Sophia	180?	A83
CHANDLER, Leanor (Brown)	187?	E1704	CHEW, William White	1803	A82
CHANDLER, May Ruth (B=)	1914	H123	CHISM, Ethel	190?	B985b
CHANDLER, Robin L.	1960	H335	CHOLLAR, Anne Lucindtte	1886	E9902
CHANDLER, Shelly Mae	1963	H335	CHOLLAR, Bessie	1877	E9900
CHANDLER, William A.	190?	H123	CHOLLAR, Ella (B=)	1855	E4201
CHANDLER, William A.	1937	H335	CHOLLAR, Estell	188?	E9901
CHANDLER, William K.	1967	H335	CHOLLAR, Frank Darby	185?	E4201
CHANDLESS, J.D.	189?	B2503b	CHOLLAR, Mary Sanford	1898	E9903
CHANDLESS, Jadine (Bobb	1931	B2503b	CHOLLAR, Walter Edward	1879	E9901
CHANDLESS, Jetta Ann	1927	B2503b	CHRISTOPHER, Carrie M.	1977	C8603
CHANDLESS, Minnie (Lewi	1901	B2503b	CHRISTOPHER, Connie (B=)	1955	C5664
CHAPEL, Caroline (B=)	1808	E309	CHRISTOPHER, Joan (Daghe	192?	C5664
CHAPEL, Francis	1836 *	E1388	CHRISTOPHER, Michael P.	1952	C5664
CHAPEL, Horace S.	180?	E309	CHRISTOPHER, Robert	192?	C5664
CHAPEL, Livia	1840	E1389	CHURCH, Addie	187?	E6685
CHAPEL, Marrion	1844	E1390	CHURCH, Emma (B=)	185?	E1622
CHAPEL, Victoria G.	1846	E1391	CHURCH, John	180?	F72
CHAPMAN, Amasa	177?	F93	CHURCH, Lydia	1776	E62
CHAPMAN, David	178?	F92	CHURCH, Monroe	183?	E1622
CHAPMAN, Ebenezer	178?	F94	CHURCH, Nancy (B=)	1804	F72
CHAPMAN, J.	184?	K2944	CHURCH, Samuel Jr.	175?	E62
CHAPMAN, Jemima	177?	F91	CHURCH, Sarah	175?	E62
CHAPMAN, Martha N. (B=)	184?	K2944	CHURCHILL, Charles	184?	E1398
CHAPMAN, Mary (B=)	1747	F18	CHURCHILL, Cora (B=)	184?	E1398
CHAPMAN, Mary	1771	F90	CHURCHILL, Edith	192?	E39009
CHAPMAN, Mary	178?	F289	CHURCHILL, John Bennie	1948	E39009
CHAPMAN, Nancy (B=)	1817	F269	CHURCHILL, Joseph Benjam	192?	E39009
CHAPMAN, Polly (Exeter)	178?	F93	CHURCHILL, Lottie	187?	E5819
CHAPMAN, Rhoda	178?	F94a	CHURCHILL, Sheila (Ridge	1948	E39009
CHAPMAN, Sylvia (???)	177?	F89	CHURCHYARD, Mary Ann E.	184?	F1210
CHAPMAN, William	174?	F18	CLAIRY, Edith	192?	E39009
CHAPMAN, William	177?	F89	CLAPP, Lucy	184?	E1567

CLARK, ??? (B=)	1748	F17	
CLARK, Abner	178?	F83	
CLARK, Abraham	172?	B7	
CLARK, Angee	185?	E1400	
CLARK, Ann	1749	B7	
CLARK, Archie	1886	F1408	
CLARK, Asubah	178?	F80	
CLARK, Blanche (Stockton	188?	F1405	
CLARK, Carina	1896	F1409	
CLARK, Caroline (B=)	1852	F588	
CLARK, Charles	178?	F85	
CLARK, Charles Elmore	1860	F1476	
CLARK, Eber	178?	F84	
CLARK, Edward S.	185?	E4203	
CLARK, Elijah	1741	F19	
CLARK, Elijah	178?	F86	
CLARK, Elizabeth (B=)	170?	A5e	
CLARK, Elizabeth(William	172?	B7	
CLARK, Gilbert {Dr.}	1849	F588	
CLARK, Grace	1884	F1407	
CLARK, Hannah (Champion)	171?	F19	
CLARK, Hannah (B=)	1750	F19	
CLARK, Hattie (Williams)	186?	F1476	
CLARK, Ida Elvira	186?	F585	
CLARK, Inez	1882	F1406	
CLARK, Iona	189?	B1194a	
CLARK, Jemima (B=)	1785	E59	
CLARK, Jennie	1862 *	F1477	
CLARK, Joshua	170?	A5e	
CLARK, Leverett	183?	F613	
CLARK, Lucy (Fortner)	186?	B1194a	
CLARK, Margaret	180?	B34	
CLARK, Milinda (B=)	1835	F613	
CLARK, Minnie (Teller)	185?	E4203	
CLARK, Nethaniel	186?	B1194a	
CLARK, Oliver	177?	E59	
CLARK, Ralph	1880	F1405	
CLARK, Rhoda	178? *	F88	
CLARK, Samuel	171?	F19	
CLARK, Susan Kay (B=)	1952	C3409	
CLARK, Walter	178?	F82	
CLARK, Wilson	180?	F87	
CLAYTON, Patricia	1947	C3332	
CLEMENT, Iva	189?	A708	
CLEMENTS, Yvonne Marie	194?	C3339	
CLENDANIEL, Pinkey	181?	H1	
CLENDANIEL, Pinkey (B=)	1861	H8f	
CLENDANIEL, Samuel	1860	H8f	
CLEVENGER, Melissa (B=)	195?	B9642	
CLEVENGER, Orville	195?	B9642	
CLINE, John Thomas	1962	B26036	
CLINE, Rachael	1983	B26036	
CLINE, Wendy (Stoll)	1963	B26036	
CLINKENBEARD, D.R.	1917	E10823	
CLINKENBEARD, Viola (B=)	1924	E10823	
CLINTON, Charles	183?	F626	
CLINTON, Edward McGary	189?	B9600	
CLINTON, Elsie (Herrings)	190?	B9600	
CLINTON, Hazel Lorraine	1927	B9600	
CLINTON, Harriet P.	183?	F626	
CLINTON, Jessie Paul	1863	F626	
CLISBY, Alma M.	1833	F259	
CLOUD, David Gilmer	189?	B1770	
CLOUD, Francis Millar	189?	B1771	
CLOUD, Margaret (B=)	1873	B592	
CLOUD, Margaret Irene	190?	B1773	
CLOUD, William E.	187?	B592	
CLOUD, William Ephraim	189?	B1772	
CLOUSE, Harriet O.(Wells	1912	J120	
CLOUSE, Mr.	190?	J120	
CLOWES, Hannah	173?	L3	
CLYDE, Colleen	1965	Q147	
CLYDE, David	1940	Q147	
CLYDE, Hester (McKee)	191?	Q147	
CLYDE, Jhon	191?	Q147	
CLYDE, Lena	1971	Q147	
CLYDE, Marjorie (McGrego	1949	Q147	
CLYDE, Ruth P.	1964	Q147	
COCHRAN, Mary (Robins)	1860	F635	
COCHRAN, Robert	185?	F635	
COCKENOWER, Eliza (B=)	1841	B297	
COCKENOWER, Michael	183?	B297	
COE, Anna (Haines)	178?	F103	
COE, Anson	178?	F103	
COE, Elijah	175?	F62	
COE, Hannah	1766	F21	
COE, Mary	1781	F62	
COE, Miles	178?	F102	
COE, Phineas	1753	F22	
COE, Polly	178?	F104	
COE, Rhoda (B=)	1761	F22	
COE, Sallie	178?	F105	
COFFIN, Enoch	172?	B8	
COFFIN, Jane	172?	B8	
COFFIN, Mercy	1753	B8	
COGGINS, Betty L.(Carter	1935	J2111	
COGGINS, Billy W.E.	1932	J2111	
COGGINS, Brenda Lee	1965	J2111	
COGGINS, Floyd	190?	J2111	
COGGINS, Floyd W.	1962 *	J2111	
COGGINS, LaDonna Lynn	1964	J2111	
COGGINS, Lorean (Huggins	190?	J2111	
COKENOWER, Elizabeth (B=	1841	B297	
COKENOWER, Michael	183?	B297	
COLBURN, Abigail	175?	X2758	
COLE, Mary Elizabeth	185?	C232	
COLEMAN, Mr. C.	188?	F1455	
COLEMAN, Nellie V. (B=)	1883	F1455	
COLEMAN, Sarah	177?	A19	
COLLINS, Bessie	1893 *	E6743	
COLLINS, Edward D.	186?	E1650	
COLLINS, Fannie (B=)	1863	E1650	
COLLINS, J.W.	184?	H6	
COLLINS, John	189?	B1014a	
COLLINS, Laurence Edward	1897	E6744	
COLLINS, Mary Elizabeth	1890 *	E6742	
COLLINS, Mary J. (B=)	1892	B1014a	
COLLINS, Nancy A. (B=)	1844	H6	
COLLINS, Viola Maxine	193?	B26008	
COLVIN, Irene A.	1835	E1606	
COLVIN, Julia (B=)	1832	E380	
COLVIN, Timothy	1827	E380	
COMBS, Joseph	184?	B186	
COMBS, Mattie (B=)	184?	B186	

COMEGYS, Elizabeth	183?	C68
COMPTON, Earl Charles	189?	F7003
COMPTON, Ethel Mae	1921	F7003
COMPTON, George	185?	B239
COMPTON, Martha (B=)	1854	B239
COMPTON, Nora M. (Edmons	189?	F7003
COMSTOCK, Albert M.	1830	E1466
COMSTOCK, Alexander	1826	E1463
COMSTOCK, Angeline	1834	E1468
COMSTOCK, Clarence Burna	187?	E12092
COMSTOCK, Claud Linn	187?	E12093
COMSTOCK, Dwight Ray	187?	E12091
COMSTOCK, Ellen M.	1832	E1467
COMSTOCK, Elodia (B=)	1852	E6400
COMSTOCK, Eugene S.	1845	E1472
COMSTOCK, Gates S.	185?	E6400
COMSTOCK, Harriet M.	1838	E1470
COMSTOCK, Jabez	180?	E420
COMSTOCK, James	1827	E1464
COMSTOCK, John	183?	E1389
COMSTOCK, Julia T.	1843	E1471
COMSTOCK, Livia (Chapel)	1840	E1389
COMSTOCK, Margaret (Broc	1805	E420
COMSTOCK, Mary E.	1828	E1465
COMSTOCK, Melinda (B=)	1806	E344
COMSTOCK, Prentice	1795	E344
COMSTOCK, Warren P.	1836	E1469
CONDRA, Alma L. (B=)	1886	B610
CONDRA, Carolyn	1908	B1826
CONDRA, Harley	188?	B610
CONE, Rebecca	169?	F6
CONGDON, Ellen (B=)	189?	E5845
CONGER, Rita C.	192?	F3082
CONKLIN, Hazel (B=)	1889	A706
CONKLIN, Oliver L.	188?	A706
CONLEY, Clarissa M.	1823	B64a
COOK, Clydelle	192?	F11988
COOK, David A.	184?	L195
COOK, Jay	18??	A72
COOK, Mable I.	191?	E19069
COOK, Margaret J. (B=)	1841	B219
COOK, Mary B. (Stones)	1845	L195
COOK, Mary	188?	E6362
COOK, William J.	183?	B219
COOPER, Alice	183?	L186
COOPER, Alta (Pierce)	1903	B2513
COOPER, Burl Lonzo	1911	B2513e
COOPER, Burl Lavon	1935	B2513e
COOPER, D. Blaine (Jackson	1925	B2513h
COOPER, Edwina F.	1934	B2513
COOPER, Emily Imogene	1904	B2513a
COOPER, Florance (Perry)	1915	B2513e
COOPER, Fred D.	1909	B2513d
COOPER, George Washin	1877	B943a
COOPER, Golda (Page)	1918	B2513
COOPER, Gwin Dee	1933	B2513d
COOPER, Irene	1921 *	B2513
COOPER, James Edwin	1901	B2513
COOPER, James E.	1930 *	B2513
COOPER, James M.	1948	B2513
COOPER, James Dudley	1952	B2513h
COOPER, Juda E. (B=)	1883	B943a
COOPER, Julia (B=)	1883	B943a
COOPER, Mary Ola	1907	B2513b
COOPER, Minnie Ester	1914	B2513f
COOPER, Myrtle E.	1929	B2513
COOPER, Nola Jane	1907	B2513c
COOPER, Nola B.	1924	B2513
COOPER, Ora Lee	1932	B2513d
COOPER, Oveta M.	1943	B2513
COOPER, Retha (Dowell)	1913	B2513d
COOPER, Ruth	1918	B2513g
COOPER, Wanda L.	1938	B2513
COOPER, William Jennings	1920	B2513h
COOPER, William Levern	1931	B2513e
COOPER, William David	1950	B2513h
CORDELL, Harlene (B=)	1926	R358
CORDELL, Homer E.	192?	R358
CORDELL, Michael Josepj	1953	R496
CORDELL, Nanci Lynn	1953	R497
CORDELL, Thomas Jamer	1951	R495
CORDIN, Caroline M.	181?	B71
CORGILL, Lillian Belle	191?	E19107
CORWIN, Clarissa	1780	E63
CORWIN, Mary (Lord)	175?	E63
CORWIN, Theophilus	175?	E63
COSBY, Judy	193?	E19046
COTHRON, Hudson	180?	B19
COTHRON, Nancy C.	1802	B19
COURTWRIGHT, Karla	194?	A3657
COUSINS, Karen	196?	H765
COUTS, Clarence Kennith	1907	C333
COUTS, Jessie (B=)	1879	C146
COUTS, Samuel Lafayette	187?	C146
COUTS, Samuel Lloyd	1904	C332
COVE, Brian Michael	1960	H836
COVE, David Francis	1957	H835
COVE, Francis H.	1930	H377
COVE, Helen Mary (Stratt	191?	H377
COVE, Jay Scott	1967	H838
COVE, Jennifer Lynn	198?	H835
COVE, Joan Louise (B=)	1932	H377
COVE, Karen Lynn	1955	H833
COVE, Kevin Peter	1963	H837
COVE, Lee Ann (Michaud)	196?	H837
COVE, Leo A.	191?	H377
COVE, Michael David	198?	H835
COVE, Patty Ann (Bloomer	1958	H835
COVE, Ryan Thomas	1987	H837
COVE, Teresa Marie	1988	H835
COVE, Valerie Ann	1956	H834
COVER, Clyde Robert	189?	H177d
COVER, Clyde Robert	1922	H177d
COVER, Clyde Robert 3rd	1947	H177d
COVER, Margaret (Ierley)	189?	H177d
COVER, Melissa Rae	1952	H177d
COVER, Verna J.(Deatrick	1924	H177d
COWDRY, Edith	178?	F67
COWDRY, Martha	1811	F70
COWLES, Aaron	177?	F91
COWLES, Jemima (Chapman)	177?	F91
COX, Adolphus	187?	B701
COX, Daisy (Lawrence)	1898	F2640
COX, James Reginald	189?	F2640

COX, James L.	192?	F2640
COX, Kerry L.	192?	F2640
COX, Lillie	1882	B263
COX, Norma	192?	F2640
COX, Pam L.	192?	F2640
COX, Regina	192?	F2640
CRAFT, Miss.	183?	A244
CRAIN, Edward W.	188?	J136
CRAIN, Etta Evelyn	1911	J136
CRAIN, Rebecca (???)	188?	J136
CRAPSEY, Daniel Burns	1848	F609
CRAPSEY, Myra (Caldwell)	1854	F609
CRAWFORD, Elizabeth	183?	X3501
CRESSWELL, Effie	192?	Q95
CRISMON, Minnie Ann	1931	E10834
CROSBY, Denney	1790	F63
CROW, Georgina (B=)	185?	X502
CROW, Henry S.	185?	X502
CROWDER, Nelda	192?	Q151
CROWELL, Barbara	192?	E19055
CROWELL, James	192?	E19055
CROWELL, Sharla	195?	E19055
CROWLEY, Aletha A. (B=)	1933	B9602
CROWLEY, Becki (Rogers)	1951	B26006
CROWLEY, David Allen	1952	B26006
CROWLEY, Don Dwyer	1930	B9602
CROWLEY, Drew Alan	1976	B26006
CROWLEY, Elizabeth	178?	F424
CROWLEY, Elizabeth Jolyn	1981	B26006
CROWLEY, Jacob Edward	1978	B26006
CROWLEY, Matthew David	1973	B26006
CROWLEY, Millard Earl	190?	B9602
CROWLEY, Obie Jane (Rice)	190?	B9602
CUISAK, Cynthia Priscill	184?	G18
CULKIN, Margaret F.	1891	F1412
CULLEN, Mary E.	185?	X1508
CUNNINGHAM, Arthur	187?	G88
CUNNINGHAM, Arthur Cam	190?	G224
CUNNINGHAM, Donald Shelt	190?	G225
CUNNINGHAM, Ella M. (B=)	1881	G88
CURTIS, Angelica	1832	B64
CURTIS, Elizabeth (Bird)	1811	B64
CURTIS, Elizabeth	1820	B93
CURTIS, Elizabeth	1848	B64
CURTIS, Emily	1834	B64
CURTIS, George Washingto	1838	B64
CURTIS, John Spencer	1836	B64
CURTIS, Jonathan Bird	1845	B64
CURTIS, Josiah Askew	1810	B64
CURTIS, Mary Pauline	1804	B62a
CURTIS, Mary	182?	A247
CURTIS, Mary R.	1843	B64
CURTIS, Miss.	187?	E5805
CURTIS, Moses Hightower	1852	B64
CURTIS, Washington Lafay	1841	B64
DADLEY, Jane	1816	A74
DAGHERTY, Joan Marie	193?	C5664
DALE, Joshua	177?	X2997
DALE, Mary	177?	X2994
DALE, Nancy (B=)	1774	X2997
DALL, Charles	182?	L127
DALL, Elizabeth (B=)	1792	L28

DALL, Elizabeth	182?	L132
DALL, George	182?	L136
DALL, James Hartley	182?	L134
DALL, John Wesley	179?	L28
DALL, John	182?	L133
DALL, Joseph	182?	L130
DALL, Margaret	182?	L135
DALL, Maria	182?	L137
DALL, Mary Ann	182?	L131
DALL, Robert	182?	L128
DALL, William	182?	L129
DALTON, Dorothy	191?	B997d
DAMMEIER, Jodie Lynn	1973	C3340
DAMMEIER, John Earl	194?	C3340
DAMMEIER, John Earl	1970	C3340
DAMMEIER, Lynnette (Hert	1947	C3340
DAMON, Lucina (Brockway)	1795	E417
DAMON, Nathan	179?	E417
DANIEL, Mary	1834	B70
DANIEL, Robert	180?	B70
DANIELS, Agatha	184?	E1403
DANIELS, Daniel	168?	E2
DANIELS, Franciel(Carter	1940	J2114
DANIELS, Johnny	193?	J2114
DANIELS, Mary (???)	1690	E2
DARLINGTON, Charles	193?	H332
DARLINGTON, Norma (B=)	1932	H332
DAVIDSON, Laura (Noyes)	1875	E6316
DAVIDSON, Robert C.	187?	E6316
DAVIES, James E.	189?	Q42
DAVIES, Lyla Jean	1915	Q42
DAVIES, Myrtle (McDermid	1895	Q42
DAVIS, Charlotte	1829	E312
DAVIS, Emma (B=)	185?	E1622
DAVIS, George B.	188?	I388
DAVIS, Harriet	183?	B223
DAVIS, Henry	187?	E6686
DAVIS, Jane	1837	B89
DAVIS, Lizzie (B=)	1856	I73
DAVIS, Martha	188?	Q27
DAVIS, Mary (Johnson)	181?	B89
DAVIS, Peter F.	185?	E1622
DAVIS, W.H.	180?	B89
DAVISON, Cornelia (???)	1830	X3800
DAVISON, Delilah F.	184?	B236
DAVISON, William P.	182?	X3800
DAWSON, Jennie L. (B=)	1903	J140a
DAWSON, Leo	190?	J140a
DAY, Ansell	187?	E6683
DAY, Burt	187?	E6684
DAY, Emma (B=)	185?	E1622
DAY, Grace	190?	C865
DAY, William	185?	E1622
DE LONG, William Columbu	183?	A237
DE LONG, Sophia (B=)	1834	A237
DE LONG, Norton Sheldon	1857 *	A678
DE LONG, Blucher	1858 *	A679
DE LONG, Birdie Maria	1860	A680
DE LONG, Frank Banning	1865	A681
DE LONG, William Columbu	1874	A682
DE SHASIER, Henry Clint	185?	B205
DE SHASIER, Julia E.(B=)	185?	B205

DE VERE, Ann (B=)	164?	X2012	DETERMAN, Jack	192?	P143
DE VERE, Aubrey	163?	X2012	DETERMAN, Jean	192?	P143
DEVORE, Minnie	186?	B1193a	DETERMAN, Josephine (Lyn	190?	P143
DE WOLF, Benjamin	168?	E5	DETERMAN, Leland George	1912 *	P146
DE WOLF, Margaret (Smit	1696	E5	DETERMAN, Lewis T.	1891	P141
DE WOLF, Margaret	1717	E5	DETERMAN, Marcille	191? *	P141
DEARMAN, Dorothy (Rust)	1911	H174	DETERMAN, Margaret T.	1894	P142
DEATRICK, Aldena (Laucks	186?	H58c	DETERMAN, Maria (Elskamp	1824	P32
DEATRICK, Charles	1928	H177e	DETERMAN, Patsy	192?	P143
DEATRICK, Edward	186?	H58c	DETERMAN, Raymond Ber	1906	P145
DEATRICK, Emily Aldema	1913	H177	DETERMAN, Sarah Theresa	1900	P144
DEATRICK, Frances R.	1922	H177c	DETERMAN, Tennie (Anders	189?	P141
DEATRICK, Gladys I.	1916	H177a	DETMEYERS, Anna Elizabet	166?	N1
DEATRICK, Grace C.(Offne	1919	H177b	DEWEY, Charles S.	188?	C557
DEATRICK, Harry E.	1888	H58c	DEWEY, Kathleen	1916	C1841
DEATRICK, Harry Mark	1919	H177b	DEWEY, Neva Pearl (B=)	1885	C557
DEATRICK, Joyce Ann	1951	H177b	DEWIT, Maud	187?	B1031
DEATRICK, Lenora (B=)	1890	H58c	DIBBLE, Mr.	169?	E10
DEATRICK, Marie (Keller)	192?	H177e	DIBBLE, Mrs. (B=)	1701	E10
DEATRICK, Michael James	1947	H177b	DIBBLE, Thomas	1727	E33
DEATRICK, Verna Jane	1924	H177d	DICK, Mary	184?	G17
DEHART, Betty Ethel	1901	J181	DICKEY, Alice	187?	E5697
DEHART, Clarence Ogden	1875	J30	DINKIN, Jeffrey A.	194?	B19000
DEHART, Clarence	1899 *	J180	DINKIN, Kathryn (Haymes)	1945	B19000
DEHART, Gaylord Ogden	1905	J183	DINKIN, Sophy Allison	1987	B19000
DEHART, Jessie Blanch(B=	1878	J30	DIXON, Avis (B=)	1880	A670
DEHART, John Wesley	185?	J30	DIXON, Edgar	187?	A670
DEHART, Mary Eliz. (Rank	1854	J30	DOLY, Eunice B. (B=)	1818	E349
DEHART, Muriel Patrice	1907	J184	DOLY, Martin	181?	E349
DEHART, Ruby Lucille	1909	J185	DOMINEE, Ludia	185?	E1645
DEHART, Zora Irene	1903	J182	DONE, Dorothy (Lay)	1953	Q154
DELANO, Diana (Miller)	1935	A3658	DONE, Jeremy Robert	1976	Q154
DELANO, Elizabeth Chris	1966	A3658	DONE, Joann Lois	1974	Q154
DELANO, George Broughton	1931	A3658	DONE, Mr.	194?	Q154
DELANO, Sylvia Rose	1960	A3658	DONE, Raymond A.	1972	Q154
DELORME, Ida	1896	Q56	DONICA, Debra Kay	195?	E19124
DENNIS, Polly J. (B=)	182?	C80a	DONOHUE, Clara (Nichols)	188?	B1136
DENNIS, Stephen R.	182?	C80a	DONOHUE, Mr.	188?	B1136
DENNY, Ann (B=)	177?	A28a	DORMAN, Darlene (Betts)	1954	H760
DENNY, Catherine B.	180?	A66d	DORMAN, Daryl Anderson	1967	H760
DENNY, James Earle	177?	A28a	DORMAN, Douglas Aldon	1971	H760
DENNY, Mary	180?	A66c	DORMAN, Robert Blackston	195?	H760
DERBY, Arthur	186?	E1695	DORRELL, Linda	195?	H767
DERBY, Henry	183?	E410	DOTICE, Theadocia	179?	E84
DERBY, Lila	186?	E1696	DOTY, Ada (???)	189?	B2703
DERBY, Mary (B=)	1839	E410	DOTY, Cecil Griffin	1898 *	B2704
DESLAURIER, Edna (B=)	1909	Q60	DOTY, Donna (Stonecipher	189?	B2701
DESLAURIER, Hilma	1939	Q108	DOTY, Elizabeth (Patters	189?	B2701
DESLAURIER, Irene	1931	Q104	DOTY, Eunice (B=)	1818	E349
DESLAURIER, Kenneth	1934	Q106	DOTY, Gladys (???)	190?	B2705
DESLAURIER, Marlyn	1942	Q109	DOTY, Isaiah Jones	1857	B1025
DESLAURIER, Melvin	1932	Q105	DOTY, Isaiah Donald	1900	B2705
DESLAURIER, Shirley	1935	Q107	DOTY, Jennings Bryan	1896	B2703
DESLAURIER, William	1904	Q60	DOTY, Katie (???)	190?	B2703
DETERMAN, Benjamin	1888 *	P140	DOTY, Laura Mabelle	1894	B2702
DETERMAN, Bonita (Shire)	190?	P145	DOTY, Lucille	1907	B2707
DETERMAN, Donna Lou	193?	P145	DOTY, Martin	181?	E349
DETERMAN, Grace	1912 *	P147	DOTY, Mary Jane (Cavanee	1819	B1025
DETERMAN, Henry Herman	1852	P32	DOTY, Mercy	1785	E302
DETERMAN, Henry Clem	1897	P143	DOTY, Moses	1816	B1025
DETERMAN, Herman Berna	1823	P32	DOTY, Owen Leslie	1892	B2701
DETERMAN, Ida Jane (B=)	1869	P32	DOTY, Sarah A. (Tipsword	1863	B1025

Name	Year	Code
DOTY, Victoria Regina	1904	B2706
DOUD, Adlaide	185?	E1641
DOUD, Charlotta (B=)	1824	E400
DOUD, Elizabeth	185?	E1639
DOUD, Emma	185?	E1642
DOUD, Emory	185?	E1638
DOUD, Frank	185?	E1640
DOUD, Jane (Lewis)	185?	E1638
DOUD, Phineas	182?	E400
DOUGLAS, Shelli	195/	J505
DOUGLASS, Achsah	1812	E253
DOUGLASS, Eliza	1812	E253
DOUGLASS, Eliza (Post)	1824	E259
DOUGLASS, Nancy	182?	E256
DOUGLASS, Nathan	182?	E259
DOW, Betsey (Phelps)	178?	E100
DOWELL, Cora Alice	1883	B883
DOWELL, Millie (Askins)	186?	B883
DOWELL, Retha Edith	1913	B2513d
DOWELL, William M.	185?	B883
DOWERS, Perlina	183?	C560
DOWLING, Adam Timothy	1983	H1009
DOWLING, Betty J.	1949	H499
DOWLING, Laurin Pinkney	192?	H499
DOWLING, Natalie Yvonne	1969	H1007
DOWLING, Orillo M. (Trul	192?	H499
DOWLING, Thomas Allen	1944	H499
DOWLING, Thomas Allen	1972	H1008
DOWNEY, Menolia	1900	H118
DOWNEY, Samuel	189?	H118
DOWNING, Annie Lyndia	1870	F3376
DOWNS, Charles	191?	E19052
DOWNS, Martha I.	191?	E19052
DOWNS, Patrica L.	1940	E19052
DOYLE, Helen	191?	C1866
DRAKE, Arthur W.	187?	K2936
DRAKE, Charles Milton	185?	A629
DRAKE, Mary B. (Pugh)	183?	K2936
DRAKE, Rachel (Seymour)	185?	A629
DRAVES, Neva Pearl (B=)	1885	C557
DRAVES, Wayne	1908	C1840
DRAVES, William H.	188?	C557
DRECHSLER, Heidi	1991	J507
DRECHSLER, Thomas	195?	J507
DREDHSLER, Vicki (Ohls	1957	J507
DRIVER, Mary	176?	L7
DRUCE, Annie Laura	184?	L138
DU PONT, Anna (Ridgely)	1815	C61
DU PONT, Charles Irenee	181?	C61
DU PONT, Amy E.	184?	C61
DUDLEY, D. Wilson	170?	A5c
DUDLEY, Harriet	1807	L31
DUDLEY, Lucy Bell	192?	E10809
DUDLEY, Richard	169?	A5c
DUKE, Lorraine A.(Wells)	1917	J121
DUKE, Mr.	191?	J121
DUNCAN, Andrew William	186?	L468
DUNCAN, Josephine (Rea)	1870	L468
DUNHAM, Fred L.	185?	E6401
DUNHAM, Mary Druscilla	182?	X3515
DUNHAM, Mary Ester	188?	E12094
DUNHAM, Nellie (B=)	1857	E6401
DUNLAP, Harmon	191?	B2513g
DUNLAP, Ruth (Cooper)	1918	B2513g
DUNN, Lillian	189?	C1859
DUNN, Nancy J. (B=)	1842	B332
DUNN, Thomas B.	184?	B332
DUNNIGAN, Mary	1882	Q36
DUNNING, Nancy (B=)	1819	A228
DUNNING, Silas	181?	A228
DUNSHEATH, Ethel I. (B=)	1882	G84
DUNSHEATH, John H.	188?	G84
DURHAM, Annette Coker	194?	C5661
DUNHAM, Beverly (Ward)	1951	B26002
DUNHAM, Jim	194?	B26002
DUNHAM, Jimmy	1975	B26002
DUNHAM, Molly	1973	B26002
DURHAM, Pamela D.	196?	C5661
DURHAM, William Bryan	193?	C5661
DUSENBERRY, Maude (Cars	188?	B747
EADS, Mr.	18??	X1007
EAGEN, Brian Patrick	1980	H1490
EAGEN, Christopher M.	1979	H1489
EAGEN, Doris (Foster)	192?	H823
EAGEN, Elizabeth Ann	1985	H1491
EAGEN, Mary Ellen (B=)	1952	H823
EAGEN, Mary Courtney	1989	H1492
EAGEN, William F.	192?	H823
EAGEN, William Francis	1952	H823
EARP, Emma (Salt)	179?	L53
EARP, Mr.	178?	L53
EAST, Ida May (B=)	1878	E5695
EAST, William B.	187?	E5695
EASTER, Jasper	170?	K236
EASTER, Susannah (B=)	1712	K236
ECELES, Mary	186?	B1193a
EDGAR, Jane	182?	A232
EDGERTON, Maria (Bryant)	184?	E1578
EDGERTON, Perry L.	184?	E1578
EDISON, Cyrus F. {Dr.}	182?	F495
EDISON, Julia (B=)	1829	F495
EDMOND, Bill	194?	J503
EDMOND, Don	196?	J503
EDMOND, Joanne (B=)	194?	J503
EDMOND, Von	196?	J503
EDMONDSON, Nora Mae	189?	F7003
EDMUNSON, Sophia Charlot	177?	A25
EDSON, Grace	188?	B601
EDWARDS, Carl Jr.	1938	J511
EDWARDS, Debra	1960	J511
EDWARDS, Janet Lee	1962	J511
EDWARDS, Jimmy Earl	1967	J511
EDWARDS, Melba (Allen)	1939	J511
EDWARDS, Isaac	171?	A34
EDWARDS, Rachel (B=)	1723	A34
EELLS, Amelia (Vinning)	1804	F236
EELLS, Osiah Sheldon	180?	F236
EGERTON, Elizabeth (Murr	165?	X2016
EGERTON, Randolph	165?	X2016
EINSENHOWER, Thelma Iren	1926	E10828
ELBERT, Harriett Troth	178?	A66b
ELBERT, John Lodman	177?	A66b
ELBERT, Martha B. (Watts	177?	A66b
ELDRIDGE, James	187?	B1033

453

ELDRIDGE, Minda (Tipswor	1874	B1033
ELINE, Rachel	1822	I11
ELKIN, Parthenia	1844	B117
ELLIOT, Donald	191?	C1830
ELLIOTT, Bobbie Nell	193?	E39012
ELLIOTT, C.M.	187?	C554
ELLIOTT, Eliza	185?	C108
ELLIOTT, Elizabeth (B=)	181?	C21
ELLIOTT, Fanny Banning	185?	C109
ELLIOTT, Grace (B=)	1879	C554
ELLIOTT, Isaac	181?	C21
ELLIOTT, Isaac L.	181?	C22
ELLIOTT, Isaac C.	185?	C110
ELLIOTT, James Kelly	193?	E39012
ELLIOTT, Kari	1956	E39012
ELLIOTT, Marie (Wright)	192?	J405
ELLIOTT, Mr.	192?	J405
ELLIOTT, Sallie (B=)	1822	C22
ELLIS, Dennis	195?	H768
ELLIS, Erica	1978	H768
ELLIS, Jessica	1974	H768
ELLIS, Penny D. (Furroug	1953	H768
ELLISON, Annie (Wilson)	1870	X3807
ELLISON, Eliza (Berry)	184?	X3807
ELLISON, Gertrude	187?	A673
ELLISON, John	184?	X3807
ELLISON, John	1871	X3807
ELLISON, Robert John	1891 *	X3807
ELLISON, Walter Joseph	1892	X3807
ELSHARKAWI, Nadra	193?	H826
ELSKAMP, Maria M.	1824	P32
ELWYN, Sarah	174?	X2755
ELY, Betsey (Brockway)	179?	E414c
ELY, Jean J.	1919	F3081
ELY, Semillius B.	179?	E414c
EMERSON, George	177?	X2998
EMERSON, Roxalina (B=)	1776	X2998
EMERSON, Virginia	181?	C62
EMERY, Maude J.	186?	J10
EMORY, Ann (B=)	186?	X1509
EMORY, Arthur	188?	X1541
EMORY, Charles	186?	X1509
EMORY, George	188?	X1542
EMPERSON, Amelia	184?	L452
ENGDOHL, Sharon (B=)	1946	Q195
ENGDOHL, Waren	194?	Q195
ENNIS, Charles D.	193?	H497
ENNIS, Joyce L. (Powell)	1933	H497
ENNIS, Susan Pamela	1966	H497
EPTING, Dana Patrick	196?	H1007
EPTING, Natalie (Dowling	1969	H1007
ERICKSON, Ann (Schwams)	191?	C1907
ERLING, Deborah	194?	J2115
ERRETT, Banning	187?	A703
ERRETT, Blanch (Robinson	18??	A704
ERRETT, Charles	1868	A704
ERRETT, Elizabeth (Tudor	1866	A705
ERRETT, Geophry	190?	A705
ERRETT, Harry	187?	A705
ERRETT, Isaac	184?	A260
ERRETT, Isaac	1876	A702
ERRETT, Jane	1885	A701

ERRETT, Minnie (Breutlin	18??	A703
ERRETT, Sarah (B=)	1846	A260
ERRETT, Virginia	1902	A704
ESCHENBURG, Emily	1825	A51
ESTER, Gail Claire	1937	Q43
ESTER, Lillah (McDermid)	1897	Q43
ESTER, Marion	1914	Q39
ESTER, Raplh G.	1887	Q39
ESTER, Violet (McDermid)	1885	Q39
ESTER, Walter	1897	Q43
ESTER, Walter Kenneth	1923	Q43
ESTES, Ann (Fullwood)	180?	B61e
ESTES, John	180?	B61e
EUERLE, Mary K.	187?	H133
EVANS, Joseph	181?	C85
EVANS, Marie (Moore)	191?	H380
EVANS, Mary	1940	H380
EVANS, Matilda (Turner)	1820	C85
EVANS, Paul	191?	H380
EVENSON, Dennis Warner	1943	C3337
EVENSON, Elmer	188?	C1828
EVENSON, Ramona (Gasser)	1945	C3338
EVENSON, Tilda G.(Tolrud	189?	C1828
EVENSON, Verda Irene (B=	1913	C1828
EVENSON, Vernon Harold	1945	C3338
EVENSON, Warner Merton	1913	C1828
EVERHEART, Mary (B=)	1871	A665
EVERHEART, Mildred	1904	A1593
EVERHEART, Milton	186?	A665
FAIRBANKS, Mary	174?	X2756
FARENS, Nancy (B=)	1944	H331
FARENS, Roy	194?	H331
FARENS, Shannon Renee	1964	H778
FARENS, Tonya F.	1962	H777
FARRINGTON, Clinton	189?	F1417
FARRINGTON, Jessie O. (B=)	1896	F1417
FARRINGTON, Jessie L.	191?	F3105
FARRINGTON, Lydia Banning	192?	F3106
FARRIS, Alice (B=)	1865	C144
FARRIS, Charles H.	186?	C144
FARRIS, Edna W.	1889	C326
FARRIS, John	1885	C325
FAULKNER, Alpha Lulu	187?	A628
FAULKNER, George Washing	184?	A628
FAULKNER, George Seymour	187?	A628
FAULKNER, Rhoda (Seymour	1849	A628
FAULKNER, Rhoda Evangeli	187?	A628
FAULKNER, Stella Martin	187?	A628
FELL, Jesse Benjamin	187?	F3375
FELL, Sarah E. (Parson	187?	F3375
FELL, Velma Lucille	1900	F3375
FERGUSON, Donald	193?	Q148
FERGUSON, Ruby (Reid)	193?	Q148
FERGUSON, Valerie	1957	Q148
FERRY, Edgar W.	185?	E1623
FERRY, Ida (B=)	185?	E1623
FERRY, Sarah A.	183?	E1644
FIDLER, Ina (B=)	1907	B2119
FIDLER, Mr.	190?	B2119
FINER, Irene Emma	190?	F1419
FISH, Mae. E.	189?	C590
FISHER, Alfred	1853	A643

FISHER, Almary	188?	A643		FORESTER, Heman W.	1908	E19052
FISHER, Althea	188?	A643		FORESTER, Leona (Miaman)	1911	E19052
FISHER, Anthony Banning	1848	A640		FORTNER, Addie Mae	187?	B986a
FISHER, Asa	178?	A230		FORTNER, Alfred	186?	B1194
FISHER, Bertha	187?	B930		FORTNER, Carrie (Burris)	186?	B1194
FISHER, Blucher	1858	A644		FORTNER, Douglas	186?	B1192a
FISHER, Blucher	188?	A643		FORTNER, Edith	189?	B1193a
FISHER, Clara	1852	A642		FORTNER, Edna Estella	1911	B1195
FISHER, Edwin	1814	A230		FORTNER, Eliza Jane (Wood)	187?	B1195
FISHER, Edwin Banning	1844	A638		FORTNER, Estella (Koster)	186?	B1194
FISHER, Ella Butler	186?	X129		FORTNER, Ethel	185?	B1192
FISHER, George	1858	A645		FORTNER, Eva Elnora	1899	B1195
FISHER, Idella (Robbins)	1864	A644		FORTNER, Fred	189?	B1193a
FISHER, John	188?	A643		FORTNER, John M.	183?	B314a
FISHER, Joyce Darlene	1931	E10810		FORTNER, Josephine	186?	B1193
FISHER, Mary R. (Haley)	185?	A643		FORTNER, Jossie Banning	1901	B1195
FISHER, Merton Lyle	190?	E10810		FORTNER, Lola	188?	B1193a
FISHER, Michael	174?	X2759		FORTNER, Lucy	186?	B1194a
FISHER, Rachel (B=)	1822	A230		FORTNER, Mary (Eceles)	186?	B1193a
FISHER, Ray	1845	A639		FORTNER, Minnie	186?	B1193a
FISHER, Raymond	188?	A643		FORTNER, Nancy M. (B=)	1837	B314a
FISHER, Rebecca	178?	A230		FORTNER, Raleigh	189? *	B1193a
FISHER, Roxalina (B=)	1748	X2759		FORTNER, Raymond	1904 *	B1195
FISHER, Sallie	1850	A641		FORTNER, Robert	187?	B1195
FISHER, Vivian J.(Flisra	190?	E10810		FORTNER, Steve	188?	B1193a
FLEMING, Abner	180?	C87		FORTNER, William	186?	B1193a
FLEMING, Mariah Ann	1831	C87		FOSTER, Doris	192?	H823
FLEMING, Mary Ann	180?	C87		FOSTER, Mr.	196?	E39028
FLEMING, Mary	183?	G11		FOSTER, Sally	181?	E209
FLETCHER, Malinda Jane	1870	C114		FOSTER, Sheryl (Mathews)	1964	E39028
FLICK, Clarence	1900	F3315		FOUGERE, Lynda (B=)	1953	R494
FLICK, Cora Marie	1898	F3314		FOULK, Hilda Ann	183?	C29
FLICK, Elvira Maud	1896	F3313		FOWLER, Agnes (B=)	1860	E1360
FLICK, Eva Mildred	1905	F3316		FOWLER, Edwin M.	185?	E1360
FLICK, Frank	187?	F1475		FOWLER, Jessie	186?	E4204
FLICK, Georgiana B. (B=)	1875	F1475		FOWLER, Niki C. (McNeal)	1950	H338
FLISRAM, Vivian Joyce	190?	E10810		FOWLER, Robert	194?	H338
FLOOD, Ellery	187?	E6738		FOX, Eliza	183?	E403
FLOOD, Gertrude	190?	E6738		FOX, Martha E.	184?	E1628
FLOOD, Harley	190?	E6738		FOX, Sadie	178?	X3000
FLOOD, Mary Annette Hayd	1830	E401		FRANCIS, Harriet (Warner	182?	E384
FLOOD, Nellie (Huntley)	1879	E6738		FRANCIS, Mr.	182?	E384
FLOOD, Phoebe Ann Johnso	180?	E401		FRANGLER, Mary	187?	D51
FLOOD, Richard	180?	E401		FRANKLIN, Asa Banning	1864	B560
FOCKE, Maria	169?	N2		FRANKLIN, Clarence	187?	B564
FOERSTER, Chase Banning	1990	B26036		FRANKLIN, Donald	1835	B130
FOERSTER, John G.	1959	B26036		FRANKLIN, Edith	187?	B565
FOERSTER, John G.	1989	B26036		FRANKLIN, Elizabeth (B=)	1843	B130
FOERSTER, Wendy (Stol	1963	B26036		FRANKLIN, Emma	186?	B562
FONDREN, Debbie (Hill)	195?	F11994		FRANKLIN, Ida May (B=)	1876	E6740
FONDREN, Mr.	195?	F11994		FRANKLIN, Ira	186?	B559
FORD, Fanny Ann	1883	E1147		FRANKLIN, Irving	187?	E6740
FORD, Florence	185?	L454		FRANKLIN, James	187?	B566
FORD, George	182?	E1147		FRANKLIN, John	187?	B563
FORD, Helen	186?	G76		FRANKLIN, Laura (Carney)	1870	B560
FORD, Louis Milton	1890	E1147		FRANKLIN, Margaret	186?	B561
FORD, Marion (???)	182?	E1147		FRANKLIN, Ward Burdette	1890	B560
FORD, Milton George	1849	E1147		FRANKLIN, William	186?	B558
FORD, Nancy (Jackson)	1856	E1147		FRAY, Edgar	1880	B2096
FORD, Pearl Etta	1899	E1147		FRAY, Estell	1890	B2097
FORD, Violet V.	188?	E1147		FRAY, John E.	185?	B772
FORESTER, Betty Lou	1938	E19052		FRAY, Susan (B=)	1859	B772

FRAZIER, Angelica	1726	A8		GABLE, Arthur M.	1906	F7007
FRAZIER, Benony	169?	A8		GABLE, Beulah B.	1909	F7007
FRAZIER, Cecilah	169?	A8		GABLE, Paula N.	1940	F7007
FRAZIER, Louise	188?	B594		GALLOWAY, Mary Catherin	1938	J509
FREDERICKS, Irminda Jane	1846	A235		GANNON, Charles	180?	A34c
FREEBORN, Jane Thurston	1878	E6587		GANNON, ???	183?	A34c
FREEBORN, Katherine (Big	188?	E6568		GANT, Cecil	189?	C1864
FREEBORN, Margurite	1888 *	E6569		GANT, Myrtle E. (Sams)	1899	C1864
FREEBORN, Matilda (B=)	1854	E1584		GARDNER, Emily (B=)	1837	E1384
FREEBORN, Thomas Weaver	185?	E1584		GARDNER, Erastus H.	183?	E1384
FREEBORN, Thomas Laurenc	1879	E6568		GARRETT, Amy Agnes	193?	E19120
FREEMAN, Grace M.	187?	E6303		GASKELL, Bruce	196?	J497
FRENCH, Harriet	1806	F203		GASKELL, Gwendolyn	195?	J497
FRENCH, Rachel	178?	F203		GASKELL, Jill	196?	J497
FRENCH, William	177?	F203		GASKELL, Kirk	195?	J497
FRIEDLANDER, Caleb Gard	1982	F6012		GASKELL, Liss	195?	J497
FRIEDLANDER, Catherine	1953	F6012		GASKELL, Margaret	1932	J497
FRIEDLANDER, David Gard	1982	F6011		GASKELL, Mark	196?	J497
FRIEDLANDER, Elizabeth	1984	F6011		GASKELL, Paul	196?	J497
FRIEDLANDER, Gardner L.	1919	F3089		GASKELL, Sally	196?	J497
FRIEDLANDER, Gardner L.	1951	F6011		GASKELL, Tiim	195?	J497
FRIEDLANDER, Karen (Hof	1951	F6011		GASKELL, Tom	1927	J497
FRIEDLANDER, Margaret	1949	F6010		GASKELL, Trudy	196?	J497
FRIEDLANDER, Mary (B=)	1915	F3089		GASSER, Ramona Louise	1945	C3338
FRIEDLANDER, Peter Mark	1983	F6012		GATES, Moses C.	182?	F278
FRIEDLANDER, Rebecca An	1980	F6012		GATES, Lida H.	186?	E6404
FRIEDLANDER, Thomas W.	1954	F6012		GATES, Philura (B=)	182?	F278
FULLER, Celestina	1838	J27		GATES, Ruth Adelia	1823	F254
FULLWOOD, Ann	179?	B61e		GATLIN, May Berdie	189?	J413
FULLWOOD, Ann Bell (Howa	1812	B61b		GATLING, Constance (B=)	1923	F3108
FULLWOOD, Elizabeth (B=)	1772	B14		CATLING, Irene Banning	1956	F6036
FULLWOOD, Elizabeth	179?	B61c		GATLING, James Moore	192?	F3108
FULLWOOD, Elizabeth (How	180?	B61		GATLING, James Moore	1951	F6035
FULLWOOD, John Mason	179?	B61		GAUTHIER, Evangeline Rut	187?	C102
FULLWOOD, John	183?	B61b		GAYLORD, Elizabeth (B=)	1830	B108
FULLWOOD, Martha	179?	B61f		GAYLORD, Henry	182?	B108
FULLWOOD, Robert	183?	B61		GEBHEIM, Larae A.	193?	E19119
FULLWOOD, Robert	183?	B61b		GEDDES, Henry	175?	A23
FULLWOOD, Samuel	179?	B61b		GEDDES, Margaret Laatime	175?	A23
FULLWOOD, Samuel M.	1811	B61b		GEDDES, Sarah	177?	A23
FULLWOOD, Sarah	179?	B61d		GEER, Sarah (B=)	1685	X2540
FULLWOOD, Sarah Elizabet	184?	B61b		GEER, Shubael	168?	X2540
FULLWOOD, William	1773	B14		GENTRY, Pat	191?	E10813
FULLWOOD, William	178?	B61a		GENTRY, Velma (B=)	1914	E10813
FULLWOOD, William	183?	B61b		GEORGE, Mary	172?	X2636
FULMER, Lila E.	1930	E19049		GIBBS, Lusannah	183?	G15
FURROUGHS, Bonnie Kay	1955	H769		GIBSON, Jane Lucinda	182?	X500
FURROUGHS, Cherry Lynn	1982	H767		GIBSON, Edith Gay	1954	F6037
FURROUGHS, Christopher	1980	H770		GIBSON, Henry Taylor	193?	F3109
FURROUGHS, Davis Wayne	1952	H767		GIBSON, Henry Taylor Jr.	1956	F6038
FURROUGHS, David Wayne	1980	H767		GIBSON, Joy Banning	1957	F6039
FURROUGHS, Denise Lynn	1968	H763		GIBSON, Sarah (Marshall	195?	F6038
FURROUGHS, James Eugene	1950 *	H766		GIBSON, Theodora (B=)	1933	F3109
FURROUGHS, Jeanette (B=)	1932	H327		GIBSON, Theodore Banning	1962	F6040
FURROUGHS, Linda (Dorrel	195?	H767		GIDDINGS, Affiah	179?	F67
FURROUGHS, Penny Diane	1953	H768		GIDDINGS, Asenath (B=)	1846	F627
FURROUGHS, Richard Allan	1956	H770		GIDDINGS, Frank A.	184?	F627
FURROUGHS, Richard Allan	1978	H770		GIDEON, Appa	179?	F67
FURROUGHS, Robert E.	1926	H327		GIDEON, Benjamin	176?	G67
FURROUGHS, Shirley (Mere	195?	H770		GILLAMORE, John Alex	183?	B279
FUSCH, Helena	189?	C1829		GILLAMORE, Julia A.	185?	B279
GAARDER, Gladys	1912	C1912		GILLAMORE, Mary (Mintz)	183?	B279

GILLESPIE, Effie (B=)	1868	C115	GOODWIN, Abbie (B=)	1825	F271
GILLESPIE, Emily Gladys	1895	C307	GOODWIN, Abigail	1833	F497
GILLESPIE, Frederick Ban	1892	C306	GOODWIN, Edwin Ozias	182?	F271
GILLESPIE, James H.	186?	C115	GOODWIN, Edwin Ozias	182?	F497
GILLESPIE, James Arthur	1890	C305	GOODWIN, Eunice (B=)	1818	E349
GILLETT, Linda	185?	F632	GOODWIN, Wyllys	181?	E349
GILLFER, Keziah	180?	B12	GORDIN, John	172?	A12j
GILLFER, Thomas	178?	B12	GORDIN, Susannah (B=)	170?	A5g
GILLISPIE, Judy (???)	194?	E38976	GORE, Wanda Ann	195?	H501
GILLISPIE, Kassey	197?	E38976	GORE, William Leon	192?	H501
GILLISPIE, Kelley	197?	E38976	GORDON, Darlene (Parker)	191?	C1911
GILLISPIE, Kim	197?	E38976	GORDON, Evelyn (Jennings	191?	C1909
GILLISPIE, Lynn D.	194?	E38976	GORDON, Julita Stella(B=	1884	C576
GILLISPIE, Mary A. (Bess	1926	E19041	GORDON, Ralph	191?	C1909
GILLISPIE, Mr.	192?	E19041	GORDON, Roy	191?	C1911
GINDER, Barbara E. (Gish	188?	G169	GORDON, Velma	191? *	C1908
GINDER, Effie Kathryn	1910	G169	GORDON, Viola	191?	C1910
GINDER, Seth	188?	G169	GORDON, Willmer	1883	C576
GIPSON, Binda	1854	B686	GOSSAGE, Clementina T.	177?	A24
GIPSON, Catherine (B=)	1823	B153	GOSSAGE, Freeborn	1777	A23
GIPSON, D. B.	1860	B690	GOSSAGE, Helen Louise	1927	E10826
GIPSON, Elijah	1856	B687	GOSSAGE, Julia (Sanders)	190?	E10826
GIPSON, Grace	1842	B677	GOSSAGE, Lite	190?	E10826
GIPSON, Grant	1866	B693	GOSSAGE, Mary	173?	A10
GIPSON, James	1851	B684	GOSSAGE, Robert	1776	A22
GIPSON, Louisa	1857	B688	GOSSEY, Carolyn	194?	J2119
GIPSON, Margaret	1841	B676	GOTTL, Elsa	193?	E19119
GIPSON, Martha	1847	B681	GRAHAM, Kenneth L.	192?	B19001
GIPSON, Mary	1843	B678	GRAHAM, Michael Paul	1948	B19001
GIPSON, Melissa	1846	B680	GRAHAM, Norma (Whiteside	192?	B19001
GIPSON, Nannie	1847	B682	GRAHAM, Pamela (Haymes)	1948	B19001
GIPSON, Sarah	1844	B679	GRAHAM, Patrick Edward	1983	B19001
GIPSON, Smith	181?	B153	GRAHAM, Sarah	1670	E5
GIPSON, Smith	1868	B694	GRAHAM, Sarah Kathryn	1980	B19001
GIPSON, Stephen	1849	B683	GRANDISON, Mary	163?	X2010
GIPSON, Susie	1864	B692	GRANDISON, William	162?	X2010
GIPSON, Thomas	1852	B685	GRANGER, Henry	183?	F578
GIPSON, William	1862	B691	GRANGER, Mary (B=)	180?	F240
GISH, Barbara Ellen	188?	G169	GRANGER, Mary	183?	F579
GLAD, Hester (B=)	184?	D17	GRANGER, Mr.	180?	F240
GLAD, Katie	188?	D98	GRAY, Priscilla (B=)	1807	A73
GLAD, Mr.	184?	D17	GRAY, Sewell	1806	A73
GLADDING, John Jr.	187?	E6567	GREAVES-BANNING	-	L33
GLASS, Nancy	1798	B21	GREEN, Christina	183?	B156
GLASSELL, Susan	183?	C125	GREEN, George	182?	B155
GLENHAM, Ann	15??	X2005	GREEN, Mary	182?	E397
GLENHAM, Henry	15??	X2005	GREEN, Mary	190?	B2037
GOFF, Elizabeth (Doud)	185?	E1639	GREEN, Matilda (B=)	1831	B155
GOFF, Mr.	185?	E1639	GREEN, Matilda	185?	B697
GOLDMAN, Eugene P.	183?	E1606	GREEN, Melissa	187?	E1698
GOLDMAN, Irene (Colvin)	1835	E1606	GREENLEAF, Mace E.	187?	C133
GOLDSBROUGH, Elizabeth	16??	A5	GREENO, Camelia Gayle	1945	B2513f
GOLDSBROUGH, Jane(Spenc	170?	A5	GREENO, Eddie Ruth	1938	B2513g
GOLDSBROUGH, Nicholas	1704	A5	GREENO, Edgar Wayne	1909	B2513g
GOLDSBROUGH, Robert	16??	A5	GREENO, Edgar Wayne	1937	B2513g
GOLDSBROUGH, Robert	1704	A5	GREENO, Edgar Bruce	1947	B2513g
GOLDSMITH, Mary	162?	X2501	GREENO, Elizabeth W.	1944	B2513g
GOODMAN, Frank	187?	X516	GREENO, George Edward	1943 *	B2513f
GOODMAN, Jim	187?	X515	GREENO, Judy Carol	1951	B2513g
GOODMAN, John Wesley	185?	X503	GREENO, Malcolm Lynn	1935	B2513f
GOODMAN, Len	187?	X517	GREENO, Minnie (Cooper)	1914	B2513f
GOODMAN, Mary E. (B=)	1857	X503	GREENO, Oliver Millard	1913	B2513f

GREENO, Peggy Angelina	1939	B2513g	
GREENO, Roger Dale	1949	B2513f	
GREENO, Rowena Jean	1939	B2513f	
GREENO, Ruth (Cooper)	1918	B2513g	
GREENO, Wynella Karen	1953	B2513f	
GREENSLIT, Catherine D.	1853	F1200	
GREER, Fannie	190?	H496	
GRIAGAR, Mr.	194?	E19044	
GRIAGAR, Sharon E. (Bess	1947	E19044	
GRIAGAR, Stephanie Micha	1971	E38981	
GRIER, Evangeline	189?	C299	
GRIFFAN, Rebecca	179?	B48	
GRIFFIN, John	16??	K234	
GRIFFIN, Mary (White)	16??	K234	
GRIFFIN, Mary	170?	K234	
GRIFFITH, Anna Mae	189?	E10832	
GRIFFITH, Kenneth	190?	R150	
GRIFFITH, Mary F. (B=)	1879	R42	
GRIFFITH, Meredith	190?	R151	
GRIFFITH, Thomas E.	187?	R42	
GRISWOLD, Marion	185?	F630	
GROTE, Augusta W.	180?	N267	
GROVES, Francis Porter	188?	C298	
GROVES, Jackson A.	185?	C298	
GROVES, Katherine (B=)	1891	C298	
GULLICKS, Oscar	189?	C1863	
GULLICKS, Verna Mae(Sams	1896	C1863	
GULLIFER, Kezian	177?	B10f	
GULLIFER, Thomas	174?	B10f	
GUSTIN, Donna Maxine	192?	J162	
GUSTIN, Leslie Vernon	192?	J162	
GUSTIN, Margaret (Hopkin	1895	J162	
GUSTIN, Margaret Ilene	192?	J162	
GUSTIN, Verle Wilson	192?	J162	
GUSTIN, Vern	189?	J162	
GUTHRIE, Clarence	190?	B2706	
GUTHRIE, Victoria (Doty)	1904	B2706	
HAAJANEN, Barbara	192?	H825	
HABERMANN, Olga L.	189?	B3000	
HAENER, Addie	186?	E5689	
HAHN, Eva	177?	A68	
HAINS, Elizabeth	181?	B16	
HAINES, Miss.	176?	L7	
HALE, Dorothy	172?	X2639	
HALEY, John	182?	A643	
HALEY, lydia Myrtle	1905	F7006	
HALEY, Mary Rose	185?	A643	
HALEY, Sarah Lurinda	182?	A643	
HALL, Alemna	1819	E372	
HALL, Alexander	182?	C77	
HALL, David	176?	C16	
HALL, Elizabeth Wolcott	179?	F262	
HALL, Garnette (B=)	1869	E5803	
HALL, Georgia Mary	1858	E6403	
HALL, Helen L. (B=)	1833	E1508	
HALL, Horace	188?	F1406	
HALL, Inez (Clark)	1882	F1406	
HALL, Jane	1891	Q47	
HALL, Joseph	186?	E5803	
HALL, Lois M.	191?	E10825	
HALL, Margaret	187?	C138	
HALL, Nancy	1796	C16	
HALL, Nathan	179?	F262	
HALL, Nettie	190?	E19050	
HALL, Orphania	1813	F261	
HALL, Rachael	1830	C77	
HALL, Rachel (Veach)	176?	C16	
HALL, Rexford R.	183?	E1508	
HALL, Sarah	164?	X2502	
HALL, Sarah	176?	X2993	
HALL, Sarah Maria	1821	F262	
HAMILTON, Cora (B=)	1868	B768	
HAMILTON, Thomas R.	186?	B768	
HAMLYN, Clay Justin	1959	E39014	
HAMLYN, John Harold	193?	E39014	
HAMLYN, Marjorie J.	193?	E39014	
HAMLYN, Rhonda (Ridge)	1959	E39014	
HAMMEL, Carolyn Regina	188?	H177a	
HAMMETT, Margaret	182?	B151	
HAMMOND, Albert H.	189?	E6712	
HAMMOND, Lillias (B=)	1894	E6712	
HAMNER, Celia Ann	1894	J136	
HANDLIN, Nettie	187?	A674	
HANKEY, Anna (B=)	1875	A687	
HANKEY, Philo	187?	A687	
HANSEN, Cora	1890	C1860	
HANSEN, Curt	188?	C1860	
HANSEN, Mr.	195?	F11997	
HANSEN, Pamela (Hill)	195?	F11997	
HAPGOOD, Adeline (B=)	1847	E1569	
HAPGOOD, George	184?	E1569	
HARBER, Earl P.	189?	C663	
HARBER, Winifred (B=)	1899	C663	
HARDING, Arthur	1912	Q14	
HARDING, Elsie Edna	1901	Q14	
HARDING, Frederick J.	1869	Q14	
HARDING, Lilda	1906	Q14	
HARDING, Malissa (Roy)	1871	Q14	
HARDING, Roy Channings	1903	Q14	
HARDMAN, Mary E.	184?	B109	
HARDY, Eleen	190?	Q59	
HARDY, Frances Emily	187?	L469	
HARING, Kathy Jane	189?	H177b	
HARLAN, Benayce	196?	E39008	
HARLAN, Benny	194?	E19048	
HARLAN, Brandon	196?	E39007	
HARLAN, Brenda (B=)	1941	E19048	
HARLAN, Bryson	196?	E39006	
HARMON, Mary J.	184?	E1509	
HARPER, Caroline (B=)	182?	A57	
HARPER, Elizabeth W.	188?	A688	
HARPER, Christopher C.	182?	A57	
HARPER, Susan Antonia	18??	A147	
HARR, Emanule	190?	E19050	
HARR, Nettie	190?	E19050	
HARR, Wilma Leona	1932	E19050	
HARRINGTON, Matilda	186?	X1512	
HARRIS, Alexander	18??	A144	
HARRIS, Alva	193?	F2628	
HARRIS, Alvin	193?	F2629	
HARRIS, Charles B.	186?	F1210	
HARRIS, Charles A.	1903	F2628	
HARRIS, Charles	194?	F2628	
HARRIS, Clairice (???)	191?	F2631	

HARRIS, Conn	185?	A643	HAYMES, Albert Howard	1883	B1140
HARRIS, Dolly (???)	190?	F2629	HAYMES, Albert Burke	1916	B3000
HARRIS, Donald B.	1909	F2631	HAYMES, Andrew B.	1858	B310a
HARRIS, Doreen	193?	F2629	HAYMES, Charles K.	1903	B1141
HARRIS, Eileen	193?	F2629	HAYMES, Cynthia Ann	1945	B3001
HARRIS, Ellen M. (B=)	1867	F1210	HAYMES, Dwight William	1922	B1141
HARRIS, Elsie Margaret	1900	F2626	HAYMES, Esther (Redmon)	1896	B1143
HARRIS, Emma	184?	A144	HAYMES, Ethel D.	1890	B1142
HARRIS, Estella Marie	1907	C1827	HAYMES, Eva Dora (B=)	1857	B310a
HARRIS, Eugene {Dr.}	1880	A1567	HAYMES, John Clarence	1896	B1143
HARRIS, Evelyn	1899	F2625	HAYMES, Kathryn Nelle	1945	B19000
HARRIS, Evelyn	193?	F2629	HAYMES, Mark Burke	1960	B3001
HARRIS, Fay	194?	F2629	HAYMES, Nancy Jane	1927	B1143
HARRIS, Frank	1944	F2631	HAYMES, Nelle I. (Smith)	1893	B1140
HARRIS, Grace Lillian	1911	F2632	HAYMES, Norma J. (Simons	1925	B3001
HARRIS, Helen {Nell}(???)	190?	F2628	HAYMES, Pam	188?	B1140
HARRIS, Irene Ellen	1901	F2627	HAYMES, Pamela Jeanne	1948	B19001
HARRIS, Joan	193?	F2631	HAYMES, Paul Warren	1926	B3001
HARRIS, Joseph	184?	F1210	HAYMES, Paul Howard	1954	B3001
HARRIS, Judith	193?	F2628	HAYMES, Sarah (Waugh)	1884	B1141
HARRIS, Leonard	1907	F2629	HAYMES, Stella Marjorie	1919	B1141
HARRIS, Leonard	193>	F2629	HAYMES, Sylvia C. (Popp)	1916	B3000
HARRIS, Maria Spencer	18??	A144	HAYMES, William E.	1881	B1141
HARRIS, Marrianne	194?	F2629	HAYWARD, Ernest Waler	1865 *	E6302
HARRIS, Mary (Churchya	184?	F1210	HAYWARD, Frances (B=)	1836	E1473
HARRIS, Maureen	193?	F2628	HAYWARD, Frances Stella	1861 *	E6300
HARRIS, Neil	194?	F2631	HAYWARD, Grace (Freeman)	187?	E6303
HARRIS, Robert	193?	F2631	HAYWARD, Harriet	183?	B223
HARRIS, Shirley	193?	F2628	HAYWARD, Harry Bradbury	1871	E6303
HARRIS, Sophia (B=)	1855	A634	HAYWARD, Waldo Banning	1861	E6301
HARRIS, Tempy	181?	B85	HAYWARD, Wales A.	183?	E1473
HARRIS, Tom	194?	F2628	HEBERN, Berton	184?	E1643
HARRIS, William C.	187?	C1827	HEBERN, Mary (B=)	185?	E1643
HARRISON, J.M.	187?	B798	HEGGART, Barbara Louise	1953	Q152
HARRISON, Lora G.	1880	J32a	HEGGART, Eric William	192?	Q152
HARRISON, Margaretta (O	1874	B798	HEGGART, Marjorie (Assel	192?	Q152
HART, Patience	1810	F243	HEIBECK, Alison Marie(B=	1955	H825
HARTE, Lucy (B=)	190?	F2633	HEIBECK, Barbara (Haajan	192?	H825
HARTE, Ned	190?	F2633	HEIBECK, George	192?	H825
HARTMAN, Pearl B.	188?	C553	HEIBECK, Jason Michael	1982	H1496
HARVEY, Joanna (Sill)	172?	E17	HEIBECK, Matthew William	1983	H1497
HARVEY, John B.	182?	C228	HEIBECK, Michael W.	1951	H825
HARVEY, Joshua	172?	E17	HEIBECK, Sean Patrick	1986	H1498
HARVEY, Mary Ellen	1849	C228	HELLENS, Alexander	184?	H7
HARVEY, Sarah	1752	E17	HELLENS, Mary (B=)	1846	H7
HARVEY, Sarah (Wheeler)	182?	C228	HEMMONMDS, Nina {or Ann	1882	H29
HATCHELL, Alice E. (B=)	1948	H498	HENDERSON, Jerry Don	194?	J2116
HATCHELL, Clyde William	192?	H498	HENDERSON, Wanda (Carter	1944	J2166
HATCHELL, Eunice (Langst	192?	H498	HENDRICKS, Leonard	1936	Q187
HATCHELL, Gena Dalaine	1969	H1005	HENDRICKS, Maureen (B=)	1938	Q187
HATCHELL, Gene Langston	1945	H498	HENDRIX, George Lewis	191?	J413
HATCHER, Minnie N.	192?	H500	HENDRIX, Grace B. (B=)	1917	J413
HAVEN, Vera	188?	J414	HENRY, Jessie Lee	1897	E5617
HAWK, Anetta	186?	E1361	HENRY, Laura Anna	187?	E5617
HAWK, Florence (B=)	1852	E1357	HENRY, Wylie	186?	E5617
HAWK, Mr.	184?	E1357	HENSHAW, Charlotte L.	185?	B109
HAYES, ----? (Nugent)	183?	L190	HEPNOR, Annie	187?	D65
HAYES, Francis	182?	L190	HERALD, Frances	194?	E19069
HAYES, Hannah (B=)	1796	L45	HERBERT, Ann (B=)	164?	X2013
HAYES, James {Rev.}	1???	E1477	HERBERT, John	164?	X2013
HAYES, Margaret	1822	L191	HERREGODST, Marie Louise	188?	H135
HAYES, Thomas	179?	L45	HERRING, Elsie Helen	190?	B9600

Name	Year	Code		Name	Year	Code
HERRINGTON, Charlott	184?	B225		HILMES, Scott Jerome	1959	B14000
HERRINGTON, Mary E.	184?	B225		HILMES, Sherri (Holley)	1959	B14000
HERRMANN, Helen	192?	E19118		HILMES, Tarlyn Holley	1985	B14000
HERTH, Brian Robert	1978	C3339		HILTON, Addie Frances	1894	E11024
HERTH, Helena (Fusch)	189?	C1829		HILTON, Cora (B=)	1861	E5690
HERTH, Jacob George	189?	C1829		HILTON, Ethel Alberta	1882	E11023
HERTH, Janet Marie(Nordi	194?	C3339		HILTON, Eva	1896	E11026
HERTH, Lois R. (B=)	1922	C1829		HILTON, Mable	1899	E11027
HERTH, Lorayne Kae	1955	C3341		HILTON, Richard M.	185?	E5690
HERTH, Lynnette Lee	1947	C3340		HILTON, Ruth Bell	189? *	E11025
HERTH, Robert Eugene	1923	C1829		HIMES, Martha E.	183?	B243
HERTH, Robert Eugene	1943	C3339		HIRZ, Mary	188?	C1827
HERTH, Tracy Marie	1967	C3339		HISE, Jane L. (Gibson)	182?	X500
HERTH, Yvonne M. (Clemen	194?	C3339		HISE, John B.	182?	X500
HICKOX, Harriett (B=)	1854	B121A		HISE, Thomas Banning	185?	X504
HICKOX, Lewis M.	185?	B121A		HISSEY, Emma B. (B=)	1860	R37
HICKS, Dolly Nelly	192?	E19113		HISSEY, Ethel M.	1887	R133
HICKS, Lillian J.	192?	E19051		HISSEY, Howard M.	1890	R134
HIGH, Angelina (B=)	1838	G16		HISSEY, John Andrew C.	1850	R37
HIGH, Peter	183?	G16		HISSEY, Namomi V.	1884	R132
HILAND, Earl Jackson	1928	B9609		HISSEY, Violet M. (???)	189?	R134
HILAND, James Edward	1929	B9610		HITCHENS, Ida	188?	H58a
HILAND, Linda Sue	1948	B9608		HOFFMAN, Karen	1951	F6011
HILAND, Mable A.M. (B=)	1906	B2038		HOKENSON, Bertha Hannah	185?	C234
HILAND, Peggy Lee	1951	B9608		HOLCOMB, SEBA (B=)	176?	F56
HILAND, Rose Mary (Lewis)	192?	B9608		HOLCOMB, Truman	176?	F56
HILAND, William	190?	B2038		HOLDEN, Foy	191?	B998
HILAND, William Eugene	1926	B9608		HOLDEN, Mary (B=)	1916	B998
HILL, Abram	177?	B16		HOLIDAY, David	190?	B997a
HILL, Absolem	1833	B67		HOLIDAY, Edith (B=)	1906	B997a
HILL, Angeline	185?	E1601		HOLLANDER, Callie R.(B=)	1960	C5666
HILL, Carrie	185?	E1600		HOLLANDER, Peter	195?	C5666
HILL, Charles	181?	B65a		HOLLEY, Addie Mae (Fortner	187?	B986a
HILL, Charles L.	182?	E379		HOLLEY, Annie Mae (B=)	1904	B986a
HILL, Charles	186?	E1604		HOLLEY, Bradley Gene	1960	B14001
HILL, Debra	195?	F11994		HOLLEY, Caroline (Pearce)	193?	B2576a
HILL, Elizabeth (Hains)	181?	B16		HOLLEY, Charles Franklin	1933	B2576a
HILL, Elizabeth (Stephen	181?	B65a		HOLLEY, Cheryl (Jones)	194?	B2577a
HILL, Elizabeth	1829	B66a		HOLLEY, Clara Mae	1927	B2575a
HILL, Elizabeth (Crawford)	183?	X3501		HOLLEY, Darlene (Phillips)	1932	B2576
HILL, Estella	185?	E1599		HOLLEY, Gerald Dean	1925	B2575
HILL, Esther Louise	193?	E19125		HOLLEY, Gerilyn (Meier)	196?	B14001
HILL, Hazel P. (B=)	1903	J203		HOLLEY, Glen Dewey	1898	B986a
HILL, John	1801	B16		HOLLEY, Henry	187?	B986a
HILL, Laura A. (B=)	1829	E379		HOLLEY, Joan (Smith)	194?	B2577
HILL, Linda Sue	195?	F11995		HOLLEY, Julie Ann	1961	B14002
HILL, Lulu	185?	E1602		HOLLEY, Larry Phil	1941	B2577
HILL, Mary (Stewart)	182?	B66		HOLLEY, Patsy Lou	1939	B2576c
HILL, Nancy A.	1836	B67a		HOLLEY, Ronald Eugene	1929	B2576
HILL, Nancy	1945	J496		HOLLEY, Sherri Frances	1959	B14000
HILL, Pamela L.	195?	F11997		HOLLEY, Shirley Jean	1937	B2576b
HILL, R. B.	181?	B65		HOLLEY, Steven Joe	1947	B2577a
HILL, Robert M.	182?	X3501		HOLLEY, Wanda (Williams)	192?	B2575
HILL, Roy	190?	J203		HOLLISTER, Dezell E.	184?	F615
HILL, Sandra Jo	195?	F11996		HOLLISTER, George E.	1862	F1478
HILL, Sarah (B=)	1778	B16		HOLLISTER, Gertrude (Hunt	1877	E6739
HILL, Shirley (B=)	1928	F7005		HOLLISTER, Hanyes	187?	E6739
HILL, Stephen	1821	B66		HOLLISTER, J. Spencer	1868	F1479
HILL, Swinfield	177?	B16		HOLLISTER, Martha (B=)	1843	F615
HILL, William	186?	E1603		HOLLISTER, Mary	1846	C27
HILL, William	193?	F7005		HOLLISTER, Maud (Carnack	186?	F1478
HILMES, Ryan Scott	1982	B14000		HOLLISTER, Pearl Louise	1877	F1480

HOLMES, Lucretia	171?	E16
HOLMES, Lydia E. (B=)	1893	F1416
HOLMES, Richard	189?	F1416
HOLSTINE, Ardis (B=)	1934	F7006
HOLSTINE, Carolyn Kay	1963	F11999
HOLSTINE, Deborah (Weis)	196?	F11998
HOLSTINE, Hugh Washingt	1901	F7006
HOLSTINE, Kirk Michael	1960	F11998
HOLSTINE, Lydia (Haley)	1905	F7006
HOLSTINE, William Clem	1932	F7006
HOLT, Ann	181?	L51
HOLT, Constance Daisy	188?	L467
HOOD, Zakery	17??	A10
HOOPER, Dawn	194?	E19061
HOOVER, Lois	191?	E19053
HOPKINS, Benjamin Frankl	1835	J26
HOPKINS, Bertha (Scovern	190?	J164
HOPKINS, Caroline (Cloud	1841	J26
HOPKINS, Carrie Rachel(B	1869	J26
HOPKINS, Clementina (B=)	177?	A24
HOPKINS, Donald	193?	J164
HOPKINS, Florence (???)	190?	J164
HOPKINS, George Arthur	1902	J164
HOPKINS, George Jr.	192?	J164
HOPKINS, Jeremiah	177?	A24
HOPKINS, Lulu Minerva	1892	J161
HOPKINS, Margaret Blanch	1895	J162
HOPKINS, Mary Agnes	1886	J159
HOPKINS, Nellie May	1905 *	J165
HOPKINS, Vera Elizabeth	1899 *	J163
HOPKINS, Viola Caroline	1888 *	J160
HOPKINS, Wilson Nathanie	1863	J26
HORN, Alexander E.	187?	C138
HORN, Fanny (B=)	1833	C28
HORN, Henry John	186?	C137
HORN, John	183?	C28
HORN, John H.	186? *	C134
HORN, Josephine (Robinso	186?	C137
HORN, Laura B.	187?	C140
HORN, Lydia Ann	184?	C260
HORN, Mable B.	188?	C141
HORN, Margaret (Hall)	186?	C138
HORN, Mary B.	186? *	C135
HORN, Priscilla F.	187?	C139
HORN, William Banning	186? *	C136
HORRICKS, Earl	192?	Q145
HORRICKS, Judy	1947	Q145
HORRICKS, Muriel (White	192?	Q145
HORSLEY, Mary (Denny)	180?	A66c
HORSLEY, ?Samuel?	180?	A66c
HOSTLER, Elizabeth	181?	C83
HOSTOS, Anna	190?	H374
HOUGHTON, Elizabeth	184?	L455
HOWARD, Ann Bell	180?	B61b
HOWARD, Cecillia	183?	B61f
HOWARD, Edward	183?	B61f
HOWARD, Elizabeth	180?	B61
HOWARD, Laurel Lee	1946	C3422
HOWARD, Margaret	183?	B61f
HOWARD, Martha (Fullwood	181?	B61f
HOWARD, Mortimer	183?	B61f
HOWARD, Robert	183?	B61f

HOWARD, Sarah Ann	1825	Q1
HOWARD, William M.D.	180?	B61f
HOWARD, William	183?	B61f
HOWE, John Calvin	188?	B931
HOWE, Ottie F. (Severe)	1883	B931
HOWGATE, Henry Otis	190?	H373
HOWGATE, Margaret Ann	1931	H373
HOWGATE, Mary (Wallace)	190?	H373
HOYLER, Erika Louise	191?	C1826
HUBBARD, Benjamin	172?	X2638
HUBBARD, Fred Adriel	1888	E6737
HUBBARD, Gertrude Lillia	1877	E6739
HUBBARD, Harriet C.	183?	B175
HUBBARD, Mary (B=)	1726	X2638
HUBBARD, Nellie Georgia	1879	E6738
HUBBARD, Sarah Jane	1854	B140
HUCKSTEP, Dorothy Irene	190?	Q71
HUDSON, Charles Raymond	188?	H137
HUDSON, Christine	196?	H382
HUDSON, Edith Evelyn	188?	H137
HUDSON, Jann Lynn (Small	1946	H382
HUDSON, Lydia Elizabeth	1913	H137
HUDSON, Nancy Ann (Linds	1945	H382
HUDSON, Raymond R.	1913	H137
HUDSON, Richard Banning	1944	H382
HUDSON, Roberta Sue	1946	H383
HUGGINS, Lorean R.	190?	J2111
HUGHES, Frank	174?	X2761
HUGHES, Mary Serene	196?	H844
HUGHES, Tabitha (B=)	1751	X2761
HUMPHRES, Rachel	171?	A12e
HUNGERFORD, Annie (B=)	1904	R147
HUNGERFORD, Mr.	190?	R147
HUNTLEY, Benjamin B.	185?	E1646
HUNTLEY, Edith (Chase)	188?	E6737
HUNTLEY, Frederick A.	1888	E6737
HUNTLEY, Gertrude L.	1877	E6739
HUNTLEY, Henry	184?	E1628
HUNTLEY, Lucy S.	1868	E1628
HUNTLEY, Martha E. (Fox)	184?	E1628
HUNTLEY, Mary (B=)	1855	E1646
HUNTLEY, Nellie Georgia	1879	E6738
HURBERT, Martha (B=)	1724	X2637
HURBERT, Martin	172?	X2637
HURD, Jean	192?	Q96
HURD, Mary (Norton)	1817	A220
HURD, Rollin {Judge}	181?	A220
HURST, Anna	1847	B117
HUTCHEN, Benjamin	17??	F16
HUTCHINS, Flora	184?	F582
HUTCHISON, Anita	193?	H300
HUTCHISON, Joseph	193?	H300
HUTCHPATH, Peggy Jean	193?	E19106
HUTTON, Annie Evelyn	184?	L142
IERLEY, Margaret	189?	H177d
INGRAHAM, Lucy	178?	E346
INGRAM, Jane	194?	H333
INGRAM, Joshua P.	184?	B334
INGRAM, Sarah E. (B=)	1846	B334
IRVINE, Carloine (Best)	191?	Q144
IRVINE, Deborah Ann	1961	Q144
IRVINE, Howard D.	1937	Q144

IRVINE, Julie Kathleen	1966	Q144	
IRVINE, June (Lippiatt)	1942	Q144	
IRVINE, Kevin Mark	1963	Q144	
IRVINE, Livingston	191?	Q144	
ISAACS, Mary	184?	H4	
ISAACS, Minos	181?	H4	
ISHAM, Almira (Riddell?)	180?	E361	
ISSACS, Mary Ann	185?	H58c	
IVALL, Cathy	195?	Q96	
IVALL, Cecil Robert	1917	Q94	
IVALL, David	195?	Q96	
IVALL, Doreen Ruth	1940	Q94	
IVALL, E.	191?	Q92	
IVALL, Effie (Cesswell)	192?	Q95	
IVALL, Grace	1930	Q96	
IVALL, Hilda J. (B=)	1900	Q57	
IVALL, Jean (Hurd)	192?	Q96	
IVALL, Lloyd	1925	Q96	
IVALL, Norman	1918	Q95	
IVALL, Rhoda Ruth	1918	Q94	
IVALL, Robert	1895	Q57	
IWANSKI, Evelyn (Nichols	189?	H1137	
JABLONSKI, Bruce Edward	1952	E19120	
JABLONSKI, Chester	192?	E19120	
JABLONSKI, Darr Ann (Und	1951	E19120	
JABLONSKI, Mary	192?	E19120	
JACKSON, Alonzo	185?	B577	
JACKSON, Andrew	181?	E255	
JACKSON, Anson G.	1836	E1144	
JACKSON, Browynne	193?	F2632	
JACKSON, Charles E.	1845	E1145	
JACKSON, Charlotte (B=)	1825	B132	
JACKSON, Charlotte	185?	B574	
JACKSON, Daniel	193?	E19126	
JACKSON, Della Blaine	1925	B25134	
JACKSON, Donald	191?	B998b	
JACKSON, Elizabeth	177?	X2996	
JACKSON, Ephraim	185?	B576	
JACKSON, Fanny (Post)	1818	E255	
JACKSON, Grace (Harris)	1911	F2632	
JACKSON, Ida G. (McDermi	1878	Q37	
JACKSON, Ina (B=)	1922	B998b	
JACKSON, Jasper {Joseph?	182?	B132	
JACKSON, Jeanne Clara	1962	E19126	
JACKSON, Lee	186?	B579	
JACKSON, Lewis	190?	F2632	
JACKSON, Nancy Ann	1856	E1147	
JACKSON, Orange	185?	B578	
JACKSON, Oscar	186?	B580	
JACKSON, Ronnie	193?	F2632	
JACKSON, Samuel	186?	B581	
JACKSON, Thersa	185?	B575	
JACKSON, Todd	193?	F2632	
JACKSON, Velma (Norris)	193?	E19126	
JACKSON, Vista	186?	B582	
JACKSON, William A.	1847	E1146	
JACKSON, William I.	187?	Q37	
JARBOE, Frank	190?	B2047	
JARBOE, Pearl (Turbin)	1911	B2047	
JARRATT, Mathew	172?	C3	
JARZABEK, Victoria Franc	193?	E39021	
JAY, Donna	194?	Q182	

JEFFERIES, Mr.	189?	F2623	
JEFFERIES, Sylvia (B=)	1899	F2623	
JELANIE, Boris	194?	Q196	
JELANIE, Patricia (B=)	1947	Q196	
JENKINS, Arabella	185?	X3509	
JENKINS, Okemah	195?	H504	
JENKINS, Virginia	182?	C62	
JENKINS, William Jr.	192?	H504	
JENNE, Emilie Bartlett	185?	B139	
JENNE, Hannah Amelia	183?	B139	
JENNE, Otis Bartlett	183?	B139	
JENNEY, John	15??	B139	
JENNINGS, Evelyn	191?	C1908	
JENSEN, Alma	187?	E6503	
JENSEN, Henry	184?	E1568	
JENSEN, Janette (B=)	1845	E1568	
JENSEN, Sarah	187?	E6504	
JESSUP, Charity (B=)	183?	X3503	
JESSUP, Isaac	183?	X3503	
JESSUP, Martha J.	1851	X3521	
JESTER, Barbara (Parkhur	195?	H771	
JESTER, Bernadette (Sehn	195?	H772	
JESTER, Christopher D.	1981	H773	
JESTER, Cora	1900	H58d	
JESTER, Delmea M. (B=)	1927	H329	
JESTER, Donald W.	1949	H772	
JESTER, Donna L.	1955	H774	
JESTER, Katherine Ann	1986	H773	
JESTER, Kimberly M.	1976	H771	
JESTER, Lee Ann (welch)	195?	H773	
JESTER, Rachael Joy	1983	H771	
JESTER, Ronald E.	1955	H773	
JESTER, Rose (Sehn)	194?	H771	
JESTER, Ryan M.	1977	H771	
JESTER, Samuel	187?	H58d	
JESTER, Stephanie M.	1969 *	H772	
JESTER, William P.	192?	H329	
JESTER, William P.	1945	H771	
JOHNSON, Alexander	182?	C67	
JOHNSON, Alma E. (B=)	1907	H175b	
JOHNSON, Asa H.	1816 *	E524	
JOHNSON, Asa Sanders	1866	J27	
JOHNSON, Asa Earl {Jack}	1901	J171	
JOHNSON, Benjamin L.	1818	E525	
JOHNSON, Bertha	1886	H58b	
JOHNSON, Catherine (Wrig	182?	E526	
JOHNSON, Cheri L.	1949	E19102	
JOHNSON, Chester	192?	J428	
JOHNSON, Clestina (Fulle	1838	J27	
JOHNSON, Dora Mae	1889	J166	
JOHNSON, Edith Bessie	1903	J172	
JOHNSON, Elizabeth (B=)	1811	B58	
JOHNSON, Elizabeth H.	1826	E527	
JOHNSON, Elizabeth	185?	B278	
JOHNSON, Frances Marie	1897	J170	
JOHNSON, George W.	1829	E528	
JOHNSON, George Merrill	1905	J173	
JOHNSON, Gladys E.{Babe}	1910	J175	
JOHNSON, Glen	191?	C1910	
JOHNSON, Glenn Everett	1912	J176	
JOHNSON, H. G.	188?	B1014	
JOHNSON, Harold Albert	1895	J169	

JOHNSON, Hattie M. (B=)	1871	J27
JOHNSON, Horace F.	1832	J27
JOHNSON, Hulda J. (B=)	1894	J138
JOHNSON, James Lloyd	1893	J168
JOHNSON, Jane (Van Brunt	192?	J428
JOHNSON, Joan	193?	P321
JOHNSON, Jo Ellen	192?	E19102
JOHNSON, Joe	189?	J138
JOHNSON, John Nathaniel	1906	H175b
JOHNSON, Julia Edna	185?	B207
JOHNSON, Junior R.	192?	E19102
JOHNSON, Lawrence	178?	E112
JOHNSON, Leona (Lemker)	1913	P321
JOHNSON, Lloyd R.	191?	P321
JOHNSON, Maggie (Sylvest	188?	H175b
JOHNSON, Mamie Louise	188?	C589
JOHNSON, Martha (Yontlae	1821	B87
JOHNSON, Mary (B=)	1806	B55
JOHNSON, Mary	181?	B89
JOHNSON, Mary Ann	184?	B235a
JOHNSON, Mary Myrtle	1891	J167
JOHNSON, Merle Ervin	1916	J177
JOHNSON, Mr.	180?	B55
JOHNSON, Nancy	1813	B57
JOHNSON, Nancy (Mack)	182?	E525
JOHNSON, Nathaniel	188?	H175b
JOHNSON, Nathaniel Ross	1990	H1476
JOHNSON, Patsy	193?	P321
JOHNSON, Ransom	180?	F210
JOHNSON, Rebecca P. (B=)	1889	B1014
JOHNSON, Sarah (Pratt)	1789	E112
JOHNSON, Sarah	1814	E523
JOHNSON, Tillman A.	182?	B87
JOHNSON, Uda Ollivene	1908	J174
JOHNSON, Useba M. (B=)	1810	F210
JOHNSON, Viola (Gordon)	191?	C1910
JOHNSON, Wanda Lee	1931	H496
JOHNSON, William	180?	B58
JOHNSON, William P.	1823	E526
JOHNSON, Williamina (Rid	1827	C67
JOHNSTON, Florence Lewer	1895	C314
JOHNSTONE, Clifford	1909	Q86
JOHNSTONE, Donald Hugh	1938	Q86
JOHNSTONE, Henrietta (Mc	1908	Q86
JONES, Addie	184?	A239
JONES, Alice E. (B=)	1948	H498
JONES, Allen	1958	J498
JONES, Ben	195?	J498
JONES, Bessie R. (Ward)	192?	H498
JONES, Beth	196?	H498
JONES, Betsy	1789	F66
JONES, Cheryl {Sherry}	194?	B2577a
JONES, Claude	1903	J203a
JONES, Cora F.	1881	R128
JONES, Edward Floyd	191?	H498
JONES, Eliza E. (B=)	1857	R36
JONES, Ella	186?	C143
JONES, Fred	184?	A239
JONES, Gertrude	184?	A239
JONES, Goshen A.	182?	A239
JONES, Hannah	169?	A5d
JONES, James Marion	1888	R130

JONES, James Arthur	1943	H498
JONES, Jason Ward	1982	H1006
JONES, John R.	180?	F216
JONES, Lila E.	190?	E19049
JONES, Louler Virginia	1879	R127
JONES, Margaret	1932	J497
JONES, Maria	1831	F216
JONES, Mary	184?	A239
JONES, Mary Blanche	1884	R129
JONES, Mary Louise	1930	E19049
JONES, Patricia (Clayton	1947	C3332
JONES, Robert Paul	1934	J498
JONES, Ruby M. (B=)	1906	J203a
JONES, Sally May	1895	R131
JONES, Samuel	176?	F66
JONES, Sarah (Raymond)	1820	A239
JONES, Sarah	196?	J498
JONES, Sophronia (Bowen)	180?	F216
JONES, Thomas Lirty	185?	R36
JONES, William	166?	A5d
JONES, William Alton	190?	E19049
JORDAN, Mary	187?	D54
JUMP, Eliza Ellen (B=)	1857	R36
JUMP, Margaret	167?	A5a
JUMP, Robert H.	1821	R36
JURGENSON, Gladys	1930	C1883
JUSSEN, Louise	188?	E6322
KANDELHARDT, Henriette	180?	N226
KANDELHARDT, Sophia E.	180?	N266
KEENEY, Selinda C.	1834	E388
KEENY, Fanney	1800	E81
KEEVIN, Vivian Virginia	193?	E19121
KELLAIN, ???	164?	X2504
KELLER, Cynthia	195?	H781
KELLER, Marie	192?	H177e
KELLEY, Ruby	191?	H493
KELLY, John	179?	B22
KELLY, Margary (B=)	187?	G63
KELLY, Mr.	187?	G63
KELLY, Philadelphia (B=)	1794	B22
KELLY, Rose Ann	185?	H28
KEMP, Glynn	1955	Q97
KEMP, Grace (Ivall)	1930	Q97
KEMP, Morris	192?	Q97
KEMPER, Robin (B=)	1967	H1302
KEMPTON, Rosemary	1923	H1672
KENT, Nathan	177?	F59
KENT, Ruth (B=)	177?	F59
KEPNER, Amelia	1821	F215
KERBY, Julia	183?	A251
KERBY, Timothy	18??	A251
KERR, Eleanor (B=)	1950	Q151
KERR, Lynn Tracy	1972	Q247
KERR, Nelda (Crowder)	192?	Q151
KERR, Rhonda Eleanor	1974	Q248
KERR, Ronald	1948	Q151
KERR, Thomas	192?	Q151
KERRISK, Beryl Jean	191?	F2643
KESTER, Mina	187?	F1504
KEYS, Arminda	182?	G10
KEYS, Mary (B=)	1813	B36
KEYS, Morgan	181?	B36

KILLIAN, Robert Charles	1952	E39021		KNUTSON, Arlene Ann	1931	C1882
KILLIAN, Susan (Ridge)	1957	E39021		KNUTSON, Carl	191?	P321
KILLIAN, Victoria France	193?	E39021		KNUTSON, Laura A. (Walla	190?	C1882
KILLIAN, Walter Lawrence	193?	E39021		KNUTSON, Leona (Lemker)	1913	P321
KIMBALL, Richard	164?	X2506		KNUTSON, Melvin Benheart	190?	C1882
KIMBALL, Sarah (B=)	1646	X2506		KOGE, Alice Carol	193?	E19129
KINDLESIDE, Nettie	186?	F636		KORNANDOSKY, Hedwig E.	192?	E39010
KING, Bessie (Chollar)	1877	E9900		KOSTER, Estella	186?	B1194
KING, Charles Hamlin	1901	C1825		KRANTZ, Opal	192?	C1907c
KING, Charles Hubert	1935	C3331		KRAUSE, Elizabeth	195?	F6007
KING, David Charles	1961	C3331		KREIGE, Wilhelmeine	179?	N266
KING, Duane Eugene	1949	C3332		KROHMER, Helen M. (B=)	1940	E10825
KING, Ella Evelyn	1856	E1644		KROHMER, Lois M. (Hall)	191?	E10825
KING, Florence	191?	Q89		KROHMER, Marla Ann	1964	E19106
KING, Harvy L.	187?	E9900		KROHMER, Russell Eugene	1936	E10825
KING, John M.	187?	C1825		KROHMER, William F.	191?	E10825
KING, John Thomas	1959	C3331		KRUM, Jerusha (B=)	1839	F614
KING, Joseph Edward	1963	C3331		KRUM, Peter H.	183?	F614
KING, Lila Marie (B=)	1906	C1825		KRUMVIEDA, Inola Grace	1921	C1907c
KING, Margaret M. (Moore	1935	C3331		KRUMVIEDA, Rose Marie	1925	C1907b
KING, Mary (B=)	185?	E1634		KUHL, Mary Ann	1850	P142
KING, Mr.	184?	E1634		KURZROCK, Ernest August	185?	B614
KING, Patricia (Clayton)	1947	C3332		KURZROCK, Olga	188?	B614
KING, Sarah A. (Ferry)	183?	E1644		KURZROCK, Theresa Alvina	185?	B614
KING, Timothy	1968	C3331		LACY, H.L.	177?	L32
KING, William Andrus	182?	E1644		LACY, Helen	181?	L32
KINGSBURY, Hannah (B=)	1750	X2760		LAKE, Mary	183?	A250
KINGSBURY, Samuel	174?	X2760		LAMMERS, Martha M.	194?	P322
KINSEY, Anna Ellis	186?	B1030		LAMPSON, Clara May	1887	P322
KIRBY, Benjamin K.	186?	I367		LANDE, Mildred Maxine	192?	E19120
KIRBY, Burch	187?	B778		LANDREVILLE, mary	181?	Q2
KIRBY, Evlyn	187?	I372		LANE, Alice M.	188?	E1684
KIRBY, Harriet	187?	I369		LANE, Carrie M.	184?	E1475
KIRBY, Josephine (B=)	1844	I70		LANE, Florilla	187?	F208
KIRBY, Lizzie	187?	I370		LANE, Sarah	181?	F209
KIRBY, Martha (B=)	1874	B778		LANGON, Tom	185?	E4213
KIRBY, Maud	186?	I368		LANGSTON, Eunice	192?	H498
KIRBY, Myrtie	187?	I371		LARSON, Catherine M.M.	1941	C3336
KIRBY, O. T.	186?	I366		LARSON, Louie Jr.	191?	C1910
KIRK, Adeline	190?	C664		LARSON, Viola (Gordon)	191?	C1910
KIRKENDALL, Jenny	187?	E5618		LASTER, Dorris V.	1940	E19047
KISSELBERG, Bonnie L.(Mc	1943	E19103		LASTER, Erzula May	191?	E19047
KISSELBERG, Paul Ralph	1938	E19103		LASTER, Orie	191?	E19047
KISSELBERG, Rayma Lynn	1961	E19103		LASTER, Venetta	1940	E19047
KISSELBERG, Renetta Kaye	1962	E19103		LATIMER, Margaret	175?	A23
KISSINGER, Carolyn (Hamm	188?	H177a		LAUCKS, Aldema	186?	H58g
KISSINGER, George W.	188?	H177a		LAW, Charles Nathan	188?	E5807
KISSINGER, Kathy Regina	1959	H177a		LAW, Mary Ora (B=)	1885	E5807
KISSINGER, Maggie E.(B=)	1872	B518		LAWRENCE, Alan Andrew	1905	F2643
KISSINGER, Theodore	186?	B518		LAWRENCE, Alan	193?	F2642
KISSINGER, William F.	1913	H177a		LAWRENCE, Allison (???)	190?	F2641
KNEAS, Mary Emma	186?	H23		LAWRENCE, Amy (???)	190?	F2642
KNIGHT, Archibald	1896	Q54		LAWRENCE, Beryl (Kerrisk)	191?	F2643
KNIGHT, Charles Archibal	1922	Q54		LAWRENCE, Charles W.	1870	F1213
KNIGHT, Darlene M.	1938	Q150		LAWRENCE, Charles Banning	1902	F2642
KNIGHT, Donna	1942	Q142		LAWRENCE, Daisy Irene	1898	F2640
KNIGHT, Hazel (Workman)	191?	Q142, 150		LAWRENCE, Dawn	193?	F2641
KNIGHT, Hubert	191?	Q142,150		LAWRENCE, Denise	194?	F2643
KNIGHT, Ida E. (Moors)	1903	Q54		LAWRENCE, Glenda	192?	F2642
KNIGHT, Lydia Ann	1845	E408		LAWRENCE, Harriet (B=)	1873	F1213
KNIP, Christene Ann	189?	C1835		LAWRENCE, Kay	194?	F2643
KNOWLTON, Mary	164?	X2503		LAWRENCE, Laurie	194?	F2643

464

LAWRENCE, Marjorie	193?	F2642		LEMKER, Viola Jennie	1915	P322
LAWRENCE, Nancy Jean	1914	F2644		LEONARD, Charles S.	187?	F762
LAWRENCE, Nancy	192?	F2642		LEONARD, Clara J. (B=)	1873	F762
LAWRENCE, Rita	193?	F2641		LEONARD, Deforest	1897	F1795
LAWRENCE, Wilford Wallace	1904	F2641		LEONARD, Elizabeth (B=)	163?	X2011
LAWTON, George Augustas	1829	B144		LEONARD, Francis	162?	X2011
LAWTON, George Augustas	1862	B144		LEONARD, Lloyd Earl	1901	F1796
LAWTON, George Augustas	1893	B623		LEPLEY, Horace C.	188?	P135
LAWTON, Grace	1890	B620		LEPLEY, Susan D. (B=)	189?	P135
LAWTON, Helen Margaret	1889 *	B619		LEWIS, C. W.	1859	B940b
LAWTON, Martha (B=)	1860	B141		LEWIS, Clarissa (B=)	1845	E413
LAWTON, Ruth	1903 *	B626		LEWIS, Elmer	186?	E1716
LAWTON, Sophia Pauline	183?	B144		LEWIS, Homer Osmer	1893	B2503
LAWTON, Sophia Louise	1888	B618		LEWIS, Jane	185?	E1638
LAWTON, Twin boys	1891 *	B621		LEWIS, Lillian Omegia	1904 *	B2503c
LAWTON, Walter Banning	1899 *	B625		LEWIS, Lizzie	185?	E1009
LAWTON, William Ephraim	1896	B624		LEWIS, Lorin	184?	E413
LAY, Albert John	190?	Q71		LEWIS, Minnie Ola	1901	B2503b
LAY, Cindy P.	1978	Q153		LEWIS, Monnie E.	1900 *	B2503a
LAY, David	178?	E346		LEWIS, Rose Mary	192?	B9608
LAY, David	189?	Q69		LEWIS, Sinda Ann (B=)	1868	B940b
LAY, Donald W. J.	1929	Q71		LILLEY, Jeff	190?	B2707
LAY, Donald Roy	1951	Q153		LILLEY, Lucille (Doty)	1907	B2707
LAY, Donna K. (Williams	1942	Q142		LILLY, Anna W.	184?	F642
LAY, Dorothy (Huckstep)	190?	Q71		LINDSAY, Mary Ellen	1883	J33
LAY, Dorothy Lena Ann	1953	Q154		LINDER, Olive S.	1868	J9
LAY, Eilleen (Villeneuv	1954	Q153		LINDSLEY, Caroline L.P.	182?	B139
LAY, Erastus	178?	E82		LINDSLEY, Lucretia Thali	1853	B139
LAY, Erastus	182?	E393		LINDSLEY, Myron B.T.	1818	B139
LAY, George	182?	E396		LINDSLEY, Thales	1818	B139
LAY, Jean Lois (B=)	1930	Q71		LINDSTROM, Bernice (Warr	192?	H382
LAY, Julius A.	1827 *	E392		LINDSTROM, Elmer E.	192?	H382
LAY, Kevin Roy	1975	Q153		LINDSTROM, Nancy Ann	1945	H382
LAY, Kim Albert	1956	Q155		LINGO, Albert	185?	A642
LAY, Krista D.	1977	Q142		LINGO, Clara (Fisher)	1852	A642
LAY, Lemira	1819	E391		LINGO, Edna	188?	A642
LAY, Lucy (Ingraham)	178?	E346		LINGO, James	188?	A642
LAY, Lucy	1816	E346		LIPPIATT, Ernest E.	1914	Q69
LAY, Margaret (Moffatt)	1944	Q143		LIPPIATT, Gerald Edward	1939	Q143
LAY, Mary	182?	E394		LIPPIATT, Harvey Ernest	1938	Q142
LAY, Michelle A.	1975	Q142		LIPPIATT, June Shirley	1942	Q144
LAY, Nancy (B=)	1790	E82		LIPPIATT. Seth M.	1969	Q143
LAY, Nancy	182?	E395		LIPPIATT, Stefanie M.	1967	Q143
LE DUC, James	182?	A255		LIPPIATT, Verna E. (B=)	1919	Q69
LE DUC, Mary (Bronson)	1829	A255		LITTLETON, Deborah A.(Ti	1962	E19109
LEE, Edwin	188?	A701		LIVERSON, Jane A.	1807	B69
LEE, Ellen (O'Keefe)	181?	F498		LOBDELL, Betty Lou	1929	C1918
LEE, Fitz Hugh	18??	B591		LOCKETT, Ruth	190?	C316
LEE, Jane (Errett)	1885	A701		LOCKWOOD, Jessie T.	1860	F589
LEE, Lori (Stephenson)	1965	E39039		LOGSDON, Nancy A. (B=)	1859	C235
LEE, Margaret	1840	F498		LOGSDON, Thomas Perry	185?	C235
LEE, Patrick	181?	F498		LONGON, Minnie (Merry)	186?	E4213
LEE, Rickey Joe	1965	E39039		LONGON, Tom	186?	E4213
LEFLER, David Donald	1946	E39010		LONGSHAW, Gary	194?	H776
LEFLER, Hedwig Elizabeth	192?	E39010		LONGSHAW, Linda M. (B=)	1949	H776
LEFLER, Lenard Doak	192?	E39010		LORD, Bessie	1883	H25
LEFLER, Sherry (Ridge)	1949	E39010		LORD, Mary	175?	E63
LEMKER, John B.	1844	P142		LORING, Mary	162?	X2501
LEMKER, Joseph A.	1891	P142		LOUD, Viola May (Smith)	185?	B600
LEMKER, Leona Mary	1913	P321		LOUDERBACK, Anna G.(B=)	1931	E10824
LEMKER, Margaret (Determ	1894	P142		LOUDERBACK, George W.	190?	E10824
LEMKER, Mary Ann (Kuhl)	1850	P142		LOUDERBACK, Leslie Earl	1925	E10824

LOUDERBACK, Reba Ann	1953	E19105
LOUDERBACK, Virgina (Whi	190?	E10824
LOW, Mary S.	1844	E1493
LOWBER, Alice (Ponder)	176?	C12
LOWBER, Daniel	17??	C14
LOWBER, Elizabeth (B=)	17??	C14
LOWBER, Elizabeth	1794	C12
LOWBER, Peter	1???	C12
LOWBER, William	176?	C12
LOWE, Mary Josephine	1869	Q9
LOWER, Amanda	183?	J7
LOWRY, Annie	189?	D168
LOWRY, Clair (B=)	1864	D50
LOWRY, Joseph	186?	D50
LOWRY, Joseph	188?	D167
LOWSING, Bertha Mae (B=)	1872	C561
LOWSING, William	186?	C561
LUMMIS, Betty Esther	1921	Q40
LUMMIS, Effie (McDermid)	1887	Q40
LUMMIS, William H.	1889	Q40
LUMMIS, William W.	1921	Q40
LUTHER, Albert	184?	E1406
LUTHER, Catherine (B=)	1820	E314
LUTHER, Dell	184?	E1408
LUTHER, Ellen	185?	E1410
LUTHER, Leora	184?	E1407
LUTHER, Mittie	185?	E1409
LUTHER, Monroe (Orin?)	181?	E314
LUTHER, Orin	181?	E314
LWERSON, Jane A.	1807	B69
LYMAN, Elizabeth (Peters	1886	N3687
LYMAN, Oscar	188?	N3687
LYNCH, Frances A.	183?	G10
LYNCH, Josephine	190?	P143
LYONS, Alanson P.	184?	E1394
MABRY, Joann Marilyn	1940	C3333
MacDONALD, Addie	1879	Q22
MacGREGOR, Harold H.	1914	Q69
MacGREGOR, Marjorie Lois	1949	Q147
MacGREGOR, Robert Alan	1957	Q148
MacGREGOR, Ronald Leslie	1947	Q146
MacGREGOR, Verna E.	1919	Q69
MacGREGOR, William James	1946	Q145
MACK, Hannah	177?	F95
MACK, Jonathan	170?	F17
MACK, Jonathan	1731	F17
MACK, Mary	185?	B131
MACK, Nancy	178?	E110
MACK, Nancy M.	182?	E525
MACK, Sarah (Bennet)	171?	F17
MACK, Sarah (B=)	1745	F17
MACK, Sarah	177?	F96
MACKY, Mary	177?	A22
MAHONEY, Jennifer P.	1970	H1305
MAHONEY, Sean M.	1973	H1306
MALLOY, Peggy L. (Carter	1946	J2117
MALLOY, Vernon	194?	J2117
MALONEY, Jack	189?	P144
MALONEY, Sarah (Determan	1900	P144
MANHART, Miss.	185?	F646
MANN, Emily L. (B=)	1842	F584
MANN, Tompkins	184?	F584

MANNING, Mable E.	1877	J210
MANSON, Alpha (B=)	191?	B2120
MANSON, Mr.	190?	B2120
MANWARRING, Hepsy Estell	187?	E1681
MAPLE, Charlotte (B=)	1871	B572
MAPLE, Clair	189?	B1756
MAPLE, Howard	189?	B1757
MAPLE, Jessie	189?	B1753
MAPLE, Lulu	189?	B1755
MAPLE, Mark	189?	B1754
MAPLE, Stephen	186?	B572
MARA, Alice	1909	H136
MARCHANT, Abigail	177?	B16
MARCHANT, Abigail	1804	B16
MARCHANT, George	177?	B16
MARKHAM, Alice	186?	E1710
MARKHAM, Almira (B=)	1842	E412
MARKHAM, Flora	186?	E1711
MARKHAM, John	186?	E1712
MARKHAM, Martha E.	1857	F603
MARKHAM, Theron	183?	E412
MARKS, Bryant	181?	F267
MARKS, Bryant	184?	F672
MARKS, Cornelius	184?	F670
MARKS, Maria	184?	F671
MARKS, Ruth (B=)	1813	F267
MARLOW, Carolyn (Holst	1963	F11999
MARLOW, Kelly Kay	1993	F11999
MARLOW, Richard Roy	196?	F11999
MARLOW, Taylor Ray	1993	F11999
MARSDEN, Edward	186?	X14
MARSDEN, Emma F. (B=)	1867	X14
MARSH, Eunice (B=)	181?	F204
MARSH, Wyllys Goodwin	1814	F204
MARSHALL, Sarah	195?	F6038
MARSHELL, Sara Jane	170?	A12e
MARTIN, Charles	184?	A118
MARTIN, Elizabeth	181?	B69
MARTIN, Elizabeth A.(B=)	1837	B224
MARTIN, Emma (Doud)	185?	E1641
MARTIN, George	185?	E1642
MARTIN, James	188?	D171
MARTIN, Joseph	186?	D52
MARTIN, Josiah	183?	B224
MARTIN, Lizzie	189?	D173
MARTIN, Mamie	188?	D172
MARTIN, Mary (B=)	1869	D52
MARTIN, Mr.	18??	A147
MARTIN, Susan (Harper)	18??	A147
MARTIN, Susan (B=)	1846	A118
MARTINDALE, Amanda Nic	1985	E19121
MARTINDALE, Bill Eugene	193?	E19121
MARTINDALE, Diana Lynn	1960	E19121
MARTINDALE, Vivian (Keei	193?	E19121
MARVEL, Anita	193?	H300
MARVEL, Edna (B=)	19??	H114
MARVEL, Florence (B=)	1870	D63
MARVEL, L. Baynard	19??	H114
MARVEL, Watson	187?	D63
MARVIN, Jemima	1711	E5
MARVIN, John	1665	E5
MARVIN, Sarah (Graham)	1670	E5

MASON, Elizabeth	174?	A29
MASON, Eliza (Chew)	1798	A80
MASON, James M.	179?	A80
MASON, Orrill (B=)	1803	F207
MASON, Orris	179?	F207
MATHEWS, Ethel	189?	E10808
MATHEWS, Florence	189?	E10806
MATHEWS, Florence (Sossa	189?	E10806
MATHEWS, James Earl	1954	E19057
MATHEWS, James Buckley	1977	E39035
MATHEWS, Jason James	1973	E39030
MATHEWS, Jerry Lee	1948	E19055
MATHEWS, Joe Marvin	1944	E19054
MATHEWS, Joey	1980	E39032
MATHEWS, Joseph	189?	E10806
MATHEWS, Justin Rutherfo	1975	E39031
MATHEWS, Linda Joy	1951	E19056
MATHEWS, Mamie Alice	1980	E39037
MATHEWS, Marvin Lonnie	1920	E10806
MATHEWS, Melanie Jane	1979	E39036
MATHEWS, Patricia Ann	1940	E19053
MATHEWS, Patsy (Roberson	1945	E19054
MATHEWS, Ruby (B=)	1920	E10806
MATHEWS, Sharla (Crowell	195?	E19055
MATHEWS, Sheryl Nadine	1964	E39028
MATHEWS, Todd Marvin	1967	E39029
MATHEWS, Virginia (Carte	1958	E19057
MAYO, D. F.	187?	Q30
MAYO, Elsie	1895	Q79
MAYO, Stella (B=)	187?	Q30
MAYOR, Kathryn Alice (B=	1962	H841
MAYOR, Steve	196?	H941
McCARTNEY, Irene	190?	Q58
McCAULEY, Charles H.	185?	H58a
McCAULEY, Emma	186?	X1511
McCAULEY, Lizzie	1883	H58a
McCAULEY, Mary Ann (Issa	185?	H58a
McCLAIN, Beth (McGraw)	191?	E10828
McCLAIN, Jessie	191?	E10828
McCLAIN, John	194?	J496
McCLAIN, John M.	196?	J496
McCLAIN, Louise Anna	1932	E10828
McCLAIN, Nancy (Hill)	1945	J496
McCLAIN, Scott	196?	J496
McCLAIN, Shelley	197?	J496
McCLAIN, Sherri	196?	J496
McCLAIN, Travis	197?	J496
McCLUEN, Carl	189?	J162
McCLUEN, Margaret (Hopki	1895	J162
McCUNE, Karen	194?	J2118
McCLURE, Hannah Amelia	183?	B139
McCORMICK, Elizabeth C.	187?	H134
McCOY, Bridget Agnes	1842	Q3
McCRAKEN, Martha A.(B=)	1858	J22
McCRAKEN, Mr.	185?	J19,22
McCRAKEN, Sarah Jane	1855	J19
McCREARY, Emma	185?	A647
McCREARY, Ida Augusta	1855	A259
McCREARY, Jacob	182?	A259
McCREARY, Mary M. (Skeen	1825	A259
McCUAIG, Leslie J.	189?	Q70
McCUAIG, Mary (Wigney)	189?	Q70

McCUAIG, Muriel Emma	1924	Q70
McCULLOUGH, Lena	1886	Q25
McDERMID, Arthur	192?	Q41
McDERMID, Beryle	1918	Q41
McDERMID, Birdie (Bidgoo	190?	Q44
McDERMID, Cletta Esther	1904	Q45
McDERMID, Colin	193?	Q44
McDERMID, David	192?	Q41
McDERMID, Doris	191?	Q41
McDERMID, Douglas	1917	Q41
McDERMID, Effie Genevive	1887	Q40
McDERMID, Esther A. (B=)	1859	Q7
McDERMID, Esther	190?	Q38
McDERMID, Esther	192?	Q41
McDERMID, Florence	1905	Q38
McDERMID, Ida Grace	1878	Q37
McDERMID, J. Sturart	191?	Q38
McDERMID, James Earl	1892	Q41
McDERMID, James	192?	Q41
McDERMID, Jean (Campbell	188?	Q38
McDERMID, Lillah Claire	1897	Q43
McDERMID, Mamie (Stewart	189?	Q41
McDERMID, Murray	191?	Q38
McDERMID, Myrtle Dean	1895	Q42
McDERMID, Pauline	192?	Q41
McDERMID, Peter Albinas	1883	Q38
McDERMID, Violet May	1885	Q39
McDERMID, William	1852	Q7
McDERMID, William Jr.	1899	Q44
McFARLAND, Eleanor A.(B=	1893	C315
McFARLAND, John	188?	C315
McFARLAND, Selma A.	1859	F552
McGAHEY, Bonnie	1943	E19103
McGAHEY, Henry	189?	E10823
McGAHEY, Lester Charles	1917	E10823
McGAHEY, Lorene J. (B=)	1924	E10823
McGAHEY, Marieta	1946	E19104
McGAHEY, Viola (Orsborn)	189?	E10823
McGRAW, Beth	191?	E10828
McGREGOR, Harold H.	1914	Q69
McGREGOR, Judy (Horrick	1947	Q145
McGREGOR, Kelly Dean	1969	Q146
McGREGOR, Marjorie Lois	1949	Q147
McGREGOR, Michael James	1973	Q145
McGREGOR, Patricia (Vil	1948	Q146
McGREGOR, Rebecca (Thom	188?	Q69
McGREGOR, Robert Alan	1957	Q148
McGREGOR, Robert James	1979	Q148
McGREGOR, Ronald Leslie	1947	Q146
McGREGOR, Scott Alan	1971	Q145
McGREGOR, Shelley Ann	1972	Q146
McGREGOR, Valerie (Ferg	1957	Q148
McGREGOR, Verna E.	1919	Q69
McGREGOR, William A.	188?	Q69
McGREGOR, William James	1946	Q145
McGUIRE, Gary Wayne	1952	E19116
McGUIRE, Merrick K.T.	1987	E19116
McGUIRE, Tamara Kay (Tac	1954	E19116
McGWIN, Mary E. (Sams)	1893	C1862
McGWIN, Rolland	189?	C1862
McHANON, Sadie M. (B=)	1886	C566
McHANON, Walter	188?	C566

Name	Year	Code
McKEAN, Elizabeth	184?	E1393
McKEE, Dr. William	174?	C5
McKEE, Elizabeth (Alford	174?	C5
McKEE, Hester	191?	Q147
McKENZIE, Eldon	1888	Q55
McKENZIE, Gray	191?	F2644
McKENZIE, Henrietta	1908	Q86
McKENZIE, Holland	1892	Q55
McKENZIE, Jennifer Rae	194?	F2644
McKENZIE, Nancy (Lawren	1914	F2644
McKENZIE, Stella M. (B=)	1892	Q55
McKERROW, Margaret (B=)	1904	F2623b
McKERROW, Mr.	190?	F2623b
McKILLAP, Maxine	191?	C1902
McKINNIE, Ella C. (B=)	1852	F629
McKINNIE, Thomas	185?	F629
McKINNIE, Willow	189?	F1481
McLOUD, May	187?	C559
McMAHON, Anna (Hostos)	190?	H374
McMAHON, Dorothy Ann	1928	H374
McMAHON, William E.	190?	H374
McNEAL, George M.	191?	H124
McNEAL, Myrtle (B=)	1916	H124
McNEAL, Niki C.	1950	H338
McNEELEY, Marion	185?	B1026
McNEIL, George A.	187?	Q37
McNEIL, Ida G. (McDermid	1878	Q37
McNEIL, Ralph	1910	Q37
McVAIN, Isabel	1836	E1382
McVEY, Rosa	1877	B941
McWATTERS, Donald C.	1905	Q67
McWATTERS, Mildred (B=)	1910	Q67
MEIER, Gerilyn	196?	B14001
MELCALF, Clara	189?	E10827
MELLEN, Abner	182?	E1480
MELLEN, Helen Louise	182?	E1480
MELLEN, Helen Josephine	1850	E1480
MELOTT, Letha	190?	E10829
MELRIEN, Floyd Bryan	196?	E19103
MELRIEN, Renetta K.(Kiss	1962	E19103
MELVIN, Amanda Doris	193?	H503
MELVIN, Arthur	184?	A641
MELVIN, Arthur	188?	A641
MELVIN, Minerva	183?	A243
MELVIN, Sallie (Fisher)	1850	A641
MENDOZA, Nancy U.	196?	E39024
MENDOZA, Pauline	193?	E39024
MERCHANT, Abigail	178?	B28
MERCHANT, Abigail	1804	B28
MERCHANT, George	178?	B28
MEREDITH, Nancy Jane	181?	X1500
MEREDITH, Shirley	195?	H770
MERRICK, Elizabeth Rayn	1828	A224
MERRICK, William H.	182?	A224
MERRY, Albert	185?	E4212
MERRY, Bertha	186?	E4214
MERRY, Clara	185?	E4209
MERRY, Florence	186?	E4215
MERRY, George	183?	E1005
MERRY, George	186?	E4216
MERRY, Ida	185? *	E4211
MERRY, Jennie	186?	E4217
MERRY, Jessie	185?	E4210
MERRY, Mattie (B=)	1841	E1005
MERRY, Minnie	185?	E4213
MESSENGER, Cynthia	178?	F81
MIAMAN, Leona	1911	E19052
MICHAUD, Lee Ann	196?	H837
MICHAUD, Lillian (Ruszcz	193?	H837
MICHAUD, Louis	193?	H837
MICHELSON, Grace	191?	H134
MICKELSON, Doris Lenora	1912	C1838
MIFFLIN, Mary	182?	C65
MILES, Daniel L.	185?	H28
MILES, Lydia Elizabeth	1877	H28
MILES, Rose Ann (Kelly)	185?	H28
MILLAR, Alice	1878	Q17
MILLARD, Mary	178?	E78
MILLER, Agusta (B=)	1908	A1654
MILLER, Almira (Patterso	183?	B141
MILLER, Arra	1908 *	B793
MILLER, Aurilla	1806	F69
MILLER, Barbara T.	193?	F7004
MILLER, Bascomb	1889 *	B793
MILLER, Charles Raymond	192?	B2575a
MILLER, Clara (Holley)	1927	B2575a
MILLER, Cora (B=)	183?	E1398
MILLER, Diana	1935	A3658
MILLER, Edward	180?	F73
MILLER, Edwin Sheppard	1904	A1654
MILLER, Elizabeth J.	1859	B792a
MILLER, Elmina (B=)	1807	F73
MILLER, Emily	1806	F69
MILLER, George	179?	F71
MILLER, George	183?	F274
MILLER, Jamea R.	1867	B793
MILLER, Joseph	1816	B193
MILLER, Letitia Ann	1850	B136
MILLER, Margaret	187?	B136
MILLER, Mary (B=)	1839	F274
MILLER, Mary E.	1850	B792
MILLER, Maxine	191?	C1842
MILLER, Mr.	183?	E1398
MILLER, Nancy Ellen	1861	B141
MILLER, Polly (B=)	1798	F71
MILLER, Roda	1801	F68
MILLER, Thomas	187?	B136
MILLER, Thomas J.	183?	B141
MILLER, Vianah	1830	B193
MILLER, Victoria (???)	186?	B793
MILLIE, Harriet (Kirby)	187?	I369
MILLIE, Mr.	187?	I369
MINER, Annah L.	1856	E1535
MINER, Caroline (Brockwa	178?	E416
MINER, Caroline	181?	E416
MINER, Caroline	1836	E1528
MINER, Charles	181?	E416
MINER, Charles Carol	1844	E1530
MINER, Daniel S.	181?	E366
MINER, Emerette (Brockwa	184?	E1530
MINER, Harriet	181?	E416
MINER, Harriet P.	1851	E1534
MINER, Janette (Brockway)	183?	E1529
MINER, Janette	1846	E1531

468

MINER, Jared S.	178?	E416	MOORS, Sarah Jane (Sadie	1900	Q53
MINER, Laura F.	1846	E1531	MOORS, Thomas H.	1857	Q8
MINER, Mae	187?	H176	MOORS, Thomas William	1885	Q47
MINER, Orrin Southmayd	1837	E1529	MOORS, William Herbert	1922	Q47
MINER, Sarah (B=)	181?	E366	MORAN, Frank J.	1881	F1200
MINER, Sarah E.	1848	E1533	MORAN, Grace D. (Allen)	1883	F1200
MINER, Southmayd	181?	E366	MOREY, Ada Elizabeth (B=	1867	J25
MINNER, Annie (B=)	1875	D64	MOREY, Clara	1890	J154
MINNER, Helen	190?	D224	MOREY, Edith	1888	J153
MINNER, Joseph	187?	D64	MOREY, Ellis	1893	J155
MINNER, Laura	189?	D223	MOREY, George Henry	1856	J25
MINNER, Lawrence	190?	D225	MOREY, Georgie	1898 *	J156
MINNER, William	190?	D226	MOREY, Mildred	1900	J157
MINTZ, Mary	183?	B279	MOREY, Theo Pearl	1884	J152
MITCHELL, Mr.	194?	H404	MOREY, Vernon E.	1902	J158
MITCHELL, Sophia Pauline	183?	B144	MOREY, William Arthur	1882	J151
MITCHELL, Virginia A.	194?	H404	MORGAN, Edward	184?	C257
MITCHNER, Virginia	1937	J510	MORGAN, Elizabeth (B=)	1843	C257
MOFFATT, Dorothy (Patter	191?	Q143	MORGAN, George Elmer	189?	H175c
MOFFATT, George	191?	Q143	MORGAN, June E. (Caldwel	189?	H175c
MOFFATT, Margaret M.	1944	Q143	MORGAN, Leatha Elizabeth	1919	H175c
MOFFITT, Estelle	191?	B997c	MORGAN, Lee	1931	J508
MOHS, Donna	1951	C1841	MORGAN, Shirley (Vandev	1931	J508
MOHS, Harry J.	1908	C1841	MORIARTY, Isabel M.	1862	K2931
MOHS, Karen Kay	1939	C1841	MORRELL, Florida	184?	F585
MOHS, Kathleen (Dewey)	1916	C1841	MORRIS, Amanda D. (Melvi	193?	H503
MOLYNEAU, Ann	181?	L182	MORRIS, Anna	1885	B747
MONICK, Mary C.	1836	J2	MORRIS, Charles L.	1863	J12
MONTGOMERY, Donna Gayl	195?	E19066	MORRIS, Edith Lucille	195?	H503
MOON, Donavan	1987	E39069	MORRIS, John Henry	185?	B747
MOON, John Henry	195?	E19068	MORRIS, Lydia E. (B=)	1865	J12
MOON, John 3rd	1983	E39068	MORRIS, Lynnette (Herth)	1947	C3340
MOON, Lori Lee (B=)	1961	E19068	MORRIS, Melissa Dawn	1977	B26009
MOOR, Rachel (B=)	1723	A34	MORRIS, Michael Terry	194?	C3340
MOOR, William	171?	A34	MORRIS, Nora Casandra	189?	H58d
MOORE, Ann	175?	C13	MORRIS, Rachel Ann	1978	B26009
MOORE, Charles Alfred	184?	E1358	MORRIS, Randy K.	195?	B26009
MOORE, Ethel Kate	1909	H121	MORRIS, Raymond	192?	H503
MOORE, Eva Nita	1943	E19051	MORRIS, Sarah (McCollum)	185?	B747
MOORE, Hannah	1817	E387	MORRIS, Theresa (Swope)	1957	B26009
MOORE, Huldah Ann	1906	H119	MORRIS, Walter	187?	H58d
MOORE, Laura (B=)	1856	E1358	MORRIS, William	17??	A10
MOORE, Levi	183?	E1564	MORROW, Effie	187?	J150
MOORE, Lillian J.	192?	E19051	MORSE, Alice M.	189?	C297
MOORE, Lillian	193?	H502	MORSE, Louise	186?	B1028
MOORE, Malora (B=)	1849	E1356	MORTON, Helen	1898	B932a
MOORE, Margaret Mary	1935	C3331	MOZAN, May (B=)	189?	J150
MOORE, Marie	191?	H380	MOZAN, Mr.	189?	J150
MOORE, Mary Ann (B=)	1838	F1564	MUNGER, Gordon L.	184?	E1391
MOORE, Millord	192?	E19051	MUNGER, Mary	1791	F62
MOORE, Mr.	184?	E1356	MUNGER, Victoria (Chapel	1846	E1391
MOORE, W. E. {Mr.}	187?	X518	MURPHY, Alice	1906	H134
MOORS, Arthur	1883 *	Q46	MURPHY, Anna	172?	A12
MOORS, Bessie M. Elizabe	1892	Q50	MURPHY, Anne (???)	174?	A29
MOORS, Charles Henry	1895	Q51	MURPHY, Elizabeth (Mason	174?	A29
MOORS, Della	1887	Q48	MURPHY, Elizabeth C.	187?	H134
MOORS, Hubert	1896	Q52	MURPHY, Jacob	174?	A29
MOORS, Ida Ethel	1903	Q54	MURPHY, Jessie D.	188?	H174
MOORS, Jane M. (Hall)	1891	Q47	MURPHY, Mercy (Doty)	1785	E302
MOORS, Luch {Dollie}	1889	Q49	MURPHY, Michael	187?	H134
MOORS, Lucy M. (B=)	1863	Q8	MURPHY, Noah	178?	E302
MOORS, Marguerite Della	1926	Q47	MURPHY, Sarah	1766	A29

MURPHY, Susan Malora	1820	E302	NORDEN, Susan	15??	X2003
MURRAY, Ann (B=)	162?	X2008	NORDI, Janet Marie	194?	C3339
MURRAY, Elizabeth	165?	X2016	NORIS, Jane	182?	F262
MURRAY, Henry	161?	X2008	NORRIS, Mary H. (B=)	1871	C131
MURRAY, Mary Jane	183?	B88	NORRIS, Velma	193?	E19126
MURPHY, William	174?	A29	NORRIS, Wilt Watseman	186?	C131
MURRISH, Bertha M. (B=)	1881	R122	NORTHCUST, Elizabeth M.	178?	K610
MURRISH, George Martin	187?	R122	NORTHWAY, Lavinia A.	1808	F288
MYERS, Evelyn (Nichols)	189?	B1137	NORTON, Abram Baldwin	1819	A221
MYERS, Joseph	193?	B1137	NORTON, Ann (Baldwin)	1762	A67
MYERS, Steven	193?	B1137	NORTON, Anthony Banning	1820	A222
NAOTA, Diana Rae (B=)	1960	C5669	NORTON, Daniel Sheldon	1788	A67
NASH, Emily P.	1847	C25	NORTON, Daniel Sheldon	1829	A225
NAUNTON, Penelope	161?	X2006	NORTON, Dorothy	191?	E19051
NAUNTON, Robert	15??	X2006	NORTON, Elizabeth (Merri	182?	A224
NEAL, Frances	1752	K351	NORTON, Elizabeth (Sherm	183?	A225
NEEDHAM, Sarah	165?	X2508	NORTON, Ellen (Burr)	182?	A222
NEEL, Timpie	186?	B237a	NORTON, George	182?	A242
NEELY, Jason	185?	X501	NORTON, George Kenyon	1827	A224
NEELY, Laura J. (B=)	185?	X501	NORTON, Maria Banning	182? *	A223
NEILSON, Eliza (B=)	181?	L116	NORTON, Mary Banning	1817	A220
NEILSON, Mr.	181?	L116	NORTON, Philo	1760	A67
NELSON, Doyle	192?	C1943	NORTON, Sarah (B=)	1792	A67
NELSON, Louise	191?	C1826	NORTON, Sarah (Davidson)	182?	A221
NELSON, Mavis L. (B=)	1926	C1943	NORTON, Sarah Banning	1831	A226
NELTE, Carolyn J.	193?	H334	NOTA, Kirby	195?	C5669
NESTER, Mildred	191?	B2037	NOYES, Charles Reginald	1883	E6317
NEWARK, Ann	165?	X2014	NOYES, Clarissa Dutton	1866	E6311
NEWARK, Cecilia (B=)	161?	X2007	NOYES, Elizabeth	167?	K126
NEWARK, Grace	165?	X2015	NOYES, Enoch	183?	E1477
NEWARK, Henry	161?	X2007	NOYES, Enoch	1864	E6310
NEWHOUSE, Edna A. (Chand	1942	H336	NOYES, Francis B.{Frank}	1874	E6315
NEWHOUSE, Scott C.	1964	H336	NOYES, Harry Dutton	1871	E6313
NEWHOUSE, Theodore M.	194?	H336	NOYES, Jonnie Banning	1867 *	E6312
NEWHOUSE, Theodore M.	1962	H336	NOYES, Josephine (Sylves	186?	E6309
NEWMAN, Ruby Lorena	193?	E39015	NOYES, Laura (B=)	1841	E1477
NEWSOM, Hannah T.	181?	E254	NOYES, Laura Banning	1875	E6316
NICHOLS, Clara	188?	B1136	NOYES, Lucy (Bancroft)	1884	E6317
NICHOLS, Eliza	182?	J1	NOYES, Martha	187?	E6314
NICHOLS, Ella (B=)	1858	B310	NOYES, William Curtis	1862	E6309
NICHOLS, Elma (Parmeter	1891	B1135	NUGENT, {Monseingor}	182?	L190
NICHOLS, Esther (???)	189?	B1138	NUGENT, Miss.	182?	L190
NICHOLS, Eunice	1779	F56	O'BRIEN, Luch{Dollie}(Mo	1889	Q49
NICHOLS, Evelyn	1900	B1137	O'BRIEN, Thomas Herbert	1879	Q49
NICHOLS, Greenville F.	1854	B310	O'CONNELL, John D.	193?	E19119
NICHOLS, Herman E.	1882	B1135	O'CONNELL, Larae A. (Geb	193?	E19119
NICHOLS, Lena Ann (Waggo	183?	B310	O'CONNELL, Mary Ann	1957	E19119
NICHOLS, Levi D.	1827	B310	O'DAY, Clattie	187?	H175a
NICHOLS, Lewis	1890	B1138	O'DOWELL, Cecily (Arnold)	1934	F5291
NICHOLS, Maria E. (B=)	1858	B310	O'DOWELL, Ken	193?	F5291
NICHOLS, N.A.	185?	B198	O'KEEFE, Margaret	181?	F498
NICHOLS, Norman Eugene	1916	B1135	O'NEIL, Virginia	1922	F3090
NICHOLS, Paul L.	1911	B1135	OAKLAND, Donald Bayard	192?	E19118
NICHOLS, Robert	188?	B1139	OAKLAND, Donald Bayard	1950	E19118
NICHOLS, Stephen D.	185?	B310	OAKLAND, Helen (Hermann)	192?	E19118
NICHOLSON, Maria	1782	A25	OAKLAND, Katherine (Schl	1953	E19118
NILES, Abigail	166?	E1	OAKLAND, Melissa Maxine	1985	E19118
NOBLES, Martha Elizabeth	1949	E19050	OAKLAND, Sarah Katherine	192?	E19118
NOBLES, Pauline F.	192?	E19050	OFFNER, Arthur Andrew	189?	H177a
NOBLES, Woodie Parr	192?	E19050	OFFNER, Grace Christine	1919	H177a
NONAST, Floyd E.	193?	E39023	OFFNER, Katie J. (Haring	189?	H177a
NONAST, Rhonda Sue	196?	E39023	OGDEN, Mahala	181?	X3500

OGLE, Marguerite (B=)	191?	B2052		OWENS, Mary	185?	E5614
OGLE, Roy	191?	B2052		OWENS, Mary E. (Brand)	193?	B26007
OHLSEN, Carrie Beth	197?	J505		OWENSBY, Blanche I. (B=)	1888	C660
OHLSEN, David Lee	1949	J506		OWENSBY, James L.	187?	C660
OHLSEN, Diane (Ace)	194?	J504		OXFORD, A. V.	1891	B796a
OHLSEN, Edna B. (B=)	1919	J205		OXFORD, Albert S.	190?	B796a
OHLSEN, Gerald Wayne	1947	J505		OXFORD, Alonzo	1890	B795
OHLSEN, Kimberly	196?	J504		OXFORD, Amanda	1902	B796a
OHLSEN, Kyle Thomas	197?	J506		OXFORD, Carl B.	1905 *	B796a
OHLSEN, Lawrence	191?	J205		OXFORD, Carrie	1905	B796a
OHLSEN, Marian (Stovall)	195?	J506		OXFORD, Catherine (B=)	1832	B194
OHLSEN, Michael	196?	J504		OXFORD, Charles	1891	B795
OHLSEN, Robin	196?	J504		OXFORD, Elgins	1894	B795
OHLSEN, Ronald Lee	1944	J504		OXFORD, Emily Jane	1859	B794a
OHLSEN, Sarah Nichell	197?	J506		OXFORD, Emma A.	1903	B796a
OHLSEN, Shawn	197?	J505		OXFORD, Frank G.	1916	B796a
OHLSEN, Shelli (Douglas)	195?	J505		OXFORD, George T.	1900	B796a
OHLSEN, Vicki Jean	1957	J507		OXFORD, Ida (Orsteen)	1855	B795
OITMAN, Harriet Elizabet	182?	E376		OXFORD, Iley Erwin	1907	B796a
OLIVER, Albert	1896	C328		OXFORD, James Richard	1868	B796a
OLIVER, Charles	1894	C327		OXFORD, James G.	1880	B795
OLIVER, Daniel Lawrence	1965	E19128		OXFORD, James R.	1889	B796a
OLIVER, Dean Edward	1957	E19125		OXFORD, Jessie C.	1865	B796
OLIVER, Delilah Ann (Por	1958	E19125		OXFORD, Jessie J.	1895	B796a
OLIVER, Elizabeth Ann	1976	E19125		OXFORD, John C.	1833	B194
OLIVER, Esther L. (Hill)	193?	E19125		OXFORD, John W.	1870	B797
OLIVER, Hellen	183?	C29		OXFORD, John Wesley	1885	B795
OLIVER, Joshua Lawrence	1986	E19128		OXFORD, John Henry	1888	B796a
OLIVER, Justin Edward	1989	E19128		OXFORD, Joney	1898 *	B796a
OLIVER, Mammie (B=)	186?	C145		OXFORD, Joseph H.	1871	B797a
OLIVER, Mr.	186?	C145		OXFORD, Laura G.	1882	B795
OLIVER, Ollie	1898	C329		OXFORD, Lora A.	1893 *	B796a
OLIVER, Otis Oren	193?	E19125		OXFORD, M. L.	1862	B795a
OLIVER, Wallace	1902	C331		OXFORD, Margaretta E.	1874	B798
OLIVER, Walter	1901	C330		OXFORD, Martha	1886	B795
OLLER, Arwilda	187?	B308		OXFORD, Mary Will	1856	B794
OLLER, Clara Mae	1866	B243		OXFORD, Mary (McCan)	1869	B796a
OLLER, Henry	183?	B243		OXFORD, Mary Elizabeth	1881	B795
OLLER, Martha (Himes)	183?	B243		OXFORD, Mollie (Cates)	186?	B796
OLSZOWY, Catherine Ann	1953	F6012		OXFORD, Oscar Lee	1895	B795
ONDROZECK, Anna (???)	185?	C569		OXFORD, Robert W.	1887	B795
ONDROZECK, Florence (B=)	1886	C569		OXFORD, Sallie (Todd)	186?	B796
ONDROZECK, Fredrick Char	1873	C569		OXFORD, William Jerry	1860	B795
ONDROZECK, Jerry Nathani	1911	C1902		OXLEY, Catherine Mahala	1849	C227
ONDROZECK, Joy Julia	1914	C1903		OXLEY, Eliza Jane (Blue)	182?	C227
ONDROZECK, Karl	185?	C569		OXLEY, George Washington	182?	C227
ONDROZECK, Waldo Russell	1919	C1904		PACE, Annie Lydia (Downi	1870	F3376
ORDWAY, Mary E.	184?	F585		PACE, Annie L. (B=)	1924	B998c
ORENDORF, Catherine	196?	H764		PACE, Howard	192?	B998c
ORR, May Belle	191?	B997b		PACE, Loretta Lucile	1906	F3376
ORTMAN, Irene Bernice	1925	C1907d		PACE, William Hayden	1867	F3376
OSBORN, Viola	189?	E10823		PACK, Brownlow Morris	189?	B1014b
OSTEEN, Ida	1855	B795		PACK, Rose Edna (B=)	1895	B1014b
OTA, Lucy T. (B=)	1876	C133		PAGE, Golda Marie	1918	B2513
OTA, Setsuya	187?	C133		PAINTER, Jeanetta	193?	E39019
OTTO, Nancy	194?	F3110		PAINTER, Jr.	193?	E39019
OUTLAW, Lela Nadine	192?	E19054		PAINTER, Remau	1956	E39019
OUTTEN, Delma (Paskey)	192?	H494		PALMER, David	195?	F6039
OUTTEN, Karen Mary	1950	H494		PALMER, Joy B. (Gibson)	1957	F6039
OUTTEN, Tilghman	192?	H494		PALMITER, Manly	181?	E373
OWENS, Buddy Richard	193?	B26007		PALMITER, Mary (B=)	1817	E373
OWENS, Deborah L.	1958	B26007		PANOS, Maesimund (B=)	191?	F1404a

PAOLINI, Helen	1908	Q81	PEEPLES, Jefferson W.	192?	H502
PARKER, Darlene	191?	1911	PEEPLES, Jefferson W.	1954	H502
PARKER, Sadie	184?	A631	PEEPLES, Lillian (Moore)	193?	H502
PARKHURST, Barbara	195?	H771	PEEPLES, Rose Marie (B=)	1955	H502
PARKHURST, Nellie (B=)	185?	E1019	PEET, Maud (B=)	187?	E6305
PARKHURST, Thomas	185?	E1019	PEET, Robert A.	187?	E6305
PARKINSON, Mary P.	185?	B1026	PEILE, Lydia (B=)	1851	P26
PARMELEE, Philo	181?	E523	PEILE, Lydia J.	187?	P127
PARMELEE, Sarah (Johnson	1814	E523	PEILE, Minnie E.	187?	P126
PARMETER, Elma H.	1891	B1135	PEILE, Myrtle	187?	P129
PARNELL, Richard	168?	A5a	PEILE, Robert Moore	1853	P26
PARROTT, Eliza	18??	A66	PEILE, Robert Moore	187?	P128
PARROTT, Jane (B=)	177?	A28	PERDON, Doris	191?	X3581
PARROTT, Richard	177?	A28	PERDON, Madora (B=)	1893	X3547
PARROTT, William Henry	179?	A66a	PERDON, Mr.	189?	X3547
PARSONS, Debra N.(Betts)	1956	H761	PERINE, Minnie (B=)	186?	E1626
PARSONS, Jaime Rae	1975	H761	PERINE, Oscar	186?	E1626
PARSONS, Nicole Renee	1975	H761	PERKINS, Exa (B=)	1904	B997
PARSONS, Randy Elious	195?	H761	PERKINS, Frances M.	182?	X2
PARSONS, Sarah E.	187?	F3375	PERKINS, Walter	190?	B997
PASKEY, Delema	192?	H494	PERRIN, Iva	1899	A708
PASSWATERS, Sally (B=)	1842	H5	PERRY, Albert Alonzo	1891 *	X3515
PASSWATERS, Samuel	184?	H5	PERRY, Anna Amanda	1885	X3515
PATE, Karen (Thompson)	1940	Q189	PERRY, Charles	1894 *	X3515
PATE, Robert	193?	Q189	PERRY, Charlotte	1820	E348
PATON, Maryon	186?	X1007	PERRY, Clara (Ross)	1880	B551A
PATTERSON, Almira	183?	B141	PERRY, Cora Elizabeth	1882	X3515
PATTERSON, Dorothy	191?	Q143	PERRY, Deborah	172?	A9
PATTERSON, Elizabeth	189?	B2701	PERRY, Ebenezer	187?	B551A
PATTERSON, Minta (B=)	186?	F648	PERRY, Edna May	1888	X3515
PATTERSON, Mr.	186?	F648	PERRY, Florance Mae	1915	B2513e
PATTON, Beatrice (Ayer)	188?	C290	PERRY, George Edwin	1878	X3515
PATTON, George S. 3rd	1885	C290	PERRY, Kizzie Banning	1889	X3515
PATTON, Ruth	1913	C290	PERRY, Mary (Dunham)	182?	X3515
PATTON, Susan (Glassell)	183?	C125	PERRY, Mary Ann	185?	X3517
PAULEY, Clara (Lampson)	1887	P322	PERRY, Mary Eliz (Stim	1853	X3515
PAULEY, James Leroy	1889	P322	PERRY, Samuel	182?	X3515
PAULEY, James L.	1916	P322	PERRY, William Edwin	1856	X3515
PAULEY, James D.	1941	P322	PERSON, Bertha E. (B=)	191?	J411
PAULEY, Martha (Lammers)	194?	P322	PERSON, Dorothy Ann	1936	J2109
PAULEY, Richard J.	1946	P322	PERSON, LeRoy	1913	J411
PAULEY, Shirley (Stringe	194?	P322	PERSONS, Barbara	193?	F7004
PAULEY, Viola J. (Lemker	1915	P322	PETERS, Elizabeth	1886	N3678
PAULI, Martha	194?	F6013	PETERS, Elli (B=)	186?	N1677
PEABODY, Benjamin H.	1825	F257	PETERS, Friedrich	1894	N3689
PEABODY, George Lee	1851	F630	PETERS, Lathen	1891	N3688
PEABODY, Marion (Griswol	185?	F630	PETERS, Wilhelm	186?	N1677
PEABODY, Mary Ann (B=)	1826	F257	PETTY, Nancy C.	1802	B19
PEABODY, Mary A.	1857	F631	PFEIFFER, Eva	187?	A666
PEABODY, Sarah	1824	F255	PFISTER, Abnie	186?	B780
PEARCE, Caroline	193?	B2576a	PHELPS, Benjamin	180?	E100
PEARSON, Mehitable	176?	E67	PHELPS, Betsey	178?	E100
PEASE, Mary	169?	X2541	PHELPS, Betsey	180?	E100
PECK, Alice	176?	E76	PHELPS, Beulah	179?	E100
PECK, Charles	178?	F242	PHELPS, David	1762	E100
PECK, Elizabeth (Crowle	178?	F242	PHELPS, David	179?	E100
PECK, Franklin	181?	F245	PHELPS, Dora (B=)	1875	B748
PECK, James L.	189?	P144	PHELPS, Frank	191?	B2043
PECK, Jemima Marvin	1711	E5	PHELPS, Goldie	190?	B2041
PECK, Lydia Humston	1811	F242	PHELPS, Hannah	180?	E100
PECK, Sarah (Determan)	1900	P144	PHELPS, Henry	187?	B748
PECK, William	1709	E5	PHELPS, Irena	179?	E100

PHELPS, Joseph	179?	E100		PISCATELLI, Meghan Seren	1983	H844
PHELPS, Louise E.	184?	E1003		PISCATELLI, Pamela	1972	H847
PHELPS, Orville	191?	B2042		PISCATELLI, Robert	1942	H381
PHELPS, Parnal	180?	E100		PISCATELLI, Robert T.	1959	H844
PHELPS, Pearl	190?	B2040		PISCATELLI, Robert G.	1987	H844
PHELPS, Temperance (Wil	1768	E100		PITCHFORTH, Sarah Eleano	188?	B609
PHELPS, Temperance	180?	E100		PITTS, Juanita	1944	J512
PHILLIPS, Alma E.	189?	E9907		PLANT, Charlotte Warner	1866	E6677
PHILLIPS, Bessie L.	189?	B1742		PLANT, Edwin Thomas	1860	E6676
PHILLIPS, Carl Ivan	189?	B1746		PLATT, Ida May	187?	E1681
PHILLIPS, Cleo Frances (???)	190?	B2576		PLATT, Julia (Allen)	1852	F1201
PHILLIPS, Cora E. (B=)	1891	C301		PLATT, Stiles T.	1844	F1201
PHILLIPS, Custer	188?	B1741		PLATTS, Lydia	1757	E57
PHILLIPS, Darlene Faye	1932	B2576		POCTIERS, Hannah	183?	L197
PHILLIPS, Elda M.	188?	B1740		POE, Joseph W.	193?	H497
PHILLIPS, H. Melvin	189?	B1743		POE, Joyce L. (Powell)	1933	H497
PHILLIPS, Homer	188?	B1739		POLLARD, Julia Ann	1834	B536
PHILLIPS, Howard	189?	B1745		POLLOCK, Ada S.G. (B=)	183?	L140
PHILLIPS, James	185?	B568		POLLOCK, Charles Stewart	1875	L364
PHILLIPS, Joseph Kenneth	190?	B2576		POLLOCK, Douglas William	1872	L363
PHILLIPS, Lucille (Doty)	1907	B2707		POLLOCK, Hilda Louise	1876	L365
PHILLIPS, M. L.	186?	E4205		POLLOCK, Hubert Charles	1878 *	L366
PHILLIPS, Maletha (B=)	1860	B568		POLLOCK, Joseph Keating	183?	L140
PHILLIPS, Minnie (B=)	1870	E4205		POND, Gwendolyn (Kisselb	1958	E19103
PHILLIPS, Pearl	189?	B1744		POND, William Arthur	1954	E19103
PHILLIPS, Roy	189?	E9908		PONDER, Alice	176?	C12
PHILLIPS, Thomas	190?	B2707		POPP, Bruno Walter	188?	B3000
PHILLIPS, William August	189?	C301		POPP, Olga (Habermann)	189?	B3000
PHIPPS, Gertrude	191?	B1792		POPP, Sylvia Corrine	1916	B3000
PICKETT, Caroline Elizab	187?	E1682		PORTER, Aaron Marie	1981	E19124
PICKUP, Alfred	182?	L185		PORTER, Amy Suzanne	1980	E19124
PICKUP, Alfred Edwin	185? *	L463		PORTER, Debra Kay (Donic	195?	E19124
PICKUP, Izetta (B=)	1825	L185		PORTER, Delilah Ann	1958	E19125
PICKUP, James	1850	L462		PORTER, Earl Edward	1959	E19126
PICKUP, Louise (Richards	185?	L462		PORTER, Gary Allen	1978	E19124
PICKUP, Margaret Ann	1854 *	L464		PORTER, Hazel Joyce (B=)	1928	E10833
PICKUP, Thomas Hartley	1849 *	L461		PORTER, Jeanne C. (Jacks	1962	E19126
PIDCOCK, Ann Burton	1801	L43		PORTER, John	189?	E10833
PIEPER, Doris (Perdon)	191?	X3581		PORTER, Maria Abigail	1962	E19128
PIERCE, Alta F.	1903	B2513		PORTER, Mary Ann	1853	C259
PIERCE, George	17??	A29		PORTER, Mary Frances	1965	E19129
PIERCE, Mary (B=)	184?	D14		PORTER, Mathew Wayne	1976	E19124
PIERCE, Mr.	184?	D14		PORTER, Minnie (Radar)	189?	E10833
PIERCE, Rebecca	169?	X2541		PORTER, Murl Edward	1922	E10833
PIERCE, Sarah Murphy	1766	A29		PORTER, Patarica Lynn	1960 *	E19127
PIERSON, Caroline Lucert	183?	B139		PORTER, Sampson Wayne	1955	E19124
PIERSON, William P.	182?	B139		PORTER, Sandra Kay (Wals	1954	E19124
PINKLEY, Beaulah (B=)	1922	J414		PORTER, Shanna Marie	1987	E19126
PINKLEY, Carolyn (Gossey	194?	J2119		PORTER, Timmy Rae	1989	E19126
PINKLEY, Jackie Dewayne	1944	J2119		POST, Achsah (Douglass)	1812	E253
PINKLEY, James Carl	1917	J414		POST, Adin	178?	E385
PINKLEY, James Warren	1943	J2118		POST, Alonzo	181?	E257
PINKLEY, Karen (McCune)	194?	J2118		POST, Ann (???)	1812	E253
PINKLEY, Lilla R.(Arnold	194?	J2119		POST, Betsy (B=)	177?	E57
PINKLEY, Maxine J.(Battl	194?	J2118		POST, Charles	182?	E260
PINKLEY, Vera (Haven)	188?	J414		POST, Catherine (Windsor)	181?	E252
PINKLEY, William Elbert	188?	J414		POST, Eliza (???)	181?	E254
PISANI, Therisa	188?	H177		POST, Eliza (Douglass)	1812	E253
PISCATELLI, Claire M.(B=	1941	H381		POST, Eliza	1824	E259
PISCATELLI, Dawn	1970	H846		POST, Fanny (B=)	1786	E57
PISCATELLI, Maria	1961	H845		POST, Fanny An	1818	E255
PISCATELLI, Mary S. (Hug	196?	H844		POST, Hannah (Newsom)	1823	E254

POST, Ida	185?	E1150	
POST, Janet Kirby	189?	C299	
POST, Josiah	1761	E57	
POST, Josiah Jr.	1784	E57	
POST, Josaiah	1814	E252	
POST, Juane M.	184?	E1130	
POST, Lorenzo	1817	E254	
POST, Lydia (Platts)	1757	E57	
POST, Lydia	1821	E258	
POST, Mary E.	184?	E1131	
POST, Nancy (Douglass)	182?	E256	
POST, Nathan	181?	E260a	
POST, Philo	1819	E256	
POST, Sylvia Minerva	1808	E385	
POST, William H.	1815	E253	
POTTER, Mary	181?	B35	
POTTS, Almary (Stevens)	1838	A626	
POTTS, Edwin	183?	A626	
POUNDRIS, Connie Lea (B=	1955	C5664	
POUNDRIS, Constantine D.	1943	C5664	
POVAH, Alfred	1886	K6906	
POVAH, Edith S. (B=)	1860	K2932	
POVAH, Frederick G.	1855	K2932	
POVAH, Martha Spencer	1886	K6907	
POWELL, Aimee (B=)	1911	H176	
POWELL, Baswell	1853	B672	
POWELL, James	1859	B674	
POWELL, James Thomas	187?	H176	
POWELL, John	1865	B675	
POWELL, Joyce Louise	1933	H497	
POWELL, Louise	1855	B673	
POWELL, Mae (Miner)	187?	H176	
POWELL, Marion A.	1968	B26037	
POWELL, Nancy (B=)	1820	B152	
POWELL, Peter	1846	B670	
POWELL, Samuel James	1901	H176	
POWELL, Thomas	1850	B671	
POWELL, William B.	181?	B152	
PRATT, Albert	1812	E506	
PRATT, Alfred	1812	E505	
PRATT, Almira	1818	E510	
PRATT, Alphus	1816	E520	
PRATT, Alva	1822 *	E522	
PRATT, Amanda	1818	E515	
PRATT, Benjamin	178?	E113	
PRATT, Btsey	1817	E509	
PRATT, Blanch (B=)	1865	A675	
PRATT, Blanch	188?	A1632	
PRATT, David B.	175?	E77	
PRATT, David Beebe	175?	E21	
PRATT, David	1784	E111	
PRATT, Eli	1830	E516	
PRATT, George	1810	E504	
PRATT, Gilbert	1813 *	E507	
PRATT, Hepsibah	176?	E111	
PRATT, Hepsibah	1820	E521	
PRATT, Howard	188?	A1633	
PRATT, Josiah	1808	E503	
PRATT, Julia	1815	E508	
PRATT, Lafayette	1824	E514	
PRATT, Maria	1820	E511	
PRATT, Mary	1779	E77	

PRATT, Mary	1779	E109	
PRATT, Nancy (Mack)	178?	E110	
PRATT, nancy	1805	E501	
PRATT, Noah	1781	E110	
PRATT, Noah	1804 *	E500	
PRATT, Noah	1807	E502	
PRATT, Phebe	1826	E514	
PRATT, Philo	1814	E519	
PRATT, Phineas	175?	E111	
PRATT, Phineas	1812	E518	
PRATT, Sally	1833	E517	
PRATT, Sarah	175?	E77	
PRATT, Sarah (B=)	1753	E21	
PRATT, Sarah	1789	E112	
PRATT, Submit	178?	E111	
PRATT, William	1822	E511	
PRATT, William	186?	A675	
PRATT, Zebdial	179?	R7	
PRESTON, Cora A.	187?	B311	
PRICHARD, Jeanne	193?	E19110	
PRINCE, Henry	183?	X3504	
PRINCE, Mariana (B=)	1834	X3504	
PRITCHARD, Eugene	1931	A3591	
PRITCHARD, Janith	1938	A3592	
PRITCHARD, Margaret (B=)	1906	A1643	
PRITCHARD, Maud	191?	Q78	
PRITCHARD, Olin	190?	A1643	
PROSCHLING, Louis	183?	C256	
PROSCHLING, Lydia A.(B=)	1841	C256	
PUGH, Alice Jane	186?	K2939	
PUGH, Ann Caroline (B=)	172?	K1269	
PUGH, Arthur Lyon	186?	K2942	
PUGH, Caroline Elizabeth	185?	K2938	
PUGH, Charles	1804 *	K1275	
PUGH, Charles	1805	K1277	
PUGH, Edward	1809	K1278	
PUGH, Edward	1809	K1269	
PUGH, Edward Stuart	185?	K2937	
PUGH, Elinor Stuart	186?	K2943	
PUGH, Elizabeth (B=)	1781	K611	
PUGH, Elizabeth Annie	1853	K2941	
PUGH, Emma (Waters)	181?	K1276	
PUGH, Emma	1851	K2946	
PUGH, Florence Martha	185?	K2947	
PUGH, Mary Banning	185?	K2936	
PUGH, Walter Thomas	186?	K2940	
PUGH, William	177?	K611	
PUGH, William	1805	K1276	
PUGH, William Carrington	185?	K2945	
PURDY, Bertha (B=)	191?	Q91	
PURDY, Herman	191?	Q91	
PURDY, Martha	1872	Q19	
PURINTON, Lydia (B=)	1858	E1359	
PURINTON, Mr.	185?	E1359	
PURNELL, ???	168?	B3	
PURNELL, Margaret (Jump)	167?	A5a	
PURNELL, Margaret	171?	A5a	
PURNELL, Richard	165?	B3	
PURNELL, William	167?	A5a	
QUALLS, Kenneth Edwin	1927	E2513c	
QUALLS, Nola Jane (Cooper)	1907	B2513c	
QUALLS, Robert	190?	E2513c	

QUANT, Adderine (B=)	1862	R30
QUANT, Charles	1859	R30
RACCIO, Betty (Waldorf)	192?	H378
RACCIO, Peter W.	192?	H378
RACCIO, Sharon Joy	1943	H378
RADAR, Minnie	189?	E10833
RALPH, Elbert Elam	1902	Q12
RALPH, Ethel Lucindia	1896	Q12
RALPH, Eunice (B=)	1837	F499
RALPH, Gordon Francis	1894	Q12
RALPH, Hiram Walter	1869	Q12
RALPH, Robert F.	1867	Q12
RALPH, Samuel W.	1858	F499
RALPH, Sarah L. (Roy)	1869	Q12
RALPH, Victor Denzil	1904	Q12
RALSTON, Eva	185?	E5688
RAMSEY, Louise (B=)	18??	A1562
RAMSEY, Mr.	18??	A1562
RANDOLPH, Lillian	186?	B2702
RANKIN, Mary Elizabeth	1854	J30
RANSOM, Betsy (Chadwick)	1782	E311
RANSOM, Elizabeth (Johnso	1826	E527
RANSOM, Jane	172?	F15
RANSOM, Mary Ann	1816	E311
RANSOM, Richard Ely	1773	E311
RANSOM, Richard E.	182?	E527
RANSOME, Alice	178?	E81
RAPKIN, Sandra	195?	A3660
RASSELL, Jane (B=)	177?	A28
RASSELL, William	177?	A28
RATHBONE, Cynthia (Messe	178?	F81
RATHBONE, Daniel	171?	F16
RATHBONE, Daniel	1767	F75
RATHBONE, Denzian (Rice)	1764	F75
RATHBONE, Didy	177?	F79
RATHBONE, Diorama	1765	F74
RATHBONE, Dorotha (Rock	177?	F77
RATHBONE, Elijah	1783	F81
RATHBONE, Frances	1768	F76
RATHBONE, Hannah	1773	F78
RATHBONE, Jonathan	1780	F80
RATHBONE, Lucy (B=)	1743	F16
RATHBONE, Mary	1760	F21
RATHBONE, Thankful (Higgi	171?	F16
RATHBONE, William	168?	F16
RATHBONE, William	1740	F16
RATHBONE, William	1770	F77
RAVEN, Ann	15??	X2001
RAVEN, Robert {Sir}	15??	X2001
RAYMOND, Anthony Banning	1823	A241
RAYMOND, Delia Maria	1832	A243
RAYMOND, Elizabeth	1828	A242
RAYMOND, Elnathan	179?	A69
RAYMOND, Fanny	1861	A263
RAYMOND, George Elnathan	1834	A244
RAYMOND, Mary Banning	1821	A240
RAYMOND, Rachel (B=)	1796	A69
RAYMOND, Sarah Banning	1820	A239
RAZELL, Jane (B=)	177?	A28
RAZELL, William	177?	A28
REA, Daniel	183?	L188
REA, Daniel Arthur	1871	L469
REA, Emma (B=)	1839	L188
REA, Frances (Hardy)	187?	L469
REA, Josephine Banning	1870	L468
REA, Mary Beatrice	1873	L470
REA, Muriel Amy	1879	L472
REA, William Lawrence	1876	L571
REDMON, Ann	180?	B20
REDMOND, Esther	1896	B1143
REED, Beverly Ann	1947	H763
REED, Brandi Elizabeth	1983	H765
REED, C. James	1960	H764
REED, Catherine (Orendor	196?	H764
REED, Carlyn Danielle	1982	H764
REED, Caroline	173?	E26,E86
REED, Charles	191?	Q78
REED, Clarence James	192?	H326
REED, Clarence James	1979	H764
REED, Debora	173?	E14
REED, Elizabeth J. (B=)	1929	H326
REED, Ella Frances	189?	R125
REED, George	171?	F7
REED, George	174?	F25
REED, John H.	188?	Q28
REED, Karen (Cousins)	196?	H765
REED, Kenneth	194?	Q78
REED, Kenneth Lee	1945	H762
REED, Lawrence	193?	Q78
REED, Mary (B=)	1718	F7
REED, Maud (Pritchard)	191?	Q78
REED, Minnie	188?	Q28
REED, Ralph	193?	Q78
REED, Richard Allen	1963	H765
REED, Ruth	183?	B131
REED, Ryan Dennis	1986	H765
REEDE, Lydia	1782	F57
REESE, Loree J. (B=)	1896	B992b
REESE, Walter	189?	B992b
REEVES, Irene	192?	E19060
REID, Ruby	193?	Q148
REISZ, Patty Louise	1953	B26000
RENO, Emeline	186?	G77
RENO, Mary L. (B=)	1920	C1879
RENTH, Edith Evelyn	19??	H137
REPPLIER, Dorothy (B=)	1881	E6321
REPPLIER, Francis Ewing	187?	E6321
RERICH, Anton	191?	E19069
RERICH, Mable I. (Cook)	191?	E19069
RERICH, Rose Juanita	1942	E19069
REVES, Nancy	184?	B235b
REYNOLDS, Allen	188?	B1731
REYNOLDS, Arthur	188?	B1734
REYNOLDS, Clarence	188?	B1738
REYNOLDS, Clemon	188?	B1732
REYNOLDS, Daphen J.(Burn	1963	E19104
REYNOLDS, Earl	188?	B1737
REYNOLDS, Floyd	188?	B1736
REYNOLDS, Laura (B=)	185?	B557
REYNOLDS, Minnie	188?	B1733
REYNOLDS, Mira	188?	B1735
REYNOLDS, Steven T.	196?	E19104
REYNOLDS, Wiley	185?	B557
RICE, Antoinette	1839	F496

RICE, Deziah	1764	F75
RICE, Fisher	181?	B150
RICE, Frances (Rathbone)	1768	F76
RICE, Jennie	185?	E1571
RICE, Mr.	182?	C78
RICE, Obie Jane	190?	B9602
RICE, Pricilla (B=)	1832	C78
RICE, Sally (B=)	1815	B150
RICH, Almeda M.	185?	E1645
RICHARDS, Mary E.	197?	H115
RICHARDSON, Alfred Gordo	184?	L147
RICHARDSON, Anna (Carint	183?	L143
RICHARDSON, Charles Bann	184?	L146
RICHARDSON, Christina(B	1967	F10000
RICHARDSON, Freddie	193?	E19110
RICHARDSON, Geoffery D.	196?	F10000
RICHARDSON, James Aitken	1845 *	L145
RICHARDSON, Jeanne (Pric	193?	E19110
RICHARDSON, John	181?	L34
RICHARDSON, John William	1838	L143
RICHARDSON, Louise	185?	L462
RICHARDSON, Mary (B=)	1811	L34
RICHARDSON, Tammy L.	1964	E19110
RICHARDSON, Thomas Banni	1841 *	L144
RICHIE, Josephine	186?	F1202
RICHMOND, Helen E.	190?	E5844
RICKEY, Lydia	183?	B172
RICKMAN, Sarah A.	183?	B79
RIDDELL, Lucetta	180?	E361
RIDGE, Anetta (B=)	1908	E10803
RIDGE, Charles William	1926	E19049
RIDGE, Charles Russell	1955	E39012
RIDGE, Chester Leroy	1932	E19050
RIDGE, Chestina Louise	1962	E19015
RIDGE, Clifford Alan	1965	E39016
RIDGE, Eltha Lennis	1913	E10802
RIDGE, Eva N. (Moore)	1943	E19051
RIDGE, Isaac Henry	1906	E10803
RIDGE, Jeffrey Lee	1954	E39020
RIDGE, Jewel	1910	E10811
RIDGE, Kari (Elliott)	1956	E19051
RIDGE, Katrina (Smith)	1952	E39019
RIDGE, Kevin Tracy	1960	E39022
RIDGE, Marilyn Sue	1951	E39011
RIDGE, Martha E. (Nobles	1949	E19050
RIDGE, Mary L. (Jones)	1930	E19049
RIDGE, Mary A. (Brake	1936	E19051
RIDGE, Randall Dean	1952 *	E39013
RIDGE, Remau (Painter)	1956	E39019
RIDGE, Rhonda Lea	1959	E39014
RIDGE, Richard Lee	1934	E19051
RIDGE, Richard Scott	1953	E39019
RIDGE, Roy Dean	1974	E39018
RIDGE, Sandra Lee	1971	E39017
RIDGE, Sarah Melissa	1874	E10802
RIDGE, Sarah (Cassel)	188?	E10803
RIDGE, Sarah (Cassel)	188?	E10811
RIDGE, Sheila Jean	1948	E39009
RIDGE, Sherry Lynette	1949	E39010
RIDGE, Susan Gail	1957	E39021
RIDGE, William Jacob	1878	E10802
RIDGE, William Jacob	1878	E10811
RIDGE, Wilma L. (Harr)	1932	E19050
RIDGELY, Abraham	1811 *	C59
RIDGELY, Ann (Moore)	175?	C13
RIDGELY, Anna	1815	C61
RIDGELY, Charles Greenbu	175?	C13
RIDGELY, Charles	177?	A81
RIDGELY, Charles G.	1804	C55
RIDGELY, Edward	1831	C68
RIDGELY, Elizabeth (Brin	180?	C55
RIDGELY, Elizabeth	1813	C60
RIDGELY, Elizabeth (Come	183?	C68
RIDGELY, Eugene	1822	C65
RIDGELY, Harriet	180?	A81
RIDGELY, Henry Moore	1779	C13
RIDGELY, Henry	1817	C82
RIDGELY, John Banning	1807 *	C57
RIDGELY, Juliet	1819 *	C63
RIDGELY, Mary (Tilden)	1827	C64
RIDGELY, Mary (Mifflin)	182?	C65
RIDGELY, Mary	1824 *	C66
RIDGELY, Mary Tilden	184?	C64
RIDGELY, Nicholas	1806 *	C56
RIDGELY, Nicholas	1820	C64
RIDGELY, Ruth Ann	184?	C62
RIDGELY, Sarah (B=)	178?	C13
RIDGELY, Virginia (???)	182?	C62
RIDGELY, Williamina	1809 *	C58
RIDGELY, Williamina	1827	C67
RIED, Deborah	177?	F57
RIGGS, Elizabeth	1819	B43
RIMES, Solomon	1841	B235
RIPPY, Abigale (B=)	177?	B11
RIPPY, Henry	177?	B11
RIVERA, Donna L. (Jester	1955	H774
RIVERA, Michael	195?	H774
RIVERA, Michael	1980	H774
ROACH, Brenda Gay	196?	E39025
ROBB, Bessie	186?	B775
ROBBINS, Frances A.	193?	H335
ROBBINS, George	187?	F1453
ROBBINS, Idella {Del}	1864	A644
ROBELAITTO, James	186?	C265
ROBELAITTO, Ruth L. (B=)	1868	C265
ROBERTS, Albert W.	183?	E1576
ROBERTS, Helen (Ackley)	1839	E1576
ROBERTS, Hetty J.	184?	B134
ROBERTS, Jennie	185?	G20
ROBERTS, Lulu Belle	1883	Q16
ROBERTSON, Clara G. (B=)	1885	R124
ROBERTSON, Elwood	1905	R356
ROBERTSON, Fred George	188?	R124
ROBERTSON, Helen H.	192?	R357
ROBERTSON, Mary S. (B=)	1905	B2118
ROBERTSON, Mr.	190?	B2118
ROBINS, Alice A. (B=)	1879	F1453
ROBINS, Burt	1863	F636
ROBINS, Carrie (Starrett	187?	F637
ROBINS, George	187?	F1453
ROBINS, John	179?	F61
ROBINS, Laura (B=)	181?	F244
ROBINS, Lee C.	1869	F637
ROBINS, Malinda	1815	F238

ROBINS, Mary	1860	F635
ROBINS, Melinda (B=)	1834	F260
ROBINS, Mr.	181?	F244
ROBINS, Nettie (Kindlsid	186?	F636
ROBINS, Newton	1832	F260
ROBINSON, Blanch	18??	A704
ROBINSON, Howard G.	192?	E19054
ROBINSON, Josephine	187?	C137
ROBINSON, Lela Nadine	192?	E19054
ROBINSON, Leslie	189?	C1864
ROBINSON, Myrtle E.(Sams	1899	C1864
ROBINSON, Nancy M.	1813	E386
ROBINSON, Patsy Nadine	1945	E19054
ROBSON, Mary	1923	Q84
ROCKWELL, A.	177?	F78
ROCKWELL, Dorotha	177?	F77
ROCKWELL, Hannah (Rathb	1773	F78
ROGERS, Ann E. (B=)	1827	B91c
ROGERS, Betty M. (B=)	1942	E19112
ROGERS, Becki	1951	B26006
ROGERS, Eli	180?	E345
ROGERS, Henry F.	183?	E1390
ROGERS, James F.	182?	B91c
ROGERS, Jane E.	181?	B90a
ROGERS, Joshua	182?	B172
ROGERS, Lydia (Rickey)	183?	B172
ROGERS, Marrion (Chapel)	1844	E1390
ROGERS, Mehitable (B=)	1808	E345
ROGERS, Ruth (Wantland)	190?	E19112
ROGERS, Sarah Ann Eliz.	1856	B172
ROGERS, Thomas S.	190?	E19112
ROGERS, Thomas S.	1930	E19112
ROLAND, Dora (B=)	1875	B742
ROLAND, Buddy	19?	B2039
ROLAND, Henry	168?	E2
ROLAND, John	187?	B748
ROLAND, Mary	1690	E2
ROLPH, Eunice (B=)	1837	F499
ROLPH, Samuel W.	1858	F499
ROOT, Sarah	172?	X2632
ROS, Ann (Newark)	165?	X2014
ROS, John	164?	X2014
ROSE, Melethia	183?	F601
ROSE, Morgan	1953	E19115
ROSE, Nancy E.	1875	B941
ROSS, Charles Stanley	1882 *	B552A
ROSS, Clara Belle	1880	B551A
ROSS, Ellen Gertrude	1878	B551
ROSS, George McLennan	1885	B553
ROSS, Harriett (B=)	1854	B121A
ROSS, Hattie Eliza	1887 *	B553A
ROSS, John McLennan	1844	B121A
ROSS, John Banning	1881	B552
ROSS, Lucy T. (B=)	1876	C133
ROSS, Margaret (???)	188?	B552
ROSS, Mary Jane	1866	Q11
ROSS, Robert E.	188?	C133
ROSS, Robert Anderson	1888 *	B553B
ROSSMAN, Jacob Adolph	184?	C260
ROSSMAN, Lydia Ann (Horn	184?	C260
ROSSMAN, Sarah Jane	1866	C260
ROTH, Edna	1909	A1653

ROTH, Joseph D.	188?	A1653
ROWLAND, Annie M. (B=)	1839	L458
ROWLAND, Henry	183?	L458
ROY, Alice (Millar)	1878	Q17
ROY, Bertram Stanley	1905	Q16
ROY, Beulah Winnifred	1899	Q9
ROY, Birtha C.	1890 *	Q9
ROY, Charles Albert	1867	Q11
ROY, Clinton	1903	Q17
ROY, Clayton Albert	1903	Q11
ROY, David Joseph	1878	Q16
ROY, Earle Picken	1900	Q11
ROY, Elspeth Margaret	1896	Q11
ROY, Emma Lavina	1865	Q10
ROY, Ernest	1913	Q17
ROY, Esther	1874 *	Q15
ROY, Ethel Minnie M. Ros	1881	Q18
ROY, Eve Blanch	1893	Q9
ROY, Francis Xavier	181?	Q2
ROY, Francis Xavier	1835	Q2
ROY, Frank Henry	1905	Q9
ROY, Fred	1906	Q17
ROY, George David	1908	Q16
ROY, Gladys Estelle	1893	Q11
ROY, Howard	1880	Q17
ROY, Isa Collins	1898	Q11
ROY, Iva Pearl	1912	Q16
ROY, Joseph	1870 *	Q13
ROY, Lucinda (B=)	1840	Q2
ROY, Lulu Belle (Roberts	1883	Q16
ROY, Mable sarah	1897	Q9
ROY, Malissa	1871	Q14
ROY, Mary (Landreville)	181?	Q2
ROY, Mary Jane (Ross)	1866	Q11
ROY, Mary J. (Lowe)	1869	Q9
ROY, Milfred Margaret	1917	Q16
ROY, Sarah Louise	1869	Q12
ROY, William Frank	1863	Q9
ROY, William Milton	1918	Q16
RUDESEAL, Clydelle (Cook	192?	F11988
RUDESEAL, Herman	192?	F11988
RUDESEAL, Martha Jean	1944	F11988
RUMER, Jerusha A. (B=)	1839	F614
RUMER, Peter H.	183?	F614
RUNYAN, Dora	188?	R121
RUSHTON, Susan	1947	Q150
RUSSELL, Ann (Teagarden)	184?	B551
RUSSELL, Catherine	187?	B930a
RUSSELL, Cyrenus	184?	B551
RUSSELL, Elizabeth (???)	172?	C4
RUSSELL, Ellen (Ross)	1878	B551
RUSSELL, Eugene Seward	1905	B551
RUSSELL, Florence Irene	1909	B551
RUSSELL, John A.	1873	B551
RUSSELL, John Paul	1913	B551
RUSSELL, Marion Gertrude	1917	B551
RUSSELL, Mary	174?	C4
RUSSELL, Miss.	183?	A244
RUSSELL, William	172?	C4
RUST, Beth	1980	H769
RUST, Bonnie K. (Furroug	1955	H769
RUST, Carlton	195?	H769

477

RUST, Dorothy	1911	H174		SCARGE, B.E.	185?	B792a
RUST, Mark	1981	H769		SCARGE, Elizabeth (Mille	1859	B792a
RUST, Nikki	1972	H769		SACRGE, Joseph Henry	1881 *	B792a
RUSZCZYK, Lillian	193?	H837		SCHAFER, Bruce Layne	1949	C1835
RUTHERFORD, Bell	184?	G11		SCHAFER, Celeste Sue	1942	C1835
RYAN, Louisa	1876	F1209		SCHAFER, Christine (Knip	189?	C1835
RYAN, Mary Jane	1858	Q6		SCHAFER, Christine Ann	1952	C1835
SACKVILLE, Ann	15??	X2005		SCHAFER, Dominic Gregory	1946	C1835
SAGE, Sady	185?	E1625		SCHAFER, Frederick Lloyd	1915	C1835
SALISBURY, Anna (Sanders	1904	A1639		SCHAFER, Frederick Lloyd	1943	C1835
SALISBURY, Charles	1902	A1639		SCHAFER, Ione Amanda	1918	C1913
SALT, Emma	178?	L53		SCHAFER, Norma L. (Baker	1917	C1835
SALT, Sarah (B=)	1757	L11		SCHAFER, Vincent Lee	1954	C1835
SALT, Sarah	178?	L54		SCHAFER, William A.	188?	C1835
SALT, Thomas	175?	L11		SCHARLAU, Carl Lewis	1912	C1839
SALT, Thomas	178?	L52		SCHARLAU, Jay Dean	1940	C1839
SALTFORD, Barbara Ann	193?	H835		SCHARLAU, Katherine (Wil	1912	C1839
SAMS, Bertha Mae (B=)	1872	C561		SCHARLAU, Lynn Carl	1939	C1839
SAMS, Cora	1890	C1860		SCHINGO, Earl	1904	Q18
SAMS, Etta Luella (B=)	1869	C560		SCHINGO, Ethel M. (Roy)	1881	Q18
SAMS, Grace (Day)	190?	C1865		SCHLEICHER, Carl John	190?	E10831
SAMS, Helen (Doyle)	191?	C1866		SCHLEICHER, Chris Lee	1955	E19119
SAMS, Inez	1886	C1858		SCHLEICHER, Katherine L.	1953	E19118
SAMS, John	183?	C560		SCHLEICHER, Lois V. (Fre	190?	E10831
SAMS, Kennetth Webb	1918	C1866		SCHLEICHER, Lowell	1925	E10831
SAMS, Lillian (Dunn)	189?	C1859		SCHLEICHER, Mary A.(O'Co	1957	E19118
SAMS, Mary Etta	1893	C1862		SCHLEICHER, Ruth I. (B=)	1921	E10831
SAMS, Myrtle Estella	1899	C1864		SCHLEICHER, Sylvia (Spielm	1957	B19119
SAMS, Pearl	1892 *	C1861		SCHLEICHER, Tera Lee	1974	E19118
SAMS, Pearlina (Dowers)	183?	C560		SCHOOLEY, Jennie L. (B=)	1903	J140a
SAMS, Perry Francis	1901	C1865		SCHOOLEY, John	190?	J140a
SAMS, Stephen Riley	1858	C560		SCHULL, Antonie	183?	N673
SAMS, Verna Mae	1896	C1863		SCHWAMS, Ann	191?	C1907
SAMS, Walter Abraham	1888	C1859		SCHWARTZ, Edward Jacob	194?	J2117
SAMSON, Jane A.	1807	B69		SCHWARTZ, Peggy L.(Carte	1946	J2117
SANDERS, Barbara (Buck)	193?	C5666		SCOFIELD, Kate DeWitt	184?	E1476
SANDERS, Breia Rosemarie	1978	C8609		SCOGGINS, Mr.	179?	B34
SANDERS, Callie R. (B=)	1960	C5666		SCOLES, Charles W.	1877	B882
SANDERS, Dorothy Carter	1891	E6319		SCOLES, Cora A. (Dowell)	1883	B883
SANDERS, Julia	190?	E10826		SCOLES, John William	1874	B881
SANDERS, Lewis	186?	E6319		SCOLES, Kenneth Nelson	1920	B883
SANDERS, Richard Ernest	193?	E5666		SCOLES, Martha L. (B=)	1843	B220
SANDERS, Ricky Edward	1957	C5666		SCOLES, Martha Evaline	1881	B884
SANDERSON, Anna Minerva	1904	A1639		SCOLES, Melvin	1872	B880
SANDERSON, Harry	187?	A685		SCOLES, Reuben	1837	B220
SANDERSON, Howard	1908	A1640		SCOLES, Reuben Ezra	1881	B883
SANDERSON, Priscilla (B=	1873	A685		SCOTT, Frances (Widdows)	1837	L450
SANFORD, Elizabeth	184?	E1004		SCOTT, Martha	1795	B35
SANFORD, Mary J.	183?	E1001		SCOTT, Robert	183?	L450
SANFORD, Rebecca	1836	C27		SCOVEL, Deborah (Ackley)	171?	F15
SATURNO, Emily A. (Deatr	1913	H177		SCOVEL, Edward	171?	F15
SATURNO, Gladys Elizabet	1932	H177		SCOVEL, Lydia	1735	F15
SATURNO, Gloria Theresa	1932	H177		SCOVERNER, Bertha	190?	J164
SATURNO, James David	1911	H177		SCOVIL, Rhelma Leona	1915	C1916
SATURNO, James Lewis	1937	H177		SCOVIL, Sarah	171?	E3
SATURNO, Samuel	188?	H177		SCOVILL, Lydia	1735	F15
SATURNO, Theresa (Pisani	188?	H177		SCROGINS, Ann (B=)	1795	B49
SAUNDERS, Gladys	193?	H827		SCROGINS, Mr.	179?	B49
SAWYER, Kenneth	194?	H383		SCRUGGS, N.C.	183?	B79
SAWYER, Roberta Sue (Hud	1946	H383		SCULLION, Bessie (Moors)	1892	Q50
SAXON, Emerson	188?	D68		SCULLION, Grace Kathleen	1925	Q50
SAXON, Vira (B=)	1885	D68		SCULLION, John Stewart	1890	Q50

SCULLION, John Stewart	1927	Q50	
SCULLION, Lucy Elizabeth	1919	Q50	
SEAVERNS, Dana	193?	H827	
SEAVERNS, Gladys (Saunde	193?	H827	
SEAVERNS, Lori	1958	H827	
SEIBEL, Arthur	1931	J508	
SEIBEL, Curtis	1953	J508	
SEIBEL, Michael	1951	J508	
SEIBEL, Shirley (Vandeven	1931	J508	
SEIBEL, Steven	1955	J508	
SEIBEL, Vernon	1959	J508	
SELBY, Ashbel J.	183?	F286	
SELBY, Elmina (B=)	1833	F286	
SENTELLE, Alma (B=)	1919	B998a	
SENTELLE, Frisco	191?	B998a	
SEVERE, Arene (Breece)	1820	B231	
SEVERE, Bertha (Fisher)	187?	B930	
SEVERE, Catherine (Russe	187?	B930a	
SEVERE, Cenia Josephine	1891	B931b	
SEVERE, Charles	1877	B930a	
SEVERE, Cordia May	1886	B931a	
SEVERE, George	1874	B930	
SEVERE, Gilman	1816	B70,B231	
SEVERE, Helen (Morton)	190?	B932a	
SEVERE, Jessie	1854	B231	
SEVERE, Martha J. (B=)	1855	B231	
SEVERE, Mary (Daniel)	1834	B70	
SEVERE, Mary A.	1880	B930b	
SEVERE, Ollie Grace	1895	B932	
SEVERE, Ottie Filena	1883	B931	
SEVERE, Samuel J.	182?	B70	
SEVERE, Vernon	1898	B932a	
SEWEITZER, Elsie (Turpin)	1909	B2046	
SEWEITZER, Jacob Louis	190?	B2046	
SEYMOUR, Louise Ann	1846	A627	
SEYMOUR, Nancy Banning	1854	A630	
SEYMOUR, Rachel Maria	1850	A629	
SEYMOUR, Rhoda Sophia	1849	A628	
SEYMOUR, Silas Dunning	181?	A228	
SHAFFNER, Emma	186?	A663	
SHALER, Annie	180?	E305	
SHANNAHA, James	179?	R7	
SHARP, Hattie Roberta	1910	E10804	
SHARP, Russell Kelly	1871	E10804	
SHARP, Sarah M. (Yandell	1873	E10804	
SHEILER, Ursula Maria	1813	E395	
SHELDON, Clara (Melcalf)	189?	E10827	
SHELDON, Emma (B=)	1867	B536	
SHELDON, Frank Pollard	1866	B536	
SHELDON, Isadore	189?	B1674	
SHELDON, John A.	189?	E10827	
SHELDON, Juanita Jewel	1923	E10827	
SHELDON, Julia Ann	1834	B536	
SHELDON, Lawson	1827	B536	
SHELLABARGER, Mary F.	185?	F1509	
SHELLEY, Ardeen H.	1883	J161	
SHELLEY, Lowell	191?	J161	
SHELLEY, Lulu M. (Hopkin	1892	J161	
SHELLEY, Max	191?	J161	
SHELLEY, Ruth	191?	J161	
SHEPARD, Harold	190?	E10812	
SHEPARD, Jewel (B=)	1910	E10812	
SHERMAN, Elizabeth	183?	A225	
SHERRY, Cameron Banning	1892	B1761	
SHERRY, D. B.	186?	B583	
SHERRY, Edith Hope	1891	B1760	
SHERRY, Homer Kent	1888	B1758	
SHERRY, Inez Bell	1890	B1759	
SHERRY, John	186?	B585	
SHERRY, Josephine (B=)	1863	B583	
SHERRY, Mary	1866	B585	
SHERWOOD, Catherine (Den	180?	A66d	
SHERWOOD, James	195?	R497	
SHERWOOD, Nanci (Cordell	1953	R497	
SHERWOOD, Susan	181?	A50	
SHERWOOD, Thomas	180?	A66d	
SHIRE, Bonita	190?	P145	
SHIRLEY, Barbara J. (B=)	1951	H500	
SHIRLEY, Chad Matthew	1984	H1012	
SHIRLEY, Harold J.	192?	H500	
SHIRLEY, Kenneth Laran	1952	H500	
SHIRLEY, Lance Kenneth	1977	H1010	
SHIRLEY, Minnie (Hatcher	192?	H500	
SHIRLEY, Trent Justin	1978	H1011	
SHOOK, David Wayne	1964	E19106	
SHOOK, Harry A.	192?	E19106	
SHOOK, Marla Ann (Krohme	1964	E19106	
SHOOK, Peggy J. (Hutchpa	193?	E19106	
SHOWALTER, Heather Sidon	1975	E39003	
SHOWALTER, Johnnie Danie	1949	E19056	
SHOWALTER, Linda (Mathew	1951	E19056	
SHOWALTER, Mathew Scott	1979	E39034	
SHOWALTER, Milton John	192?	E19056	
SHOWALTER, Monnie Mae	192?	E19056	
SHULL, Nora Louise	192?	E39010	
SILENCE, Mary Jane	1856	C553	
SILL, Grace (Clark)	1884	F1407	
SILL, Joanna	172?	E17	
SILL, Webester H.	188?	F1407	
SILMAN, Alphonso Bertram	1888	Q49	
SILMAN, Jack Forrest B.	1923	Q49	
SILMAN, Luch {Dollie}(Mo	1923	Q49	
SILVER, George M.	187?	F1499	
SILVER, Lilly R. (B=)	187?	F1499	
SIMMERMAN, Sarah	180?	B20	
SIMONS, Bertha (Blevins)	190?	B3001	
SIMONS, George W.	190?	B3001	
SIMONS, Norma Juanice	1925	B3001	
SIMPSON, Chestina (Ridge	1962	E39015	
SIMPSON, Douglas	1962	E39015	
SIMPSON, Emily (Cooper)	1904	B2513a	
SIMPSON, Emily	1941 *	B2513a	
SIMPSON, Harold Eugene	193?	E39015	
SIMPSON, Nancy Jane	186?	B260	
SIMPSON, Ola Wandalea	1931	B2513a	
SIMPSON, Richard	1897	B2513a	
SIMPSON, Ruby Lorena	193?	E39015	
SINGLETON, Betsy (B=)	1827	B154	
SINGLETON, Joseph	182?	B154	
SIPE, Cheryl Sue	1960	C5668	
SIPE, Darrel Donald	1956	C5567	
SIPE, Donald Dewey	1931	C3335	
SIPE, Shirley Ann (B=)	1937	C3335	
SKEEN, Mary Matilda	1825	A259	

SKEET, Annie 40	183?	R35 &
SKEETERS, Bryant	189?	J149
SKEETERS, Eva (B=)	189?	J149
SKEGGS, Mary Etta	19??	H116
SKINNER, Annie (B=)	1827	A56
SKINNER, Ella	187?	E1703
SKINNER, Gustavus	182?	A56
SKINNER, Joyce	192?	Q146
SKINNER, Lawrence Albert	18??	A146
SKINNER, Pauline F.	1949	E19050
SLOAN, Sadie M. (B=)	1886	C566
SLOAN, William	188?	C556
SMALLPACE, Miria (Dall)	182?	L137
SMALLPACE, Mr.	182?	L137
SMALLWOOD, Jann Lynn	1946	H382
SMALLWOOD, Mildred (Cam	192?	H382
SMALLWOOD, Thomas Edwa	192?	H382
SMEED, Eliza Amelia	183?	L187
SMEND, Friederike L.	176?	N60
SMITH, Abigail (???)	172?	B6
SMITH, Ada Elizabeth(B=)	1867	J25
SMITH, Alice Marion	1885	B616
SMITH, Allen Lee	187? *	B785
SMITH, Alma	187?	B776
SMITH, Alta (B=)	1869	G78
SMITH, Anna Ophelia	1871	C125
SMITH, Anna	187?	B784
SMITH, Ansoletta A.	184?	E1618
SMITH, Beatrice Whithe	188?	B600
SMITH, Benjamine F.	184?	B206
SMITH, Bessie	187?	D53
SMITH, Calvin	197?	E38977
SMITH, Catherine (B=)	1838	B180
SMITH, Celina Elizabeth	1887	Q10
SMITH, Cenia J. (Severe)	1891	B931b
SMITH, Charlotte (Thomas	1866	E6677
SMITH, Clark	1883	B931b
SMITH, Claude	189?	J148
SMITH, Cunthia Ellen	1884 *	B615
SMITH, Cynthia (B=)	1858	B143
SMITH, Dawn (Hooper)	1943	E19061
SMITH, Delila (B=)	1841	B297a
SMITH, Donnie R.	195?	E38977
SMITH, Earl	189?	J147
SMITH, Edith	1885	Q10
SMITH, Eliza A.	183?	F591
SMITH, Eliza Alice (B=)	1860	J23
SMITH, Elizabeth	1805	B52
SMITH, Elmer Lafayett	192?	E19060
SMITH, Elon	187?	A1565
SMITH, Emma L. (Roy)	1865	Q10
SMITH, Ethel	189?	E10808
SMITH, Flora June	187?	B783
SMITH, Frances A. (B=)	1927	H325
SMITH, Fred	185?	E4210
SMITH, George Hugh	183?	C125
SMITH, George W.	186?	B1140
SMITH, George	187?	G78
SMITH, George	1906	G189
SMITH, Harvey	189?	B932
SMITH, Heather	197?	E38977
SMITH, Hellen Almanson	1893 *	B617
SMITH, Henrietta (Beshea	194?	E19061
SMITH, Herman	1919	E10808
SMITH, Hiram Almason	185?	B143
SMITH, Howard	186?	E6677
SMITH, Howard	1909	Q10
SMITH, Irene	182?	E19060
SMITH, Jessie (Merry)	186?	E4210
SMITH, Joan	194?	B2577
SMITH, Jobe	1854	Q10
SMITH, Joe	193?	E39019
SMITH, Joseph Jr.	183?	B297a
SMITH, Justin Richard	1968	E39045
SMITH, Katrina Ann	1952	E39019
SMITH, Kenny Ray	1946	E19061
SMITH, Lee	189?	J146
SMITH, Lee Ann	197?	E38978
SMITH, Leona Patsy	193?	F7003
SMITH, Leroy	192?	E19041
SMITH, Lewis Levi	1887	Q10
SMITH, Lou (???)	195?	E38977
SMITH, Lulu (Tichenor)	187?	B1140
SMITH, Mabel	188?	H175b
SMITH, Madison Lee	183?	B180
SMITH, Margaret	1696	E5
SMITH, Margaret	1917	Q83
SMITH, Marshal Orlando	186?	J25
SMITH, Martha (B=)	1922	E10808
SMITH, Mary Ann (B=)	1850	B206
SMITH, Mary Amner	1876 *	B786
SMITH, Mary Alice (Bess)	192?	E19041
SMITH, Mary	193?	E39019
SMITH, Nancy	1845	A233
SMITH, Nay W.	189?	E10807
SMITH, Nelle Irene	1893	B1140
SMITH, Nellie (Strong)	1878	A1565
SMITH, Ollie Grace (Seve	1895	B932
SMITH, Paul James	1942	E19060
SMITH, Rickey D.	195?	E38978
SMITH, Rodney Brent	1969	E39043
SMITH, Ruby Lillian	1892	G188
SMITH, Sabina	1742	B6
SMITH, Sadie Helen	1903	C1826
SMITH, Sam	197?	E38978
SMITH, Sandra Lee	1942	E19060
SMITH, Shannon Lynne	1975	E39044
SMITH, Tammie (???)	195?	E38978
SMITH, Tonya Laynette	1972	E39046
SMITH, Urban Earl	1894	Q10
SMITH, Victor Boyd	1893	Q10
SMITH, Viola May (Loud)	185?	B600
SMITH, Walter	186?	E1661
SMITH, Walter F.	192?	H325
SMITH, Wilber	185?	J23
SMITH, William Sr.	172?	B6
SMITH, William Fulton	185?	B600
SMITH, Zella	189?	J137,140b
SNYDER, Bessie (B=)	1877	B422
SNYDER, Cynthia Sue	1947	H493
SNYDER, Hary A. {Dr.}	187?	B422
SNYDER, Olin	191?	H493
SNYDER, Patricia Ann	1954	H493

480

SNYDER, Ruby (Kelly)	191?	H493	STAFFORD, Frank	185?	E4209
SOLOMAN, John T.	187?	E5619	STAFFORD, George	184?	L456
SOLOMAN, Matilda J. (Bar	187?	E5619	STAFFORD, Mary (Widdows)	1848	L456
SOLOMAN, Nellie Frances	1900	E5619	STANHOPE, Amelia (Steven	18??	F617
SOMERSET, Rebecca	177?	K601	STANHOPE, Benjamin	18??	F617
SOSSAMAN, Florence	188?	E10806	STANHOPE, Philip	18??	F617
SOUTHWORTH, Jabez	183?	E1619	STANTEME, Harriet P.	183?	F626
SOUTHWORTH, Louise (B=)	1842	E1619	STANTON, Addie (B=)	186?	F684
SOWERS, Hiram	184?	A632	STANTON, Courtland A.	186?	F684
SOWERS, Nancy (B=)	1848	A632	STANTON, Edith	18??	F1566
SPAIN, Herman	189?	C796	STANTON, Grace N.	18??	F1563
SPALSBURY, Leah	189?	E6364	STANTON, Harry Albert	18??	F1565
SPARKS, Sarah	180?	D2	STANTON, Maud	18??	F1568
SPARROW, Anna (Atwood)	172?	F20	STANTON, Ralph Winthrop	18??	F1564
SPARROW, Annah	1752	F20	STANTON, Ruth Noyes	18??	F1569
SPARROW, John	172?	F20	STANTON, Winthrop	18??	F1567
SPEAK, Tommy	194?	J2116	STAPLETON, Bud	191?	B2053
SPEAK, Wanda Lee (Carter	1944	J2116	STAPLETON, Dorothy (B=)	191?	B2053
SPEES, George	187?	X519	STAR, Rilla	186?	F647
SPELLMAN, Elijah	178?	F269	STARK, Betsy (B=)	1832	E405
SPELLMAN, Elijah Chapman	1802	F269	STARK, Ella	185?	E1661
SPELLMAN, Mary	178?	F269	STARK, Lewis	185?	E16560
SPELMAN, Elijah	176?	F90	STARK, Nathan	182?	E405
SPELMAN, Mary (Chapman)	1771	F90	STARKEY, Vivian Ethel	1903	C1905
SPENCE, Cynthia (Snyder)	1947	H493	STARNES, Arthur Ray	1950	E39011
SPENCE, Franklin Merle	1950	H494	STARNES, Marilyn (Ridge)	1951	E39011
SPENCE, Gale Dean	1978	H493	STARNES, Nora Louise	192?	E39011
SPENCE, Geneva (B=)	1913	H175	STARNES, William Walter	192?	E39011
SPENCE, Hilred Jessie	1915	H174	STARRETT, Carrie	187?	F637
SPENCE, Jessie (Murphy)	188?	H174-5	STEARNS, Sarah (B=)	182?	X105
SPENCE, Karen M.(Outten)	1950	H494	STEBBINS, Hannah	185?	C260
SPENCE, Lane Kelly	1971	H493	STEELE, Dorcas	1928	Q53
SPENCE, Larry Wayne	1946	H493	STEELE, Leonard Cracraft	189?	Q53
SPENCE, Lisa Beth	1974	H494	STEELE, Samuel	1925	Q53
SPENCE, Michele Lynn	1977	H494	STEELE, Sara J. (Moors)	1900	Q53
SPENCE, Oscar Wiley	188?	H174-5	STEPHENS, Elizabeth	181?	B65a
SPENCE, Patricia (Snyder	1954	H493	STEPHENSON, Jack Reese	1942	E19058
SPENCE, Seth Ryan	1980	H493	STEPHENSON, Jack Reese J	1962	E39038
SPENCE, Walter Franklin	1916	H175	STEPHENSON, Kimberly M.	1976	E39041
SPENCER, Abigail	166?	E1	STEPHENSON, Larry	1944	E19059
SPENCER, Adlaide (Doud)	185?	E1641	STEPHENSON, Lori Ann	1965	E39039
SPENCER, Arthur	185?	E1641	STEPHENSON, Majorie (Wil	1943	E19058
SPENCER, Jane	1696	A5	STEPHENSON, Mary (B=)	1922	E10807
SPENCER, Joseph	183?	F612	STEPHENSON, Patsy (Young	1944	E19059
SPENCER, Mary (B=)	1833	F612	STEPHENSON, Robb	1969	E39040
SPENCER, Millie M. (B=)	188?	C568	STEPHENSON, Scott	1971	E39042
SPENCER, Miss.	176?	A25	STEPHENSON, Simeon Reese	1913	E10807
SPENCER, William	187?	C568	STERAT, Jane (B=)	177?	A21a
SPICER, Mildred	190?	C1907	STERAT, Mr.	177?	A21a
SPIELMANN, Elsa (Gottl)	193?	E19119	STERLING, Abigail	1742	F15
SPIELMANN, Manfred G.	193?	E19119	STERLING, Jane (Ransom)	172?	F15
SPIELMANN, Sylvia G	1957	E19119	STERLING, John	171?	F15
SPRACKLIN, Adaline F.	184?	B221	STEVENS, Addie	185?	E1636
SPRACKLIN, Pamelia A.	184?	B298	STEVENS, Alfred	185?	K2938
SPRIGGS, Elizabeth (Turn	1811	C82	STEVENS, Alice (Pugh)	185?	K2939
SPRIGGS, John	180?	C82	STEVENS, Almary	1838	A626
SPRIGGS, Mary Ann	180?	C87	STEVENS, Amelia C.	18??	F617
SPROTE, Josephine (Fortner)	186?	B1193	STEVENS, Amelia	181?	F251
SPROTE, Oliver	185?	B1193	STEVENS, Anthony Banning	1836	A625
SPRUMOUR, Loura (Horn)	187?	C140	STEVENS, Caroline (Pugh)	185?	K2938
SPRYMOUR, McNeil V.	187?	C140	STEVENS, John	181?	A227
STAFFORD, Clara (Merry)	186?	E4209	STEVENS, Jonathan	182?	E399

STEVENS, Lorraine	193?	F5290		STRIMPLE, Hilary Perry	1897	X3517
STEVENS, Louise (B=)	1817	A227		STRIMPLE, Jesse Elsworth	1891	X3517
STEVENS, Lydia (B=)	176?	F55		STRIMPLE, John W.	1865	X3519
STEVENS, Lydia (Allen)	1806	P3		STRIMPLE, Josiah	1822	X3502
STEVENS, Margaret J.	1825	P3		STRIMPLE, Keziah (B=)	1832	X3502
STEVENS, Melinda	181?	F252		STRIMPLE, Mary Ann (Perry)	185?	X3517
STEVENS, Robert	1806	P3		STRIMPLE, Mary Elizabeth	1853	X3515
STEVENS, Rosetta (B=)	1822	E399		STRIMPLE, Sarah J.	1860	X3518
STEVENS, Rowland	185?	E1637		STRIMPLE, Samual	179?	X3502
STEVENS, Seth Banning	18??	F616		STRIMPLE, Samuel William	1893	X3517
STEVENS, Stoddard C.	180?	F252		STRINGER, Shirley Ann	194?	P322
STEVENS, Sylvester	176?	F55		STRONG, Catherine (B=)	1851	A633
STEVENS, Walter	185?	K2939		STRONG, Gertrude	1880	A1566
STEVENSON, Catherine F.	193?	H505		STRONG, Nellie	1878	A1565
STEWART, Dorothy (B=)	191?	B2115		STRONG, Paul	1874	A1563
STEWARD, Hulda A. Foulk	183?	C29		STRONG, Roger Wesley	1875	A1564
STEWART, Mamie	189?	Q41		STRONG, Wesley	184?	A633
STEWART, Mary	182?	B66		STROUD, Emma	188?	H176a
STEWART, Mr.	190?	B2115		STROUGH, Charles Lester	1892	E6745
STICKNEY, A. B.	184?	C101		STRUM, Drothy Evelyn	1910	B1686
STICKNEY, Lucy	186?	C101		STRUM, Henry Peter	1865	B538
STICKNEY, Martin	176?	X2995		STRUM, Rhonda (B=)	1873	B538
STICKNEY, Sarah (B=)	1770	X2995		STUART, Ann C. L.	1785	K606
STIRLING, Abigail	1735	F15		SULLIVAN, Jane S. (???)	180?	B72
STOCKTON, Blanche	188?	F1405		SULLIVAN, Malinda C.	1827	B72
STOCKWELL, Carina (Clark	1896	F1409		SULLIVAN, William B.	180?	B72
STOCKWELL, Claude	189?	F1409		SUMMERS, Cheayl Denise	1956	B26008
STOLL, Dean Eldon	1941	B9641		SUMMERS, David Ray	1941	E19101
STOLL, Jennifer Leigh	1974	B26038		SUMMERS, Norma Lee (B=)	1942	E19101
STOLL, Joushua Daniel	1987	B26037		SUMMERS, Ray	191?	E19101
STOLL, Leann (B=)	1944	B9641		SUMMERS, Raymond Joseph	193?	B26008
STOLL, Marion (Powell)	1968	B26037		SUMMERS, Viola M. (Collins)	193?	B26008
STOLL, Mitchell Kent	1964	B26037		SUYDAM, Viola H.	185?	B142
STOLL, Nicholas Dean	1992	B26037		SWAYINGAME, Benjamin	184?	B277
STOLL, Wendy Lynn	1963	B26036		SWAYINGAME, Earl	1879	B1011
STONE, Chester Bruce	1901	B1686		SWAYINGAME, Edgebert	1877	B1010
STONE, Dorothy (Strum)	1910	B1686		SWAYINGAME, Rebecca	1816	B80
STONE, Dorothy Jean	1933	B1686		SWAYINGAME, Sophia (B=	1850	B277
STONE, Lina	184?	E1401		SWEARINGEN, Minerva	1834	F645
STONECIPHER, Donna	189?	B2701		SWEENEY, Mary Alice	1830	C20
STONER, Charles H.	1910	B2513c		SWEEZIE, Julia	184?	Q4
STONER, Nola Jane (Cooper)	1907	B2513c		SWOPE, Anna Mae (B=)	1928	B9601
STONES, Eliza (B=)	1806	L50		SWOPE, Bitha Pearl (Cleveng	190?	B9603
STONES, Eliza Banning	1848	L196		SWOPE, Catherine Renee	1963	B26004
STONES, George	180?	L50		SWOPE, Christopher Eugene	1978	B26007
STONES, Margaret Ann	1837	L192		SWOPE, Charles William	190?	B9603
STONES, Mary Beaumont	1845	L195		SWOPE, Charley Farrell	1934	B9603
STONES, Thomas Joseph	1840 *	L193		SWOPE, Cheryl D. (Summers)	1956	B26008
STONES, William Henry	1842 *	L194		SWOPE, Deborah (Owens)	1958	B26007
STOUGH, Charles	186?	E1651		SWOPE, Jessie Lee	1961	B26003
STOUGH, Lillian (B=)	1867	E1651		SWOPE, Lee Tillman	1932	B9601
STOVALL, Marian	195?	J506		SWOPE, Lois	1976	B26004
STOVER, Anna Hudson	184?	E1616		SWOPE, Michael Lee	1956	B26008
STRATTON, Helen Mary	191?	H377		SWOPE, Mindy Rachelle	1981	B26007
STRAUB, Nora	190?	H77c		SWOPE, Nathan Michael	1983	B26008
STRICKLAND, Pearl	191?	E10811		SWOPE, Peggy Lee (B=)	1937	B9603
STRIMPLE, Ada Mae	1904	X3517		SWOPE, Ronnie Eugene	1955	B26007
STRIMPLE, Amanda Belle	1871	X3520		SWOPE, Sherry Annn	1962	B26004
STRIMPLE, Asa	1854	X3516		SWOPE, Theresa Lynn	1957	B26009
STRIMPLE, Elizabeth (???)	179?	X3502		SYLVESTER, Maggin	188?	H175b
STRIMPLE, George	1851	X3514		TABER, Clauden Wellingto	1903	X27
STRIMPLE, Harry	1857	X3517		TABER, Florence E. (B=)	1877	X15

TABER, Loyal C. G.	187?	X15	THARP, Thomas J.	183?	B331
TABER, Mary Elizabeth	1900	X26	THILGHAM, William	17??	A77
TACKER, Carter James	189?	E10829	THOMAS, Bonnie J.(Carter	1937	J2113
TACKER, Carter James Jr.	1924	E10829	THOMAS, Bud	193?	J2113
TACKER, Dora Mae (B=)	1926	E10829	THOMAS, Charlotte Warne	1866	E6677
TACKER, James Phillip	1959	E19117	THOMAS, Edwin Plant	1860	E6676
TACKER, Letha (Malott)	190?	E10829	THOMAS, Ellen (B=)	1836	E1617
TACKER, Tamara Kay	1954	E19116	THOMAS, George	181?	E350
TAFT, Alma	187?	E6501	THOMAS, George Sherman	183?	E1617
TAFT, Celestine (B=)	1841	E1566	THOMAS, George C.	1842	E1495
TAFT, Jesse	183?	E1566	THOMAS, Harriett	177?	A22
TALBOT, Nancy	1783	L43	THOMAS, Lucy (B=)	1845	E1479
TALLMAN, Benjamin Frankl	1804	B242	THOMAS, Martha	184?	E1496
TALLMAN, Carl Benjamin	1884	B981	THOMAS, Martha	1888	E6318
TALLMAN, Catherine (B=)	1862	B242	THOMAS, Mathilda (B=)	1820	E350
TALLMAN, Edith Ora	1886	B982	THOMAS, Miss.	184?	F604
TALLMAN, Ernest Wells	1893	B984	THOMAS, Sarah	183?	J1
TALLMAN, Lora Estella	1890	B983	THOMAS, Susan	178?	A22
TALLMAN, Nancy C.	1824	B242	THOMPSON, Addie	186? *	G75
TALLMAN, Stella Cecil	1882	B980	THOMPSON, Albert	1858	G73
TALLMAN, Wells	1858	B242	THOMPSON, Bonnie J.(Cart	1937	J2113
TANNER, Laura	179?	F64	THOMPSON, Dorothy Ruth	193?	J2110
TANNER, Peggy	178?	F62	THOMPSON, Emily (Atherto	186?	G74
TANNER, Trial	177?	F242	THOMPSON, Harvey E.	182?	B90
TARPLEY, Alma E. (B=)	1907	H175b	THOMPSON, Helen (Glenden	185?	G73
TARPLEY, Branch	188?	H175b	THOMPSON, James	182?	G13
TARPLEY, Duward S.	1907	H175b	THOMPSON, John D.	182?	A249
TARPLEY, Mabel (Smith)	188?	H175b	THOMPSON, John Bell	1863	G74
TARRELL, Lois L.	1917	C1907a	THOMPSON, Joseph	1950	Q193
TAYLOR, Albert	186?	X1510	THOMPSON, Karen	1940	Q189
TAYLOR, Anna E. (B=)	1849	X10	THOMPSON, Louisa	1820	X3800
TAYLOR, Anna Mae	1887	F585	THOMPSON, Louisa (B=)	1836	B314
TAYLOR, Bessie (Brown)	1864	A694	THOMPSON, Margaret (B=)	1830	G13
TAYLOR, Catherine (B=)	186?	X1510	THOMPSON, Mark	1942	Q191
TAYLOR, Ella (B=)	1867	E1680	THOMPSON, Marlyn (Cheap)	194?	Q190
TAYLOR, Ethel (Fortner)	185?	B1192	THOMPSON, Mary E. (B=)	1829	B90
TAYLOR, Florence	1892	E6891	THOMPSON, Mary (B=)	1911	Q82
TAYLOR, George	186?	E1680	THOMPSON, Mary	1951	Q194
TAYLOR, George	1883	E6890	THOMPSON, Maurice	1907	Q82
TAYLOR, Gertrude	189?	X1543	THOMPSON, Mr.	183?	B314
TAYLOR, Ida E. (Clark)	186?	F585	THOMPSON, Neil	1941	Q190
TAYLOR, J. W. {Dr.}	186?	A694	THOMPSON, Nora	1948	Q192
TAYLOR, James M.	184?	X10	THOMPSON, Patsy (Holley)	1939	B2576c
TAYLOR, Mr.	185?	B1192	THOMPSON, Priscilla (B=)	1829	A249
TAYLOR, William David	185?	F585	THOMPSON, Rebecca	188?	Q169
TEAGARDEN, Ann	184?	B551	THOMPSON, Sherman A.	193?	J2113
TELLER, Emelin H. (B=)	1835	E1002	THOMPSON, William Joe	193?	B2576c
TELLER, Harvey	183?	E1002	THOREEN, Doris E. (B=)	1916	C1877
TELLER, Minnie Mary	185?	E4203	THOREEN, Kenneth	191?	C1877
TELLER, William Joseph	185?	E4202	THORNTON, Isabel	186?	E1587
TENNISON, Ann (B=)	181?	B82	THORPE, Ruby	189?	C661
TENNISON, Rutherford	181?	B82	THORPE, Ruth	189?	C662
TERRELL, James Tuttle	188?	B2036	THURSTON, Benjamin Franc	186?	E1588
TERRELL, Josie (Tomlinson)	188?	B2036	THURSTON, Donald Pitman	188?	E6571
TERRELL, Zoe Lee	1906	B2036	THURSTON, Mary (B=)	1866	E1588
TERRILL, Agnes	183?	B177	TIBBALS, Sarah	165?	X2507
TERRILL, Rebecca	182?	B175	TICHENOR, Lulu	187?	B1140
TERRY, Charles A.	186?	B700	TIFFANY, Della (B=)	186?	E1629
TERRY, Herschell Bannin	1891	B1938	TIFFANY, Elizabeth (???)	165?	E2,F2
TERRY, Susie (B=)	1867	B700	TIFFANY, Harrison	189?	E6715
TESKE, Eileen	1923	Q90	TIFFANY, Humphrey	165?	E2,F2
THARP, Martha A. (B=)	1840	B331	TIFFANY, Lucy	174?	E18

TIFFANY, Mr.	186?	E1629	TOURIGNY, Evelyn Ralme	191?	H376
TIFFANY, Nathan	177?	E18	TOWNSEND, Jesse H.	1900	B993
TIFFANY, Sarah	1683	E2,F2	TOWNSEND, Martha J. (B=)	1863	B261
TILDEN, Mary H.	181?	C61	TOWNSEND, Matthew	186?	B261
TILGHAM, Elizabeth M.	179?	A77	TRAVIS, Mary Ann	183?	L188
TILLER, Emelin H. (B=)	1835	E1002	TRICE, Mahala	180?	R2
TILLER, Harvey	183?	E1002	TRICE, Silas	180?	R2
TILLER, Minnie Mary	185?	E4203	TRICE, Willis	1825	R2
TILLER, William Joseph	185?	E4202	TRIPLETT, Mary (B=)	1917	F2624b
TIMMINS, Charles	1937	C3421	TRIPLETT, Peter	194?	F5296
TIMMINS, Eddie Daniel	1962	C5802	TRIPLETT, Tom	191?	F2624b
TIMMINS, Lasurie Danette	1964	C5803	TRIPLETT, Tom	194?	F5297
TIMMINS, Stephen Faron	1960	C5801	TROTH, Harriett	178?	A66b
TIMMINS, Vicky Rae (B=)	1940	C3421	TRUITT, Francis Emily	1856	H8c
TINKER, Laura	181?	F246	TRUITT, Nemiah	183?	H8c
TIPSWORD, Anna E.(Kinsey	186?	B1030	TRULUCK, Orillo Margarit	192?	H499
TIPSWORD, Catherine (You	186?	B1028	TUCKER, Isadore (Sheldon	189?	B1674
TIPSWORD, Christopher C.	1869	B1031	TUCKER, Marieta J. (McGa	1946	E19104
TIPSWORD, Clemit Vallandin	186?	B1194a	TUCKER, Marion	189?	B1674
TIPSWORD, Deane Wiley	1915	B2702	TUCKER, Miss.	184?	D11
TIPSWORD, Elizabeth (B=)	1834	B289	TUCKER, Robert D.	1941	E19104
TIPSWORD, Elizabeth Fae	1933	B2702	TUDOR, Elizabeth	187?	A705
TIPSWORD, Frances (Carly	1805	B289	TUFFORD, Alice M. (B=)	1871	R40
TIPSWORD, Frances Jeanne	1924	B2702	TUFFORD, Annie (Skeet)	183?	R35, R40
TIPSWORD, Franklin W.	1891	B2702	TUFFORD, Edwin William	1860	R40
TIPSWORD, Gail Lillian	1917	B2702	TUFFORD, Isaiah	183?	R35, R40
TIPSWORD, Griffin	1831	B289	TUFFORD, Mary Catherine	1857	R35
TIPSWORD, Hugh Dwight	1919	B2702	TURNAHAND, Cherry	195?	H780
TIPSWORD, Isaac Benton	186?	B2702	TURNER, Ann	182? *	C86
TIPSWORD, Isaac Vanlandi	1867	B1030	TURNER, Annie Maria	1866	C87
TIPSWORD, James Merida	1859	B1028	TURNER, Elizabeth (Hostl	181?	C83
TIPSWORD, John	1805	B289	TURNER, Elizabeth	1811	C82
TIPSWORD, John J.	1854	B1026	TURNER, Elizabeth (Wood)	182?	C84
TIPSWORD, Joseph C.	1872	B1032	TURNER, Isaac	1780	C17
TIPSWORD, Jossie (Fortner)	1901	B1195	TURNER, Isaac Banning	1817	C84
TIPSWORD, Juresin France	1862	B1029	TURNER, John	182?	C86b
TIPSWORD, Keith Warren	1914	B2702	TURNER, Mariah (Fleming)	1831	C87
TIPSWORD, Laura M.(Doty)	1894	B2702	TURNER, Mary Josephine	1851	C87
TIPSWORD, Leo C.	1900	B1195	TURNER, Matilda	1820	C85
TIPSWORD, Lillian (Rando	186?	B2702	TURNER, Minna Alice	1853	C87
TIPSWORD, Louise (Morse)	186?	B1028	TURNER, Nancy	182? *	C86a
TIPSWORD, Lucy (Fortner)	186?	B1194a	TURNER, Otis Howard	1871	C87
TIPSWORD, Marion (McNeel	185?	B1026	TURNER, Ovid Homer	1858	C87
TIPSWORD, Mary (Parkinso	185?	B1026	TURNER, Phineas	1827	C87
TIPSWORD, Mary Hester J.	1857	B1027	TURNER, Priscilla (B=)	178?	C17
TIPSWORD, Maud (Dewit)	187?	B1031	TURNER, Sally {Sarah}	1806	C81
TIPSWORD, Minda	1874	B1033	TURNER, Samuel	1812	C83
TIPSWORD, Rolland Fortner	1925	B1195	TURNER, William	175?	C17
TIPSWORD, Vera Delyne	1936	B2702	TURPIN, Adelia (B=)	1879	B749
TIPSWORD, Walter	1878	B1034	TURPIN, Elsie	1909	B2046
TIPTON, Deborah Ann	1962	E19109	TURPIN, Lola	1901	B2044
TIPTON, Jerry	193?	E19109	TURPIN, Mollie Ann (???)	190?	B2045
TIPTON, Saundra Kay	193?	E19109	TURPIN, Orlando L.	1905	B2045
TODD, Edward Edgerton	187?	L365	TURPIN, Pearl	1911	B2047
TODD, Helen Irene	1924	E10822	TURPIN, Robert	1879	B749
TODD, Hilda L. (Pollock)	1876	L365	TYLER, Ellen	1842	R7
TODD, Sallie F.	186?	B796	TYLER, Mary Ann	1840	R8
TOLRUD, Tilda Gurina	188?	C1828	TYLER, Sarah (Burrows)	181?	R7, 8
TOMLINSON, Josie May	188?	B2036	TYLER, William	181?	R7, 8
TOMLINSON, Ona Alice	1897	B752	UECKER, barbara Jane	1953	C1915
TORANEK, Christina	1938	Q186	UECKER, Berry John	1963	C1915
TORRENCE, Catherine	183?	A248	UECKER, Douglas Dale	1965	C1915

UECKER, Gregg Robert	1961	C1915		VEST, John W.	188?	B962
UECKER, Karon Sue	1915	C1915		VEST, Minnie A. (B=)	1884	B962
UECKER, Lela Mae (Weilan	1928	C1915		VEST, Nora (B=)	1892	B963b
UECKER, Robert Charles	1933	C1915		VEST, William	188?	B963b
UECKER, Ronald Charles	1949	C1915		VILLENEUVE, Eilleen	1954	Q154
ULACKY, Mr.	195?	F11995		VILLENUVE, Bill	192?	Q146
ULACKY, Susie (Hill)	195?	F11995		VILLENUVE, Joyce (Skin	192?	Q146
UMBARGER, Donna (Determ	193?	P145		VILLENUVE, Patarica	1948	Q146
UMBARGER, Robert	193?	P145		VINNING, Abner	1806	F237
UNDERWISCH, Zuneita (B=)	189?	P139		VINNING, Amelia	1804	F236
UNDERWOOD, Amanda Nico	1985	E19121		VINNING, Ellen (Benton)	180?	F237
UNDERWOOD, Anna M (Gri	189?	E10832		VINNING, John	183?	F237
UNDERWOOD, Darr Ann	1951	C19120		VINNING, Malinda (B=)	179?	F61
UNDERWOOD, Diana (Mar	1960	E19121		VINNING, Richard	179?	F61
UNDERWOOD, George	189?	E10832		VOGEL, Mr.	195?	F11996
UNDERWOOD, John George	1925	E10832		VOGEL, Sandy (Hill)	195?	F11996
UNDERWOOD, John Nelson	1959	E19121		VORHEES, Eunice (B=)	1818	E349
UNDERWOOD, Johnathan E.	1988	E19121		VORHEES, Mr.	181?	E349
UNDERWOOD, Naomi (B=)	1925	E10832		VROOM, Helen Cameron	1890	F1410
UTLEY, Julia (B=)	1829	F495		WABNITZ, Annie E. (B=)	1864	X3545
UTLEY, Lucius C.	1809	F495		WABNITZ, Edwin S.	186?	X3545
VALLANDINGHAM, A (Edw	192?	E19108		WABNITZ, Glen M.	1911	X3571
VALLANDINGHAM, Edward	192?	E19108		WADE, Larry Dean	193?	B2576b
VALLANDINGHAM, Kar(B=	1949	E19108		WADE, Shirley (Holley)	1937	B2576b
VALLANDINGHAM, William	1946	E19108		WAGGONER, Lena Ann	183?	B310
VAN BRUNT, Charlie	192?	J432		WAHRER, Clara Louise	188?	B599
VAN BRUNT, Hulda J. (B=)	1894	J138		WAHRER, Elizabeth	184?	B599
VAN BRUNT, Jane	192?	J428		WAHRER, Frank	184?	B599
VAN BRUNT, John	192?	J430		WAISHES, Harry	191?	H124
VAN BRUNT, Mae	192?	J429		WAISHES, Myrtle (B=)	1916	H124
VAN BRUNT, Robert	192?	J431		WAIT, Margaret	185?	Q5
VAN BRUNT, Todd A.	1894	J138		WAITE, Chloe	1738	F23
VANCE, Christian Jacob	185?	C236		WAITE, Rebecca (Fisher)	178?	A230
VANCE, Cora Ada	186?	C237		WALDEN, Minnie (B=)	1879	E6734
VANCE, Mary F. (B=)	1861	C236		WALDEN, Mr.	187?	E6734
VanDer MAELEN, Benoit	188?	H135		WALDEW, Jesse	186?	B940c
VanDer MAELEN, Marie L.	188?	H135		WALDEW, Sarah E. (B=)	1868	B940c
VanDer MAELEN, Margaret	1910	H135		WALDORF, Betty	192?	H378
VANDEVENTER, ADA (B=)	1878	J34		WALDRON, Linus	180?	P3
VANDEVENTER, Charles	1878	J35		WALES, Beulah Blanche	1909	F7007
VANDEVENTER, Elsie L.	1906	J211		WALKER, Annie (Wisson)	1870	X3807
VANDEVENTER, Mable (Ma	1877	J210		WALKER, Carlos Orlando	1875	X3807
VANDEVENTER, Mattie (B=	1883	J35		WALKER, Donna Rose	1934	C3334
VANDEVENTER, Mattie K.	1909	J212		WALKER, Everett Christo	1911	X3807
VANDEVENTER, Oscar A.	1877	J34		WALKER, Joseph Gilmer	179?	B35
VANDEVENTER, Shirley J.	1931	J508		WALKER, Louise Caroline	1817	B35
VANDEVENTER, Vernie V.	1902	J210		WALKER, Martha Scott	1795	B35
VanDRILLAR, Frances	183?	F602		WALKER, Melinda	183?	F611
VANDYK BERG, Peter	193?	F3109		WALLACE, Alice C. (Koge)	193?	E19129
VANDYK BERG, Theodo(B=	1933	F3109		WALLACE, Austin	192?	E19120
VanZANT, Elizabeth (Hill	1829	B66a		WALLACE, Darr Ann (Under	1951	E19120
VanZANT, James Harvey	182?	B66a		WALLACE, Jamie Frances	1990	E19129
VanZANT, John	183?	B67a		WALLACE, Kevin Robert	1963	E19129
VanZANT, Nancy (Hill)	1836	B67a		WALLACE, Kurt Alan	1948	E19120
VanZANT, Sarah	185?	B66a		WALLACE, Laura Fannie	190?	C1882
VAUGHN, Lula Edna	1887	A699		WALLACE, Leigh Ann	1973	E19120
VECH, Rachel	176?	C16		WALLACE, Mary	190?	H373
Ver STEEG, Madaline	190?	H372		WALLACE, Mary P. (Porter	1965	E19129
VERTREES, Charles H.	184?	B138		WALLACE, Mildred (Lande)	192?	E19120
VERTREES, Edwin Alfred	1882 *	B596		WALLACE, Paul Kenneth	193?	E19129
VERTREES, Elizabeth (B=)	1847	B138		WALLAR, A. C.	192?	E19105
VERTREES, Ernest	1884 *	B597		WALLAR, Allan Carl	1949	E19105

Name	Year	Code
WALLAR, Lesli Shantel	1976	E19105
WALLAR, Lois	192?	E19105
WALLAR, Mark Allen	1973	E19105
WALLAR, Rebea Ann (Loude	1953	E19105
WALLER, Joseph	178?	B84
WALLER, Minerva	181?	B84
WALSTON, Amy Agnes	193?	E19120
WALSTON, Arthur Richard	193?	E19120
WALSTON, Sandra Kay	1954	E19120
WALTERS, Amasa	181?	E258
WALTERS, Lydia (Post)	1821	E258
WANTLAND, Ruth	190?	E19122
WARD, Bessie Ruth	192?	H498
WARD, Beverly B.	1951	B26002
WARD, Elizabeth Ada	1936	Q87
WARD, Fred	1911	Q87
WARD, Freda Henrietta	1940	Q87
WARD, George {Sir}	176?	G2
WARD, Gertrude (Campbell	1911	Q87
WARD, Heather Jean A.	1946	Q87
WARD, James	173?	A102k
WARD, Littleton	171?	A36a & d
WARD, Mary (B=)	1715	A36a & d
WARD, Mary Ann	179?	G2
WARD, Mary	1838	F496
WARD, Philip	173?	A102j
WARD, Polly	181?	X3500
WARD, Rachel	174?	A102l
WARD, William	177?	X3500
WARDLEY, Edward Sherman	184?	L203
WARDLEY, Harriet (B=)	1849	L203
WARMER, John	169?	X2544
WARMER, Tabitha (B=)	1693	X2544
WARNER, Brockway {Capt.}	179?	E82
WARNER, Ebenezer Brockw	179?	E79
WARNER, Hannah Brainard	17??	E19
WARNER, Harriet {Susan}	182?	E384
WARNER, Jabez	17??	E19
WARNER, Joseph	182?	E383
WARNER, Lucinda (B=)	1795	E79
WARNER, Mary (Brockway)	1794	E414b
WARNER, Selden J.	179?	E414b
WARNER, Susanna	1753	E17
WARREN, Amelia (B=)	1848	F628
WARREN, Bernice	192?	H382
WARREN, Dennis	184?	F628
WARRINGTON, Amelia L.	1883	R41
WASHBURN, Alfred	188?	B931a
WASHBURN, Cordia (Severe	1886	B931a
WASSON, Cornealia (B=)	1815	F245
WASSON, Mary Jane	1844	F598
WASSON, Robella Bell	1851	F599
WASSON, Warren Hastings	1842	F597
WASSON, William	181?	F245
WATERMAN, Jane (Ackley)	1841	E1577
WATERMAN, Mr. {Capt.}	181?	E314
WATERMAN, William G.	183?	E1577
WATERS, Charlotte	182?	L184
WATERS, Emma	182?	K1270
WATERS, Maria Louise	183?	A117
WATERSTON, Ethel M.(Roy)	1881	Q18
WATERSTON, Inez Julia	1911	Q18
WATERSTON, Irene Ann	1914	Q18
WATERSTON, Lloyd Orville	1912	Q18
WATERSTON, Norris Everet	1912	Q18
WATERSTON, Robert Albert	1877	Q18
WATERSTON, Robert	1909	Q18
WATERSTON, William	1910	Q18
WATKINS, Frank William	184?	A254
WATKINS, Lila Banning	1878	B598
WATKINS, Lila Banning	1878	A698
WATKINS, Mary (B=)	1843	A254
WATSON, Rebecca	180?	B54
WATTERSON, Jessie	187?	Q23
WATTS, Ann (B=)	177?	A28a
WATTS, Hugh	177?	A28a
WATTS, Martha B.	179?	A66b
WAUGH, Sarah Viola	1884	B1141
WEBB, Catherine (B=)	185?	H8b
WEBB, Catherine (Stevens	193?	H505
WEBB, Charles	187?	C564
WEBB, Cyril D.	192?	H505
WEBB, Donna Sue	1956	H505
WEBB, Edith L. (B=)	1880	C564
WEBB, Ellen (B=)	184?	E1354
WEBB, George H.	184?	E1354
WEBB, George F.	1853	H8b
WEBB, Helen (Doyle)	191?	C1866
WEBB, Keneth	1918	C1866
WEBB, Sarah	1814	H1
WEBER, Sandra	194?	A3659
WEBSTER, David Clay	195?	E19067
WEBSTER, Grace (B=)	1879	C554
WEBSTER, Henry	187?	C554
WEBSTER, Jessica	1986	E39067
WEBSTER, Susan R. (B=)	1959	E19067
WEBSTER, Tiffany	1982	E39066
WEIGELT, Mary V. (B=)	1868	R31
WEIGELT, William	186?	R31
WEILAND, Ann (Schwams)	1902	C1907
WEILAND, Benjamin Rolf	1849	C553
WEILAND, Benjamin Rolf	1916	C1907b
WEILAND, Charles Merl	1905 *	C1906
WEILAND, Delores (Wilcox	1926	C1914
WEILAND, Earl Kenneth	1911	C1907a
WEILAND, Edmond	1887	C577
WEILAND, Edmond Lloyd	1953	C1914
WEILAND, Emma Lena	1889	C578
WEILAND, Garold Lee	1932	C1912
WEILAND, Gladys (Gardner	1912	C1912
WEILAND, GLoria Jean	1946	C1914
WEILAND, Grace Ann	1883	C553
WEILAND, Inola G. (Krumv	1921	C1907c
WEILAND, Ione A. (Schafe	1918	C1913
WEILAND, Irene B. (Ortma	1925	C1907d
WEILAND, Jacqueline Rose	1950	C1914
WEILAND, Julianne	1952	C1913
WEILAND, Kenneth Leroy	1915	C1913
WEILAND, Lela Mae	1928	C1915
WEILAND, Lester William	1919	C1914
WEILAND, Lois L. (Tarrel	1917	C1907a
WEILAND, Lyle Edmond	1911	C1912
WEILAND, Mary Jane (Sile	1856	C553
WEILAND, Mildred (Spicer	1914	C1907

WEILAND, Myrtle (B=)	1885	C577	
WEILAND, Nellie (B=)	1882	C575	
WEILAND, Opal (Krantz)	192?	C1907c	
WEILAND, Ray Edmond	1904	C1905	
WEILAND, Robert Lyle	1908	C1907	
WEILAND, Rolf Johnson	1879	C575	
WEILAND, Rose M. (Krumvi	1925	C1907b	
WEILAND, Russell Lloyd	1918	C1907c	
WEILAND, Stanley Arthur	1922	C1907d	
WEILAND, Vivian E. (Star	1903	C1905	
WEIRICK, Elizabeth (Raym	1828	A242	
WEIRICK, William H.	182?	A242	
WEIS, Deborah Lynn	196?	F11998	
WEITGENANT, Elizabeth(B=	1844	C230	
WEITGENANT, Joseph	184?	C230	
WELCH, Adra Adelaide	185?	E1494	
WELCH, Lee Ann	195?	H773	
WELLS, Arlo Arthur {Bill	190?	J119	
WELLS, Charles Henry	1868	J18	
WELLS, Charles henry	1868	J31	
WELLS, Charles Henry	191?	J122	
WELLS, Edna	190?	J113	
WELLS, Emily	180?	E306	
WELLS, Eva Rose	190?	J117	
WELLS, Flossie May	190?	J116	
WELLS, George {Sonny}	1908	J118	
WELLS, Harriet Opal	1912	J120	
WELLS, Henry	183?	J18	
WELLS, Henry Clay	190?	J114	
WELLS, Lorraine A.	1917	J121	
WELLS, Mary Jane	183?	J18	
WELLS, Mary Emma	190?	J115	
WELLS, Royal H.	191?	J123	
WELLS, Sarah Bell (B=)	1877	J18	
WELLS, Sarah J. (B=)	1857	J31	
WEST, Edith (W??)	187?	C565	
WEST, Frank	186?	C565	
WEST, Gertrude	1896	C565	
WEST, Marilda Hazel	1923	H495	
WEST, Olive (Burton)	190?	H495	
WEST, Paul Washington	190?	H495	
WEST, Vietta M.	193?	H330	
WESTCOTT, Edgar	185?	E6403	
WESTCOTT, Georgia (Hall)	1858	E6403	
WESTEN, Annie E. (B=)	1864	X3545	
WESTEN, John	186?	X3545	
WESTLEY, Esther	174?	K352	
WHARTON, Elizabeth (B=)	1852	H8e	
WHARTON, William	184?	H8e	
WHAT, Ellen	179?	I2	
WHEATLEY, Clattie (O'Day	187?	H175a	
WHEATLEY, Joanne	1949	H495	
WHEATLEY, Joseph	187?	H175a	
WHEATLEY, Joseph Ralph	1923	H495	
WHEATLEY, Joseph Ralph	1954	H495	
WHEATLEY, Leona C. (B=)	1903	H175a	
WHEATLEY, Marilda (West)	1923	H495	
WHEATLEY, Ralph Lufkin	1900	H175a	
WHEATLEY, Sharol Kaye	1946	H495	
WHEELER, Alice Marie	1851	A649	
WHEELER, Amos	1819	A231	
WHEELER, Amy	1862	A651	
WHEELER, Blanch	187?	A647	
WHEELER, Emma (McCreary	185?	A647	
WHEELER, Eva	185? *	A650	
WHEELER, Frank	1853	A648	
WHEELER, Frank	187?	A647	
WHEELER, Maria (B=)	1824	A231	
WHEELER, Maud	1864	A652	
WHEELER, Portius	1849	A647	
WHEELER, Rolla	187?	A647	
WHEELER, Sarah	182?	C228	
WHEELER, Sophia E.	1846 *	A646	
WHEELOCK, Helen	184?	E1614	
WHITAKER, Alice (B=)	1866	B272	
WHITAKER, Benjamin L.	186?	B272	
WHITAKER, Ethel	188?	B1001a	
WHITAKER, Maude	188?	B1001	
WHITAKER, Myrtle	188?	B1002	
WHITE, Barbara (???)	195?	H782	
WHITE, Beverly A. (Reed)	1947	H763	
WHITE, Brian Lee	1970	H763	
WHITE, Carey	1986	H780	
WHITE, Charles Lawrence	1955	H780	
WHITE, Cherry (Turnahand	195?	H780	
WHITE, Clarance	189?	F2627	
WHITE, Cody James	1986	H781	
WHITE, Cynthia (Keller)	195?	H781	
WHITE, Denise L. Furroug	1968	H763	
WHITE, Emma Elizabeth	1862	C231	
WHITE, Gary Lee	1955	H781	
WHITE, Henry Winters	183?	C229	
WHITE, Irene E. (Harris)	1901	F2627	
WHITE, John	16??	K234	
WHITE, Julia M.	185?	C229	
WHITE, Keity Lew	1957	H782	
WHITE, Larry Jr.	1977	H780	
WHITE, Lew F. Jr.	193?	H332	
WHITE, Lydia C. (Baumwai	183?	C229	
WHITE, Mary	16??	K234	
WHITE, Melissa Marie	1987	H782	
WHITE, Muriel	192?	Q145	
WHITE, Norma E. (B=)	1932	H332	
WHITE, Regina	1984	H780	
WHITE, Robert Allen	194?	H763	
WHITE, Robert Allen	1966	H763	
WHITE, Travis Lee	1984	H781	
WHITE, Virginia Emma	190?	E10824	
WHITESIDE, Michael	184?	B312c	
WHITESIDE, Norma D.	192?	B19001	
WHITESIDE, Sarah J. (B=)	1850	B312c	
WHITLOW, Louisa S.	181?	L33	
WHITLOW, Richard	17??	L33	
WHITTEN, Daniel Wesley	196?	E19103	
WHITTEN, Rayma L. (Kisse	1961	E19103	
WIDDOWS, Ada Bromley	1842	L453	
WIDDOWS, Amelia (Empson)	184?	L452	
WIDDOWS, Edward	181?	L181	
WIDDOWS, Edward	1846	L455	
WIDDOWS, Elizabeth Julia	1836	L449	
WIDDOWS, Elizabeth (Houg	184?	L455	
WIDDOWS, Florence (Ford)	184?	L454	
WIDDOWS, Frances Izzeta	1837	L450	
WIDDOWS, Joseph Banning	1840	L452	

Name	Year	Code
WIDDOWS, Julia (B=)	181?	L181
WIDDOWS, Mary Ellen	1848	L456
WIDDOWS, Richard	1839 *	L451
WIDDOWS, Richard	1846	L454
WILCOX, Amelia	180?	F63
WILCOX, Delores	1926	C1914
WILCOX, Hannah (B=)	176?	F53
WILCOX, Joseph	176?	F53
WILCOXSON, Mary P.	1842	F638
WILDER, Elijah	1752	F29
WILDER, Hannah (B=)	1720	F8
WILDER, Hannah	1759	F31
WILDER, Joseph	171?	F8
WILDER, Sarah	1762	F32
WILDER, Thomas	1756	F30
WILEY, Ann	176?	B13
WILKINS, Ruth (B=)	189?	P136
WILKINSON, Edna M. (B=)	1918	H125
WILKINSON, Jemima (B=)	1887	B943b
WILKINSON, Mr.	188?	B943b
WILKINSON, Paul	191?	H125
WILLARD, Emma	187?	E6674
WILLEFORD, Annie D.	1916	E10802
WILLEY, Barak B.	178?	E415
WILLEY, {Deacon}Joseph	1733	E16
WILLEY, Deborah (Brockway	1788	E415
WILLEY, Irena (B=)	1742	E16
WILLEY, Lucretia (Holmes	171?	E16
WILLEY, Lurana (B=)	1742	E16
WILEY, Temprence	1768	E100
WILLIAMS, Anna	1847	L457
WILLIAMS, Billie Lee	1934	B9611
WILLIAMS, Bud	190?	B2038
WILLIAMS, Carolyn Sue	1942	B9613
WILLIAMS, Dapheny Ann	1945	B9614
WILLIAMS, Donna (Knight)	1942	Q142
WILLIAMS, Edgar Eloise	1938	B9612
WILLIAMS, Elizabeth	172?	B7
WILLIAMS, Eliza (Parrott	18??	A66
WILLIAMS, Ella	1868	B1007
WILLIAMS, Elvira (B=)	1874	B275
WILLIAMS, Hattie C.	186?	F1476
WILLIAMS, Hazel M.	193?	J510
WILLIAMS, James	1871	B1008
WILLIAMS, Jerry Dean	1946	B9615
WILLIAMS, Mable A.M. (B=)	1906	B2038
WILLIAMS, Majorie	1943	E19058
WILLIAMS, Mary {Mrs.}	182?	A247
WILLIAMS, Mr.	18??	A66
WILLIAMS, Mr.	189?	E6712
WILLIAMS, Pauline	184?	B183
WILLIAMS, Sarah	183?	E1507
WILLIAMS, T. C.	1873	B1009
WILLIAMS, Taylor	184?	B275
WILLIAMS, Wanda Jane	192?	B2575a
WILLING, Winifred	190?	B1015
WILLOUGHBY, William	175?	R1
WILLOUGHBY, William	180?	R2
WILLSON, Deborah	169?	A5c
WILLSON, John	166?	A5c
WILSON, Alfred James	187?	E6320
WILSON, Alma J. (B=)	1943	H491
WILSON, Ann Janette (B=	1847	X3801
WILSON, Annie Elizabeth	1870	X3807
WILSON, Charles Harvey	1873	X3809
WILSON, Diodate G.	1830	X3801
WILSON, Ester	172?	C3
WILSON, Helen (B=)	1881	E6320
WILSON, John	16??	C3
WILSON, Lizzie	186?	B569
WILSON, Mary	16??	C3
WILSON, Melissa Dale	1963	H1001
WILSON, Ogden	181?	X3801
WILSON, Rose Rebecca	1875 *	C3808
WILSON, Ruth (Coleman)	181?	X3801
WILSON, Wendy Star	195?	F11990
WILSON, Wilmer Tull	191?	H491
WILSON, Wilmer Tull	1941	H491
WILTGEN, Calla A. (B=)	1889	C556
WILTGEN, Doris L. (Micke	1912	C1838
WILTGEN, George Andrew	1886	C556
WILTGEN, George Michael	1950	C1838
WILTGEN, Geraldine Louis	1944	C1838
WILTGEN, Jack	1914	C1838
WILTGEN, Judy Louise	1947	C1838
WILTGEN, Katherine B.	1912	C1839
WINCHESTER, Evelyn	1909	R148
WINDSOR, Catherine	181?	E252
WINN, Alma Jane (B=)	1872	C552
WINN, Fred C.	187?	C552
WINTERS, Elsa (Gottl)	193?	E19119
WIRTS, Joseph	183?	B181
WIRTS, Missouri (B=)	1835	B181
WISE, Harry	187?	E4206
WISE, Mary (B=)	1878	E4206
WISSEMAN, Alice (B=)	191?	H140
WISSEMAN, Ethel (B=)	191?	H139
WISSEMAN, Gideon	190?	H140
WISSEMAN, Leonard	190?	H139
WITTE, Clare	187?	N1679
WOLF, Mary Ann	183?	J15
WOOD, Eliza jane	187?	B1195
WOOD, Elizabeth	182?	C84
WOOD, John	171?	F7
WOOD, John	1754	F26
WOOD, Mary (B=)	1718	F7
WOOD, Mary P.	183?	C80
WOOD, Pauline	191?	B2116
WOODY, F.M.	184?	B197
WOODY, Jancy V. (B=)	1852	B197
WORK, Alice (Markham)	186?	E1710
WORK, Fred	186?	E1710
WORKMAN, Hazel	191?	Q142
WORKMAN, Menolia	1900	H118
WORKMAN, Robert	190?	H118
WORRALL, Elizabeth (Ston	1848	L196
WORRALL, Thomas	184?	L196
WORSTER, Amanda Marie	197?	H833
WORSTER, Fred Sawyer	193?	H833
WORSTER, Karen Lynn (Cov	1955	H833
WORSTER, Mona Mae(Andre	193?	H833
WORSTER, Sarah Beth	197?	H833
WORSTER, Warren W.	1953	H833
WORTH, Henry Pease	1790	B27

488

WORTH, Mercy (B=)	1790	B27
WRENSHALL, John	176?	L9
WRENSHALL, Margaret	1761	L9
WRIGHT, A. W.	188?	J134
WRIGHT, Ada (B=)	1880	E6735
WRIGHT, Alanson	180?	E364
WRIGHT, Argul	191?	J399
WRIGHT, Berth	18??	F650
WRIGHT, Catherine	182?	E526
WRIGHT, Cecil	191?	J401
WRIGHT, Clara Cone	1880	E6726
WRIGHT, Daniel Norton	1887	E6728
WRIGHT, Dick	192?	J404
WRIGHT, Emily A. (B=)	1810	E364
WRIGHT, Ethel Mary	1875	E6724
WRIGHT, Frank Benjamin	1877	E6725
WRIGHT, Fred Warren	1871	E6722
WRIGHT, Grace Annett	1873	E6723
WRIGHT, Hiram Childs	1882	E6727
WRIGHT, Ida Bell (B=)	1885	J134
WRIGHT, Lucy (B=)	177?	F58
WRIGHT, Marie	192?	J405
WRIGHT, Marshall Daniel	184?	E1643
WRIGHT, Norton	177?	F58
WRIGHT, Owen	192?	J403
WRIGHT, Pearl (B=)	18??	F650
WRIGHT, Phoebe (B=)	1848	E1643
WRIGHT, Ray	191?	J402
WRIGHT, Rhoda (Chapman)	178?	F94a
WRIGHT, Ruby	191?	J400
WRIGHT, Willis	178?	F94a
YANDELL, Sarah Margaret	1873	E10804
YORK, Estelle	1935	B1792
YORK, Gertrude (Phipps)	191?	B1792
YORK, John Willard	190?	B1792
YORK, Rutha	186?	B324
YOUNG, Harry M.	189?	F2044
YOUNG, Lola (Turpin)	1901	F2044
YOUNG, Louise (B=)	1902	F2623a
YOUNG, Mr.	190?	F2623a
YOUNGBLOOD, Patsy	1944	E19059
YOUNGER, Catherine	186?	B1028
YOUNTLAE, Martha	1821	B87
ZAHN, Alphe Mae (Bess)	1929	E19042
ZAHN, Bill	193?	E19042
ZAHN, Billy Michael	1953	E38980
ZAHN, Virginia Mae	1950	E38979
ZANDERS, Andre N.H.	1985	C3341
ZANDERS, Lorayne (Herth)	1955	C3341
ZANDERS, Richard J.A.	1951	C3341
ZELLMAN, Bonnie (Furroug	1955	H769
ZELLMAN, Carl	195?	H769
ZIERMANN, Charles H.	188?	E11023
ZIERMANN, Ethel (Hilton)	1882	E11023
ZIERMANN, Irma	1906	E11023
ZIMMERMAN, Eva (Hahn)	177?	A68
ZIMMERMAN, Gotlieb	1768	A68
ZIMMERMAN, Sophia Eva	1798	A68